REFORMED THEOLOGY

REFORMED THEOLOGY

Identity and Ecumenicity

Edited by

Wallace M. Alston, Jr.

&

Michael Welker

WILLIAM B. EERDMANS PUBLISHING COMPANY
GRAND RAPIDS, MICHIGAN / CAMBRIDGE, U.K.

Wm. B. Eerdmans Publishing Co.
255 Jefferson Ave. S.E., Grand Rapids, Michigan 49503 /
P.O. Box 163, Cambridge CB3 9PU U.K.

Printed in the United States of America

07 06 05 04 03   7 6 5 4 3 2 1

Library of Congress Cataloging-in-Publication Data

Reformed theology: identity and ecumenicity /
edited by Wallace M. Alston, Jr. & Michael Welker.
p.   cm.
Includes bibliographical references and index.
ISBN 0-8028-4776-5 (pbk.: alk. paper)
1. Reformed Church — Doctrines — Congresses.
I. Alston, Wallace M., 1934-   II. Welker, Michael, 1947-
BX9422.3.R45   2003
230'.42 — dc21
2003049061

www.eerdmans.com

Contents

PART II
How to Shape Reformed Ecclesiology

PART III
Spirit and Covenant: Reformed Pneumatology
in Very Different Contexts

Contents

PART V
Ecumenicity and Ethical Profiles of Reformed Theology:
Catholicity and Practical Contextuality

Introduction

Wallace M. Alston, Jr., and Michael Welker

Christian theology, according to its classical definition, is faith's own intellectual work of seeking understanding or intelligibility, not in order to prove its truth but to persuade those who hear it proclaimed. It is the church's continuing effort to achieve clarity about its own message and mission, but it is also the church's attempt to reckon with understanding's increasingly open and somewhat desperate quest for constituting faith. It was to this end, that faith might gain understanding and understanding be nurtured by faith, that the Center of Theological Inquiry convened a consultation of systematic theologians who are identified, explicitly or implicitly, with the Reformed tradition. The purpose of the consultation, which met at the Internationales Wissenschaftsforum in Heidelberg, Germany, on March 18-22, 1999, was to identify current trends and motifs in Reformed thought, to mine that tradition for resources that might enrich the church ecumenical, and to foster friendship and collegiality among and between theologians of the Reformed tradition throughout the world.

The thought that such a consultation might be valuable was occasioned by the publication of *Toward the Future of Reformed Theology: Tasks, Topics, Traditions* (Grand Rapids: Eerdmans, 1999), edited by David Willis and Michael Welker. In their introduction to that volume, the editors frankly admitted that their attempt to present a volume that would be representative of the entire spectrum of contemporary Reformed thought had not met with complete success. The volume as published was highly successful in documenting the liveliness of Reformed theology in Europe and North America by bringing into public discussion issues and authors of moment and promise, but it left before those who cherish the tradition the unfinished business of developing an ongoing process of bringing to light and exploring more thoroughly the rich, structured pluralism that we find in Reformed theology today.

The reader must judge whether the current volume has been more successful in the attempt to reflect a more catholic Reformed community of inquiry. In any case, it has become increasingly obvious that one consultation of this sort is insufficient if the project is to be genuinely inclusive of the broad spectrum of persons, nationalities, disciplines, and rationalities identified with Reformed scholarship today. That having been said, those who participated in the Heidelberg consultation thoughtfully engaged the issue of Reformed identity, and if the ecumenical character of the tradition received somewhat less attention, the groundwork was laid for future consultations in which that dimension of the constituting rubric might more directly be addressed.

Participants in the Heidelberg consultation included Ulrich Körtner (Austria), Douglas Farrow (Canada), Carver T. Yu (China), Milan Opocênsky (Czech Republic), Colin Gunton (England), Peter McEnhill (England), Eberhard Busch (Germany), Michael Weinrich (Germany), Margit Ernst (Germany/USA), Jan Rohls (Germany), Michael Welker (Germany), Botond Gaál (Hungary), A. van de Beek (Netherlands), David Fergusson (Scotland), Russel Botman (South Africa), Piet J. Naudé (South Africa), Dirk J. Smit (South Africa), Myung Yong Kim (South Korea), Yung Han Kim (South Korea), Jan Millič Lochman (Switzerland), Mark Achtemeier (USA), Dawn DeVries (USA), Thomas W. Gillespie (USA), George Hunsinger (USA), Gabriel Fackre (USA), William Stacy Johnson (USA), Bruce McCormack (USA), Daniel Migliore (USA), George W. Stroup, III (USA), Leanne Van Dyk (USA), and Wallace M. Alston, Jr. (USA).

Ecclesia reformata et semper reformanda: On the Way from Mere Certainties to Truth

It is characteristic of Reformed theology to be in constant search of the Reformed identity and to define this identity time and again. This is not an evasive or a paradoxical statement. The continuous search for Reformed identity is by no means a desperate and helpless endeavor. It takes place in response to the word of God and in the midst of the challenges of the world: "Hominum confusione — Dei providentia." If the "ecclesia reformata et semper reformanda" is to be true to its sources and its calling, it must live in constant search for truth, it must be ready to repent and to learn, and it must be prepared to bear witness and to give account, time and time again, for its theological convictions and certainties. It lives in a perpetual state of trust on the one hand, and critical reflection on the other, continually testing its cherished customs and convictions on the way from individual and communal certainties to the fuller disclosure of truth.

This search serves the ever richer edification of Christian faith and the life of the Christian church as it strives for a more encompassing and intelligible knowledge of God and of God's intentions for the world. This search, however, also serves human societies and cultures, which are tempted to settle for reductionistic or ideological conceptions of certainty and truth.

Vast segments of modernity have been endangered by a confusion or conflation of certainty and truth. The name of reason, the name of the moral law, the name of natural law and other names, have stood for claims to have found the truth or at least the powers which, predictably or automatically, lead one from certainty to truth. Reformed theology has been one of the major critical voices which has challenged rationalistic, scientistic, moralistic, and political ideologies which claimed to possess the truth, or the only key to it. Reformed theology has challenged individuals, associations, societies, and cultures to be sensitive to different rationalities, different morals, and conflicting truth claims, testing them in the light of the living word of God. It has challenged individuals, associations, societies, and cultures to resist totalitarian worldviews and ideologies that regard worldly norms and powers as supplements for the living word of God.

Reformed theology, in issuing this challenge, has understood itself not as the magisterial voice that tells the rest of the world where to go and where to settle for truth. It has rather understood itself as a critical and self-critical part of a "truth-seeking community," namely, the Christian church, which invites and challenges other human institutions and communal enterprises to become truth-seeking communities rather than communities within which various certainties are espoused by various interest groups.

Contextual Challenges

Today this search for, and affirmation of, Reformed identity must take into consideration the following difficult and highly sensitive constellations:

- that we share cultures, yet live in different cultures and traditions;
- that we share theological classics, yet prefer different theological classics;
- that we emphasize the same dogmatic loci, yet stress different dogmatic loci;
- that we use similar modes of thought, yet use different modes of thought;
- that we have common ethical concerns, yet have different, even conflicting ethical concerns.

This inner pluralism of Reformed theological positions is by no means a vague plurality, or even a relativistic or individualistic constellation. It was very clear at the Heidelberg consultation that we were able to understand each other to a high degree, that we were able to translate positions to one another, and that the commonalities balanced or even outnumbered the differences. A strong commonality existed not only in basic Christian beliefs but also in a high contextual sensitivity, as well as in the understanding that we must gain theological orientation in the midst of a pluralistic setting and rapid cultural transformations. The dominant factors in these developments are:

- shifts from modern to postmodern paradigms and mentalities;
- the crisis of the nation state;
- the enormous power of market, media, and technology and its threat to destroy cultural and societal pluralism;
- the weakening of cultural and canonic memory;
- the constant crisis of common orientation;
- massive injustice, poverty, and ecological destruction on this planet;
- the threat of relativism, cynicism, and apathetic moods;
- dissatisfaction with a theology and church that appear incapable of providing leadership and giving guidance.

Shared Convictions and Fruitful Differences

Most of us shared the perspective that fear or the search for a mere metatheology from an observer's point of view could not be the answer to this complex challenge. We rather need a cultural analysis that includes a subtle approach to pluralism and moralism. Pluralism has to be distinguished from vague plurality, individualism, and relativism (although they are often called "pluralism"). Pluralism, poly-contextualism, and multi-perspectivalism call for the constant transformation of mere certainties into the recognition of truth. On several levels the church itself shows pluralistic structures in the good, strong, and healthy sense of the word. These structures are informed by the symbols and narratives of the Eucharist, Pentecost, and the Body of Christ, wherein a multitude of members, who among themselves have no monohierarchical form, are many yet one.

In the same way the widespread moralism needs subtle treatment. Human societies cannot live without morals, i.e., the mutual giving and withdrawing of respect and tolerance. At the same time, personal and public morals can become highly corrupted (an effect that has become very obvious in the German and South African histories of this century, one that is less obvious but nevertheless prevails in other contexts). Over against this challenge we need above all the readiness and the ability to interpret the individual, social, cultural, and religious reality theologically and to regain the language and knowledge of faith. We will not regain the language and knowledge of faith simply by turning back to the traditions without allowing them to enter into dialogue with the current common sense and with an analysis of the current social and cultural crisis.

Some contributions to the Heidelberg consultation highlighted the fact that we must develop new concepts of theological education and "paideia." Some contributions insisted on an improvement of theological reflections on the economic order. Dogmatically we saw strong shared interests in trinitarian theology and pneumatology. We saw differences in emphasis on whether the theistic challenge, or the postmodern challenge, or pentecostalism, needs the closer attention. We saw differences in emphasis on the fact that dogmatic theology cannot be done in our time apart from an interest in ethical issues and the desire to shape moral engagement and passion. We also saw slight differences with regard to the need to draw upon the richness of the classical Reformed sources, as well as to whether Reformed theology should concern itself primarily and specifically with the theologies of Calvin and Barth.

Different Modes of Learning from Scripture

Less conspicuous than the topic of the Reformed identity was the topic of its ecumenicity. It was present, however, from the very beginning. It was present in the reflections on the multi-perspectival and poly-contextual setting of each theology. It was present in the overarching contextual sensitivity of the participants and their contributions. It was present in the concentration on trinitarian theology and pneumatology, which opened new possibilities of dialogue with other families of the Christian faith.

Above all, the ecumenical task was present in the insight that confessions and confessional profiles are modes of learning from Scripture. This topic called for further exploration, particularly in dialogue with exegetes. For that purpose a second consultation was convened at the University of Stellenbosch, South Africa, on March 30-April 3, 2001. The Stellenbosch meeting was the direct result of the strong support of the Heidelberg consultation for dialogue with exegetical scholars of the Reformed tradition, who might bring their own visions and tasks to bear on the issues addressed in Heidelberg.

The ecumenical task was also present in several differences that could not be overcome, such as whether today we primarily need to read the scriptures in confessional modes of learning, taking account of the living word and the work of the Holy Spirit; or whether today we primarily need obedience to the church and its confessions in order to overcome the threat of relativism. Some participants in the consultation viewed the latter position as a crypto-Catholic statement and an abnegation of Reformed theology; others regarded this as a necessary emergency brake in the current crisis.

There were also differences in the evaluation of the potential of the "Unio Mystica cum Christo" and in the notion of the "Ascension of the Church." Some saw here operative paths toward new understanding with Roman Catholic and Orthodox positions. Others saw the danger that this type of ecumenical openness could blur the Reformed profile.

In conclusion, it must not go without saying that the editors are profoundly grateful to the participants in the Heidelberg consultation for the faithfulness and integrity of their work, and for the commonality of mind and heart that created an atmosphere within which differences as well as similarities could be freely displayed without fear or embarrassment. We are grateful for the editorial work of Bryan Bibb of the Department of Religion at Furman University, who was at the time of his work on this volume a doctoral candidate in residence at Princeton Theological Seminary. We are grateful as well to the staff of the Internationales Wissenschaftsforum in Heidelberg, Germany, for hosting this consultation, and to Ms. Kathi Morley, administrator of the Center of Theological Inquiry in Princeton, New Jersey, apart from whom neither the consultation nor this volume would have been attempted or completed.

Princeton and Heidelberg   W.M.A., Jr., and M.W.

PART I

Reformed Identity in Historical Continuity and Contextual Awareness

CHAPTER 1

The Identity of Reformed Theology and Its Ecumenicity in the Twenty-First Century: Reformed Theology as Transformational Cultural Theology

Yung Han Kim

Preface

We Reformed Christians are now facing the twenty-first century. In this postmodern age, the information highway has been opened globally, the cyber-culture formed, pluralistic thought dispersed, secularism strengthened, ecology highly regarded, ethical issues crucially raised due to advanced gene technology, and the discussion of bio-ethics brought to the forefront.

How can Reformed theology preserve its identity and claim its ecumenicity while facing the twenty-first century? We have been challenged by postmodernism, religious pluralism, new age movements and neopaganism, astrology, reincarnation thought, new technological secularism, and cyber-culture. Reformed theology — preserving its identity on the one hand and claiming its ecumenicity on the other — needs to respond to these challenges creatively and to heal and guide the spirit of the twenty-first century.

In the days of Luther's Reformation, the gospel's proclamation was prohibited by the papacy from coming to light. In the upcoming century, Reformed churches will face the difficulties raised by the challenges mentioned above. To preserve the identity of Reformed theology and claim its ecumenicity in the twenty-first century, we must draw upon our Reformed heritage and reinterpret and develop it in today's context. To carry out this task, Reformed theology should become a transformational cultural theology.

The Spiritual Challenge of the Twenty-First Century

Postmodernism: Relativizing and Dissolving Truth and Values

Postmodernism has pursued a new paradigm of reason and science in order to overcome the crisis brought about by modernism. Based on a Cartesian rationalism that established scientific rationality as the norm for all knowledge, modernism destroyed the idea of revelation of God, authority of Scripture, and traditional doctrine. Postmodernism, by contrast, refers us to the boundaries of the modern concept of reason and science, specifically the human alienation and ecological pollution to which modernism gave rise. Postmodernism has destroyed the rationalist castle of science and reason, and the idol of scientific objectivism and rationalism.

This postmodern movement has been called the collapse of foundationalism.[1] Among others, H. G. Gadamer and P. Ricoeur have contributed to the discovery that human reason is undergirded by prerational, practical, and belief-dimensions.[2] A radical critique represented by J. Derrida in philosophy and by M. Taylor in theology has led to deconstructionism. Post-structuralists do not regard immediate, intuitive self-presence as a sensible ideal of self-knowledge.[3] According to them, the subject is dispersed like a network of diverse languages rather than the center of the world. In this kind of total mediation reason has no autonomy. They have contributed to the collapse of autonomic thinking about the human self and to disclosing the limits and boundaries of human existence. However, such thinkers as Derrida and Taylor move into nihilism, denying the reality of the self beyond its autonomy. They have insisted that there exists neither reality nor actuality but merely the text. Here, texts are narration and event, etc. Reality is nothing but text. Thus they deny reality, falling into representationalism.

Deconstructive thought has tried to demythologize Christianity and other religions. It has denied the reality of truth and the universality of morals and values, insisting that there is no truth, justice, or humanity. It is an arbitrary mixing of this and that, an anarchy of thinking and style, a methodological and moral relativism that permits everything.[4] Deconstructive thought is a

1. Nicholas Wolterstorff, *Reason Within the Boundary of Religion*, 2nd ed. (Grand Rapids: Eerdmans, 1984), pp. 46-57.

2. Herman Dooyeweerd, *Roots of Western Culture: Pagan, Secular and Christian Options* (Toronto: Wedge Publishing Foundation, 1979), p. 9; Hendrik Hart, *Understanding Our World: An Integral Ontology* (Lanham, Md.: University Press of America, 1984), p. 307.

3. Kenneth Baynes, James Bohman, and Thomas McCarthy, eds., *After Philosophy: End or Transformation?* (Cambridge, Mass.: MIT Press, 1987), p. 8.

4. Baynes et al., *After Philosophy*, pp. 19, 56.

secular ideology that challenges tradition, authority, and canon, Reformed or otherwise. In the twenty-first century such thinking will penetrate more and more into Christian churches worldwide.

Religious Pluralism

With the ideology of postmodernism, religious pluralism — which insists that other religions are also a way of salvation — has been exerting an influence on theological circles in Europe and Asia. In Korea, this problem has been an important issue in the Methodist Theological Seminary since the early 1990s, and has been discussed in Korean theological societies.

Religious pluralism appears as a religious movement in postliberal theology in a postmodern era that insists that the salvific revelation of God is not only in Christianity but also in other religions. Christianity is thus not the only way of salvation, but salvation may be found in other religions as well. Religious pluralism is culturally a postmodern liberal theology. The distinction between modern and postmodern theology is as follows. Modern liberal theology tends to deny and reduce certain parts of Christian traditional doctrine and to think christologically. In contrast, postmodern liberal theology tends to add to Christian doctrine and to think theocentrically.

Whereas traditional liberal theology denies the divinity of Jesus, postmodern liberal theology supports both the divinity and humanity of Jesus at the same time. Jesus is recognized as one among many saviors. Religious pluralists promote a spiritual freedom. Without denying the distinctiveness of each religion, they acknowledge the truth of each religion and provide a vision of the "ultimate" that connects the faith of each religion.[5]

Religious pluralism includes three theological arguments. The first is historico-cultural relativity. Religious pluralism maintains that each religion and its scripture are creations of human imagination, and come from a special human cultural viewpoint (Gordon Kaufman). Therefore, Christian theology has to give up its claim of absolute and ultimate truth (John Hick).

The second argument is experiential mystery. In every religion there is a certain experience of the transcendent beyond our perception. Our theology is merely our intellectual image of God. To absolutize our image of God is idol worship (Wilfred Cantwell Smith). Idol worship consists of the claim that there is only one way, one norm, one truth (Tom Driver).

The third thesis is practical justice. The prior choice for the poor and the

---

5. Stanley J. Samartha, *Courage for Dialogue* (Maryknoll, N.Y.: Orbis Books, 1981), p. 98.

alienated requires dialogue between the religions (Paul Knitter). The only possible criterion to judge the religions is not doctrine or mystery, but ethics.

Therefore, religious pluralists affirm that monopolizing religious truth, even though it may be Christian or biblical truth, is an enthusiastic and irrational religious fanaticism. Religious pluralists suggest a "theocentric model" that overcomes the religious exclusivism of christocentric theology advocated since Karl Barth and surpasses the christological universalism of Karl Rahner.

New Age Movement, Neopaganism, Astrology, and Reincarnation

New age thought is syncretistic, and is spreading not only in theology but also in science and culture and among the younger generation. It is a mystical thought that mixes Christianity and the esoteric ideas of Hinduism and accommodates astrology. Fritjof Capra, the science writer who preaches new age thought in the realm of science, connects physics and Hinduism. He views the image (in modern physics) of an interconnected cosmos as explaining the mysterious experience of nature in relation to Brahman, the thread that connects the cosmic web with the ultimate basis of all being.[6]

New age thought anticipates the arrival of new humans and new generations through a change of consciousness. It seeks to awaken the potential Self consciousness through mind control and to discover the true Self, that is, the Self which is divine. This Self, being the ultimate reality, has no morality.[7] The new age thinker says "The Heaven is you. Know yourself. Then you shall be free. . . . Know you are gods, and cosmos."[8] New age thought seeks the human god, and is based on the pantheistic thought of Hinduism, saying "the cosmos and I are one." New age thought is a monism of spirit or consciousness that claims that all is spirit and consciousness.

Neopaganism has also spread. The postmodern age has developed high technology but not a morality that protects against the abuse of power by different groups. Drugs, homosexuality, and the corruption of officials have spread widely, while violence and sex have become the main agenda of today's TV and multimedia.

Astrology and a belief in reincarnation have been increasing among today's younger generation. The phenomena described above have become great

6. Fritjof Capra, *The Tao of Physics: An Exploration of the Parallels Between Modern Physics and Eastern Mysticism* (Boulder, Colo.: Shambhala, 1983), pp. 161ff.; Yung Han Kim, *The 21st Century and Reformed Theology*, vol. 1 (Presbyterian Press, 1998), p. 213.

7. Shirley MacLaine, *Dancing in the Light* (New York: Bantam Books, 1986), pp. 334-35.

8. MacLaine, *Dancing in the Light*, p. 135.

challenges to the Reformed churches. Postmodernity has captured people in the chains of a neopagan worldview.

High Technological Secularism and Its By-products

High technology has brought material richness and dominion over nature. High technological secularism has become the most dynamic worldview in human history. Its ideology is "you should always have more, always better, always faster." This ideology of progress has survived among the streams of postmodernism, viewing techno-industrial development as an absolute value and deifying it.

The Third Industrial Revolution has replaced human intellectual work with the computer and telecommunications. In the information society, power is determined by the control of information. Modernization is, as Lyotard has said, an informationalization of society, seen from the viewpoint of knowledge. The distinctiveness of the information society is "a totalization through universalization of language and universal language."[9] Thus, it seems that the ideal society that once seemed fantasy is being realized due to ultramodern processes such as miniaturization and digitalization.

The technology produces centralization of theoretical knowledge and new intellectual techniques. Socially, there is the rise of a new technological elite and a shift from a production society to an information and knowledge society. Humans have developed technology but do not have the power of spirit to control its unforeseen dangers. Owing to the misuse of scientific research, humans face the many negative developments that ultramodern technology has brought.

Expectations that an era honoring humanity would automatically come with the development of technology have led to despair. Homicidal and destructive impulses remain. New hostilities follow the dissolution of old ones. For example, with the disintegration of the Soviet Union, civil war sprang up in the former Yugoslavia due to the resurgence of old nationalisms. The world has not progressed to a peaceful co-existence, and now even greater catastrophes are possible.

There is no one to raise an objection to this technological progress. The problem is that techno-industrial development has become an absolute value and a blindly worshiped idol. What is important here is whether or not one requires that technology serve humanity. A high technology has been developed,

9. Jean François Lyotard, *Das postmoderne Wissen, Ein Bericht* (Bremen: Verlag Impuls), p. 30.

but no commensurate wisdom. And this high technological secularism —
which has no place for God — will prevail in the twenty-first century, challenging the Reformed churches.

Cyber-culture

The upcoming century arrives as an age of multimedia, which has already had a
large influence on Christianity. In the information age, the church and Bible exist in a new way, in the form of an emerging cyber-church. This is no longer the
local church, but a church to which one may be electronically connected, when-
ever and wherever. The worship in this new church is not face to face, but conducted remotely by way of multimedia. It is a cyber-church rather than a spiritual church, and some think that it will become the World Wide Church.[10]
    Cyber-theological schools and cyber-theology have also been emerging.
Discussion and information exchange between theologians have become possible without limits of time or space. Preaching materials are exchanged between
ministers through the information highway, and research papers are freely exchanged between theologians. Cyber-worship and churches have begun replacing traditional Christian worship and churches. This increasing phenomenon
will result in a certain wearing away of the historical institutional churches and
worship.

The Identity of Reformed Theology

In order to respond to these five challenges creatively from a Reformed perspective, I would like to suggest that Reformed theology should reaffirm five aspects
of the Reformed heritage: "sola scriptura," "solus Christus," "the human as image of God but totally depraved," "Reformed spirituality," and "cultural transformation."

Sola Scriptura: Rehabilitation of the Word of God and Its Authority

Postmodernism, proclaiming an ethical and moral relativism, has been decons-
tructing traditional ethics and morality. Accordingly, the social spirit is disinte-
grating. Our society is losing not only a consensus about individual behavior
but also the foundation for the rational discussion of morality, values, truth,

---

10. Lyotard, *Das postmoderne Wissen, Ein Bericht*, pp. 123-39.

and meaning. Today's postmodern culture is similar to that of the time of Judges when everyone acted according to what he considered good. The modern belief that knowledge is good has collapsed. It has been discovered that there is no real connection between knowledge and its good use. For example, it is clear that knowledge may be misused in genetic engineering and in nuclear power.

We Reformed Christians cannot accept Lyotard's postmodern idea that there is no universal meaning, truth, value, or ethic. We affirm there is a universal truth that humanity should and could pursue, even given the diversity of ways of thinking, culture, and customs. Meaning, truth, value, and ethics should not be developed at will according to human thought but rather interpreted under the light of the divine created order and will. The situational context of values and ethics can be important, but this must never fall into relativism, as situationalists believe. Values and ethics should be dynamically illumined by the paradoxical relation between the infinite request of God and the human situation in which value judgments and ethical acts are required. A deconstructive postmodernism falls into an anarchistic situation vis-à-vis values and knowledge when it denies all authority, especially that of the sacred books.

The World Alliance of Reformed Churches (WARC) therefore professes the position that postmodernism does not accord with the biblical tradition. It is true that every thought has its own right, and that the era of insisting on the absolute is over. However, biblical culture opposes the postmodern culture. Postmodernism is a response to the dilemma of the modern era and a questioning of the structure of the modern era, which homogenizes and suppresses people. However, the battle between the poles of life and death, good and evil, love and hate, etc., still continues. The search for truth and for God is an issue that will never be given up. Self-justified authority and artificial sacred books should be criticized and examined again. When authority and sacred books as a whole are rejected, however, human thought and action loses its way and falls into nihilism.

I would say that we can preserve the identity of Reformed theology in the upcoming century only with the reaffirmation of *sola scriptura*: Scripture as the Word of God.[11] Today's hermeneutics of higher criticism conceals through artificial operations the truth of revelation, rather than listening to the living voice of God. Gadamer suggests that the hermeneutics of effective history, rather than methodological thinking, will uncover the meaning of texts. The true task of biblical hermeneutics consists in listening to the living voice of God who is speaking through the biblical text. We must have biblically realistic thinking that

---

11. George Lindbeck, *The Nature of Doctrine: Religion and Theology in a Postliberal Age* (Philadelphia: Westminster, 1984), pp. 113-24.

does not evaluate critically but instead accommodates what the scripture is saying. We who are listening to and interpreting the Word of God can interpret it in diverse ways. This is the surplus of meaning Paul Ricoeur discusses in his hermeneutics. The authority of Scripture as the Word of God should be rehabilitated.

Solus Christus: The Uniqueness of Jesus Christ

Reformed theology has to reaffirm, against the challenges of religious pluralism, the Reformed heritage of "solus Christus." First, it should confirm its belief in Jesus of Nazareth as the unique incarnation of God. Through his virgin birth, his messianic life and powerful mission, his suffering and death on the cross, his resurrection from the dead, and his ascension, Jesus of Nazareth revealed that he was not merely a religious genius born as natural man but the Son of God who became flesh. He is the incarnate Son of God who appeared in time and space and is the only mediator between God and humans. The Christian claim of uniqueness and finality is valid not for Christianity in its institutional and cultural existence, but only for Christ. The historical shape of Jesus of Nazareth is the criterion in the light of which all Christian affirmation is judged, and by which it stands and falls.

The event of his incarnation is absolute oneness. Incarnation, as Cullmann says in his analysis of the New Testament word "Ephapax," is "once for all."[12] Hinduism says regarding divine descension or avatars that the god Vishnu appears as Rama or Krishna. In the Bhagavad Gita Krishna says to Arjuna that he often wears human forms. In Hinduism, the avatar signifies frequent rebirth. Avatars are temporary embodiments of Vishnu in humans. However, in Hinduism it is not possible that divinity really takes human form. In contrast, Jesus taught as one having authority, not like the scribes,[13] with an authority superior to Moses, and he addressed God with the most intimate term, "abba." He died for the redemption of humanity, rose again from the dead, and ascended to heaven. He is not simply a great one among spiritual leaders in the world. He is not to be compared with Alexander the Great or Napoleon. He is absolutely unique. The early church confessed concerning Jesus that he is "our Lord and Savior, Jesus Christ" (2 Peter 3:18). The confession "Kyrios Jesous" is the earliest formulation among all the Christian confessions.

Second, Reformed theology has to reaffirm Christ as the ultimate salvific

12. Oscar Cullmann, *Christ and Time* (Philadelphia: Westminster, 1962), p. 121.
13. Stephen Neill, *Crises of Belief: The Christian Dialogue with Faith and No Faith* (London: Hodder and Stoughton, 1984); *Christian Faith and Other Faiths: The Christian Dialogue with Other Religions* (Downers Grove, Ill.: InterVarsity Press, 1984), p. 286.

revelation of God. Through his presence in nature God works among other religions. However, other religious believers do not know or reject God until God's presence is revealed in Jesus Christ (Rom. 1:19-20). Here is the limit of the knowledge of God and of salvation in other religions. The risen Jesus, giving the disciples the command to do world mission, claimed to be the unique Son of God possessing the rights of heaven and earth. Jesus himself taught the parable that the farmer sows the seeds, and then lets the wheat and weeds grow together (Matt. 13:30). This speaks of the existence of other religions. That other religions and other faiths are on this earth is due to a mysterious divine providence through which God has permitted them, in order to judge the true and false religions at the end of the world. As Peter preached, everyone must kneel down before the name of Jesus who has risen from the dead, and every lip should confess that he is the savior (Acts 10:36).

Mohammed, misunderstanding the physical language of the incarnation, wrote in the Koran as follows: "Allah forbids that he should bear a son." In early Buddhism there was no God or worship. For five hundred years after the Buddha's death neither divine title nor honor was attributed to him. Only after five hundred years had passed was Buddha worshiped as God. However, in the case of Jesus of Nazareth the contemporaries of Jesus called him Lord and God. Therefore, John Hick is not persuasive when he asserts that Buddhology and Christology developed in a comparable way, incarnation being the result of the religious dedication of followers.[14]

The Human as Image of God and Total Depravity

Facing the new age movement, Reformed theology has to reaffirm its traditional views of the human being as made in the image of God and as totally depraved. Reformed tradition views the human as created after the image of God. This means that the human is not God, but rather is a creature. He is a finite, dependent being able to live only in relationship with God. The Reformed heritage does not speak of man-god but of God-man. Humanity is fallen because of the attempt at human self-deification. Humans are totally depraved, and cannot save themselves but can only be saved by the mediator, Jesus Christ. New age thought insists that the human, having the divine nature in himself, should awaken the potential God-consciousness and come into unity with the cosmic spirit. It therefore completely disregards the total depravity of humanity, and is a second revolt that searches for self-deification. The Reformed heritage has

14. John Stott, *The Contemporary Christian: Applying God's Word to Today's World* (London: InterVarsity Press, 1992), p. 308.

taught us that humans can recover the lost image of God by believing in Christ's redemptive work, and by experiencing both rebirth in Christ and justification. This is accompanied by sanctification, through which the original humanity — made after the image of God — is recovered.

Reformed Spirituality

Reformed theology must reaffirm its spiritual heritage[15] against the challenge of high technological secularism.

First, we need a spiritual awakening that will overcome secularism. The extinction of religion that Feuerbach, Marx, and Nietzsche anticipated has not occurred even in the postmodern era. The decrease of members in traditional religions is a fact. This, however, is because of the negligence of institutional religion, not because religion itself is illusionary or impotent: "The abolition of religion modern atheists proclaimed is a great illusion."[16] American futurologist Daniel Bell, confronting the cultural conflict of capitalism, says that the moral ground of secularized society will be fulfilled only when the religious consciousness is renewed.[17]

Without the ultimate reality called God, our quest for comfort will never be fulfilled. Philosophy therefore has to defer to religion because it is unable to provide comfort, as the Jewish thinker E. Levinas has argued.[18] The mystical aspect of religion should be considered anew. "There is a fundamental development to point to God in today's philosophy and cosmology."[19] Here, the Reformed belief that a religious seed is planted in humanity should be reaffirmed.

Second, we need to correct the doctrine of the cessation of charisma. A. Kuyper, B. B. Warfield, A. A. Hoekema, J. D. G. Dunn, Frederick D. Bruner, and R. Gaffin are among the theologians in the Reformed tradition that promote the doctrine of the cessation of charisma. They insist that the pouring out of the Holy Spirit has ceased and deny its continuity to the present. Such a doctrine of charismatic cessation is not only unsuitable for the life of faith of the

---

15. Howard L. Rice, *Reformed Spirituality: An Introduction for Believers* (Louisville: Westminster/John Knox Press, 1991), p. 224.

16. Hans Küng, *Existiert Gott? Antwort auf die Gottesfrage der Neuzeit* (München: Deutscher Taschenbuch Verlag, 1978), ch. C.

17. Daniel Bell, *The Cultural Contradictions of Capitalism* (New York: Basic Books, 1976).

18. Emmanuel Levinas, *Wenn Gott ins Denken einfällt. Diskurse über die Betroffenheit von Transzendenz* (Freiburg: K. Alber, 1985), p. 107. Translation of *De Dieu qui vient à l'idée*.

19. Diogenes Allen, *Christian Belief in a Postmodern World: The Full Wealth of Conviction* (Louisville: Westminster/John Knox Press, 1989), p. 3.

church; it also lacks biblical ground. Here, we can mention four theologians, Augustine, Edwards, Wesley, and Berkouwer, as well as the 1970s report of the United Presbyterian Church, all of which testify to the continuation of charisma. (1) Augustine, in *The City of God*, abandoned his earlier thesis of the cessation of charisma and testified to many cases of charismatic continuation.[20] (2) Jonathan Edwards testified to the works of the Holy Spirit that occurred in his revival movement from 1735 to 1740.[21] (3) John Wesley experienced the work of the Holy Spirit when many fellow believers fell down on the floor, touched by the Holy Spirit coming upon them on January 1, 1739, and Wesley, seven ministers, and sixty lay people prayed through the night.[22] (4) G. C. Berkouwer, in *The Providence of God*, argues that those who think miracles no longer happen surrender to determinism.[23] (5) The United Presbyterian Church reported on the charisma phenomena in 1970, saying that it was difficult to justify the old-Princeton School's view on charismatic cessation.[24]

In the experience of the Korean churches today, the phenomenon of charisma as mentioned in 1 Corinthians 12:4-11 often appears strongly in prayer meetings and is becoming a universal tendency. We need not have an abstract understanding but rather a concrete experience of the Holy Spirit according to the scriptures. However, I do not agree with the opinion of pentecostalists who view the baptism of the Holy Spirit as an experience after rebirth. The pentecostalists, in viewing baptism of the Holy Spirit as a second experience after rebirth, neglect the salvation that is completely and ultimately won in Christ. There are only two aspects of the works of the Holy Spirit: justification and sanctification. To pursue a higher salvation than justification and sanctification is to step out of the biblical-Reformed way. There is no other way to salvation than rebirth and justification.

Cultural Transformation: Christ, the Transformer of Culture

Reformed theology must reaffirm the heritage of cultural transformation in order to respond to the cyber-culture. We need to know the positive and negative

20. Augustine, *City of God*, books 17-22, in *The Fathers of the Church*, vol. 24, ed. J. Defferrai (Washington, D.C.: Catholic University of America Press, 1947), pp. 431-45.

21. Jonathan Edwards, "A Divine and Supernatural Light Immediately Imparted to the Soul by the Spirit of God, Shown to be both a Scriptural and Rational Doctrine," in *The Works of Jonathan Edwards* (New Haven: Yale University Press, 1957-), vol. 2, pp. 12-17.

22. John Wesley, *The Journal of John Wesley*, ed. Percy Livingstone Parker (Chicago: Moody Press, 1968).

23. G. C. Berkouwer, *The Providence of God* (Grand Rapids: Eerdmans, 1980), p. 225.

24. *The Work of the Holy Spirit*, Report of the United Presbyterian Church, 1970, p. 56.

functions of informationalization, and use the information properly. The Reformed church is asked to develop a cyber-theology that anticipates the problems that will arise in cyber-culture and to prepare countermeasures to solve them.

The problems of the cyber-church are as follows. First, the cyber-church can never be a spiritual church. It risks the danger that in the electronically mediated virtual world the experience of the holy will become visual and secularized. It also faces the danger that the Word of God pervading the depth of the soul will be changed into the on-screen messages of the electronically reduced multimedia. Second, the cyber-church is not a real church. It is merely a virtual church, existing only in the electronic network of the Internet. Third, the cyber-church lacks face-to-face encounter and personal fellowship. Dialogue with a partner on-screen is not the same as dialogue with someone whom one knows personally. It is a limited kind of communication that lacks personality. Violence and pornography can dominate cyberspace. Here, Jesus Christ intervenes as the savior of cyberspace. Jesus Christ does wish to carry out his salvific work through the cyber-church and Internet-mission. Cyberspace is also the forum of God's salvific event, as long as the Internet missionaries do not retreat and surrender to cyber-secularism, but consistently engage in preaching the gospel and communicating the divine message. Jesus Christ can be a transformer of cyber-culture.

The Ecumenicity of Reformed Theology

In order to claim the ecumenicity of Reformed theology I would suggest that Reformed theology reaffirm the five Reformed heritages: "the claim of universal truth," "the seed of religion," "God's sovereignty and human responsibility," "creation doctrine and ethics," and "cultural mandate."

The Claim of Universal Truth: Reformed "Postmodern" Theology

The ecumenicity of Reformed theology responds to postmodernism by affirming that the Word of God proclaims not only salvific truth but also universal truth and value. The word "postmodern" may be used in either a chronological or ideological sense. Regarding the former, Reformed theology should be a theology that responds to this historical period in which the "modern" is passing away in deference to the "postmodern." Thus "postmodern" Reformed theology, used in a chronological sense, can respond to the negative features of modernism and creatively transmit its heritage.

Reformed Christians can use the concept "postmodern" in its sense of intending to transform culture. In this sense, "postmodern" thinking can become

14

a constructive criticism of modernism, promoting a holistic point of view. Avoiding a one-sided emphasis on rationality, it can take into account feelings, emotions, and the natural environment. To the extent that the "postmodern" is a critique of the modern, Reformed "postmodern" theology affirms the value of such thinking. Postmodernism is a struggle against modern scientific, positivistic, and metaphysical thinking.

We can describe its distinctive value in four ways. First, postmodernism employs multidimensional thinking in its analysis of politics, economy, culture, and ecology. This is important since there has developed a multi-confessional, ecumenical world community.[25] A pluralism prevails, preventing society from becoming closed. This pluralism also causes religion to become public in character.

Second, postmodern thinking is important in its change of values, that is, its emphasis on ethical responsibility. This paradigm change is not the demise of values, but rather a change of fundamental values, from a science divorced from ethics into an ethically responsible science. Technology serves humankind instead of ruling over it. New values in "postmodernity" include imagination, sensibility, emotionality, warmth, tenderness, and humanity.[26] The ethics of responsibility is not a human-centered ethics. It is an ecotopian ethics focused on maintaining humankind and nature on the earth.[27] Such an ethics is similar to the responsibility of parents to children. Parental responsibility is "an archetype of all responsible ethics." It is human love planted in the mother's womb, a maternal humanity. Such an ethics is not self-assertion but self-transcendence.

Third, postmodern thought is holistic in that it has a new environmental consciousness. It points to a thinking balanced among rational, emotional, and sensitive tendencies.

Fourth is its focus on liberation, in solidarity with the isolated, the oppressed, the poor, and the underprivileged. It has sympathy with them and attempts to liberate them from unjust social structures.

The Seed of Religion: Reformed Theology Conducting a Paradoxical Unity of Exclusivism and Inclusivism

Calvin argues that God has planted a seed of religion in all people, and this may become a basis for Reformed theology to engage in dialogue with other reli-

---

25. Hans Küng, *Projekt Weltethos* (München: Piper Verlag, 1991), p. 41.

26. Küng, *Projekt Weltethos*, p. 42.

27. Hans Jonas, *Das Prinzip Verantwortung, Versuch einer Ethik für die technologische Zivilization* (Frankfurt am Main: Suhrkamp, 1984); *Technik, Medizin und Ethik, Praxis des Prinzips Verantwortung* (Frankfurt am Main: Suhrkamp, 1987).

gions. Reformed theology is inclusive in the sense that it may have an open-minded attitude toward other believers and their relative truths and may even learn from them. Within that interreligious dialogue it testifies to the uniqueness and finality of Christ. This exclusive attitude affirms that no other savior is given under heaven but Jesus Christ, as Peter witnessed in Acts 4:12. However, this exclusive attitude takes an inclusivistic stance toward other religions, since other religions also attest to the general revelation of God. They refer to the transcendent God and also make a contribution to the nourishing of piety and morality. However, general revelation does not ultimately lead to the true God because it is distorted by human corruption.

Therefore, other religions must be illumined and complemented by the gospel of Christ as the unique incarnating revealer of God and the unique redeemer for the salvation of humans, and for the knowledge of the true God. This is a transforming thinking that asserts the uniqueness of Jesus Christ while embracing other religions. It is not arrogance but a humble and true testimony and personal confession of the unique revelational event of God in Christ.

This transforming position is not compatible with the exclusivist position adopted by the dialectical theologians represented by Karl Barth, who regarded other religions as idol worship. Their position denies the general revelation of God given in the other religions, while inclusive transformationalism acknowledges the relative usefulness and values that other religions have, even though they do not bring salvation.

At the same time, the inclusive transforming position denies the continuationalist position that says other religions are also ways to salvation. This universalistic position, represented by Rahner and Tillich, confuses God's general revelation of grace with the particular revelation of salvation. They fail to distinguish the creation-related, transcendental revelation given in human consciousness, and the historical, particular revelation of salvation given in the scriptures and Jesus Christ. In contrast, inclusive transformationalism talks with the other religions, approves their existence, undertakes beneficial projects with them, and finally testifies to them about the uniqueness of Christ's revelation.

God's Sovereignty, Human Responsibility, and the Eschatological Worldview

Today's Reformed theology must reaffirm the Reformed doctrine of God's sovereignty. This means that God, as sovereign Creator of the cosmos, must not be conceived of as impersonal spirit or equated with the fatalistic forces of the cosmos. It means that this world and humans exist as creatures of a personal Creator in his sovereign providence. This world did not emanate out of the cyclical movement of the cosmic spirit, as new age thought says. God is not dependent on the blind will of the cosmos coming to awareness of itself, as process theology affirms. Both of these surrender the concept of the sovereignty of God. According to Reformed tradition, God in his sovereignty has been carrying out his providence for all time. The alienation of the cosmos was caused not by its fatalistic course but by human sin. There is no reincarnation after death but only judgment before the sovereign God. There exists no world spirit with control over humanity, as the new age movement confesses; the sovereign God is the only one with control over humankind and its destiny during this life and the next. The sovereign God assigns humans responsibility for their acts in history. Reformed Christians, being aware of our responsibility before the sovereign God, must carry out our personal decisions in this history.

Reformed theology, in the face of reincarnational thought, presents an eschatological view of history, which is not cyclical and eternally renewing, but culminates in the eschaton of Christ's return. Human and cosmic history will end with Christ's return and the divine kingdom will be established.

Creation Doctrine and Ethics: Creation Theology and Reformed Eco- and Bio-ethics

The ecumenicity of Reformed theology in response to high technological secularism is found in its doctrine and ethics of creation. Reformed Christians affirm the created order and feel a responsibility towards preserving nature. We need a new, relational understanding of ecology. According to Genesis, what is in the cosmos is not separated or isolated but connected with everything else. Feminist environmentalism says that the relation is born with and from the feminine. Humankind cares with a relational concern for the other, a concern that is heterogenic. Human beings can exist only in relationship. We should therefore have not an egocentric, but an other-oriented attitude. Humans are, in the root sense of the word, eccentric beings.

There are two kinds of ecological ethics, technocentric and ecocentric. The former suggests an optimistic future in which the environmental crisis is to be overcome by higher technological development.[28] It does not address the human moral responsibility for pollution, and does away with the biblical Creator concept. It thus supports a value-neutral view of nature. The latter insists on the equality of nature and humankind, drawing on romanticism, pantheism, and

28. David Pepper, *The Roots of Modern Environmentalism* (London: Croom Helm, 1984), ch. 2.

evolutionism, and on the subjugation of the human to nature. Its vision of the future is pessimistic,[29] characterized by the interdependence of humans and nature. It uses an Asian pantheistic view of nature in its stress on human moral duty and respect for nature as a way of solving the ecological crisis.

Jürgen Moltmann developed an ecological theology from the viewpoint of Reformed theology. He says that nature and the world are the creation of God, and that humans take responsibility from the Creator as the guardians of nature.[30] Moltmann's chief contribution is in viewing the cosmos as an open, value-laden system,[31] since it is created for the glory of God. However, Moltmann changes the Christian ecological theology into a panentheistic one. In the biblical tradition, God is in the creation but is never identified with nature or with natural processes. God interferes in natural processes through his immanent transcendence. Reformed theology needs to preach a God who acts in the creation by his providence and as a savior, without falling into the panentheistic error.

Second, we need Reformed eco- and bio-ethics. The meaning, value, and appropriate uses of new technologies are not implicit in their existence. Therefore, Reformed theology is called to develop ethical criteria for issues such as euthanasia, abortion, *in vitro* fertilization, genetic manipulation, organ transplants, and cloning.[32] It should point the way toward the peaceful use of nuclear energy. Also, we need preventive ethics to foresee the worst possibilities and to work toward the prevention of crises, as the German Catholic theologian Hans Küng has remarked.[33]

The Cultural Mandate: Christ as the Lord of Culture

Reformed theology, claiming its ecumenicity in response to the cyber-culture, should reaffirm its cultural mandate: Christ as king of culture. Christ is the key to culture (Klaas Schilder) and is therefore also the king of cyber-culture. Cyberspace is an electronic space in which Jesus Christ also rules as king. The positive function of the cyber-church and theology can be expressed in two points.

First, it provides a forum for objective, rational critique of religious mes-

---

29. Pepper, *The Roots of Modern Environmentalism*, ch. 3.

30. Jürgen Moltmann, *Gott in der Schöpfung. Oekologische Schöpfungslehre* (München: Kaiser Verlag, 1984), pp. 16-33.

31. Jürgen Moltmann, "Schöpfung als offenes System," in *Zukunft der Schöpfung* (München: Kaiser Verlag, 1977), pp. 123-39.

32. Russell Chandler, *Racing Toward 2001*, Korean translation by Yong Kil Maeng (1993), p. 82.

33. Küng, *Projekt Weltethos*, p. 35.

sages. Dialogue on the Internet is ceaselessly open toward the best, and is developing a community not ruled by particular ideologies or powers. The Internet displays the dogmatic and closed convictions of each religion, objectifies them, and opens them for public critique. It can promote dialogue between the religions by facilitating diverse messages regarding faith and social ethics, thereby providing indirect exposure to other creeds, experiences, and religions.

Second, the cyber-church and theology are the new media for mission and theology. They send out missionaries and theologians without need of a visa into the living room of the world through the information highway.

Reformed churches therefore need to make use of this medium as a great opportunity to propagate the gospel to the end of world. On one hand, they need to build local information networks for members; on the other hand they need to connect to national and international networks of mission and theology. Mission projects and theological colleges need to have a network by means of the Internet, thereby making it a new instrument for doing missions and theology. The Reformed church may confess that Christ also rules as the king of cyber-culture.

Closing Remarks

Reformed theology must reaffirm the five Reformed heritages: "sola scriptura," "solus Christus," "the human as image of God and total depravity," "Reformed spirituality," and "cultural transformation" in order to preserve its identity. On the other hand it should stake its ecumenicity through affirming: "the claim of universal truth," "the seed of religion," "God's sovereignty and human responsibility," "creation doctrine and ethics," and "cultural mandate."

This is not simply going back to the past but is rather a revitalization of Reformed roots and origins. This postmodern age is a great opportunity for the Christian faith to transmit creatively the treasures of the Reformed tradition, preparing for the upcoming era.

Reformed theology needs to develop a concrete and experiential pneumatology to enable it to explain the works of the Holy Spirit manifest throughout the world, thereby paving a way for spiritual theology in the twenty-first century. The direction of spiritual theology, inwardly, is to experience the presence of God in the rebirth of the individual and the conviction of salvation. Outwardly, it is to nourish cultural transformers who serve as stewards of God in the society, history, and cosmos in which God is acting. Reformed spirituality should not dwell on pious inwardness, but extend outwardly into all the spheres of life through which God is carrying out his providence. This is a transforming cultural theology. The direction of Reformed theology in the new century is therefore twofold: inwardly spiritual, outwardly transforming.

CHAPTER 2

Reformed Strength in Its Denominational Weakness

Eberhard Busch

Reformed Embarrassment

In ecumenical dialogue a partner is likely to declare, "Now you know what we believe, but what is distinctive about the Reformed position?" Then ensues not a little embarrassment. Some of the Reformed have an answer, to be sure. But others contradict it because they see the matter differently. Still others content themselves with this response: "For the Reformed family it is not something particular which is distinctive, but rather a sense for ecumenicity." This kind of response hardly satisfies the other party, and they ask further: "In whose name are you speaking? And how binding are ecumenical agreements for the Reformed churches?" Even greater embarrassment arises! Reformed Christians today are inclined to ask about their identity. One usually raises questions about identity when one is unsure of it. Yet this questioning should not be confused with the questioning of so many churches today about what the Christian task is in the midst of a changing world. For this latter questioning poses itself to the Reformed in a special way. Roman Catholics normally do not ask about their Catholic identity, even if they are not content with the present pope. Lutherans do not discuss their Lutheran identity, even if they are concerned about whether or not the alleged consensus with Rome in the matter of justification corresponds to the guidelines of Luther himself. Apparently it belongs to the structure of the Reformed tradition itself to question its confessional identity. Maybe one is no longer Reformed if the problem of Reformed identity is no longer an embarrassment. And perhaps clarifying the reasons for this special

Reformed problem, rather than compounding the uncertainty so prevalent to-day about the task of the churches, will give helpful orientation.

However that may be, who shall solve for the Reformed their identity problem? The Reformed do not have a visible head or an astonishing church father as the Lutherans do. Certainly, in various regions confessions are used with joy, but there is no confession that defines as a general rule what is meant by "Reformed." Nor does the sixteenth century have the same definitive importance for the Reformed as for the Lutherans. The Reformed churches have consciously avoided appealing to such authorities. This is why the Reformed family differentiated itself into Reformed, Presbyterian, and Congregationalist branches. This is why members of this family were free enough to do what is unthinkable for Lutherans: to draw up in the last fifty years new confessions — even more than were drawn up in the sixteenth century.[1] All this does not necessarily indicate confessional weakness. Rather, the contrary is true, as these new confessions demonstrate. But this means there is nevertheless a unique confessional weakness within the Reformed tradition which gives the following signal: "One does not need to belong to the Reformed faith in order to be a member of the church of Jesus Christ." Therefore in some places Reformed churches could enter into union with other denominations, with the risk that what they have brought into the union from their own tradition is downplayed. There is also another reason why uniting with Christians of other denominations is more readily done today than in earlier times. It is because the churches stand before tasks of such elemental challenge that they can only in part be dealt with from a confessional perspective. But this does not change the picture of a specific Reformed openness for relativizing one's own denomination.

Let us remember that there was a widespread movement among the German and Swiss Reformed churches at the beginning of the twentieth century which was concerned about the confessional weakness of the Reformed tradition and sought to remedy the weakness.[2] People were troubled by the question: "Where are Reformed churches and communities to be found anymore?" Then the question arose: "Why are we Reformed people necessary?" Still, one knew a way to answer this question satisfactorily, and affirmed: "A new wave of Reformed spirit" is triumphing. Parallel to the Luther-renaissance arose a Calvin-renaissance, and groups united under the title "Friends of the Reformed

---

1. Cf. Lucas Vischer, ed., *Reformiertes Zeugnis heute. Eine Sammlung neuerer Bekenntnistexte aus der reformierten Tradition* (Neukirchen-Vluyn: Neukirchener Verlag, 1988), especially p. v.

2. Cf. H. Vorländer, *Aufbruch und Krise. Ein Beitrag zur Geschichte des deutschen Reformiertentums vor dem Kirchenkampf* (Neukirchen-Vluyn: Neukirchener Verlag, 1974). The quotations are from pp. 15ff.

Confession." In 1926 a journal committed itself to the cause that "the Reformed heritage of our fathers not simply disappear, but rather come to prominence alongside the great Lutheran heritage." But what does it mean that the so-called "heritage of the fathers" dare not "simply" disappear? And curious indeed was the eagerness to be on a level with the model of the relation of the Lutherans to their heritage — the model that one thereby stood up for! At the same time one lamented "Lutheranization" as the danger against which one battled under the slogan of "Reformed interests" that had to be protected. Today we have to say that this movement possessed much of the Reformed letter, but little of the Reformed spirit. This was demonstrated in the thirties, when the German representatives of this movement, in and with their preservation of Reformed interests, allied themselves with the so-called "German Christians," instead of lifting up the Christian confession against the brown nonsense and so demonstrating the Reformed spirit. The mistake lay in the fact that they wanted to transform the structural confessional weakness into an imposing confessional strength. They did not take seriously the sentence in the Heidelberg Catechism (for whose rebirth they fought): that the church does not gather, protect, and sustain itself, but rather Christ does all this.[3] They did not put their worry about their confession into God's hand, but rather took it into their own hands and ignored these words: "Those who want to save their life will lose it, and those who lose their life for my sake and the gospel's will keep it" (Matt. 16:25). So they carried on their Christianity in order to protect its Reformed nature, to keep it "inviolate," instead of, as Reformed Christians, keeping the witness of the gospel. I would like to propose the following thesis: The confessional weakness of the Reformed apparently belongs to the distinctiveness of this confession. This weakness need not mean that damage is involved. Rather, in naming the grounds for this weakness, we come up against the characteristic profile of this confession, which basically holds true in all its many historical and geographical variations with astonishing faithfulness. This profile is the reason not only for specific Reformed dangers, but also for the lively richness and spiritual energy of the Reformed confession. I will try to develop this claim.

About the Freedom of the Reformed Confession

Granted, there has been at times among Reformed people, as among others, a denominational narrow-mindedness, a way of judging things according to criteria that officially do not exist for them. Thereby, in addition to Scripture a holy tradition became important. This tradition was cultivated by the Re-

3. Q. 54.

formed because they were used to trying to endure the present by conserving the past. There was a sense of superiority because they basically knew only themselves, and knew others only in caricatures. A variation of this confessionalism could be a striving to be distinctive. The Reformed, as the minority, wanted to try to surpass other confessions through radicalism, in order to prove their indispensability. But in general, confessionalism is less of a problem for the Reformed. There was no such fratricidal war on the Reformed side as that of the Gnesiolutherans against the followers of Melanchthon. The exclusion of the Arminians in Dordrecht was something different. And even among the orthodox Reformed, one would have to search a long time to find such pugnacious guardians of Zion as the Lutherans produced. From the beginning, the Reformed seem to have been too schooled in humanism; their churchmanship was too international and too decentralized to have the minimal presuppositions for a monolithic confessionalism. Herein is revealed something of the Reformed freedom toward their own confession. This freedom has theological reasons, the recognition of which belongs to the alpha and omega of Reformed knowledge itself. I want to mention three typical reasons.

The Unconditional Subordination of the Confession to Scripture

Reformed confessions have been accused of substantiating their statements with passages from the Bible. But what is wrong with that? After all, the confession doesn't want to proclaim a new truth in addition to Scripture. It wants to teach how to read Scripture itself, and in order to teach this it opens Scripture and asks the congregation to do the same. From this stems what distinguishes the Reformed tradition from others: the proviso, often directly appended to their confessions, of possible better understanding in the future through Scripture. The Bernese Synod of 1532 gives a classic example of this: "If something would be brought forward to us from our pastors or others, which leads us closer to Christ and which is, according to the Word of God, more conducive to general friendship and Christian love than the opinion recorded now, we are happy to accept it and do not want to block the way of the Holy Spirit."[4] For Lutherans also, the confession intends to be subordinate to Scripture, but in the sense that the confession itself makes the claim that Scripture agrees with it. From now on it is always binding, *because* it agrees with Scripture. The Reformed confession, on the other hand, claims binding character only for Scripture and for itself only *insofar* as it concurs with Scripture. The confession seeks

4. G. W. Locher, ed., *Der Berner Synodus von 1532*, vol. 1 (Neukirchen-Vluyn: Neukirchener Verlag, 1984), p. 26.

to have its agreement with Scripture examined by the mature congregation in the light of Scripture itself. This is why it adds Bible passages to its text, so that the people will look up in their Bible to see "whether it corresponds." The confession takes into account the possibility of a mistake in its own statements. It sees itself open to improvement, and even replacement. But it is not open to being changed at will. For in the confession's subordination to Scripture it is a signpost for the church, and is to be acknowledged as an ecclesial authority. Therefore a decision made by the church is open to revision only by a new decision of the church, according to the same standard to which the confession sought to comply. Moreover, Scripture is normative for the church because it is, in a way that cannot be equaled, the witness of the "once for all" speaking and acting of the God of Israel and the Father of Jesus Christ. In this conviction, the Reformed from the beginning looked askance at a method that takes this norm into the hands of the church in such a way that certain insights are identified with core passages in Scripture while the rest of the Bible comes on behind. Certainly, there are words in Scripture that have or attain in specific situations a special importance. But even Luther's saying that Scripture becomes the Word of God in "that which proclaims Christ"[5] can become questionable if it leads to a control of the church over the canon and if, in such control, parts of the canon are cleared away. To be sure, Reformed thinking seeks for the Word of God, but is convinced that it is to be found not in a willful selection of the words, but in the words, and in principle in all kinds of words in Scripture. The witness of Scripture is there for us only in the fullness of the various witnesses, which resists our manipulating grasp. These witnesses need to be seen, each in its own particular color. So the primacy of Scripture over the church is unconditional, and this gives freedom in relation to one's own confession. At the same time it becomes clear how the criterion for this freedom includes a specific Reformed concept of Scripture.

Associating One's Own Confession with the One Ecumenical Church

The words of Calvin to Bishop Cranmer are a guide: "If my help is needed, I would like to cross ten oceans in order to help keep the body of the Church from being dismembered."[6] Certainly there is "no other bond of church unity than the fact that Christ the Lord, who reconciled us to the Father, gathers us out of the dispersion into the fellowship of his body, so that through his word

5. Cf. Martin Luther, *Erlanger Ausgabe*, vol. 63, p. 157.
6. John Calvin, *Lebenswerk in seinen Briefen. Ein Auswahl von Briefen Calvins*, trans. Rudolf Schwarz (Neukirchen-Vluyn: Neukirchener Verlag, 1962), p. 596.

and spirit we grow together to one heart and soul."[7] But this bond of unity embraces more than one's own confession. From the very outset, the establishment or maintenance of some kind of special church has been far from Reformed thinking. The Reformed sought the alliance of all Christians in the church of Christ. Calvin was free enough to believe that even in the corrupted Roman church, God has miraculously kept churches, remnants of his people.[8] And against the polarization within their movement, he reminded Protestants of the blessings that God had given through both Luther and Zwingli. He added that the mistake common to both parties lay in the fact that they did not have the patience to listen to each other and then calmly to follow the truth wherever it was to be found.[9] Also typical for this mentality was the organized cooperation of Reformed with Lutheran pastors which Lasco established in the sixteenth century in the northwestern parts of Germany under the motto "reconciled difference."[10] He took the Marburg Articles of 1529, accepted by Luther and Zwingli, about which it is wrongly said that they remained insignificant, as the basis for this cooperation. The common ground in these Articles served as the solid reason for getting together, and the differences provided the task that needed to be worked on in order to progress towards mutual understanding. I also would like to mention the fact that the Heidelberg Catechism was intended as a document of union in order to reconcile divided confessional groups in the church. And if the interpretation is right that, as a whole, it has a trinitarian structure,[11] it would by this alignment to the comprehensive action of the trinitarian God stand above the Protestant danger of reducing theology to soteriology, and would more than ever be a document of true ecumenical thinking. I call to mind also the fact that the famous Confessio Helvetica of 1566 was published "in order to seek peace and concord with the foreign Churches."[12] And similarly, in 1981 the Reformed Church of Great Britain proclaimed its confession in the one, holy,

---

7. John Calvin, *Um Gottes Ehre, Vier kleinere Schriften Calvins,* trans. and ed. Matthias Simon (München: Kaiser Verlag, 1924), p. 92.

8. John Calvin, *Institutes of the Christian Religion,* trans. Ford Lewis Battles and ed. John T. McNeill (Philadelphia: Westminster, 1960), 4.2.12.

9. John Calvin, *Kleiner Abendmahlstraktat, Studienausgabe,* vols. 1 and 2 (Neukirchen-Vluyn: Neukirchener Verlag, 1994), p. 491.

10. Cf. Jan Weerda, *Nach Gottes Wort reformierte Kirche. Beitrag zu ihrer Geschichte und ihrem Recht* (München: Kaiser Verlag, 1964), p. 88.

11. Walter Herrenbrück, "Der trinitätstheologische Ansatz des Heidelberger Katechismus," in *Warum wirst du ein Christ genannt? Vorträge und Aufsätze zum Heidelberger Katechismus im Jubiläumsjahr 1963,* ed. Walter Herrenbrück and Udo Smidt (Neukirchen-Vluyn: Neukirchener Verlag, 1965), pp. 48-66.

12. Heinrich Bullinger, *Das Zweite Helvetische Bekenntnis. Confessio Helvetica Posterior,* ed. Walter Hildebrandt (Zürich: Zwingli Verlag, 1966), p. 12.

catholic and apostolic church.[13] In brief, in their confessions the Reformed confess not their denominational distinctiveness, but rather, in their concrete location and with their own understanding, they confess a universal church. They consider themselves as part of that church, without making themselves coincident with it, much less taking over other churches. In this manner a church thinks in spiritual freedom with regard to its own confession. It does not confess its being Reformed, but rather confesses itself, as Reformed, to the one church of Christ.

Placing One's Own Confession within the Pilgrimage of God's People

The church, and much less a confession, is not the end of the ways of God. In every form, from that testified to in the Bible onward, the church is only on the way toward the goal God brings about — the fulfillment of the appearing of the kingdom of God. Calvin says, "Since we have accepted the witness of the gospel about God's free grace, we wait until God shows openly what is still hidden in hope."[14] The church knows toward whom it goes. The coming judge is the reconciler who has already come. Therefore, as the Heidelberg Catechism says, I may go to meet him, through all affliction and persecution, with head held high.[15] The church goes toward the visible emergence of the Lordship of Christ which has already begun in his ascension. But the church is only going toward this. Therefore it exists in pilgrimage, neither fleeing from nor obsessed with this world. It lives in pilgrimage, suffering, struggling, sighing, and thirsting "until we some day will be gathered into your heavenly Kingdom and receive the inheritance which is promised and won through Christ our Lord," as Calvin prayed in his last lecture.[16] And meanwhile the church has every reason to voice the petition of the Heidelberg Catechism: "Destroy the works of the devil and all power which rises up against you, and all machinations against your holy Word, until the fulfillment of your Kingdom comes, in which you will be all in all."[17] This attitude of being underway (and not a general relativism!) explains anew the free association of the Reformed with their confessions. They can deem a confession from the six-

13. Following Lukas Vischer in *Reformiertes Zeugnis heute*, p. 290.

14. Calvin, *Institutes* 3.2.41-43.

15. *The Heidelberg Catechism*, q. 52; cf. E. F. K. Müller, *Die Bekenntnisschriften der reformierten Kirche in authentischen texten mit Geschichtlicher Einleitung und Registrar* (Leipzig: A. Deichert, 1903), pp. 248-53.

16. *Johannes Calvins Auslegung des Propheten Ezechiel*, trans. Ernst Koch (Neukirchen: Buchhandlung des Erziehungsvereins, 1938), p. 348.

17. *The Heidelberg Catechism*, q. 52 and 123.

teenth century useful in worship and congregational development. But they do not have to. They may also without difficulty add new confessions to the old, such as the Barmen Declaration or statements on Israel, and can hold themselves open for further confessions. They are flexible because the confessions are not holy relics. They are articles for the use of the congregation on its way. They are directed toward a current confessing by the congregation. The purpose is not to *have* a confession, but to *confess* in the challenges of daily life. Therefore, in the journey of the people of God, what the forebears said is not something to be merely repeated. Although their decisive insights remain decisive for us, nevertheless new questions can be asked to which new answers must be given. New issues can develop, to which one must respond by either confessing or denying Christ. The Reformed tradition reckons with the Holy Spirit, who leads us into all truth. The Holy Spirit will instruct us again and again, inciting us to ask for what is agreeable to the will of God here and now. The Holy Spirit moves us to tackle what is presently necessary, and so to be on the way toward that which is more than all confessions — that great multitude which no one can number, of all nations, peoples, and tongues gathered around the throne of the Lamb (Rev. 7:9). This means once again a freedom with regard to one's own church and denomination. At the same time we see in this freedom the shaping of this church by waiting and wandering toward the coming kingdom of God.

About the Gratitude of the Reformed Confession

Where such freedom is lacking, *confessionalism* threatens. But there is another danger which is far more of a temptation for the Reformed: *liberalism*. In this case they forget that their confessional weakness has spiritual reasons, and that in this weakness they nevertheless are a confession. Then they gamble away the talent entrusted to them — of "a Church reformed according to the Word of God" — in favor of a dish of lentils, in favor of advantages that appear "Reformed," but can be had without the Word of God. Then they believe, claiming the famous "ecclesia reformata semper reformanda," that they are Reformed just because they do so much that is different from the Reformers, instead of learning with them to return ever and again to the source of faith, love, and hope. Then they store the "Reformed heritage" in a museum, which is visited sometimes with reverence, but usually is not needed. They do not take seriously the discovery that the forebears made listening to the Scripture, with which they wrestled, suffered, and struggled. Then they imagine that God is a God of the dead, and that therefore the word of their predecessors today is simply antiquated. Thus arises unspiritual arbitrariness, the inclination to make an exception for ourselves — for instance, in light of the extraordinary times in which we believe we are living — whereas for others the rule plainly applies. This is Reformed liberalism. It comes from a kind of ingratitude toward one's own confession. Gratitude is first of all the concept of the obedience in which God on the basis of his mercy wants to bind us to himself. Without this bond, there is no spiritual freedom. There is a corresponding gratitude to people, especially to those who were called as teachers of the church. In thankfulness toward them we show our preparedness to let ourselves be bound, like them and through them, to God's claim on us. And while gratitude is an action that can only be done willingly and gladly, it is an action that we should do. It has to do with our respect for ecclesial authority, which is not to be confused with Scripture, but which has, as authority under the Word of God, its own honor. It has to do with our obedience in relation to our spiritual parents. Let us hear in this context the explanation of the fifth commandment in the Heidelberg Catechism: I have to pay to my ancestors all honor, love, and loyalty and to accept all good doctrine and criticism with proper obedience and to be patient with their defects and mistakes, since it is God's will to govern us by their hand![18]

Despite their "defects and mistakes," Reformed Christians have a right to believe that they are not descended from bad parents. We honor in them especially an understanding in which they strongly emphasized our being bound to God. Reformed people should want this understanding to shine forth and not be extinguished. This understanding can be described, with a grain of salt, in the following words of Alexander Schweizer: The Lutherans preferred to stress the pure grace of God in an anti-judaistic opposition against legalistic works-righteousness. The Reformed preferred to confess the sovereignty of God in an anti-paganistic opposition against heathenism, and especially against secularization in Christianity itself.[19] To be sure, the Reformed also praise the God of grace, rejecting all contempt of grace, but they do not believe that what God expects of us is taken care of simply by a "No" to works-righteousness. Nor do they let themselves be pressured into anti-Judaism (the abusive term from the Lutheran side, "Calvinus judaizans"[20] doesn't depress us!). In fact, this is Reformed understanding: God's free grace calls us out of "heathenism" and into his congregation, in order to live under the head, Jesus Christ, no longer in conformity with a godless and inhuman world, but in the service of God in the world and in forming the conditions for life together. From this, three typical

18. *The Heidelberg Catechism*, q. 104.

19. A. Schweizer, *Die Christliche Glaubenslehre nach protestantischen Grundsätzen*, vol. 1 (Leipzig: S. Hirzel, 1863), p. 8.

20. Aegidius Hunnius, *Calvinus Judaizans*, 1595.

elements of Reformed confession can be developed. Naturally they correspond to the three aspects named in the previous section.[21]

One God Alone

The irrevocable weight of the first commandment, according to which the God of Israel, the Father of Jesus Christ, wills that we should have no other gods beside him is radicalized by Jesus in Matthew 6:24: "You cannot serve God and mammon." God necessarily precedes everything else, otherwise everything else will go wrong. Therefore all true knowledge of God is born out of obedience.[22] At this point anti-paganism has to prove itself. Sometimes heathens fight against claims of absoluteness and try to relativize them. They do not recognize that in the first commandment it is not human beings that are laying claims on other persons, but *God* claims his people totally for *himself* so that others may not rule us; we have God to obey. God's claim on us exposes as the heathens' problem that they are isolated from God, attempting to make themselves absolute. The God of the first commandment frees them from the rule of the other gods, from the tyrannies of the overbearing powers. How could humans be able to free themselves from these things? They are in fact their own products, made in their *fabrica idolorum*,[23] products of human self-absolutizing.[24] In their isolation from God they create absolute matters: that means literally matters detached from God. While humans grasp first, their own products begin to grasp them in return. They fascinate, captivate, and spellbind them, and finally the producers fall to the knees of their products, as it is shown in Isaiah 44. They are unable to free themselves from the sphere of influence of those powers. Only God is able to do that, by establishing the difference between himself and the other gods. In this work he provides a twilight of the gods who rule in a wrong world below a wrong heaven. God differs from them in this: the people do not make their god; rather, God makes them his own people. God is not the idolized creation of humans. God is the creator of those who are his creatures alone. By making this difference, God frees humans from the grip of the arro-

---

21. It should be clear: in the following text is not intended a presentation of the whole Reformed doctrine nor a description of the thoughts, in which the Reformed agree with the Lutherans — i.e., in the question of *sola gratia* and *sola fide*. But it points to the fundamental perspectives in which they are thinking and in which they accentuate also *sola gratia* and *sola fide*. The intent is to characterize the specific profile of Reformed thought. Without naming it, it would be not possible to speak of a Reformed profile.

22. Calvin, *Institutes* 1.6.2.

23. Calvin, *Institutes* 1.11.8.

24. Cf. *The Heidelberg Catechism*, q. 95.

gant powers. But the first commandment aims first at the conversion of the heathen *within* Christianity[25] — that is, those who want to gain control of God. This emphasis on the first commandment stamped Reformed thinking with an unwillingness to reduce divine truth to only *one* concept. Reformed thought does not, for instance, speak of justification without also speaking of sanctification. It does not speak of faith without also mentioning hope. It does not say that God is gracious without also speaking of his righteousness or justice. It also does not say that God became human without adding that God remains God and human remains human. Luther insists that God has bound himself, whereas Calvin keeps watch that humans cannot bind God to themselves. All that is said out of respect for the mystery and the freedom of the living God who binds himself to the human being. It is not about some abstract difference between the infinite and the finite. It is about the God of the first commandment who is the God of his covenant. This God is not an empty One beyond history. This God exists in relations, beginning within himself. Therefore this God is able to do what he does, to bind himself in his freedom within a concrete history to a certain human people, and to act, to walk, and to suffer in and with it, to deal with it in justice and grace, so that it may be a free people committed to him, so that he finally may have mercy on all. In Christ, God does not make another covenant beyond his covenant with Israel, but fulfills his one covenant of grace with reconciliation — in such a complete manner that in believing in Christ even heathen people are allowed to join it. Therefore we can say with Calvin: "He arranges everything according to His endless goodness so that nothing serves to glorify Him, which does not also at the same time work toward our salvation."[26] Yes, "where this God is honored, humanity is cared for."[27] Thus the Reformed parents taught us that we are free only in being bound to this God.

God's Claim on Our Whole Life

This is a second aspect of anti-paganism. Certainly, God's claim on us is not to be separated from his pure grace, but likewise his mercy on us is not to be separated from his claim on us. God's claim on us in his law is given to us as a signpost on the path to the coming kingdom of God. It is given to us in order to

---

25. Franz Rosenzweig, *Der Stern der Erlösung* (Frankfurt am Main: Suhrkamp, 1993), p. 317.

26. Calvin, *Um Gottes Ehre*, p. 140.

27. I quote according to a notice in Karl Barth's diary: "Ubi cognoscitur Deus, etiam colitur humanitas (Calvin)."

make us rely in this world on the just and gracious work of God and on his will, perceptible in it, and in order to guard us against the danger of conforming ourselves to the rules of a world estranged from God. Christians must not have less joy in the Torah of God than the Jews. According to Calvin the core of God's law is the one healing and authoritative principle: "Nostri non sumus, rursum, Dei sumus."[28] In a similar way, the Heidelberg Catechism takes it to be the central message of the gospel, that with my body and soul, living or dying, I belong neither to the arbitrary powers nor to myself, but to Christ, because in commitment to him I am connected with my liberator, who with his body and soul, in his life and death gave himself for me and the others. Not only all comfort and all forgiveness lie in belonging to God, but also all commandments, which bind us to God's will in thankfulness for his work.[29] Therefore gospel and law, though they are to be distinguished (otherwise God's pure grace and his gracious law would become a graceless demand) are, however, not to be separated. In contrast to the misuse of the law for human self-justification, God maintains and restores its good purpose. Reformed Christians should not engage in the Lutheran play with a *tertius usus legis*. Calvin's sentence is enough: that we have to do here with an *usus praecipuus*, the true sense of God's law.[30] It consists in the fact that God frees his people in all its members, in order that they obediently honor their redeemer in joyous willingness.[31] At the same time, divine and human commandments do not stand in simple opposition to one another (since the one who loves God's commandment also honors human rights). They are, however, to be differentiated. The Heidelberg Catechism says that good deeds are only those which are done in true faith according to the law of God and for his honor, and not those that are rooted in human laws.[32] If both God's law and human law are subsumed under the concept "law" (as in a certain Lutheran tradition), the outward use of the law of God would consist in complying with civil law. To raise an objection to it in the name of God would be nearly impossible. That leads to a splitting of life: faith for the heart, while the outward life is to be obedient to the currently reigning order of the world. The Reformed distinction between God's law and human law opposes such a splitting. We must always and everywhere obey God rather than humans. Therefore we are not simply to conform to and compromise with civil life and its laws. We are to join in the formation of life and human laws so that, in accordance with the law of God, a place for worship and for the humane practice of

---

28. Calvin, *Institutes* 3.7.1.
29. *The Heidelberg Catechism*, q. 1, 37, and 86.
30. Calvin, *Institutes* 2.7.12.
31. Calvin, *Institutes* 2.8.15.
32. *The Heidelberg Catechism*, q. 91.

justice and mercy, of public welfare and freedom, might be ensured. Therefore the classic measuring rod for the Reformed in determining whether the law of God rules the life of society, is the well-being of the weak, such as John Knox said in his time: "In the name of the eternal God and of His son Christ Jesus have respect to your poor brethren. They have been so oppressed that their living has been dolorous and bitter. Ye must have compassion upon your brethren."[33] In this way the Reformed tradition stresses that the Christian faith is inseparable from its visible witness to our belonging to God and to his Christ.

The Communal Form of the Christian Life under the One Head

According to Reformed understanding, to be a Christian means to be a member of a congregation. A Christian is a person who does not just have religious opinions, but the discipline of a life together with other believers. This also has an anti-paganist aspect. For this congregation exists only because the Son of God elects and calls them out of the entire human race.[34] Christ transfers them out of their natural surroundings into a new context. That is God's work and not the result of a sociability, rooted in the urge of like-minded individuals. But God's work is this: to transplant humans into the visible space and company of other Christians and to add them to the one people of God. And thus he is the real office-bearer, who gathers, protects, and keeps this congregation. Since he himself provides for it by the Holy Spirit and therefore needs no earthly substitutes, all members of it are sisters and brothers. The original form of church is, hence, the congregational assembly, living from the promise that here the Lord in the Holy Spirit will speak and work, so that its members will become listeners to and doers of his word, who invoke and confess him. We might well apply the following quote to the assembly: think globally but act locally. Reformed thinking is broad, ecumenical, but at the same time it is convinced that the one, holy church always is found first in the visible, concrete congregation. Therefore, Reformed thinking — and thus the Reformed contribution to the ecumenical movement — is infected by mistrust against command-centers that establish themselves above the congregational level, which then treat the congregation as a mere branch and remove from it a mature sense of responsibility and co-determination. All human leadership on the congregational level rather is derived from the actual congregation in question, and all national or international church structures are confederations of local congregations and not some kind of umbrella organization. This is the anti-hierarchical–demo-

---

33. Following a text written in the former home of Knox in Edinburgh.
34. *The Heidelberg Catechism*, q. 54.

cratic element in the Reformed understanding of the congregation. Because Christ mended the breach in the relation to God and at the same time to our human neighbors,[35] therefore God joins us in Christ together with him, in a way that is also a joining together on the horizontal level. *All* those who come in contact with him are thereby made responsible to seek contact with one another actively. Thus what the Heidelberg Catechism declares may happen in the shaping of the congregation and its missional-diaconal sending into the surrounding society: "in the congregation each is to make use of his or her gifts willingly and with joy for the well-being and salvation of the other."[36] I believe that today it is necessary to overcome the fruitless situation of an active clergy and a passive laity, in order that the whole community may be shaped as the abode in which all have and develop the gifts of grace given to them. Only then will we rightly see and take seriously the present situation of the Christian community in relation to the rest of society. It is the situation in which the whole community in all its members has the promise to be what Jesus said of it: the salt of the earth (Matt. 5:13). This element in the Reformed understanding of the church could prove to be fruitful, especially today.

35. *The Heidelberg Catechism*, q. 4 and 5.
36. *The Heidelberg Catechism*, q. 55.

CHAPTER 3

Reformed Theology — Past and Future

Jan Rohls

When making a statement concerning the future of Reformed theology, one must look to the past. And yet, such a look will reveal that it is very difficult to speak of *the* Reformed theology at all. Rather, Reformed theology appears to be not one, but rather a plurality of different theological positions. It is much easier to define what is meant by "Roman Catholic" or "Lutheran" than what is meant by "Reformed." The Reformed tradition has no institution defined by infallibility and issuing dogmas binding the teaching of the church. Yet such a characteristic defines other Protestant churches along with the Reformed. But there exists a striking difference between the Reformed and Lutheran churches, insofar as the Reformed do not possess a common confession similar to the *Confessio Augustana*. Additionally, Lutheranism is mainly a German phenomenon. The Lutheran Reformation began in Germany, and Lutheran theology was mainly shaped by German theologians during the confessional era. By contrast, Reformed theology, even in its beginnings, was not limited to the background of German culture. It was international, formed not only by Germans (in Germany, the Reformed churches played only a minor role), but also by Swiss, French, Dutch, English, and Scottish theologians. Finally, a third reason makes it difficult to speak of *the* Reformed theology — that is its history. When one compares the theology of Beza with the theology of a nineteenth-century theologian like Schleiermacher or Biedermann, one finds little in common between them. And despite Barth's break with liberal theology (starting with the Enlightenment and best represented by Schleiermacher) and his return to Reformation theology and Reformed orthodoxy, Barth's own theology is by no means a pure restoration of the latter. Only by taking into account the whole history of Reformed theology from Zwingli onwards does one get to know its

34

full character. But in this case, *the* Reformed theology dissolves into a plurality of highly different theological positions all belonging to the same family.

Reformed Confession and Pluralism

As mentioned before, one characteristic of Reformed Protestantism is its lack of a common confession. There is no equivalent to the status of the Augsburg Confession as the common confessional basis of all Lutheran churches. This fact is not without consequences. Because such a common confession was missing, Reformed Protestantism never struggled over the proper interpretation of such a confession. Early Lutheranism, on the other hand, is marked by quarrels over the adequate interpretation of the Augsburg Confession, which reached their end with the Formula of Concord. Despite the fact that this allegedly true interpretation of the Augsburg Confession was not accepted by all Lutheran churches, it remains definitive for Lutheranism, insofar as no new confession has been formulated since. Such a definitive end of the production of confessions does not exist in Reformed Protestantism. And so, there is no common confessional norm of Reformed theology. While it is true that some tried to publish a collection of Reformed confessions and harmonize them at the beginning of the orthodox era, such collections were accepted only by a very small number of Reformed churches, and even where this was the case, the acceptance did not last long. In fact, the collections were more or less private in character and cannot be compared with the official collection of Lutheran confessions in the Book of Concord. They were, rather, a reaction to the sharp line between Lutheran and Reformed churches drawn by the Formula of Concord. Because the Lutheran churches defined themselves by such a confession, the Reformed desired to do the same.

In speaking of the confessional pluralism of Reformed Protestantism, such pluralism was local and temporal. In the sixteenth and seventeenth centuries, various confessions were accepted in various territories at various times. A confession once accepted might later be put aside. But this outward pluralism was linked with an inward pluralism. For the confessions that differ as to time and space also differ as to their theology. They mirror the theology of their authors. The theology of Zwingli and Bullinger (Zurich), for example, is quite different from Calvin and Beza's (Geneva). The same holds true for other cases. The theology of Ursinus and Olevianus differs from that of Gomarus, and thus explains the difference between the Heidelberg Catechism and the Canons of Dort. Such a strong pluralism is alien to the Lutheran confessions.

The theological differences between the diverse confessions also explain why it is so difficult to find a material principle of Reformed Protestantism, al-

35

though it was not until the nineteenth century that such a principle was sought. Early in that century, questions arose concerning the underlying principles of Protestantism in general, and it was not very long before the question was raised whether such a material principle existed that distinguished Reformed Protestantism from Lutheranism. That principle, central to Calvin and Beza and the main subject of the Canons of Dort, was the doctrine of predestination. Alexander Schweizer, the Zurich theologian and pupil of Schleiermacher, identified it with Schleiermacher's assertion that total dependence was the essence of religion. The core of Reformed doctrine is that God is the only cause, whose aim is to reveal his glory. Therefore, the aim of mankind can be nothing but glorifying God, and thus gaining eternal salvation. The Reformed doctrine of predestination for Schweizer is identical with Schleiermacher's doctrine of total dependence.

But regarding the doctrine of predestination as the material principle of Reformed Protestantism brings enormous problems. The Heidelberg Catechism, a central confession of the Reformed churches, does not even mention predestination. And moving beyond the period of Reformation and orthodoxy, it becomes obvious that this alleged material principle is aggressively attacked. It totally loses the central position that it held in various Reformed churches and their corresponding confessions. Schweizer explains that the doctrine of predestination in its orthodox form can no longer be regarded as an adequate expression of faith. He does not deny that the sinner totally depends for his salvation on the grace offered by Christ. But, like Schleiermacher, he rejects the dualism of the old Calvinistic and orthodox doctrine of salvation and connects the doctrine of grace with the teaching of the *apokatastasis,* the salvation not of a part of mankind only, but of all men. If one regards the doctrine of predestination as the material principle of Protestantism, it must be recognized that it lost that function in the turn from the old Reformed Protestantism to the new one. Even Barth was not neo-orthodox in the sense that he simply restored the orthodox doctrine of double predestination. Rather, he presupposes the transformation of the doctrine of predestination inaugurated by Schleiermacher. This transformation from the old to the new Reformed Protestantism is reflected by the development of the Reformed confessions. Thus the old Calvinistic doctrine of predestination contained in the Westminster Confession was abandoned by the Cumberland Presbyterian Confession of 1829 and by the Declaratory Statement of 1903. In looking at the new Reformed confessions of this century, the doctrine of predestination no longer plays any role at all. If it had ever been the material principle of Reformed Protestantism, one would have to say that Reformed Protestantism has lost its essence and identity.

In the 1920s, when the Reformed Alliance of Churches asked whether a common Reformed confession was both desirable and possible, Karl Barth denied it. To him, a characteristic mark of Reformed confessions was their tempo-ral and spatial relativity. A Reformed confession is the answer of a local Chris-tian community at a certain time to the self-revelation of God in Jesus Christ. Barth is quite right in stressing the relativity of the Reformed confessions. But to me, he goes wrong when he declares that they explicate nothing but God's self-revelation in Jesus Christ. Whereas the relativity of Reformed confessions is a historical fact, their restriction to the revelation in Christ is part of Barth's own theological program. Barth maintains that Jesus Christ is the sole revela-tion, or the only word of God — with no other revelation, whether in nature or history, existing beside him. Barth developed this program against what he re-garded as the tendency underlying all modern theological systems since the En-lightenment (including Reformed theology). It is the new Protestant or, to put it in a more modern way, revisionist theology with Schleiermacher as hero that he sharply criticizes. As early as 1925, he regarded a new confessional statement as necessary in order to condemn what he called a new Protestant heresy. Later, Barth interpreted the first thesis of the Barmen Declaration as such a statement. For there is no revelation besides Jesus Christ, and therefore natural theology is denied, which to Barth underlies all theological systems of new Protestantism. All of Protestant theology from pietism and Enlightenment onwards presup-poses that God reveals himself in ways besides Jesus Christ. Schleiermacher es-pecially regarded religion as a universal revelation. Barth knew, of course, that the early Protestant confessions, whether Lutheran or Reformed, did not con-tain a condemnation of natural theology. But this in his eyes was a failure of those confessional statements that were otherwise so much praised by him.

As I said, Barth interpreted the Barmen Declaration as a condemnation of the whole tradition of new Protestantism, including the Reformed version of new Protestantism with Schleiermacher as its main figure. For myself, I do not accept such a condemnation. First, it implies that Barth's own theological posi-tion is correct as regards the exclusivity of God's revelation in Christ. Second, it contradicts the old confessional statements of the Reformed Church. I do not think that good Reformed theology has to be nothing but an explication of the old Reformed confessions. The doctrine of a general revelation of God, which forms the basis of natural theology, makes good sense and has a biblical foun-dation as well. It is quite obvious that it is part of the old Reformed confessions. In his Geneva Catechism, Calvin declares that the world is a mirror through which we can see God. The *Confessio Gallicana* declares that God reveals him-self through his works, that is, through the creation and conservation of the world. Because God reveals himself in the world, we are able to get natural knowledge of God through that world. The *Confessio Belgica* quite clearly thinks of the created world as a book besides the written book, the Bible. It is the natural light of reason, given to man by God when he created him, which enables us to read this book and detect the goodness, wisdom, and power of God in this creation.

But there is not only a general revelation of God in the outer world, for God reveals himself also within us. He has inscribed his own law, identical with the natural law, on our hearts and souls as the *Confessio Helvetica Posterior* remarks. Even such a document of rigid Reformed orthodoxy as the Canons of Dort declares that after Adam's fall, there remained a natural light within man by which we gain some knowledge of God and his law. So evidently, Barth's thesis that there is only one revelation of God, namely his revelation in Jesus Christ, contradicts the whole tradition of old Reformed confessions. It also lacks biblical foundation. When the *Confessio Belgica* speaks of the knowledge of God, it quotes Romans 1:20, the *locus classicus* of natural theology. If we take up this line of thought again, this would also be a rehabilitation of the new Protestant tradition of Reformed theology. It is time to free Reformed theology from the rule of Barthianism and to discover again the richness and plurality of the Reformed tradition, to which not only Barth and his followers belong, but Schleiermacher, Schweizer, Biedermann, Brunner, and the Swiss neoliberals as well.

Reformed Pluralism and Ecumenicity

What would be the ecumenical effect of stressing the plurality and diversity of the Reformed tradition? I think that the acceptance of such plurality and diversity is just the task of ecumenical theology. Ecumenicity cannot mean the total unity of doctrine, but it does mean the acceptance of different confessional and theological traditions as legitimate expressions of Christian faith. It is not very helpful for ecumenical discourse to create new confessional differences rather than reducing them. Obviously, the condemnation of natural theology by the Barmen Declaration created such a confessional difference. The same holds true of the role played by Barth's doctrine of the kingship of Christ. This doctrine is closely linked with Barth's thoughts on the relation of law and gospel. As pointed out, the old Reformed confessions spoke of the capacity of our natural reason to get knowledge not only of God but also of his will, which was identified with the natural law. Because the natural knowledge of God precedes the revealed knowledge of God, the law precedes the gospel. Law is known by natural reason, while the gospel is known only by special revelation. For Barth, there is nothing like a natural knowledge of God, so there is no natural knowledge of his will (that is, of the law). The whole notion of natural law is discarded. Neither natural theology nor natural law exists. Since God's will cannot be known apart from God's revelation in Jesus Christ, Jesus Christ is not only the gospel but also the law. So the law no longer precedes the gospel, but instead is regarded as its form.

For the old Reformed theology, the doctrine of natural law was closely connected with the understanding of state and government. Natural law was regarded as the basis of state and government, because its knowledge was assumed to be common to all reasonable persons. There was no confessional difference between Lutherans and Reformed in this regard. But if one changes the relation between law and gospel, as Barth does, one also gets a different view of the basis of the state. As the law is the form of the gospel, so the state is related not to natural law, which does not exist, but to the kingship of Christ. After the Second World War, one could get the impression that this was genuine Reformed doctrine, where in fact it was the private theological opinion of Barth. This is clearly shown by the discussion concerning the Concord of Leuenberg. Here the difference between the doctrine of the two kingdoms of God and the doctrine of the kingship of Christ is listed among the confessional differences between Lutherans and Reformed. But this is obviously not true. The only confessional differences between both Protestant denominations concern predestination, Christology, and the Lord's Supper. As in the case of Barth's condemnation of natural theology, it is not very helpful to give private theological opinions the status of confessional doctrines. Instead of multiplying the number of confessional differences by creating new confessions, it would be better to reduce the number of confessional statements in order to reduce the confessional differences.

As stated earlier, I regard this pluralism as an advantage of the Reformed tradition. Because the Reformed tradition is so manifold, it should be easier for Reformed churches to accept confessional pluralism in general, over against churches with a common doctrinal basis. It is a sign of the richness of the Reformed tradition that to it belong not only the theological systems of Calvin and Beza, but also the approaches of Zwingli and Lasco, who were deeply influenced by the humanism of Erasmus. Besides the doctrine of double predestination exists the doctrine of covenant. Beside Gomarus stands Arminius. They all form the one Reformed tradition.

It is true, of course, that those different traditions fought against each other in the past. Calvin attacked Zwingli and Bullinger's purely symbolic understanding of the Lord's Supper, and the Synod of Dort condemned Arminian teaching. But I find it strange to continue such condemnations in the twentieth century. And obviously, this is the case when, for example, Barth condemns natural theology and the whole tradition of Reformed new Protestantism.

Instead, one should realize that it has always been the merit of Reformed theology to look for a union between the Reformed churches and other traditions. The Reformed even of the old days were looking for the unity of the church. Surely, in the beginning the Reformed within the Holy Roman Empire intended a split within Protestantism. Territories that had been Lutheran suddenly became Reformed during the wave of what some have called a second reformation. It was the beginning of a process of confessional differentiation within Protestantism itself. But one must also take into account on the other hand that the Reformed were avidly interested in a union with the Protestant groups and even a union with the Roman church. Zwingli never wanted a break with Wittenberg, and Bucer's efforts concerning the eucharist finally led to the Concord of Wittenberg. Calvin too always tried to keep in touch with Melanchthon, for he had the international union of Protestantism in mind. It was Heidelberg, then, which became the center of the irenical efforts to unify the different branches of Protestantism in Europe. And it was in Heidelberg where Junius had the idea that such a union not only between Lutherans and Reformed, but also between all Christians, might be possible by returning to some fundamental articles. Just because they were convinced that they both held the fundamental articles of Christian faith, the French Reformed invited the Lutherans to the Lord's Supper. For them, there existed a unity of the church between Lutherans and Reformed. This conviction was also shared by the Prussian rulers when they initiated ecumenical conferences inviting the different Protestant parties. And it was in Prussia where the union of Lutheran and Reformed churches was finally established. From his Reformed background, it was quite natural that Schleiermacher welcomed this union. The whole idea of a union of Protestant churches may be regarded as genuinely Reformed, and the Concord of Leuenberg is nothing but the final result of the Reformed efforts to establish such a union, characterized by confessional pluralism and agreement on the fundamentals of the Christian faith. This is still a fruitful concept of church unity for ecumenical talks between the Reformed and other Protestant or non-Protestant churches.

Ecumenical talks are not restricted to Christian churches, but they include talks with non-Christian religions. For a Reformed theology like Barth's, it is rather difficult to begin such a dialogue, because it presupposes that there is no other revelation of God than that in Jesus Christ. However, if we start with the notion of a common natural knowledge of God, we are able to regard different relations as expressions of such knowledge. In this case it is, of course, easier to enter an interreligious dialogue. It is indeed the conviction of the old Reformed theology as represented by Calvin, that everyone has a certain *semen religionis*. No person is totally without any religion or knowledge of God. Of course, Calvin and his followers were by no means interested in interreligious studies, nor were they engaged in the science and history of religion. But nevertheless, an interest in both could only grow where one accepted as true that mankind as such is religious.

It is no wonder that the subject of religion as such and the history of religion became important to Schleiermacher, coming from a Reformed background. Even his own definition of the essence of religion reflects his Reformed background. To define religion as the consciousness of total dependence implies a certain concept of God, for God is conceived here as that causality upon which everything depends.

Obviously, this is a concept of God developed by Reformed philosophers and theologians who, like Clauberg and Wittich, adopted Cartesian philosophy and were in a way forerunners of Spinoza. Schleiermacher's definition of religion as feeling became very important later for the psychology of religion. But for interreligious dialogue, his idea that religion only exists as different positive religions is helpful. This idea forms the basis of comparative religious studies in the philosophy of German idealism and later in religious science. Reformed theologians such as Tiele in the Netherlands and Reville in France belong to the founding fathers of religious science in the nineteenth century. Interreligious dialogue implies a comparison between the different religions that became possible because Christianity was regarded as one religion among many. I would prefer such a view to the Barthian approach, which begins with the premise that Jesus Christ is the sole revelation of God, and religion as such is sin. This does not mean that one necessarily ends up with a pluralistic theory of religion like Hick's. But it would be the task of Reformed theology to show by arguments in what sense Christianity can be regarded as the highest form of religion. Thus, for the present interreligious dialogue, Schleiermacher's start from a definition of religion and a comparison between the different religions seems to be very promising.

Reformed Theology, Metaphysics, and Ethics

I have shown what the consequences for ecumenical dialogue are when Reformed theology discovers the plurality and richness of its own tradition, for then it becomes obvious that it is the liberal part of this tradition that seems to be helpful for ecumenical and interreligious dialogue. I now want to mention two further aspects of this openness, the first concerning the relation between theology and metaphysics and the second concerning the relation between theology and ethics.

As regards the first topic, one can realize that even during the period of Reformation and orthodoxy, the Lutheran side accused the Reformed of an excessive use of reason. At the time, the Lutherans had in mind the Reformed argument of the doctrines of the Lord's Supper and Christology. The Reformed theologians criticized the Lutheran doctrine of real presence and ubiquity by applying the law of non-contradiction. It is true that from Zwingli onwards, the Reformed were not as skeptical of the use of reason in theology as the Lutherans. And this means that for them, the relation between theology and philosophy was seen in a much more positive light. On the Reformed side, one does not find such sharp words about the use of natural reason and Aristotelian philosophy as one finds in Lutheranism. Reformed theology was heavily engaged in the reception and construction of the Aristotelian school-philosophy that soon dominated the European universities. Beza's defense of Aristotle first led to the renewal of Aristotelian philosophy at the Reformed universities. Other philosophical trends, also alive in the Reformed tradition, like that of the humanist Ramus came under severe critique. Instead, the Reformed orthodoxy took over the theory of science developed by the Aristotelian Zabarella and the metaphysics of Suarez, who was also inspired by Aristotle. The Reformed Timpler, who taught at Bergsteinfurt in Westphalia, was the first German to write a metaphysics like that of Suarez.

The Reformed theologians at that time were also philosophers, and Keckermann as well as Alsted wrote philosophical works that were famous in their time. During the time of orthodoxy, Reformed theology had a very positive relation with philosophy. And this did not change when Aristotelian philosophy was later attacked by Descartes. Reformed philosophers like Clauberg and Wittich and Reformed theologians like Cocceius were among the first to welcome Cartesianism. It was to their merit that the close connection between Aristotelian philosophy and theology was undone.

Much later, Schleiermacher promoted a new form of Platonism, and his own theology presupposes his philosophical dialectic, inspired by Plato. The Reformed theologians Daub and Biedermann, on the other hand, leaned heavily upon Hegel. For all these theologians, it was already evident that natural reason or philosophy leads to God. Barth's claim that his revelation in Jesus Christ is the sole way to knowledge of God is alien to the Reformed tradition. And despite the fact that Barth cuts the links between theology and philosophy, it is quite obvious that his own theology in its beginnings relied heavily on contemporary philosophy, especially the neo-Kantian philosophy of the Marburg school, represented by Cohen and Natorp, which forms the background of his early writings. In my opinion, Reformed theology should again take up the traditional positive relation to philosophy. And when I speak of philosophy, I mean metaphysical philosophy. For Aristotle as well as Descartes, Plato, and Hegel were metaphysicians. Instead of relying on philosophical skepticism or deconstructivism, Reformed theology should thus support philosophical metaphysics that show natural reason is able to get a knowledge of God.

Such a positive relation between theology and metaphysical philosophy dates back to the Greek and Latin churches. Western scholasticism found its expression in Anselm's famous program *fides quaerens intellectum,* which was inspired by Augustine. This program has played an important role in Reformed theology as well. It is very strange to see that the two most influential Reformed theologians of modernity, Schleiermacher and Barth, both accepted Anselm's program. Schleiermacher took it as the motto of his *Glaubenslehre,* and Barth declared that his own theological method in the *Kirchliche Dogmatik* was inspired by Anselm's famous proof of the existence of God in his *Proslogion.* Of course, when Barth refers to Anselm, he has something very different in mind from Schleiermacher. And in my opinion, Barth's interpretation of Anselm is totally wrong.

According to Barth, Anselm thinks that dogmatics has to be church dogmatics in the sense that it presupposes and only explains the creeds and dogmas of the church, which are already an answer to God's self-revelation. In contrast, I interpret Anselm's program as the program of rational theology, which wants to show the rationality of faith. Anselm wants to transform faith into knowledge. So it is no wonder that Hegel in his history of philosophy speaks of the bishop of Canterbury in high praises. For he was right when he discovered a similarity between Anselm's program and his own.

Hegel's own philosophy of religion undertakes in a similar way the task to demonstrate that there is reason in religion and faith. He was convinced that Christian dogmas could be interpreted in such a way that their rationality becomes evident. In the Reformed tradition, there were quite a number of theologians who warmly welcomed Hegel's approach to religion and Christianity. To name a few, there was Daub in Germany, Biedermann in Switzerland, Scholten in the Netherlands, and the Cairds in Scotland — all of whom took up this line of rational theology inspired by Hegel's metaphysical philosophy. So as regards the philosophical discussion, I am an epistemological foundationalist. For Hegel means of course foundationalism in a very strict sense. His epistemology is indeed far away from something like the epistemology of Plantinga and Wolterstorff, who defend epistemological antifoundationalism. But as their philosophical antifoundationalism is linked with a rather conservative theology, my own philosophical foundationalism is connected with a theological revisionism that dates back to the days of Grotius and Cappel, who first attacked the orthodox dogma of verbal inspiration and introduced humanistic historical criticism into Reformed theology. It is this liberal tradition (in a very broad sense) that dominated German and Swiss Reformed theology in the last century, and is linked with the names of Schleiermacher, Schweizer, and Biedermann, whose criticism of orthodox Reformed dogma brought Reformed theology into its modern shape.

Now to the second aspect, what does an openness to the richness and plurality of the Reformed tradition mean for the relation of theology and ethics?

Ethics always formed a central part of Reformed theology because the law played a more distinguished role for Christian life for the Reformed than for the Lutherans. Calvin regarded the third use of the divine law as the most important one, and so sanctification became a main topic of Reformed theology. That is why Schneckenberger, writing in the nineteenth century, defined Lutheranism as passive and Reformed Protestantism as active. This distinction was taken up by Hundeshagen, and from Schneckenberger and Hundeshagen, passed over to Weber and Troeltsch. Moral activity was so important for Calvin that he could even speak of a progress in sanctification. The importance of sanctification and moral activity becomes obvious when one regards the role played by the *syllogismus practicus* in Beza's theology. Closely connected with the *syllogismus practicus* is the development of introspection and moral conscience, central to English puritanism and Dutch pietism. Because the divine law and sanctification played such a central role, church discipline became very important as well, and came to be regarded as one of the distinctives of the church in Reformed tradition. The office of the elders was to keep the church pure by exercising discipline. In fact, Reformed church discipline was one part of social discipline, which characterized the early modern state in general. Reformed ethics at this very early stage of development was not only influenced by the Aristotelian ethics of virtues, but by the neo-Stoic ethics of authors like Lipsius. And indeed, as far as the control of affections is concerned, discipline within Calvinism shows a remarkable resemblance to neo-Stoic ethics, which so dominated early modern society. On the other hand, there is no direct connection between the Reformed ethics of sanctification (especially the *syllogismus practicus*), and the spirit of modern capitalism. Weber's thesis is obviously wrong in this respect, for the egocentric view, characteristic of capitalism, does not exist in Reformed ethics, and work is not regarded as the aim of life. Nevertheless, Calvinism and the Reformed tradition in general have had an enormous influence on modern culture. Unlike dialectical theology, which stressed the contrast between God and culture, Reformed theology should again find a positive relation to the culture of our world. One might think of Kuyper, who stressed such a relation, or again, of Schleiermacher, for he defines ethics as the science of culture because ethics has to do with the action of reason as regards nature. It is through this activity of reason that culture comes into existence.

Ethics also means political ethics. It would be a mistake to identify the Reformed tradition in this respect with Barth's doctrine of the kingship of Christ. For the orthodox Reformed, as the Lutherans, made a sharp distinction between church and state, Christ being the king of the church but not of the state. There is, however, a difference between Lutherans and Calvinists as far as church government is concerned. Calvin and the Presbyterians regarded the presbytery as entrusted with church discipline, thereby working together with the civil magistrate. This model presupposes a religious and confessional uniformity, which had to be upheld by the presbytery in cooperation with the civil magistrate. It was the insight of the Congregationalists that this model contradicted religious liberty. In the long run, this led to the separation of church and state. But this did not mean that Reformed theology no longer influenced political thinking. Cromwell especially defended not only religious liberty, but economic and political liberty as well, with theological arguments. So the idea of human rights was born.

Besides a tradition that defended French absolutism, there existed another Reformed tradition in Britain and the Netherlands that sharply criticized absolutistic tendencies in politics. This latter tradition was still alive in the social gospel of Ragaz and still lives in the political theology of Moltmann. In the future, I think Reformed theology should take up the line present in Hegel, which declares that religion finds its final realization in the justice of the modern state. In a way, it is the ideal of the kingdom of God that leads to the idea of a unity of nations in which freedom and justice are realized.

CHAPTER 4

The End of Reformed Theology?
The Voice of Karl Barth in the Doctrinal
Chaos of the Present

Bruce L. McCormack

The Evangelical-Reformed churches of the sixteenth century were churches whose members were bound by a common confession. It matters not whether the confessing "unit" was conceived to be a single congregation, a collectivity of congregations within a particular city, or a confederation of churches in a number of cities, unity in confession was understood to be essential to the recognition of genuine ecclesial unity. Such unity was then secured in an ongoing fashion by means of the exercise of the legitimate teaching office of the church, consisting in the explication and (as the need arose) testing of the existing confession. Essential to this process of explication and testing were the "doctors of the church" — teachers whose primary task lay in thinking through the doctrinal contents of the Christian faith "confessionally," as baptized members of a church to which they owed a relative but nonetheless real obedience. Where, today, by contrast, a common confession is not constitutive of a thoughtful and conscientious exercise of the legitimate teaching office of the church, there the theologians of the said church are not bound in any concrete way to that church. There the theologian is "free" to be self-norming in all of his/her theological work (including the education of future ministers for the churches). There the spirit of the "free churches" has triumphed on the soil of the Reformed churches, and we can no longer speak in any meaningful way of "Reformed" theology. Today, we are witnessing the demise of the "church theologian" in the classically Reformed sense. The "doctor of the church" has been replaced by the Free Church theologian.

Introduction: The Demise of Confessionalism
and Its Impact on Theology

At the dawn of the Reformation and through the course of the century or two that followed, the conviction was widespread among Reformed Christians that the subject of any genuinely ecclesial theology was the church and not, precisely not, the individual theologian. Even if the theologian in question bore the name of Jean Calvin, his personal authority[1] in matters of doctrine could never — on Calvin's view, too — attain to that of a gathering of pastors duly assembled for the purpose of resolving doctrinal controversies.

> We indeed willingly concede, if any discussion arises over doctrine, that the best and surest remedy is for a synod of true bishops to be convened, where the doctrine at issue may be examined. Such a definition, upon which the pastors of the church in common, invoking Christ's Spirit, agree, will have much more weight than if each one, having conceived it separately at home, should teach it to the people, or if a few private individuals should compose it. Then, when the bishops are assembled, they can more conveniently deliberate in common what they ought to teach and in what form, lest diversity breed offense.[2]

What they ought to teach and in what form: the principle here enunciated is that the teaching in the church which finds expression in preaching, catechizing, etc. ought to have an agreed upon form. Seen in the light of this notion, it is not surprising that the early Reformed churches sought to manifest their unity through the publication of confessions. The mind of the church, one might say,

---

1. In truth, Calvin was quite emphatic in insisting that such authority never attached itself to the person but only to the ministry performed by the person, a ministry that had a quite definite content if the authority in question was to be approved by God. ". . . we must remember that whatever authority and dignity the Spirit in Scripture accords to either priests or prophets, or apostles, or successors of apostles, it is wholly given not to the men personally, but to the ministry to which they have been appointed; or (to speak more briefly) to the Word, whose ministry has been entrusted to them." John Calvin, *Institutes of the Christian Religion*, trans. Ford Lewis Battles and ed. John T. McNeill (Philadelphia: Westminster, 1960), 4.8.2. If that is true of the prophets and apostles, it is all the more true, Calvin says, of their successors. "Yet this, I have said, is the difference between the apostles and their successors: the former were sure and genuine scribes of the Holy Spirit, and their writings are therefore to be considered oracles of God; but the sole office of others is to teach what is provided and sealed in the Holy Scriptures. We therefore teach that faithful ministers are now not permitted to coin any new doctrine, but that they are simply to cleave to that doctrine to which God has subjected all men without exception. When I say this, I mean to show what is permitted not only to individual men but to the whole church as well." Calvin, *Institutes* 4.8.9.

2. Calvin, *Institutes* 4.9.13.

was made known through the issuing of a commonly agreed upon confession to which all, ministers and lay alike, were bound.[3] This was churchly theology: theology done by the church through its properly called representatives with the approval of the people of God. "Doctors of the church," in such a frame of understanding, were those who were called by a church for a particular service, that is, "to keep doctrine whole and pure among believers" through the interpretation of Holy Scripture.[4] That such intellectual activity could also mean addressing new questions and conflicts was certainly not proscribed, though it was at least expected that such efforts would not result in the coining of "new doctrine."[5]

We have come a long way since then obviously. Some of the change that has occurred has been of a positive nature. Our confessionalism, where it still exists, is not as conservative as theirs. We recognize, for example, that doctrine — even sound doctrine — undergoes development over time and that the avoidance of coining "new doctrine," even where that is recognized as being a valuable goal, is not an easy thing. And, yet, I think there can be little question but that the pendulum has swung much too far. Karl Barth's tragi-comedic lament in the 1920s was but a harbinger of things to come. Noting that "dogmatics" ought to have, in the nature of the case, some direct connection to the dogmas of a given church, Barth wrote,

> . . . the dogmatics of present-day Protestantism has been more or less left in the lurch by its churches. For the most part they do not say what church dogma is, or they do so only with enigmatic brevity, or by means of a cheap and very general reference to the confessional writings of the Reformation. They act like Nebuchadnezzar among his wise men when he wanted them to tell him not only what his dream meant but also what it was [Dan. 2:1f.]. In face of the embarrassed mumbling or total silence of the modern

---

3. The meaning of this "binding," its proper weight and significance, will be taken up momentarily. Suffice it here to say that the exact legal status of these documents in church and civil community is not my concern in this paper (as it would require more detailed investigation than I am capable of at the moment). It does merit mentioning that the citizens of Geneva were required by a decision of the Great Council of 27 April 1537 to make public profession (in groups of ten) of their faith through swearing an oath to the Genevan Confession of 1536, and that the adoption of the Basel Confession of 1534 by that city's town council was not only accompanied by a similar oath on the part of the citizens but that oath was also solemnly reaffirmed through the public reading of that confession during Holy Week every year until 1821. See Karl Barth, "Wünschbarkeit und Möglichkeit eines allgemeinen reformierten Glaubensbekenntnisses," in *Vorträge und kleinere Arbeiten, 1922-1925*, ed. Holger Finze (Zürich: TVZ, 1990), pp. 617-18, nn. 53 and 54. But my point is a theological one. It is simply to say that the proper subject of church theology is the church.

4. Calvin, *Institutes* 4.3.4.

5. See note 1 above.

churches about their basic statements, dogmaticians can only surmise that finally the churches do not want any dogmatics. . . .[6]

In all likelihood, it was the surrender by the cantonal churches in Switzerland of all confessional standards during the course of the nineteenth century that was foremost in Barth's mind in the reference to Nebuchadnezzar. But that unfortunate circumstance by no means exhausts the possibilities. The formal act of setting aside confessional standards is not the only way to render a church, for all practical purposes, confessionless. A "conscience clause" that would allow to the ordinand liberty of opinion with respect to those matters treated in the church's confession "which do not enter into the substance of the faith" would certainly do the trick — so long as the ordinand were also granted complete freedom to define for him/herself which matters belonged to that "substance" and which did not.[7] Or a "Book of Confessions" could be adopted and even made part of the constitutional basis of the church but never, in practice, appealed to by General Assemblies or presbyteries in an effort to provide authoritative guidance in doctrinal controversies. Instead, every doctrinal question could be cynically reduced to a problem of polity management. Or we might try to convince ourselves that mere propositions can never be adequate for defining church "identity"; that what we need to focus our attention on is character formation through something like "habits of mind."[8] But, however it may come about, the situation is much the same at the end of the day. The churches play the role of Nebuchadnezzar, and their wise men (and women) are, by and large, left to their own devices, encouraged by the benign neglect with which

6. Karl Barth, "Unterricht in der christlichen Religion," Erster Band: Prolegomena, 1924, ed. Hannelotte Reiffen (Zürich: TVZ, 1985), p. 50; *The Göttingen Dogmatics: Instruction in the Christian Religion*, vol. 1, trans. Geoffrey Bromiley (Grand Rapids: Eerdmans, 1990), p. 40. See also Barth's "Kirche und Theologie," in *Vorträge und kleinere Arbeiten, 1922-1925*, pp. 655-56.

7. See Francis Lyall, "The Westminster Confession: The Legal Position," in *The Westminster Confession in the Church Today*, ed. Alasdair I. C. Heron (Edinburgh: St. Andrew Press, 1982), p. 69.

8. "Habits of mind," to borrow Brian Gerrish's phrase, cannot be divorced from serious attention to doctrinal distinctives without a serious reduction of his list. Habits 1 and 2, after all, call upon us to be both deferential and critical towards "the past" — and not just any past, but to the "apostles and fathers of the church." I would submit that neither deference nor criticism is possible where we do not take seriously what these "fathers" themselves took seriously: viz. church doctrine. The cultivation of "habits of mind" in the absence of a serious catechizing in the faith of a church could, in my judgment, only serve the "narcissism and faddism" about which Gerrish rightly worries. See Brian Gerrish, "Tradition and the Modern World: The Reformed Habit of Mind," in *Toward the Future of Reformed Theology: Tasks, Topics, Traditions*, ed. David Willis and Michael Welker (Grand Rapids: Eerdmans, 1999), pp. 3-20.

they are surrounded to function autonomously in the strictest sense of the word — as laws unto themselves.

This is not the place to raise the historical question of how the churches managed to reach this point, what the historical "causes" of the breakdown in the confessional character of Reformed Christianity have been. No doubt many factors played a role. I will content myself here with a single observation. I have long had the impression that one of the most significant roots of the death of a vital theological culture within our churches over the last two centuries has been our inability to do anything constructive about the presence in our historical confessions of the Augustinian/Calvinist doctrine of a "double predestination." Many there have been over the last two centuries and more who have found this doctrine deeply troubling, and efforts to diminish its significance through arguments about where the doctrine ought to appear in a doctrinal edifice (Calvin's vs. the later Calvinists) have not resolved the problem in the least. A problem suppressed is a problem that eats away at a sense of confessional identity. On the other hand, until very recently, most Reformed churches have not been in a position to think seriously about revising their stance on this particular head of doctrine. The strength in numbers of those who would absolutize confessional authority (making fidelity to every jot and tittle of a confession to be a requirement laid upon faith) has simply been too great to undertake a thoroughgoing reconsideration of the matter. The net effect of the stalemate that ensued was to make those who were troubled by the doctrine of predestination hold their confessions at arm's length, eventually making those confessions to be the subject of lip-service only; not serious commitment. But I am getting away from my true purpose here.

What of the theologians? What of their responsibility for the loose and disordered relationship that currently obtains between the churches and their theologians? Reformed confessional theology is in deep trouble today not simply because the church leaders have failed to exercise their proper teaching office but because theologians, in all honesty, are not all that eager to make themselves accountable for what they say and do as theologians to persons they regard as less qualified than themselves.[9] By and large, Reformed theologians today (in the mainline churches, at any rate) operate in a space that is carefully

---

9. On this point, too, as on so many others, it is well to hear Calvin: ". . . this is the best and most useful exercise in humility, when he [God] accustoms us to obey his Word, even though it is preached through men like us and sometimes even by those of lower worth than we. If he spoke from heaven, it would not be surprising if his sacred oracles were to be reverently received without delay by the ears and minds of all. For . . . who would not be confounded at such boundless splendor? But when a puny man risen from the dust speaks in God's name, at this point we best evidence our piety and obedience toward God if we show ourselves teachable toward his minister, although he excels us in nothing." Calvin, *Institutes* 4.3.1.

preserved from ecclesial interference by the foreboding sign that hangs over the entryway: "Academic Freedom!" What they teach, what they write, how they conduct themselves in their day-to-day affairs, speaks volumes of the debts they feel themselves to owe to the professional guilds to which they belong and (occasionally) to the institutions where they teach. But all too often their labor evinces so little connection with a particular church that it is not only impossible to discern which theological tradition they stand in but whether they stand in any tradition at all. But note well! It is not only so-called "liberal" theologians who have cut themselves off from a concrete relationship to a concrete church, it is the would-be orthodox who have done so as well!

One of the most conspicuous features of the theological situation today is that among those who still have a reason to care about orthodoxy ("right doctrine") and who promote ecclesiastical authority as a hedge against the chaos surrounding and permeating the life of the churches, it is the dogmas of the ancient church to which appeal is regularly made; it is not the confession of a Reformation church.[10] Most of us would find it difficult to name a single book or

---

10. The last decade or two has witnessed something of an undignified flight to the East on the part of theologians who have felt themselves disaffected from an increasingly liberal church leadership. Rather than attempting to revive Reformed confessionalism, many such theologians have looked to the ancient church for inspiration. In the realm of dogmatics, the result has been a fascination with classical Orthodox doctrinal themes like theosis. One might reasonably ask: Where is there in the soteriologies of T. F. Torrance, Colin Gunton, or Mark Achtemeier (I am deliberately picking on my friends here) any element that might responsibly be called "Reformed"? To ask this question is not at all to presume that if a doctrine is "Reformed," it is automatically true. It could well be that classically Reformed treatments of soteriology ("objective" and "subjective" — atonement and justification) are unsound (even by the standard to which they would have made appeal, viz. that of Holy Scripture) and, therefore, in need of correction. It could be that Torrance et al. are right to lift up the theme "union with Christ" (construed along lines that stand in very close proximity to the Eastern theosis doctrine) and to make it central to their soteriologies. But my question is: How can the doctrine that emerges from this procedure be justifiably called "Reformed"? The odd appeal to a few passages from Calvin will hardly suffice for making this case, not simply because the meaning of Calvin's statements on "union with Christ" is anything but self-evidently on the side of Eastern understandings but, much rather, because Calvin (as an individual theologian) does not define what it is to be "Reformed." I will say it again: the subject of church doctrine in the Reformed churches is a church, a church that exercises its teaching office through the public promulgation of a confession. Even if Achtemeier were right about Calvin's teaching (and I have many reasons for doubting it), he would be hard pressed indeed to show that the doctrine he thinks himself to find in Calvin was made part of the confession(s) of the Reformed churches. And he would be even harder pressed to show that the introduction of this doctrine today constitutes a legitimate development of the soteriologies of the early confessions rather than a decisive break with them. But the most questionable feature in the whole proceeding, it seems to me, lies here: If the soteriologies of

even an article of the last ten years, written by an ostensibly "Reformed" theologian, which grants to the Reformed confessions a constitutive role in their own doctrinal constructions[11] — though we can probably think of some well-received tomes that have made frequent appeals to the ancient church. The problem that the theologian who functions in this way creates for him/herself is that it is not the Nicene-Constantinopolitan Creed which, in theory at least, defines the doctrinal stance of the church to which any "Reformed" theologian belongs. Rather, it is the Nicene-Constantinopolitan Creed as interpreted by a Reformed confession or group of Reformed confessions. For a theologian belonging to a Reformed church body to affirm the Nicene-Constantinopolitan Creed in the absence of any discernible connection to the theology of the confession(s) of his/her church is to treat the "one, holy, catholic and apostolic church" as a Platonic ideal that hovers above all existing churches without ever touching ground. It is to evacuate one's own church membership of all concrete reality; fidelity to a creed that is not church-defining is an expression of the sheerest ecclesial idealism. It is, in short, to act as a self-norming theologian — and it really matters not a whit that the self-norming activity in this case results in a high valuation of ecclesial authority and the orthodoxy it promotes. It is to become a "free-church" theologian.

It is very important, I think, that we see and understand that there is really no difference, finally, between what Ernst Troeltsch once called the theologian of "subjective experience" and the theologian of "objective revelation" — once both have become self-norming in all of their basic theological decisions. In his *Social Teachings of the Christian Churches*, Troeltsch drew a line of connection between the mysticism of the late Middle Ages (Meister Eckhart and Sebastian Frank) on the one side and the "romantic" theology of the early

---

the Reformed confession(s) really need to be corrected, how can that be done responsibly where the confessions are simply passed by in silence? where the correction sought is undertaken under the auspices of a parachurch "renewal movement" rather than through the constitutional means afforded for such doctrinal changes by the particular churches? and where common cause is sought first and foremost with "renewal movements" in other denominations (the "evangelical Catholics," for example) rather than with confessionally minded Reformed people?

11. Presbyterian Miroslav Volf has written a highly praised volume on "ecumenical ecclesiology" that intends to be "unmistakably Protestant" while also being "enriched by Catholic and Orthodox" voices (p. xi). Obviously, there is nothing wrong with a Reformed theologian writing an ecumenical book. And there is nothing surprising about his choice of Joseph Ratzinger and John Zizioulas to be his Catholic and Orthodox conversation-partners. What is surprising is that the "Protestant" perspective which is then developed very conspicuously owes far more to the Free Church tradition than it does the Reformed tradition. See Volf, *After Our Likeness: The Church as the Image of the Trinity* (Grand Rapids: Eerdmans, 1998).

Schleiermacher of the Speeches and the speculative theologies of Hegel and de Wette on the other. Common to all of these theologies, he suggested, is the fact that in each, "salvation is not a static quality, belonging to institutional religion, but an experience of the union of the soul with God which is new every time it takes place."[12] One of the most striking features of theology today, in my view, is the convergence of interest among a good many "liberals" and the "orthodox" center party in the idea of "union with Christ." On both sides, Troeltsch has proven prophetic. Preoccupation with this theme today is an expression of the triumph of the Troeltschian "sect-type" that has become disaffected from institutional Christianity. It is also, I suspect, an expression of the rampant individualism of the consumerist societies of the West in this latest phase of their capitalist development.

In sum, we find ourselves confronted today with the confessional idealism of the orthodox party in the center that lacks a concrete relation to an existing church body and a confessionless left that would be happy to see all confessions and those who think highly of them disappear.[13] So, what are we to do in the face of such unhappy alternatives? There is, I believe, a better alternative than those we have reviewed. No Reformed theologian in this century has given greater attention to the problem of ecclesial authority, the nature of a church confession, and the obedience that is proper to such a confession than Karl Barth. In what follows, I am going to try to bring Karl Barth's voice to bear on the doctrinal chaos into which our churches have submerged themselves at the end of the millennium. We would do well, I think, to pay heed. I have heard it said — and have no reason to doubt it — that if present trends in membership decline continue, the only churches left in the West by the middle of the next century will be Roman Catholic, Orthodox, and conservative evangelical. Protestantism as we know it will have ceased to exist. The end of Reformed theology may well coincide with the end of the Reformed churches.

The organization of this paper bears forceful witness to the fact that the truly decisive issue is not the nature of confessions. Regional conferences on "the confessing nature of the church" have been sponsored in the United States these past two years by the so-called "Theology and Worship Unit" in the Office of the General Assembly of the Presbyterian Church (USA) in order to get at that issue. And since the merger of northern and southern churches in 1983, a fair number

---

12. Ernst Troeltsch, *The Social Teachings of the Christian Churches*, vol. 2, trans. Olive Wyon (Louisville: Westminster/John Knox Press reprint, 1992), p. 796.

13. There is also a third option, of course, which I have deliberately left undiscussed here: the absolutism of those confessionalists on the right who would make subscription to the letter of a confession to be an obligation for faith. But such folk are a negligible force in the "mainline" churches and, for the most part, carefully segregated out of the academy.

of books and articles have appeared, addressing themselves in one form or another to this problem. But to take up the issue of the nature of confessions without giving serious attention to the entire problem of ecclesial authority is to lay hold of a conclusion to a much larger argument without attending to the argument itself. The greatest theological problem confronting Reformed theology today — and I suspect that this is true not only for the American church but for other western churches as well — is the problem of ecclesial authority. In what follows, then, I will give the lion's share of my attention to that problem, treating the nature of confessions only briefly near the end.

I will also be confining my attention to a single moment in Barth's life, the year 1925. I do so in the conviction that the situation he confronted at that time was very much like our own. I am also convinced that he never strayed from the basic decisions that were registered in the essays published in that year.[14]

The Presupposition of Ecclesial Authority: No Immediacy That Is Not Tied to Mediation!

In the summer of 1925, Erik Peterson (until 1924, Barth's colleague in Göttingen) published a sharp criticism of the dialectical theologies of Barth and his comrade-in-arms Rudolf Bultmann.[15] The essay provoked an immediate sensation due to what was rightly perceived to be its hyper-Catholic tendencies.[16] At the heart of Peterson's essay lay the claim that Christian theology consists essentially in concrete obedience to concrete authority.[17] What is most striking about Barth's *Auseinandersetzung* with Peterson, from the standpoint of our concerns here, is that he did not at all dispute the validity of this claim. What he disputed was its meaning.

For Peterson, the concrete authority in question was dogma. Concrete

---

14. Although Barth's essay "Kirche und Theologie" will provide the focus for my reflections here, my interpretation of it will presuppose close attention to two other essays: "Wünschbarkeit und Möglichkeit eines allgemeinen reformierten Glaubensbekenntnisses" and "Das Schriftprinzip der reformierten Kirche." The bibliographical data for the first may be found in note 6, above; data for the second in note 3. "Das Schriftprinzip" may be found in Barth, *Vorträge und kleinere Arbeiten, 1922-1925*, pp. 500-44.

15. Erik Peterson, "Was Ist Theologie?" in *Theologische Traktate* (München: Hochland-Bücherei im Kösel Verlag, 1951), pp. 11-43.

16. That Peterson's Protestant critics were not wrong to see in Peterson strong Catholic tendencies was proven by the sequel to this story: Peterson's conversion in 1930 to Roman Catholicism. On this later development, see Karl Barth and K. L. Schmidt, "Zu Erik Petersons Übertritt zum römischen Katholizismus," *Theologische Blätter* 10 (1931): 59f.

17. Barth, "Kirche und Theologie," p. 653.

obedience was owed to dogma because the true subject of dogma is, ultimately, the Logos himself. Only Christ can speak of God, according to Peterson, because only Christ is God and is therefore able to truly speak from God. Dogma consists in a "prolongation of Christ's speaking of God."[18] And that can only mean that the authority of dogma is not the authority of any human but the authority of Christ. On closer analysis, however, the "prolongation" of Christ's speaking turns out not to mean that he himself is the author of dogma; not directly, anyway. "Dogma does not directly continue Christ's speaking of God, but rather in such a way that there is a teaching power which is transferred from Christ to the church"[19] so that the church is enabled to continue the speaking of God that ceased with Christ's ascension. Not all church doctrines qualify as dogma, but (apparently) only those that have been recognized by the church as such. Dogma, so understood, carries Christ's authority in a derived fashion; Christ's authority is "lent" to dogma. In that Christ is now ascended into heaven, he has "lent" his power — indeed, "all power in heaven and on earth" — to the church that now represents him in and through its teaching office.[20] Thus, the concrete obedience that is owed to dogma could not be more absolute.

Barth was placed in a somewhat awkward position by Peterson's essay. Not only was Peterson a friend (who had been wounded by the fallout surrounding this essay); but he was also, in many respects, an ally in the troubled theological and ecclesial world of Weimar Germany. Hence, Barth expressed the hope that his "no" to Peterson would not be confused with the negations of others who did not participate in their common concerns.[21]

Barth began his response where Peterson had begun: with the incarnation. Theology, he said, is an ongoing service to God's revelation in the form of conceptual thinking in a particular place and time. Revelation is Christ; on that point, he and Peterson were in agreement. But between the "there and then" of Christ's appearing and the "here and now" in which theology is done lies a gap in time. "In order to be able to become the object of theology, revelation must become contemporaneous with theology. This contemporizing of revelation is carried out, however, not only immediately, through God's direct speaking in all times, but also — though not without the witness and seal of that immediacy — in a mediated [form]."[22] The concrete form the object of theology takes in making itself contemporaneous, that through which revelation is mediated to us in the present, includes four factors which constitute "concrete authority":

18. Peterson, "Was Ist Theologie?," p. 30.
19. Peterson, "Was Ist Theologie?," p. 31.
20. Peterson, "Was Ist Theologie?," p. 31.
21. Barth, "Kirche und Theologie," p. 650.
22. Barth, "Kirche und Theologie," p. 654.

(1) the decisions of the church on the canon and text of the Bible, (2) creeds (or the decisions of the church on fundamental statements of faith that have been more or less unanimously acknowledged), (3) "fathers" or "doctors of the Church" who have been acknowledged by the church(es) as faithful expositors of those authoritative creedal statements, and (4) the "command of the hour" (the "definiteness of the moment" in which theology finds itself, which lays upon it an obligation to speak to the real needs of the present).[23] None of these in isolation from one another but all of them taken together constitute "concrete authority" — though Barth also points out that they lie on different planes and do not each possess the same significance.

But whose authority is it that theology here acknowledges? The church's, to be sure, but what kind of authority is this? What is its status in relation to the authority that is Christ's? Barth will grant that there is some kind of transferal of power and authority by Christ to the church at his ascension. But what is the nature of this transfer? And, most important of all, what are the material presuppositions on whose basis an answer to this question ought to be given? The decisive sentences in Barth's answer to the last question read:

> . . . the bestowal of power on His church cannot mean that Christ abdicated, so to speak, in favour of the church; that He placed Himself even only partially under its power; that He ceased to be wholly and completely God in relation to the church. The ascension means not only, as Peterson would have it, the transferal of representative, secondary power to the church, but also the departure of the proper, primary Holder of power, the making visible of the eschatological limit that is placed on the church. The exaltation of the Head truly means for the body a humiliation, a being placed in a position of humility and exaltation.[24]

And, hence, Barth says (rather mildly), "In order to avoid naturalistic confusion of heaven and earth, one would do better not to speak at all of an 'elongation' and 'continuation' of revelation."[25] The authority granted by Christ to the church is therefore appropriately described as "Christ's authority in a secondary sense," but given the material presuppositions that undergird this claim and give to it its significance (presuppositions that have been established above all in Barth's doctrine of revelation[26]), the church's authority can only be seen as "temporal, relative, and formal authority."

23. Barth, "Kirche und Theologie," pp. 656-57.
24. Barth, "Kirche und Theologie," p. 661.
25. Barth, "Kirche und Theologie," p. 662.
26. What I am alluding to with this remark is Barth's concept of an *indirect* revelation and, especially, his treatment of the traditional problem of the *communicatio idiomatum*

That the authority of the church is "temporal" means that it is strictly delimited by its origin and goal in the first and second comings of Christ. It means that the authority of the church is the authority of forgiven sinners; that the decisions of the church can never attain to the level of infallibility and immutability. That the authority of the church is "relative" means that it is not authority in and for itself but authority only in relation to the authority of Another (which is an authority in itself). And, finally, that the authority of the church is "formal" means that its content is not self-generated. Revelation is mediated, we have said, by the four factors named above. Mediation, more closely analyzed, means that the four factors function collectively as the form, the channel through which revelation comes to us. And the water that flows through this channel, the content that must be borne witness to if church decisions are to have authority, is a content that comes to the church from Holy Scripture.

If the distinction between the authority that is original and proper to Christ and the mediated authority of the church is to be a meaningful one, then, Barth contends, "there must be a cardinal point at which the subordination of the church to its Lord comes to expression."[27] That "point" is Holy Scripture. "This spoken and written Word, into which the Logos-revelation has entered in order to go out into all the world, is as such, as the principle of all concrete contemporizing of revelation, the origin and limit of all such contemporizing, the measure by which everything that the church 'speaks' in the name of its Lord is measured and is always to be measured anew."[28] The authority of the church, in other words, finds expression in this activity above all: in the faithful interpretation of Holy Scripture. The authority that accrues to the church in being verbally faithful to Scripture is itself the authority of Holy Scripture. That is what Barth means in speaking of the church as a channel through which revelation comes to the people of God.

In sum, the concrete authority to which obedience is owed in the church is an authority that is never simply a predicate of any of the church's institutionalized offices. And because it is not, there is no possible way to confuse this account of church authority with that found within the bounds of Roman Catholicism. The teaching office of the church on Protestant soil is a ministry of the church to the Word, a ministry that consists in a church-wide, ever to be repeated, interpretive act whose success is constantly to be measured by the judg-

---

(which allows for no divinization of the human). For a treatment of these themes, see my "Revelation and History in Transfoundationalist Perspective: Karl Barth's Theological Epistemology in Conversation with a Schleiermacherian Tradition," *Journal of Religion* 78 (1998): 18-37.

27. Barth, "Kirche und Theologie," p. 663.
28. Barth, "Kirche und Theologie," p. 664.

ment of Word and Spirit. In fact, the "immediate" speaking of God in the church in Word and Spirit of which Barth spoke is a speaking that either confirms or does not confirm the mediated form through which the Word in Scripture comes to us today. It is, therefore, an immediacy that may never be detached from mediacy; an immediacy that serves mediacy.

I will return in a moment to the question of the nature and significance of "concrete obedience" in theology. For now, I wish to point out that the material presuppositions by means of which Barth cuts off the flowering of Catholic concepts of authority at their very root also mean the cutting off of the possibility of the free-thinking individualism of the left-wing Reformation (and their "liberal" followers today) as well.

Barth was very astute in his judgment that the opponents the Reformers confronted on the right hand (the Roman Catholics) and the left (the Enthusiasts and Spiritualists, the Socinians and the later Arminians) were, in fact, the same opponent — only differently garbed.[29] Essential to both is the thought of an immediacy to revelation, though it is differently located in each case. For sixteenth-century Catholics, Christ and the church were merged in a sacerdotal understanding of the church that made the institutional church as such the bearer of revelation (not simply the channel but a bearer with the power to effect that which it bears) and, therefore, the instrumental cause of grace. For sixteenth-century Spiritualists, on the other hand, immediacy to God took the form of a mystical union which (as Troeltsch observed) by-passed the institutional church, its means of grace, and (what is more significant for our purposes here) its teaching office. For the Spiritualists, the proper interpreter of Scripture is the individual who has experienced the salvation of which Scripture speaks. No teaching can or should be laid down by the institutional church as an authoritative declaration of its mind. For the church is not a collective such that it could have a mind. It is a gathering of believers who may, as the times require, agree on a few, very brief articles of faith, but insofar as these articles are conceived to be the result of a wholly voluntary expression of minds, such expressions have validity only for the times in which they are written. I speak in typological terms, of course. I do not mean this description to be taken as accurate to each and every group located on the left-wing of the sixteenth-century Reformation. But the spirit of what is here expressed will have been found in one form or another in all of these groups. My point is simply this: what makes both Catholic heteronomy and Spiritualist autonomy possible is the same thing. It is the idea that we are able to stand in a relation of immediacy to revelation. And the corrective that Barth invoked against this error is one that has profound relevance for Reformed theology today.

29. Barth, "Kirche und Theologie," p. 651.

The abiding temptation of theologians belonging to the "orthodox" party in the Reformed churches today is to return to Rome (or to Constantinople, as the case may be); if not in fact, then at least in spirit. And the abiding temptation of "liberal" theologians is to promote the autonomous free-thinking of the Spiritualists. Neither is functioning as a "doctor of the church" in a Reformed sense. To be a "doctor of the church" in a Reformed sense is to serve the institutional church in its God-given task of interpreting Holy Scripture. This we do when, guided by the church's previous authoritative attempts to interpret Scripture, we return to Scripture and ask: How far is the church's authoritative interpretation correct? And, does the church's interpretation leave out of consideration important elements in the scriptural witness to God's self-revelation in Jesus Christ which we must today lift up for attention? The "doctor of the church," in other words, serves the church by serving its confession — in fidelity and in criticism. But this function is not performed where the confession of the church is routinely ignored.

Concrete Obedience: A Witness to Our Obedience to Christ[30]

Given the fact that the concrete authority to which obedience is owed is a temporal, relative, and formal authority, the obedience in question can never be ab-

---

30. Before proceeding, it should be acknowledged that a fairly sizable question has been begged in the preceding account. Why should the church have a priority over the individual? If neither the church as a collectivity nor the individual enjoy a relationship of immediacy to revelation, then why should one be granted even a temporal, relative, and formal authority over the other? A full answer to this question would require a far longer paper than the one I have been asked to write. But this much can and should be said. First, the church is not simply a collectivity. It is an organically related whole. And that means that the individual has no standing within the life of the church as a mere individual. He/she is a part of a whole. Second, the communion of saints is a communion that stretches not only throughout space but also throughout time. Because that is so, the *unity* of the body we call the church is not something that is invented anew in each moment. It is something that is *given* to the church. And that giving is a divine act which belongs to a *history* of other divine acts of giving. The unity of the church did not first begin to exist when we modern lovers of peace decided it might be nice to get along with one another. The unity of the church is a reality with a history, a history that is ignored only at the cost of surrendering that unity. Third, there is the matter of the power of the keys spoken of in Matthew 16:19. The fact that Calvin made the power to excommunicate rest upon an authority that belongs to the church only insofar as its ministers are rightly interpreting the Word of God in *Institutes* 4.11.2 shows just how important doctrine was in his mind for legitimizing an exercise of ecclesial power. Consistent with that claim is his belief that "the spiritual power which is proper to the church . . . consists either in doctrine or in jurisdiction or in making laws." The "doctrinal side," he adds, "has two parts: authority to lay down articles of faith, and authority to explain them." See *Institutes*

solute. Clearly, the absolute obedience that is proper to faith is an obedience that is owed only to God. If obedience is also offered to human authorities, then such obedience cannot compete with the obedience that is owed to God but must somehow be related to it. But how are we to understand this relation? The law that the four factors of canon, creed, fathers, and kairos constitute for theology is a human law, Barth says, and as such must never be identified with divine law. Obedience to the church, he would later add, is only owed to the extent that the church itself is obedient to the divine law that is constituted by God's self-revelation attested in Holy Scripture.[31] But even in that ideal situation, obedience to human law can only be a witness to our obedience to divine law. We theologians submit ourselves to the authority of the church as a fundamental act of witness to our obedience to Christ. Because church law is always human law, our obedience to it can never be identical with our obedience to Christ. There is, however, a relationship between the two, a relationship whose essence is captured in this little word *witness*.

Because obedience to the concrete authority of the church can never be more than penultimate, there is also a very real freedom within the bounds of the church. Where church authority is falsely erected, where its exercise is not productive of "pure doctrine" (i.e., doctrine that stands in conformity to the witness of Scripture), there the church stands in a relationship of disobedience to divine law. There, the theologian has no choice but to obey Christ rather than the church. But the theologian will also recognize how prone he/she is to errors of judgment and will therefore undertake to correct the church humbly and never out of self-protectiveness or a desire for self-aggrandizement. Real freedom is freedom under the Word, not over it. And the theologian must never forget that God has placed a third element between the eternal truth of God and the opinions of the individual vis-à-vis the church.[32]

We hear it said today — in a myriad of ways and from many quarters — that doctrine does not define the identity of the church. Whatever else such claims may be, they are (almost without exception) self-serving. For what will they have accomplished by claiming that the identity of the church is in no way defined by doctrine if not to make their own doctrinal labors entirely independent of the (allegedly) true being of the church, thereby purchasing for themselves complete

---

4.8.1. To these theological arguments for the pre-eminence of the church over the individual, we might add a pragmatic one. Given that neither the church as a collectivity nor the individual enjoys a relationship of immediacy to revelation, the church's advantage over the individual consists in the fact that sound interpretation of Scripture is more likely to emerge from collaborative efforts than from virtuoso performances. This is, as I say, only a pragmatic argument; it has not proven true in every case.

31. Karl Barth, *Church Dogmatics* I/2 (Edinburgh: T. & T. Clark, 1957), p. 587.
32. Barth, "Kirche und Theologie," p. 666.

freedom to pursue self-appointed tasks in accordance with self-chosen norms? Can it really escape anyone's notice that such arguments serve to further the individualism that is the chief characteristic of western theology today?

Obedience to the church is only witness; its significance can never be more than penultimate. But this witness is a service to the church's service of the Word. In the absence of concrete obedience to church authority on the part of theologians, it is very unlikely that the churches will ever come to recognize anew their God-given calling to exercise a temporal, relative, and formal authority. And if they do not, then their service of the Word will at best be a truncated, withered, and lame one.

The Nature of a Confession

All of Barth's reflections in the essay "Church and Theology" circle around the question of the nature of a confession without ever stating clearly what was meant by it. The reason was that the problem of ecclesial authority was the central issue raised by Peterson. Barth's view of confessions and their authority was presupposed but never articulated. We do not have to guess as to his views on the latter subject, however. In an address written just a few months prior to Barth's response to Peterson, he described the Reformed understanding of a confession of faith in the following words.

> A reformed confession of faith is the spontaneously and publicly formulated presentation to the Christian Church in general of a provisionally granted insight from the revelation of God in Jesus Christ attested in Holy Scripture alone by a geographically circumscribed Christian fellowship which, until further action, authoritatively defines its character to outsiders and which, until further action, gives direction to its own doctrine and life.[33]

There is much in this definition that would reward close study. Here I only wish to lift up two themes that are pertinent to the goals established for this paper.

The first is the twice-repeated element of "until further action." A confession, Barth says, authoritatively defines a church's character to outsiders and gives direction to its own doctrine and life — but it does all of this only "until further action." The significance of this "until further action" is not at all self-evident. That it underscores the provisionality of the authority of a confession is undeniably true — and Barth makes that point at some length.[34] But we must also take into consideration the fact that, for Barth, a confession is, above all other things, a

33. Barth, "Wünschbarkeit und Möglichkeit," p. 610.
34. Barth, "Wünschbarkeit und Möglichkeit," pp. 613-16.

commentary on Holy Scripture. Scripture alone, he says, is law and norm in a material sense; dogma and creed are not. Still, the creed has an "obligating power" (a few months later he would say, the power of human law) so long as the commentary it offers has not been convicted of lies by Scripture itself (as law and norm) and so long as the law that Scripture is continues to be recognized.[35] The "obligatory power" of a confession, on this view, is measured by the degree to which it presents a sound exposition of scriptural teaching. If the commentary it offered were perfectly sound, then the "until further action" would never come into play. Of course, no commentary is ever the thing itself; improvement is possible in the case of every commentary. But — and here is the decisive point — the limit placed on the "until further action" has to do with the church's ability to improve on its existing commentary. Where it is not in a position to do so, the commentary retains its force as sound exposition of an authoritative Bible no matter how neglected it may be. The only "further action" that could qualify or set aside the authority of an existing confession (and any of its parts) is a more sound exposition of Scripture. Where that has not taken place, the old confession remains in force. In the very nature of the case, neglect of a confession cannot bring an end to its authority. If its authority is a function of the degree of correctness accruing to its exposition of a Bible that is law and norm in the church, then its authority cannot be challenged by neglect. Neglect of a church confession by its members and even its leaders does not, in itself, constitute a confessional crisis. It will, eventually, constitute an educational crisis, since the church's officially promulgated, received, and adopted commentary on Scripture will no longer be understood. But the answer to an educational crisis is church-wide study of its existing confessions and catechisms, not the writing of new confessions.

The second element meriting attention here is the dialectic developed in Barth's definition between a "geographically circumscribed" Christian fellowship and the universality of its truth claims. For Barth, the proper subject of a Christian confession is a body of Christians capable of doing theology and of living the Christian life together. In the 1920s, that was still a geographically limited possibility. Communications were not then what they are now. Still, it is a definite church body which must declare its faith and when it does so, it will necessarily (unavoidably) also give expression to its theological identity (and the theological traditions which have shaped that identity). But — and here is where the dialectic makes itself felt — giving expression to that identity cannot be the goal of a confession. As Barth would later put the point,

A confession is not a Church confession which seeks only to represent the importance of one group in the Church or to declare and prove the equal

35. Barth, "Wünschbarkeit und Möglichkeit," p. 620.

justification of particular interests which may perhaps represent only the local or national peculiarity of one part of the Church. . . . However limited and oppressed the authors of a confession may be in the Church, if they really have to confess, i.e. to confess the Word of God, they cannot possibly dare to speak of themselves and from their own small corner, or in order to secure recognition for themselves and this corner. Not fearing to make the unheard-of claim which this involves, they must be confident to speak from and to the one universal Church. They must accept responsibility for expressing the voice of the *una sancta catholica.* Otherwise, they must be silent or at any rate not regard their speaking as the confession of the Church.[36]

A genuine church confession seeks to present an authentic insight from the revelation of God in Jesus Christ attested in Holy Scripture to the whole church. And because a church confession has this character its claim will be universal. But we must never lose sight of the fact that it is a particular group that is making this universal claim. Hence, even though group interests may never legitimately be made the goal of writing a document that aspires to be a genuine church confession, every such document will also give expression to the identity of its group. Its confession will offer an authoritative definition of its character to outsiders.

Obviously, the dialectic of particularity and universality that Barth seeks to uphold here is not an easy one to maintain. I would like to suggest that we can break this dialectic in two ways. On the one side, we allow the subject-matter treated in a would-be confession to become purely parochial, as described in the lengthy passage cited above. On the other hand though, and this is just as dangerous, we break with this dialectic when we seek a false universality that is the product of a willful suppression of our own particularity. Genuine universality cannot be purchased by seeking merely to be "generically Christian." Where this takes place, our desire is to emphasize only the lowest common denominator of what we share, doctrinally, with all other Christian bodies, steadfastly refusing all the while to acknowledge our own theological traditions and the ways in which they shape our attempts to define "generic Christianity" (either positively, through their ongoing but unexpressed presence in our efforts, or negatively, through our equally unexpressed opposition to our own traditions). Genuine universality is a function of the truth of the gospel we proclaim; as such it is something that must be given to us by God. We cannot establish it for ourselves through our love of benevolence, etc. A peace that we could give to ourselves is a profane, secular peace. It is not the peace that the Holy Spirit brings.

36. Barth, *CD* I/2, p. 623.

Conclusion

In this paper, I have tried to show how Karl Barth sought to address a situation very much akin to the one we face. I think it would be fitting to close with the advice with which he concluded the lament with which I began.

> In face of the embarrassed mumbling or total silence of the modern churches about their basic statements, dogmaticians can only surmise that finally the churches do not want any dogmatics, that they simply wish to preach, and go on preaching, as though the church were all right if only it could go on preaching, and did not want any reflection on God's Word, which might bring unrest to both the pastors and their flocks. If this is so, then the answer is that dogmatics must not respect these "undogmatic slumbers" of the church . . . but look out for the vital interest of the church, even against the church. The vital interest of the church may be summed up in the old war cry that the Reformers understood better and more profoundly than the humanists who first raised it: Back to the sources![37]

We cannot wait for the churches to undertake to exercise their proper teaching office in a full awareness of the human authority that is proper to such labor. The churches will die if we wait. What we can do, in an effort to shake the churches from their undogmatic slumbers, is to set a good example through submitting ourselves to churchly authority even when the churches are not actively exercising it. We can return to the sources (and thereby honor an ecclesial authority that has not been challenged by a new and improved exposition of Holy Scripture). We can do theology as Barth and Schleiermacher did it: through loving attention to and in constant conversation with the confessions of our churches. We can allow the confessions to perform their appointed function of a "first commentary" on Scripture by making them the primary conversation partner that we engage in our dogmatic labors; not slavishly following them as do those who think them to possess the absolute authority proper to God's Word alone but allowing them, as relatively binding authorities, to guide our efforts to appropriate the biblical message for constructive theological uses today. To do so will make it clear to all who read us that it is our desire to have our progress and our regress in theology measured by our churches. May God grant to us would-be Reformed theologians the grace to surrender our self-serving aims and to replace them with those that lead to the upbuilding of the church.

Amen.

37. Barth, *The Göttingen Dogmatics,* pp. 40-41.

CHAPTER 5

Theology and the Church's Mission: Catholic, Orthodox, Evangelical, and Reformed

William Stacy Johnson

Today as always the purpose of Christian theology is to embody and proclaim the gospel of grace. We are to proclaim the God who is graciously engaged to be "for" us and "with" us in Jesus Christ and who, in turn, judges us and calls us by the Spirit's power to embody this gracious engagement "for" and "with" one another. In short, Christian theology has a mission, and that human mission is meant to be a reflection of the triune God's own mission in behalf of the world.

Serving this mission, in response to the Word of God, requires theology to be reformed and always in the process of being reformed *(ecclesia reformata semper reformanda secundum verbum Dei)*. The words "reform" and "reformation" come from the Latin word *reformare*, which means literally to fashion, shape, or render something anew. To re-form the church, therefore, is not merely to retrieve something from the past in the manner of contemporary hermeneutical theologies, nor is it merely to experiment with new ideas from the present in the manner of modern revisionist theologies.[1] To retrieve and to revise one's inherited traditions are no doubt necessary tasks, but this exercise by itself falls far short of the monumental meaning conveyed by the word "reform." For to be "reformed" means that all worship, all doctrine, all practice, in short, the whole of

---

1. The distinction that many draw today between hermeneutical and revisionist theologies represents a false dichotomy. There is more revisionism at work in the hermeneutical theologies and more hermeneutical awareness in play within the revisionist theologies than is often acknowledged. Cf. George A. Lindbeck, *The Nature of Doctrine: Religion and Theology in a Postliberal Age* (Philadelphia: Westminster, 1984), with David Tracy, *The Analogical Imagination: Christian Theology and the Culture of Pluralism* (New York: Crossroad, 1981).

life, are to be called into question and transformed in the light of the living and dynamic Word of God. Reform, in other words, is not in the service of a program of our own devising (retrieving, revising, etc.) but occurs as a gift of God's own ongoing work in the world. To put it plainly, reform is an act of God.

Now this divine work of reform is not something we can coerce or second-guess. It is something real, to be sure, yet still incomplete, something present yet still waiting to be finished. In a sense, as the parables of Jesus suggest, God's work in the world confronts us as mystery. To that extent, it exceeds the language of our creeds and lies beyond the horizon of our particular aspirations for the church.

Perhaps this is why the so-called "Reformed tradition" in Protestantism, which has placed such an emphasis on the sovereignty, majesty, and glory of God, has itself proved so hard to define with finality. On the negative side, perhaps this is also why there has always been so much finger-pointing in Reformed circles as to who is truly Reformed and who is not. On the one hand, there can be no denying that there exists a distinctive Reformed tradition of theology and church life with its own particular emphases that spring from the sixteenth-century Swiss Reformation. As heirs of Zwingli, Calvin, Bullinger, and so many others, we have already inherited the reform of the church as a bequest from our past. Nevertheless, on the other hand, the Reformed tradition is ever-changing and diverse; it is nothing that we can pin down as a fixed and definable essence. Indeed, one of the hallmarks of Reformed theology is that no single creed or teaching office has been vested with the power to state definitively what the boundaries of Reformed opinion ought to be. Whereas Lutheran theology may be said to reach its summit in the Formula of Concord (1577) and the Book of Concord (1580), Reformed theology, as Jan Rohls observes, arrives at no such conclusion.[2] Its confessions are many, and it conceives the theological task as an ongoing *metanoia*, a process of everything we know about ourselves being transformed in accordance with everything we know about God.[3]

This emphasis on ongoing *metanoia* is especially necessary today. With western Christendom being dismantled before our very eyes, there is a pressing need for theologians to rethink their traditional approaches to theology. Insofar as the vocabulary and stories of the ancient tradition are no longer the common coinage on which our minds trade, the situation we face in Europe and the

---

2. Jan Rohls, *Reformed Confessions: Theology from Zurich to Barmen*, trans. John Hoffmeyer, intro. Jack L. Stotts, Columbia Series in Reformed Theology (Louisville: Westminster/John Knox Press, 1998), p. 9.

3. Cf. H. Richard Niebuhr, *The Meaning of Revelation* (New York: Macmillan, 1941), ch. 4.

United States today is less like that of the sixteenth century, when belief in God was already assumed, and more like the earliest centuries of the Christian movement, those days when every belief needed to be sifted and every plan of action examined afresh. Today our own back yard has once again reverted to a mission field, so that today the ongoing *metanoia* to which the church is called is likely to look fundamentally different from what has gone before. In this context, some of the old battles of the sixteenth and seventeenth centuries — battles pitting Lutherans against Roman Catholics, Reformed against Lutherans, etc. — may no longer seem as pressing.

With this in mind, then, we need an approach that recognizes "reform" as the task of the whole church, while not failing to lift up the distinctive concerns that have made the Reformed faith what it is. First, putting aside all attempts to reify the Reformed tradition as something to be sharply distinguished from other Christian confessions, we need to regain a holistic appreciation for the task of theology as simultaneously catholic, orthodox, evangelical, and reformed. Christian allegiance is not to a single tradition but to the gospel, not to the task of reform for reform's sake but to Christ. Therefore, one should never intend, in the first instance, to be a "Reformed" theologian; rather, one should intend to be a *Christian* theologian who is always in the process of *being* reformed. Neither catholicity, orthodoxy, evangelism, nor reformation is alone sufficient, but all four must engage in a mutually correcting conversation as we proceed together into our common missional future.

Second, recognizing the distinctive way in which we in the Reformed tradition have heard the gospel, we will need to pursue this holistic, missional theology in the light of our traditional commitments to grace alone, Christ alone, faith alone, and Scripture alone. By invoking these four rubrics today, I do not mean to signal a repristination of the past. What grace alone, Christ alone, faith alone, and Scripture alone mean today is likely to look rather different than it did in the sixteenth century. Accordingly, a church praying to be catholic, orthodox, evangelical, and reformed must receive its life like manna from the gospel of grace. Gathered afresh each new day, the gospel comes to us as more than a message, but a life. The mission of the triune God as graciously engaged in the world: God for us, Christ with us, the Spirit among us — that is the living drama of Christian proclamation to which theology seeks to bear witness.

Grace Alone: The Ground of Our Catholicity

Though it may seem to be a paradox, the aim of reforming the church is never an end in itself; reform for reform's sake is never the goal of the gospel. Instead, the protestant principle of reform, as Paul Tillich taught us, must always be linked to its catholic substance.[4] Already in the sixteenth century Heinrich Bullinger had suggested something similar in the very first of his *Sermonum Decades*. There Bullinger made it clear that a truly reformed and evangelical faith, one that seeks to be "authentic," or true to the Word of God, must also be "orthodox" and "catholic," which is to say, responsive to the faith that has been handed down through the centuries by the patriarchs, the prophets, the apostles, and the pivotal theologians of the early church.[5]

For Bullinger and the other theologians of the early Reformed tradition, being "reformed" was a task set before the whole church and not the prerogative of a single sect. Yet Bullinger's suggestion that we should link "reformed" and "evangelical" identity, on the one hand, to "catholic" and "orthodox" identity, on the other, raises a vexing problem. For it becomes frustratingly clear upon a moment's reflection that there has seldom been crafted a definition of "catholicity" that fails to operate in an exclusionary — and thus, arguably, non-catholic — way; nor any definition of "orthodoxy" that does not operate to exclude the very heterodoxy and change that ongoing reform — and thus, arguably, orthodoxy itself — would seem to require.

To find a paradigmatic example of this, one need look no further than to Augustine. According to the Bishop of Hippo the catholicity of the church meant universality, the church's wide-open embrace of the world with the gospel. When compared with the exclusionary policy of the Donatists, who viewed the church as a more narrow company of the committed, Augustine's was a vision of a church that would be an open hospital for sinners. Nevertheless, the supposed universality of Augustine's one, holy, catholic, and apostolic church included also the belief that there are some persons — notably "Jews and heretics" — who are outside the church *(extra ecclesiam)* and thus against the church *(contra ecclesiam)*.[6]

Yet how can one define Jews and others as being outside the sphere of grace when, according to ancient Christian teaching, it was the Jews through whom God made the world aware of the covenant of grace in the first place? This incongruity requires that we investigate further, and the more we examine the traditional notions of catholicity, the more we are confronted by a peculiar sort of circle: we begin to see that the concept of catholicity — when defined in terms of an inside and an outside, in terms of those who belong and those who

---

4. Paul Tillich, *The Protestant Era*, trans. James Luther Adams (Chicago: University of Chicago Press, 1948).

5. See *The Decades of Henry Bullinger*, 5 vols., ed. Thomas Harding, The Parker Society (Cambridge: Cambridge University Press, 1849), 1:45.

6. Augustine, *Epistulae ad Romanos inchoata expositio*.

do not — can gradually work to turn the very idea of catholicity itself into a contradiction. There is something exceedingly strange in a catholicity that marks off boundaries in order to define a theology whose goal ought to be precisely to break barriers down. After all, we are told by the Apostle Paul (Gal. 3:28) that in Christ "There is no longer Jew or Greek, there is no longer slave or free, there is no longer male and female; for all of you are one in Jesus Christ." Catholicity, arguably, ought to espouse a different sort of universality, one in which difference is no longer supposed to differentiate. In short, our concept of catholicity ought to be a reflection of what the Reformation theologians spoke of as grace alone.

"Grace alone" signals the belief that God's unmerited favor is alone able to redeem human life. This is a belief that also found its first systematic expression in Augustine, for whom grace is the gift of God's presence in the world to bring creatures to know God and to love God. Yet "grace alone" should not be construed narrowly as a definition of how human beings are saved, but should be seen as the very definition of who God is. Grace is not primarily an anthropological, ecclesial, or soteriological concept but a properly theological concept, a concept about God. God is not just any old "god" we may happen to dream up, but in Jesus Christ we know a God who is irrevocably "for" human beings. As Luther put it, to receive the grace that is *pro nobis* in salvation is to take hold of a promise that is rooted in God's own character, revealed in Christ, the suffering one who both forgives us and renews us.[7]

Within Reformed Christianity the articulation of God's character as grace was usually cast with an emphasis on the doctrine of election. Now to the post-Enlightenment mind, the doctrine of election may seem the least likely place to turn for an affirmation of the catholicity of grace. Especially as conceived within the relentless logic of seventeenth-century Calvinism, election may seem to represent the very epitome of all that is exclusionary and parochial. What are we to make, asks a critic such as Regina M. Schwartz, of a God who chooses some to triumph and consigns others to perdition, who blesses the few but marks the rest with the curse of Cain?[8]

To interpret election in this way, however, is to miss that its fundamental message is meant to be one of solace, good news for all humanity. Election, in both its Jewish and Christian forms, offers a sublime religious answer to one of the most pervasive questions human beings ask, namely: Who are we, and why

7. Martin Luther, *Sermo de duplici iustitia* (1519). For a contemporary rendition of this idea, see Ronald F. Thiemann, *Revelation and Theology: The Gospel as Narrated Promise* (Notre Dame: University of Notre Dame Press, 1984).

8. Regina M. Schwartz, *The Curse of Cain: The Violent Legacy of Monotheism* (Chicago: University of Chicago Press, 1997).

are we here? We are here, answers the doctrine of election, because in the exercise of grace, God knows human beings, God saves human beings, and God empowers human beings to be engaged in behalf of the "other."

First, God knows us. This means that God thought of us before we were and called us into being. Through election, God sets God's heart upon us and determines not to be God without us. Thus, to speak of "grace alone" is not only to pronounce the revelation of God's character but also the demarcation of our own calling as human beings. Just as it is God's unique character to be "for" us, so too it is our upward calling as God's people to be fundamentally "for" the other. This engagement for the other should be the test of all our social, political, and ecclesiastical relationships. Do they indeed embody this irreversible disposition for the other?

Second, God is at work to save us. This need not signal a mechanical predeterminism that eviscerates human freedom or that eliminates contingency in the drama of history. Rather, so-called pre-*destination* underscores that human beings have a *destiny* already thought of by God in advance. The New Testament letter of 1 Peter compares it to a parent who sets aside an inheritance that is waiting there for the child (1 Peter 1:4). God has set before us our destiny, if we will but live into that future and embrace that hope.

Third, through election, and through the future it projects for us, God empowers us to embody God's "yes" in behalf of the other. We misunderstand who God is and who we are, if we construe too narrowly the "us" in this phrase, "God for us." Here, I believe, the more catholic instincts of Zwingli (who emphasized the goodness above the glory of God, and who expected salvation to include Socrates and others outside the Christian fold) are superior to the more narrow perspective of the successors of Calvin.[9] The real problem with seventeenth-century Calvinism — a problem visible both in double predestination and in its Arminian shadow side — is that both these views understand the part *we* play in the drama to be determined from a point of indifference. For double predestination, it is God who chooses — inscrutably — to elect some and reject others, whereas for the Arminians it is human beings themselves who choose either to embrace or to reject God.

By contrast, the point of the biblical doctrine of election is that *God is never indifferent,* and neither should we be. Nor should indifference ever mark our social or political arrangements. This is the main point of Karl Barth's christocentric reconstruction of the doctrine of election.[10] According to Barth,

9. On the goodness of God, see Huldrych Zwingli, *On Providence* (1530). The expectation of seeing the virtuous pagans in heaven is mentioned in Zwingli's *Exposition of the Faith* (1536).

10. Karl Barth, *Church Dogmatics* II/2 (Edinburgh: T. & T. Clark, 1957).

the humanity of Jesus of Nazareth is the earthly sacrament of the living God. Jesus' life lived "for" the other, is an index of God's own engagement in our behalf. God is never indifferent concerning the humanity of a single one of us.[11] When God's election operates to invest some with a particular calling to be God's agent, theirs is not a calling to a particular status but to a special service. It is a special vocation, like that of Abraham, undertaken by the few for the sake of the many. It is a vocation like that of a beloved son, whose life is placed at risk of death, not because God is a tyrant but because just such risk-taking is the measure of God's own character.[12] It is just such a vocation, a calling in behalf of the other — and of every other — that Christians believe was enacted by God's mission to the world in Jesus of Nazareth.

Christ Alone: The Measure of Our Orthodoxy

If ever there was a generation since the Reformation needing to hear anew this message of grace alone, of a giving of oneself in behalf of the other, it is ours. The pressing religious question for so many in this self-centered era of postmodernity is not whether salvation comes by way of grace alone but whether there is any such thing as grace at all. This question of whether God is really gracious arises not only from those who are estranged from their religious traditions but from many who are searching for intelligibility within those very same traditions.

Is it any longer possible, in a postmodern, post-Holocaust world, to believe in a divine grace that is at work in human history? The many outrages that marked the history of the twentieth century — two world wars, Hiroshima and Nagasaki, the killing fields of Cambodia, "ethnic cleansing" in the Balkans, nuclear disaster at Chernobyl, and on and on — found their nadir in the mass extermination of European Jewry in the death camps of World War II. This event — the Shoah — in which every Jew in Europe was made a target for death, has shattered the faith of many religious-minded people, Jew-

---

11. As the Apostle Paul puts it in Romans 5:18, speaking of the work of Jesus Christ: "just as one man's trespass (Adam) led to condemnation FOR ALL, so one man's act of righteousness (Jesus) leads to justification and life FOR ALL." Or again, in Romans 11:32, speaking of the relationship between Israel and the Church, "God has imprisoned all in disobedience so that [God] may be merciful to all."

12. Consider, for instance, Jon Levenson's recent examination of the biblical history of the "beloved son" from Cain and Abel to Jesus of Nazareth, a history of sibling rivalry in which the elect one is inextricably bound for and in behalf of the other. *The Death and Resurrection of the Beloved Son: The Transformation of Child Sacrifice in Judaism and Christianity* (New Haven: Yale University Press, 1993).

ish, Christian, and otherwise. For many it has precipitated a monumental crisis of faith and a questioning of God's grace, a questioning that they believe must be answered, or else.[13]

For the Jewish philosopher Emmanuel Levinas, the systemic violence against Jews during the Holocaust bears lessons for all people about the dangers of unfettered ideology and the bankruptcy of naïve theodicies.[14] As Karl Barth put it, God says "no" to evil, yet in human history God seems to work to confront evil only through human agency itself. We must not wait for some superhuman act of God to overcome evil, but we must ourselves be willing to become the act of God, by the Spirit's power. As both Levinas and Barth have in their different ways argued, to know oneself as "elect" is to put aside indifference; it is to find oneself seized and placed under arrest, indeed held hostage by the claims of the other.[15] As people of faith, we must proclaim with unrelenting vigor the God who is "for" us and who calls us to be "for" the other.

In a post-Holocaust world, however, the claim that God is "for" us is not enough. We need more. We need to know that God is not content to remain aloof from humanity. We need to know that God is living out God's own life among us. The claim of the Christian faith is that God is not only "for" us but that God has determined to be "with" us as well.

In Christian confession, this is what is seen in the life, death, and resurrection of Jesus of Nazareth. God is able not only to love the "other" from afar but to actually become "other" on our behalf, and to do so without ceasing to be God. In the life and death of this suffering one, God is with us. As Dietrich Bonhoeffer once poignantly put it, only the suffering God can help. Or, as Karl Barth has put it equally well, the broken humanity of Jesus of Nazareth presents itself as the earthly sacrament of the living God.

There are many things over which Christians may disagree, but the conviction that God is truly "with" us in Jesus Christ provides the only measure of our orthodoxy. For many of us, the idea of a single "orthodoxy" is a dangerous and impossible notion. "Orthodoxy" literally means "right opinion," and one might assume that right opinion is always the goal of the quest for learning. Yet

13. See especially Richard Rubenstein, *After Auschwitz: History, Theology, and Contemporary Judaism,* 2nd ed. (Baltimore and London: Johns Hopkins University Press, 1992); Emil Fackenheim, *God's Presence in History: Jewish Affirmations and Philosophical Reflections* (New York: Harper, 1970); *To Mend the World: Foundations of Post-Holocaust Jewish Philosophy* (Bloomington and Indianapolis: Indiana University Press, 1994); Arthur Cohen, *The Tremendum: A Theological Interpretation of the Holocaust* (New York: Continuum, 1993).

14. Richard A. Cohen, *Elevations: The Height of the Good in Rosenzweig and Levinas* (Chicago and London: University of Chicago Press, 1994), p. 128.

15. See especially, Emmanuel Levinas, *Otherwise Than Being or Beyond Essence,* trans. Alphonso Lingis (Dordrecht: Martinus Nijhoff, 1991).

it is not clear that there is anyone wise enough or good enough to define what constitutes right opinion for all time.

The Reformed theologian Friedrich Schleiermacher noted that in every age the church entertains not only opinions that are orthodox but opinions that are heterodox as well.[16] If "orthodoxy" means "right opinion," then "heterodoxy" means simply "other opinion." Opinions that may be considered heterodox today, Schleiermacher observed, sometimes become orthodox tomorrow. We may even go a step further and claim that orthodoxy needs heterodoxy in order to remain true to the divine mystery of its subject matter. The quest for "right opinion" needs the challenge of "other opinion" lest it degenerate into concepts that are fixed and idolatrous.

Just as the belief that God is "for" us is the ground of our catholicity, I want to suggest that God "with" us should be the only measure of orthodoxy in the church. What we mean by God "with" us was painstakingly worked out by the seven ecumenical councils of the early church. These councils are accepted by East and West, but they were primarily the work of theologians who belonged to what we now know as Eastern Orthodoxy. To be sure, the philosophical presuppositions at work in these seven councils are no longer part of our own intellectual world. Still, these councils help us to think about the "person" of Christ, even though there is still no ecumenical consensus concerning the "work" of Christ and perhaps never will be.

The journey into orthodoxy, as is well known, was set in motion by the claim of Arius that the Word, which became flesh in Jesus Christ, was a created and not an eternal Word. In Jesus Christ, we are confronted with the highest and best of God's creation but not, in actuality, with God.[17] The Church at Nicea said "no" to this, but what Arius was teaching was hardly based on his own idiosyncrasies. From the very beginnings of the Christian movement, its theologians, *and even its Nicene theologians,* could not completely rid themselves of the Greek idea that God can have no commerce with anything that is in the process of becoming or that dies. Thus, for centuries theologians have denied that God can suffer (God is impassible, they said) or

16. Friedrich Schleiermacher, *Kurze Darstellung des theologischen Studiums,* ed. Heinrich Scholz (Leipzig, 1910). It should be noted that "heterodoxy," which is necessary to the task of theology, is not for Schleiermacher the same as "heresy," which is to embrace a view that steps outside the bounds of Christian faith.

17. The debates represented in the seven ecumenical councils were precipitated when a trinitarian religion, based in the gospel, collided with a unitarian theology, based in Greek philosophy. The question was whether the religion would properly transform the theology, or the theology would unjustly stifle the religion. Leonard Hodgson, *The Doctrine of the Trinity,* p. 103, quoted in Robert Jenson, *Systematic Theology* (Oxford: Oxford University Press, 1998), vol. 1, p. 95, n. 37.

change (God is immutable, they declared). In so declaring, these theologians were unable to embrace the God who in Jesus Christ embraces us in our fragility and brokenness, in our humanity.

Unfortunately, the Reformed theology that flows from the sixteenth century has too often been held captive to the limitations of this Greek philosophy. Reformed theology has always attempted to claim at one and the same time a God who is the eternally self-sufficient ground of all that is, and a God who is actively at work transforming the world.[18] Reformed theology has customarily asserted both sides of this twofold conviction without adequately explaining how both could really be true at once.

Consider, for example, the Reformed tendency to distinguish the divine and human natures of Jesus. Technically, both Bullinger and Calvin embraced the theology of Cyril of Alexandria and rejected Nestorius. Yet, this embrace and this rejection usually were made in name only without working through the issue systematically. Up until the days of Karl Barth, it was not clear that Reformed theology had adequately thought through what is at stake in the sharp distinction it draws between the Creator and the creature. In short, I am saying the Lutherans were not completely wrong in their suspicions that early Reformed theology had a tendency to flirt with Nestorianism.

In light of this, and for the sake of the church's mission, it is time for us in the Reformed churches to reexamine our relationship to all seven of the councils. Speaking for the Reformed tradition in the *Second Helvetic Confession,* Heinrich Bullinger endorsed the first four ecumenical councils, from Nicea to Chalcedon. At Chalcedon the church insisted that Jesus Christ is both truly human and truly divine. The Chalcedonian definition does not mean that Jesus Christ is fifty percent human and fifty percent divine, nor that some aspects of his person are human and others divine. Rather, Jesus Christ is, so to speak, both one hundred percent human and one hundred percent divine. "He is of the same reality as God [*homoousion to patri*] as far as his deity is concerned and of the same reality as we are ourselves [*homoousion hemin*] as far as his human-ness is concerned."[19] Jesus Christ shows us what it means to be divine and also what it means to be human. Chalcedon corrects our mistaken assumption that we already know in advance what true humanity and true divinity might be. Apart from Jesus Christ we are without genuine and complete knowl-

---

18. Both sides of this vision, incidently, are under assault in a postmodern world. On the one hand, following the lead of Heidegger many have repudiated the search for a highest principle that grounds the possibility and reality of everything else. On the other hand, taking their cue from Derrida, many more are suspicious that every appeal to an ultimate "presence" in human history is illusory and masks a power play in which one group is seeking to coerce another.

19. John H. Leith, *Creeds of the Churches* (Richmond: John Knox, 1973), p. 36.

edge of either God or ourselves. In the life, death, and resurrection of Jesus Christ, the life and character of God have been demonstrated for all to see. God is as Jesus is; God does as Jesus does. In that same life, death, and resurrection we also discover who we are and who we are meant to be. It is not the case that some of Jesus' actions are divine and some human, but all his public actions convey this togetherness of divinity and humanity.

By stopping at Chalcedon, however, Reformed theologians tended to underscore the distinction between the divine and human natures. After the Council at Nicea in 325 A.D., with its declaration that in the person of Jesus Christ humanity was being confronted by the act of the living God, the subsequent councils fluctuated back and forth between the Antiochene emphasis on divine unity and on the difference between the Creator and the creature, and the Alexandrian emphasis on the Word becoming flesh, assuming human nature, and transforming all humanity in the process. At Chalcedon, the church reached a compromise between the two schools that, relying as it did so heavily on the Tome of Leo, leaned somewhat in the direction of Antioch, thus underscoring the distinction between divinity and humanity.

Bullinger claimed that the councils after Chalcedon added nothing substantive to the christological discussion. Yet this is not true. Had it more clearly embraced the Fifth Council, with its endorsement of the hypostatic union of the divine and human natures in Jesus, Reformed theology could have made more explicit its affirmation of Cyril and the reality of the Word made flesh. Similarly, the Sixth Council, with its espousal of a coincidence of divine and human willing in Jesus, provides a way to speak of the divine-human togetherness in Jesus, while also preserving a proper differentiation between the two. Even the Seventh Council, with its affirmation of the human capacity and calling to bear the divine image, is arguably necessary for an intelligible theology of the triune God who is for us and with us in Jesus Christ.

The orthodoxy of the councils is germane to one of the pivotal conflicts in contemporary Reformed theology, namely the extent to which God's embrace of the other is constitutive for God's own being. This issue is raised by Barth's theology, but Barth himself did not provide a clear answer. One school of Barth interpretation emphasizes that the being of God in election must retain a logical priority over the act of God in history; divine a-seity takes precedence over divine pro-meity. To that extent, what God does in human history is not so much constitutive as it is exemplary of who God is. Another school of interpretation, however, understands God's pro-meity as constitutive of who God is in a-seity. This alternative view points to Barth's radical claim that in Jesus Christ God determined *not* to be God without the human. What has happened in Jesus Christ, and perhaps even in all human suffering, on this view, is constitutive for the being of God. The incarnation — God "with" us — was more than a thirty-three-year experiment. God would rather join us in our suffering and death, on this view, than break covenant with us.

It is the latter view, I believe, that best helps us make sense of our confession, "Christ alone," and enables us to heal the breach between the competing sides of our overall theological vision. Remember that the "Christ alone" is saying two things. It is saying, first, that what we see in the humanity of Jesus Christ provides the distinctive way of knowing what it means to be God, and, second, that the peculiar way in which Jesus is divine, namely through being truly human, shows us the way into our own humanity. To lift up what God does in Jesus Christ in this way is not to undermine our earlier claim to universal election and catholicity.

We are not saying that God's revelation in Jesus Christ prevents God from working in all times and places, including times and places outside the bounds of Christianity. Nor is the attempt here one of shutting down further discussion. Some people find it hard to declare their own identity as Christian without opposing it to non-Christian identity. They find it difficult to think of catholicity and orthodoxy without defining these matters over against something believed to be heresy. Obviously there are some beliefs that are heretical, i.e., non-Christian. Nevertheless, in opposing such beliefs, we must exercise care not to deny the gospel of grace in the process.

What I am saying is that the way God is "with" us in Jesus Christ — embracing the suffering other — is determinative for how we Christians believe God is working everywhere to save. God "with" us is also determinative for how we, who are followers of Jesus Christ, are meant to behave in the world. The primary point of advancing an orthodoxy concerning the person of Christ, in other words, is to seal God's priority, which is the priority of the other.

Faith Alone: Trusting the Gospel, Being the Church

If "grace alone" is the claim that the God of election and covenant is on a mission to be "for" us, and "Christ alone" is the claim that this mission extends so far that God purposes to be "with" us in our humanity, then "faith alone" bespeaks the way God's Spirit is made real "among" us. If God "for" us is the ground of our catholicity, and Christ "with" us is the measure of our orthodoxy, then the Spirit "among" us signals how it is that we are brought to the point of trusting the good news of the gospel. In short, theology must not only be catholic and orthodox, it must be evangelical too, partaking through faith in the dynamic, life-giving reality of the God who is.

To be "evangelical," to be rooted in the *euangelion*, is not necessarily the same thing as embracing what on the American scene today is known as evangelical*ism*. The truth of God is dialectical and cannot be reduced to any particular religious or cultural ideology, whether of the right, the left, or the middle. Christ alone is Lord, and Christ speaks through many voices as the drama of salvation continues to unfold. So then, the desire to be "evangelical" means broadly the desire to trust the gospel and thus to be the church.

In explaining what this gospel means, Martin Luther made the doctrine of justification the centerpiece, the article upon which the church stands or falls. Justification by grace through faith means that salvation and right living come to us not as a human work but as a divine gift. To be made right with God is not something we can earn through merit, nor is receiving God's grace conditioned (as was said to be the case in the *via moderna* of medieval theology) upon one first somehow doing one's best *(facere quod in se est)*. Rather, receiving the righteousness of God consists in trusting God to be true to God's promise, and being thus free to bestow righteousness upon us, even in the absence of our merit. As such, the righteousness received by faith alone is the extrinsic, "alien" righteousness of Christ himself, a righteousness that belongs to the sinner only by grace. Unlike the Augustinian view, carried forward into the Middle Ages, in which justification refers to both the *declaration* of righteousness and the *process* of being made righteous, Luther's view of justification, especially as carried forward in his successor Melanchthon, reconceived it as a forensic declaration alone. It is forensic rather than ethical.

The Reformed tradition followed Luther, but has not always made justification the article on which all else turns.[20] So much emphasis has been placed on justification by grace through faith, however, that we risk forgetting Luther's other great contribution, the theology of the cross. As Luther made clear in the Heidelberg Disputation of 1518, the faith that recognizes and trusts what God has done in Jesus Christ is precisely a faith that looks to the suffering and cross of Christ. Sometimes referred to as Luther's "humility theology," this teaching underscores that justification, in liberating us, does not constitute a freedom "from" but a freedom "for" the other. To receive grace is to receive Christ, and to receive Christ is to belong to the fellowship of Christ's suffering. Just as Christ is "for us" and thus dwells in us, says Luther in *Von der Freiheit eines Christenmenschen*, so also I must freely give myself "as a Christ to my neighbor." Justification declares one righteous, but the righteousness in question here is the righteousness of covenant relationship, the righteousness of "being Christ" for and with the other.

If this need for our own embodiment of grace was not always clear in the

20. See, e.g., Karl Barth, *Das christliche Leben. Die Kirchliche Dogmatik IV/4. Fragmente aus dem Nachlass Vorlesungen 1959-1961*, ed. Hans-Anton Drewes and Eberhard Jüngel, Gesamtausgabe II, Akademische Werke, 1959-1961 (Zürich: TVZ, 1976), 55-73.

writings of Luther, it was made abundantly clear in the theology of the Swiss reformation. Although the Reformed tradition can claim, through Zwingli, to have already arrived at "Scripture alone," "grace alone," and "Christ alone" working independently of Luther, there can be no question but that "faith alone," the recovery of a full Pauline understanding of salvation, was the unique contribution to Protestantism of Martin Luther himself.[21] Nevertheless, the Reformed tradition links the Lutheran emphasis on justification with a counterbalancing emphasis on sanctification, a recognition that the law is a form of the gospel, and a desire to see justification work itself out in the reform of church and world. In short, we Reformed theologians fully accept the Lutheran insights that true freedom is freedom for obedience, and that true obedience is freedom for the "other." Justification by grace through faith can mean nothing less.

To this must be added, however, the Reformed insistence that we can receive the gospel of grace only in obeying it. In the end, the disparity between justification as either forensic or ethical is a false dichotomy. How ironic it is that Luther, who lifted up the need for us to be Christ to one another, failed to extend the *sola fide* into a more thoroughgoing reform of church and world! To be sure, there were social and political factors that conspired to push him, both ecclesially and politically, in a more conservative direction. Still, to be evangelical is to let the gospel and not circumstances rule the day. It is to clear a path so that the gospel may be brought to bear to transform the circumstances.

As we go about this transformative task today, we do so, as noted above, with Christendom collapsing before our very eyes. Because many church leaders today seem to be fearful of the western church's apparent loss of power, the voices of a creeping sectarianism are tempting us to retreat into an insulated cocoon, to withdraw from culture, and to eschew all things secular. Often the neo-sectarian argument appeals to the biblical motif of Exile. The church has been consigned to Exile, they claim, and so we must simply be the church and forget about taking up responsibility for the secular world.

This is a strange argument coming from western Christians who, by and large, control unprecedented wealth, information, and influence in today's world. The plight of the mainline western church is not a crisis of power, as the metaphor of Exile implies, but of meaning. The people who inhabit the pews, as well as so many who have left the pews, are asking real questions about the meaning of religious faith, and they need to hear constructive Christian answers. Our situation is less like that of the Old Testament Exile and more like

21. Zwingli embraced "Scripture alone" as early as 1516, and certainly by 1523 had come to speak of "Scripture alone," "Christ alone," and "grace alone." See W. P. Stephens, *The Theology of Huldrych Zwingli* (Oxford: Clarendon Press, 1986), ch. 1.

that of the book of Ecclesiastes. We have "been there," and "done that," concluding that all is vanity, and now we wonder what is the meaning of it all.

Catholicity, orthodoxy, and the gospel itself require that we embrace the *saeculum* by speaking God's "yes" to the secular world.[22] To do this faithfully will necessitate ongoing biblically grounded dialogue with the intellectual and cultural currents of the contemporary world. The goal of the gospel is not merely the rescue of the sinner but the remaking of the church and the world. It is to embody the missionary purposes of the triune God.

Scripture Alone: Fountainhead of Ongoing Reform

God *for* us, Christ *with* us, and the Spirit *among* us must be accompanied by another belief, namely, that the living God still remains *beyond* us. The catholicity, orthodoxy, and evangelical witness to which the church is called are ongoing tasks that we never completely fulfill; the depth of God for us, Christ with us, and the Spirit among us are realities we never fully understand. For this reason, among others, the historic Reformed confessions articulated what has come to be known as the "Scripture principle." The confessions of the Reformed tradition almost always begin not with the assertion of a particular doctrine, such as justification, but with the declaration of Scripture alone as the only test of faith and practice in the church.[23]

By correlating the Reformed motto, "Scripture alone," with the equally Reformed insistence on the need for ongoing reform, I am attempting here to lean against the biblicism to which some Reformed Christians have fallen prey. Scripture alone cannot mean for us today that the Bible is the sole source of theological reflection. What it does mean is that the reality to which Scripture uniquely bears witness is the fountainhead of our ongoing engagement with the triune God. Scripture offers us the corrective lens, to put it another way, through which to perceive the ongoing work of the living God.

The time is ripe, in this postmodern, post-Christendom age, for a fresh engagement with the text of Scripture. In a grand departure from modernity, which sought emancipation from biblical textuality in favor of a religion within the limits of reason alone, postmodernity — strangely and perhaps providen-

22. Cf. R. A. Markus, *Saeculum: History and Society in the Theology of St. Augustine* (Cambridge: Cambridge University Press, 1970).

23. See especially Zwingli's confessional writings, the *Sixty-Seven Articles of Zurich* (1523), the *Ten Theses of Berne* (1528), the *Confession of Faith to the German Emperor Charles V* (1530), and the *Exposition of the Christian Faith to King Francis I of France* (1531). See also Zwingli's *Commentary on True and False Religion* (1525).

tially enough — has announced an unabashed return to the text. With its fascination over the enigma of language, its probing into the perplexities of narrative meaning, and its focus on the infinite interpretive possibilities of textuality, postmodernity has opened a strategic door to new forms of scriptural reasoning. Rather than the secular world standing in judgment over the text, it is the text, so to speak, that gives birth to the world. Accordingly, the return to Scripture is visible today in the work of both Christian (e.g., Hans Frei, George Lindbeck) and Jewish (e.g., Moshe Greenberg, Michael Fishbane, Peter Ochs) scholars.[24]

Nevertheless, if the postmodern calling into question of Enlightenment assumptions about the Bible opens a door for scriptural reasoning, it also poses a challenge to certain premodern and modernist practices of scriptural reading that are still prevalent in the churches. As a challenge to premodern readings, it will no longer do simply to reify "the Bible" as though it were a single agent that "speaks" in a univocal manner. Instead, the scriptures bear witness to the reality of God's work in the world through a bewildering variety of voices, a fact that has direct implications for theology. Rather than presuming that one already knows the meaning of the divine Word to which the scriptures bear witness, it is now time to return with a new openness to the enigma of the text itself. One of the sad ironies of the American Christian scene is that, notwithstanding two centuries of historical critical work that should have taught us otherwise, "proof-texting" is still the dominant mode of argument when theological disputes arise.

Similarly, as a challenge to modern readings, postmodernity levels a critique against the reductionism effected by some uses of the historical critical method in mainline biblical interpretation. After the work of interpreters as diverse as Gadamer, Ricoeur, and Derrida, it will no longer suffice to naïvely employ the assumption that texts have a single, objective, historically ascertainable meaning rooted in the intention of an author. For one thing, the situation is simply more complicated historically, and, for another, this way of thinking misconstrues how Scripture functions as Scripture. It is not the one, historically objective meaning distilled by the biblical scholar that gives Scripture its authenticity; rather, it is the reiterability of the biblical texts, with their surplus of meaning, in ever new contexts that enables meaning to come alive yet again in the believing community. This means that the "horizon" of present meaning is not impervious to change but is itself forever in motion. Biblical meaning is not just intratextual but intertextual.

This new postmodern situation, I submit, offers strategic opportunities —

---

24. See Peter Ochs, ed., *The Return to Scripture in Judaism and Christianity: Essays in Postcritical Scriptural Interpretation* (New York: Paulist, 1993).

and perils — for those who pray for the ongoing reform of the church. Just as God's work in the world confronts us as an unfolding mystery, so also being reformed involves a preparation for the "new thing" God is doing in the church's midst. It is this dynamic reality to which Scripture bears unique witness.

Conclusion

To sum it up, a theology that responds to the work of the living God must seek in a new way to be simultaneously catholic, orthodox, evangelical, and reformed. These four rubrics are not ends in themselves but signposts that point us to the vital drama of God "for" us, Christ "with" us, the Spirit "among" us. In addition, God is, so to speak, *beyond* us, and so theology must engage in an ongoing and mutually correcting conversation that touches base with all four concerns. Just as no one is truly reformed who does not seek also to be truly catholic and orthodox, so too there can be no catholic and orthodox rendition of the gospel that is not always also in the process of being reformed.

I have modulated these four rubrics into a different key than that which they sounded for our sixteenth-century forebears, but this is to be expected. Our calling as Christians is not to repeat the timeless "essence" of the Reformed tradition but to assume our respective roles in the great drama of salvation as it unfolds in unexpected new ways in church and world. Today that drama is being played out on a new stage, for a new audience, in a vastly new social, political, and cultural situation. Guided by grace alone as the ground of our catholicity, Christ alone as the measure of our orthodoxy, faith alone as the way we receive the gospel, and Scripture alone as the fountainhead of ongoing reform, let the whole church honor the God who is for us and with us in Jesus Christ and who calls us, by the Spirit's power at work among us, to be for and with one another.

PART II

How to Shape Reformed Ecclesiology

We Believe the One Holy and Catholic Church . . . : Reformed Identity and the Unity of the Church

Margit Ernst

> The Spirit builds *one* church,
> united in *one* Lord and *one* hope
> with *one* ministry around *one* table.
> He calls *all* believers in Jesus
> to respond in worship together,
> to accept all gifts from the Spirit,
> to learn from each other's tradition,
> to make unity visible on earth.
>
> "Our Song of Hope," 1974 —
> Reformed Church in America

How we understand ourselves has a great impact on how we relate to others, how we understand and act out our relationships. This is true not only for individuals, but also for communities, and here in particular, for communities of faith. To enter into a relationship, into a dialogue, means to bring into this relationship what and who we are — what we have in common with our partners and what distinguishes us from them.

Reformed churches have been actively involved in the ecumenical movement for more than a century. In fact, they seem to have a spontaneous inclination to advocate agreement, reconciliation, and cooperation among the separated churches.[1] And yet, when Reformed churches are challenged to formulate their convictions jointly *as* Reformed churches, their answers remain vague and often even contradictory. The dialogue partners of Reformed churches often complain that it is difficult to find out what these Reformed churches stand for today. This problem becomes even more difficult when Reformed churches themselves seek to figure out what it means to belong to this particular tradition. Is there a common "Reformed identity," and provided that there were one, what would that mean for the quest for the unity of the one holy and catholic church?

With this essay, I want to focus on one single aspect that seems to be very informative in the search for a Reformed identity: the Reformed understanding of confessions and its meaning for the Reformed understanding of the unity of the church. From the very beginning, it has been a hallmark of the Reformed tradition that there was (and still is) neither a single confession, nor a collection of confessions, that could claim any kind of authority for *all* Reformed churches. On the contrary, Reformed churches have produced an astonishingly great number of confessions throughout the centuries,[2] of which some became more important and influential (like the Westminster Standards, the Canons of Dort, or the Heidelberg Catechism), while others are long forgotten. And although there have been attempts to harmonize Reformed confessions,[3] there has never been a kind of "Reformed standard" with an authority similar to that of the Book of Concord for Lutheran churches. As a consequence, it seems to be not easy (or maybe even possible) to define a common Reformed identity by means of the confessional tradition of Reformed churches — all the more, since the writing of new confessional statements has not come to a definite end.

After several centuries of relative inactivity in the development of new confessions, the twentieth century brought a kind of "revival," in which churches of the Reformed tradition worldwide issued about fifty new confessions or statements of faith.[4] These confessions differ considerably in their

1. Cf. Lukas Vischer, "Der Auftrag der reformierten Kirchen heute," in *Gottes Bund gemeinsam bezeugen: Aufsätze zu Themen der ökumenischen Bewegung (Herausgegeben von einem Freundeskreis)* (Göttingen: Vandenhoek & Ruprecht, 1992), p. 11.

2. In 1903, E. F. K. Mueller published a collection of almost 60 Reformed confessions from 1523 to 1883 (*Die Bekenntnisschriften der reformierten Kirche* [reprint, Waltrop: Spenner, 1999]), and this collection is not even complete.

3. As early as 1581 and 1612 two collections (the *Harmonia Confessionum Fidei Orthodoxarum et Reformatarum Ecclesiarum* and the *Corpus et Syntagma Confessionum fidei*) tried to define a consensus among the most important Reformed confessions and the Lutheran Confessio Augustana Variata, but neither one gained enduring influence or authority.

4. Most of these confessions and statements of faith until 1982 are collected in Lukas Vischer, ed., *Reformed Witness Today* (Bern: Evangelische Arbeitsstelle Oekumene Schweiz, 1982).

contents as well as in their forms and intentions: there are short statements of faith, intended for liturgical use in worship; confessions dealing with one single issue on the one hand and confessions trying to summarize the Christian faith on the other hand; there are bases of church unions and declarations on human rights — and so forth. They do not speak the same theological language; they do not focus on the same doctrines. There is no list, no set of *the* essential tenets of *the* Reformed faith worldwide, no "TULIP-principle"[5] that could be defined as the basis for each and every confession. Furthermore, none of the "classical keywords" (such as predestination, for example) of the Reformed tradition appears in every confession — some of them are mentioned very rarely or never. There is also a wide diversity of churches that have issued new confessional statements over the last decades: churches in a minority situation in non-Christian societies and mainline churches in post-Christian societies, churches stemming from mission or emigration, and long-established churches. The background and history of the churches that have confessed their faith anew are as diverse as are the churches of the Reformed tradition worldwide.

Now, can we find a common Reformed identity, a common Reformed self-understanding in these confessions? Theologians, Reformed churches, and the World Alliance of Reformed Churches have struggled for quite some time to define what does make us "Reformed," what does distinguish the Reformed tradition from other Christian traditions. This is the challenge often raised by partners in interconfessional dialogues. The World Alliance, for example, held a meeting of Reformed theologians in 1981 on the theme of "Confessions and Confessing in the Reformed Tradition Today" to examine how Reformed churches confess their faith today, and what these new confessions might have to say about the "identity" of the Reformed tradition.[6] Subsequently, the WARC and other Reformed institutions have been working on these questions — especially on the search for a Reformed identity — and have issued several studies from individual theologians, organizations, and Reformed churches.[7]

Given the variety and diversity of the recent confessional statements, it is

5. According to the Canons of Dort, some branches of the Reformed tradition summarize their understanding of Reformed faith with this principle. TULIP stands for: *T*otal depravity, *U*nconditional election, *L*imited atonement, *I*rresistible grace, and *P*erseverance of the saints.

6. Cf. *Confessions and Confessing in the Reformed Tradition Today* — Studies from the World Alliance of Reformed Churches 2 (Geneva, 1982).

7. The most recent attempt to portray the "Reformed Heritage" features certain common emphases as well as unresolved issues. See Jean-Jacques Bauswein and Lukas Vischer, *The Reformed Family Worldwide: A Survey of Reformed Churches, Theological Schools, and International Organizations* (Grand Rapids: Eerdmans, 1999), pp. 26-33.

in fact not an easy task to work out something that is common to them all or could be described as a "Reformed identity." And, of course, as important and authoritative as confessions of faith are, they are by no means a sufficient base for defining and specifying a Reformed identity, since that would need to take all other expressions of faith and life of the respective churches into account. Nevertheless, confessions do hold a special authority; all other expressions of the faith and life of Reformed churches can only be considered and fully understood in their relation to the insights of faith that are expressed in confessional statements. Hence confessions have a twofold relation to all other expressions of a church's faith and life: they articulate in a distinctive way the living faith of a church, and they are guidelines for that church's faith and life. Therefore, in confining my considerations to that particular aspect of Reformed identity, I do not claim to talk about an all-embracing Reformed identity, but rather about a not insignificant *part* of it. To put it differently: I am going to talk about it from a particular perspective, the perspective of the recent confessional development.

The mere fact that Reformed churches, unlike churches from most other Christian traditions, write new confessional statements is an indicator of something *particularly and uniquely Reformed*. It is not just the wish to be "up to date," nor is it ignorance or forgetfulness (or at least for the most part it is not) of our confessional heritage, that brings Reformed churches to formulate and articulate their faith anew. Reformed churches write new confessions because they try to live and express their faith according to the motto: *Ecclesia reformata semper reformanda secundum verbum Dei*. The Presbyterian Church in the United States declares:

> We are grateful heirs of reformations and awakenings. We are faithful to the reformers of the past when we hold ourselves open in the present to the reforming and renewing work of the Spirit.[8]

That leads us to one main aspect of Reformed identity: the openness for being reformed again by the Word of God under the guidance of the Holy Spirit. Karl Barth has put this Reformed understanding of confession into an almost classical definition, stating that a Reformed confession of faith is formulated by a Christian *community within a geographically limited area, spontaneously* and *publicly*, with *provisional authority*, and is a description of the *provisional insight currently* given to the *universal Christian church*, into the

---

8. A Declaration of Faith (1976), Vischer, *Reformed Witness*, p. 44. The Declaration of Faith was not accepted as a confessional statement, but was approved as "a contemporary statement of faith, a reliable aid for Christian study, liturgy, and inspiration" (*Reformed Witness*, p. 230).

revelation of God in Jesus Christ, as he is attested in Holy Scripture.[9] Hence Reformed creeds and confessions have only *provisional, temporary,* and *relative* authority and are therefore subject to revision and correction.[10] Reformed churches formulate their faith anew, when they find themselves challenged; when they find the true preaching of the gospel is at stake; when they gain new insights from Scripture; when they must confess that they have been wrong in the past; when the average Christian no longer understands the traditional confessions and their outdated language or philosophical and cultural background. As the Presbyterian Church in the Republic of Korea says in the preamble to its New Confession from 1972:

> The truth of the Scriptures empowers us in all time through the Holy Spirit. We make it, however, our duty to articulate in a *new way* the truth of the gospel and thereby to seek *new ways* of obedience to Christ in that we face the ever changing usage of language, new insights, rapidly changing living situations, new challenges of the traditional and the newly emerging sectarian religions and the threats of various evils today.[11]

Reformed churches within a *geographically limited area* formulate their faith anew for their context and challenges, in their language and with their own philosophical background. They do not regard their contextually determined confessing as a disadvantage or admission of weakness, but rather as a point in their favor — to a certain extent they even take pride in having always confessed their faith *in tempore* and *in loco*.[12] The *coetus particularis* [particular

---

9. "Ein reformiertes Glaubensbekenntnis ist die von einer örtlich umschriebenen christlichen Gemeinschaft spontan und öffentlich formulierte, für ihren Charakter nach außen bis auf weiteres maßgebende und für ihr eigenes Lehren und Leben bis auf weiteres maßgebende Darstellung der der allgemeinen christlichen Kirche vorläufig geschenkten Einsicht von der allein in der Heiligen Schriften bezeugten Offenbarung Gottes in Jesus Christus." K. Barth, "Wünschbarkeit und Möglichkeit eines allgemeinen reformierten Glaubensbekenntnisses (1925)," in *Vorträge und kleinere Arbeiten 1922-1925,* ed. Holger Finze (Zürich: TVZ, 1990), p. 610. (English translation: "The Desirability and Possibility of a Universal Reformed Creed," in *Theology and the Church* [London: SCM, 1962], pp. 112-35; here, p. 112.) See also Barth's lecture series on the Theology of Reformed Confessions (1923): *Die Theologie der reformierten Bekenntnisschriften. Vorlesung Göttingen Sommersemester 1923 (Gesamtausgabe Abt. II),* edited by the Karl Barth-Forschungsstelle an der Universität Göttingen (Leitung Eberhard Busch) (Zürich: TVZ, 1998), pp. 1-62.

10. Cf. Presbyterian Church (USA), "The Confessional Nature of the Church," in *Book of Confessions. Study Edition,* pp. 359f.

11. Vischer, *Reformed Witness,* p. 70 (emphasis added).

12. Cf. Martien E. Brinkman, "The Will to Common Confession: The Contribution of Calvinist Protestantism to the World Council of Churches Study Project Confessing the One Faith," in *Louvain Studies* 19 (1994): 118f.

assembly] is author of the confession, but — and this is very important to notice — only as a part of the universal church at the same time, as part of the *una sancta catholica ecclesia*. That means that a *particular* Reformed church formulates the provisional insight that is given to the *universal* church. One aspect of the common identity of Reformed churches therefore is that they always confess their faith not only as this or that Reformed church in this or that area, *but* as a part of the *one* church. The quotation from "Our Song of Hope" of the Reformed Church in America, which I quoted at the beginning of this paper, is just one example for it:

> The Spirit builds *one* church, united in *one* Lord and *one* hope with *one* ministry around *one* table.[13]

Reformed confessions confess the *one* church, the *one* Lord, the *one* hope — in short: the unity of the church. And furthermore, they call the members of their church to make the given unity of the church visible on earth. The Belhar-Confession of the Dutch Reformed Mission Church (1982/86) confesses:

> We believe in one holy, universal Christian Church, the communion of saints called from the entire human family. We believe: . . . that unity is, therefore, both a gift and an obligation for the Church of Jesus Christ, that through the working of God's Holy Spirit it is a binding force, yet simultaneously a reality which must be earnestly pursued and sought: one which the people of God must continually be built up to attain; that this unity must become visible so that the world may believe.[14]

There is a second, important implication to this. While they are confessing as a particular Reformed church, they aim to confess not some kind of *Reformed faith,* but the *biblical* and *catholic* Christian faith.[15] The Church of Jesus Christ in Madagascar confesses its faith "in communion with the Christian Church

13. Vischer, *Reformed Witness,* p. 226 (emphasis added). "Our Song of Hope" received an official status as a *statement of faith* but not as a *Standard;* it was approved as "a statement of the church's faith for use in its ministry of witness, teaching, and worship" (Vischer, *Reformed Witness,* p. 220).

14. The text of the confession can be found, for example, in: *Apartheid Is a Heresy,* ed. John W. de Gruchy and Charles Villa-Vicencio (Grand Rapids: Eerdmans, 1983), pp. 179-81 (here, p. 179); it is not included in the English version of Vischer, *Reformed Witness.*

15. Sometimes churches are in danger of neglecting this aim. For example, the draft title of the most recent confessional statement of the Presbyterian Church (USA) was "A Brief Statement of Reformed Faith." The committee working on this text came to realize the problem and omitted the term "Reformed" from the title. Cf. William C. Placher and D. Willis-Watkins, *Belonging to God: A Commentary on A Brief Statement of Faith* (Louisville: Westminster/John Knox Press, 1992), p. 9.

throughout the world,"[16] and the Toraja Church in Indonesia does so "in connection with Ecumenical and Reformed Confessions, together with all the saints *of all ages* and *in all places*."[17]

When we turn from the confessional statements to the history of the involvement of Reformed churches in the ecumenical movement, the first impression one gains is that their confessions provide Reformed churches with a theological basis for ecumenical efforts. Right from the beginning many Reformed churches have been engaged in the ecumenical movement, and they are still actively committed to its goals. This commitment to ecumenical goals found its first expression within the intraconfessional realm: the foundation of the World Alliance of Reformed Churches in 1875, with its first General Assembly two years later. The WARC was to be the first alliance of a worldwide denominational family. Though the foundation of the WARC was clearly dominated by concerns about inner-denominational issues, it represented at the same time the principal existing forms of the ecumenical movement, since it gave its member churches a *new consciousness of universality* in discovering the *worldwide dimensions* of their own community.[18] Simultaneously, Reformed churches, their leaders, theologians, and lay people have been active not only in the intraconfessional arm of the ecumenical movement, but also in its interconfessional arms, the World Council of Churches, and the Christian World Communions. Many times the same persons who were working in one of the arms of the ecumenical movement could be found doing inspiring work in the other one as well.

The WARC and its member churches take part in and often initiate various bi- or multilateral dialogues with churches from other Christian traditions, on a national or worldwide level.[19] Several Reformed churches united with other Protestant churches within the last decades, forming new united or uniting churches. It could even be argued that one of the main driving forces of the ecumenical movement can be found in churches of the Reformed tradition.

Contemplating these observations, one could gain the impression that Reformed churches stand firmly within the ecumenical movement and do not

16. Statement of Faith of the Church of Jesus Christ in Madagascar (1958), Vischer, *Reformed Witness*, p. 16.

17. Confession of the Church of Toraja/Indonesia (1981), Vischer, *Reformed Witness*, p. 48 (emphasis added).

18. Cf. Harold E. Fey, "Confessional Families and the Ecumenical Movement," in *The Ecumenical Advance: A History of the Ecumenical Movement*, vol. 2, 1948-1968, ed. Harold E. Fey (London: SPCK, 1970), p. 117.

19. See, for example, Alan P. F. Sell, *A Reformed, Evangelical, Catholic Theology: The Contribution of the World Alliance of Reformed Churches, 1875-1982* (Grand Rapids: Eerdmans, 1991), pp. 112-37.

have too many problems with their attitude towards the wider Christian community or with the endeavor to make unity visible on earth. It seems as though they are well equipped for this search in two ways: by their own theological basis as it is displayed in their confessions, and by their actual engagement within the ecumenical movement.

And yet, there is still a tension between the identity and self-understanding that Reformed churches might share to a certain degree, and the quest for unity within the ecumenical movement. As the WARC study cited above puts it: "Is there enough clarity in the contemporary statements of the Reformed churches to the *Una Sancta*? As a rule, the Reformed churches claim to have a deep concern for the unity of the Church. But can the contemporary statements be regarded as a constructive contribution to the common struggle for the unity of the Church? . . . To what extent is the family of Reformed Churches prepared to accept the implications of the dialogue with other churches?"[20] In principle, Reformed churches agree with the sixteenth-century reformers' desire not to create a new church, but rather to work toward bringing about the renewal of the whole church. "But what are the implications of this conviction? Does it not mean that the Reformed Churches need to turn their attention to the renewal of *their own tradition* insofar as the Reformed heritage can lead to a renewal of the whole Church? Does it not mean that they need to deepen the awareness of the *common tradition* of all churches?"[21] To question the preparedness of the Reformed tradition from yet another angle: though they do agree *in principle* with the reformers on renewing the whole church, are they *de facto* willing and ready for it? Or is Páraic Réamonn right in his assertion that "the Reformed are no less prone to an introverted denominationalism than other Christians"?[22]

In my opinion, these questions touch the very core of the problem. How are the churches of the Reformed tradition supposed to deal with their own identity (as hard as it is to define) within the ecumenical movement, within interconfessional dialogues? How do they go about describing their own identity without falling prey to an "introverted denominationalism"?

One way to handle the tension between Reformed identity and the search for unity of the church is an attitude not exclusively Reformed, but rather typical of churches that tend be "conservative" or "evangelical" and generally not much engaged in the ecumenical movement. Representatives of this attitude claim that the Reformed tradition (or to be more exact: *their* particular vision of the Reformed tradition) holds the one and eternal truth about God. They

20. *Confessions and Confessing in the Reformed Tradition Today,* pp. 17f.
21. *Confessions and Confessing in the Reformed Tradition Today,* p. 18 (emphasis added).
22. P. Réamonn, "A Reformed Vision of Unity," in *Reformed World* 47 (1997): 85.

postulate the existence of a Reformed system of doctrine that not only categorizes the Reformed view of Christian faith, but the Christian faith itself. Churches with such kinds of categorized systems of doctrine (such as the TULIP-principle mentioned above) tend to be very certain about their own Reformed identity. Among the majority of Reformed churches this attitude, this kind of Reformed confessionalism, is not regarded as a possible solution. And since the recent confessional statements of Reformed churches do not display such an attitude, I will not discuss it further, though quite a number of Reformed churches do in fact act according to that kind of attitude — be it consciously and intentionally or not.

The second way certainly could not be described as a way of confessionalism or introverted denominationalism. As the World Alliance stated in its Basel Statement in 1951, "the purpose of the Alliance is not to promote world Presbyterianism as an end in itself, but to make the Reformed tradition the servant of God's redemptive purpose through the wider agency of the Church Universal. . . . They [the Presbyterians] believe that in their religious heritage there are treasures of thought and life which are important for the Church Universal," which they do not want to keep to themselves, but "to bring into the common heritage of the Christian Church."[23] A good forty years later, a commentary on the Brief Statement of Faith of the Presbyterian Church (USA) says with regard to the same issue and evidently with the same intention: "We [Presbyterians] have a distinctive vision, but we believe it to be a vision of the one catholic faith. We want to learn from other Christians; but we want to make sure that we too have something *special* and worthwhile to contribute to it. That means holding on to *special themes* within our Reformed tradition. . . ."[24] As Berkhof said with regard to the Basel Statement (and it would be applicable to the latter statement as well), "all that has an attractive sound,"[25] and it is quite a common attitude among Reformed churches and organizations concerning their own identity and relation toward the ecumenical movement. But Berkhof continues: "One would . . . like to know how exactly the process of 'bringing in' a 'religious heritage' into the 'common heritage' is envisaged. How is it done? How short or long does such a process last?"[26] With regard to the commentary on the Brief Statement of Faith one might ask, how might we contribute our special themes to other Christian traditions — and what are *the* special themes, anyway?

---

23. For the statement of Basel see *The Reformed and Presbyterian World* 27 (1962): 11-14.

24. Placher and Willis-Watkins, *Belonging to God*, p. 9 (emphasis added).

25. H. Berkhof, "The Reformed 'Confession' and the Oekumene," in *The Reformed and Presbyterian World* 27 (1962): 351.

26. Berkhof, "The Reformed 'Confession,'" p. 351.

We need not discuss at great length the positive aspects of this second way to handle the tension between one's own identity and the ecumenical movement. Surely the heritage of every particular confession has a theological significance, and so does the heritage of the Reformed tradition. "We are what we are as Reformed churches because of the witness of our mothers and fathers in faith. We must hear their voices and learn from their faith and faithfulness."[27] The important and decisive point now is, how or even whether "common heritage" on the one hand, and "special teaching," "special doctrines," or "special themes" on the other hand are to be linked together. It might be helpful to remember that all talk of special doctrines, of denominational heritage and partial truths as an enrichment of the universal church, is completely foreign to the reformers, be it Calvin, Luther, Zwingli, Knox, or whoever. Berkhof asks sharply, "What sort of quantitative thinking is this? Is revelation then a number of separate truths? And even if it were, would not the maintaining of particular special truths over against other special truths mean the betrayal of the Church and a deliberate decision in favor of sectarianism?"[28]

Asked from the perspective of the confessional statements: when Reformed churches confess the unity of the one church, when they confess to be part of the *una sancta,* when they confess the biblical and catholic faith — can they claim to have a "distinctive vision"? Can they hold on to "special themes"? Does the search for or a provisional definition of a common Reformed identity predetermine us to see ourselves contributing special doctrines to the wider ecumenical church? Should we aim at rediscovering or redrafting such a picture of the "real Reformed" at all? Karel Blei is very resolute on this question: "We should not try to identify a 'special' Protestant, or even Reformed identity. . . . Not 'Reformed identity,' but 'Christian identity' should be our main issue (as it was Calvin's and Luther's). We should not ask what it means to be Reformed (or Protestant), but what it means to be Christian today."[29]

I agree with Blei that the search for a Reformed identity can and should never be an end in itself. It contradicts our confession that we are part of the *una sancta,* part of the one body of Christ. Our task is not to define a Reformed identity in order to determine the boundaries around churches of the Reformed tradition. If the search for a Reformed identity merely provides a label for a particular "box" alongside other Christian "boxes" labeled "Lutheran,"

27. From the report of Section 1: Reformed Faith and the Search for Unity, Subsection 1.1: Who are we called to be? Reformed Self-Understanding, issued by the General Assembly in Debrecen/Hungary 1997.

28. Berkhof, "The Reformed 'Confession,'" p. 353.

29. Karel Blei, "Some Dutch Reflections on Reformed Identity," *Reformed World* 43 (1993): 3.

"Anglican," "Roman-Catholic," or whatever, we have clearly failed to accomplish our task. The unity of the church does not consist of several boxes, sitting neatly side by side, but is the given unity of the one body of Christ. It is helpful, though, to understand one's tradition, heritage, context, and theological background. We are indeed what we are because of our mothers and fathers in faith. To look for a Reformed identity therefore is a way to understand more deeply why we are what we are as Reformed Christians.

How then should the relation between confessional identity and the unity of the church be solved? Again I agree with Berkhof that it can be done "only by a radical return to the preconfessional and pre-denominationalist stage of Reformed ecclesiology."[30] It may sound like a step toward confessionalism, but as Reformed churches we cannot try to represent and act as anything else but the universal and catholic church. We cannot aim to confess anything else but the catholic faith; we cannot search for anything else but for our identity as Christians. It is not a step toward confessionalism, since we do not claim that Reformed churches are the *only* representatives of the *ecclesia catholica* and that all other Christian churches are not. The *ecclesia catholica* is also present in many other churches, a fact we have to acknowledge and to take seriously into account. Indeed, a real acceptance of this fact is the only starting point and basis for a real, mutually correcting and enriching dialogue between churches of different confessions. But accepting this fact does not mean that we now conclude that our task is "to specialize in 'special' Reformed doctrines"; instead, our task is "rather to represent in itself this *ecclesia catholica* as deeply and as broadly as possible."[31] It does not mean that we must hold on to special themes or to some kind of Reformed identity as the *raison d'être* for Reformed churches. Furthermore, it does lead us into real dialogue with other churches, since we expect them to hold convictions that we may not ignore if we claim to be part of the *ecclesia catholica*. What could be considered as the "special teaching" or "special themes" of other Christian traditions might be something we need to accept on our pilgrimage towards representing the *ecclesia catholica*. The more the churches that are engaged in interconfessional dialogues are aware of their own identity, not as a particular confession or denomination, but as representatives of the one church, the more these churches will be willing to learn from each other and, most importantly, from the scriptures, what the already given unity of the church means for them. As that happens, the process of unification will broaden and deepen. If we keep talking about special teachings, a special Reformed identity, while at the same time insisting on making our contribution to the ecumenical dialogue, we actually recite a monologue. We may confess

---

30. See also for the following, Berkhof, "The Reformed 'Confession,'" pp. 353f.
31. Berkhof, "The Reformed 'Confession,'" pp. 353f.

that we are called to learn from each other, we may confess that we have to make the given unity of the church visible on earth, but actually we are merely safeguarding our Reformed "box," to whose inventory these statements belong.

It goes without saying that the task ahead is not to strive for a uniform and homogeneous Christianity without any difference and distinctions. The task ahead demands of us that we represent as Reformed churches the *one* and *catholic* church: "But now are they many members, yet but one body" (1 Cor. 12:20).

CHAPTER 7

Election and Ecclesiology in the Post-Constantinian Church

Colin Gunton

The Problem

It is often enough averred that Calvin developed his doctrine of predestination in order to reassure believers of their status before God; it is even more often asserted that the overall effect of his teaching was eventually to subvert that assurance, or at any rate to turn it into a form of self-absorption that has an effect contrary to that for which the gospel frees us. Self-absorption is indeed among the besetting sins of western Christianity, from Augustine onward. In each era, it takes characteristic form. In our day, it is among the prime dangers of the post-Constantinian church, which, deprived, apparently, of its once secure social and political status and role — diminished, apparently, in numbers and influence — flounders variously in inaction, activism, and political correctness in a sometimes desperate concern not to lose the attention of the — reprobate? In this paper, I propose to bring together the related themes of election and ecclesiology, with particular reference to the beleaguered situation of the Christian church in a world which, as Robert Jenson has observed, is unique in being the first once apparently believing culture to have abandoned the Christian gospel. That throws into the limelight the problem of the, if not everywhere minority status, at least unique situation for the church of rejection by the mainstreams of intellectual and cultural life.

Augustine and Calvin were right in one thing: the elect are indeed a minority. That, surely, is the message of much of the New Testament, as also of Luther's suggestion of making persecution one of the marks of the church.[1] This is the case, however, not because the mass of perdition is going to hell (though, of course, it may be), but, I would contend, because God elects the particular in order to achieve his universal purposes. Here, the doctrine of election, properly stated, should serve the cause of a proper ecclesial self-confidence, one based not in individual assurance of future salvation, though that may be a proper part of it, but in a call to ecclesial faithfulness. That is the proposal to be explored in this paper, because in it lies the basis of a genuinely universal contribution to the church's calling that may be made on the basis of Reformed teaching.

Election and Ecclesiology

Another oft-repeated truism is that the work of the so-called magisterial Reformers still operated within an essentially Constantinian model of the relation of church and state, by which I mean, quite neutrally, a social arrangement according to which it is assumed that in certain respects church and state or church and society will be coterminous. Over against this, the thesis to be argued is that the development of the theology of dissent in England offers interesting possibilities for an ecclesiology that is yet free from the pelagianizing tendencies that seem sometimes to mark the ecclesiologies of the so-called radical Reformation. The dissenting stream of the Reformed tradition offers models of a stronger distinction-in-relatedness between the church and its social context than did Constantinianism, without falling into the voluntarist theologies of baptism and church membership that mark both Barth and modern Anabaptism alike.

Part of the resolution of the problem is to be found in the doctrine of election. Theologies of election have tended to suffer from two questionable formulations, both rooted in the same weakness. After Barth, indeed, after Arminianism, we are all too aware of the weakness of the traditional Augustinian-Calvinist form of the teaching. Under what has come to be called Constantinianism, its tendency is to conceive the elect and the reprobate as two classes *within* the church, with the true, invisible, church being known only to God. In reaction to it, a form of voluntarism tends to develop, an Arminianism stressing the free adherence of the believer and easily degenerating into a form of self-election. Barth's teaching serves as a corrective. All people are, at least *de jure*, among the elect, because they are already contained within the corporate Christ by virtue of his eternal election to be the one he is in the becoming/being

---

1. I owe this point to Ian McFarland, *Listening to the Least: Doing Theology from the Outside In* (Cleveland: Pilgrim Press, 1998), p. 70.

of the triune God.[2] It is scarcely fair to say that it was in order to compensate for the apparently universalist implications of this doctrine that Barth introduced his theology of baptism, but that is nonetheless the effect that it has in the overall weighting of his dogmatics. To counterbalance a determinist-seeming theology of election there is introduced a theology of the sacraments that over-determines the human act, underdetermines the divine.

The common weakness of the two formulations is to overweight the protological and underweight the eschatological determinants of the doctrine of election. Or rather: eschatology is so determined by protology that the end is effectively determined by the beginning, and history is, apparently, closed to the recreating work of the Spirit. To justify this thesis requires a brief and no doubt tendentious historical recitation. Augustine's view of creation as a timeless and instantaneous willing of the whole of time and space makes something like the double decree inevitable, unless he is to follow the universalist path of Origen. As we know, he does not, yet Origen's contribution is essential, for it shapes the form that western eschatology later takes. Significant here is first his insistence that God creates a *finite* number of immaterial spirits, whose pre-mundane fall requires the creation of the material world to provide a period of (re-?)training in human bodies;[3] and second the (almost) entirely other-worldly eschatology that is its consequence. Under the impact of a pre-temporal creation of a non-material being, eschatology inevitably comes to mean the return of the spirits to the pure immateriality of the beginning.[4]

Once that picture is in turn modified by Augustine's pessimistic and this-worldly view of the origin of sin, the problem of the finitude of the complement of heaven becomes acute. Eschatology continues to be other-worldly, and it comes to be taught that the end of creation, the eschatological purpose of God, is to fill the complement of heaven with a finite number of the saved. The seriousness with which Anselm enquires at length whether the number of the saved will equal the number of fallen angels is in this respect western theology's most revealing passage.[5] The foreordained complement of heaven requires to be made up, the outcome being that the new heaven and the new earth of bibli-

---

2. Karl Barth, *Church Dogmatics* II/2, ed. Geoffrey W. Bromiley and Thomas F. Torrance (Edinburgh: T. & .T Clark, 1957), especially perhaps, §33.

3. Origen, *Princ.* 2.9.6, 2.6.3.

4. Joseph W. Trigg, *Origen: The Bible and Philosophy in the Third-Century Church* (Atlanta: John Knox, 1983), p. 110.

5. Anselm of Canterbury, *Cur Deus Homo*, I.16-18. Notice the Origenist aspects of the following: "We cannot doubt that the rational nature, which either is or is going to be blessed in the contemplation of God, was foreseen by God as existing in a particular reasonable and perfect number, so that its number cannot fittingly be greater or smaller" (*Cur Deus Homo*, I.16).

cal promise give way before a view that God foreordains a limited number of the elect to complete an essentially other-worldly aim. That is, to be sure, something of a parody, and there were always counterinfluences, so long as the doctrine of the resurrection of the body continued to be confessed and taught. But it reminds us that there is little that is materially new in Calvin's doctrine of predestination, at least so far as the number and destiny of the elect are concerned. What is materially new, and it was to be developed further by Barth, is the greater orientation to Israel and Christ.[6] What later became historically new is the way the doctrine of predestination came to dominate theological controversy to such an extent that revulsion has made it almost impossible to mention the doctrine without misunderstanding.[7]

However, there are moments of truth in the received doctrine, and we must affirm on biblical grounds that election is indeed prevenient and particular. Some, and therefore presumably not others, are chosen, apart from their willing and in advance of their acceptance. "The Lord did not set his affection on you and choose you because you were more numerous than other peoples. . . . But it was because the Lord loved you and kept the oath he swore to your forefathers . . ." (Deut. 7:7-8). So it is also with the election of particular people within Israel, including especially kings and prophets. "Before I formed you in the womb I knew you, before you were born I set you apart . . ." (Jer. 1:5). Notice that Jeremiah is, on this account, created in order that he might be a prophet to Israel. Indeed, we should also remember here the insistence of Scripture that Israel's call is not only prevenient and unmerited but also irrevocable. "God did not reject his people, whom he foreknew" (Rom. 11:2) and, as that chapter of Paul's shows, the same is the case with those within Israel who remain true when all others have become apostate: "I have reserved for myself seven thousand who have not bowed the knee to Baal . . ." (Rom. 11:4, citing 1 Kings 19:18). Writing to a church that contains both Jew and Gentile, the apostle sets her election in what must be called pre-eternity: "For he chose us before the foundation of the world to be holy and blameless in his sight. In love he predestined us to be adopted . . ." (Eph. 1:4).

The most pressing systematic problem, engaged in another context by Augustine (far more rigorously, it must be said, than some of his critics), is in this context that of the relation of time and eternity. If God is the creator of time, then necessarily his acts will be "from without," and, it would seem, election "from before." Barth similarly sees that election is at once an eternal and tempo-

6. John Calvin, *Institutes* 3.21.2.

7. I once preached on election in King's College Chapel and one of the more intelligent of the listeners needed to see a copy of the script before she could be convinced that I had not propounded eternal and predestined reprobation.

100

ral act, and the greatness of his treatment is its interlocking, interweaving, of eternal and historical divine act. However, in systematic theology balance and weighting, if not everything, are undoubtedly crucial. Here, as chaos theory has taught us, a minor shift in initial conditions can have immense implications for the remainder of a system, and it is characteristic of the sensitivity of Barth's dogmatic antennae that he gives in advance indications of the weakness of his proposal and hints as to where a solution might be found. Those theologies, he says, that fail to give due weight alike to the pre-temporality, supra-temporality, and post-temporality of God fail to incorporate the overall thrust of the Christian gospel.[8] What then is the place of post-temporality in Barth's treatment of election? The crucial shift that we have already met in the history of this doctrine is Origen's, with his spiritualizing eschatology, and its reverberations are still to be felt in Barth, albeit weakly.[9] What tends to disappear from view is the kind of eschatology to be found in Scripture, for example in Ephesians, Romans 8–11, and the Apocalypse. Relevant features are: a greater orientation to the destiny of this material creation as the context which is also inextricably bound up with the goal of the human; a different conception of the way in which eschatology might be realized; and, in sum, a more concrete pneumatology.

What might this threefold cord contribute? Let us begin with one of the most important contributions of Calvin to theology, his affirmation of the unity of the Testaments and therefore of the divine economy.[10] Taken seriously, and with a stress on the promise of the resurrection displacing his tendency to prefer the dangerously ambiguous "immortality," this would involve greater attention to the historical calling of Israel construed as something more than the people from whom the Christ was born. Whatever the precise meaning of the promise to Abraham in Genesis, its meaning for Paul is clear. The descendants of Abraham were, are, and remain elect, and their rejection is not eternal like that of the Calvinists' reprobate, but temporary and instrumental. "Israel has experienced a hardening in part until the full number of the Gentiles has come in. And so all Israel will be saved . . ." (Rom. 11:25-26). The historical election of Israel is with a view to the election of representative Gentiles, after which it will be re-established and perfected. Noteworthy is (1) that we are here concerned with the election of communities, not individuals from within communities; and (2) that the realization of eschatology takes place in time in advance of its completion in eternity.

By contrast, Augustine can indeed use Israel as a model, but his problem-

---

8. Barth, *Church Dogmatics* II/1, pp. 615-20.

9. Douglas B. Farrow, *Ascension and Ecclesia* (London: T. & T. Clark, 1999).

10. "The covenant made with all the patriarchs is so much like ours in substance and reality that the two are actually one and the same. Yet they differ in the mode of dispensation." Calvin, *Institutes* 2.10.2.

atic takes him into rather different byways. As TeSelle points out,[11] "infants can be saved only through baptism or its counterpart in Israel, circumcision and membership in the chosen people." What are the problems here? Predominating are those deriving from an overemphasis on the ultimate salvation of the individual. Barth is right that the doctrine of election goes astray when much weight is borne by analysis, on the basis of observation, of the fact that some believe and others do not.[12] But what he sees to be characteristic of Calvin, others have attributed to Augustine, as the father of this way of thinking. "Predestination is viewed . . . as the ultimate explanation of the actual — at least the *observable* — course of events."[13] Bound up with this preoccupation with the faith and destiny of the individual, and distorted by it, are all those problems associated with a proper concern with attributing the gift of salvation to God. "Augustine thinks that predestination involves *two* problems . . . one of *the beginning of faith,* and another one of *perseverance to the end.* . . ."[14]

As cannot be too often recalled in discussion of this question, election has to do with definiteness — with determinateness — and not with determinism. A Reformed, indeed I would want to say a biblical, account should be able to accept that both the beginning of faith and the capacity to continue in it are the gifts of God. In the former, we cannot avoid an element of *pre*-determining, *fore*-ordaining. Otherwise, what can we make of the call of Israel and Jeremiah, let alone the first two chapters of the Gospel of Luke? The offense in the way the Augustinian tradition has construed it is clear: it lies in the fact that God's choice is rendered gratuitous rather than gracious, surely another casualty of the quantitative approach to the question of the complement of heaven that we have already met. The proper interest served by the doctrine of election concerns not the numbers, but the purpose of the election of such quantities as there are, paradigmatically for our age of ecclesial anxiety, perhaps, Elijah's seven thousand. It is that God's will continue to be done in Israel and on earth. In other words, it is an ecclesial matter before it is concerned with the individual believer: with what Israel and the church are here for rather than the fate of individuals within them.

It is in connection with the latter of the two dimensions of the life of faith — perseverance — that we are perhaps able to open the question a little. Do we not need to be able to say that this, too, is the gift of God, to a degree foreordained? And yet must that be taken to be the equivalent of absolutely preprogrammed? An answer to that will be approached by reference to another weakness of the traditional doctrine, where two disastrous shifts took place:

11. Eugene TeSelle, *Augustine the Theologian* (London: Burns and Oates, 1970), p. 323.
12. Barth, *Church Dogmatics* II/2, pp. 38-44.
13. TeSelle, *Augustine the Theologian,* p. 325.
14. TeSelle, *Augustine the Theologian,* pp. 324f.

away from an ecclesiology of *koinonia* — grace mediated communally — to one of inwardness; and away from a conception of the action of the eschatological Spirit enabling right human response to a conception of grace as a semi-substantial force causally either assisting or determining human perseverance.[15] (In the either/or is contained, in a nutshell, almost the whole Reformation debate, and, as TeSelle has pointed out, both conceptions ultimately derive from Augustine's attempt to find room for human freedom in his doctrine of perseverance.)[16]

What is lost in all this is a theology of the eschatological Spirit enabling right human action within the church and in anticipation of the final reconciliation of all things. If the Spirit is the electing God,[17] and if the Spirit is the one who gathers the church to the Father through Christ in order that his will be done on earth, then somewhere in that vast dogmatic minefield are to be found clues to the way we should take. Here we must distinguish between the Spirit's universal creating work and the way by which he perfects creation by enabling particular events to realize eschatological truth and goodness in created time and space. The Spirit "in transfusing into all things his energy, and breathing into them essence, life, and movement . . . is indeed plainly divine."[18] The Spirit's creating work is, before it is anything else, universal. However, the point of the story of Israel's election and Jesus' resurrection is that the universal end

15. See Robert Jenson's remark about the tendency to identify the work of the Spirit as a process, as the means of God's causal action upon us, rather than, say, his free personal relation with us. Robert W. Jenson, "The Holy Spirit," in *Christian Dogmatics*, vol. 2, ed. Carl E. Braaten and Robert W. Jenson (Philadelphia: Fortress Press, 1984), pp. 126f.

16. "Augustine states repeatedly that the gift of perseverance is a grace that 'cooperates' with men. . . ." TeSelle, *Augustine the Theologian*, p. 328. He appears to have bequeathed to the tradition two possibilities, inherent as both were in the ambiguities of his thinking about grace and freedom. The first is what became Calvinist double predestination, and we need not linger with it, except to say that it is preferable to its alternative. For some of the reasons why almost anything is preferable to Arminianism, see Robert W. Jenson, *America's Theologian: An Appreciation of Jonathan Edwards* (New York: Oxford University Press, 1988). The second is a development of a doctrine of cooperating grace, which muddied the waters and still muddies them, as is shown by recent debate about the Joint Declaration on Justification. All such doctrines generate a doctrine of divine-human interrelation in which the human and the divine are in some way in cooperation or competition. The doctrine of grace displaces that of the Spirit, according to which human action does not cooperate with the divine because it is enabled by it. Only thus can action be seen to be authentically human without in some way appearing either to compete with, cooperate with, or be overridden by divine action.

17. "The speaking of the gospel is the event of predestination in that the gospel gives what it speaks about, but this eschatological efficacy of the gospel is the Spirit. We must parody Barth: the Holy Spirit is the choosing God." Jenson, "The Holy Spirit," p. 138.

18. Calvin, *Institutes* 1.13.14.

of creation — "to bring all things in heaven and on earth together under one head, even Christ" (Eph. 1:10) — is achieved through particularities.

Among those particularities, and indeed, pre-eminent among them, are Israel as the people of God and the church as the body of Christ. The election and calling of the *particular* communities is rooted in the universal mediation of creation in Jesus Christ. The relation between creation, its eschatological perfecting, and the place of the church in it is perfectly expressed in the words of another Pauline letter. "He is before all things, and in him all things hold together. And he is the head of the body, the church . . . so that in everything he might have the supremacy" (Col. 1:17-18). Once again, the passage brings together heaven and earth in its eschatological promise: "to reconcile to himself all things, whether things on earth or things in heaven, by making peace through his blood . . ." (v. 20). On such an account, the elect are not primarily those chosen for a unique destiny out of the whole; rather, they are chosen out of the whole as the community with whom the destiny of the whole is in some way bound up. It follows that what is needed to correct imbalances in historic treatments of our doctrine is a stronger orientation to the bearing of post-temporality on the present than either Calvin or even Barth was able to achieve.

Election and the Post-Constantinian Church

It is at this stage that we can introduce the contribution of the generations after Calvin, particularly in England, shaped as it is by their greater involvement in discussion of the church's being over against Constantinian forms of Christianity. John Owen is, on the face of it, the last person we should expect to be of assistance. As Cromwell's chaplain, he is hardly a post-Constantinian figure; as proponent of a scheme of "federal theology" at odds with Calvin's stress on the unity of the covenant, his dual predestination often sees him placed in the class of those rigid Calvinists who are alleged to have distorted the master's theology. Yet he has contributions to make which can, taken apart from his rather rigid doctrine of limited atonement, generate an approach to election that is more christological and pneumatological, and therefore more historical and eschatological, than that of the tradition.

The first is that although Owen is not, in the modern sense, a voluntarist, he insists on the incompatibility of the gospel with any manner of coercion. ("Is there no means of instruction in the New Testament established, but a prison and a halter?")[19] This enables the formulation of a *theology* of tolera-

---

19. John Owen, "Of Toleration," in *The Works of John Owen*, 24 vols. (London: T. & T. Clark, 1862), vol. 8, p. 171.

tion — and thus of the relation of church and the social order — which need owe nothing to the individualistic rights theory of liberal modernity. Appealing to a pre-Constantinian tradition, he points out that, "For three hundred years the church had no assistance from any magistrate against heretics. . . . As the disease is spiritual, so was the remedy . . . and the Lord Jesus Christ made it effectual."[20] There is also to be heard a note of eschatological reserve that enables the church to combine confident acceptance of election with a relatively open stance to those not elect, or apparently not so.[21] That is to say, there is in this theologian of double predestination an essentially christological defense of toleration, and therefore the basis of an ecclesiology that is both Reformed, appropriately confident and "modern," even allowing for "pluralism" of a kind.

Second, and in a related way, Owen's Christology enables greater attention to be given to the humanity of Christ as the locus of divine action and election; that is to say, to concentrate attention not on a pre-temporal election, in either Calvinist or Barthian form, but on election as the genuinely historical realization of, indeed, God's actual eternal purpose, which is not the salvation of a few but something manifested in the fact that "the Gentiles are heirs together with Israel . . ." (Eph. 3:1-11). What is interesting is that Owen's Christ is indeed the eternal Son become flesh, but also the chosen one whose life is *both* predestined by God the Father *and* enabled and realized by the action of God the Holy Spirit. The Spirit is the one who, as Jesus' inseparable other, relates him to the Father and so enables his response which is both obedient and free.[22]

This has important anthropological and soteriological implications. What the Spirit performs in relation to the humanity of Christ, he can be seen also to do in relation to those who are the adopted — elect — bothers and sisters of the risen Jesus; that is to say, enable them to realize their freedom. This is an eschatological act, for it involves liberating *from* the chains of sin *to* the maturity of the children of God. It is also eschatological in that it will be perfectly

20. Owen, "Of Toleration," p. 183.

21. In dispute with Rome's overrealized eschatology, represented by Bellarmine, Owen points out that according to 1 Corinthians 11:19 "heresies" are "for the manifesting of those that are approved, not the destroying of those that are not. . . ." Quoting 2 Timothy 2:25, "Waiting with all patience upon them that oppose themselves, if at any time God will give them repentance . . . ," Owen comments: "Imprisoning, banishing, slaying, is scarcely a patient waiting" (p. 202).

22. "The Holy Ghost . . . is the immediate, peculiar, efficient cause of all external divine operations. . . ." John Owen, "A Discourse Concerning the Holy Spirit," in *The Works of John Owen*, vol. 3, pp. 160f. See Alan Spence, "Inspiration and Incarnation: John Owen and the Coherence of Christology," *King's Theological Review* 12 (1989): 52-55.

realized only at the resurrection, although from time to time that realization is anticipated through the Spirit's agency. Systematically, this provides a means of developing a more open doctrine of election than those to which I have alluded, including Barth's. Only the Spirit can relate lost human beings to God the Father through Christ — election — yet the Spirit's otherness, modeled on the New Testament depiction of his relation to Jesus, generates an openness according to which the Spirit can determine a relation through an election that is yet uncompelled because it is the means of the realization of the sinner's true being in Christ. The function of the otherness of the Spirit is thus to confirm and re-establish the true otherness of the creation in reconciled relation to God. In that way, the Spirit crowds out grace as a semi-hypostatic reality intermediate between God and the world.

It is in the words "in Christ" that we find the heart of the matter of the right relation of an electing God and a temporal world. In contrast to both Augustine and Barth it has to be taken more temporally in terms of election to the worship and life of a concrete earthly people gathered out of the peoples of the world. In other words, a stronger reference to the actual historic community is needed in place of both Augustine's other-worldly individualism and Barth's heavenly-earthly Christ. The latter is right to see election as being "in Christ" but more questionable when he tends to see the whole human race as *immediately* in Christ rather than *mediately,* as Israel and the church historically elected by the Spirit's eschatological enabling.

We now reach our third contribution from Owen, which consists in the fact that this predestinarian theologian is able to be surprisingly "voluntarist" in his doctrine of the church. Given that the church is the particular number of the elect gathered in Christ by the action of the eschatological Spirit, we are now enabled to conceive their free action as voluntary though determined. For Owen, the church takes form through human acts of free obedience, but can only do so because it is elect. "Wherefore *the formal cause of a church* consisteth in an obediential act of believers . . . jointly giving themselves up unto the Lord Jesus Christ, to do and observe. . . ."[23] What else is that obedience than response to an election to be in a particular form of relation to others, as the examples of Israel, Jeremiah, and Jesus in different ways indicate?

If, however, this account is not to run the risk of appearing to reduce election to vocation, the shape of divine action in relation to those called into the church requires further specification. Here three dogmatic focuses will enable this to take place. The first is contributed by Robert Jenson, in Lutheran mode:

23. John Owen, "The True Nature of a Gospel Church," in *The Works of John Owen,* vol. 16, p. 29.

Predestination is simply the doctrine of justification stated in the active voice. If we change "We are justified by God alone" from passive to active we get "God alone justifies us."[24]

Election therefore becomes for Jenson the other side of justification and so part of his polemic against modern Arminianism, the peculiarly but by no means solely American teaching that we elect ourselves. "It is a strict corollary of the Reformation doctrine of justification: All things happen by God's will."[25]

We shall return to the problem raised by that final assertion, but not before there has been some discussion of the means by which predestination is realized. It is sometimes charged against Calvin that he sees the church and the sacraments as the contingent rather than intrinsic means by which the purposes of God are realized. (Book 4 is after all entitled: "The external means or aims by which God invites us into the society of Christ and holds us therein.") The orientation I have been attempting, of placing greater weight on the actual historical election of Israel and the church, acts as a counterweight to the danger of divorcing the gospel from the church. If election is first of all *revealed* as and through the election of Israel and the church, can such a suspicion remain? Here, supplementing Jenson's stress on justification, a second dogmatic notion, that of incorporation, provides a more explicitly christological focus. "Those God foreknew he also predestined to be conformed to the likeness of his Son . . ." (Rom. 8:29). On this account, election is not merely vocation, because it entails also being made part of the body of Christ, incorporate in him who died and was raised. This means that election for the Gentile consists in being made in some way to share Israel's election, and that partly for the sake of Israel herself, as Paul makes clear in Romans 11, where an image he uses (vv. 17-22) is the horticultural one of engrafting. This in turn entails a relation of near identification: if the church is the body of Christ, those incorporate by baptism are more than merely called. There is an ontological change, because they have entered a new set of relationships — with God, with other people, and with the created order.

Third, the pneumatological dimensions of that incorporation are in turn provided by the notion of adoption. It is almost a commonplace of Christian theology that only one is Son of God by right; others attain that status by the grace of adoption. Adoption is the Spirit's means of realizing God's election of particular people into the body of Christ. This means again that election, for the Gentile, takes the form of being elected alongside Israel in part for the sake of Israel. The logic of this had been set out earlier in the same letter. "[T]hose who are led by the Spirit of God are the sons of God. . . . And by him we cry

24. Jenson, "The Holy Spirit," p. 134.
25. Jenson, "The Holy Spirit," p. 135.

'Abba, Father.' The Spirit himself testifies with our spirit that we are God's children" (Rom. 8:14-16). The Spirit brings particular human beings into actual and transformed relationship with God, realizing their election. The catena of Romans 8:30 brings into view something of the point being here made, that far more should be made in this context of the concrete historical event of election. "And those he predestined he also called; those he called, he also justified; those he justified, he also glorified" (Rom. 8:30).

And yet we cannot avoid here the implications of the Pauline "foreknew." Election is indeed rooted in eternity, because it is an act or acts of God. This means that from our point of view if it is to be grace, it must be prevenient, must come before the human act of obedient choice that is the proper response to it. The case stands thus. Because God is eternal, his acts, as embracing time with eternity, cannot be placed on the same time scale as ours, so that any naïve attribution of them to past, present, and future is excluded. However, that does not mean that care is not required in relating election to the timeline on which we understand that we live, in the light of the temporal structure of the economy of salvation, of which election is a part. The need is not to solve all the problems, or indeed any of the problems, of the logic of time and eternity so much as so to construe the relation of the different episodes in the economy of divine action that none is inappropriately over- or underweighted in such a way as to distort the biblical message. Here we can draw a parallel. If the notion of creation in the beginning is stressed at the expense of creation's eschatological direction and destiny, the latter can come to appear as no more than the outworking of a determinist scheme. If, similarly, as we have seen, the eschatology of the human is understood too transcendentally, too spiritualistically, too individualistically, the actual details of the biblical portrayal of election — that is to say, its historical outworking through Abraham, Israel, Jesus, and the church — become merely or mainly Platonic shadows of an eternal reality, not the actual concrete locus of God's saving action.

By contrast, the kind of eschatology envisaged here, with the resurrection conceived as the anticipation and beginning of an end that is neither this-worldly nor other-worldly, but in some sense the completion and transformation of this heaven and earth into a new heaven *and earth,* will give more weight than has hitherto been the custom to election's temporal outworking: in this case the *before* will not be stressed at the expense of the constitutive importance of what happens after the beginning and before the end. This does not even require that there can be no prelapsarian dimension to election; "he chose us in [Christ] before the creation of the world" (Eph. 1:4). Those willed to be chosen on this account are not primarily to be understood — though they may for all we know be that secondarily — as those who will end up in heaven, but those by whom God's universal purposes are to be mediated. That the purposes should be mediated by disobedient Israel and crucified messiah is indeed contingent on the fall; but it does not follow that Israel and the incarnation are not willed from eternity. The key, as the critique of the Augustinian doctrine of election was designed to suggest, is in the content we give variously to the *destination* and the *pre*, and the way we relate them. We shall not by this change of emphasis evacuate the gospel of offense, as the above quotation from Jenson will demonstrate. What we shall do is remove the false offense, that because Israel and the church are elect, it necessarily follows that all other human beings will end up on — at best — the rubbish heap of history.

In conclusion: despite the fact that the Reformed notion of obediential freedom came in time to be contaminated by secular and individualistic accounts of freedom, the ecclesiology of Dissent has much to teach us. If the church is to be the church in the post-Constantinian age, she must renew her sense of her (passively constituted) *calling* to be a particular people serving a universal end. "Who will bring any charge against those whom God has chosen? It is God who justifies" (Rom. 8:33). Only by a turning away, enabled by the Lord who is the electing Spirit, from the self-absorption of those who have lost their sense of direction to an orientation to the promised reconciliation of all things in Christ can this happen.

Concluding Apologetic Postscript

It was pointed out in discussion of this paper that there is in such an approach a danger that something from the old conception of election may be lost: the joy in believing that belongs to those who know that they are among the elect.[26] It must be conceded that if an overmoralistic conception of the servant church is the outcome, perhaps the move to a more historical conception of election is a mistake. But it need not be overmoralistic. The point about the dangers of Constantinianism does indicate a real flaw in the church's historical witness, so that the change of moral and political orientation need not entail a diminution of the doctrine's edifying effect on the life of the church. There is here, in any case, no intention to deny the grounding of election in God's eternal will for his people nor any need to treat the two movements as alternatives. Their compatibility is well expressed in Francis Watson's recent account of Trinity and community in John's Gospel:

> The movement of the Spirit towards Jesus' followers includes them within
> the scope of Jesus' relation to his Father, thereby gathering them together in

---

26. I thank Steve Holmes for this point.

koinonia with one another. But it also has the effect of directing them outwards, turning them towards the world. The comfort that the Spirit brings is not the comfort of communal self-absorption. . . .[27]

Why should not this election equally be a cause of rejoicing? So the point of the paper remains: in this doctrine, so characteristic of the Reformed tradition, there is surely something we can with profit harvest unashamedly from our Reformed tradition.

27. Francis Watson, "Trinity and Community: A Reading of John 17," *International Journal of Systemic Theology* 1/2 (1999): 181.

CHAPTER 8

Church, State, and Civil Society
in the Reformed Tradition

David Fergusson

In this essay, I attempt to characterize the typical Reformed approach to the state and civil society by reference to its Scottish expression, before raising some questions about the usefulness of this model for today. My contention will be that in a social context of pluralism and dechristianization within western societies we are likely to face calls for greater Christian authenticity and the revival of anabaptist models for the separation of the church from the civil realm. I shall seek to argue nonetheless that classical Reformed attempts to perceive the church as committed to the tasks of social transformation and critical support for the state remain valid, but that these require transposition in our more pluralist context

The distinction between the roles of church and state was set out by both Luther and Calvin in the first half of the sixteenth century. Luther could argue in 1523 for a clear separation of church and state, claiming that the state was concerned with the maintenance of law and justice whereas the church was concerned with the proclamation of divine grace and the freedom of the Christian who lived by faith.[1] Calvin likewise asserted that the Christian is under a twofold government *(duplex in homine regimen)* pertaining to the inner spiri-

---

1. "Von Weltlicher Oberkeit." New English translation in *Luther and Calvin on Secular Authority,* ed. Harro Höpfl (Cambridge: Cambridge University Press, 1991): "God has ordained the two governments, the spiritual which governs true Christians and just persons through the Holy Spirit under Christ, and the secular government which holds the Unchristian and wicked in check and forces them to keep the peace outwardly and be still, like it or not" (pp. 10-11).

tual life and the outer civil life.² This enabled the Reformers to argue both for the exclusion of the clergy from the pursuit of worldly power and the church's right to order its own affairs.

The separation of church and state, however, was strictly limited by the former's need for the protection and support of the secular authorities in their protest against the Roman church. This led Luther to appeal to the Christian conscience of the prince while Calvin stressed the responsibility of secular government in suppressing idolatry in the church. Calvin indeed claimed that the office of the civil magistrate concerned both the first and second tables of the law.³ Appealing to the precedent of Old Testament kings, he pointed to the responsibility of the magistrate to maintain the purity of divine worship. In the context of Geneva, it was understood that all citizens were under the discipline of both the religious and civil authorities.⁴ At the same time, both Luther and Calvin attempted to counter charges of anarchy and to resist the radical reformation by insisting upon the responsibility of each citizen to recognize the legitimacy of the civil ruler as ordained by God. The distinguishing of church and state was thus inevitably accompanied by a relating of the two in the quest for religious and social well-being. The tensions that are already implicit in this approach to church-state relations can be illustrated with reference to the course of the Scottish Reformation.

In Scotland prior to 1560 strong Lutheran emphases can be detected in critical approaches to the relationship between church and state. These were primarily intended to warn the state against undue interference in the affairs of the church and clergy against meddling in temporal pursuits. Henry Balnaves could distinguish the province of the magistrate from that of the church in a manner reminiscent of Luther's two kingdoms doctrine. The prince had a duty to govern justly and to defend the poor and the oppressed. While he also had a responsibility to restore the true and pure Christian religion he did not, according to Balnaves, have jurisdiction over the administration of the Word of God.⁵ Similar sentiments were expressed more forcibly in a letter of Protestant leaders

2. John Calvin, *Institutes of the Christian Religion,* trans. Ford Lewis Battles and ed. John T. McNeill (Philadelphia: Westminster, 1960), 3.9.15. This passage appears in the 1536 edition of the *Institutes* in the course of a discussion of Christian freedom where it is closely linked to the section on civil government. This connection is lost sight of in the 1559 edition.

3. *Institutes* 4.20.9. "Holy kings are greatly praised in Scripture because they restored the worship of God when it was corrupted or destroyed, or took care of religion that under them it might flourish pure and unblemished."

4. Cf. John T. McNeill, "John Calvin on Civil Government," *Calvinism and the Political Order,* ed. George L. Hunt (Philadelphia: Westminster, 1965), pp. 23-45.

5. For Balnaves's views, I am indebted to James Kirk, *Patterns of Reform* (Edinburgh: T. & T. Clark, 1989), pp. 232ff.

to the queen regent, Mary of Guise, in 1559. As queen she was entrusted with authority in the civil realm, but in Christ's kingdom as represented by the church she was merely a servant without pre-eminence and special authority.[6]

In the political writings of John Knox a theory of active resistance to the state is encountered for the first time in the Scottish Reformation. His notorious *First Blast of the Trumpet Against the Monstrous Regiment of Women* (1558) not only asserted that it was unnatural and unscriptural for a woman to hold political office but also that the citizens of the country had a duty to refuse obedience to one who was a "traitoress" and rebel against God.[7] This advocacy of active resistance was further developed in another treatise written in the same year, *Appellation to the Nobility.* Here Knox appealed to noblemen in their capacity as local rulers. They had a God-given vocation to rule justly and to uphold the practice of true religion. Thus not only the monarch but also the lower magistracy had religious responsibilities, and the possibility emerges that opposition to the monarch may be required in the exercise of these responsibilities. In other words, if the monarch prevented the local magistracy from upholding the cause of true religion then he or she would have to be resisted or even removed. "God will neither excuse nobility nor people, but the nobility least of all, that obey and follow their kings in manifest iniquity."[8]

No longer was passivity to be the stance of the persecuted. By raising the collective lower magistracy to the level of the prince, Knox could assert that the nobility must act even against the prince in the support of religion and the suppression of idolatry. He went so far as to allow that it would be legitimate action if only some of the nobility took up their swords. In 1558, the application of this imperative could have been almost everywhere in western Christendom.[9]

Knox's incitement to rebellion was a source of embarrassment to some of his fellow reformers living in very different political circumstances,[10] but it is clear, nonetheless, that he was not alone in formulating a theory of resistance to the state. He was himself strongly influenced by the Lutheran Magdeburg Confession of 1550. The activity of the Magdeburgers had come to prominence in

---

6. John Stuart, ed., *The Miscellany of the Spalding Club* (Aberdeen, 1841), vol. 4, pp. 88-92.

7. "First Blast of the Trumpet Against the Monstrous Regiment of Women," in *The Political Writings of John Knox*, ed. M. A. Breslow (London: Folger, 1985), p. 74.

8. "Appellation to the Nobility," in *The Political Writings of John Knox*, p. 127.

9. Breslow, in *The Political Writings of John Knox*, p. 30.

10. Elizabeth I had acceded to the English throne, and Knox's diatribe apparently alienated Geneva from Elizabeth. Calvin expressly disapproved of Knox's outburst, claiming he had no prior knowledge of it. Cf. The Zurich Letters. Second series comprising the correspondence of several English bishops and others with some of the Helvetian reformers during the reign of Queen Elizabeth (Cambridge: Cambridge University Press, 1845), pp. 34ff.

the 1550s, and this appears to be the most likely source of Knox's political think-ing on resistance.[11] Similar ideas can be found around the same time in Théodore Beza and Peter Martyr.

The Scots Confession (1560), composed by Knox and five colleagues, ap-pears at first sight to present a less critical view of the state. Article 24 deals ex-plicitly with the role of the civil magistrate and asserts the divine appointment of the same and the duty of all citizens to obey those whom God has set in au-thority. We know, however, that before the Confession was submitted to the Scottish Parliament in August 1560 it was amended by a government subcom-mittee that deleted a chapter discussing the conditions under which obedience or disobedience was required of subjects. Thus, a section describing the legiti-macy of civil disobedience appears to have been removed by the government-backed censors.[12] Moreover, the question of active resistance is referred to in passing in Article 14 of the Confession in the context of a discussion of the sec-ond table of the law. Here the Confession refers to the duty of all persons to "represse tyrannie." This seems to signal a muted endorsement of the position that Knox had earlier developed. It was this reference that led Karl Barth in his Aberdeen Gifford Lectures (1937/38) to say of the Scots Confession:

> I think, all things being considered, we must agree with the Confession here. . . . It could well be that we had to do with a Government of liars, mur-derers and incendiaries, with a Government which wished to usurp the place of God, to fetter the conscience, to suppress the church and become itself the Church of Antichrist. It would be clear that in such a case we could only choose either to obey God by disobeying this Government. . . . In such a case must not faith in Jesus Christ active in love necessitate our active resistance in just the same way as it necessitates passive resistance or our positive co-operation, when we are not faced with this choice?[13]

The Knoxian theory of the church-state relation was dominated by an appeal to Old Testament examples. As in ancient Israel the religious and the civil were in-extricably linked, so in sixteenth-century Scotland there had to be harmony be-tween church and state. Yet for Knox this amounted to rather more than each respecting the other's discrete province. In reforming the church Knox and his colleagues also sought to reform the life of the nation. This is illustrated by the *First Book of Discipline* which accompanied the Scots Confession in 1560. Here

---

11. I am indebted here to Ian Hazlett's discussion in "The Scots Confession 1560: Con-text, Complexion and Critique," *Archiv für Reformationsgeschichte* 78 (1987): 318.

12. Cf. Hazlett, "The Scots Confession," p. 316.

13. Karl Barth, *The Knowledge of God and the Service of God* (London: Hodder & Stoughton, 1938), pp. 229-30.

we see an attempt to inculcate the life not merely of the church but of every parish in the land with the principles of Reformed Christianity. Provision was to be made for the catechizing of the entire population, the establishment of a school in every town, the relief of the poor, and the exercise of discipline within the community by the representatives of the church.[14] This vision of a "godly nation" with its repeated appeal to the precedent of the Old Testament might indeed be perceived as distinctively Reformed in its ethos. The office of the state is not merely to limit the worst excesses of sin and to enforce the law by the use of the sword. The state is under the sovereign rule of God and plays its part in fulfilling the divine will in a community that acknowledges the Word as proclaimed by the church. This reflects a tendency to perceive the community and not merely the individual under the Word of God, and also to perceive both the law and the gospel as expressions of divine grace.[15]

Knox sought to reform not only the church but also national life. This was based solely upon his appeal to Scripture and to the model of nationhood that he found in the Old Testament. Yet his theory of church-state relations was fraught with problems that later Scottish history inevitably experienced. The relationship of church and state was too closely set. On the one side, it produced a regrettable intolerance of all those not professing the Reformed religion. This is confirmed by the vituperative rhetoric of the Scots Confession. On the other side, it created an alliance between church and state that could in a future age easily lead to the political corruption of the former. The church might thus be tempted to provide tacit approval of the political establishment instead of addressing it on the basis of the Word of God. This danger was exacerbated by the role that was assigned to the state as watchkeeper over the church. It is ironic that Knox, who championed active resistance to ungodly rulers, should be accused of failing to establish a critical distance between church and state in his writings. Yet with the benefit of hindsight we have little difficulty in perceiving the problems that his ideal of a godly nation created.[16]

---

14. Offenses worthy of capital punishment were only within the jurisdiction of the civil authority. "But drunkenness, excesse be it in apparel, or be it in eating and drinking, fornication, oppressing of the poore by exactions, deceiving of them in buying and selling by wrang met and measure, wanton words and licentious living tending to slander, doe openly appertaine to the kirk of God to punish them, as God's word commands." *The First Book of Discipline*, ed. J. K. Cameron (Edinburgh: St Andrew Press, 1972), pp. 166-67.

15. This is argued, for example, by Eberhard Busch, "Church and Politics in the Reformed Tradition," in *Major Themes in the Reformed Tradition*, ed. D. K. McKim (Grand Rapids: Eerdmans, 1992), pp. 180-95.

16. These issues are imaginatively assessed from the perspective of contemporary Scottish life in William Storrar's *Scottish Identity: A Christian Vision* (Edinburgh: Handsel Press, 1990).

The distinction between church and state needs to be drawn more sharply for at least two reasons which, if not absent from Knox's thinking, are certainly underemphasized. First, the need for a greater eschatological reserve implies a necessary differentiation between church and state. The eschatological *polis* of the New Testament cannot be identified with any earthly *polis* in the interim period. This means that the church cannot constitute itself a *polis* in advance of the eschaton, nor can the civil state be viewed as the perfect instrument of God's will. Under these circumstances, the church must maintain a critical distance from the state and recognize that the laws which govern the state and the method of their enforcement are not ultimate. This notion of an "eschatological reserve" was indeed deployed by Calvin against the Anabaptists. "But whoever knows how to distinguish between body and soul, between this present fleeting life and that future eternal life, will without difficulty know that Christ's spiritual Kingdom and the civil jurisdiction are things completely distinct."[17]

Second, the freedom of the Christian life is threatened by any attempt to create political conditions under which the Reformed religion is imposed upon a community. Commitment to the cause of Christ is offered freely through the inspiration of the Holy Spirit and cannot be coerced through civil legislation. The fruits of the Spirit that are brought forth in the life of the Christian cannot be engineered by political skill. In this respect, the alignment of church and state set out in the *First Book of Discipline* ignores the freedom of the Christian by encroaching upon the spiritual territory within which alone that freedom can be realized. Nonetheless, one cannot easily dismiss all that was sought by the Scottish reformers. The church's advocacy of comprehensive education and economic support for the poor in the land were remarkable proposals in their context and their worth will need to be acknowledged in any contemporary Christian critique of the state's responsibilities.

This commitment to the transformation of civil society has been one of the hallmarks of the Reformed tradition. From the beginning it had a political and social theology. This is reflected in lists of Reformed characteristics. Thus Hesselink notes that for Bucer not only the individual and the church, but also the whole of our social existence must be ordered according to the will of God revealed in Scripture. He thus includes the following in his inventory of Reformed emphases: the concern for the fulfillment of God's will in the wider world of culture, society, and politics.[18] Similarly, in his textbook on Christian doctrine John Leith writes of the Reformed conviction that the end of life is the

17. *Institutes* 4.20.1.
18. I. John Hesselink, *On Being Reformed: Distinctive Characteristics and Common Misunderstandings* (Ann Arbor, Mich.: Servant Books, 1983), pp. 93ff.

transformation of individuals and societies.[19] A study of the confessions bears this out and articulates the theological concern for the attainment of justice and peace in the civil realm as constitutive of the common good.[20]

This approach to civil society and the state is maintained in later sixteenth- and in seventeenth-century Reformed thought. However, other strains of political thought can be found. George Buchanan's dialogue *De Jure Regni Apud Scotos* (1579) reflected the humanist strain in Reformation thinking and an older Scottish constitutional tradition he had inherited from his teacher John Major in St. Andrews. Buchanan argued that the civil ruler should be thought of as one who has been elected to office and who has entered into a contract with the people. Justice is achieved in society where the various members function properly and in harmony with one another. The king, like a doctor, is required to maintain health in the body politic and is appointed with this end in view. He is charged with the administration of justice and the maintenance of order; this constitutes a mutual contract between the king and the people. Where the king breaks this bond he forfeits any legal right arising from the contract and therefore no longer holds lawful power over the people. He becomes their enemy against whom they are justified in waging war.[21]

This attempt to justify active resistance to an unjust ruler is constructed on more philosophical grounds than those of Knox. It appeals to something like a natural law governing the actions of rulers and their subjects, and this style of argument was not uncommon in the Scottish Reformation alongside the more Knoxian appeal to scriptural warrants.[22] It had the distinct advantage of being able to provide a theory of the state that could be understood independently of theological premises and could thus be advanced in the absence of theological unanimity. Its weakness, however, is that it could say little about the relationship of the church to the state from the perspective of the church.

It is perhaps not surprising that one of the leading Scottish theologians of the seventeenth century, Samuel Rutherford, should seek to combine these distinct approaches from the preceding century in his erudite *Lex, Rex* (1644). Here Rutherford argues against the theory of the divine right of kings by appealing

19. *Basic Christian Doctrines* (Louisville: Westminster/John Knox, 1993), pp. 3ff. This approach also informs the introduction, organization, and selection of materials in *Reformed Reader*, vol. 1, ed. William Stacy Johnson and John Leith (Louisville: Westminster/John Knox, 1993).

20. E.g., Jan Rohls, *Reformed Confessions: Theology from Zurich to Barmen* (Louisville: Westminster/John Knox, 1998), pp. 254ff.

21. *De Jure Regni Apud Scotos* LXXXVI. English translation by D. H. MacNeill in *The Art and Science of Government Among the Scots* (Glasgow: William MacLellan, 1964).

22. Cf. James Kirk, *Patterns of Reform*, pp. 248-49.

both to scriptural precedent and to the type of contractual theory grounded in natural law that was advocated by Buchanan in the previous century.

> If one lay the supposition, God hath immediately by the law of nature ap-
> pointed that there should be a Government; and mediately defined by the
> dictate of naturall light in a communitie, that there shall be one or many
> Rulers to governe the communitie; then the scriptures' arguments may well
> be drawn out of the school of nature.[23]

The principal target of Rutherford's treatise was Charles I and his supporters. The king was subsequently beheaded by his opponents in 1649.

Rutherford was also a prominent member of the Westminster Assembly and a contributor to its Confession of Faith, which was adopted by the General Assembly of the Church of Scotland in 1647. The Westminster Confession of Faith remains to this day the subordinate standard of faith in the Church of Scotland,[24] and not the least controversial of its chapters is the one dealing with the civil magistrate. Here the argument is essentially similar to Article 24 of the Scots Confession. The magistrate is appointed by God "for the defense and en-couragement of them that are good, and for the punishment of evildoers." While the magistrate may not interfere with the administration of Word and sacraments nonetheless he is given extensive powers to organize the church within his jurisdiction.

> [H]e hath authority, and it is his duty, to take order that unity and peace be
> preserved in the church, that the truth of God be kept pure, and entire, that
> all blasphemies and heresies be suppressed, all corruptions and abuses in
> worship and discipline prevented, or reformed; and all the ordinances of
> God duly settled, administered, and observed. For the better effecting
> whereof, he hath power to call synods, to be present at them, and to provide
> that whatsoever is transacted in them, be according to the mind of God.[25]

This alignment of church and state invites the same criticisms as were made above. The danger of undue political interference in the life of the church re-mains present; the persecution of nonconformist groups becomes possible through this church-state axis; and the liberty of the citizen (and therefore the

23. *Lex, Rex* (1644) q. 2.
24. A series of acts passed in the nineteenth century concerning the more controversial sections of the Westminster Confession, together with a formula of subscription for all min-isters and elders which allows "liberty of opinion on those matters not affecting the sub-stance of the faith," have reduced the *de facto* authority of the Confession in the twentieth century. However, its presence as the sole subordinate standard of faith remains problematic.
25. Westminster Confession of Faith, ch. 23, "Of the Civil Magistrate."

liberty of the Christian) to practice the faith of his or her choosing is seriously threatened.

The problem facing Reformed theology today is whether this social theology is irretrievably anachronistic. Does it reflect the context of early modern Europe? Is it available for fin de siècle western society let alone for the different polities of South East Asia or Africa? At least two problems require to be faced. One is the emergence of pluralism, with its insistence on tolerance of variations in religious practice, lifestyle choices, and patterns of association in both the household and civil society. This is particularly acute in those cases where the church finds itself as a minority religion overshadowed numerically by other faiths. A second problem, alluded to earlier, is whether the critical and prophetic voice of the church can be articulated if there is too close an alliance between the temporal and the spiritual.

Some of these difficulties were already being felt in eighteenth-century America. Thus the problematic chapter of the Westminster Confession on the civil magistrate was rewritten by the mainstream Presbyterian church. John Witherspoon, a Scotsman, president of Princeton, and the only clergyman to sign the Declaration of Independence, contributed in 1788 towards a revision of the Westminster Confession that distinguished more sharply between the provinces of church and state.

> [A]s nursing fathers, it is the duty of civil magistrates to protect the church of our common Lord, without giving the preference to any denomination of Christians above the rest, in such a manner that all ecclesiastical persons whatever shall enjoy the full, free, and unquestioned liberty of discharging every part of their sacred functions, without violence or danger. . . . It is the duty of civil magistrates to protect the person and good name of all their people, in such an effectual manner as that no person be suffered, either upon pretense of religion or infidelity, to offer any indignity, violence, abuse, or injury to any person whatsoever: and to take order, that all religious and ecclesiastical assemblies be held without molestation or disturbance.[26]

Here the influence of the standard arguments for religious liberty is apparent: the inner conscience of the individual cannot be invaded by the civil order, and to this end the natural rights of the individual must be guaranteed; the convictions of the heart cannot be coerced or destroyed by the rule of force; true religion and a just social order will always respect the independence of the other. Yet, in this last context, there lurks an inchoate *religious* element in the American notion of civic virtue that still remains problematic, and gives rise to the

---

26. *The Book of Confessions (Presbyterian Church, USA)* (Louisville, 1983), 6.129.

paradox that while Christianity is legally disestablished in the U.S.A. it remains deeply embedded in American culture.[27]

Our contemporary situation, however, is more marked by phenomena such as pluralism, dechristianization, and individualism than by the imperialist imposition of an ecclesiastical agenda on our civil authorities. The recent corrosive effects of individualism on the cultural force of the churches have been documented in a number of studies. The aspects of our social condition sometimes described as postmodern are familiar to us.[28] They include the extension of consumerist principles into our social and private lives (we choose from among competing options in leisure, work, travel, family, sex, and religion); the end of mass movements with large memberships and support across society such as the trade unions and the established churches of Europe; and the emergence of cultural pluralism in our modern urban environments. People of different races, religions, and lifestyles now co-exist in the cities of the world, and one cannot assume that any single frame of reference governs their social life. It has been pointed out that whereas once the rich contributed to social cohesion by virtue of their status as landowners and lairds, now they typically have several residences, private jets, and tax havens, and exist in relative detachment from any one society or community.[29] This deracinated élite epitomizes the atomistic forces at work in our social landscape.

The impact of this social scene, particularly in Europe, is momentous. Grace Davie, a Roman Catholic sociologist of religion, has described our religious condition as one of "believing without belonging."[30] Against the secularization thesis, she points out that the citizens of our society remain incurably religious. Today, however, their religion is expressed in more diverse, individualist, and consumerist ways than before. While we are witnessing a decline in the membership of established churches, we see a growth of interest in house churches, holistic medicine, ecological spirituality, the new age, Eastern religions, and astrology. A leading U.K. bookseller recently reported that sales from the "Body, Mind, and Spirit" section accounted for around 8 percent of total turnout, at a time when the Bible and books on traditional Christianity are found in more remote sections of their stores.

27. For a discussion of church-state relationship in American Reformed theology see David Little, "Reformed Faith and Religious Liberty," in *Major Themes in the Reformed Tradition*, pp. 196-213.

28. E.g., David McCrone, "The Postmodern Condition of Scotland," in *The Future of the Kirk*, ed. D. A. S. Fergusson and D. W. D. Shaw (Edinburgh: St. Andrew Press, 1997), pp. 11-20.

29. Cf. the introduction to the recent edition of Robert Bellah, Richard Madsen, William M. Sullivan, Ann Swidler, and Steven M. Tipton, *Habits of the Heart* (Berkeley: University of California Press, 1996).

30. *Religion in Britain Since 1945* (Oxford: Blackwell, 1994).

It is not hard to see the pressures and tensions this creates for Christian ministry in our society. How does one respond to requests for weddings, baptisms, and funerals when one is dealing with a growing dissociation from the scriptures, beliefs, and practices of the church? How does one comport oneself as a chaplain in a school, hospital, or prison? The questions are endless. David Wright has recently written,

> There is a real risk that, without a realistic re-appraisal of its position, a national-minority Church ends up with the worst of all worlds — with neither the recognition and influence appropriate to national status nor the freedom of action and initiative indispensable for a minority body. Worst of all is the pathetic impotence that results from a rejection of the latter in the deluded belief that the former still has cash value.[31]

Not surprisingly this situation has elicited some interesting theological proposals. Perhaps none is more striking than Stanley Hauerwas's colorful call for a distinctive, countercultural church that will eschew the task of contributing to a social consensus in the interests of greater Christian authenticity. He speaks to those who are conscious of the divorce between church and culture at the end of the second millennium, particularly those within liberal, western democracies. Christian theology and ethics become distorted by increasingly forced attempts to stand on common ground with those outside the colony.[32] His stress upon the distinctiveness of the Christian community and its narrative provides a stronger basis upon which ministry can be conducted. In a context of social fragmentation and moral disarray greater Christian authenticity becomes possible. Hints as to what a distinctive Christian witness might entail punctuate his writings. He suggests that the church should not admit to the Lord's Supper those who make a living from building weapons,[33] that Christians should publicly declare their income in the fellowship of the church,[34] that separate Christian schools are what we need,[35] that vegetarianism may be an appropriate witness to the eschatological vision of creation,[36] and that life-

---

31. "The Kirk: National or Christian?," in *The Realm of Reform: Presbyterianism and Calvinism in a Changing Scotland,* ed. R. D. Kernohan (Edinburgh: Handsel Press, 1999), p. 37.

32. This is argued, for example, by Stanley Hauerwas in *Resident Aliens: Life in a Christian Colony* (Nashville: Abingdon, 1993 [1989]).

33. Hauerwas, *Resident Aliens,* p. 160.

34. Stanley Hauerwas, *After Christendom: How the Church Is to Behave If Freedom, Justice, and a Christian Nation Are Bad Ideas* (Nashville: Abingdon, 1991), p. 100.

35. Hauerwas, *After Christendom,* p. 151.

36. Stanley Hauerwas, *In Good Company: The Church as Polis* (Notre Dame: University of Notre Dame Press, 1995), pp. 196-97.

long marriage is a sign of God's fidelity to us but that this essential practice may accommodate the exception of faithful relations between gay people.[37]

Hauerwas's arguments are clearly indebted in some respects to ecclesiologies redolent of the radical reformation. Thus, for example, Menno Simons's argument against the magisterial reformers was that they depended upon the coercive support of the state. Roman Catholics, Lutherans, and Zwinglians were referred to as the "great and comfortable sects."[38] The old organic unity of church and society had been maintained in the ecclesiastical polities they defended. This had the effect of making the church an institution into which one was born and to which one could belong without the costly witness of discipleship. Of six characteristics by which Menno Simons claimed the church to be known, four are explicitly ethical.[39] In addition to the purity of doctrine and a scriptural administration of the sacraments, we read of obedience to the Word, brotherly love, a bold confession of God and Christ, and a readiness to embrace suffering for the sake of the Word.

We can find similar themes in the work of Hauerwas: suspicion of the Lutheran doctrine of justification; the inherently ethical description of faith; a withering criticism of mainline Protestantism; and a desire further to distance the church from the state and civil society. It seems likely that in the short-term future we shall find support for such an ecclesiological model. The declining membership of the established churches, the loss of social influence, the dissociation of the rising generation from the precepts, traditions, and scriptures of the Christian faith — these will make it inevitable that the church is perceived as a distinct, if smaller, community that nurtures, forms, disciplines, and makes greater demands upon its members. Greater stress will be placed upon a ministry that evangelizes and upbuilds the life of the congregation. There will be a questioning of 1960s enthusiasm for the setting up of the chaplaincies in hospitals, factories, prisons, and educational institutions. There will be a loss of confidence in centralized, bureaucratic mechanisms for dealing with these problems. The widespread questioning of the practice of infant baptism should be seen as one symptom of all this.

Ernst Troeltsch once characterized the sect ideal in terms of a holy community distinct from surrounding society.[40] It maintains its purity through disciplines and excommunication. Its aim is individual holiness, and it is indiffer-

37. Stanley Hauerwas, "Gay Friendship: A Thought Experiment in Catholic Moral Theology," in *Sanctify Them in the Truth: Holiness Exemplified* (Edinburgh: T. & T. Clark, 1998), pp. 105-22.

38. Cf. Timothy George, *Theology of the Reformers* (Leicester: Apollos, 1987), p. 286.

39. George, *Theology of the Reformers*, p. 287.

40. Ernst Troeltsch, *Social Teaching of the Christian Churches*, vol. 2 (London: George Allen & Unwin, 1931), pp. 691ff.

ent to social domination. One of the most frequent charges leveled against Hauerwas and his associates is that of "sectarianism." Thus James Gustafson characterizes sectarian theology as an attempt to maintain the language and culture of a minority tribe without reference to knowledge that is available from other areas of experience and enquiry.[41] It sacrifices relevance and coherence for a misplaced notion of historical faithfulness. In doing so, it fails to take into account the theological notion that the whole world and therefore all experience and knowledge are within God's creation. It ignores the sociological fact that members of the Christian community also belong to other communities and cannot be hermetically sealed up inside the church.

The term "sectarian" is a contested notion, and one that has various applications. If, however, it suggests that Hauerwas and others advocate a withdrawal from civil society it is manifestly unfair. The call is not for retreat, but rather for the church to engage in distinctively Christian terms with the moral conundrums of the day. In doing so, it may have a greater impact than through a strategy of advocating consensus solutions to the problems we face.

James McClendon likewise points to the way in which H. R. Niebuhr, following Troeltsch, casts the "sectarian" model in an unfair light. In *Christ and Culture*, Niebuhr presents a range of thinkers from the author of the first Johannine epistle through Tertullian to Tolstoy as advocating a withdrawal from the world. Their concern is with the purity of the church, and reveals an indifference to the surrounding culture. Niebuhr castigates this type of ecclesiology for the way in which it is ensnared in contradiction — we are infected to some degree by our surrounding culture — and by its divorce of creation and redemption. In a devastating comment, he remarks that "at the edges of the radical movement, the Manichean heresy is always developing."[42] This typology, however, ignores the possibility that the development of a distinctive church may act in the interests not of withdrawal but of witness and mission. The purpose of a countercultural distinctiveness, it may be argued, is not isolationism but a proper contribution to the wider social world. Its task is to be faithful as the disciples of Christ in a world where the mission of the church is to be conducted. McClendon writes of the so-called sectarians that "engagement with the world was not optional or accidental, but lay at the heart of obedient discipleship."[43]

---

41. James Gustafson, "The Sectarian Temptation," *Proceedings of the Catholic Theological Society of America* 40 (1985): 84-85.

42. H. Richard Niebuhr, *Christ and Culture* (New York: Harper & Row, 1956), p. 81.

43. James W. McClendon Jr., *Systematic Theology: Ethics* (Nashville: Abingdon, 1986), p. 233. A comprehensive discussion of the sectarian charge can be found in Arne Rasmusson, *The Church as Polis: From Political Theology to Theological Politics as Exemplified by Jürgen Moltmann and Stanley Hauerwas* (Notre Dame: University of Notre Dame Press, 1996), pp. 231-47.

"Sectarianism" should probably be dropped as a term of criticism for it is too imprecise and loaded a concept. The criticism that the anabaptist model as currently articulated by McClendon, Yoder, and others is separationist should also be avoided. The church's orientation is towards the world, and its witness is directed to its well-being as the world. The critical and countercultural nature of this ecclesiology should caution other churches against too easy an accommodation with civil society. For the Reformed community, it might remind us of the ways in which a political theology that at one time warranted opposition to the political powers, at other times too easily lapsed into quietism.[44]

Yet there are other considerations that may require a less antithetical reading of the Reformed position of critical support for the state and the institutions of civil society. The incipient Pelagianism of the radical position has repeatedly been questioned by the Lutheran and Reformed emphasis upon *sola gratia*. This has been a theme of Christian ecclesiology at least since Augustine's rejection of Donatism. The church is a community gathered by the grace of God and not by human ethical achievement. For this reason, it has generally been willing to accord membership to those whose allegiance is faltering and intermittent. Ecclesiology has in practice often been inclusive rather than exclusive. There are ever-widening circles of formal commitment that have been tolerated in the name of grace and catholicity. This finds its theological rationale in the once-for-all, complete, and sufficient work of Christ. Thus the Lutheran Formula of Concord at Article XII criticizes the Anabaptists. It condemns as erroneous the view that "our righteousness before God does not consist wholly in the unique merit of Christ but in renewal and in our own pious behavior."

Christian theology whether of a Roman, Lutheran, or Reformed cast has generally been anxious to admit the possibility of a rudimentary moral perception without the church. It is this which makes civil society possible and which the church can endorse, correct, and extend in its own teaching. Here categories of natural law, common grace, and the orders of creation have been devised. Whatever theological and philosophical difficulties now surround them, they served a valuable function and if they are to be abandoned they will need to be replaced by some other discourse that accounts for a measure of common moral ground within and without the church. If not, the church's social witness is condemned either to silence or violence. In the absence of genuine moral perception outside Christian faith, it is difficult to know on what basis Christian social criticism is being offered. Social criticism must give way to evangelism.

44. This point is well made by John W. de Gruchy, *Liberating Reformed Theology* (Grand Rapids: Eerdmans, 1991), pp. 256-57. In this context, I have attempted to explore further Scottish examples in "The Kirk and Its Contribution to Scottish Identity," *Theology in Scotland* 5 (1998): 27-40.

The people of the church inhabit other communities and fulfill social roles beyond those of church membership. This has two consequences. On the one hand, the insights, experiences, and practices that accompany these roles will be of hermeneutical significance in the understanding of Christian belief. We can see this at work in contemporary Christian attitudes to feminism, other religions, and gay relationships. On the other hand, the church has a responsibility to provide its members with the resources by which they can live faithfully and with integrity in modern society. In some instances, support will have to be offered for the efforts of the state to maintain order, to secure its borders, to make provision for the poor, to run a national health service, and to manage a system of comprehensive education. In this respect, the ecclesiological task is not merely to prophesy against, but to support and conserve elements of the status quo.[45]

In the western context of dechristianization, where does this leave us? It is time to recognize that models of establishment derived from early modern Geneva and Scotland have to be abandoned. We can no longer assume nor aspire towards co-extensive membership of church and civil society, and shifting patterns of establishment in western Europe confirm this.[46] In this limited respect, the secularization thesis which recognizes the differentiation of civil and religious spheres must be accepted. The separation of the state, the market economy, and science from the influence of religious institutions is an undeniable feature of modernity. Yet, this entails neither the decline of religion nor its confinement to a private or sectarian sphere. The public contribution of the Christian churches has recently been apparent in a range of social contexts in Eastern Europe, South Africa, Latin America, and the U.S.A. This works not so much at the level of the state or political parties but instead through the exercise of influence upon civil society.[47] Here much depends on making common cause with other groups and movements, and articulating anxieties and aspirations that are experienced both inside and outside the church. At the same time, the public contribution of the churches will depend upon the maintenance of a

45. Cf. Nicholas Wolterstorff's remark: "If our criticisms of our fellow Christians are to fit, we will have to get down to the details of arguing that *here* the church condemned what it should have blessed, and *there* it blessed what it should have condemned." Review of John Howard Yoder, *The Royal Priesthood* (Grand Rapids: Eerdmans, 1994), in *Studies in Christian Ethics* 10 (1997): 145.

46. For a recent discussion of the church-state relationship in England see Tariq Modood, *Church, State and Religious Minorities* (London: Policy Studies Institute, 1997).

47. I am borrowing here from the thesis of José Casanova, *Public Religions in the Modern World* (Chicago: University of Chicago Press, 1994). Cf. Robert Wuthnow, *Christianity and Civil Society: The Contemporary Debate* (Valley Forge, Pa.: Trinity Press International, 1996).

distinct Christian subculture that nurtures and equips individuals for authentic service at a time of increasing moral fragmentation and confusion. While there may no longer be an organic unity between church and secular society, the Reformed vision of social transformation and critical support for the state is still relevant. It continues to offer a badly needed perspective in its intent to make common cause in search of a positive social contribution, in a hopeful though sober vision of political possibilities, in the affirmation of public service, and in the dignity of political office which, though frequently demeaned, remains a gift and a calling of God.

CHAPTER 9

"The State We're In":
A Reformed Response to Some Aspects of
John Milbank's Theory of Church and State

Peter McEnhill

The reasons for offering a response[1] to John Milbank's account of the relationship between church and civil society as outlined in his influential work *Theology and Social Theory* are many and varied.[2] First, Milbank's work, whatever one may think of some of its conclusions, is a work of considerable intellectual power, originality, and creativity; and it attempts, in a fashion barely seen since the time of Karl Barth, to wrestle the trajectory of theological discussion onto an entirely new plane. Despite, as will become apparent, my reservations about his posing of the problem, it has, like all good works in theology, caused me to wrestle with the issues it raises. Furthermore, in tandem with the related and similar projects of Alasdair McIntyre and Stanley Hauerwas, it looks set fair to capture the allegiance of many thoughtful Christians in a fragmented and confused intellectual climate.

Second, the work is self-consciously a "Catholic" work by an Anglo-Catholic writer. This is not to indulge in mere tribalism but to acknowledge that Milbank is mining a cultural and intellectual seam that is foreign to many Reformed and Protestant thinkers. Moreover, in delineating his thesis Milbank is contemptuous of modern secular liberalism, which he obviously views as the bastard offspring of liberal Protestantism. Lest we should rest assured in

1. This paper is a revised version of the one originally given to the Heidelberg conference. I am grateful to the participants for their comments.
2. John Milbank, *Theology and Social Theory* (Oxford: Blackwell, 1990).

our neo-orthodox and post-liberal Protestant souls, it is quite clear that for Milbank the whole Protestant and therefore Reformed enterprise is misconceived. The Reformation in general, Protestantism as a movement, neo-orthodox and liberal Protestantism alike, are invariably referred to pejoratively (admittedly they are not referred to very often at all). And it is clear that for Milbank all are variants of an essentially mistaken path that leads inevitably to the great Satan of modern, rational, secular society.[3] So there is an implicit challenge to Reformed patterns of thinking that has to be responded to. This is not to say that Milbank engages at any great length (in this work) with Reformed theologians. Social theorists and sages, yes, but we search in vain for a sympathetic or even a hostile engagement with Calvin, Schleiermacher, Barth, Brunner, or Moltmann.

This is somewhat surprising, as in relation to other thinkers Milbank's work is tiringly comprehensive. Moreover, at least some of the thinkers alluded to above anticipate much of the central thrust of Milbank's conclusions concerning the relationship between the church and civil society. Indeed, I would contend that the Reformed position is a more nuanced and subtle position than that offered by Milbank and that the articulation of it is an important part of what a distinctive Reformed theology has to offer the church today.

Milbank's work has a well-earned reputation for being somewhat difficult. It is perhaps best read back to front; the central thesis is revealed in the final chapter, where he engages in a penetrating analysis of Augustine's critique of the virtues of antique society as outlined in the *City of God*. In that work, Augustine contrasts human forms of society (the earthly city) with the city of God (the society of believers) primarily in terms of the assertion of power and violence that characterizes all earthly forms of society. As such, the peace of the earthly city is no real peace but only an arbitrary limitation of prior conflict and violence by the threat of yet greater violence. For Augustine neither peace nor justice nor virtue truly belong to the earthly city because the ends to which these limited goods are directed are not God. They are in this sense ends in themselves and any society that is structured in this fashion is marked by the denial of God, self-love, self-assertion, and the exercise of sheer dominion for its own sake.[4] It is on this account unambiguously the sphere of sin. Following Augustine's lead Milbank deconstructs the pagan mythos that supports this view to reveal an account of order that is only conceivable as the restraining of a prior and primal state of conflict and disorder.

Opposing this account of reality is the Christian mythos, which does not postulate a primal conflict but rather posits the creative act of God that origi-

---

3. Milbank, *Theology and Social Theory*, especially pp. 92ff.
4. Milbank, *Theology and Social Theory*, pp. 389-90.

nates all that is in an act of peaceful, gracious donation. This original creative act bestows and presupposes a peaceful, harmonious fellowship between God and his creatures and between his creatures themselves. The "heavenly city" that comprises the angels and the saints abides in this fellowship, and "their virtue is not the virtue of resistance and domination, but simply of remaining in a state of self-forgetting conviviality."[5] This Christian mythos confronts the pagan mythos with an assertion of the ontological primacy of peaceful, harmonious existence over against the inevitability of violence and conflict. This vision of peace obtained for the whole of creation, temporal society included, before the intrusion of sin, pride, and domination introduced the pervasive and destructive element of conflict.

Milbank concedes that Augustine allows a role for the state (better, "civil society") in limiting the effects of sin, but for Milbank this is a form of resignation on Augustine's part, as it allows for a concept of worldly peace that is merely "a bare compromise between competing wills."[6] Milbank takes Augustine to task for acknowledging even this limited role and validity on the part of the state in establishing a compromised peace (which is really no peace) and argues that at this point Augustine himself contributes to the invention of liberalism![7] Augustine's true insight, according to Milbank, is that it is the church alone which forms the true society, the true civitas, marked by "absolute consensus, agreement in desire and harmony among its members and this form of existence is itself the locus and the means of salvation — the restoration of being."[8] The church itself is nothing other than the realized heavenly city, the "telos of the salvific process."[9]

From this perspective the "earthly society" can only be regarded as the realm of sin. There is no sphere in which it has its own autonomous role. Yet Milbank again recognizes a breach in the pattern of Augustine's thought. For Augustine did argue that the church can and must make use of the false peace that civil society establishes, the excessive force, the economic compromises and exploitations that the earthly society engages in. It must make use of these and never derive them from its own order but instead use them to further its own particular and legitimate end — the heavenly peace. "Within this sphere of ambiguity alone, the earthly city must continue to have a separate identity."[10] However, Milbank is skeptical about the possibility of laying down Christian

---

5. Milbank, *Theology and Social Theory*, p. 391.
6. Milbank, *Theology and Social Theory*, p. 402.
7. Milbank, *Theology and Social Theory*, p. 402.
8. Milbank, *Theology and Social Theory*, p. 403.
9. Milbank, *Theology and Social Theory*, pp. 402-3.
10. Milbank, *Theology and Social Theory*, p. 407.

norms for an area that is intrinsically sinful. Thus this determinedly "Catholic" portrayal of the relationship between church and civil society rejects the categories of nature and supernature, natural law and universal reason that traditionally have formed the bridge between these two spheres in Catholic thought. There is no separate legitimate order outside the society of the church. (One can therefore understand why one Catholic commentator has said of Milbank's thesis, "Non tali auxilio.")[11]

If we ask what this means in practice, then Milbank's account becomes very hazy. He calls for fuzzy boundaries between church and state so that a social existence of complex interlocking powers might prevent either an absolutist state or a hierarchical church. But the clearest examples of where this might be taking place are resolutely local in that "base communities" are offered as the nearest contemporary equivalents.[12] If the question is posed as to how difference and conflict are to be overcome in the fallen world that we inhabit, then the answer is given that this can only be overcome through charity and forgiveness. This is not, however, "a Protestant resignation to sinfulness."[13] The task of the church is to extend this sphere of truly harmonious social relationships "within the state where this is possible . . . but of a state committed by its very nature only to the formal goals of dominion, little is to be hoped."[14]

This is an all-too-brief account of what is a stimulating, complex, and rigorous work. Its breadth of reference theological, philosophical, and sociological is literally staggering, and its imaginative construal of the cultural situation we find ourselves in is profoundly thought provoking. Milbank's ontology of a primal peaceableness is undoubtedly a benign and attractive vision that merits serious attention. However, despite my admiration for many things about this work, its basic description of the relationship between the church and civil society is one that I find disturbing. Its treatment of this relationship tends towards what might be called the anabaptist and sectarian tendency in Christian theology — the imagining of pure oases of perfected communities living in a detached, reflective, and somewhat self-absorbed isolation from the rest of society.

This is not to say that the work is without value from a Reformed perspective. Many in the Reformed community will welcome Milbank's implicit rejection of the nature/supernature distinction. The Reformed tradition has

11. Aidan Nichols, "An Ecclesial Critique of Milbank," in *Theology and Sociology*, ed. R. Gill (London: Cassell, 1996), p. 445.

12. Milbank, *Theology and Social Theory*, p. 408.

13. Milbank, *Theology and Social Theory*, p. 411.

14. Milbank, *Theology and Social Theory*, p. 422.

long maintained that the nature/supernature distinction prejudices the truth of God's presence in the world as Creator and Preserver by speaking of nature as a separate and autonomous sphere. Similarly, many Reformed theologians will applaud Milbank's recognition of the sinful nature of the state's coercive power and its tendency towards absolutism. Indeed, it is precisely at this point that Milbank's work shows its closest affinity with the powerful and voluble protests that have issued forth many times in the twentieth century from Reformed theologians who have thundered against all idolatrous and totalizing accounts of the state and its powers.

Yet had Milbank paid more attention to these theologians I think that he would have found a more nuanced position which takes more seriously what he terms the "sphere of ambiguity" that alone allows for the earthly city to have its separate identity. Yet attending to such thinkers as Barth and Brunner would, perhaps, have deflected Milbank from the simplistic trajectory through liberal Protestantism to secular society that he attempts to draw. Indeed a sub-theme of this paper might be to show that Milbank's position bears a striking resemblance to the early social and political thought of Karl Barth and that Barth breaks with what might be termed the Augustinian/Reformed pattern at precisely the same point. However, world events did not allow Barth the luxury of remaining in this position, and it will be argued that although his attempts to formulate a new position are ultimately unsatisfactory he nevertheless presents a position that is more subtle in its understanding of church and civil society than that offered by Milbank.

If we attend to civil society first — that "sphere of ambiguity" we have to exist in — then the Reformed tradition is not to be found wanting in its description of the fallen, sinful, and violent character of the state. As Barth would say, in almost identical terms to Milbank,

> civil community is spiritually blind and ignorant. It has neither faith, nor love nor hope. Civil community can only have external, relative and provisional tasks and aims and it is consequently defaced by that which the Christian community can characteristically do without: physical force . . . the polis has walls.[15]

Emil Brunner also argued that in contrast to antiquity, primitive Christianity recognized that the state was ordained by God in spite of the somewhat paradoxical fact that it was actually "without God."[16] Traversing essentially the same trajectory as Milbank, Brunner contends that the autonomous state is a prod-

---

15. Karl Barth, *Community, State and Church* (Gloucester, Mass.: Peter Smith, 1968), p. 151.

16. Emil Brunner, *The Divine Imperative* (London: Lutterworth Press, 1937), p. 440.

uct of the Enlightenment, prepared by the Renaissance, deriving ultimately from a Stoic/Christian fusion of Natural Law doctrine. (This is in essence Milbank's thesis.)

Brunner is quite clear that the state represents something of a riddle to Christian theology and one that it is not called to solve by anything like a Christian theory of the state. The riddle comprises of the fact that the state has the power to compel obedience. Indeed this force of compulsion is the state's very reason for existing, as it is through its compulsive power that it establishes a limited and fragmentary social order. Yet this force of compulsion, which is the *raison d'être* of the state, is a contradiction of the law of love and in its compulsive aspect is sinful and not an expression of the will of the Creator.[17] Therefore, for Brunner, every state exercises nothing other than a demonic power of compulsion and represents human sin on a large scale.[18]

In faithfulness to the Augustinian and classical Reformed pattern Brunner recognizes the paradoxical fact that it is this power of compulsion that creates peace within the social sphere and suppresses the anarchic conflicting forces present within society. Without this compulsive power all peaceful creative activity would ultimately be impossible in a fallen world. As such, in the necessity of the state we see and experience the consequences of sin. For Brunner the refusal to recognize the necessity of the state is a sign of arrogant sentimentality! For the state in all its sinfulness realizes the possibility at least of some form of community in accord with the divine purpose. Augustine's "sphere of ambiguity" is perfectly reflected in Brunner's idea that over every state there broods something of the light of the divine creation and also a heavy cloud of anti-divine forces. This divine light, of course, forms the basis of the Reformed understanding that human society is part of the order of creation and that the state or organized society is part of the order of preservation necessary after the fall. These orders, so prevalent in much of the classical Reformed tradition, are almost completely absent from Milbank's account. In this the Reformed tradition is a more accurate and faithful follower of Augustine, who clearly argued that the good at which earthly societies aim (earthly peace) is a real good and no sham and was not to be despised or disturbed but to be used.[19] That civil government is necessary is due to the fall, but that it exists at all is a gift of divine providence.

To state the faithfulness of the classical Reformed thinking in this matter to Augustine is not, of course, a powerful refutation of Milbank's position since

17. Brunner, *The Divine Imperative*, p. 445.
18. Brunner, *The Divine Imperative*, p. 445.
19. J. N. Figgis, *The Political Aspects of St. Augustine's "City of God"* (London: Longmans, Green & Co., 1921), p. 167.

Milbank has distanced himself from Augustine at precisely the point at which the Reformed tradition remains faithful. But the weakness in Milbank's theory is in imagining that the church can so exist in isolation from society that all it has to do is to concern itself with its own lived performance of its metanarrative of primal peaceableness. That the church has to do at least this, and to do so faithfully, is not denied. Instead it is being suggested that to truly live out its primal narrative requires much greater care for *all* forms of social life than Milbank seems to contemplate.

Perhaps the closest thinker in the Reformed tradition to Milbank's position is Karl Barth. Barth was famously unable to accept the classical Augustinian/Reformed pattern on the relationship between church and state because in his view it depended solely upon a general and somewhat vague category of providence.[20] He sought instead to view this relationship in christological terms, as part of the order of redemption instead of preservation.[21] The early Barth had declared that all forms of existing social order, both conservative and radical, were called into question by the divine No![22] The result was that political questions lost any absolute sense of importance for the Christian who viewed them from the ultimate perspective. From this perspective politics was judged to be "fundamentally uninteresting" and consequently political activity was possible only when carried on as "essentially a game; that is to say, when we are unable to speak of absolute political right . . . and when room has perhaps been made for that relative moderateness or for that relative radicalism in which human possibilities are renounced."[23] Barth, of course, had been heavily politicized during his time as pastor at Safenwil, but the second edition of *Romans* and certainly his Tambach lecture seem to mark a break with his early involvement with Ragaz and Religious Socialism.[24] It was in this lecture that he argued that the kingdom of God is the revolution before all revolutions that says "No" to both the forces of conservatism and revolution. But as Will Herberg has pointed out, this is a position that perhaps can only be held in a country and at a point in time when the rule of law is relatively speaking just and society on the whole stable.[25] The

20. Karl Barth, *Community, State and Church*, p. 104.

21. Karl Barth, *Community, State and Church*, p. 140.

22. Karl Barth, *The Epistle to the Romans* (London: Oxford University Press, 1933), p. 479.

23. Karl Barth, *Church Dogmatics*, IV/1 (Edinburgh: T. & T. Clark, 1936), p. 307; and Barth, *The Epistle to the Romans*, p. 489.

24. Eberhard Busch, *Karl Barth* (London: SCM, 1975), p. 111. Tim Gorringe, "Eschatology and Political Radicalism," in *God Will Be All in All*, ed. R. Bauckham (Edinburgh: T. & T. Clark, 1999), p. 99, notes the same possible break in Barth's thought but he is inclined to see more continuity than I do.

25. Will Herberg, "Introduction," in Barth, *Community, State and Church*, p. 24.

early Barth's influence on much of contemporary Christian ethical theory at this point can be clearly seen and is perhaps to be lamented.

Barth, however, was forced from this position by the crisis that confronted him in Germany in the 1930s. In the totalizing and absolutist claims of the Nazis, which made an inward claim upon the individual, Barth discerned a challenge to the freedom of the church to proclaim its message of divine justification that was essentially the challenge of an anti-church.[26] Barth saw that the freedom of the church to proclaim this message is the source and guarantee of all other freedoms and the foundation of all human law.[27] From this realization Barth called for the resistance of the church against the claims of the Nazi state. Whereas the early Barth dismissed political questions as being in the final analysis fundamentally uninteresting, in the crisis of the moment he was now moved to declare that the democratic form of the state was a justifiable implication of New Testament teaching.[28] It was not possible, Barth thought, for the church in the light of the contemporary situation to live in relation to the state as though it lived "in a night when all cats are grey."[29] The function that the church had to render to the state was that of the prophetic service of Watchman by praying for it in all circumstances.[30] Yet tellingly, he argued,

> Can serious prayer in the long run, continue without the corresponding work? . . . Can we ask God for something which we are not at the same moment determined and prepared to bring about, so far as it lies within the bounds of our possibility? Can we pray that the state shall preserve us, and that it may continue to do so as a just state, or that it will again become a just state, and not at the same time pledge ourselves personally, both in thought and action, in order that this happen, without sharing the earnest desire of the Scottish Confession. . . . thus without, in certain cases, like Zwingli, reckoning with the possibility of revolution, the possibility, according to this strong expression, that we may have to "overthrow with God" those rulers who do not follow the lines laid down by Christ?[31]

Thus Barth issued forth this clarion call for resistance and the right of resistance which was to form the basis of his famous later wartime letters to French Protestants and British and American Christians calling for full-scale support

26. Barth, *Community, State and Church*, p. 143.
27. Barth, *Community, State and Church*, pp. 141, 147.
28. Barth, *Community, State and Church*, p. 145.
29. Barth, *Community, State and Church*, pp. 119-20.
30. Barth, *Community, State and Church*, p. 107.
31. Barth, *Community, State and Church*, p. 145.

for the war effort against Hitler. A clearer call for political action based squarely on the demands of the Christian gospel would be hard to find. Yet, famously, or infamously, Barth refused to condemn the later abuses and totalitarian claims of postwar communist regimes, arguing that the situation was not the same as that which confronted the church in the war years and that the task of the church now was to "stand quietly aloof and tread the 'narrow path midway between Moscow and Rome.'"[32] It is unfair, with the benefit of hindsight, to charge Barth with inconsistency (although there were many including Brunner who thought so at the time) even though it seems clear that if ever an ideology made totalizing and inward claims upon the individual it was the Marxist Leninism of the Soviet era. Barth's failure to see this does him no credit, but it does not in itself constitute a theological problem. Indeed, he was perhaps wiser than we know in refusing quite clearly to join in the Western denunciation of all things communist during the cold war. He certainly cannot be accused of being a mouthpiece for either side even if from this side of history it is hard to make the same absolute distinction between Stalinism and Nazism that Barth clearly drew. However, Barth's failure at this point and his reversal to his prewar position is not, I believe, simply due to a lack of knowledge or understanding on his part of the situation pertaining in Soviet Russia. It is related, rather, to the narrow base on which he founds his political thought.[33] By attempting to ground everything christologically, that is, as part of the order of redemption, Barth succumbs to that pervasive Christomonism so characteristic of his thought — which tends to separate his whole theology from the reality of human experience.

In detaching his position from the concept of providence and the order of preservation Barth finds himself unable to address the middle ground between a position in which political questions are fundamentally uninteresting and that in which they are posing an absolute and fundamental threat to the existence of the church. In other words, there is no median point between an eschatological indifference on the part of the church and a moment of apocalyptic crisis. Given that most human lives are lived, and most societies are organized, somewhere between these two extremes, it is clear that for the most part Barth's social thought is largely redundant.

This is not to say that Barth was wrong when he argued against the idea of Christian political parties or specifically Christian theories of the state or Christian solutions to each and every problem that confronts us. Coming from a church that has a Church and Nation committee prone to comment on every-

---

32. Karl Barth, "The Christian Community in the Midst of Political Change," in *Against the Stream: Shorter Post War Writings* (New York: Philosophical Library, 1954), p. 117.
33. Charles West, cited by Herberg, "Introduction," pp. 62-66.

thing from the size of holes in fishing nets to nuclear waste, I am particularly sensitive to the demand that the authority of the Christian gospel should not be invoked to support each and every passing issue of the day. However, a theological position that can posit quiet disinterest unless faced with the extreme horror of something as catastrophic as Nazism has to be viewed with some suspicion. Where, on Barth's scale of things, might we place slavery, segregation, apartheid, or the economic injustice that condemns many to servitude, illness, and early death today? Are these matters about which we should be indifferent, or is the message of divine justification challenged in various forms by these too? Barth the young pastor quite clearly held such matters to be of considerable importance and perhaps, on a personal level, Barth the professor did too. However, theologically and ecclesiologically his response seems to be quite different.

Barth, of course, has many positive things to say about the forms of communal life, but I would agree with the assessment that far from the express intention of these being grounded christologically in an analogy or correspondence between the heavenly *polis* and the earthly *polis* they are in fact the postulates of natural law surreptitiously smuggled back into the christological analogy by a theological sleight of hand.[34]

To his credit Barth did recognize that the state was an order of grace relating to sin and a necessary remedy for the corruption of nature, and that as part of God's providential order there was a proper Christian obedience to state with the proviso that this obedience is always subject to a prior obedience to God.[35] Had he followed this classical Reformed pattern and his own best insights that, "(T)he Church lives in expectation of the eternal state, and therefore honours the earthly state, and constantly expects the best from it, i.e., that, in its own way amongst 'all men,' it will serve the Lord whom the believers already love as their Saviour," he would, perhaps, have had greater theological resources to secure his political thought in a way that would have made it much more vital and connected to everyday social existence.[36]

By following this line of thought Barth would have been led to a recognition of the pervasive activity of Christ throughout his creation, activity that is not simply confined to the sphere of the church as in Milbank. By linking our social and political thought to the order of preservation we understand that the whole of creation is under Christ's dominion and is claimed for him, and this means the state no less than the church. This is to grant the state a legitimate place in the providential ordering of the world but not a separate auton-

34. Herberg, "Introduction," p. 36.
35. Karl Barth, *Ethics* (Edinburgh: T. & T. Clark, 1981), p. 519.
36. Barth, *Community, State and Church*, p. 140.

omy. Ultimately, it is subject to the same lordship of Christ as the church. Barth, I believe, would also reject Milbank's idealized view of the church, having a much stronger sense that the church though healed remains a scarred and disfigured community and that redemption is not simply our retrieval of a primal innocence but the future transformative act of God for which we long and hope.

The Reformed recognition of the paradoxical nature of the state means that the church cannot leave the state to its own devices. As Barth recognized, we must expect the best from the state without blinding ourselves to the reality of its distorted and sinful nature. To be sure, the first and prior way that the church confronts the state is simply to be the church as faithfully and purely as it can. It must pray for and confront the state with the gospel of the kingdom of Christ and call the state to conform itself to that gospel in the name of Christ who is its lord. But simply to be the church as purely as we can is not enough. The field of the political and the social is too important to be left to the state alone. Indeed, as Barth (and I think Milbank) would argue, if the state can only ultimately recognize its proper purpose and role because of the proclamation of the church, then it becomes ever more important for the church to participate constructively in the formation of communal and civic life.

To truly appreciate the sinful distorted nature of the state and the fallen world in which we live does not lead inevitably to Milbank's terminal pessimism: that from a state which is by its very nature committed to the formal goals of dominion, little is to be hoped. On the contrary, unless sin is to have the final word, then much is to be hoped because God is providentially active in and through the state as well as the church. As Barth reminded us, there is no reason for supposing that the ordained state of Romans 13 inevitably has to become the "beast" of Revelation since it too has been created in, through, and for Christ.[37]

The failure to recognize a place for the state in God's providential order has important implications for Milbank's ethical proposal, just as the attempt to transfer it completely into the christological sphere had for Barth's. For one finds little serious engagement with the question as to how, in a mixed community, in which the *civitas terrena* and the *civitas dei* are always inextricably linked, one advances and engages in any type of social and political activity; how one performs the exchanges and the compromises that actually increase and establish harmonious relationships in the world.[38] In short, there is rarely found an ethical, social, or political problem in the world that is not mirrored

37. Barth, *Community, State and Church*, p. 119.
38. R. Williams, "A Theological Critique of Milbank," in *Theology and Sociology*, ed. R. Gill (London: Cassell, 1996), p. 438.

in some way in the church. The insistence that the church should simply live out as purely as it can its communal life inevitably leads to separation and fragmentation as faith communities seek to be ever more pure, ever more perfect realizations of a separated Christian ideal. The visible/invisible distinction advocated by Augustine and picked up by the Reformed tradition is a vital safeguard against all forms of Christian perfectionism and sectarianism.

This failure to see the providential activity of the Spirit at large in the world is surely a major failing in Milbank's vision. It fails to take seriously (as Barth in his deepest insights clearly did) the ways in which the sovereign God takes the sphere of the state in all its imperfection and sinfulness and makes its broken, fragmented, and flawed order and form of community a provisional (more provisional than the church, yes — but still a provisional) embodiment of that *polis* which is yet to come — the heavenly city.[39]

In short, there has to be a position that allows for a variety of positions on a continuum the church can inhabit in relation to the state. Milbank can only see the state as a sphere of sin from which little is to be hoped. This is perhaps the most resigned aspect of the pole tending inevitably towards separation and disinterest in political and social life. The early Barth inhabited this pole theologically for a time, but within the totality of his theological position there is room for a more positive view as well, and it is this aspect of his thought that has been the most constructive politically and ethically. In some ways this is due to the lingering remnants in his theology of the classical Augustinian/Reformed position which he inherited and which, despite his intentions to ground everything christologically, he could never quite fully escape from. This position allows for a range of positions accommodating themselves to the actual form of the state that is being confronted at any given time. We might describe these as the critically neutral, the critically supportive, and the critically resistant. The critically neutral is perhaps self-explanatory. There are many forms of government and society that are compatible with the Christian gospel, and the church may on a whole range of issues have little to say that distinctively emanates from its gospel message. The critical function is ever present as it recognizes the coercive and sinful aspect of the state's nature that has always to be carefully monitored and safeguarded. The critically supportive is for those forms of government and social arrangement that are deemed to be positive manifestations of the way in which God desires his creatures to live. I would not suggest any particular political arrangement per se but let us say that those institutions and forms of life that promote peaceableness, justice, freedom, and the ability to worship might be especially commended. The critically resistant is, of course, called for in relation to those forms of society and communal living that

39. Barth, *Community, State and Church*, p. 155.

threaten and deny the integrity of the gospel. It will, as Barth clearly saw, take a moment of prophetic discernment to realize when and what conditions justify such a decision and what form of particular action is called for on the part of the church.

In concluding this piece I would simply like to note that much of the debate on church/state relationships in the twentieth century has focused upon the overwhelming claims to absolute power and authority that have been made by the state and of the need to reject these claims in the name of the sovereign lordship of Christ. This has been and remains a fundamental emphasis. However, faced with the phenomenon of globalization with its effective consumerization of all human existence and the consequent reduction in the power of the state to organize communal life in the face of anonymous multinational corporations and the movement of massive amounts of money in the global markets, we are conscious of seeing the disastrous and anarchic effects of the total absence of any effective ability to organize equitable social living. The disastrous effects of mass unemployment, widespread hunger, and the forms of civil war that rage in societies decimated and bereft of social structures after the effects of colonialism and economic neo-colonialism should give us cause to stop and think before we too cavalierly dismiss the proper role and function of the state. In ways that Barth perhaps could not have imagined (but curiously in ways that Calvin, who seems to have been particularly troubled by the possibility of anarchy and societal breakdown, might have) we now see the hazardous and deleterious effects of a lack of society, a lack of social order. In this situation there may well be a gospel imperative laid upon us in our time to nurture and sustain that which leads to harmonious living, that which promotes civil order and justice as an anticipation of the kingdom. This is not say that we can recover the Reformation paradigm of church and Christian magistrate, or that we can recreate Calvin's Geneva, nor even to say that the modern form of the nation state is the best or only way to organize "civil society," but it is to argue that the conviction that the gospel has transformative implications for *all* social and political life has always been, and remains, a vital part of Reformed and indeed Christian identity.

CHAPTER 10

The Communion of the Triune God: Towards a Trinitarian Ecclesiology in Reformed Perspective

Daniel L. Migliore

Theologians of many traditions are rethinking the doctrine of the church and its relation to the doctrine of the Trinity.[1] My aim in this essay is to explore this theme from a Reformed theological perspective. The thesis is that trinitarian doctrine provides the key to a proper theology of community. Genuine human community has its ultimate basis in the communion of the triune God.

I begin with a brief description of the challenge of pluralism to modern society and especially to the life of the church today. I then sketch a trinitarian ecclesiology that incorporates three classical themes of Reformed theology: the church is a community of faith rooted in the free grace of God, a community of love centered on the servant lordship of Christ, and a community of hope in which diverse gifts of the Holy Spirit are shared and celebrated as first fruits of

---

1. See Jürgen Moltmann, *The Trinity and the Kingdom* (New York: Harper & Row, 1981); John Zizioulas, *Being as Communion: Studies in Personhood and the Church* (Crestwood, N.Y.: St. Vladimir's Press, 1985); Colin Gunton, "The Church on Earth: The Roots of Community," in *On Being the Church: Essays on the Christian Community,* ed. Colin Gunton and Daniel Hardy (Edinburgh: T. & T. Clark, 1989); Medard Kehl, *Die Kirche: Eine Katholische Ekklesiologie* (Würzburg: Echter, 1992); Michael G. Lawler and Thomas J. Shanahan, *Church: A Spirited Communion* (Collegeville, Minn.: Liturgical Press, 1995); Christoph Schwöbel, "The Quest for Communion," in *LWF Documentation* 41 (1997): 227-85; Miroslav Volf, *After Our Likeness: The Church as the Image of the Trinity* (Grand Rapids: Eerdmans, 1998).

God's promised reign. A final section of the paper summarizes the promise and the limitations of a trinitarian ecclesiology.

Pluralism and the Postmodern Crisis of Human Community

Uncertainty about the meaning and possibility of community is evident in modern societies in countless debates about pluralism, diversity, and multiculturalism.

Pluralism has both creative and destructive potential.[2] On the positive side, pluralism espouses respect for individuality, particularity, and difference, and resists the drive toward total control and homogenization of life by dominant cultures, ideologies, and political powers. On the negative side, pluralism can be debilitating and disintegrative. A pluralist society completely indifferent to common beliefs, norms, and values is a society at grave risk. Even the minimal ideals of tolerance and civility that some philosophers commend as a unifying framework for pluralist societies depend on a tacit consensus regarding the fundamental principles and values governing the common life.[3] The church today experiences pluralism in its own life as well as in the surrounding society and culture. The present challenge of pluralism to the church follows two earlier epochal challenges.[4] The first of these was the challenge of disestablishment. At least formally, disestablishment is now a familiar feature of the life of the church in North America. For European churches, too, the so-called era of Christendom is over and the future will bring new tasks and opportunities for a disestablished church.

While many ecclesial traditions made peace with legal disestablishment long ago, a second epochal challenge to the church — marginalization — is a reality with which many churches still struggle. The once mainstream North American Protestant denominations, for example, find themselves increasingly on the margins of American culture and society. This has posed a major challenge to the self-understanding of these denominations. Once wielders of considerable influence in the public domain, they must now discover their vision and mission as a minority community of faith with far less influence and power than they once possessed.

Beyond disestablishment and marginalization, pluralism outside and inside the church constitutes the third epochal challenge to the church in the mod-

2. See Michael Welker, *Kirche Im Pluralismus* (Gütersloh: Kaiser Verlag, 1995).
3. Christoph Schwöbel, "The Quest for Communion," p. 233.
4. See Douglas John Hall, *An Awkward Church: Theology and Worship Occasional Paper No. 5* (Presbyterian Church [USA]).

ern period.⁵ To many Christians today, pluralism seems an even greater threat than either disestablishment or marginalization. Rightly understood, however, pluralism challenges the church to achieve greater clarity about Christian identity and the meaning of Christian life in community. This challenge is often missed by some familiar responses of the church to the pluralism of our time.

One response is to engage the reality of pluralism within a framework of competition and to emphasize the importance of increasing the size of the church lest it diminish while other religious groups expand. A second response is for the church to withdraw into self-imposed isolation in hope of avoiding all corrupting outside influences. Still a third response is to adopt authoritarian attitudes and structures to defend the identity of the church against the surrounding world. A fourth response is simply to accept current legal, economic, and political understandings of pluralism with uncritical enthusiasm.⁶ Such responses are bound to fail because they do not wrestle with the reality of pluralism as a genuine theological challenge. The church must learn to distinguish between forms of pluralism that enrich and enhance life in community and forms of pluralism that weaken and destroy community.⁷ The theological challenge of pluralism to the church cannot be adequately answered by more favorable membership statistics, by simplistic withdrawal into self-imposed isolation, by the adoption of authoritarian strategies that contradict the gospel message, or by sheer accommodation to prevailing cultural norms.

In a pluralist context where the reality of community is elusive and the quest for community acute, the church must dare to speak concretely and specifically about what God has done to establish new community in Jesus Christ by the power of the Spirit. In the light of the gospel, human community has its basis and promise in the life and activity of the triune God.⁸

Discerning the connection between the trinitarian reality of God and ecclesial life cannot be a matter of directly and mechanically deriving an understanding of the church as communion from dogmatic descriptions of intra-trinitarian relationships.⁹ This would lead to an ecclesiological idealism or ro-

5. K. Rahner writes: "It is of the utmost importance to recognize that the problem of pluralism in theology really does exist, and that it is new." See "Pluralism in Theology," *Theological Investigations XI* (London: Darton, Longman & Todd, 1974), p. 4.

6. According to Oliver O'Donovan, "Much Christian enthusiasm for 'pluralism' has . . . to do . . . with the church's yearning to sound in harmony with the commonplaces of the stock exchange, the law-courts, and the public schools." *The Desire of the Nations* (Cambridge: Cambridge University Press, 1996), p. 226.

7. See Michael Welker, *God the Spirit* (Minneapolis: Fortress, 1994), pp. 22-23.

8. See Schwobel, "The Quest for Communion," p. 234.

9. See Ulrich Körtner's warnings in his essay in this volume about facile moves from statements about the immanent triune life to ecclesiological affirmations.

manticism that ignores the imperfection of the actual church. Rather, we must think through the meaning of communion as an anticipatory sign of and partial correspondence to the life of the triune God as made known in the economy of salvation. Calvin indicates the proper basis of a trinitarian ecclesiology in his statement: "by the kindness of God the Father, through the working of the Holy Spirit, [we] have entered into fellowship with Christ."[10]

The Church as Communion in Faith

The church is a people who share a common faith. That faith centers on the God who has entered into covenantal relationship with the people of Israel and has acted decisively in Jesus Christ for the reconciliation and renewal of the world.

According to the New Testament, Christians "share in the gospel" of God's free grace (Phil. 1:5). The good news is that the free grace of God in Jesus Christ is extended to all people: sinners and strangers, Jews and Gentiles, men and women. Christ brings peace to a divided world, and in him one new inclusive people of God has been established (Eph. 2:13-15).

Communion in faith, according to the Reformed tradition, finds expression in common confession. The truth of the gospel is not an esoteric truth to be concealed but a public truth to be joyfully shared. Faith in the gospel seeks public expression and communication with others. The confessional character of Christian faith is rooted in the nature of God and in the nature of humanity created in the image of God. Just as the triune God is eternally communicative rather than solitary and silent, so human beings created in the image of God are meant for communication and fellowship. There can be no genuine fellowship where truth is ignored or withheld from others. Hence, from a Reformed perspective, to be a Christian is to be "a confessing Christian in a confessing community."[11] For the Reformed tradition, the confessional task of the church is always twofold. First and foremost, the task is to share the gospel humbly but without shame (Rom. 1:16). The church is a community of faith where the crucified and risen Lord is joyfully preached, praised, and obeyed in the power of the Holy Spirit.

Reformed Christians respect the confessions of the church and the central doctrines they contain as indispensable guides for sound preaching and teaching. Church confessions are valued in the Reformed tradition as impor-

10. John Calvin, *Institutes of the Christian Religion*, trans. Ford Lewis Battles and ed. John T. McNeill (Philadelphia: Westminster, 1960), 4.1.3.

11. Karl Barth, *Church Dogmatics* IV/1 (Edinburgh: T. & T. Clark, 1956), p. 779.

tant ways by which the community of faith declares what it believes to be true and what it resolves to do in response to God's word. Thus, for Reformed faith and theology, faithful confession and sound doctrine are primary responsibilities of the church in every cultural and historical context.

The second aspect of the confessional task, equally emphasized within the Reformed theological tradition, is to acknowledge the incompleteness and reformability of all confessional statements. While the confessional tradition of the church is to be approached with respect and even deference, it is not to be invested with absolute authority. In the Reformed view, the latter would be tantamount to idolatry. No single confession and no inherited church practice is to be absolutized. All confessions and practices are subordinate to the living Word of God and open to reform. This twofoldness of the confessional task — faithfulness to the gospel and openness to new insight from the living Word of God — requires that the church make room for and learn from a diversity of receptions of the gospel.

Of the great confessional traditions, the Reformed is marked by its commitment to the Word of God proclaimed and heard in diverse times and places. Reformed faith and theology are guided by a singularly rich confessional history that includes the Apostles' and Nicene creeds, the Reformed confessions of the sixteenth and seventeenth centuries, and many other confessional documents of Reformed churches forged in diverse social and cultural contexts. In a Reformed understanding of communion in faith, the confession of one and the same crucified and risen Lord requires bold and fresh expression in particular times and places. Reformed identity is thus not to be found in a fixed or finished corpus of doctrine even though there are unquestionably distinctive emphases in the Reformed theological tradition. The identity of Reformed faith rests on the ever new hearing and obeying of the living Word of God. From a Reformed perspective, a right understanding of the church as communion in faith calls for openness to different and often disturbing voices, both inside and outside the church, that serve to challenge narrow or calcified understandings of the Word of God.

This dynamic of identity and diversity in the Reformed understanding of communion in faith is not explainable solely in terms of the different cultural and historical contexts in which the gospel is proclaimed and heard. It is not just the varying contexts of Christian faith and confession that require a multiformity of receptions. The multiformity of confession is required also by the richness and inexhaustibility of the object of faith and confession. Barth explains: "The recognition of Christian faith can and should be varied. Although its object, the Jesus Christ attested in Scripture and proclaimed by the community, is single, unitary, consistent and free from contradiction, yet for all His singularity and unity His form is inexhaustibly rich, so that it is not merely legitimate but obligatory that believers should continually see and understand it in new lights and aspects. For He Himself does not present Himself to them in one form but in many — indeed, He is not in Himself uniform but multiform. How can it be otherwise when He is the true Son of God who is eternally rich?"[12]

Barth's reference to the God who is "eternally rich" points to the trinitarian basis of the unity and diversity that mark Christian communion in faith. The life of the one triune God is differentiated and rich rather than uniform and fearful of difference. Differentiated communion is not strange to the eternal life of God. The communion of the triune God includes otherness and difference that does not destroy but deepens community. In the eternal divine life, there is difference that does not divide, otherness that does not separate, and encounter that does not become opposition. The richness of the triune life is the basis of all genuine life in community.[13] If communion in faith is rich and multiform because God is eternally rich, it is a mistake to equate communion in faith with a monolithic system of doctrinal statements. Calvin describes faith as far more than assent to doctrinal formulae. Faith is trust in the faithfulness of the triune God. For Calvin, faith rests on the scripturally attested promise of God decisively confirmed in Christ and sealed on our hearts by the Holy Spirit.[14] Christian communion in faith is thus God-centered, Christ-focused, and Spirit-empowered. Because the God of the gospel is always more than we can grasp or exhaustively comprehend, communion in faith must be open and self-critical. It knows that all confessional statements and theologies this side of the promised reign of God are *semper reformanda.*

This does not mean there are no limits of confessional pluralism, ecclesial inclusivity, and ecumenical openness. Unquestionably, there are boundaries that mark off the Christian communion of faith. Yet Reformed confessional sensibility, while unashamed and unapologetic about the specific content of the gospel, remains teachable. It is open to new light from the witness of Scripture under the guidance of the Spirit and attends to the particularities of context in the effort to rightly understand and proclaim the gospel here and now.

Within the Reformed tradition, therefore, communion in faith and its confessional expression require both faithfulness and openness, both freedom and responsibility. Freedom in the Reformed tradition is always accountable rather than arbitrary freedom, accountable to the scriptural witness to the freely gracious God made known in Jesus Christ by the power of the Holy Spirit. Jesus Christ is the living and inexhaustibly rich Word of God. It is in re-

---

12. Barth, *Church Dogmatics* IV/1, p. 763.

13. See Barth, *Church Dogmatics* IV/2 (Edinburgh: T. & T. Clark, 1958), p. 343.

14. See John Calvin's trinitarian definition of faith in the *Institutes* 3.2.7.

lation to this word attested in Scripture that the church is a communion in faith that remains *semper reformanda.*

The Church as Communion in Love

The church is not only a communion in faith but also a communion in love. United with Christ by the power of the Spirit, Christians are called to participate in and act in correspondence to God's eternal self-giving love decisively revealed in the ministry, cross, and resurrection of Jesus Christ.

While the Reformed tradition emphasizes the sovereignty of God, it defines divine sovereignty and power not as sheer omnipotence but as the very particular power revealed in the servant lordship and costly love of the crucified and risen Jesus. Because the word "love" is often used in a loose and sentimental way, one is tempted to avoid it altogether in attempting to express the depth of the biblical proclamation of the grace of God in Jesus Christ. Christian theology does not define God in terms of love but defines love in terms of the being and acts of the God attested in Scripture.

There are at least two distinctive features of the love of God manifest in God's relations with Israel and God's incarnate presence in the life, ministry, and passion of Jesus. The first is hospitality. Hospitality means showing welcome to strangers. The summons to hospitality is deeply etched in the Torah and in the prophetic tradition of the Old Testament. Israel is called to show hospitality to strangers because she too was once a stranger in the land of Egypt (Exod. 23:9).

In the New Testament the theme of hospitality is writ large in the stories of Jesus' welcoming of the poor and his table fellowship with sinners and the outcast (Mark 2:15-17). As he hangs on the cross, Jesus extends hospitality to the thief who asks to be remembered (Luke 23:42-43). Paul exhorts us to "Welcome one another as Christ has welcomed you" (Rom. 15:7). The author of Hebrews encourages the church to show hospitality to strangers (Heb. 13:2). A people who participate in the life of God made known in the ministry of Jesus will be a hospitable community, open to the other, the stranger, the alien, the outcast.

A second mark of the life and ministry of Jesus that helps to define the particularity of Christian love is compassion. According to the gospel narratives, Jesus had compassion on the crowds and took their plight to heart (Matt. 9:36). Compassion means suffering with others. There is no genuine love where the readiness to enter into solidarity with others in need is missing. The apostle Paul sees the evidence of love in the act of bearing each other's burdens (Gal. 6:2). The primary instance of God's bearing our burdens is of course the passion and death of Christ wherein God takes the burdens and consequences of our sin and misery into the divine life and overcomes their power at great cost.

That the church is a communion in love certainly cannot mean that we replace Christ in showing compassion to the needy and in bearing the heavy burdens of our neighbor. Christ is irreplaceable in this respect as in every other. But Christians are called to participate in the compassion of Christ for others and in the life of bearing each other's burdens. That is surely an important part of what is meant when the church is described as a communion in love. One of the ways the Reformed tradition has underscored the nature of the church as a communion marked by hospitality and compassionate love is the high honor it has ascribed to the office of diaconate among the ministries of the church.[15] Just as the doctrine of the Trinity points to the ultimate basis of the wealth and breadth of Christian communion in faith, so there is light from trinitarian doctrine for reflection on the meaning of the church as communion in love. The ultimate basis of the church's hospitality to strangers and its readiness for costly compassion and the bearing of one another's burdens is the free grace of God decisively present in Jesus Christ to whom we are united by the Holy Spirit.

According to classical trinitarian doctrine, the way God relates to us in the economy of salvation, in the missions of Christ and the Spirit, corresponds to the divine depths of God from all eternity. The triune God is the hospitable God, the God who lets another be, who eternally makes room for another. From all eternity there is an exchange of love between Father and Son in the Spirit. For Christians, God is not the great exemplar of life in splendid solitude but the one who eternally exists in the triune communion of self-giving love. As triune, God is the act of boundless, mutual, ever new sharing of life and love of Father, Son, and Spirit. The triune love of God has been freely extended to the world in the works of creation, reconciliation, and redemption.

This trinitarian understanding of God has as its corollary a radical redefinition of personhood and community. By concrete participation in the self-giving love of the triune God, we learn that "persons" and "community" are mutually dependent realities. Whatever the prevailing cultural definitions of personhood, "persons" as defined theologically are not self-enclosed, autonomous individuals, and true "community" is something quite different from an aggregate of individuals. As created and redeemed by God, persons are constituted by communion with God and each other, and true communion respects and nurtures persons. The dilemma of community-disintegrating individualism on the one hand and of person-destroying collectivism on the other is overcome in the communion of mutual love and mutual service that begins

15. For further development of this theme, see Daniel L. Migliore, *Faith Seeking Understanding* (Grand Rapids: Eerdmans, 1991), pp. 56-79.

here and now in Christ by the power of the Spirit even if the completion and fulfillment of this communion is eschatological.

At every celebration of the Lord's Supper, Christians participate in a special way in the hospitable, self-giving love of God in Christ by the power of the Spirit. We partake of the body of Christ broken for us and the blood of Christ shed for us, and we are thereby strengthened for costly service to each other and to the world (1 Cor. 10:16-17). Christian spirituality and Christian ethics are built on the foundation of God's act of self-giving love in Christ proclaimed in the gospel and made palpable in the Lord's Supper, where all are invited to eat and drink.

Within the Reformed theological tradition, the church as communion of love grounded in and shaped by the self-giving love of God has unmistakable implications for the order of the church's life. As Barth contends, there is no evading the question of the proper form and true order of the *communio sanctorum* in the world.[16]

Sometimes in reaction to rigid and hierarchical conceptions of the institutional structures of the church, the need for order and leadership in the church is rejected altogether. This results in ecclesiological romanticism. The question is not whether order and leadership are needed in the church but what kind of order and leadership are appropriate to the gospel.[17] If the church is based on the free grace of God, marked by the servant lordship of Christ, and enlivened by diverse gifts of the Spirit, then whatever particular structures and orders are adopted by churches in particular times and places, they are to be continuously examined, and when necessary reformed, in the light of the gospel of the costly love of the triune God.

The organization of the church into a fixed and sacralized hierarchy of clergy and laity is incompatible with the church as *koinonia*. From a Reformed faith perspective, offices in the church are provisional and diaconal rather than permanent and honorary. All members of the church are ordered to minister to each other in mutual love and service. To be sure, there are different forms of service and different ways of expressing love. Just as in the triune life of God the divine persons are differentiated as well as united by love, so in the church as a communion of love there is differentiated equality rather than a fixed hierarchy. There is "mutual subordination" (Eph. 5:21) rather than a unilateral superordination and subordination. Barth describes the order of the church as "christocratic brotherhood."[18] We do not intend to say less but to say the same thing more fully when we speak of the church as the communion ruled by the triune God.

---

16. Barth, *Church Dogmatics* IV/2, p. 686.
17. See Volf, *After Our Likeness*, p. 235.
18. Barth, *Church Dogmatics* IV/2, p. 680.

Because Jesus Christ is the servant Lord, because the life of the triune God is defined by what God does in the acts of creation and election, cross and resurrection, Pentecost and commission, the church enters into its true identity and discovers its appropriate order by its anticipatory participation in and always imperfect reflection of God's hospitable, compassionate, community-seeking way of being. The church becomes an ambassador of God's transforming love in the world when in its very life it bears witness to the spirit of generous hospitality and joyful service to all in need.

The Church as Communion in Hope

The church is a communion in hope as well as a communion in faith and love. In the Spirit, Christians already share a foretaste of the glory yet to be revealed (1 Peter 5:1) and have a common hope of sharing fully in the glory of God (Rom. 5:5). The Spirit who awakens us to faith in Christ and who pours the love of God into our hearts is also the Spirit who fills us with hope. Because communion with God and others is realized only partially now, the Spirit continuously directs us to the promised future when God will be all in all.

For the Reformed tradition, the work of the Spirit is never ancillary or secondary. Pneumatology is crucial in all aspects of Reformed doctrine: in the understanding and use of Scripture; in the interpretation of the doctrines of providence, the person and work of Jesus Christ, and the sacraments; and not least, in the understanding of the church and Christian hope. Barth's definition of Christian communion is evidence of the importance of the Holy Spirit in Reformed ecclesiology: "Communion is an action in which on the basis of an existing union many persons are engaged in a common movement towards the same union. This takes place in the power and operation of the Holy Spirit, and the corresponding action of those who are assembled and quickened by him."[19]

Barth's definition of communion holds together the reality and the promise of communion in the power of the Spirit. Christian communion in hope made possible by the work of the Holy Spirit is both real and provisional. The reality of communion in Christ is guaranteed by the Holy Spirit whose presence and gifts are the first fruits of God's reign (Rom. 8:23). The Spirit is God's power and promise of new life.

How do we know that the Spirit is at work among us? In many ways, but this one in particular: The life-giving Spirit of God builds a new community in Christ, a new people of God marked by an enriching diversity of gifts. The Spirit of God gives gifts (charisms) to all members of the church (1 Cor. 12–14).

---

19. Barth, *Church Dogmatics* IV/2, p. 641.

As giver of many different gifts, the Spirit at one and the same time differentiates us and makes us completely interdependent. The differences among members of the body of Christ no less than their unity in Christ is the work of the Holy Spirit. Because each member of the community has distinctive gifts, no member should assume he or she has no need of the others. The communion that defines the church includes both a multiplicity of gifts and a mutual sharing of gifts for the well-being of all.[20]

But while real, communion in Christ is still provisional. To speak of Christian communion as provisional is to say that the church must not claim to be already the reign of God. The church must not be captivated by triumphalistic self-adulation. Neither should the church be utterly dispirited or immobilized by its past betrayals of its Lord or by its present fragmentation and failures. Provisional communion is proleptic communion. The church is not God's reign but bears witness to the coming of God's reign and the completion of God's redemptive purposes for the whole creation. As a communion in hope, the church prays and works ceaselessly for the coming of God's reign. It is the Holy Spirit who again and again awakens and sustains this great hope.

Here again we can speak of a deep connection between Trinity doctrine and ecclesiology. The differentiating and unifying work of the Spirit of God whereby we are united to Christ and to each other is grounded in the eternal triune life. The Spirit binds together Father and Son in a love that creates, welcomes, and sustains personal differences. The exchange of love between Father and Son in the Spirit is always living, new, and fresh. There is nothing stale, rigid, or lifeless in the triune life of God because it is a communion in the Spirit of perfect love.

Usually we think of the gifts of the Spirit as strictly "spiritual" gifts such as teaching, preaching, healing, and leading. But just as the love of God in Christ is incarnate love, so the gifts of the Spirit are worldly as well as spiritual. Not only a variety of spiritual gifts but also a variety of natural and social gifts are necessary in a community that anticipates God's coming reign. "Race, sex, and age are all differences which must be included in the diversity of communion. No one should be excluded because of racial, sexual or age differences. . . . This is true about social differences as well: rich and poor, powerful and weak, all should be accommodated in the community."[21]

According to the story of Pentecost in Acts 2, the Spirit empowers communication of and communion in the gospel across all linguistic, ethnic, racial, and other barriers. The event of Pentecost contains a promise of enormous sig-

20. The best recent treatment of the doctrine of the Holy Spirit is by Michael Welker in *God the Spirit.*

21. Zizioulas, *Being as Communion,* p. 9.

nificance for the mission of the church today in a world of deeply engrained and often deadly divisions. As Michael Welker writes, "The action of God's Spirit is pluralistic for the sake of God's righteousness, for the sake of God's mercy, and for the sake of the full testimony to God's plenitude and glory."[22]

Because the communion of the Holy Spirit here and now is fragmentary and provisional, there is always a need to "test the spirits" (1 John 4:1). Only the Holy Spirit enables the confession that Jesus is Lord (1 Cor. 12:3). This is the deep truth of the classical western filioque doctrine: it underscores the christological criterion necessary for the discernment of spirits in a pluralistic world. At the same time, the filioque doctrine fails to express adequately the reciprocal relationship of Spirit and Christ. According to the New Testament witness, Jesus is both bearer and giver of the Spirit.[23] Recognition of this reciprocal relationship of Christ and Spirit opens new possibilities of Christian discernment of the work of the Spirit in a pluralistic world without relinquishing the christological criterion. Because they belong to a community that hopes in Christ by the power of the Spirit, "when Christians encounter vitality, truth, and justice in their pluralistic world, the first issue may be not Baptism but doxology."[24]

When the church encounters others who do not confess Christ, it has an opportunity not only to proclaim the gospel but also to discover new dimensions of the reality of Jesus Christ. In mission we live in the hope not only of giving but also of receiving, not only of teaching but also of learning. Because communion with God in Christ by the Spirit is ever new, it will always be open to truth from unexpected sources. It will welcome strangers who bring gifts of new friendships, new challenges, and new insights. Jesus Christ is the same yesterday, today, and forever (Heb. 13:8), but our knowledge of him grows deeper as we are led by Word and Spirit in fellowship with Christians in other contexts and also in our encounters with those who do not confess Jesus as Lord.[25]

The Spirit empowers us to pray and labor fervently for the coming of God's reign of justice and peace rather than resigning ourselves to the way things are, or identifying God's reign with some utopian society of the future that we will build by ourselves. We know that the Spirit is at work in the church when the church acknowledges that it is not itself the reign of God. It is instead, by the power of the Spirit, the first fruits, the concrete promise and provisional

22. Welker, *God the Spirit*, p. 25.

23. See Hendrikus Berkhof, *The Doctrine of the Holy Spirit* (Atlanta: John Knox, 1976).

24. George W. Stroup, "The Spirit of Pluralism," in *Many Voices, One God: Being Faithful in a Pluralistic World*, ed. Walter Brueggemann and George W. Stroup (Louisville: Westminster/John Knox, 1998), p. 176.

25. See Daniel L. Migliore, "Christology in Context: The Doctrinal and Contextual Tasks of Christology Today," in *Interpretation* 49 (1995): 242-54.

representation of the coming reign of God for which the church ceaselessly prays, waits, and works.

Christian communion is communion in hope. We hope and pray for the time of the great messianic banquet when people will come from north and south and east and west to celebrate together (Luke 13:29). Christian communion in hope transcends boundaries of time as well as boundaries of space. Christian hope includes not only those now alive but also those who have gone before us and those who will come after us.

The church becomes an ambassador of God's coming reign when it not only proclaims in words but also shows in its own life that there is a power at work in the world that brings together an astonishingly diverse people — young and old, women and men, people of all classes, races, cultures, and languages — in the praise and service of God. In this way the church becomes an ambassador of hope in the midst of the world's cynicism and despair about the possibility of new and lasting community.

The Promise and Limits of Trinitarian Ecclesiology

I have attempted to show that a trinitarian ecclesiology, properly understood, can prosper on Reformed soil.[26] Whether this emphasis constitutes a new paradigm for ecumenical theology that can help heal the divisions of the church remains to be seen.[27]

The value of a trinitarian ecclesiology is that it explicitly connects what Christians affirm about the triune God, the lordship of Christ, and the presence of the Holy Spirit with what they affirm about the nature and mission of the church. In its faith, love, and hope, the church established by the free grace of God shares, albeit now only brokenly, in the communion of the triune God. This participation is real but only partial and provisional. The church lives by "the grace of our Lord Jesus Christ, the love of God, and the communion of the Holy Spirit" (2 Cor. 13:14).

A trinitarian ecclesiology reminds us that the God of the Christian gospel is relational and calls us to life in relationship with God and with others. It emphasizes that the church is not primarily a juridical or hierarchical institution but a communion established by "the God who is triune communion and who

---

26. For another effort in this direction, see Philip W. Butin, *Reformed Ecclesiology: Trinitarian Grace According to Calvin* (Princeton: Princeton Theological Seminary, 1994).

27. See Konrad Raiser, *Ecumenism in Transition: A Paradigm Shift in the Ecumenical Movement?* (Geneva: WCC Publications, 1991). For a critical response see the article by Ulrich Körtner in this volume and the literature cited therein.

calls men and women to communion with one another and with God."[28] Trinitarian ecclesiology makes clear why both community-eroding individualism and person-disregarding collectivism distort the true nature of human life as created by God and as revealed in God's dealings with the people of Israel and definitively in the ministry, death, and resurrection of Jesus Christ.

In addition to the promise of trinitarian ecclesiology there are also limits that must be recognized. The church is not the promised reign of God but bears witness to and provisionally represents the coming reign of God. While Trinity doctrine points to the divine life of communion as the ultimate ground and hope of ecclesial life, a trinitarian ecclesiology becomes distorted if it is pressed into the service of an ecclesiological triumphalism or is expected to provide a detailed blueprint for the life and order of the church here and now.

The limits of trinitarian ecclesiology would be overstepped if we claimed to know more about the inner life of God than has been revealed to us, and then on the basis of our own ideas and ideologies portrayed the innertrinitarian relations as a model to be emulated by the church.

This danger is more than hypothetical. A glaring example of the misuse of a trinitarian ecclesiology is the projection of hierarchical relations to the trinitarian persons (for example, the superordination of the Father to the Son) with the aim of pointing to this supposed heavenly hierarchy as justification of a fixed hierarchical order in the relationship between clergy and laity in the life and organization of the church. A similar misuse of trinitarian ecclesiology is the claim that man and woman are related in a hierarchical manner analogous to the relation of Father and Son in God's eternal life. According to this view, women are destined to a state of perpetual subordination because this reflects the putative hierarchy in God's own being. Still another misuse of trinitarian doctrine would be the sacralizing of ideologies of racial superiority and inferiority by referring to a supposed trinitarian hierarchy. In such theories, distortions of trinitarian ecclesiology and trinitarian anthropology are put in the service of ideologies of clerical, patriarchal, and racial superiority.

In response to these distortions it is necessary to reaffirm the ontological equality of the trinitarian persons. According to both Scripture and creeds, the relationships of Father, Son, and Spirit are defined by a reciprocity of love in which each person both gives to and receives from the others. Beyond that, Reformed Christians do well to learn from the strong patristic emphasis on the incomprehensibility of God. We should not pretend to know the inner life of God in minute detail. We are to proclaim only what is firmly rooted in the biblical witness and what the church has consistently confessed: that Jesus Christ and the Spirit are one in essence with the Father; that neither Son nor Spirit is a

---

28. Lawler and Shanahan, *Church: A Spirited Communion*, p. 6.

subordinate deity; that Father, Son, and Spirit are together to be worshiped and glorified; that the triune God is boundless self-giving love.

To summarize: In a pluralistic world marked by the quest for community yet threatened by fragmentation in all areas of life, the church is called to bear witness to God's gift of new community in Jesus Christ by the power of the Spirit.

Trinitarian ecclesiology understands the church as a communion in faith based on the good news of the free grace of God in Jesus Christ. Communion in faith is rooted in God's living word and not in our own piety or in what we think we can accomplish by our favorite schemes of orthodoxy and orthopraxis.

Trinitarian ecclesiology understands the church as a communion in love centered on the servant lordship of Christ. Special marks of this love are hospitality to the stranger and compassion toward those in need. All Christians are summoned to participate in God's own person-making and community-forming life of love and service that reaches out to all both inside and outside the church.

Trinitarian ecclesiology understands the church as a communion in hope energized and enriched by the many diverse gifts of the Holy Spirit who empowers all members for their distinctive service of God and neighbor. When the church manifests such communion, its life becomes a witness to and an anticipation of the eschatological reign of the triune God.

PART III

Spirit and Covenant: Reformed Pneumatology in Very Different Contexts

CHAPTER 11

Charismatic Movement, Postmodernism, and Covenantal Rationality

Carver T. Yu

To consider the future of Reformed theology in an ecumenical way, we have to wrestle with the challenge of both the charismatic movement and post-modernism together. At first glance they may seem unrelated. At closer look, however, they point to the same condition of our present age, the seeming triumph of subjectivity — with the human subject struggling to pull itself back from dissolution or dissipation under the grip of ruthless functional rationality. For most of the twentieth century, human beings have been plagued by a deep sense of crisis about themselves. "Liberated" from traditions or communal control, the human person is said to be free. Yet he/she finds what is central to his/her freedom — his/her self — fragmented. The sense of ambiguity in personal identity, the loss of inwardness, the failure of meaningful relation, and the oppressiveness of the structure of objectified functional values is pervasive. Everywhere in modern literature and cultural reflections, the human person is portrayed as a dissolved entity of introspective skepticism or narcissistic withdrawal caught in a mechanized socio-economic process based on "objective" principles that completely disregard his/her personal and (especially) emotional qualities. The "objective" becomes abstract and oppressive.[1] There is thus a deep yearning for a sense of immediate presence of the real. This problem is still with us today, and will continue to beset us well into the twenty-first century. Have theologians in the Reformed tradition paid enough attention to this?

1. "Modern man . . . does not 'live in society.' . . . This society has lost more and more of its reality and meaning and seems to be hardly able to function as the holder of human freedom." A. C. Zijdervald, *The Abstract Society* (London, 1972), p. 49.

This needs critical reflection. The problem about the erosion of the personal has been brought into the open for many decades, but unfortunately, the issues have often been obscured by debates centering around the existentialist movement. Reactions against the existentialist method and its philosophical implications tend to obscure the issues even further.

From the historical-sociological perspective, both the charismatics and the postmodernists strive in their different ways to respond to the stifling rationalization of modernity. The postmodernists do so by unmasking and thus discrediting the modern form of totalizing rationality, while the charismatics answer it with recourse to an immediate experience of the transcendent. In making this historical-sociological observation, we do not intend to reduce charismatic experiences to sociocultural causes. We are merely trying to point out that whatever happens in history has a historical context. Even the Holy Spirit would work in a way that addresses the spiritual needs of a particular context.

It is no use pointing out to them the dangerous implications of subjectivism, religious or secular. We need to ask, has Reformed theology taken seriously the erosion of the personal in a world of impersonal functional rationality? Or have we been rather insensitive to the problem? Is our insensitivity due precisely to the fact that our theology has itself been hijacked by such a mode of rationality and become part of the rationalization process? Is it not true that the way we respond to issues somehow reflects our theological frame of mind? What has been our frame of mind? We should not forget that the objectivistic, propositional, and impersonal approach to truth of Protestant orthodoxy brings about the pietistic reaction, and its quest for inner spiritual certainty in turn anticipates the enthronement of reason in the Enlightenment. Reason as the ground for objective certainty rests on an inner immediate sense of coherence. Here we see subjectivism and objectivism interplay intricately as necessary correlates. As philosophical discussion in the last several decades unfolds, we see radical objectivism giving rise to a reaction that aims at unmasking the subjective foundation of all formulations of objective truth. Ironically it was at the height of logical positivism, when the verification principle reigned supreme in philosophical discourse, that the subjective revealed itself to be all pervasive and fundamental. Objectivism aims at distilling pure objective truth, and in so doing, it regards the subject as an obstacle to be cleared, to be disposed of. Yet the subject simply refuses to go away. Objectivism tends to beget subjectivism, and radical objectivism begets radical subjectivism. Heidegger summarizes the situation most aptly:

> Certainly the modern age has, as a consequence of the liberation of man, introduced subjectivism and individualism. But it remains just as certain

that no age before this one has produced a comparable objectivism and that in no age before this has the non-individual, in the form of the collective, come to acceptance as having worth. Essential here is the necessary interplay between subjectivism and objectivism. It is precisely this reciprocal conditioning of one by the other that points back to events more profound.[2]

The profound events that Heidegger refers to are the events leading to western man's defining the human self as subject.

What I am trying to say is, if postmodern subjectivism and relativism arise out of the reaction against radical objectivism and positivism, then objectivists could see themselves as the reverse mirror image of the subjectivists. If that is the case, then the subjectivist approach to truth, problematic as it may be, really has something significant to say to the objectivists: that they may be forgetful of something truly fundamental. By the same token, those who lament the sweeping success of the charismatic movement, seeing it as no more than a subjectivization of faith, would have to reflect whether the movement has something significant to say to them. In reacting against the movement without self-reflection, are they not missing something? They may perhaps need to reflect on how the rise of the movement could be something of their own making. Let me use another analogy from the history of philosophy. As Husserl puts it, the crisis of European science (note: not science as such, but the particular mode of science developed in recent European history) lies in the forgetting and disregarding of the self in objectivistic scientistic pursuit. However, the self would ultimately take revenge by popping up in the form of subjectivism, for the self is the meaning-foundation of all scientific pursuits.[3] Perhaps the situation in theology is comparable. The self is of course not the meaning-foundation; it is, however, the locus where the Word became flesh, and it is ignored with serious consequence. To many Reformed theologians, the charismatic movement represents the manifestation of subjectivism in faith. Even if this is true, we still have to understand that the challenge of subjectivism cannot be answered by a pure objective formulation of truth. The outbreak of subjectivism may point us back to our forgetfulness, and may serve to compel us to understand afresh the meaning of objectivity with the full view of the irreducible reality and conditions of the self. Perhaps, in this way, we may see both the charismatic movement and postmodernism in a different light.

It is our conviction that the Reformed tradition has the theological re-

---

2. Martin Heidegger, "The Age of World Picture," *The Question Concerning Technology and Other Essays*, trans. William Lovitt (New York: Harper & Row, 1977), p. 128.

3. Edmund Husserl, *The Crisis of European Sciences and Transcendental Phenomenology*, trans. David Carr (Evanston, Ill.: Northwestern University Press, 1970), pp. 60ff.

sources for developing an understanding of truth relevant to the spiritual predicament of the present age. It is also our conviction that covenant, a theological truth central to the Reformed tradition, is highly relevant for the healing of the crisis of the personal as well as the subjectivist-objectivist rift, and may help us understand the meaning of the emergence of postmodernism and the charismatic movement.

Covenantal Rationality

The theological magnetic center of the Reformed tradition is the sovereignty and glory of God. Reformed spirituality is thus directed away from the self to the glory of God. The spiritual anchor is on the objective reality of God's sovereignty and grace. Faith, the personal coordinate of salvation, is grounded on, determined by, and directed toward this objective reality. This anchor has to be held onto fiercely, for it is the hope with which the church and the world may weather this raging storm of narcissism and relativism.

I totally agree with John Leith as he succinctly lays out the ethos of Reformed faith:

> the theocentric character of Reformed faith sets it over against every ethic of *self-realization,* against *inordinate concern* with the salvation of one's own soul, against *excessive preoccupation* with the questions of personal identity.[4]

However, we need to make a qualification here. Indeed, self-realization, the inordinate concern and excessive preoccupation with the self, has to be rejected. Yet even in the deepest theocentric commitment, the concern with the self and its identity has to be there. Calvin is most insightful in pointing out the reciprocal relation between the knowledge of God and the knowledge of the human person. Even from the perspective of the glory of God, the human person has a significant place. The glory of God is not something for contemplation. It is meant to shine through the human person as it shines through the universe. The human person is the arena where the glory of God is to be unfolded. He/she does not contemplate God's glory as a detached beholder. He/she is part and parcel of the manifestation of the glory of God. H. R. Niebuhr defined the Reformed principle of Christian life as the principle of the kingdom of God in contrast to the principle of the vision of God. He observed,

---

4. John H. Leith, *Introduction to the Reformed Tradition* (Atlanta: John Knox, 1981), p. 99.

> To call the vision man's greatest good is to make contemplation . . . the final end of life; to put the sovereignty of God in the first place is to make obedient activity superior to contemplation, however much is *theoria* necessary to action. The principle of vision suggests that the perfection of the object seen is loved above all else; the principle of the kingdom indicates that the reality and power of the being commanding obedience are primarily regarded.[5]

The being of the human person as the image of God is ontologically implicated as the very reflection of the glory. He/she is involved in the most fundamental way in making God's glory real, real in his/her life, and real for the world. The "reality and the power of God" are not something detached from man but should be something intimate to his/her being. Here certain Reformed theologians may have shifted, without their own knowing it, from the principle of the kingdom to the principle of the vision. The glory of God, to be truly objectively grasped, has to be subjectively real at the same time. That does not imply that without man God's glory is in any way diminished. That we do not have to worry about. What we need to worry about is whether the glory of God is real in *us*, for insofar as God has chosen us to be the temple of his presence, his glory is supposed to shine in us and through us.

The sovereign God is none other than the covenantal God. His sovereignty can only be truly understood from the covenantal perspective. God in covenant does not intend his sovereignty to be declared and appropriated as a mere objective fact. His sovereignty is "infused" with covenantal love, with his determination to be present with his covenantal partner. In this light, God's sovereignty may best be understood in terms of his absolute freedom, a freedom to be *with* the human person and *for* the human person. To characterize the divine-human relation in terms of covenant, God intends to reveal that the divine-human relation is to be a relation coming out of freedom. Therefore, to create the human person as a covenantal partner, God has given him/her a mode of freedom that reflects the very nature of God's freedom. Thus freedom of the human person is freedom for covenanting with God. Freedom in humanity has meaning only in the covenantal context. Similarly, insofar as God chooses to be a covenantal partner to his creature, the only true meaning of God's freedom can be realized in his covenantal relation with his creature.

Covenant is real only in its being fulfilled. And such fulfillment calls for mutual presence, reciprocal engagement, dynamic involvement. God's will to be with his partner determines the way he reveals himself as God, even in his sovereignty. Insofar as God has chosen to be a covenantal God and not otherwise, his

---

5. H. Richard Niebuhr, *The Kingdom of God in America* (New York: Harper Torchbook, 1959), p. 20, cited in Leith, p. 71.

sovereignty is revealed in its truest form as sovereignty in covenant only, in his presence with his creature — even if that means self-limitation of his absolute power. Thus the sovereignty of God is not to be adored at a distance as an objective fact, but as God's freedom and power in loving the human person, in overcoming the distance between the human person and himself. Despite the ontological distinction between them, the presence of God with the human person is a constant theme in God's revelation. God's declaration in Hosea 11:9 — "For I am God and not man; the Holy One in your midst" — expresses this most clearly. "Holiness," which symbolizes ontological distance, and God's closeness to the human person are brought together here. Snaith is right in qualifying the meaning of *qdsh* (holiness) as "ontological separateness":

> It is true that the root stands for the difference between God and man, but it refers positively, and not negatively, to that "Wholly Other," of whom Rudolf Otto writes. It refers positively to what is God's and not negatively to what is not man's. . . . When we use the word "separated" as a rendering of any form of the root *qdsh*, we should think of "separated to" rather than "separated from."[6]

God as the Holy One is determined to be "separated to" the human person, and the human person as something holy is that which is "separated to" God. Here, we are in complete agreement with Karl Barth when he says,

> Creation itself . . . is already a seeking and creating of fellowship. This seeking and creating is heightened in the work of revelation itself. . . . If it is right and necessary to bring together the purpose and meaning of this act in order to understand it, and therefore to understand God, we must now say that He wills to be ours, and He wills that we should be His. He wills to belong to us and He wills that we should belong to Him. . . . He wills as God to be for us and with us who are not God.[7]

In this light,

> the absoluteness of God . . . means that God has the freedom to be present with that which is not God, to communicate Himself and unite Himself with the other, and the other with Himself, in a way which utterly surpasses all that can be effected in regard to reciprocal presence, communion and fellowship between other beings.[8]

6. N. H. Snaith, *Distinctive Ideas of the Old Testament* (London: Epworth Press, 1957), p. 30.

7. Karl Barth, *Church Dogmatics* II/1 (Edinburgh: T. & T. Clark, 1957), p. 274.

8. Barth, *Church Dogmatics* II/1, p. 313.

If the act of revelation has its *telos* not in the mere understanding of the human person but in his/her union with God, or the presence of God in his/her being, then revelation is not complete when it stops short at that. The problem of the human person is not ignorance but alienation from God. And so revelation and reconciliation always belong together. The truth of God is attained only when the human person is united with God. The truth is attained in Jesus Christ.

The sovereignty of God carries within itself a "logic of self-involvement." Where we see God's sovereignty revealed, we also see his being-with and being-for the human person. There is no "pure" sovereignty of God where sovereignty is not to some extent "tinged" by God's binding himself to finite and sinful humanity, even to the point of self-limitation. One cannot "see" the sovereignty of God without "seeing" at the same time his freedom for the human person, nor can one "see" the "objectivity" of the divine Being without "seeing" at the same time his self-involvement in making it subjectively real to him/her. His objectivity involves the subjectivity of the human person in a covenantal mutual presence. Taking his/her subjectivity seriously does not mean to allow his/her selfish needs to have their way. Barth is right when he says,

> "For us," of course, does not mean the selfish desire for salvation of those who will accept Jesus Christ as a good man because they think that they find in Him the satisfaction of the private religious needs of man. . . . Pietism is quite right. We speak of real revelation only when we speak of the revelation which is real to us. . . . An objective revelation as such, a revelation which consists statically only in its sign giving, in the objectivity of Scripture, preaching and sacrament, a revelation that does not penetrate to man: a revelation of this kind is an idol like all the rest, and perhaps the worst of all idols.[9]

The Holy Spirit as the Subjective Reality of Revelation

How then are we to describe the state of our being united with God through Jesus Christ? In what sense is God's presence with us and our presence with him real to us? In what way may the power of his presence be manifested? What role does the Holy Spirit have in making the presence of God, his love, and his sovereignty real to us?

Barth refers to the subjective reality of revelation as the reality of the outpouring of the Holy Spirit. Barth makes it very clear that even the most inti-

9. Barth, *Church Dogmatics* I/2, p. 237.

mate subjective reality has its objective anchor in God's initiative. The work of the Holy Spirit reveals the freedom of God for man. Barth's theological scheme in expounding the revelation of God is clear. Objective reality of revelation always precedes subjective reality. The objective is the source of energy that makes what takes place in the subjective real. Barth's approach is in fact nothing new. It is an approach long used by Calvin.

After expounding the objective reality of revelation in Jesus Christ, Calvin emphasizes the significance of the indwelling of Christ in us. He also points out that in order to understand the indwelling of Christ, we have to "examine into the secret energy of the Spirit, by which we come to enjoy Christ and all his benefits."[10] It is obvious that Calvin takes the subjective dimension very seriously in expounding the various aspects of faith, and he would emphasize that "the knowledge of *faith consists in assurance rather than in comprehension.*"[11] Faith as the subjective reality of revelation is the work of the Holy Spirit.

John Hesselink's article is extremely helpful in succinctly bringing out the scope and depth of Calvin's doctrine of the Holy Spirit. He is certainly right in echoing Warfield's conviction that Calvin is "the theologian of the Holy Spirit."[12] Calvin not only delineates the work of the Holy Spirit in redemption, but also the work of universal providence in upholding the order of the universe and in showing forth God's goodness to the world.[13] However, as Hesselink puts it,

> the question arises as to whether the Reformed churches have been aware of and faithful to this magnificent theology of the Holy Spirit developed by Calvin. Unfortunately, the answer, for the most part, has to be No. In the seventeenth century a scholastic orthodoxy on the one hand and a one-sided pietism on the other dealt crippling blows to Calvin's balanced presentation of the work of the Spirit.[14]

Evidently Reformed orthodoxy has formalized the magnificent theology of the Holy into a logical part of a cognitive system. The charismatics are quite right when they insist that it is not enough to have the right doctrine of the

10. Calvin, *Institutes* 3.1.1.
11. Calvin, *Institutes* 3.2.14.
12. I. John Hesselink, "The Charismatic Movement and the Reformed Tradition," *Reformed Review* 28 (Spring 1975): 147-56, reprinted in *Major Themes in the Reformed Tradition,* ed. Donald K. McKim (Grand Rapids: Eerdmans, 1992), pp. 377-85.
13. Cf. Ford Lewis Battles, *Interpreting John Calvin* (Grand Rapids: Baker Books, 1996), pp. 168-78.
14. Hesselink, "The Charismatic Movement," p. 380.

Holy Spirit. The "real thing" is the presence of God, which should have vital impact in our life. Larry Christenson puts it forcefully,

> This accent on the person of the Holy Spirit is linked to the experiences of receiving or being filled with His presence. Precisely because He is a person, He must be received. The effectual presence of the Holy Spirit cannot be assumed simply because a person agrees to correct doctrine. It is possible to hold the doctrine on the Holy Spirit, yet not experience His presence and power.[15]

This remark needs to be taken seriously. To do so it may mean that we have to re-examine our position in regard to the experience of the Holy Spirit. We may need to admit that our experience of the presence of the Holy Spirit has been truncated, perhaps due to an all-too-objectivist approach to truth, or by a wide variety of theological assumptions. Recently I have felt challenged in reading Jon Ruthven's *On the Cessation of the Charismata — the Protestant Polemic on Postbiblical Miracles.*[16] The book examines Warfield's philosophical presupposition in formulating his cessationist thesis. It shows convincingly the incoherence in Warfield's argument as well as problems in his biblical exegesis. I find this kind of exercise very important. It challenges us to read the Bible afresh continually. It is only then that channels for genuine dialogue with the charismatics are open. It is all too easy to dismiss the charismatics as shaky in biblical-theological grounding, regarding their spiritual experience as purely subjective and not sufficiently informed by the Word of God. It is much more difficult to open ourselves up and see that our own interpretation of the Bible is not always unbiased.

Despite certain excesses in claims, the charismatic movement has nevertheless brought not only into the church but also into modern cities a new religious intensity in the midst of secular indifference, a great sense of celebration of God's presence, a joyful experience of communion, and a strong sense of mission. It seems to address the spiritual thirst of modern man in an effective way. Of course, one may point out that the "power vocabulary" of the movement appeals most effectively to the deprived, marginalized, and maladjusted. But the point is, modern man feels deprived and marginalized in a fundamental way; it is his humanity that is at stake. When we dismiss the movement as biblically and theologically unsound, we need to ask ourselves: How should we help the church understand the Holy Spirit in such way that it is open to his work and power, so that the world may know the glory of God at work in us?

15. Larry Christenson, *The Charismatic Renewal Among Lutherans* (Minneapolis: Bethany Fellowship, 1976), p. 35.

16. Jon Ruthven, *On the Cessation of the Charismata: The Protestant Polemic on Postbiblical Miracles* (Sheffield: Sheffield Academic Press, 1993).

This is not a challenge to silence ourselves if we cannot come up with an effective alternative. Rather, it is the challenge of asking ourselves whether indeed the rationalist-objectivist inclination in our theological approach has been averting by default the kind of experience we should have, in view of our sound doctrine of the Holy Spirit.

Jonathan Edwards is an example of such openness to and creative researching of something not new but always there in our tradition. He reminds us that faith is not merely "an exercise of the understanding." Indeed, faith is knowledge, but a "loving knowledge of God's truth" that involves the mind and heart as a unified whole. Our reason, in the exercise of knowing God, is infused by our love for God. The act of faith is "the sense of the heart."

> To be sure, the sense of the heart, the "tasting" of divine reality, is not "reasoning" if reasoning is narrowly defined as "ratiocination," or the power of inferring by arguments. For the sense of the heart is not in its essence a judgment regarding the truth *about* an object, wherein the judging subject is detached as an observer from his object in order to infer that object. One is intimately bound up with the object in an attitude of love and adoration.[17]

In knowing the divine truth, one is not only illuminated but also infused by the Holy Spirit. By that Edwards means, "The Spirit of God is given to the true saints to dwell in them, as his proper lasting abode; and to influence their hearts, as a principle of new nature, or as a divine supernatural spring of life and action."[18] Reason is therefore bound to be affected by feelings and experiences due to such influence of the heart. To Edwards, many theological understandings stop short at notional and speculative knowledge. This kind of knowledge cannot open the deeper level of consciousness that touches the fundamental experience of sin, alienation, faith, grace, and holiness. Edwards proposes another form of knowledge — sensible knowledge, which "creates within the mind a sense of things, an intuited conviction, a sight that transforms abstract truth into 'actual ideas' inseparable from feelings."[19] Here aesthetics and imagination have their place in theological understanding. The soundness of theological ideas is no longer tested merely by attestation of Scripture and logical coherence, but also by how much they can be translated into living experience.

17. Conrad Cherry, *The Theology of Jonathan Edwards: A Reappraisal* (Bloomington: Indiana University Press, 1990), p. 22, with reference to Edwards's "A Divine and Supernatural Light."

18. Jonathan Edwards, "Treatise on Religious Affections," cited in Cherry, p. 28.

19. Harold P. Simonson, *Jonathan Edwards: Theologian of the Heart* (Macon, Ga.: Mercer University Press, 1982), p. 69.

Edwards opens up a mode of theological reason that is not automatically averse to experiences that may appear "unreasonable" in the judgment of common sense. He is well aware of the fact that imagination, and thus sensible knowledge, has its danger. It may provide the room for all kinds of error to operate. Nevertheless, instead of rejecting what could be truly the signs of the Holy Spirit for fear of errors, he carefully delineates "the distinguishing marks of a work of the spirit of God."

Re-examining our theological approach to make room for the experience of the gifts of the Holy Spirit is a challenge. Another challenge is in drawing out our theological resources for the sake of the charismatics. It is true that there are genuine experiences of the gifts of the Holy Spirit among them. However, it must be acknowledged at the same time that there is a need for solid theological grounding and undergirding for their renewal experiences. A truncated theology will give a truncated or one-sided understanding to their experiences. The richness of the Christian faith can be seriously compromised by a noncomprehensive or one-sided theology.

Going back to covenantal thinking, the manifestation of the presence of the sovereign God in our life should not be confined to the power of the Holy Spirit as experienced in signs and wonders. First, a comprehensive understanding of the works of the Holy Spirit is called for. Here, Calvin and Kuyper would be very enriching. In studying the theology of the Holy Spirit in Calvin and Kuyper, charismatics may come to distinguish the works of the Holy Spirit in believers' life for sanctification and the gifts of the Holy Spirit for enhancing ministry. At the same time, the God who is present with us is also the God who died on the cross. The sign of God's presence carries with us the signs of the cross. The Holy Spirit is also the Spirit of Christ. What about the power of the suffering of Christ, the power in not exerting and displaying power? What about the symbol of the paschal lamb meeting sacrifice in silent submission? The primary work of the Holy Spirit is to guide believers into truth, the truth of Christ, so that they may know the power of his suffering and resurrection. And so the theology of the Holy Spirit is to be undergirded by Christology. How can we develop our theology in such a way that charismatics do not feel rejected but attracted by the richness of our tradition, which can sustain and give direction for their renewal experiences? That is a real challenge. But first, let us open ourselves and be ready to learn from the charismatics.

The Postmodernist Challenge

Postmodern thinkers shatter the idealization of pure objective truth. Truth, they remind us, carries within it the subjective horizon, including pre-understandings, historical situatedness, and interests. The subjective is real. This affects and even determines the mode in which truth appears. This is a great insight, an insight that we seek to bring out in our discussion on covenantal rationality. Incidentally, this insight expresses something not altogether different from Calvin's idea of accommodation, and it has deep implications. On the one hand it unmasks the presumptuousness of the claims of certain systems of explanation. This engenders critical reflections on widely accepted beliefs. Discomforting as it may be, theologians are reminded to review their formulations critically, to understand their "situatedness," their "accommodatedness," and perhaps even their bias. Postmodernism has opened up space in hardened frameworks for a certain degree of imaginativeness. The postmodernist critique of the Enlightenment is refreshing. Yet on the other hand, some of the implications are deeply disturbing.

In striving to deconstruct the Enlightenment project, the postmodern critique nevertheless radicalizes some of its basic assumptions, the most central of which is the understanding of man as subject. The starting point is still the consciousness of the subject. In fact, the subjective is amplified into a logic of suspicion and skepticism. Before, the subjective is to be overcome in order to arrive at pure objectivity. Now the subjective is embraced, with narcissism and relativism celebrated. The subject threatens to sink into solipsism, and we are confronted with infinite ways of world-making. What started out with great philosophical promise in the phenomenology of Husserl and Heidegger, and out of which came Gadamer's hermeneutics, is now directed towards a regress into radical subjectivism and constructionism. This however seems inevitable. When human consciousness is made the starting point, when the transcendent is in principle "exiled," the integrity of the objective realm is questionable, and in the long run it stands to be reduced into a mere coefficient of the subjective, as seems to have happened now.

The possible way out lies in taking the covenantal nature of reality seriously. The objective and the subjective have their own irreducible integrity. They are joined together in mutual engagement in the drama of unfolding reality. The subject is indeed the limiting condition in which the object has to "accommodate." But accommodation is no compromise. What is revealed as real indeed has a distinctive quality of accommodatedness; nevertheless, the irreducibility of its being the objective truth remains. The subject, by giving the objective a distinctive character of its (the subject's) particularity, does not necessarily distort the objective. It serves as the horizon in which the objective reveals itself. The particular frame of reference of the subject will give a particular mode of appearing of the objective. Nevertheless, the objective has a stubbornness that cannot be dissolved. This sets the limit to its accommodatedness. The Principle of Relativity can be extremely helpful here.

The Reformed tradition puts tremendous emphasis on the absoluteness, irreducibility, and priority of the transcendent. This cannot be compromised. In fact, it is the only hope that postmodernists can bank on to get them out of their narcissistic predicament.

CHAPTER 12

Reformed Pneumatology and Pentecostal Pneumatology

Myung Yong Kim

There was controversy in the twentieth century between the Pentecostal churches and the Reformed churches about the work of the Holy Spirit such as speaking in tongues, divine healing, and miracles. There was also conflict between the two sets of churches about the doctrine of the baptism of the Holy Spirit. It is often insisted that Pentecostal churches are full of the Spirit, while Reformed churches ignore the work of the Spirit. It is, however, also insisted in response that Pentecostal churches are too enthusiastic and have a biased view of the Holy Spirit's work. We will study and discuss Reformed and Pentecostal pneumatologies, analyzing positive and negative aspects of both to make clear their contours. Both pneumatologies, it seems, err in many ways. After this study and analysis we will try to build a holistic pneumatology to which both churches must pay attention.

Reformed Pneumatology

Outline of Reformed Pneumatology

It is not easy to summarize Reformed pneumatology, but it is generally held that it has five important features:

1. According to Reformed pneumatology, the Holy Spirit first of all unites us with Jesus Christ. We become Christians through the Holy Spirit. Christ dwells within us. This union is obtained by the power of the Holy Spirit.

Through the power of the Holy Spirit we are regenerated and become children of God. We are justified by God in the grace of the Holy Spirit. In this sense, we call the Holy Spirit the Spirit of regeneration or justification.

2. Sanctification is the second work of the Holy Spirit. John Calvin develops and views the whole doctrine of Christian life from the perspective of the Holy Spirit. Sanctification is possible only by the dominant role of the Holy Spirit. According to Calvin not only calling, conversion, regeneration, and justification but also sanctification are the work of the Holy Spirit. The Christian life originates in and is continually renewed and sanctified by the power of the Holy Spirit. The Holy Spirit fashions us in the image of Jesus Christ. Sanctification refers to the transformation of human life into the image of Christ. This work is always attributed in Reformed pneumatology first of all to the Holy Spirit.

3. The Holy Spirit is active not only in the order of spiritual salvation but also in nature and human history. The Spirit of God is at work in the world, preserving, restoring, and guiding. Without this general work of the Spirit, the world would soon be in chaos, and humankind would degenerate into bestiality.[1] According to Abraham Kuyper the creative work of the Holy Spirit affects the upholding of things, of men, and of talents, through the providence of God. He bestows gifts and talents on particular people, talents and abilities upon artisans and professional men that are relative to their work. Kuyper insisted that the Holy Spirit even bestows artistic skills and talents upon a nation at one time and withdraws them at another.[2] According to Calvin all that is good, true, and beautiful is due to the Spirit of God.[3] In the view of Calvin, those who depreciate the arts and mathematical sciences "dishonor the Spirit of God."[4] Calvin also stresses the cosmic dimensions of the Spirit's work in a way rarely found in studies of the Holy Spirit.[5] Later Reformed theologians developed a doctrine of common grace that is active in all creation and human history, in addition to the special grace that is operative in the order of salvation. Reformed pneumatology has classically emphasized that the Spirit works in all creation.[6] In this sense we call the Holy Spirit the Spirit who preserves creation.

---

1. I. John Hesselink, "The Charismatic Movement and the Reformed Tradition," in *Major Themes in the Reformed Tradition*, ed. D. K. McKim (Grand Rapids: Eerdmans, 1992), p. 379.

2. Abraham Kuyper, *The Work of the Holy Spirit* (Ann Arbor, Mich.: Cushing-Malloy, 1975), p. 42.

3. John Calvin, *Institutes of the Christian Religion*, trans. Ford Lewis Battles and ed. John T. McNeill (Philadelphia: Westminster, 1960), 2.2.12-20.

4. Calvin, *Institutes* 2.2.16.

5. Hesselink, "The Charismatic Movement," p. 379.

6. John H. Leith, *Basic Christian Doctrine* (Louisville: Westminster/John Knox, 1993), p. 165.

4. The fourth work of the Holy Spirit is testimony. We come to know Scripture as the Word of God through the testimony of the Holy Spirit.[7] Calvin's most original and enduring contribution to an evangelical understanding of the nature and authority of Scripture was his doctrine of the internal witness or testimony of the Holy Spirit. Calvin pointed out that all that Christ did for us would be of no avail unless the Spirit makes Christ present to us and unites us to him. The work of the Spirit is to create faith in us by means of the Word.[8] Neither the written word nor the proclaimed word has any power of persuasion apart from the secret, inner working and witness of the Spirit. According to Karl Barth God is acknowledged only through the Holy Spirit. The Word of God becomes Word of God only through the Holy Spirit. The written word without his testimony is meaningless. Although Scripture is self-authenticated, it is not accepted in the heart of men and women as the Word of God without the inner working of the Holy Spirit. Its majesty and mystery are revealed only by the testimony of the Spirit.

5. It is important to note that Calvin put pneumatological emphasis on his doctrine of church and sacraments. It is well known that Calvin repeated the famous words of the early church father Cyprian: for those to whom God is Father the church may also be mother. For Calvin the church is the mother "because there is no other means of entry into life, except she should . . . feed us at her breast, and then preserve us under her guardianship and guidance until we have put off this mortal flesh."[9] The church is the visible means of God's grace. The Holy Spirit protects and guides the people of God through the church as the mother. It is the instrument through which the Holy Spirit guides the people of God to heavenly salvation. According to Barth the church is the sacrament of the Holy Spirit.[10] It is the visible human instrument of the Holy Spirit for the unity of men and women with God. The Spirit of Christ appears in the social existence of the church. Jesus in today's history is seldom discovered apart from the existence of the church. For Barth it is the instrument of the Holy Spirit for Jesus in today's history. For Reformed pneumatology not only Scripture but also church and sacraments are means of the Holy Spirit for the grace of God. Sacraments are also visible signs of God's grace manifest in Christ. They have no efficacy unless God works in us by invisible grace through the Holy Spirit.[11] The Reformed view of the church and sacraments can accord-

7. Leith, *Basic Christian Doctrine*, p. 164.

8. Calvin, *Institutes* 3.1.1.

9. Calvin, *Institutes* 4.1.4.

10. Thomas Freyer, *Pneumatologie als Strukturprinzip der Dogmatik: Überlegungen am Anschluss an die Lehre von der "Geisttaufe" bei Karl Barth* (Paderborn: Schöningh, 1982), p. 221.

11. Calvin, *Institutes* 4.14.18.

ingly best be described as a pneumatocracy. They are visible means of the Holy Spirit to reveal the grace of God and save people.

Positive Aspects of Reformed Pneumatology

1. According to Reformed pneumatology, Christian life begins and continues in the Holy Spirit. The Holy Spirit regenerates, justifies, and sanctifies us. This teaching of Reformed pneumatology is biblical and very significant. We are born again of the Holy Spirit. Jesus said to Nicodemus, "Except a man be born of water and of the Spirit, he cannot enter into the Kingdom of God. That which is born of the flesh is flesh; and that which is born of the Spirit is spirit" (John 3:5, 6). The new spiritual life is imparted to us through the indwelling Holy Spirit, which is the mark of a Christian. One of the most comprehensive definitions of a Christian is that of a person in whom the Holy Spirit dwells. A Christian's body is a temple of the Holy Spirit, in virtue of which experience he/she is sanctified as the Tabernacle was consecrated by Jehovah's indwelling. It is correct that Reformed pneumatology sees the entire salvation process of individuals in the light of the work of the Holy Spirit.

2. The emphasis on the deep relationship between the Word of God and the Holy Spirit is a strong point of Reformed pneumatology. Reformed tradition points out that the Holy Spirit guides us by means of the Word of God. The activities of the Holy Spirit and the Word of God are inseparable. According to Barth the Holy Spirit is the subjective reality of revelation,[12] while Jesus Christ is the objective reality of revelation.[13] Reformed pneumatology doesn't like a loosening of the ties between the Spirit and the historical Christ or between the Spirit and the letter of the Scripture or between the Spirit and institutional church life. It does not permit an enthusiastic church. It is difficult to find in Reformed churches the arbitrary subjective prophecies that are often discovered in Pentecostal churches.

3. Compared with Pentecostal pneumatology, Reformed pneumatology has a wider perspective on the work of the Holy Spirit. I. John Hesselink writes, "in Reformed theology there is a greater appreciation, deeper understanding, and more comprehensive and balanced presentation of the full power and work of the Holy Spirit than in any other tradition, including the Pentecostal tradition."[14] In Pentecostal pneumatology believers' baptism plays a very important role, but the Lord's Supper appears to receive little attention. In Pentecostal

---

12. Barth, *Kirchliche Dogmatik* I/2 (München: Kaiser Verlag, 1938), pp. 1-49.
13. Barth, *Kirchliche Dogmatik* I/2, pp. 222-304.
14. Hesselink, "The Charismatic Movement," p. 378.

pneumatology supernatural gifts of the Holy Spirit play very important roles, but natural gifts of the Holy Spirit appear to receive little attention. Many pneumatologies including Pentecostal pneumatology pay little attention to the cosmic work of the Holy Spirit, but Reformed pneumatology is well aware of it. Reformed pneumatology is aware of the work of the Holy Spirit in preserving, restoring, and guiding humanity and the creation. It also has a good spiritual understanding of the sacraments and the church. We can find abundant pneumatological interpretations of baptism (including infant baptism), the Lord's Supper, Scripture, preaching, and the installation of pastors and elders in Reformed pneumatology. While Pentecostal pneumatology is concentrated on the supernatural gifts of the Holy Spirit, Reformed pneumatology has a wider perspective on the work of the Holy Spirit. It knows the works of the Holy Spirit not only in the spiritual life of individuals but also in the church, sacraments, Scripture and preaching, human history, and creation. In this sense the evaluation of Hesselink about the Pentecostal charismatic movement is correct. He insists that it does not "stress the work of the Holy Spirit too much, but too little! Its viewpoint is too narrow and myopic. . . . The charismatic theologians have much to learn from Calvin in particular and the Reformed tradition in general, about the Spirit and creation, the relation of the Word and the Spirit, the Spirit and the church and sacraments, the Spirit and tradition, the Spirit and the Christian life."[15] Although Reformed pneumatology is weak on individual-spontaneous aspects of the Holy Spirit, it must be appreciated because of the broad perspective that the Bible gives us on the work of the Holy Spirit.

Negative Aspects of Reformed Pneumatology

1. Although we can find an abundant number of references to the work of the Holy Spirit in Calvin, pneumatology in the Reformed tradition gradually lost its importance. In the books of too many important Reformed theologians there is no chapter on pneumatology, and pneumatology plays only the role of an assistant to the doctrine of salvation. As Presbyterian theologian Lewis Mudge argued in 1963, creeds and confessions of the Reformed tradition do not do justice to the biblical emphasis on the work of the Holy Spirit, and the result is that in reading what the Bible says about the Spirit we are blind and deaf.[16] The eclipse of pneumatology in Reformed doctrine leads Reformed churches to ignore the work of the Holy Spirit. The result is the danger of a rigid church, with no mission and no *diakonia*.

15. Hesselink, "The Charismatic Movement," pp. 383-84.
16. Lewis Mudge, *One Church, Catholic and Reformed: Toward a Theology for Ecumenical Decision* (Philadelphia: Westminster, 1963), p. 68.

2. The great mistake that can be seen in the Reformed tradition of pneumatology is the belief that miracles ceased. Miracles mean so-called supernatural manifestations such as speaking in tongues, dramatic healings, prophecy, and the like. Calvin insisted that the "gift of healing, like the rest of the miracles, which the Lord willed to be brought forth for a time, has vanished away in order to make the new preaching of the gospel marvelous forever."[17] Centuries later the American Presbyterian, Benjamin B. Warfield, maintained that miracles ceased with the end of the apostolic age. In the late twentieth century a professor of Calvin Theological Seminary, Anthony A. Hoekema, also emphasized that miracles ceased. According to his view miraculous gifts were intended to authenticate the apostles and are no longer needed.[18] But this argument is too skeptical.

3. In Reformed pneumatology the Holy Spirit is conceived of as the Spirit of salvation of individuals. But what is meant here by salvation is spiritual salvation. The Holy Spirit is working for spiritual regeneration and sanctification. The renewal of the Holy Spirit is the spiritual renewal of individuals. The cosmic dimension of the Spirit in Reformed pneumatology is mainly linked with his preserving the work of creation. According to John Owen the office of the Spirit of God is "to preserve the creation."[19] The renewal of the political and social world, however, is excluded here. The saving work of the Holy Spirit exists in the realm of religion and church. Liberation from political oppression and freedom from economic poverty are seen as having no relation to the work of the Holy Spirit. The pneumatology in the Reformed tradition has no social, political dimension of liberation.

Pentecostal Pneumatology

Outline of Pentecostal Pneumatology

There are many similarities between Reformed pneumatology and Pentecostal pneumatology. According to the doctrine of the Holy Spirit in pentecostalism

17. Calvin, *Institutes* 4.19.18.

18. Anthony A. Hoekema, *Holy Spirit Baptism* (Grand Rapids: Eerdmans, 1985), pp. 56-129. But Rev. Cephas Omenyo reported in his paper under the topic "Work of the Spirit in Proclamation and the Manifestation of Charisms of the Spirit within the Church" (at the conference for Reformed-Pentecostal Dialogue at McCormick Theological Seminary, May 10-16, 1997) that many Reformed churches in the world today disagree with Calvin on his position on the cessation of certain gifts of the Holy Spirit.

19. John Owen, *The Holy Spirit: His Gifts and Power; Exposition of the Spirit's Name, Nature, Personality, Dispensation, Operations and Effects* (Grand Rapids: Kregel, 1977), p. 57.

the Holy Spirit witnesses to the redeeming work of Christ and convicts the world of sin, righteousness, and judgment. Through the work of the Holy Spirit we are born again and baptized into the body of Christ.

After the justification of believers the Holy Spirit sanctifies them, enables them to mortify the flesh, transforms them into the image of Christ, strengthens them for greater revelations of Christ, leads them, performs the office of Comforter, and brings forth fruits in their life. And in connection with ministry or service the Holy Spirit baptizes believers, reveals and gives understanding of the Word of God, helps them to pray, and gives power for preaching the Word of God. All of these teachings of the work of the Holy Spirit in pentecostalism are also found in Reformed pneumatology.

We can find the special characteristic of Pentecostal pneumatology in the doctrine of the baptism of the Holy Spirit.[20] In pentecostalism the baptism of the Holy Spirit is a definite experience subsequent to salvation. The purpose of the baptism of the Holy Spirit is to get power for service, power for spiritual warfare, and power for other abilities. The immediate evidence of the baptism of the Holy Spirit is generally considered to be speaking with other tongues, although there are other evidences. The conditions for obtaining the baptism of the Holy Spirit are repentance from sin, experience of salvation, water baptism, full yieldedness of the entire being, deep conviction of need, and faith without doubt.[21] Another important characteristic of Pentecostal pneumatology is the doctrine of divine healing. According to Pentecostal pneumatology atonement was made for healing. Pentecostals think that the great redemption chapter of the Old Testament, Isaiah 53, teaches that Christ bore our sickness as well as our sins on Calvary. It is significant in Pentecostal pneumatology that physical diseases and afflictions are solved in the redemptive suffering of Christ. Christ has redeemed us from sickness. Therefore the power of the Holy Spirit saves us from all physical diseases and afflictions.

Positive Aspects of Pentecostal Pneumatology

1. Pentecostals are correct in challenging the spiritual neglect of traditional churches. According to Dutch theologian Hendrikus Berkhof pneumatology was neglected in traditional systematic theology. In the preface of his famous book *The Doctrine of the Holy Spirit* he notes that "pneumatology is a

20. Frederick D. Bruner, *A Theology of the Holy Spirit* (Grand Rapids: Eerdmans, 1985), pp. 56-129.

21. Guy P. Duffield and Nathaniel M. van Cleave, *Foundations of Pentecostal Theology* (Los Angeles: L.I.F.E. Bible College, 1987), pp. 313-20.

neglected field of systematic theology."[22] Pentecostals make it clear that pneumatology is a very important field of theology. The discovery of the significance of pneumatology and the development of pneumatology in today's churches is influenced by the Pentecostal movement. It has led traditional churches to rediscover powerful works of the Holy Spirit.

2. Pentecostals want themselves filled with the Holy Spirit. The desire for life to be filled with the Holy Spirit is the symbolic expression of the Pentecostal movement. We can discover vitality in the Pentecostal churches. This vitality is linked with their understanding of life filled with the Holy Spirit. According to traditional Reformed pneumatology, only these two aspects of life — justification and sanctification — were important. The Holy Spirit was the Spirit of justification and the Spirit of sanctification A third aspect — being filled with the Spirit — was not fully emphasized in Reformed pneumatology. But the church must be filled with the gifts and power of the Holy Spirit. Church growth is strongly linked with being filled with the Holy Spirit. Pentecostal emphasis on life filled with the Holy Spirit is a strong point of Pentecostal pneumatology.

3. The reason why pentecostalism has great influence on the poor and the sick is its preaching on the worldliness of the gospel. Pentecostalism has discovered the link between worldly affliction and the gospel of Jesus Christ. According to the Korean Pentecostal preacher Rev. Yong Yi Cho, the atonement of Jesus through his blood is linked not only with the remission of every sin of every sinner but also with the healing of the sick and the overcoming of poverty.[23] The blood of Jesus has been shed for our sins, our illnesses, and our poverty. This christological relation between the religious atonement and salvation from worldly afflictions is the firm ground on which Pentecostal pneumatology moves toward worldly salvation. Pentecostalism emphasizes that salvation becomes apparent in our body and in our earthly life. Illness and poverty are areas where the power of the Holy Spirit is concretized. The Holy Spirit affects our body and earthly life, and the sick can be healed and the poor can be rich. This preaching of pentecostalism has been the hope of the poor and the sick. This is the reason why Pentecostal churches can get many church members from among the sick and the poor.

4. Pentecostal pneumatology is correct in insisting that speaking with tongues is a gift of the Holy Spirit and can be found in present-day churches. Many Reformed theologians including B. B. Warfield and A. A. Hoekema insisted that speaking with tongues disappeared after the end of the apostolic age.

22. Hendrikus Berkhof, *The Doctrine of the Holy Spirit* (Atlanta: John Knox, 1977), p. 10.

23. Y. K. Cho, *The Doctrine of the Holy Spirit* (Korean) (Seoul: Seoul Books, 1985), pp. 243-47.

But speaking with tongues is now a worldwide phenomenon. In Korean churches we can find this gift of the Holy Spirit easily, and it should not be thought of as a psychological disorder. People who have the gift of speaking with tongues speak and act very healthily, not as people with a psychological illness. In the rapid twentieth-century growth of Korean churches, the gift of speaking with tongues played an important role. Church members who had this gift were very active, moved by the personal conviction that God exists and is with them.

5. Longing for miracles and for the healing of sickness by prayer is an important characteristic of pentecostalism. Pentecostals believe in the supernatural power of the Holy Spirit. They believe that miracles happen. Under the influence of the Enlightenment and liberalism, antisupernaturalism developed in the eighteenth and nineteenth centuries. Reformed theology in the nineteenth century was also too rationalistic. The rise and growth of pentecostalism in the twentieth century was a rediscovery of the supernatural element in the Christian faith. If the faith is merely rational, it is possible that the scientific worldview may replace it in the long run. The place on which faith stands becomes ever narrower, and eventually the church dies. However, as the leaders of the charismatic movement have preached, God is the God who makes the impossible possible. The preaching of positive thinking and belief in miracles has moved people to have courage in the midst of disappointment and despair, and has probably been the main cause behind the budding megachurches in Korea.

Negative Aspects of Pentecostal Pneumatology

1. The unfortunate significant error of Pentecostal pneumatology is "the Pentecostal misunderstanding of the so-called baptism of the Holy Spirit as something that is subsequent to and distinct from becoming a Christian."[24] This misunderstanding is based on a mistaken exegesis of Acts 2:1-4; 8:14-17; and 19:2-7. Luke doesn't know of a second baptism apart from the baptism received at the time of conversion. The intention of Luke is that everyone who believes in Jesus Christ receives the Holy Spirit, including those who were formerly heathens.[25] This means that everyone who believes in Jesus Christ becomes part of God's people and comes to salvation. This intention of Luke is written clearly in the preface of Acts: "Repent, and let each of you be baptized in the name of Jesus Christ that your sins may be forgiven, and you will receive the gift of the Holy Spirit" (Acts 2:38).

24. Hesselink, "The Charismatic Movement," p. 383.
25. Myung Y. Kim, *Open Theology, Right Church* (Korean) (Seoul: Presbyterian College & Theological Seminary, 1997), pp. 232-61.

The baptism of the Holy Spirit is a personal encounter with Jesus Christ in the Holy Spirit. According to Paul, "no one can say, 'Jesus is Lord!' except under the influence of the Holy Spirit" (1 Cor. 12:3). There is no difference between Paul and Luke about the relation of regeneration and the baptism of the Holy Spirit. The baptism of the Holy Spirit is related to regeneration. It is false to separate the baptism of the Holy Spirit from regeneration. As Billy Graham has rightly written: "the moment we received Jesus Christ as Lord and Savior we received the Holy Spirit. He came to live in our heart."[26]

2. The overestimation of speaking in tongues is the second important error of Pentecostal pneumatology. To be sure, according to a number of New Testament testimonies, speaking in tongues is regarded as a gift of the Spirit. Paul notes that speaking in tongues is a gift of the Spirit. Those who speak in tongues speak to God, speak mysteries in the Spirit, and edify themselves. "I would like all of you to speak in tongues" (1 Cor. 14:5). "Do not forbid speaking in tongues" (1 Cor. 14:39). Yet the gift of speaking in tongues is not the first, the central, or the highest gift of the Spirit, and still less the only and decisive gift of the Spirit.[27] Paul repeatedly emphasizes that prophetic speech and the person who speaks prophetically are more important and stand higher than speaking in tongues and the person who speaks in tongues.[28] "How will I benefit you unless I speak to you in some revelation or knowledge or prophecy or teaching?" (1 Cor 14:6). "In church I would rather speak five words with my mind, in order to instruct others also, than ten thousand words in a tongue" (1 Cor. 14:19). In Paul the reasonable words of God are more important than unclear speaking in tongues. Therefore Reformed theology, which puts the focus on the reasonable words of God, has a deeper relation to the work of the Holy Spirit than pentecostalism, which puts the focus on speaking in tongues. It is a great mistake on the part of Pentecostal pneumatology that it so highly regards speaking in tongues, which is not a central and indispensable gift of the Spirit.

According to Michael Welker the reason for this mistaken evaluation "certainly lies in part in an understanding of God's Spirit that sees the Spirit as something numinous."[29] Pentecostals regard God's Spirit "as a force that evokes numinous feelings and corresponding experiences."[30] This misunderstanding of God's Spirit tends to lead Pentecostal churches toward becoming mystical churches in which mystical gifts and experiences are placed at the center of piety and ecclesial life.

---

26. Billy Graham, *The Holy Spirit* (Waco, Texas: Word Books, 1978), p. 103.
27. Michael Welker, *God the Spirit* (Minneapolis: Fortress, 1994), p. 266.
28. Welker, *God the Spirit*, p. 267.
29. Welker, *God the Spirit*, p. 268.
30. Welker, *God the Spirit*, p. 268.

3. Suspicious miracles are another questionable practice in the Pentecostal movement. Pentecostal churches insist on the occurrence of many miracles. Sometimes they insist that the dead will be resurrected. Walter J. Hollenweger reported:

> William Branham, an American Baptist preacher, died on Christmas Day in 1965 as a result of a head wound — as he had prophesied — which he received when he was putting petrol into his car, and another car full of drunken youths ran into him. But he had announced that a great miracle evangelization campaign would begin on 25 January of the following year. His followers had his body embalmed and refrigerated, because they expected him to rise from the dead on 25 January. When this did not happen, the date was put off until Easter 1966. This postponement of his burial is probably the reason why European Pentecostals heard nothing about Branham's death. When he did not rise at Easter 1966 either, he was buried.[31]

In Korea's Yoido Full Gospel Church, the biggest church in the world, it was rumored that a young dead girl had risen from the dead. But it was not true. Numerous miracles are reported in Pentecostal churches, but most of them are very questionable. They cannot be verified.

The rapid growth of Korean Pentecostal churches in the twentieth century has a deep relationship to practices of miracles and healings. Because of rumors about miracles and healings innumerable people went to Pentecostal churches. But more recently, during the past ten years, reporters from the press, radio, and TV have investigated whether the miracles and healings in the Pentecostal movement were really true. The outcome was very negative. The Pentecostal churches in Korea have stopped growing nowadays. Mistrust of Korean churches is also deepening in the heart of the Korean people, and church growth has come to a halt.

4. Pentecostal pneumatology pays a great deal of attention to the power of the Holy Spirit. Powerful evangelization and powerful ministry are symbolic expressions of the Pentecostal movement. Pentecostals want to drive out devils with the power of the Holy Spirit. But they pay little attention to love, which is the best way and also the best gift of the Holy Spirit. They also pay little attention to the theology of the cross. It seems that they do not know where the real power of God exists. The struggle of power against power is characteristic of the Pentecostal movement. Pentecostals believe that the greater power of the Holy Spirit destroys the power of the devil. But they do not know that love is the power of the Holy Spirit that destroys the power of the devil. Remember the way of Jesus on the cross in order to overcome the dark power of

31. Walter J. Hollenweger, *The Pentecostals* (London: SCM, 1976), pp. 354-55.

death! According to Welker love is the public force field in which God and life in God's presence become known.[32] Love is "a world-changing force field."[33] We must take into consideration that a naked power struggle without love is a satanic struggle. Pentecostals must pay much more attention to love. Not only faith and prayer but also love is the force field in which the forceful power of the Holy Spirit becomes a reality. We must remember that resurrection and the cross are deeply related. The power of resurrection hides in the love of the cross.

5. Pentecostal pneumatology concentrates on speaking in tongues, divine healing, and prophecies. Here a critical question occurs. Jürgen Moltmann criticizes the Pentecostal pneumatology: "Where are the charismatic persons for the life of everyday, in politics, in the peace movement and in the ecological movement? Why don't they protest with us against nuclear missiles?"[34] The charismatic movement tends to flee from the conflicts of the real world into the world of religious individual hope. If it has nothing to do with the liberating power of God in the concrete conflicts of the real world, it exists only in the realm of private religion. According to Moltmann, the charismatic movement must not reduce Christian faith to an apolitical, private religion. "The standard of life in the Holy Spirit is and will be following Jesus."[35] We cannot find in the charismatic movement people who follow Jesus in politics, in the peace movement or the ecological movement.

The Right Path for Pneumatology

The right kind of pneumatology on the right way is a holistic pneumatology.[36] The word "holistic" here does not mean to separate soul from body, individual from society, human beings from the cosmic world. Pneumatology must not be limited to the area of spiritual salvation and it must not be limited to the area of individual salvation as well. The Holy Spirit is working not only for the salvation of individuals but also for the establishing of the kingdom of God. Holistic pneumatology means that the Holy Spirit is the Spirit establishing the kingdom of God. Neither individual salvation nor social salvation should be excluded

---

32. Welker, *God the Spirit*, pp. 239-58.

33. Welker, *God the Spirit*, p. 250.

34. Jürgen Moltmann, *Die Quelle des Lebens. Der Heilige Geist und die Theologie des Lebens* (München: Kaiser Verlag, 1997), p. 66.

35. Moltmann, *Die Quelle des Lebens*, p. 66.

36. Moltmann calls his pneumatology "a holistic pneumatology" ("eine ganzheitliche Pneumatologie"). See Moltmann, *Der Geist des Lebens. Eine ganzheitliche Pneumatologie* (München: Kaiser Verlag, 1991).

from the work of the Holy Spirit. What is important is that the Holy Spirit aims at the universal fulfillment of God's will of cosmic salvation. The salvific work of the Holy Spirit includes establishing justice and peace on the earth and giving life to the whole creation. Justification and sanctification are important for the work of the Holy Spirit. But the Holy Spirit is not only the Spirit of individual salvation but also the Spirit of the world and the cosmos. Traditional Reformed pneumatology as well as Pentecostal pneumatology have neglected the work of the Holy Spirit in the world and cosmos.

The Holy Spirit and the Salvation of Individuals

The Holy Spirit is working for the salvation of individuals. But the salvation of individuals must be seen as holistic. The concentration of Reformed pneumatology on spiritual rebirth and spiritual sanctification should be widened. The Holy Spirit is working to save the body as well as the spirit. The Pentecostal doctrine of physical healing has a better perspective at this point compared with the limited spiritual regeneration and sanctification doctrine of Reformed pneumatology. The liberating power of the Holy Spirit protects life from physical sickness as well as spiritual sickness. This work of the Holy Spirit is deeply related to the ministry of Jesus who healed all the sick who came to him.

The resurrection is the highlight expressing bodily salvation through the Holy Spirit. The Holy Spirit will raise us up by his own power. It should be noted that the New Testament proclaims not the immortality of the soul but the resurrection of the body. The power of Christ's redemption is working in our body. According to Moltmann the healing of the sick is the proleptic sign of the resurrection in the future.[37] Sickness is the tool of the power of death. The kingdom of God begins in the place where the tools of death are destroyed. The Holy Spirit is working to save us from all kinds of afflictions such as diseases, poverty, debts, and a distorted mentality. He saves the whole person from the power of death. Karl Marx criticized a Christian church that pursued only the happiness of the soul. For Marx a religion of the soul is an opium. A spiritualized church at the time of Marx did not know the holistic salvation about which the Bible teaches. Spirit and body must not be distinguished according to an escapist model.[38] The liberating power of the Holy Spirit protects life from perplexity, joylessness, poverty, anxiety, insecurity, illness, and death. Without the action of the Holy Sprit, what is fleshly is helplessly handed over to the

37. Moltmann, *Der Geist des Lebens,* p. 203.
38. Welker, *God the Spirit,* pp. 258-64.

power of death. With the action of the Holy Spirit, what is fleshly experiences God's gracious earthly salvation in the midst of an afflicted world. God's earthly salvation is the proleptic sign of eternal salvation. In this sense eternal life begins in the midst of the earthly world.

The Holy Spirit and the Kingdom of God

The Holy Spirit and Justice

Luke 4:18-19 is very significant for today's pneumatology. It opens the social dimension of pneumatology.

> The Spirit of the Lord is upon me, because the Lord has anointed me to bring good news to the poor. The Lord has sent me to proclaim release to the captives and recovery of sight to the blind, to let the oppressed go free, to proclaim the year of the Lord's favor.

This is a quotation from Isaiah 61:1-2. The Spirit of the Lord who is with Jesus makes the oppressed free. He proclaims release to the captives. It is important to note that the year of the Lord's favor in Luke 4:19 is the year of jubilee.[39] In the year of jubilee slaves are freed and people return to their ancestral property. It is really the year of delight to the poor who lost their land and became slaves. It is the year of social and economic liberation. It is important here to see the deep relationship between the work of the Spirit of the Lord and social, economic liberation.

We see another important text of pneumatology for justice in Matthew 12:18-21, which is quoted from Isaiah 42:1-4. Here the bearer of the Spirit proclaims justice. This justice is the hope of the Gentiles. According to Isaiah 42:1-4 the bearer of the Spirit, who is called God's servant, is the one who creates the universal establishment and fulfillment of God's justice.

We see a very important, definite relationship between the work of the Spirit and justice in Isaiah 11:1-5, as well.

> A shoot shall come out from the stump of Jesse and a branch shall grow out of his roots. The Spirit of the Lord shall rest on him. . . . with righteousness he shall judge the poor, and decide with equity for the poor in the land; he shall strike the earth with the rod of his mouth, and with the breath of his lips he shall kill the wicked.

39. K. S. Lee, "The Value of the Year of Jubilee as the Year of Delight and Grace in the Old Testament," in *A Study on the Theology of Jubilee* (Korean) (Seoul: KNCC, 1997), pp. 11-35.

The bearer of the Spirit establishes righteousness on earth and returns equity to the poor. The wicked disappear before him. The land will be full of justice and equity.

There is no doubt that the work of the Holy Spirit as well as the work of Jesus are deeply linked with establishing and creating the universal fulfillment of God's justice. The bearer of the Spirit chosen by God brings good news to the oppressed and proclaims liberty to the captives. He is the ground on which liberation and justice are created in the world. It is, therefore, a great error to say that a chapter on justice is lacking in the pneumatology of Reformed theology as well as of pentecostalism. According to Moltmann and Welker the liberating work of the Holy Spirit for justice is the basic chapter of pneumatology. In this connection it must be noted that Dr. Martin Luther King, Jr. and Archbishop Romero were persons filled with the Holy Spirit. It is spiritual ignorance not to know that they are persons of the Holy Spirit.

The church must take part in the liberating work of the Holy Spirit for justice. The Korean Catholic Church has been growing rapidly for the past twenty years, and still is growing. The main reason for the rapid growth of the Korean Catholic Church is its action for justice in the time of the dictators' regime and its practice of love. The Korean people trust the Korean Catholic Church because it is the church of justice and love. Church growth is deeply linked with social trust in the church. While the Korean Protestant church lost social trust because of shamanistic beliefs, suspicion about miracles, and neglect of social responsibility, the Korean Catholic Church earned it because of its action for justice and its actions of *diakonia*. The Korean Catholic Church has worked hand in hand with the Holy Spirit for the establishing of justice in Korean society. It must be noted that the church will grow only if it does the work of the Holy Spirit.

The Holy Spirit and Peace

The fruit of the Holy Spirit is peace (Gal. 5:22). "Happy are the peacemakers; they will be called God's sons" (Matt. 5:9). The Holy Spirit brings about not only justice but also peace on earth in order to establish the kingdom of God. In contrast to the work of the devil who causes hatred, war, killing, and death on this earth, the Holy Spirit establishes life, love, and peace. Where was the devil, when six million Jews were murdered by Adolf Hitler? It is sure that the devil was laughing and dancing on the six million dead Jewish bodies. Jesus said that the devil was "a murderer from the beginning" (John 8:44). Where was the devil, when the Second World War broke out? It is sure that the devil was monitoring the Second World War.

If we think of the work of the Holy Spirit only in regard to the spiritual world, we have a fatal, false understanding of the Holy Spirit. It is unfortunate that traditional Reformed pneumatology didn't know about or acknowledge the work of the Holy Spirit in establishing peace and preventing the world from killing, from war and death. Spiritual regeneration is an important work of the Holy Spirit, but establishing peace on earth is an important work of the Holy Spirit too! The work of the Holy Spirit must be extended beyond the limitations of a spiritual inner world.

It was fortunate that Pentecostal pneumatology understood the Holy Spirit as the saving power from sickness that has at its root the devil's power of death. But it was unfortunate that Pentecostal pneumatology did not extend the work of the Holy Spirit into those social relations in which war, killing, and murder take place. The structure of death on earth must be changed and destroyed. The Holy Spirit is the destroying power of the structure of death and the power to establish a world of life and peace.

The Holy Spirit in the Creation

The Old Testament is aware, even more than the New Testament, of the work of the Holy Spirit in creation. We begin with Genesis 1:2: ". . . the Spirit of God was moving over the face of the waters." But it is difficult from Genesis 1:2 to get a clear understanding of the work of the Holy Spirit in creation. We can find further understanding in Job and the Psalms. "By the word of the Lord the heavens were made, and all their host by the *ruach* of his mouth" (Ps. 33:6). "When thou sendest forth thy Spirit they are created; and thou renewest the face of the ground" (Ps. 104:30). "The Spirit of God has made me, and the breath of the Almighty gives me life" (Job 33:4). From these passages Reformed pneumatology understood the Holy Spirit as the Spirit preserving creation. The Holy Spirit also inspires human culture. The Old Testament connects the gifts of the Spirit with agriculture, architecture, jurisdiction, and politics. In general, all human wisdom is the gift of God's Spirit.

Reformed pneumatology was fortunately aware of this relationship between the Holy Spirit and creation. Calvin and, following him, Abraham Kuyper are the representative ones who tried to do justice to this cosmic aspect of pneumatology. But it was unfortunate that the Reformed tradition understood the work of the Holy Spirit in the creation only in the framework of general revelation. The work of the Holy Spirit in the creation is only the background against which the salvation history takes place.

Jürgen Moltmann's book *God in Creation*, published in 1985,[40] was a turn-

---

40. Jürgen Moltmann, *Gott in der Schöpfung. Ökologische Schöpfungslehre* (München: Kaiser Verlag, 1985).

ing point in understanding the creation. Moltmann developed in this book a cosmic pneumatology. The creation is according to Moltmann not the background against which the salvation history takes place. God's salvation is the salvation of the whole creation. The salvation history of human beings is a part of the salvation of the whole creation. The Holy Spirit liberates the whole creation from the prison of death's power. For Paul the creation hopes to be "freed from its enslavement to decay and receive the glorious freedom which belongs to the children of God" (Rom. 8:21). The whole created world is waiting with eager expectation for the liberating work of the Holy Spirit. Isaiah 11:6ff. describes a universal condition of peace that even includes animals. "The wolf shall live with the lamb, the leopard shall lie down with the kid" (Isa. 11:6). The eschatological image of creation is peace. There is no misery like eating flesh and being eaten. The salvation of the whole creation must be accomplished. The Holy Spirit is the Spirit that gives life and establishes peace for the whole creation.

The Holy Spirit and the World of Love and Life

For Paul the best gift of the Holy Spirit is love (1 Cor. 12:31). According to Galatians 5:22 the fruit of the Holy Spirit is also love. The love of the poor is the beginning of Christian love. Mercy for the poor and weak is a gift of the Holy Spirit (Rom. 12:8). The Holy Spirit establishes therefore *diakonia*, which works worldwide for the poor and weak. It can be a critical error if we think *diakonia* is a worldly affair that does not belong to the spiritual task of the church. This error was commonplace in both the Korean Reformed churches and the Korean Pentecostal churches. *Diakonia* did not belong to the primary task for these churches because their pneumatology was too religious and "spiritually" oriented.

So too, *diakonia* must not be confined to a circle of persons or to the realm of individual mercy. It must be established socially and universally. It needs laws of justice and mercy.

Anchoring ordinances of mercy in laws is inevitable for the routinization of mercy and the continuing protection of the poor and weak. Without routinized protection of the poor and weak, they will be virtually dehumanized because they cannot survive by occasional acts of mercy. The world of love and mercy is deeply related to the establishing of socially rooted mercy laws. The Holy Spirit is the ground on which laws of mercy and justice stand. The church of the Holy Spirit is a church that is continually sensitive to the poor and weak, trying to make society reflect mercy and justice, and building a humanized community. A society of justice and love is a proleptic image of the eternal kingdom of God. The Holy Spirit that establishes the kingdom of God also establishes a society of justice and love.

The Holy Spirit establishes not only a world of justice and love but also a world of life. The love of life is the core of the work of the Holy Spirit. He wants to destroy death's tools — in all their forms. In this connection medical developments relate to his works. He wants to destroy cancer and AIDS and bring people to life. The arduous struggle of medical scientists to overcome cancer and AIDS has a connection to the task of the Holy Spirit. His power of healing comes to reality not only through prayer but also through medical developments. Pastors and doctors can work hand in hand to establish the kingdom of God, where no death will remain. Pastors proclaim words of God and doctors cure the sick to establish the kingdom of God, just as Jesus proclaimed words of God and cured the sick to bring in the kingdom of God. The activities of doctors must not be excluded from their connection with establishing the kingdom of God. The Holy Spirit urges pastors to pray for the sick and doctors to become real tools of life through which he wants to bring about life on earth.

The Spirit of life establishes on earth the culture of life. Cynicism has nothing to do with the culture of life. Literature and music that motivate young people to despair and death also have nothing to do with the culture of life. Ideologies that urge young people to sacrifice their lives to meaningless revolutions have no connection to the culture of life. The culture of black and gray that can be found in practices of asceticism is far from the culture of life. The culture of life is colorful and joyful. It has a connection with feeling a colorful and meaningful creation. Augustine wrote in *Confessions* X.6: "What do I love, as I love Thee? Neither the beautifulness of bodies nor the rhythm of the moving time, nor the sparkling of light . . . nor the honey melodies with all kinds of tones in the world." However, as Moltmann responded to Augustine we must echo: "If I love God, then I love the beautifulness of bodies, the rhythm of the moving, the sparkling of eyes, embraces, feelings, odors, tones of this colorful creation."[41] The culture of life is a culture that makes the joy of life abundant. It is not a culture to motivate spiritual piety in the soul in a way that oppresses bodily life. The Holy Spirit establishes on earth a culture of joy and meaning.

The Holy Spirit and the Knowledge of Jesus Christ and God

The Holy Spirit is "the Spirit of knowledge and the fear of the Lord" (Isa. 11:2). According to Isaiah 11:1-5 the bearer of the Spirit brings justice. Righteousness is the belt around his waist. He judges the helpless righteously. He helps the poor. He wants the earth filled with righteousness. But the earth filled with righteousness is not the end of the work of the bearer of the Spirit. He wants the

41. Moltmann, *Die Quelle des Lebens*, p. 89.

earth to "be full of the knowledge of the Lord as the waters cover the sea" (Isa. 11:9). Righteousness and knowledge of God are deeply linked. They stand in strict reciprocal interconnection. The bearer of the Spirit establishes on the earth not only justice but also knowledge of God. He wants the earth to be full of the glory of God.

The New Testament connects in a profound way the work of the Holy Spirit with knowledge of Christ. Jesus says, "The Spirit of truth . . . will bear witness to me" (John 15:26). According to Acts, with the descent of the Holy Spirit the last days have dawned. The meaning of these last days is that the Spirit is poured out on all flesh and that the gracious presence of God will be acknowledged by people of all languages, races, classes, and ages (Acts 2). The knowledge of a gracious God, including his saving act in Jesus Christ, is the center of the church's mission. "You are . . . God's own people, that you may declare the wonderful deeds of him who called you out of darkness into his marvelous light" (1 Peter 2:9). For Karl Barth the goal of Christian life is not personal salvation but being a witness. The Holy Spirit establishes churches in order to let them proclaim the saving act of Christ and the knowledge of a gracious God. The knowledge of God apart from the saving act of Christ can be dangerous. It cannot be the knowledge of the real God who revealed himself in the cross of Christ. For Barth the knowledge of God without Christ is heathen. It is the knowledge of idols.

According to the New Testament the Holy Spirit is the Spirit of God (Rom. 8:9) and the Spirit of Christ (Rom. 8:9). The Spirit points to Christ, Christ's proclamation, Christ's action, and Christ's cross and resurrection. He draws people into the community of Christ, and thus brings God closer to human beings and human beings closer to God. He leads people to know and glorify Christ and God.

The Holy Spirit wants to witness and glorify Christ and God. He wishes that the name of God and Jesus Christ is praised through all the creation as well as all human beings. The kingdom of God is a place that is filled with the knowledge of a gracious God. The salvation of individuals is not the end of the work of the Holy Spirit. The end is the glory of God and the praise of God's grace and love. The salvation of the whole creation is also not the end of the work of the Holy Spirit. The end is the everlasting thanksgiving given to God on the basis of the knowledge of God's grace and love.

Conclusion

The mission of the Holy Spirit is the mission of new life. It is the new life of the whole cosmos as well as the whole person. Traditional Reformed pneumatology as well as Pentecostal pneumatology was too narrow in understanding the work of the Holy Spirit. "We must find ways from religion to the kingdom of God, from church to world, from anxiety of self to hope of the whole world."[42] The mission of the Holy Spirit is a mission against death and all the powers that create death. The afflictions in Bosnia and Rwanda are deeply related to the power of death. Instead of the hope of a solely spiritual, private salvation we must develop the hope of the whole world and creation. Pneumatology in the twenty-first century must be conceived accordingly.

---

42. Moltmann, *Die Quelle des Lebens*, p. 28.

CHAPTER 13

A Reformed Theological Perspective Based on the Characteristic Past and Present of Debrecen

Botond Gaál

I must confess that this topic made me sit down at the school desk again and think over the essence of our Reformed theological heritage, with a view to showing how it has been enriched over the course of history and how it may open toward the future. I am going to do this job from a specific point of view, namely that of the Reformed way of thinking characteristic of Debrecen. One of the old and beautiful Debrecen hymns says that "the past has to be taken for a mirror"[1] if we wish to see our present and plan our future. In other words, if we want to get to know ourselves better we should see where we come from, where we are now, and where we are heading. This is what I call an identity check, and I intend to do it by embedding our Reformed existence, determined by its manifold tradition, into the universal context of Christianity while keeping ecumenicity in mind. To start with, I will explain what I mean by the Reformation's universal importance, and will then attempt to predict the future of the Reformed perspective from the special viewpoint of Debrecen's past and present. In other words, I would like to describe how the particular, Reformed way of thinking characteristic of Debrecen can contribute to the enrichment of the universal Reformed heritage and thus the theological strengthening of universal Christianity. We will get to the crucial problem, too, of whether it is sufficient or right to base our future solely on past heritage and present condition.

Many people, including church historians, say that the essence and aim of the Reformation was to restore the church in its ancient, pure, and original form.

---

1. *Reformed Hymnal*, 1948. Hymn 280, v. 6.

Others take it for a kind of intention of reform in which new theological princi-ples arise. Still others would say that the Reformation was only a single moment in a gigantic intellectual movement aimed at the liberation of the human mind from its medieval authoritarian constraints. In their opinion, this movement started with the Renaissance and Humanism, came to a relative standstill in the age of Enlightenment, and was finally accomplished in the modern, scientific way of thinking. The Reformation was one of the links in the chain of this pro-cess. It accomplished the liberation of mind in both the religious and canonical sense of the word by proclaiming the freedom of conscience and claiming free speculation in terms of faith. A variant of this concept is that the Reformation gave birth to a modern way of respecting the individual. A similar approach is reflected in the field of political history, where the Reformation is seen as one of the most important factors in the national idea that broke through the ecclesias-tical and political universality of the Middle Ages, or as the first major victory of democracy in the history of Christendom. Parallel to these notions, there is an-other that regards the whole world of ideas of the Reformation as an ideological superstructure whose true driving force does not lie in intellectual or moral springs but economic ones, i.e., the rise of early capitalism.

There is a lot of truth in the above; yet it must be admitted that these ideas and approaches do not investigate the root of things but rather interpret the results that are already at our disposal. Briefly speaking, the items we have listed here are the fruits, the mere facts made visible for the world! Thus, *a decisive step in the Reformation's breaking out of medieval thinking was made when a new, personal link between God and man was brought about.* In fact, it was the discovery of a new kind of attitude. The believing mind stood face to face with its living, omnipotent, and gracious Lord who had been hidden and separated by the religious world or "religious institution." Martin Luther strug-gled with himself for this very reason; that is, he searched for his identity be-cause he did not know "how to find his Gracious Lord." Eventually he realized that the "righteousness of God" was not what was thought to be righteousness in the human or legal sense but ". . . the righteousness of God is that by which the righteous lives by a gift of God, namely by faith."[2] We can thus understand what the Apostle Paul says in his epistle to the Romans (1:17): "In the gospel a righteousness from God is revealed; as it is written, 'he who through faith is righteous shall live.'" This served as a basis for the doctrine so strongly empha-sized by the Reformers, i.e., according to Holy Scripture, the salvation of man was "by grace — through faith," which meant nothing else but the acceptance of the fact that, except for Christ, there was no need for another mediator.

2. *Luther's Works* 34, pp. 336ff. Cited by Eugene M. Osterhaven in *The Faith of the Church* (Grand Rapids: Eerdmans, 1982), p. 107.

Man's life was an obedient life by his own will; it was a happily confessing life full of loving and acting and suffering in the hope of victory; it was life filled with faith. Thus, by rediscovering this kind of personal relationship with a gracious God, the Reformation gave back to European people the courage to survive, thereby giving new hope for the future.

As a result, man had a different view of *himself*, looked at his *fellows* in a different way, and observed the *world* differently because this "wretched man" (Rom. 7:24) was liberated by his gracious Lord to get into a direct relationship with him. This change in attitude resulted in a new kind of identity. Calvin put the knowledge of God in first place, which then gave rise to the knowledge of ourselves.[3] It was regarded as dogma that the knowledge of God enriched self-knowledge, knowledge of others, and knowledge of the world. Very closely, it related to the problem of identity that Calvin emphasized when he tried to interpret Jesus' knowledge of God (John 7:17) by saying *"omnis recta cognitio ab obedientia nascitur,"* that is, *all true knowledge originates from obedience.*[4] **The radical change in the relationship towards God has fundamentally transformed our view of ourselves, of other people, and of the created world.** It has resulted in far-reaching consequences for theology and all fields of life.

I would now like to show how these Reformed ideas manifested themselves in my country, and especially in Debrecen, which is the largest intellectual center of Hungarians of the Reformed faith. I was brought up in this specific spirit. I grew up in small villages where my father worked as a minister, but when it was time, he had me enrolled in the Reformed College of Debrecen, where I received my secondary education. Afterward I studied physics and mathematics at the University of Debrecen. Upon graduation I went back to teach at the Reformed College, where in afterwork hours I studied theology, thus becoming an ordained Reformed minister. I have always worked at the Reformed College of Debrecen, which also houses the Debrecen University of Reformed Theology. My career allowed me to familiarize myself thoroughly with the heritage of the Reformation in which I had been completely immersed. My work and way of thinking have naturally been shaped and determined by the spirit of my ancestors who shared the same Reformed faith.

The Reformation in Hungary started in the 1520-30s in hard, or even cruel, historic times, on the verge of national existence and nonexistence, amidst continual warfare. The European "superpower" that flourished just half a century earlier was now divided into three; one part had been occupied by the Turks, the second third was under Hapsburg rule, and Transylvania remained a

---

3. John Calvin, *Institutes of the Christian Religion,* trans. Ford Lewis Battles and ed. John T. McNeill (Philadelphia: Westminster, 1960), 1.1.1.

4. *Calvin's Commentary on John,* ch. 7, v. 17.

Hungarian principality. Debrecen was located at the meeting point of these three powers and enjoyed a bit of support from Transylvania. In the sixteenth century, between 1558 and 1572, Debrecen had one of the most outstanding personalities of the Hungarian Reformation, Péter Méliusz Juhász, also known as the "Hungarian Calvin." Juhász labored tenaciously in this town. Owing to his powerful theological and church-organizing activities the Hungarian Reformed Church became a church based on unified theological principles. Once and for all, I learned and confessed his spiritual heritage, which consisted of three major principles: *(1) a high level of morals at work, (2) scientific openness originating from confessional commitment, and (3) responsible service of the whole church and the whole of the nation.* In that century and historic situation these principles were crucially important. Debrecen also saw the period of *Protestant orthodoxy* but, interestingly enough, the citizens of the town, who had all belonged to the Reformed faith by then, were ready to accept the theology of the *puritan movement* too, due to their openness. In my opinion, it was a good decision on the part of Debrecen citizens, as I have been deeply impressed by the views of seventeenth-century puritans. It was later that I realized our present religious life grew from the ancient tree planted by the puritans, a tree that yielded fruit such as *(1) biblicity, (2) insistence on the sacredness of life, and (3) public responsibility of the church.* I can also understand the *"rational orthodoxy"*[5] of the eighteenth century. Although that period was characterized by a number of strange ideas, concepts, and practices, in our region rational partiality was softened by the spirit of orthodoxy while orthodoxy was refreshed by rationalism. Moreover, this peculiar alignment of orthodoxy and rationalism yielded an unexpected result in the pressing political situation of the Counter-Reformation, when our greatest colleges — especially Debrecen — turned out to be the most important citadels of science. These colleges matched the European standards for the study of science, and they linked the whole Hungarian nation with European civilization. If we consider the reform period of the nineteenth century and the expression of national feeling that sprang from it, namely the Revolution and War of Independence of 1848-49, we can also find relevant teaching in some of the especially important events in our heritage. Almost all of the teachers and students of my school, the Reformed College of Debrecen, took part in the battles for independence.[6] However, they were not driven primarily by Rousseau or the slogans of the French Revolution. They were motivated by the predestination idea of Reformed orthodoxy, part of the

5. In the German Protestant theological literature it is often referred to as "vernünftige Orthodoxie."
6. Cf. Sándor Czeglédy, "Teaching Theology at the College," in *History of the Reformed College of Debrecen* (Budapest: Zsinati Iroda, 1988), p. 562 (in Hungarian).

heritage by which they lived their lives. They were also impelled by a living puritanism that encouraged them to live according to the Bible in a responsible way. In Debrecen there were no grounds for nationalism in the negative sense of the word.

Our grandparents told us about the events of this era, and we ourselves witnessed the last decades of the twentieth century. Memories of the humiliating measures and anti-Christian attitudes of the proletarian dictatorship, introduced according to the Soviet pattern, are still fresh in our minds. But believe me, even these four decades of bad memories have had their importance. If we look at history from God's viewpoint, we see that he tried our faithfulness and confessing behavior and taught us that there has always been and always will be "a remnant according to the election of grace" (Rom. 11:5). There were fewer ministers and theological students, but even in this diminished state, we were the "remnant" to represent in this period everything we had inherited from our confessor ancestors. The remnant consisted of those who took Jesus' question in all seriousness when he asked, "Will you also go away?" (John 6:67). The remnant remained faithful to the Lord Jesus.

This history has much to teach us. First of all, we Christians of the Reformed faith do have a mission in our own country, among our own people, in the mental and spiritual frame of our own church, but we can serve together with our brothers and sisters from other Christian faiths. Moreover, our place of service was appointed here exactly, according to the merciful choice of our Lord. If we believe this, we have to prepare for this mission. If someone has a mission he should be sure of his own identity, because the whole of his service stands or falls on it. From a theological point of view, the essence and distinctive feature of identity is not just what I profess or how I interpret the universe theoretically. It is not just what I believe about the creation of the world and its redemption by Christ, or what the Holy Scripture means for me according to the *Testimonium Spiritus Sancti Internum,* or how I interpret the principle of *Sola Scriptura* together with the other basic principles of the Reformation. This is not full life yet. My own identity also includes how I act according to the gospel of Jesus Christ, how I live up to my faith in my congregation, how I participate in church life, and how everything that is a consequence of personal belief is put into practice. *If my faith and visible actions are in harmony, if my faith is justified by my deeds, then my personality is alright because it is my Christian identity. I have been searching for that identity in myself because I would like to give evidence of that identity when I follow Christ.* In other words, my proper identity is found when I can say "it is no longer I who live, but Christ who lives in me" (Gal. 2:20), and through this belief I can find my authentic place "under the Sun" (Eccles. 6).

In the following, I will attempt to demonstrate what I mean by man's proper identity in the Reformed sense, in three distinct but still connected areas or situations. First, I will examine how a Christian interprets himself, next, how he relates to his fellow human beings, and finally, how he looks at the universe vis-à-vis what was done for him by Jesus Christ through redemption.

How Does a Man of the Reformed Faith Interpret Himself?

It was said earlier that according to the Reformed approach, the knowledge of God is preceded by the knowledge of ourselves. The two are inseparable, according to Calvin at the beginning of his *Institutes of the Christian Religion*. As the Apostle Paul says in Colossians 3:3, our "life is hidden with Christ in God," which means that we understand our own place in the world correctly if we consider that the reality of the world is inseparable from its Creator, who has obtained immanence in the form of Jesus Christ. So the biblical view is that the part should be approached from the whole. In the citation from Colossians, the fact of incarnation is included after all, together with all those gracious works that belong to us in Christ. Barth identifies these godsends by listing the words that follow "I believe in the Holy Spirit" in the Apostles' Creed: the holy catholic church, the communion of saints, the forgiveness of sins, the resurrection of the body, and the life everlasting. A certain kind of chronological approach can be seen in this list, namely our future observed from the viewpoint of Christ. As Oscar Wilde would say, "The only difference between the sinner and the saint is that the sinner has a past whereas the saint has a future!"[7] The same idea was expressed by Thomas F. Torrance in the language of science when he stated that we live in two real times simultaneously. The theory of relativity also knows this approach, as two different times are rendered to the same event in relation to the system of coordinates, and both of these times are real. That is how a Christian person can look at himself: he still lives in this world, but at the same time, the future era to come in Christ is reflected in the present. In Jesus' words, "the kingdom of God is within you" (Luke 17:21). If we examine our existence from the viewpoint of God, then this secret may be interpreted as God's regarding us as having obtained eternal life in Christ. "And the life which I now live in the flesh I live by the faith of the Son of God, who loved me" (Gal. 2:20). Luther said the same: "*Simul iustus et peccator.*" Therefore, a Christian person, especially one who thinks according to the Reformed faith, does not judge his significance in terms of the past and present, but in terms of the future that is visible in Christ. For such a person, the reference to Moses in the book of Hebrews has become reality: "as seeing him who is invisible" (Heb. 11:27).

7. I read the citation in Hungarian.

As for the personal, direct relationship between man and God, man, in his created finite reality, does not possess the object of cognition just because he knows God. Instead, the "existential being in the object"[8] takes place through faith as expressed earlier in the statement by Paul, that "our life is hidden with Christ in God." This does not mean that we have exceeded the limit of time or even that we have left time in some metaphysical sense, but the other way round: through Christ it is God who enters our real, historic, contingent, and temporal world. In other words, by simultaneously living in two planes of chronological reality, it is not we who step over into the realm of some unchangeable state or timeless reality, but on the contrary, we remain in a chronological world that can be changed. But this world is a transcendent one in the sense that "God hides himself in history (incarnation) or raises history to himself (resurrection) via his love expressed through Christ."[9] His act of love is at the same time an expression of his existence. Speaking in up-to-date language, this is the new thing the Reformers recognized and proclaimed to be the personal relationship between God and man. Man can recognize his identity in this state as he permanently lives in the presence of God and acts according to the powers of God's kingdom. This is what is usually called "Calvinist activity." In my opinion, that is the way a person of the Reformed faith interprets his own identity and lives up to it.

How Does a Christian Man Look at His Fellow Men?

Harmony of Faith and Practice in the Life of the Congregation

According to Reformed doctrine, a Christian man lives his life as a member of Christ's body, the church. The church itself is the community of those who have gained new identity, because "if any man be in Christ, he is a new creature" (2 Cor. 5:17). If the church is regarded as the congregation of Christ, and if we try to reveal from the standpoint of the ecumenical and generally accepted Christian confessions how it becomes one, holy, catholic, and apostolic church, then we reveal the conditions of how it changes into a community in which the "new man" becomes manifest and where "there is neither Greek nor Jew, circumcision or uncircumcision, Barbarian, Scythian, bond nor free, but Christ is all, and in all" (Col. 3:11). In Christ, the Greek, the Jew, the Scythian, the Barbarian, the servant, and the free citizen all disappear; that is, the social, racial, historical, and religious identities of individuals lose their importance in the con-

8. Csaba László Gáspár, *Metaphysics and Theology*, *Confessio*, vol. 2 (1984), p. 55 (in Hungarian).

9. Gáspár, *Metaphysics and Theology*, p. 51.

gregation. The new rules of Christ's community, based on completely different premises, are brought to the foreground. The rule of the congregational community rooted in the power of Christ is the rule of new life within the old one; it is the rule of true life in a world full of imperfection, fighting against immorality. Jesus refers to this new order when, in contrast to his disciples' expectations, he says "But so shall it not be among you" (Mark 10:43). Jesus Christ is present in the congregational community through his Holy Spirit and the force of his promise, "Behold, I make all things new" (Rev. 21:5). This "new" now has its effects on the new world, and works for this new world as the manifest and visible reality. Thus the life or teaching of a congregation is certified by a seal: Is it for itself or does it serve others? If the forces of the kingdom of God are present there, then this future dimension will determine the identity of the congregation. In a congregation like this, all the regulations that are in harmony with Holy Scripture can be enforced. They are as follows: life based on the rules of love, the principle of universal priesthood, and a biblically based church government. In this interpretation, the church is *communio sanctorum,* the manifestation of Christ's body. It is not a body in the biological sense, or a community in the social or legal sense, or an institution in the philosophical sense; but it is a functioning body in the pneumatic truth of the power of Christ.

Close-Up of Faith and Practice in Interdenominational Relationships

I have often faced the conclusion that there is a significant shift of stress in the theological activities of the various denominations. In the view of many, Orthodox Christians emphasize the importance of true faith, Roman Catholics concentrate on the loyal church, and Protestants focus on authentic teaching. There is no doubt some truth in this slightly forced division. If so, we can even learn from one another, which, although most of us cannot even imagine it, will be the future, when we mutually take more and more of one another's teaching, religious life, and example-setting through serving. In fact, no church makes such distinctions in their pure sense. In the 1950s, Thomas F. Torrance strongly warned the member churches of the World Alliance of the Reformed Churches that, "Around [the doctrine of our unity in Christ] Calvin builds his doctrine of faith, of the Church as the living Body of Christ, and his doctrines of the Christian life, Baptism, and the Lord's Supper. Apart from *union with Christ,* Calvin says, all that Christ did for us in His Incarnation, death and resurrection, would be unavailing."[10] It sounds nice this

10. Thomas F. Torrance, "Our Witness Through Doctrine," *Proceedings of the Seventeenth General Council of the Alliance of the Reformed Churches Throughout the World Holding*

way, and in theory we can fully accept it; moreover, we should do our best that this theological truth should become reality in proper interdenominational conduct. As far as Debrecen is concerned, it is not as simple as one would think. Identity and ecumenicity are in practice closely linked, and that is why our situation in Debrecen is worth telling about.

We should immediately begin with the second name for Debrecen, *the "Calvinist Rome."* It is a telling name, and is known all over the country and used in a positive sense. Only few people know that it was a nickname given to the town by the Transylvanian followers of the Unitarian faith in the sixteenth century. At the beginning of the nineteenth century this nickname was reintroduced mockingly by Ferenc Kazinczy, our famous writer. Also at the turn of the previous century, a Debrecen student and one of our greatest Reformed poets, Endre Ady, at that time used this "title" again to tease the "old-fashioned" town. Now the term "Calvinist Rome" is used almost proudly by everybody. When I hear this name I can hear the past talking. The name "Calvinist Rome" carries both the identity and ecumenicity of the contemporary Reformed people. In the age of Reformer Péter Méliusz Juhász, in the sixteenth century, it was really hard for the town of Debrecen to stand the comparison with Rome. From 1552 on, the Debrecen Reformers, who had turned towards the radical or Helvetic branch of the Reformed faith, were combating several Roman Catholic dogmas, but at the same time they were fighting a desperate battle against the deniers of the Holy Trinity. On the one hand they opposed Rome; on the other they defended the greatest values and common treasures of universal Christianity. As Imre Révész, our greatest church historian and a member of the Hungarian Academy of Sciences, said in 1940, "Debrecen has become Reformed to fully live up to Christianity and completely possess it, and not because it wanted to segregate from the unity of Christianity by all means."[11] Undoubtedly, there were times when only followers of the Reformed faith were allowed to settle in the town. But in this fact we must see not only the toughness that enabled them to preserve their Reformed heritage, but also their refusal to forget the injustice of the Counter-Reformation and the brutal "Christian" solution of sending Protestant ministers to the galleys. Among the forty-one Hungarian ministers who served as galley slaves, twelve are known to have been students of the Reformed College of Debrecen. Later, in the eighteenth century, Debrecen was ready to take Slovakian and German students of the Lutheran faith as well as Romanian and Serbian youth of the Greek Catholic religion. To be honest,

---

the *Presbyterian Order* (Geneva: World Presbyterian Alliance, 1954), p. 130. Cited by Alan P. F. Sell, *Our Unity in Christ and Our Differences from One Another* (Manuscript, 1996).

11. Imre Révész, *Yesterday and Today and Forever . . .* (Debrecen: Coetus Theologorum, 1944), p. 358 (in Hungarian).

really good relationships with Roman Catholics had not developed before the turn of the previous century. Even today, we do not understand everything in the history of the Reformed people of Debrecen. They insisted on the Second Helvetic Confession that was accepted in 1567, and then took up and spread the Heidelberg Catechism quickly, no doubt with the words of Jesus in mind: "And other sheep I have, which are not of this fold . . ." (John 10:16). The people of Debrecen might have become cautious or even distrustful because of their own historical memories, and it took some time before they let Jesus' warning turn into practice.

The situation is completely different today. The walls have been broken through, but they are not broken down yet. Ecumenicity has been making progress in the right direction, taking huge steps forward, and now we have occasions, events, and masses jointly organized by the denominations, which we would not have dreamed of two or three decades ago. Identity and ecumenicity have now become a harmonizing factor in our everyday lives. Furthermore, the more we define our identity, the better we can live up to our ecumenical openness in practice. But in Hungary, and therefore in Debrecen, too, we still lack the dialogue with Roman Catholic theologians that would clarify basic questions concerning church unity, such as issues arising from the recent papal encyclical letter, *Ut Unum Sint,* and its interpretation — which, it appears to me, goes back to the period before Pope John XXIII.[12] It seems as if it renewed the age-old concept of *Ubi papa, ibi ecclesia!,* which essentially interprets ecumenicity in a way that means all the other churches should give up their own identity. However, the very essence of ecumenicity is that it originates from the preeminent unity of the pluriform church and accepts the identity of the parts. At the practical level of the congregations it is also understood in a similar fashion, but official Roman theology sees the unity of the church differently. Supposedly, the discussion will be about the principle of whether we should proceed *from the whole towards the parts or from the parts towards the whole.* I believe the former one is the right way to be followed! Anyway, Christianity, which broke up into small confessional units, can only become Euro-compatible again if it undertakes the job of finding unity in ecumenicity and creating special individual values in its identity.

---

12. Encyclical *Ut Unum Sint,* 96-97. In Sell, *Our Unity in Christ,* p. 6: ". . . the communion of the particular Churches with the Bishop of Rome . . . is an essential requisite of full and visible communion."

The Example of Faith and Practice to Nonbelievers

As far as the colorful crowd of nonbelievers is concerned, identity and ecumenicity turn out to be relevant after all. It is an extremely complicated problem in our country. Political lines of force, emotion, and intention are still difficult to get to know, with respect to who wishes to support or hinder the activities of the church, and when, why, or how they want to do it. The scientific respect for Reformed theology has been preserved thus far in the frame of the *universitas scientiarum*. However, it has been a major problem that, in a mistaken social approach, Christianity is seen as a system of ideological and moral principles, and therefore each political system has tried to find favor with the church. Certain groups even outlined their expectations of the church, although this is now gradually disappearing. At present it seems there are no spectacular results in the missionary destiny of the church, in all likelihood because there are evident political, historical, social, economic, and moral problems, and the resulting disturbance of identity in a nation in transition. Unfortunately the church, too, has been unable to deal adequately with these problems. Even so, the church should be aware that it does not exist for itself alone; it does not have its mission for itself, but for the glory of God and the good of the world. In the present situation, the Apostle Paul's words — "a wide door for effective work has opened to me . . ." (1 Cor. 16:9) — can serve as a directive for the church in the service of those, too, who do not live in faith. In other words, there is an opportunity here to preach the true gospel.

How Does a Person of the Reformed Faith Look at the World?

The biblical account according to which God created the world out of nothing has been extremely useful in the development of scientific thinking and has had far-reaching consequences. In fact, natural science is indebted to the Christian approach to nature, and it is due to science that European civilization could become a power with a strong impact on all other civilizations. All the peoples of the world are in a hurry to acquire this scientific culture, and it seems that the better they can apply it in their own contexts, the more successful they are. There will come a time when it will be taught why such a civilization first developed in Europe. It will also be asked what is behind this "European miracle." And it will be impossible to answer this question if Christian theological notions are ignored.

Classical mechanistic science could not have been developed on the basis of Greek thought alone. The Greek dualistic way of thinking held that the only things existing in reality were necessary and timelessly true conceptual forms, which were associated with divine character. The natural world was degraded into a realm of existence insufficient for and unworthy of the intellect. Christianity, on the basis of biblical teaching, brought a new approach in which the material world is also truly real, as God created the world out of nothing and endowed it with a rational order of its own. Moreover, God appreciated this world so highly that he entered into its full reality in incarnation. Theologically this idea was elaborated in detail by Thomas F. Torrance, who explained it by saying that the created universe has a contingent rationality; i.e., due to the Christian approach, nature had become reality, which could be investigated by the human mind, interrogated by way of experiments, and recognized empirically. Newton had the same opinion, but in his system, too, there was a certain kind of dualism: an identification of space and time with the omnipresence and eternity of God, respectively. In the Reformed Maxwell's electromagnetic theory this mechanistico-dualistic approach had already disappeared to open the way towards Einstein-type thinking. Thus the "invention of the temporospatial object" resulted. But the formation of adequate concepts about the universe is not over yet. It is the theologians professing the Reformed heritage, headed by Karl Barth, who have most strongly emphasized that, by being a creation itself, the human mind comprehending the world also belongs to this spatio-temporal material world. This kind of relationship is an original Christian idea. The world is not its own cause; it is not a self-explaining reality. Its laws are contingent in the same way that human intelligence is contingent. To use a philosophical term, the twentieth century's "epistemological revolution in theology" was accomplished by Reformed theologians demonstrating the biblical idea that our intelligence is congruent with the created universe and the Word is congruent with God, the Creator and Savior. Consequently, the order of the universe, its beginning in time, the teleological nature of its laws, and a unified approach to the universe make us see the consonance between modern scientific interpretation and Christian intuition. Each component of the universe is itself composed in such a way that it has an inherent order and an upwardly open structure. As the human intellect is of a similar nature, the truth comprehended by intellect will take us closer and closer to the reality of the world, but it will not be able to reach this reality in its perfect form. It is clear that this approach will not only bring disparate fields of science closer to one another, but will also eliminate the discontinuities between them, resulting in higher development of all fields of science — and of theology too.

The openness of high level, global European culture has given rise to such rapid development in all fields of science that it has had a favorable effect on Christian intuitions. Reformed theology has been exceptionally sensitive to this change. On the one hand, it has had to rethink what roots it feeds from and what values it represents within the sphere of the one catholic church. On the other hand, it has had to inspect its theological structure to see if it can meet the requirements of future development. Let us meditate for a short while on what enormous progress has been seen in medicine, space research, and informatics! Compared to twenty or thirty years ago, our human habitat, or in a bit broader sense, our microenvironment, has turned into a real laboratory. But if we consider our macroenvironment, we see that we live in a huge laboratory in which events are broadcast by satellite into every home from all corners of the globe and beyond. We are also knit together by informatics.

Unfortunately, the situation is not rosy in every aspect. Seeing this kind of relationship between man and the universe, theologians should think seriously about Einstein's warning: that mankind lives from the laboratories and not the oratories. But Einstein also wanted to show that we need to get back the oratories if it did not want to die in the laboratories.[13] Various twentieth-century events have proven him right. Intellectually, man has grown up to his own technical and scientific creation in many respects, but from a moral point of view he has remained a child. Today, this gap is characteristic of billions of people.

Unfortunately, Debrecen, my hometown, is no exception. High morals in the workplace, which were set as a goal over four hundred years ago, are still lacking in many areas. Individual interests have rendered the service of the people, nation, and immediate community as fifth-rate. I do not even dare to mention biblicity, as it is understood only by faithful members of the congregation and appreciated only by a small segment of the educated secular layer. In both individual and public life, there are only fragments of what was once called the sacredness of life. Today everyone thinks in terms of democracy and plurality, but in many cases they conceal a mediocre moral sense and a shallow desire for individual success. By now the number of active church members has decreased, to about 10 to 15 percent of the town's population. This figure includes all denominations. This "remnant" should remind the citizens of the town of the ancestors' exemplary faith, diligent work, love of country, spirit of sacrifice, and morally pure ambitions. They should also mention that Debrecen has become a significant town through its cultivation of science and its love for culture, having given Hungary its greatest number of poets and writers. Debrecen was perhaps the most respected town in Hungary from the beginning of the second half of the sixteenth century until the end of the first quarter of the nineteenth century, because of its school, the College of Debrecen. This school, out of which the university eventually grew, was founded and maintained by the Reformed citizens of Debrecen. The town thus became one of the greatest cultural centers of Hungary as a result of its Reformed spirit. To become an ex-

13. Cited by Ferenc Mádl in "The Responsibility of Professors," *Debreceni Szemle* 2 (1998): 183 (in Hungarian).

emplary town again, a modern, Reformed way of thinking, an authentic Christian way of life, and ecumenical relations based on love and moral strictness would be necessary, accompanied by basic changes that could renew public thinking and bring back some of the puritan sanctity.

Closing Thoughts

I would like to place two citations here, one by Comenius and the other from the Second Helvetic Confession.

> All the reformations of the church up to the present time (originated by Wiclef, Hus, Luther, Calvin, Menno, and Socinus, and even several times by the pope), were just the first act of the healing of the blind man by Christ (Mark 8:19, 22-23); now it is necessary to have a perfect and universal reformation, which would represent the second act of Christ's healing, by which the blind man was restored to sight, so that he saw everything clearly (vv. 24 and 25); or, at least, the next one should be as perfect as the church of Philadelphia giving to the whole world light, peace and salvation. . . . When and who will try to bring about such a universal reformation? I answer the question: By the will of God and with general consent all will try to bring about such a universal reformation as we long for, a reformation of all in all by all means in that universally expected Council of the Church. . . .[14]

> We solemnly announce in the presence of everybody, that . . . we are ready to obey and thank all those who use the Word of God to improve us and follow them, glory be to God! March 1st, 1566[15]

The Reformation that took place in Debrecen fulfilled its historic mission, and as we have seen, it has been changed over the centuries in hard times. Its inwardness has been modified in several ways, and there are congregations that still preserve the values of this heritage. This is the "remnant according to the election of grace" (Rom. 11:5) who will face an even more serious and more difficult mission in the future, as the Reformation is not a chronologically limited period or a completed historic action. It is not even a special and unique event, but a long historic process; only its most apparent and brightest events took place in the sixteenth century. The Reformation was only a start, as may be

14. Jan Amos Comenius (1592-1670) is cited by Milan Opocensky, General Secretary of the WARC, in his 1999 New Year's circular (source not identified).

15. *Second Helvetic Confession,* Preface, Református (Budapest: Zsinati Iroda, 1965). (Translated into Hungarian by Béla Szabadi.)

noted in the spirit of Comenius and the Reformers who composed the Second Helvetic Confession. Since then, undeniably, continual reformation has been going on in both the Roman Catholic and the Protestant churches. Owing to the openness of the principle, *semper reformari,* the reformation of modern, twenty-first-century Christianity is attained as we better understand the Word of God. The identity and ecumenical nature of theology carrying the Reformed heritage is found in this openness, and the correlation of these two features determines its view of the future, which is correct only if it projects within us a continual reforming process — from the future to the prevailing present.

CHAPTER 14

Calvinism as an Ascetic Movement

A. van de Beek

When engaged in thinking about topics that touch on Calvinism's identity and ecumenicity, it must be made clear from the very beginning that Calvin's theology is deeply rooted in the ecumenical tradition. Even a seemingly apparent singularity such as the "extra calvinisticum" is not at all specific to Calvinism, as the whole of orthodox patristic tradition supports it.[1] Nevertheless, Calvinism does have its own accents and contributions to ecumenicity. Sensibility to freedom could be considered one example.[2] In this article I will highlight another aspect that, in my opinion, is not only characteristic of Calvinism, but also of importance for the whole church and ultimately for the whole world: the ascetic nature of Calvinism.

This article reflects my own position on this subject. But I have formulated it as a person coming out of the Reformed heritage, being strongly influenced by Reformed tradition and finding words and concepts in Calvin's texts. However, it is not my intention to study Calvin, but rather to express that which, in my opinion, is important to offer ecumenicity as a contribution from a Reformed theologian. Thus I am not so much looking to the past as to the future. Starting with Calvin, I will develop my own thought, which in a different cultural and theological context has its own Reformed shape.

---

1. See A. van de Beek, *Jezus Kurios: de christologie als hart van de theologie* (Kampen: Kok, 1998), pp. 49-53.
2. See A. van Egmond and D. van Keulen, eds., *Freedom*, Studies in Reformed Theology 1 (Baarn: Callenbach, 1996).

What Sort of Asceticism?

If we consider Calvinism from the perspective of asceticism, it is important to keep clearly in mind what the nature of the asceticism is that we are talking about. By asceticism here we do not mean withdrawal from the world. It is not the asceticism of the hermit, who can devote himself to piety (or at least make a try at attaining it) in splendid isolation. It is not the asceticism of the monk, who in his vows renounces certain things. Calvinism is in principle at odds with exactly this sort of asceticism, because it distrusts it. Because our whole life lies under the power of sin, we have no option of renouncing certain things, as if by doing so the rest automatically would be consecrated. On the contrary, pious asceticism arises from the sin of pride. When people want to keep the world at a distance by retreating into splendid isolation, they take the whole world along within themselves. Every attempt to escape from the world is doomed to failure before it begins, because as human beings we can never escape from ourselves. You are the world. No fiber of your being can be withdrawn from it.

Thus asceticism in the Calvinistic sense has nothing to do with withdrawing from the world or abstaining from certain things. On the contrary, Calvinism stands completely in the world. But it stands there in a certain way. It is the way of "innerweltliche Askese"[3] or as Calvin used to say: of "renouncing the world."[4] A Calvinist cannot uncritically indulge himself in the world, not even in one part of his life after having freed himself from another part. Our best works are still defiled by sin,[5] through which all is sullied. With this, we come to a crucial point: the evil that we would have to abstain from is not a quality of the world outside us, or of certain aspects of it, but is intrinsic in ourselves. We make the world evil. Every action with regard to the world, every thought about the world has something of evil in it, not because the world is evil, but because it is an action or thought of a person who has something of evil within him or herself. That requires distance in our dealing with the world, because if we go our merry way uncritically, then we will spoil everything. Thus every act and every thought with respect to the world must be accompanied with a critical

---

3. Max Weber, "Die protestantische Ethik und der Geist des Kapitalismus," in *Gesammelte Aufsätze zur Religionssoziologie*, vol. 1 (Tübingen: Mohr, 1920), pp. 84-163. Cf. also Dietrich Bonhoeffer, *Widerstand und Ergebung: Briefe aus der Haft*, ed. Eberhard Bethge (München: Kaiser Verlag, 1970), p. 176.

4. Cf. Oepke Noordmans, *Herschepping: Beknopte handleiding voor godsdienstige toespraken en besprekingen* (Zeist: NCSV, 1934), p. 173: "Indulgence in life of any description, the so-called 'full life' of a modern, of a modern Calvinistic and culture-moral world too, is an impiety."

5. Heidelberg Catechism, q. 62; cf. also q. 13: "We increase our debt each day."

second thought. That is true for myself as an individual, for people as a group or humanity as a whole, and that is also true for other individuals.

God and Humankind

Now, this self-knowledge on the part of humankind does not stand in isolation. It is closely connected with true knowledge of God. Knowledge of God and knowledge of oneself are, according to Calvin, two sides of the same coin.[6] If I know God as my Creator, to whom I am indebted for everything, then I see myself as a tiny and even more impious human being. And if I see myself as such a human being, then I realize the goodness of the God who sustains my life.[7]

In Calvin's theology, the greatness of God comes before all else. Only by proceeding from that can one understand his thought. This is not just the greatness of God's power, but also of his goodness and grace. From the side of humankind, this means complete dependence and surrender. We honor God in the recognition of this dependence. That is precisely the destiny of humankind: to honor God. We must not think of that in the sense of a harsh ruler standing on his honor and demanding tokens of his good will from his subjects. It is rather the opposite: if we know God, we can not help but praise Him for the greatness of his power, which is the power of his grace.[8] Anyone who lives with this God can only adore his goodness and love, because God concerns himself with insignificant human beings. They are never out of his mind.[9]

Calvin's anthropology reflects the understanding of the beginnings of the new era after the Middle Ages, which Pascal so powerfully put into words: insignificant man in endless space.[10] Calvin, however, does not shudder as Pascal, because though a small human, he knows himself secure in the care of God. To the degree that the universe becomes larger, human beings become smaller — but at the same time, for Calvin, the God who has created the heavens and the earth, the entire universe, becomes all the greater.[11] This greatness is not premised alone on his being Creator of this ever-expanding universe, in which the earth can only become relatively smaller. Rather, God is especially great because as the mighty Creator he knows and preserves humankind, so that not a hair

6. John Calvin, *Institutes of the Christian Religion,* trans. Ford Lewis Battles and ed. John T. McNeill (Philadelphia: Westminster, 1960), 1.1.

7. Calvin, *Institutes* 1.1 and 2.1.

8. Calvin, *Institutes* 1.17.6.

9. Calvin, *Institutes* 1.16.3.

10. Blaise Pascal, *Pensées, d'après l'édition de M. Brunschvigg,* ed. É. Boutroux and V. Giraud (Paris: Dent), no. 206, p. 94.

11. See Calvin's Commentary on Genesis 1:16.

falls from my head without him. Whoever recognizes this situation, learns as a human to honor God humbly. Like Augustine, Calvin does not tire of calling for humility.

This call is also desperately necessary at the end of the twentieth century, as humans have little inclination to humility. They rather seek after greatness. They constantly nourish the delusion of human power and potential. People want to get ahead. They want that at the expense of each other, at the expense of creation, at the expense of God. Anyone with an eye for human history and for human behavior can offer examples by the dozen. Anyone who knows themselves has noted the hidden mechanisms that shape our decisions. For Calvin, the root sin is human pride.[12] And I think he is right.[13] Humans want to be like God. They want to shape their own lives. They do not wish to be dependent. They wish to be free, and it is precisely in this urge for independence that they lose everything. They lose their social relations, because every other person degenerates into a resource for one's own self-realization. God too becomes only a means to that end. Religion becomes a form of self-realization. God becomes the transcendent fulfillment of our constant urge to self-transcendence. Therefore it is precisely in religion that the highest form of pride, and thus of sin and godlessness, lies. Anyone knowing the true God knows nothing of self-realization anymore, but only of his or her own insignificance — which is inseparably linked with the praise of the God who desires to love these little human beings and sustain their lives from day to day.

The Cross of Christ

How does one learn humility? Having knowledge of the Creator should be sufficient in itself. Anyone who kept their eyes open as they went through the world would see the signs of God's creative power throughout creation, and feel their own littleness.[14] But because of sin we no longer see this.[15] There is a mist

12. Calvin, *Institutes* 2.1.

13. This does not repudiate the study of Judith Plaskow, *Sex, Sin and Grace: Women's Experience and the Theologies of Reinhold Niebuhr and Paul Tillich* (Washington, D.C.: University Press of America, 1980), who exposes the Reformed stress (shared by most other theologians) on sin as pride, which tends to humiliate women. Certainly she is right. But pride can very well take on the shape of humility. In the cultural context of Christianity the role of women was to be dependent and humble. It was the pride of women to behave in that way. As the Dutch theologian O. Noordmans once said: "Nowadays every Pharisee prays with the words of the tax collector." Cf. Calvin, *Institutes* 2.1.2.

14. Confessio Belgica 2.

15. Confessio Belgica 14; Calvin, *Institutes* 1.4; 1.5.15; 1.6.1; 2.2.19.

before our eyes that prevents us from being able to see in things anything but a means to our own goal: power, and pleasure as an expression of it. In the world where sin rules over people, we learn of ourselves and God only through Scripture. And Scripture witnesses to Christ. Only in relation to him does the true life before God take shape.

It is usual in Calvinistic theology to separate the doctrine of creation and Christology from each other.[16] The doctrine of creation thus has its own structures,[17] which are revealed again in the law so that they might be clear to us. Christology then comes after that, to atone for sin. It thus defines neither the structures of the commandments, nor, still less, those of created reality. There is a difference on this between Calvin himself and neo-Calvinism. Not only are the distinctions he makes less sharp, but also in his theology creation, commandments, and Christ are intrinsically involved with each other. John Hesselink previously demonstrated that for the relation between law and Christology,[18] but the same is true for creation and Christology, as Hesselink has recently shown.[19] Against the Anabaptists, Calvin has to stress that the world, as God's work, was created good. But in their daily life Christians are guided by their relation with Christ.[20] Our experience of the world and knowledge of Christ go hand in hand. That is concentrated in the cross.[21] As Christ was crucified, we are crucified with him. That is most focused when we are persecuted for our faith, but it reaches much further. God deliberately lets us bear the cross, so that we may be freed from our pride. In bearing the cross we learn to see how far down the wrong track we were with our plans, impious or pious as they may have been. We see that we are not able to realize our own lives. Thus our ideals become sin for us, because we did not know ourselves. Therefore, like the law, bearing the cross has an educational function. That only becomes perfectly clear when we see that the cross of Christ stands in the middle of our lives: He must save us, because we cannot save ourselves. Like Calvin I would stress that knowledge of Christ and

---

16. Calvin also makes a clear distinction between knowledge of the Creator and knowledge of Christ (*Institutes* 1.2.1). But Calvin says in the same paragraph that only through Christ we can effectively know God as our Father, just as we can know the Creator clearly only through Scripture even though we should know him through his creatures. In the real situation of sin, as sketched in 1.1, Christ is the only way to God.

17. Calvin, *Institutes* 1.2.1.

18. I. John Hesselink, *Calvin's Concept of the Law* (Allison Park, Pa.: Pickwick, 1992), pp. 155-70.

19. I. John Hesselink, *Calvin's First Catechism: A Commentary*, Columbia Series in Reformed Theology (Louisville: Westminster/John Knox, 1997), pp. 62-68. Hesselink rightly states that it is impossible to play off the theses that Calvin is theocentric, christocentric, or pneumatocentric against each other (p. 118).

20. Calvin, *Institutes* 3.7.1. Cf. also the end of 2.2.1.

21. See specially Calvin, *Institutes* 3.8.

knowledge of ourselves goes hand in hand. Here too it is impossible for us to say which comes first. As with the knowledge of God and self-knowledge, they belong together, inseparable, because knowing Christ is knowing God, and knowing God is knowing Christ. How shall we ever be able to know God without him? As the Dutch theologian Oepke Noordmans put it, "Outside of Christ, the riddle of creation offers only dread."[22] The relation between Christology and anthropology is even stronger than between knowledge of God and knowledge of ourselves. For Christ is not only the revelation of God, but also the true human being. According to Calvin, it is not that Adam is the first image of God, which had to be restored by Christ, but that Christ is God's first image, in which Adam was created.[23] "The true image, therefore, is more clearly seen in Christ than in Adam, even in his pristine state."[24] So it is impossible to set up a separate anthropology first, and later a Christology. Anthropology is rooted in Christology. And as He is the image of God in whom all people are created, how could we develop an anthropology without Christology?

The cross that we are given to bear is thus goodness from God. Through the cross we are linked all the more deeply to Christ. Through the cross we learn to understand our human situation all the more deeply. And through the cross we learn all the more to worship God, who teaches people who were and are themselves lost in pride to discover their true state — and who continues to sustain them, despite their misunderstanding of themselves, of the world, and of God.[25]

In this, it is not just a matter of Christians bearing the cross, because all people have their own cross. All human beings participate in suffering, just as all are subject to sin. The difference between the Christian's life and the lives of others is not that bearing the cross is reserved for Christians, because God's goodness extends to everyone. Through the cross he would teach all people what true life is. All are called in Christ. But many wave the cross aside. They do not take it to heart. It is precisely the successful people in the world who are the most able to hide themselves and deny the cross. They shut their eyes to the true reality. They have success in the world, but ultimately they dehumanize themselves. In the end, others shovel sand on their coffin, and that is it.[26] You may be thankful, then, if the weight of the cross in your life was so great that you came to repentance. Thus you can give thanks to God for the cross.

Now, that is precisely the manner in which God deals with his children.

22. Noordmans, *Herschepping*, p. 63.
23. Hesselink, *Calvin's First Catechism*, pp. 67f.
24. Hesselink, *Calvin's First Catechism*, p. 68.
25. See also Irenaeus, *Adversus Haereses* 5.3.
26. Pascal, *Pensées*, no. 165.

So that they do not become haughty, he gives them much to bear. And because they know him who was crucified for their guilt, their eyes are open to what is wrong in the world. In the sight of the cross of Christ, we no longer have to deny our sins and the futility of our lives. We can recognize them. Therefore we become vulnerable. We see the cross in the world, not only among ourselves, but everywhere. We no longer look on in amazement when someone slips up, because we know ourselves with our own weakness — and we know the Lord who died for the sins of humankind.

In bearing the cross we learn:

1. that God loves us in our littleness and in the futility of our haughty aspirations and their sins. God looks after those who are lost.
2. to love God, not for any advantage, but purely for himself. When we lose all, we meet God in Christ on the cross. And he is abundant in grace.

Thus faith is a matter of the deepest relation of love, without conditions, without ulterior motives, without it being a step to something more. The only thing that matters to us is God, and the only thing that matters to God is us. This is not a question of a God who grants prosperity, but of a God who loves us, even if we bring him no offerings. The only offering is we ourselves, living by the grace of Christ alone. And that is the way we love other human beings.[27]

Thus the cross becomes a joy to bear.[28] That also means, then, a Christian asceticism: not exclusively critical distance, but at the same time accepting with joy what is taken away from us, and even being so free of what we might want to acquire that it is no longer our first goal, and we can fittingly do without it. A Christian can never dedicate him or herself totally to anything — not even to him or herself. God alone is a Christian's ultimate concern. And God meets you at the cross, in the midst of the loss of everything.

Being Christian does not involve the realization of an ideal. It is not following Christ in order to reach a higher and nobler form of being human. Christ is not the highest form of human achievement. "He is not the flower of creation, but He is God Himself, who has followed us in our fall."[29] We live as Christians in this low estate. And according to Irenaeus, a Christian's first task is to live constantly with death.[30] Or as the classic instruction for Baptism of the

---

27. Calvin, *Institutes* 3.7.7.

28. Petrus Dathenus, *Instruction for Baptism.*

29. Noordmans, *Herschepping*, p. 115.

30. "The business of the Christian is nothing else than to be ever preparing for death." Fragment XI from the Lost Works of Irenaeus, trans. A. Roberts and W. H. Rambaut, *The Writings of Irenaeus,* vol. 2 (Edinburgh: T. & T. Clark, 1871), p. 164.

Dutch Reformed Churches puts it, "This life is nothing other than a continual dying." But with that it says that we at last, comforted for Christ's sake, may leave that life, that we may appear without fear before him who is no stranger to us, but in whom we are secure in both life and in death. To live with Christ is to live under the cross, and you rejoice in the life to come that, as Paul says, is the best by far,[31] because we can then be with Christ in peace. The trouble we now experience is not so much the cross, as that which tempts us to avoid the cross — our worldly pursuit of greatness.

Resignation?

Does this not all lead now to quietism or even to seeking out suffering? This accusation is often leveled against orthodox Calvinism. It is even leveled against the whole of Christianity. It has been called a religion with a slave ethics.[32] I think that the latter is true. Being a Christian is so very much linked with service that it always has the form of a slave.[33] But it is the form of the slave that Luther described in *Von der Freiheit einen Christenmenschen*. Precisely because we are totally free from everyone and everything in belonging to Christ, we can give ourselves totally in service for the benefit of others. That this would lead to quietism is not correct. It is not so much a case of resignation as of being at rest: the peace of God which passes all understanding preserves our hearts and minds, even when the fiercest distress strikes us. It preserves us also from chasing the wind.

That does not say that suffering is a pleasure. Calvin is very clear about that.[34] Anyone who talks cheerfully about faith and the cross that we must bear has not learned their profundity.

Therefore Calvin is also happy with that which we receive in our cross-bearing, relative life. It is God's goodness when we receive bread.[35] It is God's goodness when we have clothing on our back and a roof over our head. It is God's goodness if we live in a well-ordered society, without violence or oppression. But this is all relative. That is not what it is all about. It is only about God. But precisely when we know that, we can be intensely thankful that he gives us so many other gifts too — and moreover gives us people around us who love us.

31. Philippians 1:23.
32. Friedrich Nietzsche, "Jenseits von Gut und Böse: Zur Genealogie der Moral," in *Nietzsche, Werke: Kritische Gesamtausgabe* 6.2, ed. Giorgio Colli and Mazzino Montinari (Berlin: de Gruyter, 1968), pp. 218-35.
33. Cf. Philippians 2:5-13.
34. Calvin, *Institutes* 3.8.9f.
35. Calvin, *Institutes* 3.20.44.

We know all too well that their love is not perfect, but we are also not living in the realm of ideals. Anyone seeking an ideal in another person is not living with real people, and is always disillusioned in the other. But those who know of the sinful nature of mankind can rejoice intensely, even be amazed at the love that another bestows on you. This amazement becomes yet greater when you note that the spell of sin and the will to power equally are broken, and that you love them for no reason — although it is but for a moment. But it is a moment that is no less than a gift of God.

With this we arrive at the following: God gives us possibilities. His gifts that we receive become possibilities, not for self-realization, but for expression of selfless, unconditional love. God gives us our bodies to give to one another. God gives us children that we may share with them the mystery of Christ. God gives us hands with which to work for our daily bread, and with it the strength to sing his praises. He gives us work so that we may earn our livelihood and that of those entrusted to us. And, as is found in the classic Dutch instruction for the wedding service, in order to have something to share with the poor.

Money

We now flush out a sensitive point in Calvinism: money. According to the wedding service instruction, money is not an object in itself, but a means for sustaining life and giving shape to our love for others. Actually, it is striking that the worship service is not mentioned here: your worship of God is not something special and apart, but is of one piece with your whole life, including your acts of charity.

In the history of Calvinism, however, money has taken on another significance. Max Weber has powerfully demonstrated the relationship between Calvinism and capitalism. Nor is he wrong.

Two aspects play a role in this:

1. The reserved attitude in life with regard to the world leads to Calvinism renouncing ostentatious display. That saves a load of money, so you can become rich. And once you are rich, you enjoy your wealth. That's just how people are — including Calvinists. Therefore Calvinists too must not save money up, but must give it away. One who begins to save is not merely going, going, but gone.
2. The emphasis on God's good creation, in which the Lord has given us, ungrateful humankind, so many gifts, assigns value to this creation. Life is worth the effort. It is a source of glory for God. Before we know it, life

here becomes worth the effort in itself — or, to put it a bit more cautiously, until we die, life here rather than eternal life becomes the primary reason to thank God. And then it is not the cross which is the true Christian life, but abundance. Then Calvinism and capitalism, Reformed theology and greed, can suddenly go together very well. The United East India Company was a colonial trading firm under the flag of the Calvinist Netherlands. They became rich from God's good gifts from Indonesia, and they left it poor. Its present rulers learned all too well from us. One of the few Dutch loan words in Indonesian is "rekening" — "bill."

The Puritans in America do not come off much better. They saw the new world for themselves: all gifts of God, to possess a new land. They got rich off of it, and now think that they can share in mastery over the world.

Even the Protestant churches do not escape from this shift from the cross to greatness. When Von Weizsäcker perceived that things were not going well with the world because of our immoderate greed and exploitation (Calvin would have fully agreed with him), he called for worldwide reflection on the part of the churches.[36] The World Council, chiefly at the urging of Calvinists, has picked up the theme and made it into a program — as if we must save the world! The only result has been a lot of airplane flights to consultations and trees felled to produce the paper for documents.

One cannot say that this is all exclusively attributable to later Calvinism, and that Calvin had no part in it. It is evident that Calvin's theology opposes worldly power and wealth. But he was no stranger to them. Only one who recognizes in himself the pride and the desire for wealth as security in an unstable world can so authentically oppose it. That is why he was so happy with what God still gave him, a doubting, ungrateful sinner, and why he was so attached to it. Daily he had to learn to die, because if you leave your desires unchallenged for a couple of days, you're all the way back to square one. Just like wild horses that at last have become used to the rein, if left out to graze for three days without feeling a harness, they are again as wild as they were before.[37]

Yet there is an essential difference between Calvin and all forms of neo-Calvinism. For Calvin, abundance was considered among the temptations. You had to constantly watch out for it and hope that God would give you enough of a cross to bear and deprive you of your wealth — if necessary that which you most love — to keep you humble, and thus that you would not lose your true

36. C. H. von Weizsäcker, *Die Zeit drängt: eine Weltversammlung der Christen für Gerechtigkeit, Frieden und die Bewahrung der Schöpfung* (München and Wien: Hanser Verlag, 1986).

37. Calvin, *Institutes* 3.8.5.

humanity.[38] Gifts are always seen from the perspective of "despite our evil"[39] and "alongside the all-important blessing He gave us in Christ." In neo-Calvinism this "despite" is no longer discernible. It sees a world that is good, by divine providence, thanks to general grace or thanks to the inspiration of the church, the individual believer, or the Spirit given to the world. The world can only have gotten better for these. With God's help we will get somewhere yet. As the Dutch saying puts it, "Thrift, with industry, builds houses like castles." At that rate, very quickly there's absolutely no need for God anymore. There is quite a difference between Calvin's continuous stress on renouncing[40] and the three heavy volumes on general grace by Abraham Kuyper. Calvin too knows of general grace. But in his short paragraph[41] on this subject he does not develop a theory about human possibilities and culture, but remembers the goodness of God who gives us what we need for our lives.

Government

The difference between classical Calvinism and its modern forms can be seen most clearly in the relation between church and government. For Calvin, government is a gift of God for the purpose of keeping the world livable.[42] People in a fallen world are inclined to all sorts of evil. If left unrestrained, they would decline into barbarianism. Governments serve to keep them in check.[43] This is a danger to which we must constantly be alert, because wild horses quickly forget the discipline of the bridle. For this reason we must accept and obey governments with thanks.

There is one exception to this: if a government moves to forbid the confession of God in Christ as our only salvation.[44] Then one must obey God rather than humans. Even then, one may not overthrow the government, because it is God's servant. The medicine would be worse than the disease.[45] One can only call the government to an understanding of its task of restraining evil

38. Calvin, *Institutes* 3.7.4: "If God has bestowed on us something not to be repented of, trusting to it, we immediately become elated, and not only swell, but almost burst with pride" (trans. H. Beveridge).

39. Calvin, *Institutes* 2.1.1.

40. Calvin, *Institutes* 3.7.2ff.

41. Calvin, *Institutes* 1.14.22.

42. Calvin, *Institutes* 4.20.1.

43. Calvin, *Institutes* 4.20.2: During our pilgrimage on earth we need laws and government in order not to lose our humanity.

44. Calvin, *Institutes* 4.20.32.

45. Calvin, *Institutes* 3.20.29.

and not doing evil itself. Here government can oppose government: out of its responsibility for the people that are entrusted to it, a lower government can resist the measures of a higher one.[46] Here, too, however, it is not a matter of abjuring the government, but of protecting people who wish to obey God rather than humans. In principle, that can cost you everything, and result in nothing more than bearing the cross. William the Silent is a classic example: out of responsibility for the people in the Low Countries, he opposed Philip II of Spain. But nonetheless Marnix of St. Aldegonde can have him say, "I have always honored the king of Spain." Far from rebelling, he seeks to preserve Philip and his government from a fatal error. That is similar to the sentiment of the letter that Guido de Bres wrote as the introduction to the Belgic Confession.

In neo-Calvinism as it was developed by Abraham Kuyper, government is a facet of common grace.[47] However, it is no longer a gracious gift of God that gives us room to breathe in the history of the cross, but a possibility for the development of the world and culture. Christians may contribute fully to this. They may stand up for their rights in society and politics. They may participate in these, and God gives them the possibilities to do so. Here we are clearly talking about emancipation. It is not a matter of losing yourself in love for others, but of self-realization.

Karl Barth's neo-orthodoxy denies the distinction between common and particular grace. There is only the one, particular grace of God. But this is certainly intended for the whole world. It is given with an eye to the kingdom of God, which is revealed in the royal man, Jesus Christ. In him we are called to a renewal of the world. We are called to become who we are: a consecrated people. Consecration here becomes something positive. It implies growth, in a positive sense.[48]

The perspective here is totally different from Calvin's. With Kuyper and Barth it is a matter of changing the world, which will become better. We can — with God's help — achieve something. We are put to work to that end. With Calvin it is a matter of restraining evil and keeping the world in the obedience to God. For him the kingdom of God is not realized in this world, but in future life. In modern thought regarding the kingdom of God, one often finds the idea that we can erect signs of it in the world. In a just society, with justice, peace, and integrity of creation, we see the beginnings of the kingdom. Calvin, however, reserves the idea of "beginnings" to the life of Christ in communion with

46. Calvin, *Institutes* 4.20.31.

47. See especially Abraham Kuyper, *De gemeene gratie III. Het practisch gedeelte* (Kampen: Kok, 1931).

48. See especially Karl Barth, *Christengemeinde und Bürgergemeinde* (Zollikon and Zürich: Evangelischer Verlag, 1946).

Christ, clearly to be distinguished from the public realm.[49] This can be shown by the core concepts used by Calvin with respect to the calling of governments and to the kingdom of God: equity *(aequitas)* and humility. Government must strive for equity, which is the goal, limit, and rule of all laws.[50] Civil society is not about the humility of Christian life, for wicked people would use this calling for their own purposes. In this world the government has to keep human interests in balance. That makes human life run smoothly and prevents us from becoming frustrated with all its consequences. But this is quite different from the reign of God in the life of his children, who die to the world and live in Christ. Equity is not about good and wrong, but a natural quality. The kingdom of God is of a different nature. There the concern is not equity, but humility. God sets up his kingdom by humbling the world and for this he uses the church,[51] in the same way as he cares for this world through equality, using government for that purpose. The only growth of a Christian is not for the purpose of building a better society, but is an effort to learn to love God. As my father put it, "A Christian certainly does grow, but like a cow's tail." I think that that is quite in line with Calvin.

Idealism

Now we come to the point upon which I think this ultimately all turns: the rejection of idealism. Modern theology (much more than modern philosophy) has the inclination to look at the world and at humankind idealistically. Only a handful of contrary figures escape from this tendency. They have, however, never gotten far in the church, because the church, like politics, wants to chalk up successes. Even if success does not put in an appearance, we must maintain the ideology that says tomorrow things will be better. In the church we agree with Immanuel Kant that God is involved with ethics. As churchmen and women we translate that as justice. But we forget what this same Kant had to say about change for the better. According to him we are often like the doctor who comes to the patient every day and says, "Today I have a medicine for you that will make you better tomorrow," until the patient finally says, "I'm dying of getting better."[52] Nor do Calvinistic churches escape this illusory ideology of improvement. Again and again we conceive programs that will make the world a

---

49. Calvin, *Institutes* 4.20.2.

50. Hesselink, *Calvin's First Catechism*, pp. 171-73.

51. Hesselink, *Calvin's First Catechism*, p. 135.

52. Immanuel Kant, "Die Streit der Fakultäten," in *Werke*, vol. 6, ed. Wilhelm Weischedel (Wiesbaden: Insel Verlag, 1964), p. 367.

better place. But in fact the patient is dying of our ministrations. The world suffers more from the medicines than from the illness. Or perhaps we should say that the greatest sickness of the world is that there are so many do-gooders making the rounds with medicines. All ideologies have wanted to improve the world. Colonialism was going to bring people the benefits of civilization, communism equality, apartheid individuality of culture. Time after time, churches and theology play an important role in this. But things do not get better in the world. They are, rather, made worse by ideologies, even that of a democratic society. And things will not get better. For generations God sent lawgivers and prophets, but it did not help things, wrote Athanasius in the fourth century.[53] I am not under the illusion that now, about sixteen hundred years later, things are any different.

As churches and theologians, we should all just shut up about this. We must acknowledge our fallen state, acknowledge that it is God who saves the godless world — or as Athanasius says, God did not come to improve the world morally, but to bear it.[54] From its very inception, Calvinism had to do battle with the Anabaptists. The Anabaptists wanted a kingdom of God on earth. They saw themselves as the vanguard of a new humanity. Such an inclination has always been around in the church. We are drunk on ideals. But let us exercise the sobriety that is in keeping with faith: ideals come to nothing. There is no new humanity and no better world. There is but one humanity, and that is the one which from the very start, from the primordial Adam, has lived under sin. This is the humanity that God took to himself in Christ. This is the world that God will save as his own. The world of God is not an ideal world, but a concrete world, as we know it from politics, from economics, from the thoughts of our own hearts and those of our opponents. Christ came, not as the flower of humanity — what would that be? — but as God who wished to share our life.

Here we come to the heart of Calvin's belief in providence: the concrete world, with its concrete history, is guided by God. There is no antithesis between the pure church and the godless world. There is no antithesis between people who live under the rule of God and people who live outside of it, because from the very beginning the whole world has been under God's dominion. He wishes to be king of this concrete world, not because it turned out better than expected, but in its most abject failure. In all the dark valleys in which we find ourselves, the Lord is with us. That is true for the dark valleys of unbearable fate, and also for the dark valleys of unbearable guilt. There the kingship of God is kingship veiled in mystery. It expresses itself in the dark fate of the cross, in dying to our own values, through which we grow in the worship of God.

53. *Contra Arianos* 3.31.
54. *Contra Arianos* 3.31.

Asceticism here means that we distance ourselves from our ideals and so-berly accept this broken world as the world willed by God. We seek no high things, but content ourselves with the simple: the world and life as we have received them, concretely, from the hand of God.

The Critique of the Cross

Calvin gave expression to this critical sobriety particularly in his theology of creation. Against the dualism of the Anabaptists and the emphasis on the church in Roman theology, that was salutary. In our time this same critical sobriety demands a shift of emphasis, because the doctrine of creation functions differently in theology. For Calvin it was a matter of the great God and dependent creation. In his doctrine of creation it is a question of insignificant humankind which nevertheless is God's glory. In contemporary theology a theology of creation means much more that humankind conducts itself according to, and may be inspired by divine might. God is the guarantee of at least the possibility of a better future. Faith in the Creator does not bring modern Christians to an ascetic distance as it did Calvin ("renouncing the world"), but rather to complete acceptance of life, which is good in itself. The doctrine of creation stands apart from the *meditatio futurae vitae,* unless that *futurum* is the historical future of our earthly history. In this context it is necessary to move to center stage accents that are certainly present in Calvin, but less central. That is true especially for the connection between the doctrine of creation and Christology. In order to let the critical notes sounded by Calvin be heard again in our day, in which theology is deeply involved with the ideology of improving the world, we must centrally emphasize that the Creator is no other God than we know in Christ.[55]

That, too, however, must be further qualified. We do not mean here a mediatorship with creation as this is taught chiefly in Anglican and Eastern theology. There Christ is the highest principle of creation, and he stands for power or might. I am talking about Christ the Crucified, God come down to bear our affliction and guilt. It is there that we know God and know ourselves. It is thus very concretely a matter of a worldview in the perspective of the cross, the cross being understood as a place of suffering, of sin and of judgment.

We look at the world in that perspective. That implies a critical stance at all times. The world is never entirely what it seems, because people seek the beautiful illusion. The cross always digs behind that. Therefore you are, as a Christian, always an outsider — but at the same time you are not, because you

55. On this, in extenso, see A. van de Beek, *Jezus Kurios.*

are just as much a part of the world as anyone else. You are also a critical outside observer of yourself, because you have heard the Word of God, which works to strip masks away. The final say no longer belongs to your surroundings, but rather to the Word which the Spirit teaches us to understand is the ultimate Truth.

Flip Theron, from Stellenbosch, South Africa, has expressed this situation in the idea of "paroikia." The church consists of resident aliens. Being a resident alien is something different from being a pilgrim. Pilgrims have a destination, toward which they make their way. Resident aliens live in the midst of others, and at the same time that is where their home is. They do not belong to the society, but it is still the only place they have to live. As a Christian, you are entirely a part of this world, and yet you are always a bit at odds with it. That is the typical Calvinistic attitude toward life,[56] and that is also the distinction from neo-Calvinism.

This implies that we cannot build a Christian society, let alone a Calvinist one. Cromwell's experiment did not become Calvinist. It was certainly critical of others, but not of itself. It also means that we can develop no theological program that will offer a perspective for a good church or a good society. Rather it means we must have a critical stance in our theological thinking. A critical stance also means one that keeps all things in proper perspective. That is really true asceticism. We accept that our exegesis of Scripture is relative, that we cannot subject it to any system or method. We look critically at the church, which accentuates its offices and structures too heavily. We look critically too at "free" Christians, who think they can live without structures, or who think that through the Spirit they have truth wholly in their possession.

Calvinism is by nature distrustful. It distrusts well-presented ideals. It distrusts tight systems. It distrusts idols. It distrusts the pious. It distrusts the world. It distrusts the church at least as strongly, because it consists of fallible people. It distrusts the church particularly if the church does not constantly give the appearance of being critically conscious of itself. But a Calvinist most of all distrusts himself, especially if he begins to think things are going reasonably well with himself — because this is not a matter of our goodness. Only one is good, and that is God. Only one thing matters, and that is that God is honored. A Calvinist even distrusts the proposition that God is good or that God is love, if these are not further qualified, because before you know it we have created our own concept of God, who is not the Creator of this concrete world, so that we do not have to bear the very real cross within it. We are not done with God that easily. Calvinism knows the disputation of the Psalms and of Job. It is

56. Cf. Calvin speaking of Christians being aliens in the realm of human society, *Institutes* 4.20.2.

no stranger to the question, "Oh God, where is your fidelity, where is your glory?"

Now, all this distrust would seem to lead to a negative attitude in life. That is anything but the case, because it is precisely *this* world that God loves. He came into this world.[57] He has borne this world, and bears it still, for all time. This world is God's world. Therefore we can accept ourselves. I do not have to hide my failures, my guilt. Nor will I flaunt them. On the contrary, in the sight of God I am too deeply wounded by them to do that. But I know that in the middle of death I am bound to Christ. If I know myself in that way, I will no longer be surprised at the guilt of others. I will not be surprised if someone who appears to be an ideal Christian is unmasked as a scoundrel. He is not the less Christian for that, because God can even use evil — most of all, to free people from their pride. And let us have no illusions: when your pride is crucified, that is a deep pain, and only in that comes the joy of the glory of God.[58]

Those who assume a critical attitude toward the world like this have no need to practice asceticism as a particular virtue. Life for them is asceticism enough. One could even argue that organized asceticism is a flight from the hardest asceticism of all: seeing normal reality for what it is. One who sees the refugees of Africa, the orphan children of Romania, the devastated lives of incest victims, the degeneracy of tyrants, the powerlessness of his or her own ideals, does not need to seek further disengagement. Rather, it becomes a matter of finding acceptance: that it is this world, and no other, which is loved by God.

If I know myself and others in this way, I can also deal with others in acceptance. I will not let the world pull the wool over my eyes — although it always happens to me again, just like him, who knew what sort of character Judas was, to let himself be betrayed by Judas.[59] I will not hate others because they have deceived me, because I know myself. But what is more: I know myself to be accepted by Christ as a sinner, and so can accept the other, even if he or she bears the fine semblance of the Pharisee.

Calvinistic theology for the twenty-first century has no other task than to set forth that God has come into the world in Christ and that he came to his own.

Calvin took aim at the Anabaptist idea of a church that already lives in glory now through the Spirit. The Anabaptists wanted a church that was free from the darkness of the world. Calvin opposed that with his theology of creation: this world is God's world. In the dark course of history, God moves in

57. See on this idea Irenaeus, *Adversus Haereses* 5.2.
58. Hebrews 12:1-13.
59. Hippolytus, *Contra Noetum* 18.

mysterious ways. Therefore life can be joyful. At the same time, through his emphasis on creation Calvin took aim at the Roman Catholic idea that the church and God's revelation to the world coincide. With regard to that assertion, the Anabaptists and the Roman Catholics were actually close to one another, since they both too closely identified God and the church. It's just that their ideas about the church were different. For the Anabaptists the true believers were the church; for the Romans it was the official hierarchy. Calvin, in contrast, argued the kingship of God over the whole world. God is not tied to the church or to true Christians. Even the Scripture is not tied to the church, but precedes it, even as the Spirit is bound to the Word. Also, though it does so more clearly and transparently, the Scripture witnesses to nothing other than the witness about God found in the whole of creation. As we already said earlier, the problem does not lie in creation, but in ourselves, specifically in our understanding blinded by sin.

Calvin's emphasis on God as the mighty Creator thus serves to combat a *theologiae gloriae*. It focuses on making us understand that we, as poor, tiny, and sinful human beings, live only thanks to this God, who will be God of the whole world. His theology has been cleansed of every form of idealism.

If we would carry forward the Calvinist tradition for the twenty-first century, we cannot just pass on the same theologoumena at the same place. If we would do that, we would lose sight of the fact that our situation is wholly different from Calvin's. For a large part of the world, secularism has become or is becoming the dominant culture. Moreover, the church has become worldly. If the Calvinist tradition wants to have a unique contribution to make in worldwide ecumenical theology, it will have to reflect on what, in fidelity to its roots, its gift could be in worldwide Christian theology.

Before all else, this contribution is the critical distance with respect to all-too-easy identifications and claims.

CHAPTER 15

A Proposal for Pedagogical Strategies in Theological Education in the Reformed Tradition

Leanne Van Dyk

Tolerance is very low in these supposedly postmodern times for universal claims and generalizing statements. The particular is in. The common or collective is out. The thesis of this paper concerning theological education is thus a modest one. No claims for completeness are made; rather, the approach is exploratory and suggestive. The paper proposes an approach to theological education that takes seriously both the doctrinal and confessional continuities of the Reformed tradition as well as certain contemporary challenges for theology, challenges faced not only by theologians but by the seminary student as well. The concern of this paper is focused primarily on the seminarian and the pedagogical strategies best suited to engage the interests and commitments of the seminarian. The proposal is made that an ecumenical, global Reformed identity can be best nurtured by a pedagogy that takes a contextual, dispositional, and missional approach. Each of these concepts will be articulated in turn.

Generational Markers of the Seminary Student

Because my interest in this paper is primarily the seminary student and the pedagogy best suited to reach that student, a brief précis of recent cultural and sociological analyses of the so-called Generation X is needed, the group widely represented in seminary populations.[1] The literature of analysis for this genera-

1. Generational labeling, intended to clarify cultural analysis, is itself a disputed issue. La-

tion is both vast and varied.[2] Any account of a whole generation, even a thorough one, relies heavily on generalizations and oversimplifications. The purpose of this brief synopsis is only to indicate the geography of the literature and investigate its relevance to theological education.

One useful summary of Generation X is the "four primary themes" of the generation identified in a book by Tom Beaudoin. These themes — antiinstitutionalism, experience, suffering, and ambiguity — deeply shape religious attitudes, expectations, and practices.[3] Sociologists are not the only ones interested in generational characteristics and identities. Marketing specialists and advertisers study the characteristics of each generation of consumers. For maximum profits, they have learned to pitch blue jeans and cars differently to the Boomers than to the X-ers.

The generational "markers" of Generation X, as W. Smith and A. Clurman point out, are those events that shape a collective experience and influence generational attitudes and values.[4] For Gen X-ers, those markers include the explosive growth of computer technology and online information, the initial euphoria over the dismantling of the Berlin Wall and subsequent disillusionment over continued global conflicts and tensions, Waco, Texas, and Oklahoma City, Jack Kevorkian, O. J. Simpson, and the Central Park jogger. These generational markers have influenced today's twentysomethings and thirtysomethings in ways that theological education would be wise to acknowledge. Influences include fragmentation, suspicion of tradition and authority, and uncertainty. As a response to uncertainty and ambiguity, seminary students in this generation sometimes seek overly simplistic paradigms for thinking and evaluating. Deep, often unexamined, wounds from family breakdowns also inhibit critical, nuanced thinking within the seminary context.

Faced with these broad cultural influences that shape, and even hinder, some seminary students' abilities to engage in the kind of honest, careful, rigor-

---

bels include Boomers, Busters, Gen X-ers, Gen Y-ers. For the purpose of this paper, I will use the term Gen X-ers to refer to young adults in their twenties and early thirties.

2. A sample of such literature includes George Barna, *Baby Busters: The Disillusioned Generation* (Chicago: Northfield, 1994); K. Bergeron, "The Virtual Sacred," *New Republic* 212, no. 9 (1995): 29-34; Douglas Coupland, *Generation X: Tales for an Accelerated Culture* (New York: St. Martin's Press, 1991); William Mahedy and Janet Bernardi, *A Generation Alone: Xers Making a Place in the World* (Downers Grove, Ill.: InterVarsity, 1994); and Wade C. Roof, *A Generation of Seekers: The Spiritual Journeys of the Baby Boom Generation* (New York: HarperCollins, 1993).

3. Tom Beaudoin, *Virtual Faith: The Irreverent Spiritual Quest of Generation X* (San Francisco: Jossey-Bass, 1998), p. xvii.

4. J. Walker Smith and Ann Clurman, *Rocking the Ages: The Yankelovich Report on Generational Marketing* (New York: HarperBusiness, 1997).

ous theological reflection expected for preparation for ministry, the theological educator has two choices. The one is to persist in traditional models of pedagogy, transmitting the riches of the Reformed tradition and hope the students will claim these riches as their own. Sometimes, of course, this happens. Every teacher knows that moment when the light bulb goes on in a student's eyes. Theological learning and reflection has its own inner coherence and beauty that is bound to ignite even culturally jaded and cynical students.

The other choice, however, is to think carefully about alternative pedagogies that might more directly address the challenges of Generation X. Teaching the great doctrines of the Reformed tradition, even in ways that are creative and committed, bumps up against thick barriers of suspicion of tradition and indifference to authority. This paper is intended as a pedagogical strategy — how to engage the interests, motivate the passions, and incubate the seminary student into a theological view of the world informed by the deep currents of the Reformed tradition. The three themes identified — contextual, dispositional, missional — are, of course, only partially and suggestively sketched. Nothing like a complete and detailed educational theory with these themes is attempted. Specialists in educational theory may well find these themes too abstract for any helpful pedagogical strategy. Their own work does the hard work of evaluating concrete practices of pedagogy, including multimedia instruction, various learning styles of the student, goals, objectives, and assessments. My pedagogical suggestions are more perspectival than material. They are motivated by my goal to make the biblical and theological foundations of the Reformed tradition accessible to a generation of theological students that will then further the future of Reformed theology in an ecumenical, global context.

The Theme of Context

The first pedagogical strategy to further the Reformed tradition is a keen awareness of context. There has been much discussion about contextualization in recent years. Far from a passing fad, the inherently contextual nature of all theological reflection informs the critical task of theology. This task not only takes into account the context in which theological reflection operates, but also the context of the learner of theology, the seminary student.

A keen contextual awareness must be appropriated most directly by the dominant traditions and voices of the broad Reformed tradition. Dominant theological voices cannot aspire to voice all contexts of faith and witness. Heidelberg, Tübingen, Edinburgh, Chicago, and Princeton, for example, justly proud of their long heritage in Christian theology, must practice the skill of scrutinizing their own contexts and the shaping influences such contexts exert on theology and theological education. They must identify their own context. For an American contextualized theology, this means identifying the particular influences of American history, ethos, privilege, and power on ecclesial identity and theological attitudes.

In his book, *Thinking the Faith*, Douglas John Hall recalls the 1975 conference in Detroit, Michigan, of South American and North American theologians.[5] The conference issued a report, a manifesto for contextualized theology, which stated, "The future of North American theology concerns many people today, especially those who are preoccupied with the concepts of pluralism and the contextualization of theology. . . . This seems for many Christians the right time to develop more authentic North American theologies . . . the U.S. dominates a large part of the world in economic and technological power. There must be a critical Christian word addressed to the great human issues that arise just from that fact. . . . North American theology has to be concerned with the deeper questions of how to speak of Christ in the midst of the ongoing moral crisis of the U.S."[6] Hall continues in his own words, "What the moment demands of us is not that we produce theologians capable of competing in the intellectual Olympics of the world church, but that we raise up a community of thinking Christians who are able to bear prophetic witness to the truth of God as it manifests itself in the life of the world — not some theoretical world, and not somebody else's world, but our world, the problematic First World."[7]

What Hall — and others — see as the unique challenge of a North American theology is to face the imposing implications of a specifically North American context. The implications of an American and Canadian contemporary identity are acute — more acute, in many ways, for the American context than the Canadian one. Such an identity includes the features of a Promethean optimism, a stubborn triumphalism, an isolated individualism — all of which have shaped the ecclesial and theological context in North America. Such a legacy, far from producing a people happy and fulfilled, at home in their own skins and in their own land, has resulted in a violent society, deeply disillusioned, profoundly cynical, thoroughly suspicious. There is no commitment to the common good, the good society. It is a society divided, rootless, cynical, soul-less, utterly secular. It is in this context that a contemporary Reformed theology must find voice.

Douglas John Hall suggests four guidelines for a contextual theology in a North American setting. They are framed in the form of questions. First, who are the victims of our society? Hall notes that this question is profoundly

---

5. Douglas John Hall, *Thinking the Faith* (Minneapolis: Augsburg Press, 1989).
6. Hall, *Thinking the Faith*, p. 18.
7. Hall, *Thinking the Faith*, p. 20.

threatening to First World people — including First World Christian theologians. For if this question ought to guide our theologies, it means that we must become witnesses against our own nation, our own class, our own privilege. It is far easier to take refuge in abstract and timeless formulations than engage in this hard work.

Second, how is our society depicted by its most reflective members? How is the *Zeitgeist* expressed by the artists, the poets, the playwrights, the philosophers, the social scientists? These people are not, of course, immune to the pressures that shape the cultural ethos — but theologians ought to pay attention to these cultural commentators. The voice of William Finnegan, for example, in his recent book *Cold New World,* gives a chilling and alarming portrayal of the economically disadvantaged youth in America's inner cities.[8] Such a portrayal of hopelessness, aimlessness, apathy, and pessimism ought to notify theologians that "business as usual" is not possible. The contrasts of American privilege and power with American apathy and nihilism are acute. A contextualized theology must respond to such a context explicitly.

Third, how do the pursuits and values of our society compare with the images of the human person in our authoritative sources — our Scripture and our tradition? In short, what is the difference between the dominant cultural vision of American society and the vision of shalom and human flourishing in the scriptures? In her book *By the Renewing of Your Minds,* Ellen Charry proposes a compelling resource for employing this guideline. She mines the rich vein of biblical, patristic, and Reformation sources for instruction in theological reflection — this for the purpose of reclaiming the vision-forming, virtue-developing, person-shaping scope of Christian theology. Her book is, implicitly, a contextual theology. Charry challenges the prevailing cultural standards of happiness and success. These things are not indexed to wealth, prestige, success, power, status, or possessions. Rather, happiness is indexed to character formation, specifically, to knowing, enjoying, and loving God. Here the rich traditions of the past can serve as markers and guides in a contextual theology.[9]

Fourth, what is the problem of our culture? There is, as one might expect, a range of problems identified by cultural interpreters of North American culture — both American and Canadian. Douglas John Hall identifies the cultural malaise in North America as a prison of optimism. Optimism has reached its end, yet the culture has no other vision — optimism and the bitter despair that results when optimism does not achieve its promise is the culture predicament that a contextualized theology must address.

8. William Finnegan, *Cold New World* (New York: Random House, 1998).
9. Ellen Charry, *By the Renewing of Your Minds: The Pastoral Function of Christian Doctrine* (New York: Oxford University Press, 1997).

Other cultural interpreters identify postmodernism as the prevailing cultural problem — the fragmentation, the relativism, the loss of meaning, the absence of community. Others refute this diagnosis and suggest instead that, far from being postmodern, North American culture is hyper-modern. Anthony Giddens, for example, in his book *The Consequences of Modernity*, argues that the increasing speed of technological developments puts pressure on contemporary culture in ways that intensify modern patterns, not replace them.[10]

The variety — even contradiction — of cultural diagnoses is not surprising.

Contextual theology must, however, demonstrate that it has been shaped by its attention to the problems of the culture. Likewise, contextual theologians must be genuinely aware of cultural problems and patterns and be able to give an account of how their theological reflection is informed by that awareness. In addition, theological education that is attentive to context must make cultural particularity vivid to seminary students — not only so they can better understand themselves but, even more, so they can understand the challenges and joys of their Christian witness to the culture.

The Theme of Disposition

If contemporary theology is contextualized theology, then what meaning does the term "Reformed theology" have? In the wide array of situation-specific theologies, it may appear that the whole notion of tradition is undermined and dismissed. Is there any common link for contemporary Reformed contextualized theologies?

One approach to this sort of question would be to present doctrinal or confessional content to the Reformed tradition. On this approach, the common link is a list of major tenets of the faith, a core of confessional affirmations. Such an approach is helpful in that it clarifies the continuities of proclamation throughout the history of the church and across cultural divides. Surely, one of the reasons why the Barmen Declaration and the Kairos Document have such prophetic power is not only that they were contextualized documents in a time of great danger for the church's witness, but that they express powerfully the perennial claims of the church, the timeless confidence of Christians in God and the enduring witness of Christians to Jesus Christ.

The proposal made in this paper, however, is that essential tenets may not be the best way to "hook" theological students for the task of thinking the faith.

10. Anthony Giddens, *The Consequences of Modernity* (Stanford, Calif.: Stanford University Press, 1990).

As important as clear, conceptually rigorous theology is for the health of the church, pedagogical strategy suggests a modified approach. This approach presents first the dispositions and virtues of Christian theological reflection and then the doctrinal content of the Christian faith.

A clarification is required. The dispositions that may serve as entrée to identity in the Reformed tradition for theological students are not "mere" dispositions. They are dispositions, or virtues, indexed to Christian convictions. For example, a Christian is not merely prayerful, but called to pray by God's act of generous hospitality and faithful provision. She is not merely grateful, but grateful to God who has dealt graciously with her. An approach to the Reformed tradition via dispositions in no way circumvents the confessional and doctrinal content of the Christian faith. Brian Gerrish remarks in an article on a dispositional approach to the Reformed tradition, "It certainly does not follow that we do not need doctrines, or even lists of fundamental doctrines. It would be mere feeblemindedness to say: 'We must cleave to Christ. Let's leave it at that.'"[11] Virtues and dispositions of the Christian community are the fruits that are ultimately rooted in Christian conviction.

Gerrish's perspective on the fundamentals of Christian faith is that transformation is more basic than doctrine, that virtues are more characteristic of Christian authenticity than tenets expressed in propositional form. He suggests five habits of mind and heart that are foundational to the Reformed tradition.

First, the Reformed habit of mind is *deferential.* We defer to the past. We are not better than our forebears. The call for contextualization recommended in the first part of this paper is not a veiled excuse for wholesale rejection of a tradition. The deferential habit of mind is a clear element of continuity in the Reformed tradition.

Second, and in good Reformed dialectic, the Reformed habit of mind is *critical* — even of our forebears. To find a way forward in this tension, we listen carefully to each other; we correct our perceptions; we learn to think critically of ourselves. Here, surely, is an area of challenge and correction for First World Reformed theology — to learn to listen carefully, not to correct, judge, or categorize, but rather, to be corrected.

Third, the Reformed habit of mind is *open* — not only to other expressions of Reformed faith, but also open to wisdom and insight wherever it may be found. Gerrish's remarks refer specifically to the academic disciplines, including sociology, psychology, economics, anthropology, and other scholarly disciplines that illuminate the human condition. He says, "I don't see how the

---

11. Brian Gerrish, "Tradition in the Modern World: The Reformed Habit of Mind," in *Toward the Future of Reformed Theology,* ed. David Willis and Michael Welker (Grand Rapids: Eerdmans, 1999), p. 12.

seminaries can responsibly address social, economic, medical, legal, moral, or ecological problems, as the church surely must, without the knowledge that comes chiefly from the academy."[12]

Fourth, the Reformed habit of mind is *practical:* knowledge of God is for the sake of personal and social change. Not just for personal change — for the care of souls — as some versions of pietism, evangelicalism, and pentecostalism would have it, and as some versions of contemporary spirituality suggest. Not just for social change, as some liberal theological traditions would have it. A Reformed theology that finds its source in the Incarnation of God in Jesus Christ will promote an utterly practical, incarnational theology in its own contextualized setting.

Fifth, the Reformed habit of mind stands *before the Word of God.* Gerrish says that we do not discover the Word, read about it, or decide to listen to it. It comes to us in freedom and in power. It calls us, shapes us, and sends us. A Reformed habit of mind and heart is one of humble submission and obedience to the Holy Scripture as primary witness to the Word, Jesus Christ.

A dispositional approach to Reformed theology, it must be emphasized, does not threaten the great classic doctrines of the faith. On the contrary, a dispositional approach is intended as an entrée into formation shaped by the doctrine of the faith. It is intended as a pedagogical strategy, a way of avoiding generational suspicion of tradition and authority, a way of incubating students into Spirit-initiated transformation of which the doctrines speak. Not only at the level of seminary students, these habits and dispositions of Reformed theology must be nurtured, shaped, and disciplined among professional theologians as well. They do not come easily in the competitive academic environment, which resists the planting, hoeing, and harvesting of such virtues.

The Theme of Mission

The final part of my thesis suggests that a contemporary Reformed theology must purposefully orient its reflection in the wide vision of the mission of God. Here, I explore the resources of contemporary ecclesiology. In order to develop very briefly this section, I will draw on the recent work of the "missional church" scholars.[13] Many of these scholars identify themselves in the Reformed

12. Gerrish, "Tradition in the Modern World," p. 17.
13. I think, for instance, of George Hunsberger, James Brownson, and Craig Van Gelder and others in the Gospel and Culture Network. Cf. Darrell Guder, ed., *Missional Church: A Theological Vision for the Sending of the Church in North America* (Grand Rapids: Eerdmans, 1998). Jürgen Moltmann, although not connected with the North American mis-

tradition. They draw from earlier Reformed theologians such as A. A. van Ruler[14] and J. C. Hoekendijk.[15]

This current discussion is focused on articulating the church as the embodiment of the gospel in a pluralist context. One feature of this pluralist context is the end of Christendom. The mutually reinforcing dynamics of Christendom, by which church, state, and the dominant powers of society often unreflectively legitimated each other, have faded away. No longer can there be an easy correlation between church and cultural power. The church in today's world is often a minority group, a group that does not have hold of the reins of power. This situation calls the church to a re-envisioning of its place and call in the world.

Missional church theologians have reclaimed what is an old and deep theme in ecclesiology — a vision of the church as a part of the wide mission of God. God's mission, or God's reign, is wider than any given church organization, denomination, or tradition. God calls the church to join in the *missio Dei*, to enter into a divine mission that will, by God's grace, be eschatalogically fulfilled. God's focus, then, is not primarily on the individual Christian, the organizational structures of the churches, or the specifically Christian culture. God's focus is on the world. The church is called to be the community that authentically embodies a radically alternate way of being in the world, the gospel way of being, the community shaped by the Spirit in service to the mission of God in the world.

The late David Bosch gave a broad theological framework when he said,

> Mission is understood as being derived from the very nature of God. It is thus put in the context of the doctrine of the Trinity, not of ecclesiology or soteriology. The classical doctrine of the *missio Dei*, as God the Father sending the Son, and God the Father and the Son sending the Spirit is expanded to include yet another "movement": Father, Son, and Holy Spirit sending the church into the world.[16]

---

sional church group, develops similar themes. Cf. *A Passion for God's Reign* (Grand Rapids: Eerdmans, 1998). Other important voices in this discussion include the late David Bosch and the late Lesslie Newbigin.

14. For a readily available collection of English translations of some key articles, see A. A. van Ruler, *Calvinist Trinitarianism and Theocentric Politics: Essays Toward a Public Theology,* trans. John Bolt (Lewiston, Maine: Edwin Mellen Press, 1989).

15. Johannes C. Hoekendijk, *De kerk binnenste buiten* (Amsterdam: W. ten Have, 1964). Van Ruler and Hoekendijk can be considered precursors of the current missional church perspective.

16. David Bosch, *Transforming Mission: Paradigm Shifts in Theology of Mission* (Maryknoll, N.Y.: Orbis, 1991), p. 390.

Reformed theology can learn from the missional church conversation. These perspectives do not signal a rejection or dismissal of classical Reformed ecclesiology. But they do signal an emphasis — an emphasis on the character of the church as representing the mission of God in the world. These perspectives also signal a call — a call to the church to shed old assumptions about the church's status and power, the church's privilege and institutional identity. The church is, by definition, sent. It is oriented to the world, not to its own self-perpetuation or its own self-definition.

A missional self-understanding is deeply congruent with historical Reformed theology. It may also be fruitful in theological education, especially for those students who resist tradition and are negative about the perceived authoritarian self-protectiveness of denominations. Might a missional approach capture the imaginations of seminary students, building their Christian identities as part of God's cosmic mission to all the world? Might a missional approach, with its reminder that no ecclesial setting is the normative bearer of Christian identity, encourage commitment to ecumenical and global conversations? Might a missional approach give students a new vision of the multiplicities of God's pursuit of shalom?

The approaches suggested in this essay may help prepare a generation of Christian leaders that will be ready and willing to serve God in contexts more deeply ambiguous than old, familiar paradigms so taken for granted even a generation ago. For seminary students with genuine calls to ministry, but certain generational resistances to formation in a tradition of faith, theological educators are responsible to mine whatever resources are available to prepare students for faithful, authentic witness and service.

CHAPTER 16

Can We Still Be Reformed?
Questions from a South African Perspective

Dirk Smit

Doubt Concerning the Reformed Vision for Public Life

The most characteristic difference between Lutheran and Calvinist views of obedience to the word and will of God, however, lay outside the area of church dogma, in what has been called, with reference to Bucer, his "Christocracy": *the question of whether, and how, the law of God revealed in the Bible . . . was to be obeyed in the political and social order.* That difference, when combined with the Reformed doctrine of covenant and applied to the life of nations, was to be of far-reaching historical significance, for it decisively affected the political and social evolution of the lands that came under the sway of Calvinist churchmanship and preaching.[1]

With these words Jaroslav Pelikan describes not only the main difference between Calvinist and Lutheran convictions, but, according to many, one of the most characteristic traits of Reformed identity itself. It may also be the Reformed tradition's most important contribution to ecumenism and catholicity and, consequently, to the future of Christianity. It is "the question of whether, and how, the law of God revealed in the Bible was to be obeyed in the political and social order."

The importance of this aspect of the Reformed vision can be demonstrated both historically and theologically. It has been practiced and imple-

---

1. Jaroslav Pelikan, *Reformation of Church and Dogma (1300-1700). The Christian Tradition*, vol. 4 (Chicago: University of Chicago Press, 1984), p. 217.

mented, in varying degrees, in diverse historical contexts. It comes to the fore in the typically Reformed way of appropriating fundamental Christian doctrines and themes. It is deeply embedded in what could be called Reformed spirituality. Quite understandably, major twentieth-century commentators have emphasized this aspect in describing the Reformed identity and in locating the Reformed position within the spectrum of Christian worldviews — including Troeltsch and Richard Niebuhr and all those following their seminal ideas.

The Reformed intuition is not merely that the church itself should be continuously reformed in obedience to God's revealed word and will, but in fact the whole of life, the political and social order, history and the world. Again in Pelikan's words:

> In contrast not only to Roman Catholicism, but eventually also to Lutheranism, they were to denominate themselves "Reformed in accordance with the word of God (*nach Gottes Wort reformiert*)." . . . [T]he designation "Reformed in accordance with the word of God" contained the implicit judgment that although the word of God had been affirmed also by Luther and his followers, it had not been permitted to carry out the Reformation as thoroughly as it should have.[2]

Few observers would challenge the claim that South African society today urgently needs a religious, spiritual, and moral renewal. Politicians from all perspectives, businesspeople, cultural and public leaders from diverse spheres, including religious spokespeople, all seem to agree. In his last opening speech before Parliament on February 5, 1998, the retiring icon President Nelson Mandela said, "Our nation needs, as a matter of urgency . . . an RDP of the Soul."[3] President Thabo Mbeki has repeatedly spelled out his vision for the nation's renewal and rebirth.[4]

---

2. Pelikan, *Reformation of Church and Dogma*, pp. 183-84. Both quotes are from the chapter "The Word and the Will of God," which deals specifically with the characteristics of Calvinism in the wider context of Protestantism and Roman Catholicism.

3. This is a reference to the economic Reconstruction and Development Program of the Government. He explains: "[We need] discipline — the balance between freedom and responsibility: Quite clearly, there is something wrong with a society where freedom is interpreted to mean that teachers or students get to school drunk; warders chase away management and appoint their own friends to lead institutions; striking workers resort to violence and destruction of property; business-people lavish money in court cases simply to delay implementation of legislation they do not like; and tax evasion turns individuals into heroes of dinner-table talk. Something drastic needs to be done about this. South African society — in its schools and universities, in the work-place, in sports, in professional work and all areas of social interaction — needs to infuse itself with a measure of discipline, a work ethic and responsibility for the actions we undertake."

4. See his volume of selected speeches, among others developing his theme of an Afri-

Several high-level conferences and meetings have been organized to further this cause. Representatives of the state and organized religion are meeting in a series of public Moral Summits to address the "deep moral crisis" in which the nation finds itself and to commit themselves to moral responsibility and duty, to values and ethical principles of faith.[5] They have called on all sectors of society to join them in initiatives and projects on all possible levels to advance this venture of transforming and building the spiritual and moral fabric of South Africa. A major week-long "Multi-Event" was held in Cape Town from 14 to 20 February 1998, with national and international representations from a wide variety of sectors, to help "reconstruct a language of religion in public life" and to contribute to "the reconstruction of a civic moral fibre."[6] From February 21 to 23 delegates from a large number of South African churches gathered for a historical Rustenburg II-meeting to join hands in this present struggle for the soul of the nation.[7]

It seems only reasonable to expect that all of this should challenge and encourage Reformed Christians in South Africa to fulfill their own calling and to contribute to the ongoing reformation of this society — as far as they are concerned "nach Gottes Wort." In a country where roughly two-thirds of the population confess to be Christian, and in which the Reformed churches of Dutch origin form the largest single Christian denomination, it seems reasonable to expect the Reformed presence and influence in political and social life,

---

can Renaissance, *Africa, the Time has Come* (Cape Town and Johannesburg: Tafelberg and Mafube, 1998), but also several other key speeches, for example on the responsibility of all South Africans to help "encourage and protect a system of social morality" on which the infant democracy can build: "The task faces all of us to confront this enormous challenge, to restore to our communities the system of social values which create a climate hostile to criminal and other anti-social behaviour" (Speech of Deputy President Thabo Mbeki at the National Assembly during the Debate on Budget Vote No. 2, 10 June 1997).

5. See "A Code of Conduct for People in Positions of Responsibility," from the September 1998 Moral Summit (unpublished). It discusses causes for the moral breakdown in the country (a lack of individual moral responsibility, the wider social climate, the struggles of the past, the effects of a stage of deep transition, a gross economic imbalance, materialism, a garrison mentality placing ourselves and our own group above others, the legitimation of violence, lack of responsibility), moral principles for a secular society, and a specific code of conduct for persons in public positions of responsibility. Political and church leaders actually signed this code of conduct. Deputy President Mbeki called on business leaders to join them in this process. During 1999 a national summit followed.

6. See the document "Constructing a language of religion in public life," the summary analysis of the proceedings of the preparatory workshop from 30 September to 2 October 1998. At the conclusion of the Multi-Event a joint statement will again be issued.

7. This is a follow-up of the earlier Rustenburg-conference of churches. See *The Road to Rustenburg: The Church Looking Forward to a New South Africa,* ed. Louw Alberts and Frank Chikane (Cape Town: Struik, 1991).

especially in initiatives of this nature, to be widespread and evident.[8] If the ecumenical church should really accept this as an urgent challenge, then, on the basis of its own identity and faith, the Reformed tradition and community could be expected to be wholeheartedly involved.

However, this is not the case — and the question is: *Why?* Why does it seem as if Reformed Christians in South Africa, in spite of their own faith and in spite of their numbers, seem to shy away from calls to participate in public reconstruction?[9] Using Pelikan's depiction again, it seems they have retreated from asking *how* to asking *whether at all* the will of God revealed in the Bible can be obeyed in the political and social order. Many of them seem to deny this possibility — thereby denying the very heart of the Reformed identity itself.

How did this happen? What is the story behind this negative answer to the question whether it is indeed possible to be "Reformed"? In the second section of this paper a few of the most important reasons for this apparent denial are briefly mentioned. The third part refers to some of the obvious manifestations of these developments and some of the implications for Reformed identity in South Africa. The final part draws conclusions and makes tentative suggestions regarding challenges facing Reformed theology in South Africa today.

8. The exact calculation of religious adherence in South Africa has always been problematic and controversial. It may be that the still unpublished statistics of the 1996 Census may again change the picture somewhat. For very useful general surveys of the history and state of religion, including Christianity, in South Africa, see e.g., *A History of Christianity in South Africa,* vol. 1, ed. J. W. Hofmeyr and Gerald Pillay (Pretoria: Unisa, 1994); *Christianity in South Africa,* ed. Martin Prozesky (Johannesburg: Southern Book Publishers, 1990); John de Gruchy, *The Church Struggle in South Africa,* 2nd ed. (Grand Rapids: Eerdmans, 1986); *Living Faiths in South Africa,* ed. Martin Prozesky and John de Gruchy (Cape Town: David Philip, 1995); David Chidester, *Religions of South Africa* (New York: Routledge, 1992); and the extremely valuable *Christianity in South Africa: A Political, Social and Cultural History,* ed. Richard Elphick and Rodney Davenport (Cape Town: David Philip, 1997).

9. It is impossible to talk about all Reformed churches and believers in South Africa in the same breath. This is precisely an integral part of the problems faced by Reformed people in South Africa. For some distinctions, see Dirk J. Smit, "Reformed Theology in South Africa: A Story of Many Stories," *Acta Theologica* 21, no. 1 (1992): 88-110. Very informative and helpful is John de Gruchy, *Liberating Reformed Theology* (Cape Town: David Philip, 1991).

For the purpose of this paper I generally refer to the member churches of the Dutch Reformed Church-family, which represent the single largest denomination in South Africa (with the possible exception, since the 1996 Census, of the Zionist Christian Church, an Independent African Church), constituting approximately 16 percent of all Christians, as well as the Afrikaans-speaking Nederduitsch Hervormde Kerk (1.3 percent) and the Gereformeerde Kerk (0.8 percent), together, therefore, 18 percent of all Christians. Sometimes, the comments will also apply to the Presbyterian (2.2 percent) and Congregational (1.9 percent) churches, which play a more important role in de Gruchy's analysis.

The Story behind This Doubt

The complex question obviously needs a long and careful answer. However, a few general reminders about well-known facts and trends will have to suffice.

A *first* difficulty may lie in the Reformed vision itself. It is fair to say that this idea, that the revealed law and will of God must be obeyed in political and social life, has never been without problems or without fierce critics. Even otherwise sympathetic believers question it. Irrespective of the images, notions or *Leitmotifs* used in diverse sociohistorical contexts and by different Reformed figures, traditions, and documents, they have all been ambiguous and controversial, at best, and have met with severe skepticism, criticism, and rejection. That is true of the notion of the kingdom of God, of diverse covenant and federal theologies,[10] of ideas about a Reformed commonwealth, of theocratic ideals,[11] of Christocracies and Lordship of Christ theologies,[12] of claims to be a prophetic church and religion,[13] of comprehensive philosophical worldviews, claiming every inch of this world to belong to Christ (and Calvinism),[14] and of church-and-state constructions like Article 36 of the *Confessio*

10. The World Alliance of Reformed Churches has played a major role over the past two decades in revitalizing the notion of covenant, often in the form of the verb "to covenant (with)" within the ecumenical movement. For a careful and enthusiastic attempt to reappropriate the religious notion of covenant and federalism in constitutional and social language and thought, see the studies by William J. Everett, who worked for the first semester of 1998 as visiting scholar in South Africa, *God's Federal Republic: Reconstructing Our Governing Symbol* (New York: Paulist Press, 1988), and *Religion, Federalism, and the Struggle for Public Life* (Oxford: Oxford University Press, 1997).

11. See the impressive study of the inspiring work of the Dutch theologian Arnold A. van Ruler by Christo Lombard, Reformed professor of systematic theology and director of the Ecumenical Institute at the University of Namibia, *Adama, Thora en Dogma: die samehang van aardse lewe, Skrif en dogma in die teologie van A. A. van Ruler,* diss., University of the Western Cape, 1996.

12. See, e.g., for a South African Reformed perspective Willem D. Jonker, "Die koningskap van Christus en die staat in 'n godsdienstig-pluralistiese land," *Scriptura* 12 (1984): 1-19.

13. In South African struggle circles, particularly within black and contextual theological circles, the notion of a "prophetic Christianity" was extremely popular and often intensely discussed and debated.

14. The influence of the Dutch theologian and political figure Abraham A. Kuyper in South Africa has recently been analyzed and discussed in multiple forums. See, e.g., J. J. F. Durand, "Kontemporêre modelle vir die verhouding van kerk en samelewing," *Teks binne konteks* (Belleville: UWK, 1986), pp. 13-37, as well as several recent contributions by H. Russel Botman, e.g., "'Dutch' and Reformed and 'Black' and Reformed in South Africa: A Tale of Two Traditions on the Move to Unity and Responsibility," in *Keeping Faith: Embracing the Tensions in Christian Higher Education,* ed. Ronald A. Wells (Grand Rapids: Eerdmans, 1996), pp. 85-105.

Belgica.[15] The best-known historical examples seem to suggest that every attempt to implement this transformative vision has been controversial and
deeply problematic.

A *second* reason obviously lies within South Africa's own past. South Africa has become notorious as one of the countries where this Reformed experiment was taken seriously — and where it failed dismally. It has become common wisdom to relate apartheid and its theological legitimation directly to the
influence of Reformed theology and faith. In reality, the relationship is much
more complex. The story of Reformed Christianity in South Africa is in fact a
story of many stories. John de Gruchy has argued that South Africa did not
have too much Reformed theology and influence but not enough! Many popular accusations leveled against Reformed theology in this regard, for example,
that the notion of covenant played a major role in propagating apartheid, are
historically inaccurate, to put it mildly.[16]

However, it is impossible to deny the close links between a particular
form of so-called and self-acclaimed Reformed Christianity and the ideology of
apartheid. One cannot ignore the overall impression that Reformed convictions played a major role in this oppressive, immoral, and unjust system. Today
it is difficult to overestimate the negative effect of this history on the self-image
of Afrikaans-speaking Reformed Christians. To many of them, the Reformed
tradition and identity seem to be a major part of the tragic and shameful history from which they want to be free as soon and as completely as possible. It is,
therefore, a small wonder that they are to a large extent absent in the present
struggle for the soul of the nation. They have learned a lesson and now refuse to
have anything to do with politics. Christianity and politics should not be
mixed, is the popular slogan. It cannot be denied that, both within the Reformed communities and from the perspective of outsiders, apartheid has
given the Reformed tradition, and even Christianity itself, a bad reputation in
South Africa and has caused a lack of credibility and even self-confidence.[17]

A *third* reason is closely related. Many Reformed Christians were deeply
involved in the anti-apartheid struggle. Reformed church leaders and theologians played prominent roles. Powerful decisions were taken by synods and

15. See Willem D. Jonker, *Bevrydende waarheid: die karakter van die gereformeerde
belydenis* (Wellington: Hugenote-Uitgewers, 1994), pp. 49-91.

16. See Dirk J. Smit, "Covenant and Ethics? Comments from a South African Perspective," *Annual of the Society of Christian Ethics* (1996): 265-82.

17. For critical questions raised about the Reformed tradition and identity in South
Africa today, see the introductory essay by Dirk J. Smit, "Vraagtekens oor die gereformeerde
integriteit?," pp. 5-19, and the rest of the essays dealing individually with some of these questions, in the recent volume *Vraagtekens oor Gereformeerdheid?*, ed. Willem A. Boesak and
Pieter J. Fourie (Kaapstad: LUS, 1998).

strong declarations issued. Apartheid ideology and theology and the laws and practices of the apartheid state and apparatus were opposed in the name of the gospel and the authority of the Bible, in typically Reformed fashion. The struggle years did not, however, prepare these Reformed Christians for the present situation and for the new challenges of a radically transformed, secular, democratic, and pluralistic society. All their attention was given to politics and to church-state relationships, with the result that the suddenly changed circumstances caught these churches unaware. How the revealed will of God should now be obeyed in the fullness of social life was no longer as clear. In fact, whether this is still a challenge at all is unconsciously being questioned. Many Reformed believers from these churches that opposed apartheid seem to feel satisfied that the right people, including many (former) ministers, are now in Parliament or other positions of political power. They seem to trust that everything is therefore in good hands and that the public responsibility of the church is something of the past.[18]

This, again, is closely related to a *fourth* reason, namely the nature of the radical transformation that is still taking place in South Africa. With broad strokes this can be characterized as an overnight transformation from a basically pre-modern society to a typically modern one. The shift represents the rapid institutionalization of modernity. The major institutional carriers of modernity are being implemented in South Africa at an accelerated and unprecedented pace: a secular constitution with a far-reaching bill of rights, protected by an independent constitutional court, democratic government, liberal economy, a strong civil society, freedom of speech and press, and the formation of an independent public opinion. Many of those carriers of modernity that have been present in South Africa are radically changing their roles and becoming more typically modern institutions.

Former multi-functional institutions, so characteristic of earlier, pre-modern societies, are dissolved and replaced by specific, independent systems, each only interested in efficiently fulfilling its own task within society. Modern societies produce effectiveness through the accelerated functional differentiation of their dominant subsystems. Politics, economy, the law, education, even religion, become increasingly independent from one another. They all increase their own effective functioning by seeking to limit their own spheres of operation, by loosening or even doing away with the interconnections between themselves, and by giving up any orientation and loyalty to an overarching order.

---

18. See the two essays on the new role of the church in a changed South Africa, Dirk J. Smit, "Oor die kerk as 'n unieke samelewingsverband," *Tydskrif vir Geesteswetenskappe* 36, no. 2 (1996): 119-29 and "Oor die unieke openbare rol van die kerk," *Tydskrif vir Geesteswetenskappe* 36, no. 3 (1996): 190-204.

The sacred canopy provided by religion or metaphysics no longer exists. The typically modern society no longer has a center. Society is organized pluralistically or polycentrically. In modern societies there are many tasks, performed with competence and efficiency by different institutions in differentiated spheres or subsystems, but there is no longer a central task. Individuals can freely choose whether and how they will relate to the different institutions and the different subsystems. This paves the way for narcissistic individualism and radical arbitrariness.

Major implications for religion become clear. It becomes almost impossible to fulfill the overarching, integrating role that religion typically plays in premodern societies. Society becomes secularized. This does not mean that there is no place for religion. On the contrary, religion can still be extremely valuable, important, and popular, but it must restrict itself to playing its so-called proper role, which means it must restrict itself to the private sphere of the individual's personal, intimate life. Religion is privatized. It loses its place in public life — often voluntarily and gladly. Its connections to other subsystems, like politics, economic life, the public media, the legal system, and public education, are seriously threatened, and often made impossible by walls of separation.

This is an extremely superficial and general description, yet its one-sidedness is perhaps helpful for understanding some of the implications for Reformed faith in South Africa today. These dramatic changes are certainly not only restricted to South Africa. Bishop Wolfgang Huber recently provided a very instructive and helpful analysis of similar changes in Europe, discussing them under the three rubrics of secularization, a dramatic change in values, and increasing individualization.[19] However, because of their radical, overnight implementation in South Africa, they have affected the consciousness of Christian people, and particularly of Reformed believers, in a very profound way. These tendencies seem to run counter to the very heart of the Reformed claim that the law of God should be obeyed in every sphere of life. To many Reformed Christians and churches this claim has simply lost any possible meaning.

This situation is further complicated by a *fifth* reason, typical of South African society, namely the utter lack of unity both within the Christian church itself and among the different so-called members of the Dutch Reformed family. To talk about a lack of unity is in fact to put things mildly. South African Christianity is scattered over literally thousands of churches, denominations, and groups. The historical reasons are complex and manifold, but the implications for any possible public witness on the part of the churches are disastrous.

---

19. Wolfgang Huber, *Kirche in der Zeitenwende: gesellschaftlicher Wandel und Erneuerung der Kirche* (Gütersloh: Verlag Bertelsmann Stiftung, 1998), pp. 41-96. The whole study, together with many of his earlier essays and books, has been extremely helpful in South Africa.

During the years of struggle, ecumenism was kept alive by the joint cause of fighting apartheid. Since the change to a democratic society, ecumenism has lost almost all its impetus and enthusiasm. Within Reformed circles itself the issue of church unity has been a major stumbling-block and cause of division for decades, and at present the hopes for any real unity have almost disappeared. The net result for the Reformed vision is obvious. It is impossible to see who will speak God's Word for public life on behalf of these radically divided churches. This in itself constitutes a major difference from, for example, the situation in Germany (and several other European countries). It is impossible for any church or even a cluster of churches to speak with any authority on public issues, simply because there is no large church or body of churches representing the Christian, not to mention the Reformed, perspective.

This becomes even more acute when one considers a *sixth* reason, which follows directly from the previous two. Because of the implementation of modernity, the Reformed churches have lost their access to those institutions that were traditionally regarded as vehicles of the Reformed faith and tradition. This includes in particular educational institutions, like schools, colleges and universities, and the diverse forms of public media. It is also true of many other spheres of society, like social welfare, medical services, law, and several cultural activities in which the religious presence, and in particular the Christian, including the Reformed, presence is much less than before;[20] but it is probably in *education* and *public opinion-making* that the impact for the Reformed tradition and community will be the most dramatic. The Reformed vision has always, albeit under diverse circumstances and in many different ways, taken teaching, study, education, and formation very seriously. In the new South African order it has become much more difficult, if not impossible, to fulfill this calling, whether in church schools, public schools, or tertiary education. The place of religion and morality within public education has been gravely threatened through a series of recent policy decisions.[21] The study of theology within

20. A possible exception may be social welfare, where the state is still involving religious communities as major role players in civil society. In response to the government's October 1996 White Paper for Social Welfare, a National Religious Association for Social Development (NRASD) was formed in August 1997. The official structures of the URCSA and the DRC are also involved in processes of cooperation with government, but very often these services in the churches have been completely severed from the life of and within the congregations, and members are hardly aware of the participation of their churches.

21. Education in South Africa has been radically transformed and is still undergoing fundamental restructuring.

The Government, with the approval of the Minister of Education and the Minister of Labour, passed a new South African Qualifications Authority Act (1995) and in terms of that Act established a new National Qualifications Framework (Government Gazette No. 6140, 28

universities has already been terminated at several universities, and the few faculties and departments still left are all under extreme pressure. The same atti-

---

March 1998). This framework (NQF) covers all qualifications, divided into three levels, namely General Education and Training (GET), Further Education and Training (FET), and Higher Education and Training (HET).

The whole field of education and training has been divided into twelve so-called organizing fields, in which future education and training will occur, through all these levels, from general education to higher education. Religion, theology, and/or morality is not mentioned in these fields.

Each of these fields will have its own National Standard Body (NSB), which will assure that the content and standards of all education and training in the particular field is nationally coordinated and accepted. On each of these NSBs six categories of stakeholder organizations will be represented, including state departments, organized business, organized labor, providers of education and training, critical interest groups, and community and learner organizations. Religious groups and churches are not regarded as stakeholders in any of these fields.

Each of these fields is furthered divided into subfields. The field in which to look for religion, theology, and morality is Field 07, on Human and Social Studies. This Field 07 is furthered divided into 8 subfields, including Environmental Relations, General Social Science, Industrial and Organisational Governance and Human Resource Development, People/Human-Centred Development, Public Policy, Politics, Democracy and Citizenship, Rural and Agrarian Studies, Traditions, History and Legacies (also global/local relations), and "Religious and ethical foundations of society." Under this rubric, everything that has to deal with the different religions in the country, with morality, and with Christianity and the churches, is subsumed.

Each of these subfields will be governed by a national Standards Generating Body (SGB), still to be appointed in terms of the Act. Although promises were originally made that sub-subfields, like Christian theology, would be allowed to form their own SGBs, this has now been retracted. All the stakeholders in "Religious and ethical foundations of society" in the country will therefore be represented jointly, together with other people, on a relatively small SGB, which will report to the NSB for Field 07, covering the whole encyclopedia of Human and Social Studies. It is obvious that religious bodies, seminaries, theological schools or faculties, and churches will effectively have no say at all — not merely with regard to education in general, but also very specifically with regard to the role of religion and morality in future education and training.

But will there be any role for religion and morality in the future curriculum and qualification system? The answer is still not clear.

With regard to general (GET) and further (FET) education and training, the Government has approved a new so-called Curriculum 2005 to be implemented gradually over the next few years. It seemed as if religion and morality would be totally excluded from these levels. In response to a public outcry, the Minister of Education appointed a Ministerial Committee on Religious Education in Curriculum 2005. The Committee handed a 62-page report to the Minister late in January 1999. The report suggests that schools will be given a choice between four different options. Responses have now been invited and the Minister will issue his decision later this year.

With regard to higher (HET) education and training, the situation is still even more

tude applies in the sphere of the public media and public opinion.[22] This process of the secularization of society has been accelerated by economic realities

---

confused. It seems as if institutions, like universities, will have some freedom to decide on what to offer. However, general degrees will disappear and be replaced by selected programs that must be defined and approved in terms of very specific outcomes. State subsidy will in future only be given for a limited number of student places within approved programs. It may therefore be that universities will increasingly decide to offer only such programs that offer graduates in line with the state's (and the market's) priorities — which will certainly be disadvantageous to theology and ethics.

Whatever the outcome will be, it is clear that Christian churches and believers, and specifically also Reformed churches, who put such a high premium on education, will have little say in public schools in the future, both with regard to education in general as well as with regard to religious and moral education specifically.

Observers increasingly point to the anomaly that political and business leaders are calling for religious communities to strengthen the moral fabric of the nation, but when they have to support and subsidize these activities, nothing seems to be forthcoming.

22. Religious broadcasting — i.e., the religious programs on public radio and television — in South Africa during the apartheid years projected a very restricted, privatized picture of Christianity. A research project, self-initiated but done with the assistance of the HSRC, into the Afrikaans religious programs of the SABC during the late eighties produced remarkable information in this regard. Seven different kinds of programs were analyzed, representing broadcasts over an eight-month period during 1987. The content of these programs was analyzed from a variety of perspectives, i.e., in an attempt to describe their doctrinal or beliefs-content *(lex credendi)* and their ethical content *(lex convivendi)*. A list of general ethical categories was used in order to classify the ethical thrust of the programs. Almost 60 percent of the programs had no ethical content at all. The only category worth mentioning is love (13 percent), mostly understood in an individualistic and vertical sense. A list of traditional categories, dealing with moral issues, was developed from the Decalogue in order to classify moral topics addressed in the broadcasts. This time, 91 percent of the programs had no reference whatsoever, whether direct or indirect, to any moral issue traditionally dealt with under these wide-ranging rubrics. The only issue worth mentioning was the 3.7 percent referring to marriage. From yet another perspective, scholars in journalism developed a list of the ethical issues that were at the forefront in the public media over the same period of time. This list of burning issues, reflecting the story of the dominant culture at the same time, was then used to see which of those issues were addressed in these public worship services as well. Even the most indirect references, in passing, were counted. Only one was mentioned in more than 1 percent of the programs, namely "armoede, honger, behuisingsnood," taken together, in 1.3 percent. The overall picture was clear and alarming. The public worship of the Afrikaans religious programs of the SABC was completely separated from church and society, from faith and morals, from doctrine and ethics. It was directed solely at "religious individuals," with inner-religious needs only, living without church and society. Religion, better: Christianity, as far as the public media go, had been privatized. See Bethel A. Müller, Dirk J. Smit, "Public Worship: A Tale of Two Stories," in *The Relevance of Theology for the 1990's*, ed. Johann Mouton and Bernard C. Lategan (Pretoria: Human Sciences Research Council, 1985), pp. 385-408.

Obviously, as far as the influence of the public media is concerned, the church should

and technological advances. The publication of books, including theological books, in Afrikaans has decreased dramatically in recent years. It is almost impossible to find a publisher for any theological work in Afrikaans. Although, therefore, the market for popular spiritual literature is experiencing a period of remarkable flourishing — probably because of the personal anxieties brought about by these very changes — an informed Christian (including a Reformed) voice is almost completely absent from public debates about the soul of the nation.

The overall picture emerging from all these factors, developments, and influences is obvious. Reformed Christianity no longer plays a meaningful role in the present reconstruction and transformation of South African society. We do not contribute in any significant way to the public language, not even to debates about the moral confusion after Babel.[23] What is perhaps even more significant is the fact that it seems as if no one cares, as if Reformed churches and believers accept this situation, not only as a reality but as proper and completely in order. We seem to doubt *whether* it is indeed true that the revealed will of God should be obeyed in the public and social order.

Manifestations of This Doubt

It is impossible to distinguish clearly between causes and consequences of this radical self-doubt in Reformed circles. However, a few obvious implications of this attitude deserve attention.

Both Bishop Wolfgang Huber and Michael Welker have argued convincingly that the public activity of the church — at least in Germany and other industrial nations in the West — is characterized by uncertainty concerning its proper roles ("Das öffentliche Handeln der Kirche ist durch Rollenunsicherheit

---

be interested in far more than merely the religious programs. The media themselves play an extremely important role in the formation of public life — some observers claim that it can easily become *the* religious role in society. The future role of the public media, including the Broadcasting Policy of the SABC, is at present debated in South Africa (a new Bill is being finalized, based on A Green Paper for Discussion, by the Ministry of Posts, Telecommunications and Broadcasting, November 1997), but, although individual theologians and religious leaders may be involved, the churches once again do not play meaningful roles as discussion partners in these debates.

23. On our present situation as situation "after Babel" see my series of four essays, "Etiek na Babel? Vrae rondom moraliteit en die openbare gesprek in Suid-Afrika vandag," *NGTT* 1 (1994): 82-92; "Etiese spraakverwarring in Suid-Afrika vandag," *NGTT* 1 (1995): 87-98; "Het Suid-Afrika 'n gemeenskaplike morele taal nodig?," *HTS* 51, no. 1 (1995): 65-84; and "Oor die skepping van 'n grammatika van saamleef," *HTS* 51, no. 1 (1995): 85-107.

geprägt").[24] This is most certainly also true of Reformed churches in South Africa. For Reformed people, however, this suggests a potential crisis, because it implies an uncertainty about our very *identity*. For Reformed people, because of our faith, lack of clarity about our vocation, calling, mission, and purpose implies uncertainty about our identity. Again, this is clearly the case in South Africa. The doubt concerning our public role and responsibilities both reveal and constitute a radical crisis of identity.

This crisis of identity is manifested in a variety of ways. In many ways it seems as if we have lost our *confidence in the Word of God* and in our knowledge of the will of God. Church members are disillusioned with the claims of the church concerning the Bible and in particular the church's ability and authority to interpret the Bible. Many people prefer to see this trend as a form of innocent postmodernism — it is becoming increasingly popular to embrace all kinds of attitudes and activities in the church as liberating postmodernism — but the causes are obviously much deeper and complicated. They hang together with the disillusionment with the apartheid era and the way in which the Bible was used, by theologians, ministers, and churches, to legitimate a system that they themselves now reject as sin.

Many members and ministers seem to have lost their loyalty to the *verband,* to the broader structures of the church, the many ties of unity and mutual service between congregations and even to their denomination itself. Many congregations seem to grow increasingly independent from the rest of the church, in a variety of respects. It seems as if the general lack of interest in larger institutions in modern societies and the radical freedom of choice on the religious market cooperate to strengthen a form of *congregationalism* in Reformed churches. Small wonder that enthusiasm for church unity within the Dutch Reformed Church-family is perhaps at its lowest in many years, and interest in ecumenism has dramatically declined. It has been replaced by arbitrary cooperation on specific ventures and projects with like-minded believers and congregations, with scant regard for traditional church structures.

Even congregations themselves are often experienced as too large and oppressive. Many ministers in Reformed churches are styling their ministries around small so-called care groups or friendship groups. These *small groups* of families or friends meet regularly during the week and often experience the fullness of ecclesial community in these meetings, sometimes even administering the sacraments there.

A very visible demonstration of these tendencies is the impact on *liturgy*

---

24. Michael Welker, *Kirche im Pluralismus* (Gütersloh: C. Kaiser, 1995), quoting W. Huber, "Öffentliche Kirche in pluralen Öffentlickeiten," *Evangelische Theologie* 2 (1994): 157-80.

in Reformed churches and congregations. A wave of liturgical innovations has swept many traditionally Reformed congregations, often inspired by the experiences of members in Pentecostal or charismatic congregations, by ministers on visits and study tours to well-known megachurches in the United States of America, by strong competition from nearby local megachurches, and by television broadcasts of local and American religious services on recently established channels. A sense of complete arbitrariness has taken hold of many worship services, under the complete discretion of the local minister and with scant regard for traditionally Reformed forms of worship. Since success becomes the criterion — and success is primarily measured by growing membership, increased financial contributions, and more impressive projects — the emphasis easily shifts towards entertainment.

The net effect of these changes is generally observed in a dramatic shift in *spirituality*. If spirituality is seen — in Geoffrey Wainwright's words[25] — as the particular combination of praying and living, it is understandable why Reformed Christians in South Africa are increasingly experiencing their spirituality in ways that are fundamentally different from more traditionally Reformed forms of spirituality.

This becomes very evident from our obvious difficulties in dealing with *the moral life and ethics*. Reformed churches have characteristically been more interested in morality and ethics than perhaps most other Protestant communities and traditions, precisely because of our vision of God and the will of God. This is true of all the traditional ways of approaching the moral life, as is demonstrated when one uses the helpful distinctions of the Joint Working Group between the Roman Catholic Church and the World Council of Churches on morality.[26] They distinguish between four inseparable distinctions of the moral life, namely moral vision, virtue, value, and obligation. Reformed theology and faith characteristically regard all four approaches as important.

Reformed believers, ministers, and theologians are well known, if not notorious, for their firm convictions about moral *visions* for communities and societies. Normally these are transformative visions — in Niebuhr's famous description — both affirming the importance of society, politics, culture, and creation in the divine will and therefore the human calling, and at the same time criticizing the sinful aspects of a particular situation.[27] This has often been

---

25. Cheslyn Jones, Geoffrey Wainwright, and Edward Yarnold, eds., *The Study of Spirituality* (London: SPCK, 1986), p. 592.

26. *The Ecumenical Dialogue on Moral Issues: Potential Sources of Common Witness or of Divisions*, Faith and Order Paper (Geneva: WCC, 1996). For similar distinctions, Dirk J. Smit, "Reformed Ethics and Economic Justice," *NGTT* 37, no. 3: 438-55.

27. Still very instructive is Nicholas Wolterstorff's 1981 Kuyper Lectures from the Free University in Amsterdam, *Until Justice and Peace Embrace* (Grand Rapids: Eerdmans, 1983).

called the prophetic role of the church, but many other biblical motifs and sym-bols have also been appropriated. The influential examples include the Reformed claim about the Lordship of Christ, Reformed views on justice and freedom, Reformed usage of the social and political categories of covenant and election, and Reformed claims concerning the first use of God's law.

Reformed Christianity is equally well known for its keen interest in moral *virtues.* Teaching and teachability, instruction and education, personal forma-tion and character-building have received serious attention in the Reformed tradition, often to the dismay of other Protestant communities. Reformed views on justification and sanctification, on calling and vocation, on edification and teaching, and on the third use of the law, all play a major role in this regard. Reformed liturgy has a strong formative function.[28]

Reformed communities have been the advocates and defenders of powerful moral *values* in the past. John de Gruchy, for example, in his study on *Christianity and Democracy,* reminds us of the intimate historical connections between Re-formed faith and central democratic notions and ideas, including the rule of law, principles of equity and justice, covenantal or contractual relationships between rulers and the ruled, the sovereignty of the people, and the theory of resistance against tyranny. It is no wonder that the World Alliance of Reformed Churches has been deeply involved in human rights discussions for several decades.[29]

Finally, the Reformed mindset has often been more interested in ques-tions of moral *deliberation and decision-making* than most other Protestant tra-ditions. The Reformed emphasis on the Ten Commandments and the revealed will of God, in fact on the normative authority of the whole of the Bible — however problematic it may be to ascertain "what the Bible says" in a particular situation — has always strengthened this focus.[30] Reformed handbooks in eth-

---

28. For South African discussions, see Dirk J. Smit, "Liturgy and Life? On the Impor-tance of Worship for Christian Ethics," *Scriptura: Christian Ethics in South Africa,* ed. D. Etienne de Villiers, 62: 259-80, with references to valuable and very insightful contribu-tions by Nicholas Wolterstorff on Reformed liturgy, holiness, and justice. Also Dirk J. Smit, "Church and Civil Society?," EFSA Conference Proceedings, ed. Renier Koegelenberg (un-published), with references to valuable insights from John Leith on the importance for social and public life of Reformed preaching and Christian worship. See also the volume on the preaching of virtue, *Riglyne vir prediking oor die Christelike deugde. Woord teen die lig III/4,* ed. Bethel A. Müller, Coenraad W. Burger, and Dirk J. Smit (Kaapstad: Lux Verbi), with con-tributions by several Reformed theologians, including Russel Botman, Piet Naudé, J. J. F. Durand, Willem D. Jonker, and D. Etienne de Villiers.

29. See, e.g., the overviews and essays in "Reformed Faith and Economic Justice," *Re-formed World* 46, no. 3 (1996); "Theology and Human Rights I," *Reformed World* 48, no. 2 (1998); and "Theology and Human Rights II," *Reformed World* 48, no. 3 (1998).

30. For South African controversies regarding the use of the Bible in ethics, see D. E. de Villiers and Dirk J. Smit, "Waarom verskil ons so oor wat die wil van God is? Opmerkings oor

ics, sermons, and synodical documents often tended to be almost casuistic in their attempts to clarify and prescribe exactly the moral decisions to be taken and the actions to be followed regarding specific so-called moral issues or questions. Notions like moral obligations, moral responsibility, respect for moral standards, and moral behavior are commonplace in Reformed language and thought.

Given the present moral crisis in South Africa, often described as a complete tearing apart of the moral fabric of society, it is again reasonable to expect that Reformed Christians should be alarmed and deeply involved in addressing these challenges. However, there is — again generally speaking — a remarkably uncharacteristic silence and absence, almost an apathy, on the part of the Reformed churches regarding this moral crisis.[31]

Our Reformed churches seem to lack all vision for social, political, economic, and cultural developments and to exercise no prophetic voice at all. We seem to practice a kind of personal piety and spirituality with increasingly less

---

Christelike morele oordeelsvorming," *Skrif en Kerk* 17 (1996): 31-47; "Hoe Christene in Suid-Afrika by mekaar verby praat. . . . Oor vier morele spreekwyses in die Suid-Afrikaanse kerklike konteks," *Skrif en Kerk* 15 (1994): 228-47; as well as Dirk J. Smit, "The Bible and Ethos in a New South Africa," 37 (1991): 51-67 and "Wat beteken 'die Bybel sê'? 'n Tipologie van leserskonstrukte," *HTS* 47, no. 1 (1991): 167-85.

31. Generally speaking, the Reformed churches were also silent and absent during the process of the Truth and Reconciliation Commission, without doubt the most important public initiative addressing the moral fabric of the South African nation. The Commission was appointed by an Act of Parliament and commenced its work on 15 December 1995. It had three separate committees: an amnesty committee which considered applications for amnesty from perpetrators of gross human rights violations; a human rights committee which heard the stories of victims of gross human rights violations; and a reparations committee which sought to provide reparation to victims where possible. On 29 October 1998 it handed over its five-volume set of findings to the President, although the amnesty hearings are still continuing.

Under the chairpersonship of Archbishop Desmond Tutu it often showed a very religious, Christian, spiritual face. One member of the Commission, Prof. P. J. G. Meiring, was from the DRC. However, the DRC itself refused to make the invited submission during the hearing on the responsibility of the religious communities and appeared with a document. During this appearance, they only acknowledged, like the URCSA, their "silence" in the face of apartheid's atrocities. For theological perspectives, see the volumes *To Remember and to Heal: Theological and Psychological Reflections on Truth and Reconciliation,* ed. H. Russel Botman and Robin M. Petersen (Cape Town: Human & Rousseau, 1996); and *Faith Communities Face the Truth,* ed. James R. Cochrane, John W. de Gruchy, and Stephen Martin (Cape Town: David Philip, 1998); as well as Charles Villa-Vicencio, "The Burden of Moral Guilt: Its Theological and Political Implications," in *Questions About Life and Morality: Christian Ethics in South Africa Today,* ed. Louise Kretschmar and Len Hulley (Pretoria: J. L. van Schaik, 1998), pp. 185-98.

emphasis on teaching and formation. We are absent from the public debate about the soul of the nation and about common values and norms. And we are silent about the urgent social and moral crises our society is facing, both in our congregations and churches as well as in the public sphere.[32]

Due to our awareness of our lack of credibility and our sense of shame and guilt on the one hand and our satisfaction with recent social and political developments on the other hand, we appear to be happily and willingly retreating to a sphere of private religion. This, combined with the fact that we are overwhelmed by the nature of this radical shift to a modern, democratic, and pluralistic society and that we have lost our access to our traditional spheres and vehicles of influence, further exacerbated by our own divisions and total lack of unity, leaves many Reformed Christians in South Africa at a loss regard-

---

32. Within the South African ecumenical movement the Reformed churches, and even individual Reformed figures, do not play any leading or significant role any longer.

The URCSA's synodical commission dealing with topical, urgent, and moral issues — the equivalent of the EKD's Kammer für soziale Ordnung — has not met once to discuss a single topic since its inception in the early 1990s. This is all the more remarkable if one remembers the series of outspoken and prophetic political decisions and declarations made by the former DRCA and the DRMC during the years of apartheid and the intense political involvement of many of the ministers and members during those years.

The DRC's October 1998 General Synod adopted a few important decisions concerning the public role of the church on the basis of an insightful report, but one could hardly claim that these decisions have been properly debated in the church beforehand or in any serious way received by the church, in the form of its members or congregations, afterwards. (For a plea for an ethics of dialogue in these churches, see D. Etienne de Villiers and Dirk J. Smit, "'Met watter gesag sê u hierdie dinge?' Opmerkings oor kerklike dokumente oor die openbare lewe," *Skrif en Kerk* 16 (1995): 39-56. For a plea to take the notion of "reception" more seriously, see Piet J. Naudé and Dirk J. Smit, "Reception: Opportunity or Crisis for the Churches?," *Scriptura* 73 (2000): 175-88.

In Parliament many Green Papers, White Papers, and laws with radical moral implications have been discussed and debated over the last few years. The South African Council of Churches has a representative at Parliament, who participates in some of the hearings and who is a minister of the URCSA, Rev. Malcolm Damon, but he is not representing his own church and the Reformed churches are completely absent from these proceedings and public debates.

According to recent surveys citizens are deeply alarmed by crises related to unemployment, security (crime and violence), housing, and education. Racism and discrimination, sexism and sexual violence, and violence against children are all rife in society. Cases of public corruption come to the fore at an astounding rate. Just to deal with corruption, the government has appointed a Public Protector, an investigating Commission under Judge Heath, and an Auditor-General, and has established an Office for Serious Economic Offences — but seemingly without much success in stemming the tide. See "Combat corruption collectively," the 1997/1998 report by TI-SA, Transparency International — South Africa, 3 September 1998.

ing our sense of identity and calling. We are losing our trust in the ordering and liberating power of God's Word and in the traditional structures, forms, and activities of the church. This is both exemplified and strengthened by dramatic changes in liturgy and spirituality within the Reformed tradition, and in an uncharacteristic lack of interest in the moral life, including a moral vision, virtues, values, and responsibilities.

Possibilities for Dealing with This Doubt?

To return to Pelikan's depiction, it is not quite clear why he claims that this most characteristic thrust of the Reformed vision "lay outside the area of church dogma." It could certainly mean that the "reformation according to God's will" intended by the Reformed believers dealt with much more than merely the church itself. It extended beyond the scope of ecclesiology alone, of the dogma *about* the church. However, what was at stake most certainly concerned the fullness of the dogma *of* the church. It was an issue at the heart of the Reformed faith and theology itself.

The notion that the will of God was to be obeyed in the political and social order is not primarily or merely a moral and ethical issue, but *a fundamentally theological issue*. This conviction is not something that Reformed people could also choose to ignore while retaining their identity. It is deeply embedded in *our particular form of faith in the living triune God, God's dealings in history and with creation, and our lives* coram Deo.

It seems to me that the way into the future for Reformed theology and faith is to return to our own fundamental convictions concerning the creative and liberating power of God's Word and to revisit central claims and insights of Reformed faith and doctrine. The most serious reason for concern about the state of Reformed Christianity in South Africa, I believe, is not the alarming proportions of our moral crisis and our lack of responsibility, but the integrity of our own identity and the credibility of our own life and witness. We face a theological — not primarily a moral — crisis, and we need a theological response.

I believe that the Reformed faith inspires us to answer Pelikan's *whether*-question with an affirmative yes. The will of the triune God should be obeyed in the political and social order. This answer leads us back to Pelikan's much more difficult *how*-question. What does this claim mean within the complexities of a modern, democratic, and pluralistic society? To use contemporary parlance: What does it mean to be a public church in a civil society?

This would entail difficult questions and call for serious theological reflection. The public church in a civil society needs — among others — responsible public *theology*. The particular contribution of Reformed theology to this essentially ecumenical task would include, among others, reminders to keep searching for *a fully trinitarian theology, responsible biblical hermeneutics, a faithful church*, and *socially involved and responsible believers*. Reformed spirituality is about life *coram Deo*, but specifically before the face of the *living and speaking triune God*. Because we claim that we hear this God's word in and through the Bible, it is crucial that we *read and interpret this Bible in responsible ways*. And because we claim that the content of this word and will calls the church to obedience and to continuous reformation according to the message of this Bible, we should be concerned about how that is *implemented in the concrete, everyday life — order, structure, worship, ministries, services — of the real church*. As the continuously transformed members of this continuously reformed church, we are called to live *soli Deo gloria*, to enjoy and to serve the honor of the living God in the theater of God's glory, God's history and world, among God's creatures.[33]

This calls for the overcoming of two major forms of alienation within theological scholarship in our country, namely the alienation between theologians from the different theological disciplines as well as the alienation between theological scholarship and everyday life in church and society.

First, systematic theologians, biblical scholars, practical theologians, and ethicists should return to serious *dialogue with one another*. One of the most tragic developments in South African theology, and in particular in Reformed theological circles, has been the disastrous fragmentation of the theological enterprise into isolated scholarly disciplines.[34] The reasons are obviously manifold and complex, and many of them reflect, and in fact follow, similar trends in the rest of Christianity, but to a large extent this alienation was also caused or at least strengthened by the shameful and painful history of Reformed churches in our country.[35] Reformed doctrine and particular forms of biblical scholarship,

---

33. This fourfold task follows from my understanding of the — albeit complicated — characteristics of Reformed spirituality. See Dirk J. Smit, "Kan spiritualiteit beskryf word?," *NGTT* (1989): 83-94 and "Wat is Gereformeerde spiritualiteit?," *NGTT* (1988): 182-93.

34. On the fragmentation of theological studies into different disciplines in South Africa, see Dirk J. Smit, "What Makes Theological Education Theological? Overhearing Two Conversations," *Scriptura* (1993): 147-66 and Phil J. Robinson and Dirk J. Smit, "What Makes Theological Education 'Theological'? A South African Story on the Integrity of Theological Education," *Skrif en Kerk* 17 (1996): 405-19.

35. For a discussion of the effects of modernity on Reformed theological education at two typical institutions in South Africa, see Dirk J. Smit, "Modernity and Theological Education: Crises at 'Western Cape' and 'Stellenbosch'?" Forthcoming volume on the impact of modernity on religion in South Africa, ed. A. Balcomb, to be published by Regnum Books, Oxford.

practical theology, and ethical teaching were increasingly blamed for the apartheid ideology. Leading biblical scholars, practical theologians, and ethicists from the Reformed tradition therefore deliberately distanced themselves from their Reformed identity and from one another.[36] At least in South Africa, the immediate task would be for Reformed theologians to face and acknowledge the failure and the complicity of our tradition, not by fleeing away from it, but by a renewed commitment to liberating Reformed theology — in De Gruchy's deliberately ambiguous formulation.

Second, we have to take our alienation from the realities of church and society seriously. It will be of no use if we reappropriate trinitarian theology and the believers in the congregations are not served by our insights; if we agree on the intricacies and liberating potential of responsible hermeneutics and church members are fed with biblicism and fundamentalism;[37] if we share exciting knowledge about the nature and role of the church and congregations are organized according to ad hoc recipes for success and entertainment; if we master complicated moral theories and believers do not share in moral visions, form moral virtues, prize moral values, and practice moral discernment and decision-making.[38]

---

36. The debates between systematic theologians and New Testament scholars have been particularly fierce, see e.g., Dirk J. Smit, "Ethics and Interpretation — and South Africa," *Scriptura* 33 (1990): 29-43 and "Ethics and Interpretation: New Voices from the USA," *Scriptura* 33 (1990): 16-28, two essays that inspired heated discussion, as well as "A Story of Contextual Hermeneutics and the Integrity of New Testament Scholarship in South Africa," *Neotestamentica* 28, no. 2 (1994): 265-89, "Saints, Disciples, Friends? Recent South African Perspectives on Christian Ethics and the New Testament," *Neotestamentica* 30, no. 1 (1996): 169-86 and "Reading the Bible and the (Un)official Interpretive Culture," *Neotestamentica* 28, no. 2 (1994): 309-21.

On the relationship between ethics and biblical scholarship in South Africa, see, e.g., Dirk J. Smit, "Oor 'Nuwe Testamentiese etiek,' die Christelike lewe en Suid-Afrika vandag,'" *Geloof en opdrag*, ed. Cilliers Breytenbach and Bernard C. Lategan (1992), pp. 303-25, and "The Future of Old Testament Studies in South Africa: An Ethicist's Perspective," *Old Testament Essays*, 1994, Supplement 7/4, pp. 286-92.

37. On hermeneutics in South Africa, see Dirk J. Smit, *Hoe verstaan ons wat ons lees? 'n Dink- en werkboek oor die hermeneutiek* (Kaapstad: NGKU); "Responsible Hermeneutics: A Systematic Theologian's Response to the Readings and Readers of Luke 12:35-48," *Neotestamentica* 22 (1988): 441-84; "Those Were the Critics, What about the Real Readers? An Analysis of 65 Published Sermons and Sermon Guidelines on Luke 12:35-48," *Neotestamentica* 23 (1989): 63-82; and the two essays "Biblical Hermeneutics: The 20th Century," and "Biblical Hermeneutics: The First 19 Centuries," *Initiation into Theology: The Rich Variety of Theology and Hermeneutics*, ed. Simon Maimela and Adrio König (Pretoria: Van Schaik), pp. 275-96 and pp. 297-317 respectively.

38. An important and inspiring South African illustration of the enriching potential of a new dialogue between the disciplines of systematic theology, practical theology, and ethics,

It is imperative that Reformed theology should take these challenges seriously, in order that the Word of God can be obeyed in the political and social order. Reformed theology should be both serious scholarly theology *and* churchly reflection.

---

is the work of Coenraad W. Burger and H. Russel Botman over recent years, often born from joint projects. Burger has published works in practical theology that were deliberately taking biblical scholarship and in particular systematic theology seriously and that have all been very influential in church circles. They include *Die dinamika van 'n Christelike geloofs-gemeenskap* (Kaapstad: Lux Verbi, 1991), and *Gemeentes in transito. Vernuwingsgeleenthede in oorgangstyd* (Kaapstad: Lux Verbi, 1995). His latest manuscript, *Gemeentes in die Kragveld can die gees: Oor die uniebe identitat, taale en bediering van die Keole van Christus* (Stellenbosch: Buvton, 1999), combines practical ecclesiology with doctrinal teaching about the church and again promises to be well received and influential. He wrote this while on sabbatical at the Center of Theological Inquiry in Princeton, together with Russel Botman. Botman, a trained dogmatic theologian and ethicist, who teaches practical theology at the UWC, is also working on a manuscript on the formative practices of discipleship and citizenship in Reformed churches in South Africa today.

PART IV

Affirming and Questioning Reformed Doctrines in Ecumenical Conversation

CHAPTER 17

Reformed Identity in an Ecumenical World

George W. Stroup

When Christians from the Reformed tradition participate in ecumenical conversations with other Christians (and with representatives from other religious traditions), it is important they understand their own theological identity — that is, who they are as Reformed Christians and what it is they bring to ecumenical conversation. The conviction, however, that ecumenical conversation is more productive if the participants have a clear understanding of their own theological identity raises the question as to what, if anything, constitutes "Reformed identity." Although there have been many different responses to that question, the answer is not self-evident.

Not everyone agrees that questions about Reformed identity are important. Karel Blei speaks for many when he writes, "Not 'Reformed identity,' but 'Christian identity' should be our main issue (as it was Calvin's and Luther's). We should not ask what it means to be Reformed (or Protestant) but what it means to be Christian today." And perhaps even the question of Christian identity is a mistake, Blei concludes, because the Christian "cannot and should not aim at self-maintenance, for we are called to follow our Lord, who himself did not seek his own identity, but, on the contrary, risked it, sacrificed it for the sake of humankind."[1]

It is also not clear that Reformed identity is a practical possibility. Lukas Vischer argues that the question "What is Reformed?" cannot be answered today because the Reformed tradition has "diversified considerably over the centuries and it has become increasingly hard to articulate the common elements

---

1. Karel Blei, "Some Dutch Reflections on Reformed Identity," *Reformed World* 43, no. 1-2 (1993): 3-4.

among the variety of voices. . . . There are no firm statements or signs allowing a clear-cut definition of Reformed tradition."[2] As Reformed churches outside of Western Europe and North America have begun in the last half of the twentieth century to write their own confessions, the diversity and plurality in Reformed theology have increased exponentially.

Finally, in light of the criticisms of various postmodernists concerning western logocentric and essentialist thinking, it is no longer clear that any concept of identity — much less Reformed identity — is intelligible or defensible in a world that distrusts universals and metanarratives and celebrates pluralism and relativism.

Although these are significant reasons to think carefully about the pitfalls surrounding the topic of Reformed identity, the fact remains that people from Reformed churches are currently involved in important bilateral and multilateral ecumenical discussions, and it will not do for them to participate by saying to their conversation partners, "We are glad you have some sense of who you are and what tradition you represent, but we do not have a clue as to our own theological identity!"

In this essay I will examine briefly five ways of interpreting Reformed identity. The first describes Reformed identity in terms of polity and church structure. A second uses the language of "essential tenets" of doctrine to interpret Reformed identity, while a third backs off the language of essential tenets and adopts the more modest language of "themes" and "emphases." A fourth moves away from explicitly doctrinal language and appeals to a Reformed *habitus* or character. A fifth interprets Reformed identity in terms of theological grammar, family resemblances, forms of life, and a cultural-linguistic model for theology.

Finally, I will argue that in an increasingly diverse and pluralistic world, Reformed identity is best understood in terms of a combination of the last three proposals — that is, certain general theological themes and emphases; the *habitus* or disposition, practices, and character of a community; and a cultural-linguistic model that focuses on the relation between the language and life of a church.

2. Lukas Vischer, "The Bilateral International Dialogues of the World Alliance of Reformed Churches: Achievement and Follow-Up," in *Bilateral Dialogues*, ed. H. S. Wilson (Geneva: World Alliance of Reformed Churches, 1993), p. 20.

Interpretations of Reformed Identity

Polity

One way to interpret Reformed identity is by means of polity and church structure. One version of this proposal would appeal to the themes of ecclesial connectionalism, the role of the "ruling elder," and representative polity as distinctive features of Reformed identity. One strength of this interpretation is that although church order and structure in the Reformed tradition are rooted in theological convictions, the appeal to polity and structure avoids some of the ambiguity and continual change that characterize the history of Reformed doctrine. The appeal to polity, however, cannot avoid altogether the reality of change. A church's polity undergoes as much change as does its theology and doctrine. The major weakness in this model is that given the emphasis on theology in the Reformed tradition it seems odd to interpret Reformed identity non-theologically. And yet the appeal to polity and policy remains widespread.

For example, a church applying for membership today in the World Alliance of Reformed Churches is asked to fill out a form consisting of eighteen questions. The first ten ask for factual information about the church (name, address, number of members and congregations) and a brief history of the church. The next five questions request information about the number of female deacons, elders, and ministers and other ways in which women exercise leadership in the church. If the church does not have women in these offices, it is asked to explain why it does not. The last three questions ask how ministers are trained, what magazines the church publishes, and whether the church is a member of other ecumenical and international organizations. The questionnaire does not ask a single question about the church's theology or its use of Reformed confessions. Apparently, a church's policy on the role of women is more definitive of its Reformed identity than its understanding of Reformed theology and its use of Reformed confessions.

Essential Tenets

A second response to the question of Reformed identity utilizes the language of "essential tenets" of doctrine. The *Book of Order* of the Presbyterian Church (USA) is the second part of that church's constitution and includes the *Form of Government*, the second chapter of which discusses the significance of the first part of the church's constitution — the *Book of Confessions*. The second chapter affirms that by means of its confessions the church declares to its members and to the world "who and what it is, what it believes, what it resolves to do." In other words, the church declares that its <u>confessions, which are subordinate to</u> <u>"the authority of Jesus Christ,</u> the Word of God, as the Scriptures bear witness to him," are the church's identity documents.[3]

In response to those who ask who Presbyterians are and what they believe, the church directs attention to its confessions, and within those confessions it emphasizes the Nicene and Apostles' Creeds (especially their definitions of the Trinity and the incarnation), the affirmations of the Protestant Reformation (especially "the rediscovery of God's grace in Jesus Christ as revealed in the Scriptures"), and the "watchwords" or "principles of understanding" of Protestantism (grace alone, faith alone, Scripture alone). Central to the Reformed tradition, according to the *Form of Government*, "is the affirmation of the majesty, holiness, and providence of God." In addition to this central affirmation of God's sovereignty are "other great themes of the Reformed tradition," including election for service as well as for salvation, covenant life marked by a disciplined concern for order, a faithful stewardship, the recognition of the human tendency to idolatry and tyranny, and the calling of the people of God "to work for the transformation of society by seeking justice and living in obedience to the Word of God."[4]

The same *Form of Government* also lists nine questions that are to be asked at the ordination of elders, deacons, and ministers of Word and sacrament. The third of those questions is: "Do you sincerely receive and adopt the essential tenets of the Reformed faith as expressed in the confessions of our church as authentic and reliable expositions of what Scripture leads us to believe and do, and will you be instructed and led by those confessions as you lead the people of God?"[5] The *Form of Government* does not explain what these essential tenets are. One might assume they are the material discussed in Chapter II on the status of the confessions — ecumenical statements about Trinity and incarnation, the watchwords of the Protestant Reformation, and the Reformed affirmations concerning the sovereignty of God, election, covenant life, faithful stewardship, the recognition of idolatry, and the call to work for the transformation of society. But such an assumption is at best an inference. The term "essential tenets" does not appear in Chapter II and the ordination question in Chapter XIV does not specify which tenets are essential. Furthermore, no list of essential tenets can be found in the *Book of Confessions*. The list of affirmations in Chapter II is an interpretation of the *Book of Confessions* and not something that can be found in the confessions.

3. "Chapter II: The Church and Its Confessions," in *The Form of Government of the Book of Order of the Presbyterian Church (USA)* (Louisville: The Office of the General Assembly, 1994), G-2.0100.

4. *The Form of Government*, G-2.0300 to G-2.0500.

5. *The Form of Government*, G-14.0207 and G-14.0400.

Chapter II does affirm that the Presbyterian Church (USA) is "open to the reform of its standards of doctrine" because the church affirms *ecclesia reformata, semper reformanda,* which, unfortunately, is mistranslated as "the church reformed, always reforming" rather than "the church reformed, always being reformed" by the Word of God. The mistranslation erroneously suggests that it is the church rather than sovereign God who is the agent of transformation.[6]

Although the *Form of Government* nowhere clarifies what it means by the words "essential" and "tenet," it would appear difficult to reconcile that language with the claim that the church is *semper reformanda* or "open to the reform of its standards of doctrine." If "tenets" refer to the central affirmations in the *Book of Confessions* or the church's "standards of confession," then in what sense are they "essential"? Clearly, the affirmations in the *Book of Confessions* are not essential in the sense that they are unchanging. The Westminster Confession of Faith and the Confession of 1967 differ significantly in their interpretation of such basic or essential tenets as the sovereignty of God and the authority of Scripture. And the problem is not just that of shifting interpretations of essential tenets. Essential tenets come and go. The language and affirmations in the well-known Chapter III of the Westminster Confession on "God's Eternal Decrees" cannot be found in the Confession of 1967. What is essential to one age is dispensable to another.

William Christian makes a helpful distinction between a community's "primary doctrines" and its "governing doctrines." While the former are "doctrines about the setting of human life and the conduct of life in that setting," the latter are "the principles and rules to govern the formation and development of its body of doctrines."[7] It is in this latter sense that *semper reformanda* may function as a governing principle in Reformed theology. That governing principle, however, would seem to mean that no tenet or primary doctrine can be "essential" in the sense that it is unchanging or beyond re-formation. As a governing principle, *semper reformanda* implies that no tenet or primary doctrine is as "essential" as is the living God who continues to transform a recalcitrant creation.

A final problem with essential tenets and their role in the description of Reformed identity is theological. As a governing doctrine, *semper reformanda* reflects the Reformed awareness of "the human tendency to idolatry," which can be just as pervasive in theology as in any other human endeavor. The attempt to construct essential theological tenets may be an understandable response to a deep-seated anxiety concerning religious identity in the midst of

6. *The Form of Government,* G-2.0200.

7. William A. Christian, Sr., *Doctrines of Religious Communities: A Philosophical Study* (New Haven: Yale University Press, 1987), p. 2.

expanding cultural pluralism, but it would also not be the first time that religious anxiety has led to the construction of golden calves. Essential theological tenets may be enticing in that they offer a more tangible security than does trust in a God who continues to do "new things" that are surprising and often disturbing to God's people. But essential tenets would also appear to be irreconcilable with a governing doctrine that affirms that everything, at least in principle, can be reformed and transformed by the living God. That is, how can one, in the words of the Scots Confession, cleave to God alone and at the same time affirm essential, unchanging tenets or doctrines? Rather than speaking of the "essential tenets of Reformed faith," it may be that Reformed identity is a choice between "essential tenets" and "Reformed faith."

Themes and Emphases

It might be argued that the third response to the question of Reformed identity — one that adopts the more modest language of "themes" and "emphases" — is simply a different version of the second model of essential tenets. It is possible, though, to interpret this third model as a distinctive form of Reformed identity. Themes and emphases are more like symbols and metaphors than they are doctrines and propositions and are open to — indeed, even invite — multiple interpretations.

For example, a pamphlet published by the World Alliance of Reformed Churches, Confessions and Confessing in the Reformed Tradition Today, examines several contemporary Reformed confessions and in so doing lists "some features which have tended to characterize Reformed thinking."[8] While there are many features that might be said to be typical of Reformed theology, the pamphlet lists three as particularly important: the sovereignty of God; God's gracious covenant with humanity in Jesus Christ; and the special significance commonly ascribed to the Old Testament revelation and to the law of God. To argue that it is distinctive of Reformed theology "to attach high value specially to the Old Testament" does not specify a particular interpretation of the Old Testament.[9] It simply acknowledges a prominent, general theme or emphasis, which has assumed various forms in Reformed theology.

There are several advantages to the language of "themes" and "emphases" over that of "essential tenets." First, "themes" sound less propositional than "tenets," and are more elastic, more susceptible to multiple interpretations. Sec-

8. "Confessions and Confessing in the Reformed Tradition Today," Studies from the World Alliance of Reformed Churches, vol. 2 (1983), p. 14.
9. "Confessions and Confessing," p. 15.

ond, they suggest something that cannot be reduced simply to doctrine. While the theme or emphasis of the sovereignty of God can be interpreted as doctrine, it can also be understood as a more general feature of Reformed worship, spirituality, and ethos. On the other hand, the appeal to themes and emphases does not evade the problem that they, like essential tenets, are not constant, either historically or culturally. The major themes and emphases in one Reformed confession or church are not necessarily the same as those in another.

Habitus

A fourth interpretation of Reformed identity moves more in the direction of *habitus,* character, and ethos than of doctrine. As Schleiermacher once argued, theology may perhaps best be understood in its relation to the affective dimension of human existence rather than the cognitive or volitional dimensions. In an essay subtitled "The Reformed Habit of Mind," Brian Gerrish argues that those in the Reformed tradition "appeal to something more constant and even more fundamental than fundamental beliefs; namely, good habits of mind, all of which rest finally on the one foundation which is Jesus Christ."[10] Gerrish describes "five notes of the Reformed habit of mind": it is, first, deferential (that is, it respects tradition); second, the Reformed habit is critical (especially of the tradition it reveres); third, it is open to wisdom wherever it can be found; fourth, the Reformed habit of mind is unabashedly practical (truth is in order to goodness); and, fifth, the foremost note is "the evangelical habit" ("the overwhelming prophetic sense of standing, as Jeremiah was, under a Word of the Lord that we dare not tamper with, and which does not let us remain silent").[11]

Gerrish's description of the Reformed *habitus* is appealing in several respects. There is more to the identity of a Reformed community than its polity or what it believes. There is also the question of its practices and disciplines — the way it worships, its hymnody, piety, how it lives, what kind of community it is.

On the other hand, it is perhaps significant that Gerrish refers repeatedly to "the Reformed habit of *mind*" (italics mine). His five notes describe a Reformed disposition, but it is a disposition heavily weighted in the direction of the intellect. The Reformed *habitus* is both respectful and critical of tradition, and open to all forms of wisdom. But is it also characterized not only by what it affirms concerning the authority of Scripture, but also by its practices of read-

10. Brian Gerrish, "Tradition in the Modern World: The Reformed Habit of Mind," in *Toward the Future of Reformed Theology: Tasks, Topics, Traditions,* ed. David Willis and Michael Welker (Grand Rapids: Eerdmans, 1999), p. 12.
11. Gerrish, "Tradition in the Modern World," p. 19.

ing Scripture, not only by what it says about prayer, but also by its practices of prayer? This *habitus* is characterized by simplicity, and, according to the Heidelberg Catechism, by thanksgiving or gratitude, not simply gratitude as something that is believed, but also as something that is lived.

The Cultural-Linguistic Model

Finally, Reformed identity can be described formally in terms of a theological grammar, "family resemblances," "forms of life," and a cultural-linguistic model for theology. The concepts of grammar, family resemblances, and forms of life are borrowed from Ludwig Wittgenstein.[12] Family resemblances is a helpful and attractive metaphor that can be used to describe identity in the midst of diversity. A Reformed church in West Africa may differ in many respects from Reformed churches in other parts of the world, but they can be said to have a family resemblance not because their polities are identical or because they use the same confessions or hold the same essential tenets or affirm the same themes and emphases, but because there is a discernible similarity between their grammars of faith and the forms of life that accompany them.

This interpretation of Reformed identity has obvious parallels with Dietrich Ritschl's notion of "regulative statements" in the logic of theology and George Lindbeck's use of rule theory in his cultural-linguistic interpretation of doctrine.[13] In this model what is significant about a Reformed interpretation of Christian faith is not propositionally formulated truths nor inner experience, but the story the church tells and lives and "the grammar that informs the way the story is told and used."[14] The claim that there is a discernible grammar in Reformed faith might mean, for example, that Reformed churches share a grammar concerning the relation between grace and faith that is reflected in their practices of baptism. In a Reformed community one cannot baptize the children of believers and at the same time affirm that we are saved by what we believe and do, rather than by God's grace. Nor can one say that grace is God's response to faith rather than faith being a gift of God and the work of the Spirit. Both are "mistakes" in theological grammar — not just in terms of what is believed, but in terms of the incoherence between what is said and what is done.

12. Ludwig Wittgenstein, *Philosophical Investigations,* trans. G. E. M. Anscombe (Oxford: Basil Blackwell, 1967).

13. Dietrich Ritschl, *The Logic of Theology: A Brief Account of the Relationship Between Basic Concepts in Theology,* trans. John Bowden (Philadelphia: Fortress Press, 1987), pp. 108-11; George Lindbeck, *The Nature of Doctrine: Religion and Theology in a Postliberal Age* (Philadelphia: Westminster, 1984).

14. Lindbeck, *The Nature of Doctrine,* p. 80.

Much of the current discussion concerning which forms of baptism (infant or believers) are appropriate to Reformed identity can be understood as a discussion about which baptismal practices are appropriate to a particular theological grammar.

One advantage to this interpretation is its recognition that Reformed identity cannot be restricted to theology and that Reformed identity is best understood in the larger context of the stories by which a community worships and lives, the grammar it derives from those narratives, and the forms of life that attend those narratives. That does not necessarily mean that a Reformed church in West Africa will express its faith in the same way as do Reformed churches in other parts of the world. It might mean that because they share a similar grammar they might be members of the same theological family.

The disadvantages to this way of construing Reformed identity are at least twofold. First, this cultural-linguistic model benefits from the insights of cultural anthropology, but its emphasis on the themes of language and community neglects the affective dimension of identity. What are the affective consequences of participating in the language and life of a particular community? To what extent does the affective dimension provide an important point of encounter between language and communal life? The grammar in a community's forms of life is as much a grammar of the heart as of the mind.

A second disadvantage to the cultural-linguistic model is its neglect of history. Both communities and language are embedded in history, and neither can finally be understood only functionally. Words, to use a favorite metaphor of Wittgenstein's, are not only tools, but they are tools that have a history, and the meaning of a word is not just a matter of knowing how it functions in the context of a particular form of life, but also understanding the history of its usage.

Reformed Identity: A Proposal

If Reformed identity is not to be understood in terms of polity or essential tenets of doctrine, how should it be construed? Perhaps the appropriate metaphor for understanding Reformed identity is not so much that of a grocery list of communal rules or tenets that must be believed as that of a family photograph album that spans several generations. The confessional heritage of Reformed churches can be understood in similar terms. It may take considerable study, but after a while the careful and discerning "reader" of the photograph album may be able to identify the distinctive features of the family. There may be few, if any, identical twins in the family. No two individuals may look exactly alike, but there are similarities or "family resemblances" that stretch across the generations.

For example, there are some exceptions, but over several generations not many Stroups have been over six feet tall. They tend to be short, nearsighted, slightly overweight, and have gray hair much too prematurely in life. It may take leafing through the Stroup family photograph album several times, but after a while we develop an ability to identify Stroups, to pick out who does and does not belong to the family. One learns to recognize a certain profile — a common shape of the nose, tilt of the head, gait of walk. These family resemblances are not primarily a matter of belief and commitment. Some Stroups are liberal Democrats while others are conservative Republicans. But there is a certain family resemblance, which is more a matter of shared features than of essential tenets.

In addition to leafing through a family photograph album one might also attend a family reunion in order to understand a family's shared identity. At a family reunion it quickly becomes apparent that while there may be some similar physical features, not everyone looks alike. However, there are often shared personality features and family practices. Most members of a family do or do not have a sense of humor. There is a shared discourse that may include everything from jokes that everyone has heard countless times before to familiar stories anyone in the family can begin or finish. There are also shared family secrets that are known by most of the family, but by common consent never discussed. There are also certain family customs and practices that are part of the ritual of a family reunion. It would not be a proper Thanksgiving without the traditional touch football game afterwards. It is in this family gathering that one discerns not only a shared discourse, but a common disposition, ritual practices, and forms of life.

The Reformed confessions are something like the different generations in a family photograph album or the participants at a family reunion. They do not look alike. They certainly do not say the same things. They do not have in common an essence or single tenet, but similar contours and shapes — a certain shape of the nose, tilt of the head, gait of walk.

The interpretation of the authority of the Bible in the Westminster Confession of Faith differs significantly from that in the Confession of 1967. Although they do not say the same things about the authority of Scripture, their shared family resemblance is that they both understand the Bible to be authoritative for the interpretation of Christian faith and life. So too, even though the Westminster Confession has a different interpretation of the sovereignty of God than does the Confession of 1967, their shared family resemblance is that they both affirm the priority of God in God's relation to human beings.

There is also a shared discourse in the family of Reformed confessions. While the language in the sixteenth- and seventeenth-century confessions differs from that in the twentieth-century documents, they do share a common "grammar." Although the confessional documents differ in their understanding and interpretation of topics such as the sovereignty of God and the authority of the Bible, they share a theological grammar in which, among many other things: the subject and primary agent in the drama of salvation is always God and not human beings; people are forgiven their sins not because of who they are or what they have done, but because of God's prior grace in Jesus Christ; sin is such a pervasive reality that human beings are unable to extricate themselves from it; and human beings, when illumined by the Holy Spirit, are told in Scripture the truth about God, themselves, and their world. Although the Reformed confessions use different language to express these convictions, they share a common grammar, and as a whole they constitute a kind of "textbook" by which one learns to speak, feel, and understand the Reformed faith. In this sense the Reformed confessions are not so much a series of tenets one must believe as they are a language, a grammar, and a way of speaking, feeling, and living. It may be that the grammar of the Reformed confessions not only enables one to name religious and theological realities in one's experience, but the language and grammar may themselves create or at least mediate that experience.

This notion of similar features, a shared grammar, and a common *habitus* in the Reformed family helps to interpret what does and does not constitute a "mistake" in the life of Reformed churches. When a candidate for ordination to the ministry of Word and sacrament is examined on the floor of a presbytery, the issue is not whether his or her theology agrees with that of one or more members of the presbytery. The only relevant issue is whether the members of the presbytery, as they listen to the candidate talk about his or her faith and theological understanding of the gospel, can discern how the candidate is a part of the photograph album of Reformed theology as that is depicted in the Reformed confessions. From this perspective it is not a mistake for the candidate to prefer the interpretation of God's sovereignty in the Westminster Confession of faith to that in the Confession of 1967 or vice versa. The candidate can still be a member of the family even though he or she is drawn to part of the family that some members of the presbytery do not appreciate as much as they do others. What does matter is whether the candidate participates in the shared grammar and the disciplines and practices that constitute the *habitus* of the Reformed family. If he or she does not, if the candidate speaks a "foreign tongue," the problem is not simply that he or she will be difficult to understand, but the fragile relation between language and life will be confused, if not sundered. In the Reformed tradition one cannot baptize the children of believers and at the same time affirm that we are saved by what we believe and do rather than by God's grace. That is a "mistake" in theological grammar for which there is no precedent in the Reformed confessions. No one in the Reformed family looks or sounds "that way."

One of the reasons theological education has become so difficult recently in North American Reformed seminaries is that increasing numbers of students are unfamiliar with the grammar and *habitus* of the Reformed tradition. They either come from churches in which little or no attention has been given to the grammar of Reformed discourse (that is, they have not been "catechized" or taught to speak the faith as their own language) or they come to seminary as "new Christians" with a faith that has not been tutored in the language, practices, disciplines, and forms of life of the Reformed tradition. Theological education is much more difficult and the stakes much higher if the task is not simply a matter of mastering facts and information and learning to think critically about the Bible and Reformed theology, but learning for the first time to speak the grammar and live by means of the practices and disciplines of the Reformed tradition.

An Ecumenical Context

As representatives of Reformed churches today enter into bilateral and multilateral conversation with Christians from other traditions, the question of Reformed identity is both more urgent and more complex than it ever has been. It is one thing to ask what constitutes Reformed identity in the context of the diverse confessional literature of the sixteenth and seventeenth centuries. The challenge is even greater when the question is the relation between "classical" European Reformed confessions and those written in North America in the twentieth century. And the situation is still more complex when the issue is not simply historical diversity, but cultural diversity as well. In what sense are Reformed churches in West Africa and Korea members of the same family as Reformed churches in Germany and the United States?

When representatives of Reformed churches from different parts of the world enter into conversations with Roman Catholics, Baptists, Anglicans, Mennonites, Methodists, Disciples of Christ, Lutherans, and Orthodox, in what sense, if any, do the Reformed representatives speak with one voice or as one church?[15] There is much to be said for the position that our identity — both individually and communally — is altered by our encounters and conversations with those who are "other" than us. Those Christians who enter into conversation with Christians from other traditions and churches but who are left un-

---

15. For summaries of these discussions see Wilson, *Bilateral Dialogues;* Lukas Vischer, ed., *Agreed Statements from the Orthodox-Reformed Dialogue* (Geneva: World Alliance of Reformed Churches, 1998); and H. S. Wilson, ed., *Oriental Orthodox-Reformed Dialogue: The First Four Sessions* (Geneva: World Alliance of Reformed Churches, 1998).

changed by that experience may have been involved in an exchange of views, but they have not been in a conversation. On the other hand, it is also unlikely that such encounters will be productive if one or more participants enter the conversation with little or no sense of who they themselves are. How one understands one's own theological identity is an important issue in ecumenical conversation.

A common procedure in ecumenical conversation is to attempt to discover common ground or some basis for agreement in theology and doctrine. The underlying assumption in that strategy is that if the parties can first reach some form of agreement about what they believe, they can then turn to the more difficult issues of worship and polity. In terms of the five identity models we have reviewed in this essay, many ecumenical conversations seem to assume that the focus should be on essential tenets or at least common themes and emphases. This strategy raises several questions. First, can theology be reduced to official confessional statements? As we have seen, does this strategy not ignore the important relation between theology and the practical, daily life of Christian communities? Second, if it were possible to agree on a confession or set of themes and emphases, to what would one have agreed? And what would be the relation between such an ecumenical agreement and the language, life, character, and worship of the communities represented in the confession?

Consider, for instance, the recent conversations between representatives from Reformed and Orthodox churches. Those conversations, which took place between 1988 and 1994, culminated in two statements of agreement — one on the Trinity and the other on Christology. While those statements are significant accomplishments, one must wonder about the assumptions beneath the dialogue, the strategies involved, and the dialogue's consequences and implications. In his helpful introduction to the agreed statements, Lukas Vischer writes, "From the beginning it was clear that the dialogue should concentrate on central affirmations of the Christian faith."[16] And why was that so self-evident? Perhaps because the underlying assumption was that agreement on doctrine must precede more difficult questions about life and practice. Having reached agreement on the Trinity and Christology, Vischer writes, "The expectation is now that, on the basis of this firm common ground, the differences in the understanding of the church and the ministry can be dealt with in a new perspective."[17] But can they? Having reached apparent agreement on what they believe about the Trinity, do those representatives from Orthodox and Reformed churches indeed now have "firm common ground" on which to address questions about authority in the life of the church, the church's relation to its

16. Lukas Vischer, "Introduction," in *Agreed Statements*, p. 9.
17. Lukas Vischer, "Introduction," in *Agreed Statements*, p. 9.

social and political context, and the ordination of women? One hopes so, but it is difficult to quiet the suspicion that there may be a large train wreck waiting down the tracks laid by these two common agreements.

Neither religious identity in general nor Reformed identity in particular can be understood only in terms of doctrine. Doctrine cannot and should not be separated from issues of grammar and *habitus*. The issue of the ordination of women in ecumenical conversation is an important example. The issue has never been a matter simply of polity. It has always been a matter that concerns a church's theological identity. But the issue is not simply a matter of determining the appropriate doctrinal tenets or theological themes and affirmations that might serve as the basis for the conversation. It is much more profoundly a question of what kind of communities ordain women and what kind do not, and what are the differences between their grammars, character, disciplines, and practices.

While the question of the ordination of women is a significant issue for the contemporary life of many churches, a far more important question is how churches, and Reformed churches in particular, understand their theological identity. How a church answers this broader, more basic question will have a great deal to do with its ability to respond to issues like the ordination of women and countless other challenges that are waiting in the wings for ecumenical discussion.

CHAPTER 18

Sovereignty and Sanctification: Reformed Accents in Ecumenics

Gabriel Fackre

Dialogue with Lutherans on proposals for full communion "concentrates the mind" on the subject at hand — or so I discovered in ten years on the Reformed team in the North American Lutheran-Reformed Conversation. Who are we vis-à-vis our interlocutors? What do we have to share? Are there things we have to learn?

As the specifics of Reformed identity were significantly shaped by sixteenth-century exchanges with the Lutheran tradition, they continue to come into bold relief in contemporary encounters. What follows relives historic debates. Yet this time around, like the Leuenberg Concord, important steps are taken beyond the polarization of another day. The advance is reflected in the formula of the North American Lutheran-Reformed accord consummated in 1997: "mutual affirmation and mutual admonition."[1]

---

1. The formula appears initially in Keith F. Nickle and Timothy F. Lull, ed., *A Common Calling: The Witness of the Reformation Churches in North America Today* (Minneapolis: Augsburg Fortress, 1993), and was at the heart of the Formula of Agreement (FOA) adopted in 1997 by the Evangelical Lutheran Church in America, the Presbyterian Church (USA), the Reformed Church in America, and the United Church of Christ. An exploration of the mutuality theme in the Lutheran-Reformed Conversation, and also in the proposed North American Lutheran-Episcopal Concordat and the international Lutheran–Roman Catholic dialogue on "justification by faith" appears in Gabriel Fackre and Michael Root, *Affirmations and Admonitions* (Grand Rapids: Eerdmans, 1998). On the Lutheran-Reformed exchange about the same see the writer's "What the Lutherans and the Reformed Can Learn from One Another"; Alan E. Johnson, "Seeking a Common Ground: A Response to Gabriel Fackre"; and "Gabriel Fackre Replies," in *The Christian Century* 114, no. 18 (June 4-11, 1998): 558-61, 563-64.

In this laboratory of learning I discerned two aspects of the Reformed contribution to ecumenics. One has to do with its ecumenical predisposition as such, and the other with the specific charisms the Reformed tradition brings to the ecumenical arena, "sovereignty" and "sanctification." At the same time, keeping in mind the associated admonition, a Reformed reductionism can hurt ecumenism and close our ears to the contributions and critiques of others.

Sovereignty

A critical Lutheran word repeated in the dialogue, ever and again: We're not sure that you Reformed people believe in the Real Presence. And you're too casual about the church and too wrapped up in the world. When it comes to Christology, you are Nestorius *redivivus*. Bonhoeffer sums up for us just where the Reformed went wrong. As Bethge put it:

> Bonhoeffer suspects here [in Barth] the old extra-Calvinisticum which does not allow the glory of God to enter entirely into this world. *Finitum incapax infiniti*, the Calvinists say. Bonhoeffer protests with Luther against this all his life. *Finitu capax infiniti. . . .*[2]

Bonhoeffer's point?

> God is *there,* which is to say: not in eternal non-objectivity [but] "haveable," graspable in his Word within the church. . . . It is the honour and glory of our God . . . that, giving himself for our sake in deepest condescension, he passes into the flesh, the bread, our hearts, our mouths, entrails, and suffers also for our sake that he be dishonourably *(unehrlich)* handled, on the altar as on the Cross.[3]

That's why Luther judged you Reformed to be of "a different spirit."

This charge, expressed in one way or another by our North American Lutheran critics, made for much soul-searching.[4] Some of us — both Lutheran

---

2. Eberhard Bethge, "Bonhoeffer's Life and Theology," in *World Come of Age,* ed. Ronald Gregor Smith (Philadelphia: Fortress Press, 1967), pp. 36-37.

3. Dietrich Bonhoeffer, *Act and Being,* trans. Bernard Noble (New York: Harper and Bros., 1961), pp. 81, 90-91 (Bonhoeffer quoting Martin Luther, WA 23.157).

4. For a sample of the back-and-forth on these matters see Mark E. Chapman, "Why Can't We Get This Right?," *Lutheran Forum* 27, no. 2 (1993); Gabriel Fackre, "Response to Chapman: A Common Calling," 27, no. 3 (1993); Mark A. Chapman, "Response to Gabriel Fackre," 27, no. 4 (1993). On the Lutheran critique see Robert Jenson, "Comment on A Common Calling," *Pro Ecclesia* 1, no. 1 (1992): 16-20.

and Reformed — could not forget that Bonhoeffer and Barth were allies in making a faithful witness in the German church struggle. Doesn't this suggest the presence of underlying convergences, and even more, possible mutual learnings? In the dialogue, we needed to be clear about what prompted the Lutheran judgments, then weigh their validity.

In sacramentology, Christology, ecclesiology and ethics, the Lutherans perceive the Reformed to be distancing God from the divine *haveability*. Deity seems always out of reach in a Zwinglian memorialism, a Nestorian severing of the natures, and an unstable, humanized church and mission. Where are the promises of Christ to be *with* us . . . *in* us . . . *under* us?

Lutherans, past and present, because of their "haveable" tenets, do spot something. We fight against the domestication of Deity. The sovereign God is not to be "handled" by humans. And so we, in turn, suspect Lutheran eucharistic theology of such control temptations, discover Monophysite tendencies in Lutheran Christology, and charge its ecclesiology with an uncritical "continuing of the Incarnation" devoid of the *semper reformanda*. Yes, the Reformed tradition stands unapologetically for the divine freedom! God will not be bound by our human hands, even by the holiest of claimants. The early Barth had it right when he showed how this Reformed commitment works itself out in matters of confession and creed:

> To our fathers the historical past was something which called not for loving and devoted admiration but for careful and critical scrutiny. . . . There are documentary statements of their beliefs . . . but . . . our fathers had good reason for leaving us no Augsburg Confession authentically interpreting the word of God, *no* Formula of Concord, *no* "Symbolic Books" which might later, like the Lutheran, possess the odor of sanctity. . . . It *may* be our doctrinal task to make a careful revision of the theology of Geneva or the Heidelberg Catechism or the Synod of Dort or . . . it *may* be our task to draw up a new creed. . . .[5]

All of this is of a piece, according to Barth, with the Reformed *Deo Sola Gloria* and thus its resolute refusal to deify any created thing . . . its *finitum non est capax infiniti*. . . .[6]

Just because of this "resolute refusal to deify any created thing," Reformed sensibility encourages a light touch on inherited ecclesial things. The givens of

5. Karl Barth, *The Word of God and the Word of Man,* trans. Douglas Horton (Boston: Pilgrim Press, 1928), pp. 229, 230.

6. Barth, *The Word of God,* p. 231. See also Barth's self-critical Reformed comments on these matters in Karl Barth, *Church Dogmatics* IV/2, trans. Geoffrey W. Bromiley and Thomas F. Torrance (Edinburgh: T. & T. Clark, 1958), pp. 68-69.

church life are corrigible, always reformable under the Word. The *incapax* and the *semper* predispose the Reformed to challenge the ecclesial status quo. Especially so where denominational claims are made that here and here alone is Christ's true Body. In the sixteenth century this took the shape of a reforming movement *within* the church catholic. In the twentieth century it took the shape of an ecumenical reforming movement *toward* the church catholic. The temptation in the first context was the corralling of deity into ancient homogeneous givens. The temptation in the second context was the delimited association of deity with modern heterogeneous givens.

Ecumenism as the quest for a re-formed life together beyond our multifarious tribal enclaves cannot help but find a home in the Reformed witness to the divine sovereignty. Is it any accident that Reformed theologian W. A. Visser 't Hooft, the first General Secretary of the World Council of Churches, called the churches out of their historic divisions toward the "Una Sancta" based on loyalty to the *"ecclesia reformanda, qui reformata"* mandate of its one Sovereign and thus obedience to the "kingship of Christ"?[7] The history of Reformed initiatives and involvement in the ecumenical movement reflects Visser 't Hooft's mandate.

But wait a minute. There is plenty of evidence also for Reformed footdragging, of resistance to the ecumenical impulse, indeed of reversing it by spawning division, by the claims of one or another fissiparous Reformed denomination to be the sole custodian of the treasures of the gospel. Ironically, such Reformed rigidities have a Lutheran cast to them, a defense of the "haveable," a treatment of "the theology of Geneva" and the "Synod of Dort" as if they were an unalterable Augsburg Confession, a deification of "created things" and thus creatures of the *capax.*

But wait a minute . . . again. Is it possible that the Lutherans have something to teach the "always reforming" people? Do the status quo Reformed themselves represent a reminder to us of something we revisables may forget?

When a Reformed church writes only *semper* on its banners, and neglects the criterion by which it must assess the call to reform — *under the Word* — the charges of our critics do strike home. We are too easily seduced by the *au courant.* Our eagerness to change makes us too ready to abandon the historic givens in order to "keep up with the times." Called to *relate* to the culture under the freedom of the Word, we instead *capitulate* to it. Taking up Pastor Robinson's Reformed cry of "ever-new light and truth shall break forth . . . ," we are tempted to omit the criteriological "from his holy Word."

Reformed involvement in the ecumenical arena illustrates the foregoing.

7. W. A. Visser 't Hooft, *The Kingship of Christ: An Interpretation of Recent European Theology* (New York: Harper & Bros, 1948), pp. 89-116.

The sovereignty commitment makes us ever-ready to challenge tribal givens and attempt new ventures in structural church union — for example, the United Church of Christ and the United Church of Canada in North America. At the same time, critics point to tendencies in each of these churches to succumb to an ideological religious pluralism ready to abandon the Christology that forms both their identity and their ecumenical commitments.[8] This has sparked controversy in both churches and the formation of protest groups that have raised questions about the cultural captivity of their denominations.[9]

Missing in a one-note Reformed stress on sovereignty is the Lutheran witness to *solidarity,* God's solidarity with us in the givens. The Word to which we are accountable in our right commitment to reform the corrigible past comes to us through the givens of Scripture, tradition, church, and sacrament. Ecumenism that undercuts these "haveables" is false to the very means of grace the Holy Spirit used to bring it to be. And theology devoid of them will be seduced by every claimant Now that purports loyalty to the *semper* and *incapax.*

Of course, mutual admonition works both ways. Lutherans who have little to show in their history of actual ecumenical advance have acceded in their turn to a one-note stress on "solidarity." The givens of inherited creed and cult have so dominated their tradition that even a slightly "altered" Augsburg Confession (1540) is cause for clamor, and small ecumenical initiatives in the direction of close Reformation companions evoke outrage among the self-appointed custodians of Lutheran identity.[10] How much that Lutheran ear needs to hear the Reformed word of sovereignty! Without it, Lutherans fall prey to the same reductionism they rightly criticize in Reformed history. In both cases, "the eye cannot say to the hand, 'I have no need of you.'" Paul's Corinthian admonitions are as timely as ever.[11]

8. See, for example, the United Church of Christ's Board for Homeland Ministries "Pluralism Principles" and its "foundation paper" on the subject by Daniel F. Romero, *Our Futures Inextricably Linked,* Division of Education and Publication, 1994. Latitudinarian christological statements of the moderator of the United Church of Canada evoked recent controversy in that church.

9. A case in point is the "Confessing Christ" movement in the United Church of Christ. See "The Church of the Center," in Gabriel Fackre, *Restoring the Center* (Downers Grove, Ill.: InterVarsity Press, 1998), pp. 27-45.

10. So the Department of Systematic Theology, "A Review of 'A Common Calling,'" *Concordia Theological Review* 57, no. 3 (1993): 193-213.

11. The difference in Lutheran and Reformed sensibility vis-à-vis both "sovereignty/ sanctification" and "solidarity/simultaneity" is illustrated in the approach to hymnody on new challenges of inclusive language. A comparison of the modest alterations made in the ELCA *Lutheran Book of Worship* to those that press the Reformed *semper reformanda* of inclusivity through increasing alterations in *The Presbyterian Hymnal* (USA), *The Book of Praise* (Presbyterian Church of Canada) and in *The New Century Hymnal* (A UCC agency) is

The promise of the present ecumenical developments is evidence of mutualities in listening. Certainly the remarkable role of current Lutheran ecumenics is evidence of an openness to the *semper*. The secular press in the form of *US News & World Report* captions a news story, "An Ecumenical Summer." The report had to do with three Evangelical Lutheran Church in America (ELCA) initiatives up for 1997 vote: the international Lutheran–Roman Catholic proposal to lift mutually the sixteenth-century condemnations on justification, a Lutheran-Episcopal Concordat, and the aforementioned Lutheran-Reformed Agreement. While only the last has been approved by all parties, the others may yet achieve their goals in one way or another. And, as for the Reformed contingent (including the Reformed strain in the Episcopal tradition), the Lutheran witness to classical doctrine has been heard and commitments made to the same, as in key sections of both the FOA and the Concordat.[12]

The success of the FOA was due, in part, to the rereading of one another's particularities as charisms *within* a common Body, not occasions for excommunication from it. A case in point was the eucharistic controversy. Lutherans in the current dialogue saw that all the classical Reformed confessions and contemporary liturgies affirm the "Real Presence," but do so in the characteristic Reformed framework of sovereignty and not the Lutheran mode of "solidarity" (the concept of ubiquity). Thus Reformed language of "spiritual Presence" refers to the work of the Holy Spirit in bringing the believer, in eating and drinking, into communion with the glorified humanity of Christ.[13]

Sanctification

The 1919 steel strike was long and bitter. The company "coal and iron police" and strikers fought one another in ways reminiscent of the historic 1892 shoot-

---

instructive. Here the two traditions need each other: Lutherans are too tradition-bound and the Reformed may imperil the best of tradition by eagerness for change without careful doctrinal scrutiny. On these mutualities see Richard Christensen, ed., *How Shall We Sing the Lord's Song?: An Assessment of the New Century Hymnal* (Pittsburgh: Pickwick Press, 1997).

12. For example, the inclusion in the final version of the FOA of 14 "affinities in doctrine and practice" of the two traditions appropriated from the 1983 North American "Invitation to Action" cited in James E. Andrews and Joseph A. Burgess, eds., *An Invitation to Action: The Lutheran-Reformed Dialogue, Series III, 1981-1983* (Philadelphia: Fortress Press, 1984), pp. 2-3.

13. In the nineteenth century when similar debates wracked the Reformed churches, John Williamson Nevin surveyed the Reformed catechisms to make just this point. See *The Mystical Presence and Other Writings on the Eucharist,* ed. Bard Thompson and George Bricker, Lancaster Series on the Mercersburg Theology 4 (Philadelphia: United Church Press, 1966).

out between Pinkerton detectives and Homestead steelworkers. Why these recurring conflicts in Pittsburgh's "Steel valley"?

A budding ecumenical development early in the century, the "Interchurch World Movement," took it upon itself to find out what lay behind worker unrest. Its Commission on Inquiry produced the Interchurch Steel Strike Reports that "served to present facts surrounding the employment of men in the steel industry that aroused a sense of resentment against this great corporation throughout the civilized world."[14] Church involvement of this sort in the steelworkers' struggle for justice was a factor in leading the writer to a ten-year ministry in the steel valley in mission churches earlier established by the Reformed Church in the U.S. to share in the workers' plight. The configuration here of ecumenism, the Reformed tradition, and social struggle illustrate our second motif, "sanctification."

The impetus for ecumenism has often been the strength that such alliances give for making a witness in the public arena. "Social issues" — such as the wage, hours, working and living conditions in steel towns investigated by the Interchurch World Movement — could be confronted more effectively when churches joined together. The "Life and Work" aspect of world ecumenism is the institutionalizing of the impetus. Local, regional, and national conciliar ecumenism is often best known for its social witness, and is frequently funded . . . or defunded . . . for stands taken on one or another social issue.

Sanctification in subjective soteriology is the doctrine that deals with grace as "power in" the believer that keeps company with the grace of "favor toward" the same, the impartation of grace inextricable from its imputation. *Becoming* holy as the outworking of the sinner being *declared* holy by a forensic grace has been a Reformed staple, especially so in give-and-take with Lutherans. And the more intense the conversation becomes, the more the Reformed insistence on both the *possibilities* of genuine growth in grace and the imperatives of grace with its "third use of the law."

What obtains in the personal Christian life carries over in Reformed teaching and practice in the political, economic, and social spheres — a *public* sanctification commensurate with the *personal.* From Calvin's Geneva forward, the Reformed tradition has held the civil order accountable to the regency of Christ (the conjunction of *sovereignty* with *sanctification*) with good hopes for its improvement. Nicholas Wolterstorff identifies it as its characteristic "world-formative" impulse to be contrasted with the "avertive" tendencies of other traditions. (Then-Lutheran Richard Neuhaus took offense in a response to the

14. Arthur Wharton, "What the Church Needs to Be Saved," in *Labor Speaks for Itself on Religion* (New York: Macmillan, 1929), p. 95.

book.)[15] Reinhold Niebuhr was partial to the later Calvin and the later Calvinists (Cromwell) for their world-formative commitments and critical of Luther and the Lutherans for both their privatizing of Christian faith (insufficient "sovereignty") and a stress on moral ambiguity that tended to neglect the possibilities in soul and society (insufficient "sanctification").[16]

The call to, and hope for, the world's sanctifying reform predisposes Reformed churches to look for ecclesial instruments of sufficient strength to take on the secular principalities and powers. In modern times, ecumenical agencies appeared as a likely candidate. The support by Reformed denominations for "interchurch" movements for "life and work" purposes was a natural result. Along with the urgings of *semper reformanda,* the imperatives of *sanctificatio* contributed to the major role they played in the North American conciliar efforts at all levels. And it is quite possible that, whatever the announced rationale for two major union efforts in structural ecumenism in North America (the United Church of Christ and the United Church of Canada), the chance for a more effective church witness on social issues surely played a role.[17]

Along with enthusiasm for ecumenism as such because of its potential for social witness, the Reformed tradition within that movement brought to the fore ever and again the concerns of social sanctification. In the Lutheran-Reformed conversations in both Europe and North America, the Reformed "mode of thinking"

> begins with the assumption that the obedience of faith in state and society is a matter of the church as a whole also [not just the individual] . . . and that the acting of the Christian must not be separated from this relation.[18]

Echoes of admonishing Lutherans for their "avertive" inclinations can be heard in this Reformed self-definition.

But admonition goes both ways. The strength of the sanctification charism carries with it weaknesses, as Lutherans are quick to point out. Niebuhr in his Lutheran moments said it this way:

> The theologies which have sought to do justice to the positive aspects of regeneration have usually obscured the realities of sin which appear at every

15. Nicholas Wolterstorff, *Until Justice and Peace Embrace* (Grand Rapids: Eerdmans, 1983), pp. 3-22 and passim.

16. Reinhold Niebuhr, *The Nature and Destiny of Man,* vols. 1 & 2 (New York: Charles Scribner's Sons, 1945), 1:222-23; 2:1, 192, 196.

17. See Theodore Louis Trost, *The Ecumenical Impulse in Twentieth Century American Protestantism: A Study of Douglas Horton's Illustrative Career (circa 1912-1968)* (Cambridge, Mass.: Harvard University, Ph.D. dissertation, 1998), passim.

18. *A Common Calling,* quoting the Driebergen Report, 60.

level of virtue. . . . Calvin's . . . doctrine of sanctification arrives at conclusions hardly distinguishable from Catholic ones . . . the Christian in which sin is broken "in principle" claims that the sins which remain are merely incidental . . . without realizing that the sin of self-love is present in its most basic form (Calvin) assuming a *prevailing* inclination to submit to (God's) will.[19]

The susceptibility of the Reformed tradition to illusions along the trail of sanctification has played out in both its ecumenical impulse and its social concern.

While strengthening the will to ecumenism by stressing its ethical fruits, the sanctification side of Reformed faith can so control its understanding of ecumenism that it diminishes the role of doctrinal accord so crucial to considered and lasting ecumenical agreements. In our North American dialogue, the accusation by Lutherans that my own church, the United Church of Christ, had no theology and was "only a social action agency," "the religious cheering section of the Democratic party," etc., was frequent, with many references to standard media reports of political stands taken by our officialdom. It was not easy both to defend our legitimate "world-formative" commitments and at the same time point to the confessional solidities in which our church is grounded. Hence the formation by doctrinally grounded social activists in our church of the "Confessing Christ" movement to reclaim these fundaments and call them to the attention of both our critics and the theologically indifferent within our own ranks.

A similar case might be made for the impact of a sanctification rationale for ecumenism on such conciliar ventures as the U.S. National Council of Churches and the World Council of Churches. When such bodies define themselves essentially in "world-formative" terms, without warrants in the theological substance that was critical to their birth, ecumenical momentum itself is put in jeopardy. Recent efforts of both these councils to reshape their agendas and retrieve their foundations suggest that admonitions about reductionist temptations are being heard. But again, let them be a two-way street, one in which the social sanctification dimension of ecumenism is not replaced by yet another reductionism, this time accession to apolitical pieties and theologies.

Reformed sanctification needs the partner gift of simultaneity, another learning from the Lutheran-Reformed dialogue. The Calvinist trust in "the prevailing inclination" of new states of grace in both soul and society has to be sobered by a realism that recognizes the corruptibility of every advance in either of those locales. Simultaneity has to do with the Lutheran *simul iustus et peccator*. The *sanctificatio* must walk with the *simul*. When the former goes it

19. Niebuhr, *The Nature and Destiny of Man*, 2:125, 199, 200.

alone, Reformed faith breeds utopian expectations and self-righteous fury in both the life of the believer and in movements of social protest. Sin persists in every sanctifying move forward. The failure to attend to this Lutheran sobriety in matters of social sanctification has resulted in the naïvetés of "righteous" activisms that silence internal criticism, the neglect of checks and balances within them, and the framing of social issues as simplistic "us and them" battles.[20] May we hear these Lutheran-like admonishments. And, again, vice versa: Lutheran absorptions in the ambiguities of soul and society and inclinations to retreat to the private realm must hear of Reformed hope for the work of sanctifying graces under the Lord of both soul and society.

Conclusion

A refrain of this paper is the importance of both affirmation and admonition in ecumenical matters. The toughest of the two is receiving admonishment from the ecumenical other. In this conversation on the Reformed contribution to ecumenics can we "take it" as well as "give it"? Here, finally, in this matter of vulnerability, the motif of sovereignty has a counsel for its stewards. To believe that no human opinion can be equated with the divine Word means that no Reformed accent itself can ever be exempt from self-criticism. The willingness to hear and learn from admonitions, therefore, is built into a Reformed tradition always ready to re-form in accord with the one Word. So our *semper* can walk together with another's *simul* — and yet other companions on the ecumenical path.

---

20. See the writer's critique of political fundamentalism with its strong Reformed influences, *The Religious Right and Christian Faith* (Grand Rapids: Eerdmans, 1983).

CHAPTER 19

Reconsidering the Doctrine of Providence

Jan Milič Lochman

Today, the classical ecumenical theme of providence comes under critical fire, or, worse still, moves into a shadowy area of disinterest. Some pointers: for years I have been aware of the phrase "the end of providence." It is the title of a well-known book by Carl Amery, with the subtitle "the merciless consequences of Christianity."[1] Amery offers an analysis of the philosophical premises of modern-day environmental destruction and the truly merciless way we humans deal with our fellow creatures. He puts biblical thought, in particular Christianity, on trial. The biblical "demythologizing" of creation, as established in the very first chapters of Genesis, has led to the excessive claim on the part of humans to rule recklessly over the whole of creation.

This "mandate" becomes fatal once the doctrine of providence is involved: providence enables people to salve their consciences; it allows them to have no scruples about pursuing their own interests — divine providence will sort things out. Thus the doctrine of providence leads to a dogmatic mercilessness. One can hear similar arguments — explicitly, or, more often, implicitly — in another context from Marxists, especially in relation to the philosophical premises of capitalism. Adam Smith, the "Luther of economics" as Karl Marx described him, combined the idealization of the market economy's promising future with a secular doctrine of providence: the negative effects of the division of labor and the dynamic market economy would in the end be covered up by the "invisible hand" of the Lord of history. The contradictions of the market cannot be isolated and viewed in and for themselves: providence, the healing

1. Carl Amery, *Ende der Vorsehung: Die gnadenlosen Folgen des Christentums* (Rowohlt: Reinbeck, 1972).

potency of every power mechanism, "guarantees" the eventually irresistible progress. Marxists uncover this kind of "pseudo theology" as a disguising of economic contradictions and clear class interests.

It is not just declared critics of Christianity who are articulating their concerns, but also thinkers who are kindly disposed towards Christianity. That has not always been the case. In particular, the doctrine of providence has been one of the mainstays of an "everyman's theology" (E. Brunner) for centuries, which was maintained even in circles that dismissed many other doctrines of faith, as an article that still formed a core of Christianity in secularized times. One need only to think of the religiosity of the Enlightenment period to see this.

The impression of well-ordered harmony in nature and history, and in particular the providential progress founded on this, can hardly be comprehended in the twentieth century. Many worse things have happened in our time than the earthquake in Lisbon in 1755 which threatened the optimism of the Enlightenment; not just in the area of natural catastrophes, but also "home-made" ones: through actions of human destructiveness that have led not just humanity, but the whole of creation to the edge of an apocalyptic abyss.

The old question of the mystery of obvious evil and suffering, which has always confronted the doctrine of providence, is now being asked with an unanticipated edge to it. What about the doctrine of providence? Has it not become discredited?

Even in academic circles doubting voices can be heard. In the seventies, we made an attempt at a three-volume *Dogmatics in Dialogue* with Heinrich Ott and Fritz Buri. It was Fritz Buri in particular who in relation to the subject "God's accompanying presence in the covenant" stated categorically that although amongst all the *loci* of dogmatics, the doctrine of the *concursus divinus* was to him the "most beautiful and favoured," this had a categorical restriction. This was that its rational core was the phenomenology of human presence with one another in all its myriad forms of possibilities and impossibilities. For us, in its traditional form — as God accompanying mankind — it now belongs to the past.[2]

This was a voice of extreme free-spirited Protestantism. However, theologians such as C. H. Ratschow who are more aware of their denomination can come to the same conclusions from different premises. He, too, maintains that "theological talk of providence should cease, both with regard to the term itself as well as with regard to the theological consequences it brings with it."[3]

What is the result of this variety of critical-skeptical questioning for us?

2. Fritz Buri, *Dogmatik im Dialog, Bd. 3, Schöpfung und Erlösung* (Gütersloh: G. Mohn, 1976), pp. 122f.

3. C. H. Ratschow, "Das Heilschandeln und das Welthandeln Gottes," *NZSTh* 1 (1959): 71.

Should we distance ourselves from the doctrine of providence? Of course, I do not think so. But we cannot dismiss the critical questions: they all, and the atheistic ones perhaps more so than the others, have their reasons. In other words: not every form of the doctrine of providence can be justified today, neither in a biblical nor in a contemporary context. Both of these aspects require further clarification.

Farewell to the *articulus mixtus*

Many problems associated with the doctrine of providence are related to the fact that in many parts of the history of doctrine it has been interpreted as being an, if not the, *articulus mixtus*. In other words, it has been seen as a doctrine in which the specifically biblical and general worldviews flow into one another in harmony. This already applies to the early Christian theologians (especially the Apologists) in their attempts to reconcile their message of joy with the religious-philosophical thought of the time: a humanly understandable, yet theologically dubious attempt. The doctrine of providence lends itself particularly well to such things. The terms *pronoia* and *providentia* in use in the ancient world at the time were readily adopted to describe the intended biblical topics of divine provision and care.

However, it was not just in the beginnings of Christianity, but also throughout the Middle Ages and well into the modern era, including in Reformed thought, that the doctrine was proclaimed as an *articulus mixtus*, at times with noticeable pride. Orthodox Lutheran and Reformed theologians understood the doctrine of providence as *primarium caput fidei et religionis* (Fr. Turretini). This is evidenced by the great authorities of the ancient world from Socrates to Aristotle through to Seneca, Cicero, and beyond — the overwhelming *consensus populorum*. But such references to philosophical authorities, and the starting point with the general *consensus populorum* only make sense if a general understanding of God is presumed. The doctrine of providence is therefore directed onto a "theistic track." The traditional predicates of theistic thought — the Godhead as omnipotent, all-knowing, beyond all time and space, and in particular, as having absolute power without the ability to suffer — become dominant. To be sure, at times they undergo a "Christian" baptism and are modified. The act of providence is thus seen as "the act of a superior and absolutely omniscient, omnipotent and omnioperative being whose nature and work do of course display such moral qualities as wisdom, righteousness and goodness, etc."[4]

---

4. Karl Barth, *Kirchliche Dogmatik* III/3 (Zürich, 1950), p. 34. (ET: Church Dogmatics III/3 [Edinburgh: T. & T. Clark, 1957], p. 31.)

Setting the course in this way shapes the traditional problems of the doctrine of providence. With regard to God: How is the omnipotence of God to be reconciled with his goodness? With regard to his providential presence: How do the sovereign freedom of God and the relative freedom of humankind mix? (The doctrine of providence should in no way be confused with an undifferentiated determinism.) And most importantly, put in a critical, exaggerated form: Does the doctrine of providence — the provision of a basically apathetic God — not play down the onslaught of destructive evil? Does it not pass on by the suffering of innocent people, the unbearable reality of our world? Does it not hear the cry of an Ivan Karamazov who feels obliged to return the "ticket" for the world of God, where children suffer, to the Creator who in reality acts like a cruel demon?

God's Presence in the Covenant

A resolute farewell to a doctrine of providence understood as an *articulus mixtus* is, in my opinion, not just permitted, but absolutely necessary. But it would be wrong to throw the baby out with the bathwater. "God's presence in the covenant" is undeniably a topic that is biblically founded — and with that the notion of "providence" suggests itself.

In the Reformed tradition we have a classical text that shows the way for a "different" doctrine of providence. I am thinking of the Heidelberg Catechism in its questions 26-28. It is no coincidence that it is precisely in our times, a time of challenge, that our Reformed fathers such as Karl Barth and our brothers such as Eberhard Busch begin their thoughts on the doctrine of providence with this "theological jewel" (Karl Barth). I quote the first two questions:

> *Question 26:* **What do you believe when you say: "I believe in God the Father Almighty, Maker of heaven and earth"?**
>
> Answer: That the eternal Father of our Lord Jesus Christ, who out of nothing created heaven and earth with all that is in them, who also upholds and governs them by his eternal counsel and providence, is for the sake of Christ his Son my God and my Father. I trust in him so completely that I have no doubt that he will provide me with all things necessary for body and soul. Moreover, whatever evil he sends upon me in this troubled life he will turn to my good, for he is able to do it, being Almighty God, and is determined to do it, being a faithful Father.
>
> *Question 27:* **What do you understand by the providence of God?**
>
> Answer: The almighty and ever-present power of God whereby he still

284

upholds, as it were by his own hand, heaven and earth together with all creatures, and rules in such a way that leaves and grass, rain and drought, fruitful and unfruitful years, food and drink, health and sickness, riches and poverty, and everything else, come to us not by chance but by his fatherly hand.

What is to be found in these sentences that is important for our deliberations? We can start with the approach Eberhard Busch pointed out: the Catechism speaks "of providence, as well as of creation, in a sub-clause, whilst the main clause is not about what God does, but about who the God is who acts."[5] That means that the doctrine of providence is not formulated in the manner of natural theology or historical speculation, but as a reply to the first sentence in the Apostolic Creed.

In this way the general understanding of God in the doctrine of providence is unmistakably clarified: this is no general theistic principle with its abstract qualities, but "the eternal Father of our Lord Jesus Christ — for the sake of Christ his Son my God and my Father." The name Jesus is mentioned twice: the doctrine of providence is therefore about his Father: the Emmanuel of the Old Testament, the Emmanuel of the story of Jesus of Nazareth. This is where the God of providence can be looked for and found, in this story of friendship and joy, of blood and tears, under the cross and in the encounter with the Risen One. This then means that the God of the Christian doctrine of providence is not an authoritarian principality in heaven, not a cosmic police officer, but the God who suffers, carries, and struggles with others.

From this position some of the traditional problems and difficulties of the doctrine of providence can be seen in a new light. I am thinking straight away of the question about the relationship between the omnipotence and the goodness of God. We have already encountered this question. It remains a burning question. It is powerfully evoked in an essay by Hans Jonas. He calls with real passion for a clear decision: "After Auschwitz we can say with more determination than ever before that an omnipotent God is either not all-good or (in his rule over the world, this being the only place where we can question this) completely incomprehensible." There is an "either-or" here; with the term "omnipotence" doubtful in itself, this is the one that must give way.[6]

This answer should be heard with respect and deep concern. It is founded historically (Auschwitz) as well as in the history of thought (under the premise of the general concept of omnipotence). But is the alternative valid if we follow the Heidelberg Catechism and in the thinking of the creed consider the two

---

5. *Reformierte Kirchenzeitung* 135, no. 6 (1994): 8.
6. *Reformierte Kirchenzeitung* 135, no. 7 (1994): 206.

themes of "omnipotent" and "father"? The two themes interpret each other, make each other more concrete. There is no abstract understanding of omnipotence supported here. The power of God, the Father of Jesus Christ, reveals itself in the Emmanuel story of the old and new covenants, and eventually in the fate of Jesus of Nazareth, in his life, his cross, and his resurrection. What marks this way is not the love of power but the power of love. It is in the light of this that we should reflect on the acts of divine providence: not actions of a *deus absconditus* for whom simply "everything is possible," but the omnipotence of nonviolent love, which in life, as in death, has the final word.

In rethinking this area I have found not just my theological teachers, such as Karl Barth, J. L. Hromádka, and J. B. Soucek to have been of significant help, but also my philosophy teacher, Emanuel Rádl. In 1942, in a situation of personal and political powerlessness, on his deathbed in his home city of Prague which was dominated by the occupying Nazis, he asks himself in a manuscript for a book, *Comfort from Philosophy,* the question about God, about his providence. He offers a "bold daring answer" as he finds it in the gospel: "God acts the way Jesus acted. He forces no one; he is a completely powerless being, he does not interfere with events with force; he produces no miracles, does not send lightning nor floods nor pestilence, he does not protect wheat from weeds. . . . He acts as Jesus acted: God takes no offence and suffers everything, including the crucifixion. But he is exceedingly fond of people and helps in the way defenceless people help: he teaches, sets an example, admonishes, warns. . . ."[7]

These are certainly impressive, rousing, and in part irritating and contestable words. But Rádl's moving sentences are not the voice of a faith that has given up, that has lost hope of God's truth securing a victory, that has fallen prey to feelings of powerlessness. This is not about God's absence, but about how he is present, about how he really acts: in other words not as a *deus ex machina,* but in that power which is eschatologically legitimized in the gospel and to which therefore *sub specie aeternitatis* belongs the true future.

Therefore Rádl closes with the following words: "The defenceless God; the defenceless moral world order; defenceless philosophy — I am seized by holy enthusiasm in the same way I experienced it in my childhood, when I stood in a church filled with people dressed in festive clothing and they all, all sang, until the windows and walls shook with devout reverence: 'Great God, we praise you.'"[8]

---

7. Emanuel Rádl, *Utěcha z filosofie* (Praha, 1946), p. 23.
8. Rádl, *Utěcha z filosofie,* p. 24.

Praising God from the Depths

A doctrine of providence that is justifiable in the Protestant context is precisely about such praise of God from the depths, including and particularly in times of doubt. I would like to follow up some of the questions arising from this in three sections.

The Gospel of Creation

That belief in providence is intimately connected with belief in creation is confirmed not only by the sentences quoted above from the Heidelberg Catechism, but has also been the *opinio communis* throughout the history of dogmatics, and certainly of the Reformers.

Creare et conservare, creation and conservation, are an inseparable part of God's work of Creation. The idea and doctrine of Creation would be diminished, indeed spoilt, if the conserving providence of God were to be omitted. The opening sentence of Calvin's chapter on providence points this out to us: "Moreover, to make God a momentary Creator, who once for all finished his work, would be cold and barren. . . ." Luther is equally explicit: "He has not created the world in the way that a carpenter builds a house and then goes, leaving it standing as it is, but rather stays with it and sustains everything as he has created it, since otherwise it could neither remain standing nor last."[9]

It is impossible to ignore the grateful, happy tone of these statements: the biblical doctrine of providence is fed by a "warm stream." After his work of six days, God did not withdraw, but remains present, accompanying his creation. The doctrine of providence strengthens the gospel of creation.

Simultaneously, the theme of providence protects and encourages the relationship of faith with creation and the world. Of course, the doctrine of providence is hardly the *primarium caput fidei;* it is the covenant, the *Heilsgeschichte* of Israel, the history and fate of Jesus Christ that occupy that role. This is at the heart of biblical faith. But this heart would be paralyzed were it not to be understood and lived within the horizons of the whole creation, the history of the peoples. The people of God would always be tempted to live within such a stricture, self-centered, circling around the salvation of their own soul. The Christian doctrine of providence protects against this from a very concrete, unmistakable starting point: it widens the perspective and discipleship of faith into something encompassing all humanity, indeed, all creation. If the words of Jesus are to be valid, that God "makes his sun rise on the evil and on the good,

9. WA 21, p. 251.

and sends rain on the righteous and the unrighteous" (Matt. 5:45), if we pray with the Psalmist "the eyes of all look to you, and you give them their food in due season. You open your hand, satisfying the desire of every living thing" (Ps. 145:15f.), then this faithfulness of provision and care by God urges us to do likewise. The "integrity of creation" is not simply a phrase that has come to the church from the outside. It intrinsically belongs to the arena of care of our faith.

In this context the doctrine of providence attains increased relevance. Wolf Krötke is right when he writes that "the whole of the Christian life would be . . . abstract if this dimension of faith in God were to fall away."[10] And it would not simply be an essential element of faith that would be endangered without the doctrine of providence, but the special *comfort* of the "gospel of creation." This theme speaks to us; we are fellow beings, not just in the human sense, as immeasurably important as this is, but also in the essentially theological sense, from the point of view of God.

This is important on a personal as well as on a cosmic level. As for the personal, when human fellowship fails or ends, it helps to believe that there is a covenant and a presence that, even when all other covenants fail, can hold and carry us even in the face of death. And with respect to the fate of our world, it is an encouragement to hold onto a "nevertheless" position of faith, one that in the midst of all the explosions that threaten creation will not simply allow it to slide into the abyss. It hears that this world, despite all its dead ends, may be a fallen world but not a deserted one; it remains that which it was from the beginning until the eschatological end, a world where God is present and that we should accompany in intercession and in action.

Human Confusions and God's Providence

This touches on the other complex of questions: those surrounding our fate and our responsibility in history. Especially in modern times, this topic has been recognized and developed as a classical topic of the doctrine of providence, both with theologians and philosophers. I will name just Schleiermacher and Hegel, who viewed God's *Heilsgeschichte* and world history within one another and who saw the process of civilization in history as a "moral process," as evolution towards the kingdom of God as the "highest good" (Schleiermacher), or thought that world history could be interpreted as the "plan of providence that was to be realized" (Hegel).[11] Hegel's project in particular had worldwide

10. *Reformierte Kirchenzeitung* 135, no. 6 (1994), *Theologische Beilage* 12.
11. Helmut G. Fritzsche, *Lehrbuch der Dogmatik*, vol. 2 (Berlin, 1967), p. 324.

historical consequences. He tore this piece of teaching out of the hands of timid theologians who no longer dared to support a strong doctrine of providence, and reclaimed it for strong philosophy: "It is one of the central doctrines of Christianity that providence has ruled and continues to rule the world, and that everything which happens in the world is determined by and commensurate with the divine government." Our pious-speculative reasoning should not capitulate even in the face of destruction and negativity: providence prevails even in negativity. "Reason cannot stop to consider the injuries sustained by single individuals, for particular ends are submerged in the universal end."[12]

This main point of Hegel's doctrine of providence, his "theodicy," the justification of God in the face of evil through the insight of speculative reason, has justifiably been met with protest, that of Jacob Burckhardt being particularly impressive. Providence should not be used too quickly to "justify" the victims of historical change. "Just because good comes out of evil, relative fortune comes out of misfortune, does not mean it follows that evil and misfortune are not originally that which they always were." There are "absolute destructive powers, under whose hoofbeats no grass will grow any more . . . each true individual life that is taken away through violence and, in our opinion, before its time should be seen as totally irreplaceable."[13] These are sentences that continue to be valid, a warning against any kind of triumphalistic speculation on providence and history!

A theologically justifiable doctrine of providence should think in a more differentiated manner in relation to its (indisputable) reference to history, remembering that the God of providence is not a general historical principle, but the Father of his son Jesus Christ. For this God, the victims of history are by no means a matter of indifference. He is not the same as humans, whereby the end justifies all means. World history is not a world or even a divine judgment. What Hegel emphasizes in relation to the idea of providence, that "Christians are initiated into the mysteries of God, and this also supplies us with the key to world history,"[14] is not legitimate. The cross stands at the center of time, and there is therefore no unbroken light that illuminates the process of history. Any doctrine of providence must reflect the ambiguous character of historical events.

A saying from an old Helvetian coat of arms can be helpful in this: *Hominum confusione Dei providentia Helvetia regitur.* The first time I heard

12. G. W. F. Hegel, *Die Vernunft in der Geschichte*, ed. Johannes Hoffmeister (Hamburg: F. Meiner, 1955), pp. 46ff.

13. Jacob Burckhardt, *Weltgeschichtliche Betrachtungen*, ed. Rudolf Marx (Stuttgart: A. Kröner, 1935), pp. 263ff.

14. Hegel, *Die Vernunft in der Geschichte*, p. 46.

this was in a lecture of Karl Barth's (later published as KD IV/3), and I have never forgotten it. If not the key, it has certainly been a pointer along the way to understanding history theologically. The saying does not idealize the human world. It describes it as that which it historically is, the story of human confusions. These are to be taken seriously, to be analyzed rationally, and to be viewed with eyes (and grasped with hands) without any illusions. But faith does not stop at this point, no matter how justifiable it might be or how often experience might confirm this assessment. *"Es wird regiert"* (Christoph Blumhardt) — God, the Father of Jesus Christ, remains the ruler. This is a statement of faith, and therefore not a principle of historical theology. But as a statement of faith, looking towards the providence of God is the strength of the Christian life. In this way, Christians try to orient themselves in history. "We live within the realm of the penultimate — we believe in the ultimate." The differentiation (not division) that Bonhoeffer makes also applies to our doctrine of providence.

In the course of the last decades I as well as, I am sure, *mutatis mutandis,* some of my contemporaries, have experienced something of the truth and pragmatic impact of this viewpoint. I am thinking of the sociopolitical context of my life in its different stages; the carefree youth in the democratic and cultural climate of the first Czechoslovakian Republic; its collapse due to the treacherous agreement in Munich 1938 and subsequent Nazi domination; the liberation at the end of the war; the setback through the communists taking power in 1948; the political hopes in the course of the Prague Spring; the tanks in the autumn of 1968 and the "winter" of the years of "normalization"; and the "miracle" of the completely unexpected "gentle revolution" of 1989! *Hominum confusione — Dei providentia.*

It must be made clear that the two parts of the saying on the coat of arms cannot be separated and isolated from one another in order to classify and attribute the happy coincidences of human history to providence, while the human catastrophes are assigned to human confusion. One may in certain times and for certain periods dare to make clear judgments. I will never forget the enthusiasm with which we followed the events of November 1989 and how it moved me when I was reading the Moravian daily text for one of the crucial days of that period: "Let justice roll down like waters and righteousness like an ever-flowing stream" (Amos 5:24).

We pray in supplication and intercession; we take sides in history, and are allowed to do so. But it is good not to lose sight of the two parts of the text of the coat of arms. For times of political joy there is the sobering reminder of human confusion, and for depressing setbacks the faith in the providence of God. Thus the doctrine of providence means and creates, in both directions, a piece of freedom in history.

Can God Be Justified?

The most burning problem facing the doctrine of providence is the mystery of evil and suffering in a world in which God is present. This is a real *crux*, not just the *crux interpretum*, but of the doctrine of providence itself; it is also the test case of the question asked earlier about the God of providence: How can he be justified — the question of *theodicy*.

In my attempts to approach this subject I would like to start with a New Testament text. Jesus is confronted head on with the mystery of suffering and evil at the beginning of the thirteenth chapter of Luke. The question is consciously presented to him as a "riddle." Two typical theodicy situations give rise to this confrontation: a brutal act of injustice on the part of Pilate who massacred a group of Galileans, and a catastrophe at the Pool of Siloam, where eighteen people were killed when a tower collapsed. How can such events be explained? And more urgently, how can the cruel fate of those affected be reconciled with the actions of divine providence? The theodicy question breaks out into the open.

One traditional answer is close at hand, and is probably assumed in the background of the argument: the absolute power and justice of God is declared to be an unshakeable principle of universal explanation. The history of humanity — the world's history and the history of individuals — is measured against this universal law. It must be possible to derive and explain every concrete "case" on the basis of this assumption. If that is difficult for us in one concrete case or another, then that is because we do not have access to all the information. But God has all the information. Therefore we must hold on to the belief that he has his reasons with regard to all mysteries of suffering and evil. In this way, all purely arbitrary acts or catastrophes are unintelligible only when seen from a limited perspective; *coram Deo* they will have their educational or forensic logic. Thus they are to be accepted by us as educational or punitive measures of divine providence.

Such arguments remind us of the dogmatic thought patterns that we mentioned in connection with the general theistic understanding of providence. But Jesus refuses to deal with this on the level of logical explanations or moral calculations. His heavenly Father is not to be had for such an approach. He also contradicts the distanced position of the questioners. He turns the argument around and addresses the speculative questioners directly and existentially. Twice he repeats that those in Galilee or at the Pool of Siloam were in no way greater sinners than any other people. "No, I tell you; but unless you repent, you will all perish, just as they did" (Luke 13:3, 5).

This means that the question about evil and suffering is never abstract, to be answered neutrally as a case for moral analysis, and is never even to be asked in this way. Jesus demands and practices another attitude, the attitude of personal involvement, entering into the suffering, and more than anything else, of *metanoia*. Repentance, turning around, solidarity with the fate of those suffering — these are what Jesus calls his disciples and fellow human beings to do in the light of the mystery of suffering and evil. The question of *"theodicy"* is indissolubly transformed to one of *"egodicy,"* about *my* justification, *my* readiness to carry the burden of others.

This is essential to the entire doctrine of providence. It is never to be developed as a pure theory, but as a committed witness of faith.

Despite this, however, the question remains. It is not just a question of uncommitted theoreticians, it is also a question for people of faith. After all, it was not just a question asked by Job's friends, but also by Job himself. In a concentrated form, it is unfolded at the center of the New Testament. In particular, the crucifixion acquires a key role here. The question of the saving rule of God is suffered at its ultimate extreme by Jesus himself: the messenger of the accompanying presence of the heavenly Father in the midst of our earthly fate is plunged into the incomprehensible distance of being forsaken by God: "My God, my God, why have you forsaken me?" (Mark 15:33f.; Matt. 27:45). Here, the theodicy question is literally nailed to the cross.

At the same time, the New Testament points to the other dimension of the fate of Jesus. For the disciples in the experience of Easter, the cross becomes the final confirmation of God's commitment to us humans until death, indeed beyond this last boundary. In the power of this experience of faith the Apostles recognize and confess that God was not absent on Golgotha. He was there, and (this is decisive for the theodicy question), not just there "from above" or "from outside," but "from below" and "from inside": not an apathetic principle of providence, but the God who suffers and struggles in solidarity with us.

This reveals the binding and liberating perspective of the Christian doctrine of providence. It has, inseparably, *ethical* components. The New Testament *memoria passionis* and *spes resurrectionis* invites no apathetic spectators of oftentimes confused lives and world history; it mobilizes for resistance to occurrences of evil and suffering. God did not capitulate before evil in the crucifixion and resurrection fate of Jesus. We must not capitulate either.

However, the primary and decisive message that the New Testament perspective offers is the liberating promise: we are not simply acting and suffering just on our own in our lives. We are people accompanied by God; we do not live off our own bat, but rather as the Apostles expressed it in countless variations — *"in Christ."* We are taken up into the Easter story of Jesus Christ. There is no power of evil — as real and oppressive as it may still affect us — that could separate us from the love of God which was completed on the cross (Rom. 8:38f.).

This is the gospel in our doctrine of providence. Here we may dare to say sentences that occur time and again in the Christian teaching, such as the sentence from Paul, that "we know that all things work together for good for those who love God" (Rom. 8:28). This does not formulate a cosmic law, nor does it guarantee a "happy end" to our personal or collective story. This is the encouragement for those who are under attack, *the* comfort in the light of which the Heidelberg Catechism (Question 1) places not just the doctrine of providence, but our whole lives: That I belong — body and soul, in life and in death — not to myself but to my faithful savior Jesus Christ, who at the cost of his own blood has fully paid for all my sins and has completely freed me from the dominion of the devil; that he protects me so well that without the will of my Father in heaven not a hair can fall from my head; indeed, that everything must fit his purpose for my salvation. Therefore, by his Holy Spirit, he also assures me of eternal life, and makes me wholeheartedly willing and ready from now on to live for him.

CHAPTER 20

Rethinking the Scripture Principle:
Friedrich Schleiermacher and the Role
of the Bible in the Church

Dawn DeVries

In an address delivered to the Union of German Reformed Churches
(*Reformierter Bund*) in 1923, Karl Barth argued powerfully for the centrality of
the Scripture principle to the definition of Reformed identity. "Reformed doctrine," he said, "in order to be itself at all, needs the free winds wherein the word
of God is recognized in Scripture and Spirit; it needs the vastness and energy of
untamed nature whereby once the Reformed churches, as by a volcanic erup-
tion, were 'born' — or, as Christian churches, born again. 'Reformed *by God's
word*' is the ancient and real meaning of the name we bear."[1] To lose this emphasis is to lose Reformed identity. And yet, Barth was also clear that the time
had come to rethink the *meaning* of the Scripture principle and its relation to
the theological concept of revelation.[2] Barth himself contributed to the creative
appropriation of this classical Reformed principle in the masterly first volume
of his *Church Dogmatics:* Jesus Christ is *the* Word of God, witnessed by Scripture and preaching. But after more than half a century of living with Barth's
doctrine of Scripture, many of our Reformed churches find themselves para-

---

1. "Reformierte Lehre, ihr Wesen und ihre Aufgabe," in Karl Barth, *Vorträge und
kleinere Arbeiten, 1922-1925,* ed. Holger Finze (Zürich: Theologischer Verlag Zürich, 1990),
pp. 202-47, 227-28; English translation, "The Doctrinal Task of the Reformed Churches," in
Karl Barth, *The Word of God and the Word of Man,* trans. Douglas Horton (New York: Harper
& Row, 1957), pp. 218-71, 247.
2. Barth, "Reformierte Lehre," p. 229; ET, pp. 249-50.

lyzed by conflicts that the Scripture principle — even as Barth reinterpreted it — apparently cannot resolve. The power of the Scripture principle, its ability to criticize tradition and culture, reason and experience, seems increasingly to be lost to contemporary theological debate.

In his book *What Is Scripture? A Comparative Approach,* Wilfred Cantwell Smith offers a helpful analysis of the transformation that is going on in the Christian religion as well as in other scriptural faiths. He writes:

> Most religious communities living scripturally have indeed produced over the centuries theories, for their members to explain — to themselves, to each other, to their children — how it is that their scriptures are so important and mean so much to them. The formulations have served also to nurture and to strengthen a continuing involvement. At the present time, at least for thoughtful and knowledgeable people, these theories from earlier eras are no longer calculated to serve either of these purposes: neither the informative nor the corroborative. They no longer give scripture a clear firm place within the total awareness of those concerned, no longer integrate its role into the coherent living of its devotees. Commitment proceeds more from momentum than from renewal.[3]

A doctrine of Scripture tells us why Scripture is important, and for this very reason it strengthens commitment to Scripture's ongoing significance in the life of the community. In the twentieth century we lived through the decline of one theory and the struggle to discover a new one. Specifically, we lived through the decline of the "classical" doctrine of Scripture, which in America reached its apex in the Princeton School.[4] This approach discovered the importance of the Bible in its divine origin and its correspondingly infallible content. Scripture, according to Hodge and Warfield, is the verbally inspired, inerrant Word of God. Although many of us would deny ever being attracted by this theological paradigm, it still exists in our churches. In my own denomination, the Presbyterian Church (USA), it was only in 1967 that the Princeton theology of Scripture was quietly laid aside in a new confession (a confession that is still heartily disliked by many evangelicals). Plenary inspiration ceased to be the church's official doctrine, but it survives as one party line within the church. For a time, perhaps, it seemed that the Princeton consensus on Scripture would be re-

---

3. Wilfred Cantwell Smith, *What Is Scripture? A Comparative Approach* (Minneapolis: Fortress Press, 1993), p. 215.

4. A classic statement of biblical inerrancy appeared earlier in Geneva, in François Samuel Robert Louis Gaussen's *Theopneustia* (1841). A revised concept of infallibility was advocated by the Dutch theologian G. C. Berkouwer in his study *Holy Scripture*, ed. Jack B. Rogers (Grand Rapids: Eerdmans, 1975).

placed by a new Barthian consensus. But that looks increasingly unlikely, at least in the North American circles that I move in. Barth's challenge to Reformed theologians — to rethink the Scripture principle in relation to the concept of revelation — remains an unfinished task.

I'd like to explore the resources for rethinking the Scripture principle in a neglected figure in the Reformed tradition — Friedrich Schleiermacher. Although he is the greatest Reformed dogmatician between Calvin and Barth, he has been largely written out of the Reformed consciousness of our century because of Barth's and Brunner's criticisms of him. Nonetheless, I believe he has a carefully constructed position that deserves a fresh hearing in a setting such as ours, devoted to rethinking Reformed identity for a new century.

The Word of God and the Treasure of Scripture

Although Schleiermacher works out a sophisticated doctrine of Scripture in several of his writings, and although he himself lectured more frequently on New Testament than on dogmatics, he is often presented as a theologian who radically subordinated Scripture to experience, and severely limited the role of the Bible in theology and church. Since little attention has been given to his observations on Scripture, a close reading of at least some of them is where we have to begin.

The Dogmatic Function of the Doctrine of Scripture

The discussion of the doctrine of Scripture in the *Glaubenslehre* falls under the rubric of ecclesiology in the second part. Scripture is identified, along with ministry of the Word, the sacraments of Baptism and the Lord's Supper, the power of the Keys of the Kingdom, and prayer in the name of Jesus, as one of the essential and unchanging marks *(Grundzüge)* of the Christian church as a fellowship "animated" *(beseelt)* by the Holy Spirit. These are contrasted with the changeable characteristics of the empirical church, which arise from its coexistence with the world and, under the sway of the kingdom of God, are destined to disappear: namely, the plurality and fallibility of the Christian churches.[5]

---

5. Friedrich Schleiermacher, *Der christliche Glaube nach den Grundsätzen der evangelischen Kirche im Zusammenhange dargestellt*, 7th ed. based on the 2nd German ed., ed. Martin Redeker, 2 vols. (Berlin: de Gruyter, 1960), 2:278-84, 384-91. Cited hereafter by paragraph number (§) and subsection as *CG*.

Schleiermacher begins his discussion with the assertion that the first essential and invariable mark of the church is the witness to Christ in Scripture and the ministry of the Word.[6] His assumption, fundamental to his entire dogmatic project, is that Christian faith is always and everywhere brought about in the same way, namely, by the personal impact of Christ on the believer.[7] For the apostles, this impact was direct, while for us it is mediated. Whatever may be the actions of Christ on us that produce our faith, the only way we can be certain that they come from him is to demonstrate their identity with the original faith-evoking activity of Christ. Thus, all subsequent generations of Christians are continually led back to the original representation of Christ's person in the apostolic witness. Furthermore, Schleiermacher contends, without the faith-evoking influence of Christ even the disciples themselves could not have become active agents of the kingdom of God through the communication of the Holy Spirit. The efficacy of the representations of Christ is always an indispensable condition of the communication of the Holy Spirit.

Schleiermacher is quick to point out that, if in the first instance what we seek in turning to the apostolic witness is to discover the same personal impact of Christ that produced the first disciples' faith, it seems impossible to read the whole of the New Testament with this intention. The representation of Christ that creates faith does not extend to the entire text of the canonical New Testament, and there are many doctrines that could be developed from the canonical scriptures that are not contained in or implied by it. Indeed, an appeal to an authorizing witness — an evangelical core of Scripture — does not even require a fixed written text. We must admit the possibility of a preached or oral propagation of the witness to Christ, provided only that an unimpaired identity of transmission *(Überlieferung)* can be guaranteed. Thus, we can conclude that the particular written form in which the person of Christ is represented to us (i.e., the canonical New Testament) does not belong unavoidably to the essence of the church *(Sein)* but to its well-being *(Wohlsein)*.[8] While the church truly is for Schleiermacher, as it was for Luther, the *creatura evangelii*, it is not constituted by the canonical scriptures in their final form, for this would be to place the apostles and the first several generations of Christians outside the church.

The greater part of the New Testament which is not, properly speaking, evangelical *(evangelistisch)* — that is, not part of the four Gospels — performs two functions. First, it shows that the church-forming activity promised by Christ really did proceed from his own efficacious actions and from the testi-

---

6. *CG*, §127.
7. *CG*, §127.2; cf. §14.1.
8. *CG*, §127.2.

mony he commanded from his disciples. And thus it is Christ's actions and the apostolic testimony that provide the "deed of title," as it were, for our inheritance. Second, it provides a supplement to the immediate utterances of Christ. We can look at the ordinances and actions of the disciples, and trace them back to their source in the instructions and declarations of the will of Christ.

Scripture as we now have it, both the individual books and the collection of the canon as a whole, is a treasure preserved for all later generations of the church, and must be seen as a work of the Holy Spirit.[9] It is, however, only a particular instance of the more general category "testimony about Christ," to which the ministry of the Word also belongs. To speak of the general category as "testimony" captures the truth that originally the oral and written teaching and narratives about Christ were the same and only came to be distinguished from each other fortuitously, through the vicissitudes of historical development. Now, however, Scripture constitutes a special case *(ein Besonderes)*, for its preservation without changes establishes the identity of our testimony with the original witness to Christ in a special way. Yet, without the living witness to Christ, which is the common duty and calling of all Christians — a witness that refers back to Scripture to be sure, or at least harmonizes with it — the canonical scriptures would be a dead possession. These two taken together, then, Scripture and the ministry of the Word of God *(Dienst am göttlichen Wort)*, are constitutive of the essence of the church.[10]

The Authority of Scripture

Having established the appropriate function of a doctrine of Scripture, Schleiermacher moves on to a discussion of the doctrine itself. Following a pattern he uses throughout the *Glaubenslehre*, he distinguishes his own constructive treatment of the questions from a critical engagement with the confes-

9. Schleiermacher's reference to Scripture as a "treasure" echoes his reading of Matthew 13:52 in his sermon, "The Effects of Scripture and the Immediate Effects of the Redeemer." He comments: ". . . at no time does he [Christ] fail to produce in his church those students of scripture, well-educated in the Kingdom of Heaven, to whom God's Spirit gives from his *treasure,* along with the old and proven things, new insights. . . . that enlighten us and make our hearts burn within us" (*Servant of the Word: Selected Sermons of Friedrich Schleiermacher,* trans. and ed. Dawn DeVries [Philadelphia: Fortress Press, 1987], p. 103, emphasis added). Cf. Martin Luther, for whom the treasure is not Scripture per se, but Christ hidden in Scripture, as an infant wrapped in swaddling clothes (*Vorrede auff das alte Testament* [1545 (1523)] in *D. Martin Luthers Werke: Kritische Gesamtausgabe* [Weimar: 1883-], 8.12.5).

10. *CG,* §127.2.

sional tradition of the Protestant church.[11] Positively, he argues that Scripture is not the foundation of faith in Christ, but rather faith in Christ is the foundation of the authority of Scripture. Thus Scripture is regarded as an expression of faith in Christ — the first in a series of such expressions, but normative in a way that later presentations of faith are not (§§128-129). Critically, he gives an interpretation of what the confessions mean when they speak of the inspiration of Scripture and the canon, and of Scripture's authenticity and sufficiency (§§130-131). The discussion closes with an addendum on the role of the Old Testament in Christian Scriptures (§132).

Schleiermacher argues that confusion about the relationship between biblical authority and faith is a widespread problem. Insofar as textbooks or confessions actually begin with the doctrine of Scripture, they invite the thought that Scripture is the source of faith. But if faith in Christ were in fact based on the authority of Scripture, on what would the authority of Scripture be based? One approach might be to prove the authority of Scripture by reason. But there are at least two problems with this approach. First, it would involve a kind of intellectual exercise that not all people are capable of, and hence the ground of faith would not be immediately available to all in the same way. Some would believe because they could demonstrate the authority of Scripture; others would have their faith second-hand. Second, if it really were possible to prove the authority of Scripture through reason alone, it would seem that any right-thinking person could be reasoned into belief. And yet, it is conceivable that such a person might "believe" without ever having felt the need of redemption, without ever having experienced repentance or conversion. But such a conviction would not really be faith at all, since it would not of itself lead to living communion with Christ. On the other hand, where the need for redemption makes itself felt, faith arises from a message about Christ that is in no way connected to convictions about how the writings of Scripture were produced.[12]

If we come to faith in the same way as the apostles, however, perhaps it will be admitted that they came to faith as a result of their belief in the Old Testament Scripture. Schleiermacher avers that this reasoning is just as flawed. The disciples did not believe in Christ because, after careful study, they came to recognize that he was the promised Messiah foretold by the Prophets. Rather, precisely because they believed in Jesus, they applied the prophetic writings to him. The faith of the apostles arose from Christ's own proclamation of himself, and

---

11. Schleiermacher develops his own constructive position under propositions he calls *Glaubenssätze*, literally, "faith statements," whereas the confessional tradition is located under propositions he identifies as *Lehrsätze*, or "doctrinal statements." See the discussion in *CG*, §27.

12. *CG*, §128.1; cf. §14.2-3.

in the same way all Christian faith has taken rise from the preaching of Christ. The New Testament itself is a collection of such preaching come down to us, and insofar as it is a collection of preaching, it too produces faith. But this is not the result of special doctrines concerning Scripture, attributing its beginning to a special divine revelation or inspiration. And it must be admitted that Scripture could produce faith in this way even if it contained many errors alongside the essential witness to Christ. Thus, just as the apostles had faith before they were able to produce Scripture, so we must have faith before we are led, through our reading of it, to accept the truth of propositions concerning its unique character. Doctrines such as the inspiration of Scripture are only credible to those who already believe. Scripture, then, must be seen primarily as the expression of the apostles' faith in the form of testimony about Christ.[13]

The Normative Character of Scripture

The next step in Schleiermacher's constructive argument is to identify more precisely the kind of normativity exercised by the New Testament. Although Scripture as an expression of faith in Christ is simply the first in a series of similar *(gleichartig)* presentations of Christian faith, it is not superseded by what comes later. This is because, within the apostolic age, at least some of the teachings about Christ were actually not properly Christian but rather were particular modifications of Jewish or Hellenistic religious ideas. Alongside this material, the preaching of the immediate disciples of Christ stood as a corrective, for their proximity to him, and to his own teaching, purified their testimony of alien elements. Thus within the apostolic age itself, the distinction between the *canonical* and the *apocryphal,* as respectively the most perfect and the most imperfect elements of the original witness, began to be drawn. This distinction cannot arise in precisely the same way in any other age. This is so, Schleiermacher argues, partly because the liability to corruption through foreign elements decreases in proportion to the number of Christians who are born and raised in the church. (He apparently trusts the efficacy of the religious formation of children far more than we are likely to do today.) Further, it is impossible for later Christians to generate truly canonical materials since their representations cannot be purified through an immediate encounter with Jesus.

The normative authority of Scripture, then, extends primarily to what might be called its canonical elements. Schleiermacher maintains that the peculiar normative dignity *(normale Würde)* granted to the canonical does not extend to every word of the New Testament. It is reserved for materials pro-

---

13. *CG,* §128.2.

duced to restrain error or corruption, so that many occasional remarks *(gelegentliche Äusserungen)* and merely subsidiary thoughts *(bloße Neben-gedanken)* do not share the same normativity as the chief subject matter. Further, the normative authority of Scripture does not imply that every later presentation of Christ must be derived from the canon in the same way, or that every later idea be contained in it, at least in germ. Since the Spirit has been poured out on all flesh, no age can be without its own peculiar originality in Christian thought. Scripture norms these later presentations in two ways. First, all later proclamation must be able to be harmonized with the original (canonical) teaching. And second, the original Scripture can guarantee the Christian character of a representation or expose what is non-Christian with a degree of certainty granted to no later presentation.[14]

The Meaning of Inspiration

As he turns to a critical conversation with the confessional heritage of the Evangelical churches on the question of Scripture, Schleiermacher takes up in turn a number of concepts connected with the traditional presentation. The first of these is the concept of inspiration. He notes that the term is not, strictly speaking, a scriptural one, though two passages in the New Testament are commonly mentioned in connection with it. The first, 1 Timothy 3:16, refers only to the Old Testament writings and speaks of them as *theopneustos,* "God-breathed." This could lead to the idea that in the act of writing the Holy Spirit had a special relationship with the writer that was otherwise nonexistent. Such an interpretation does not follow as easily from 2 Peter 1:21, which speaks of "men moved by the Holy Spirit" who "spoke from God" — a passage that seems to suggest a more stable state of being so moved.

Since the term "inspiration" is not strictly scriptural and moreover is a figurative term, it needs to be illuminated by other, related terms that describe the ways in which persons arrive at ideas. Schleiermacher contrasts the inspired *(das Eingegebene),* the learned *(das Erlernte),* and the excogitated *(das Erson-nene).* Often the first two types are contrasted with the last, as the products of outside influences over against the self's own activity. At other times, however, usage distinguishes the inspired from the learned. In this usage, what is inspired is understood to depend on a purely inward communication, as opposed to something learned from external communication, in which case the inspiration of Scripture would not be mechanical but might include the whole freedom of an individual's productivity.[15]

14. *CG,* §129.1-2.
15. *CG,* §130.1.

At this point in the argument, Schleiermacher makes a distinction that is crucial for his entire doctrine of Scripture. He states: "The general custom of calling Holy Scripture 'revelation' not infrequently causes the two concepts to be used interchangeably; but this cannot occur without confusion."[16] If it is taken to mean that God made known to the authors of Scripture in detail what they were to write, this is a totally unfounded assumption, because they themselves trace everything in their teaching back to Christ. Thus, God's original act of disclosure *(Kundmachung)* of everything contained in Scripture must already be in Christ himself — not as a series of discrete bits of inspired information, but rather as a single and indivisible revelation that develops organically (that is to say, under the conditions of space and time). The conclusion is that "the speaking and writing of the apostles moved by the Holy Spirit was thus at the same time simply a communication from the revelation of God in Christ."[17]

The church ascribes to the Holy Spirit not only the composition of the individual books of Scripture, but also the collection of them into the canon. The formation of the canon, however, is the result of the complex interaction of cooperative and competitive forces in the church, and not everything that has been achieved in this way can be attributed in the same measure to the Holy Spirit. For this reason, some refer to the collection of the canonical scriptures not as a case of inspiration, but as a product of the guidance *(Leitung)* of the Holy Spirit.

Now since the Holy Spirit is the source of all spiritual gifts and good works, all thinking about the kingdom of God must be attributed to, and inspired by, the Holy Spirit. Schleiermacher argues that this holds true both of the apocryphal and of the canonical elements of the thinking of the apostolic age. Yet it is also true that the efficacious work of the Spirit is most perfect and penetrating in the circle of those singled out by Peter (Acts 1:21ff.) as men who had accompanied Christ from the beginning of his public ministry. Inspiration, in the case of these individuals, extends beyond the writing of Scripture to the whole exercise of their office as apostles. In this sense, the peculiar inspiration of the apostles is not something that belongs only to the New Testament writings — on the contrary, these books only share in it. Dogmatics can ignore a whole set of questions about the extent of inspiration in the production of the text. Only dead scholasticism would try to draw lines of distinction within the process or would focus on the final form in its sheer externality *(Äusserlichkeit)* as a special product of inspiration.[18]

The most suitable analogy for understanding the mechanics of inspira-

16. *CG*, §130.1.
17. *CG*, §130.1.
18. *CG*, §130.2.

tion, Schleiermacher argues, is provided by Christology. The divine essence unites with the human nature of Jesus in a person-forming way, but it does not, thereby, destroy the true humanity of the Redeemer.[19] So, too, *mutatis mutandis*, the divine Spirit indwells the Christian church, inspiring the thoughts and actions of the apostles, but in a way that does not wipe out their full humanity. This is why Schleiermacher rejects a special hermeneutics for the New Testament.[20] Although the texts are truly disclosures of God's self-communication, they may be understood at the very same time as completely human compositions, susceptible of being understood in the same way any other human writings are understood. And the difference between God's incarnation in Christ and in the church should not be overlooked: only in Christ was the God-consciousness absolutely powerful; in the church, in its struggle with sin in the historical process, the permeation of the Holy Spirit is never complete. Thus, even the church's witness to the revelation of God in Jesus Christ can be tinged with error.[21]

The Formation of the Canon

Schleiermacher does not assail the credibility of Scripture in the manner of the Deist or rationalist skeptics. Such a stance was not possible for a man who confessed in public that his highest goal was to be a "servant of the divine Word."[22] Yet woven throughout his treatment of Scripture, even in the *Glaubenslehre*, is an account of how errors and unworthy elements can creep into the text. Scripture itself, as we have seen, must not be understood as a direct and immediate product of divine revelation. The apostolic authors were reporting out of the revelation of God in Christ. And although Christ's own life and teachings might be presupposed to be a perfectly transparent case of divine revelation, the human witnesses could, and *did*, interpret it in various ways. The movement towards distinguishing canonical from apocryphal accounts witnesses to just such a variety of interpretations. Even under the best of circumstances, it must be conceded that the scriptural authors were reproducing their memories, and such an act is a form of historical composition. The conclusion is this: "The effort to make the Redeemer appear [in the bibli-

---

19. See the discussion of Christology in *CG*, §94 and §96.

20. *CG*, §130.2. Cf. Fr. D. E. Schleiermacher, *Hermeneutik: Nach den Handschriften neu herausgegeben und eingeleitet*, ed. Heinz Kimmerle, 2nd ed. (Heidelberg: Carl Winter Universitätsverlag, 1974), p. 81.

21. Cf. *CG*, §153.

22. See his "Sermon at Nathanael's Grave," in *Servant of the Word*, p. 211.

cal narratives] as he really was is likewise the work of the Spirit of Truth, and it is only insofar as they are this that such narratives have a place in Holy Scripture."[23]

Schleiermacher was an early pioneer in historical-critical New Testament scholarship, and he was one of the first to suggest that independent fragments of tradition were later woven together into the larger narrative of a gospel.[24] Inspiration, he argues, must also be thought of as extending to the collection of stories and sayings and their incorporation into larger accounts. But once again, it is important to remember that this does not, in itself, remove the possibility of the introduction of errors.

The fallibility of the text is gradually regulated and minimized through the canonization process, which takes place under the leading of the Holy Spirit. But the process must be understood at the same time as a thoroughly human and historical one. Schleiermacher introduces as an analogy for understanding the Spirit's work in the church the model of an individual's regulation of his or her own thinking. Just as individuals know how to distinguish their ideas — identifying excellent ones, reserving others for further thought, rejecting some — so the Holy Spirit works through the whole Christian body in distinguishing the canonical from the apocryphal. The debate that occurred in the early church about the inclusion or exclusion of individual books shows that the process was one of gradual approximation to an ideal. The same kind of process persists in the church to this day as it carefully weighs the different degrees of normative dignity to be attributed to individual portions of Scripture, and decides how to interpret all kinds of gaps and interpolations. Thus, "the judgment of the Church only approaches closer and closer to the complete exclusion of the apocryphal and the pure sanctioning *(Heilighalten)* of the canonical."[25] Whatever contributes to the achievement of this ideal is from the leading of the Holy Spirit; whatever prevents its realization comes from the persisting influence of the world on the church.

Schleiermacher rejects any attempt to see the canon as irrevocably fixed. For one thing, since the determination of the canon as we have it was made after the age of the apostles, there is no genuinely apostolic indication for how to distinguish what is normatively canonical. But even more, through the natural, gradual process of sifting the early church writings, many things could have

23. *CG*, §130.3.

24. Friedrich Schleiermacher, *Einleitung ins neue Testament,* in *Friedrich Schleiermachers sämmtliche Werke,* ed. G. Wolde (Berlin: Georg Reimer, 1834-1864), I/8:217-54.

25. *CG*, §130.4; cf. the discussion on the formation of the canon in the *Einleitung ins neue Testament (SW* I/8:32-75).

crept into the sacred books that could be recognized and definitely proved as uncanonical in a later age. "The sense for the truly apostolic is, as history teaches, a gift of the Spirit that is gradually increasing in the Church."[26] Thus, it would be a mistake to try to prevent further unrestricted research into the matter — even though several of the confessional standards represent the canon as closed. It can only contribute to the well-being of the church if what does not truly belong to Holy Scripture is distinguished clearly from it.

The Sufficiency of Scripture

Holding an open canon, and positively encouraging critical investigation of the New Testament texts, it is not surprising that Schleiermacher, whose skills as a classicist had been honed in his translations of Plato's dialogues, turned his own pen to biblical criticism. In 1807, he published an essay "On the So-Called First Letter of Paul to Timothy," which argued, on internal grounds, that the text could not have been written by Paul himself.[27] He was a good enough New Testament scholar to know that more, not fewer, questions would soon be raised about other books of the New Testament. So his reading of the confessional tradition on the authenticity of Scripture starts from the presupposition that authenticity is not a matter of each book's actually coming from the author to whom it is attributed. Manuscripts could be wrongly attributed quite unintentionally and still come from a circle in which we look for canonical writings. Moreover, a biblical author may have written under someone else's name — a convention that his contemporaries did not consider reprehensible. There is nothing "inauthentic" about such a text. What the confessions are denying when they speak of "authenticity" is the thought that the texts were written with the intention to mislead. As Schleiermacher puts it:

> [The Confessions assert] that we trust universal Christian experience as the testimony of the Holy Spirit that the canon we have received through the tradition of the Church has not absorbed, through deceit or ignorance, elements belonging to a region of Christianity that is apocryphal or suspected of being heretical. . . . Nevertheless, we admit that not all these books are

---

26. *CG*, §103.4. For this reason Schleiermacher argues that the peculiar task of the part of historical theology that deals with the Bible, exegetical theology, is to establish the canon. See the discussion in Friedrich Schleiermacher, *Kurze Darstellung des theologischen Studiums zum Behuf einleitender Vorlesungen*, 3rd, critical ed., ed. Heinrich Scholz (1910; reprint, Darmstadt: Wissenschaftliche Buchgesellschaft, 1961), §110; trans. Terrence N. Tice as *Brief Outline on the Study of Theology* (Richmond, Va.: John Knox Press, 1966), pp. 50-60.

27. "Über die sogenannten ersten Brief des Paulos an den Timotheos," *SW*, I/2:221-320.

equally suited in content and form to assert their canonical dignity effectively.[28]

We can make good our confidence in the authenticity of Scripture, he argues, by approaching the canon with the utmost freedom as well as with the most rigorous conscientiousness. No prejudice should hamper free inquiry into the authorship of the texts. And interpretation should not be diverted from the purest hermeneutic out of fear that the resultant reading of the text would uncover an unworthy view of the Christian faith.

The normative sufficiency of Scripture is of two kinds: constitutive and critical. As a *constitutive* norm, the New Testament actually creates Christian thought and language. Through the use of Scripture, the Holy Spirit is able to lead into all truth. In this way Scripture is sufficient to form the language of Christian piety. Thus, if one day the church came to possess a complete image of Christ's living knowledge of God, we could with perfect right understand this to be the fruit of Scripture. The proper utterances of Christian piety take rise from Scripture and its interaction with the peculiar linguistic and intellectual environment in which individual readers of Scripture live, and the common Christian orthodoxy of every age is formed this way by the reigning interpretation of Christian faith called forth by Scripture.[29] Thus for Schleiermacher, the language of piety is not created anew by each individual believer, or chosen to freely express inner experiences — it is not, in short, "experiential-expressivist."[30] Rather, it is formed in every age through the encounter with Scripture, and each age's articulation of the faith must be appropriate to *(gemäss)* the distinctive expressions of the Bible.

The *critical* sufficiency of Scripture — which is often the only kind of normativity one has in mind when discussing the concept of sufficiency — relates to the constitutive as a strictly subordinate function, almost as a shadow. As a critical norm, Scripture tests the adequacy of religious thinking that means to be Christian, though not produced under the influence of the Holy Spirit in Scripture. As the constitutive use of Scripture grows, and as more perfect un-

---

28. *CG*, §131.1.

29. In his discussion of the use of Scripture in catechesis, Schleiermacher maintains that a genuine "living in" the language of Scripture is the foundation of all religion education *(Bildung)*. See Friedrich Schleiermacher, *Die praktische Theologie nach den Grundsätzen der evangelischen Kirche im Zusammenhange dargestellt, SW* I/13:399.

30. George Lindbeck calls Schleiermacher's view of Christian doctrine "experiential-expressivist" in his influential study, *The Nature of Doctrine: Religion and Theology in a Post-Liberal Age* (Philadelphia: Westminster Press, 1984), pp. 16, 20-21, 30-45. *Pace* Lindbeck, Schleiermacher held that even the "feeling of absolute dependence" — the abstracted core of all religious experience — is awakened by speech (*CG*, §6.2.4, §15.2).

derstanding of the text renders its misinterpretation less likely, this critical use should decrease.

If Scripture truly is sufficient, there can be nothing superfluous in it. That material is repeated in the New Testament is completely understandable given the way in which the text took shape. But the repetition has only the appearance of superfluousness. The doctrine of sufficiency articulates the conviction that cases of repetition ought to be taken as significant: they provide further assurance of the authenticity of particular traditions or teachings, and they provide potentially complementary material.[31]

The Status of the Old Testament in the Christian Canon

In an addendum to the doctrine of Scripture, Schleiermacher sets out a view that has been regarded, alternatively, either as prescient or as heretical (making him Marcion *redivivus*): that the Old Testament cannot be seen as possessing the same normative authority for Christian faith as the New.[32] He was well aware that this view was not yet generally recognized by church theologians, but he felt sure that it was destined in some future time to be widely shared. The argument against the authority of the Old Testament rests on three grounds. First, the inspiration of the Old Testament texts, with the possible exception of Messianic prophecies, was not the activity of the same Spirit of Christ at work in the church. Schleiermacher develops his case through a reading of Paul's treatment of the Law in Galatians and Romans, but he also notes that Christ himself does not represent the sending of the Spirit as the return of One who had been present already. Second, the Old Testament cannot, strictly speaking, serve as a productive or language-forming norm for Christian piety. Even in the noblest Psalms, ideas are present that Christians cannot appropriate as pure expressions of their piety, and only by deceiving oneself through unconscious ed-

31. *CG*, §131.2-3.

32. *CG*, §132; cf. *Kurze Darstellung*, §§128-31; Friedrich Schleiermacher, *Schleiermachers Sendschreiben über seine Glaubenslehre an Lücke*, ed. Hermann Mulert, Studien zur Geschichte des neueren Protestantismus, Quellenheft 2 (Giessen: Alfred Töpelmann [J. Ricker], 1908), pp. 41-42. For a discussion of Schleiermacher's view of the Old Testament, see Horst Dietrich Preuss, "Vom Verlust des Alten Testament und seinen Folgen: dargestellt anhand der Theologie und Predigt F. D. Schleiermachers," in *Lebendiger Umgang mit Schrift und Bekenntnis: Theologische Beiträge zur Beziehung von Schrift und Bekenntnis und zu ihrer Bedeutung für das Leben der Kirche*, ed. Joachim Track (Stuttgart: Calwer Verlag, 1980), pp. 127-60; Martin Stiewe, "Das Alte Testament im theologischen Denken Schleiermachers," in *Altes Testament Forschung un Wirkung: Festschrift für Henning Graf Reventlow*, ed. Peter Mommer and Winfried Thiel (Frankfurt: Peter Lang, 1994), pp. 329-36.

iting or supplementation could one construct a Christian doctrine of God from the Psalms and the Prophets. Finally, the Old Testament is also ill-suited to function as a critical norm. Even though one could find throughout the history of the church attempts to prove virtually every Christian doctrine from the Old Testament, why should we use the less clear premonitions of the prophets alongside the clear self-proclamation of Christ? The history of Christian use of the Old Testament makes clear just how such use has actually hindered honest exegesis and raised a myriad of complex problems that Christian theology had no need to address. The best course of action, then, would be to give up Old Testament proofs for specifically Christian doctrines, and to lay aside those doctrines that rest primarily on such proofs.[33]

One might ask why the Old Testament is in the Christian scriptures at all. Schleiermacher argues that there are primarily two reasons for its inclusion. First, the preaching of Christ himself and of the apostles was based on portions of the Old Testament read aloud, and this practice continued in the early Christian community before the formation of the New Testament canon.

Second, Christ himself and the apostles refer to the Old Testament books as divine authorities favorable to Christianity. In both cases, the mere fact that they were so used by Christ is not in itself sufficient to establish that they should continue to be used in this manner. Because the connection between the apostolic proclamation and Hebrew scriptures is a historical one, it could be expected that gradually the need for references to the Old Testament would diminish, and accordingly it would retreat behind the New Testament in the church's usage. Although he did not recommend the removal of the Old Testament from the Christian Bible, Schleiermacher thought it would perhaps be better to include it as an appendix after the New: then it would be clear that it is in no way necessary first to work through all of the Old Testament in order rightly to understand the New.[34]

Schleiermacher's argument about the place of the Old Testament in the Christian faith did not prevent him from adopting the familiar *munus triplex* as an ordering structure in his Christology. And as a preacher, Schleiermacher preached on and referred to Old Testament texts. But he remained convinced that a Christian reading of the Old Testament did not do justice to these texts as the scriptures of Judaism, and that Old Testament "proofs" for Christian doctrines were superfluous.

33. *CG*, §132.2.
34. *CG*, §132.3.

Conclusion

Undoubtedly much more could and should be said about how Schleiermacher constructs his doctrine of Scripture. The materials I have laid out here are primarily from the *Glaubenslehre*. I have provided a step-by-step analysis of the pertinent sections because they are seldom considered in present-day discussions either of Schleiermacher or of biblical authority. This could be filled out by examining what he has to say about the task of exegetical theology in the *Brief Outline on the Study of Theology* (1811; 2nd ed. 1830) as well as in his posthumously published *Lectures on Introduction to New Testament* and *Hermeneutics*. Moreover, it is important to remember that Scripture is, for Schleiermacher, only one of two forms of testimony to Jesus Christ that are essential marks of the church. His views on the other form, the ministry of the Word, would require at least as much exposition as I have given to the doctrine of Scripture here. In the posthumously published *Lectures on Practical Theology*, he discusses the uses of Scripture in preaching, catechesis, and church hymnody. And we can test how the theory is put into action in several technical exegetical works and ten fat volumes of published sermons. But for now I must be content to conclude by highlighting what I take to be some significant factors in Schleiermacher's approach to Scripture for rethinking the Reformed Scripture principle.

First, Schleiermacher is crystal clear that simply to equate Scripture with revelation is impossible. The biblical texts are human reports of the revelation of God in Jesus Christ and not, strictly speaking, the Word of God.[35] I realize that for some that is still a radical proposition. However, I do not see how we can go on appealing to Scripture as the "written Word of God" and face in all honesty the history of abuse associated with such appeals. While an appeal to biblical authority enabled the Reformation of the sixteenth century, it also justified the institution of slavery, the persecution of Jews, the oppression of women and children, and other practices that our churches now solidly condemn. If the words of Scripture *per se* are God's revelation, why does our hearing of them keep changing?[36] In the most contentious debates in our present-

---

35. When this paper was discussed in Heidelberg, one theologian present exclaimed at this point, "There is nothing in Schleiermacher's view on this that one could not already find in Barth." Actually, it might be more accurate to say that Barth's doctrine of the Word of God in fact borrowed heavily from Schleiermacher's understanding of Scripture and preaching as testimony to the Word incarnate in Jesus of Nazareth.

36. When this essay was discussed in Heidelberg, one of the theologians present asserted that it is precisely through the struggle with Scripture that the truth about sinful structures and practices is discovered. Thus, we can still claim Scripture *alone* as the source of God's liberating judgment on human culture. My response at the time still seems right to me. I asked: Why did it take so long for the church (or at least some parts of it) to discover the full

day North American Reformed churches, single biblical texts are quoted (usually out of context) as if they epitomized once and for all the divine verdict on complex moral issues. In a fight, we tend to fall back on the view that the Bible is the inerrant, inspired Word of God, revelatory in each and every word. Reformed theology, if it is to survive and contribute to an ecumenical future, has to do better than this.

Second, if Scripture is *not* strictly speaking the Word of God, Schleiermacher has a way of helping us to understand better what it is: it is a treasure we regard as holy *(heilighalten)*, or set apart. It is not like any other book. It is the irreplaceable witness of those who knew Jesus in the flesh. But more than that, it is the source that actually creates or *constitutes* the language of Christian piety. Without Scripture, we have no way of coming to faith and no way of speaking of faith, for there is no truly Christian *experience* in our time that is not born from the encounter with *Scripture* — Scripture creates Christian experience. What stronger normative role could Scripture have in the life of the church? This is a clear affirmation of the Reformed *sola scriptura*.

Third, it is interesting that Schleiermacher locates the doctrine of Scripture under the doctrine of the church, where Calvin's *Genevan Catechism* also locates the doctrine of the Word.[37] I have argued elsewhere that Schleiermacher, like Calvin and Luther, understands the Word as sacrament — as the *viva vox evangelii*.[38] Scripture, especially as proclaimed in preaching, is the vehicle through which Christ gives himself to us. It is like the elements of water or bread and wine in the sacraments, an instrument that unites us with Christ in the power of the Holy Spirit. To approach Scripture in this way is to be clear that its authority lies not in some property of the texts themselves that historians or unbelievers could take away, but in our faith that *through* them we have met Christ and will do so again. I think this is a particularly helpful way of looking at biblical authority in a world that includes groups like the Jesus Seminar.

---

humanity of women? Why was it only with the rise of feminism as a movement in history that theologians discovered that many plain texts of Scripture that speak against women's equality with men (like 1 Cor. 11:7 or 1 Timothy 2:11-15) should be interpreted through the lens of more egalitarian texts (like Galatians 3:28)? It seems clear in this case that culture has critiqued Scripture, not the other way around.

37. *Catechismus ecclesiae Genevensis* (1545), in *Joannis Calvini opera selecta*, ed. Peter Barth, Wilhelm Niesel, and Doris Scheuner, 5 vols. (München: Chr. Kaiser Verlag, 1926-52), 2:127.

38. Dawn DeVries, *Jesus Christ in the Preaching of Calvin and Schleiermacher* (Louisville: Westminster/John Knox Press, 1996).

CHAPTER 21

Social Witness in Generous Orthodoxy:
The New Presbyterian "Study Catechism"

George Hunsinger

The twentieth century has witnessed a number of initiatives to encourage political responsibility in the church. Each achieved a measure of success before hitting on diminishing returns. Religious socialism of the '10s and '20s in Switzerland and Germany, the American social gospel of about the same era, the worker-priest movement in postwar France, Latin American liberation theologies in the '60s and '70s with their base communities, the black theologies of the same decades in the U.S. and Africa, and the slightly later feminist and womanist theologies in industrialized nations — these and other efforts were progressive campaigns that made a mark but did not prevail. The recurring pattern of early promise broken by arrest and eventual decline surely had causes that were various and complex. Yet these campaigns all had at least one thing in common. Each in its own way forced the church to choose between progressive politics and traditional faith. Each made it seem as though the two were mutually exclusive. Each therefore forged an unwitting alliance with its opposition, which shared the same diagnosis, only from the opposite point of view. Each failed to see that confronted with a forced option, the church will inevitably choose not to abandon traditional faith. Equally tragically, each failed to see that the forced option between progressive politics and traditional faith is false.[1]

The falsity of the option might have been plain from the existence of any number of prominent figures. Dorothy Day, William Stringfellow, Fanny Lou

---

1. I do not mean to suggest that combining progressive politics with traditional faith will guarantee success, only that forcing the church to choose between them virtually guarantees failure.

Hamer, Oscar Romero, André Trocmé, Marietta Jaeger, Helmut Gollwitzer, Lech Walesa, Kim Dae-jung, Ita Ford, Desmond Tutu, and not least Karl Barth are among the many twentieth-century Christians known for their progressive politics. They saw no reason to choose between their love for Jesus Christ as confessed by faith and their love for the poor and the oppressed. They had learned from initiatives for political responsibility while refusing the fatal choice. Traditional faith was for them not a hindrance but an incentive for progressive political change. It sustained them in struggle through their darkest hours. It was not for them something disreputable to be hidden from those in need. Nor was it something to be rejected because dishonored by injustice and failure in the church. It was rather the hard-won and priceless deposit of truth that withstood every effort to discredit its relevance.

In 1998 the 210th General Assembly of the Presbyterian Church (USA) adopted two new catechisms. In a church wracked by divisions over various social issues, the catechisms passed the Assembly by an impressive 80/20 margin, with the drafting committee receiving a standing ovation after the vote.[2] Answering a questionnaire when the Assembly was over, a strong majority of the delegates (60 percent) said they regarded the new catechisms as the most important item they had acted upon. The catechisms have since been published in a number of forms. Assisted by study guide materials, they are slowly seeping into the life of the church, being used for confirmation classes, leadership training programs, and congregational education. They are not proposed as tests of orthodoxy, but simply as much-needed teaching tools for those who wish to use them. They can be employed flexibly and creatively in a variety of different settings. The real test will be the extent to which the catechisms are actually taken up and used.

The longer of the two documents, called the Study Catechism, on which this essay will concentrate, is distinctive in that it seeks to combine — in however rudimentary a form — traditional faith with progressive politics. This combination of both traditional and progressive motifs would seem to make the Study Catechism relatively unique in the history of Reformed catechisms and confessions, not to mention other Reformation or ecumenical symbols. The new catechism endeavors to balance concern for the church with concern for the world. Taken as a whole, it aims to be both traditional and contemporary, both evangelical and liberal, both Reformed and ecumenical. It casts a broad yet careful net in an attempt to be as inclusive with integrity as possible.

---

2. The catechisms were approved for use over a five-year period. A Consultation to evaluate the church's experience with them has been established through the PCUSA's Office of Theology and Worship. The catechisms will eventually be resubmitted to the General Assembly in revised form for final approval. The currently approved documents were written by a Special Committee of the General Assembly that worked over a four-year period.

"Generous orthodoxy" might be used to sum up the balance that both catechisms seek to strike. A remark from the one theologian whose work in particular, more often than not, brought the drafting committee into unity, illustrates the term. We ought not to exclude anyone from our hearts and prayers, this theologian advised, but rather to embrace "all people who dwell on earth. For what God has determined concerning them is beyond our knowing except that it is no less godly than humane to wish and hope the best for them." Although these are not always the sentiments associated with John Calvin, they appear in his work more often than commonly supposed (see *Inst.* 3.20.38). Certainly they represent the Reformed tradition at its best. When asked about the term "generous orthodoxy," which he coined, the late Hans Frei of Yale once commented: "Generosity without orthodoxy is nothing, but orthodoxy without generosity is worse than nothing." The new catechisms offer the broad center of the PCUSA the vision of a generous orthodoxy that can embrace its diversity, help to heal its wounds, and equip it for faithful service to Christ in the century that lies ahead.

Before turning to the theme of social witness, I will provide a sketch of the new catechisms, followed by some brief reflections on how catechisms have functioned in the Reformed tradition.

The shorter of the two adopted by the 1998 General Assembly, called the First Catechism, aims to reach children who are nine or ten years old. With sixty short questions and answers, it surveys the biblical narrative in outline. After a short prologue designed to draw the children in, it traces the following sequence: creation and fall, Israel as God's covenant people, Jesus Christ as Lord and Savior, and the church in the power of the Holy Spirit, concluding with an explanation of the Lord's Prayer. For the sake of simplicity in the flow of questions, the Ten Commandments, though listed, are not expounded. Elementary teachings about Scripture, the sacraments, worship, and mission appear in the section on the church. For each question and answer, specific Bible verses are attached. This method is designed to help pupils gain a basic grasp of the biblical material on which the answers are based. (A similar correlation of Scripture with the questions and answers of the Study Catechism has also been prepared.) It seemed advisable not to call this document a "children's catechism," since it may also be useful for some adults.

While the First Catechism has a narrative structure, the Study Catechism unpacks the basics of the Christian faith by examining the Apostles' Creed, the Ten Commandments, and the Lord's Prayer. Lengthier and more detailed than the narrative catechism, it is suitable for use with ages 14 and up. Traditional topics like the creation of the world "out of nothing" or like Jesus Christ's incarnation, saving death, and resurrection receive significant attention. At the same time, more contemporary concerns like faith and science, the problem of evil, and Christianity's relation to other religions are also touched upon. Openly affirming key Reformation themes, such as justification by faith alone and the Scripture principle, the catechism is "evangelical." Yet in an equally open way, social concerns, biblical criticism, modern scientific findings, and hope for the whole creation find glad affirmation as well, ensuring that the catechism is also "liberal." Finally, distinctive Reformed convictions (for example, on providence, covenant, and adoption as God's children) are balanced by a deliberate ecumenism (for example, on the Trinity, the sacraments, and "anti-supersessionism").[3]

The use of catechisms was revitalized by the Reformation. In normal Protestantism a minister could enter the pulpit and presuppose a fully catechized congregation — a situation that prevailed for at least three hundred years. Today this level of Christian education is almost beyond imagination, at least for the PCUSA. In the continental Reformed tradition it was common to preach throughout the year on the Heidelberg Catechism. Two services would be held each Sunday, with the evening service focusing on a question and answer from the catechism. The evening service presupposed that most people in the congregation had been through confirmation where the catechism was thoroughly studied. Sometimes, notwithstanding the Heidelberg's length, confirmands had memorized the whole thing. In the Reformed tradition's Anglo-American branch from which Presbyterian churches come, the Westminster standards were used in a similar way. Young people studied them for confirmation and instruction, sometimes memorizing the Shorter Catechism, though a preaching service directly on the Westminster standards was not as common.

Luther is the figure whose vision was formative. He and his followers had no idea what was going to happen in the dangerous period after the German Reformation took wing. Never far from his mind from one year to the next was whether he would be alive or murdered. Eventually, various theologians set out from Wittenberg to visit the local congregations. What they found was not encouraging. Luther once came across a priest who could not recite the Lord's Prayer. (We think things have declined for us in the PCUSA, and they have, but there is a point we haven't reached yet.) Luther revitalized the church through the catechisms. His shorter catechism, which is very simple, has lasted right down to the present day. He saw catechisms as a way of reversing the church's decline, and it worked for hundreds of years.

Luther thought that the catechism should be taught at home. He did not see the Christian household as a part of the church. He saw it as a form of the

3. Like the Heidelberg Catechism (but unlike the Westminster standards), it might be mentioned, the Study Catechism gives little prominence to "predestination," thus taking a moderately Calvinistic position.

church. It was a school for faith. Parents used the catechism to teach their children around the dinner table. Note that the word *catechesis* means oral instruction, not memorization. Luther and the Reformation believed that all Christians needed a basic understanding of the Apostles' Creed, the Ten Commandments, and the Lord's Prayer. As much as anything it was the catechisms that were responsible for the success of Protestantism. They made it possible to transmit a lively, well-informed faith from one generation to the next. When the catechisms were used as the Reformation intended, memorization was secondary to understanding.[4] Robert Wuthnow, the Princeton sociologist of religion, has said that the biggest reason why "mainline" Protestant churches in the United States are no longer retaining their young people is that they have failed to teach them a clear, compelling set of religious beliefs. The new catechisms could contribute to reversing this contemporary decline.

"Today in all dimensions of life," Jürgen Moltmann has written, "faith is urged to prove its relevance for the changing and bettering of the world. Under the pressure to make itself useful everywhere, Christian faith no longer knows why it is faith or why it is Christian."[5] Social relevance, as Moltmann suggests, will continue to elude a church that fails to fulfill its primary vocation as a community of faith. Christian faith that no longer knows why it is faith or why it is Christian has little to offer anyone. The half-hearted, low-commitment religion of much middle-class American church life corresponds to the safe, domesticated deity so devastatingly described by H. Richard Niebuhr: "A God without wrath brought men without sin into a kingdom without judgment through the ministrations of a Christ without a cross."[6] Wrath, sin, judgment, and the cross are difficult themes that require responsible retrieval in the church today, without which there will be no liberation from mediocre Christian niceness. Shallow and pernicious notions of "self-esteem," pervading every sector of the church, whether "evangelical" or "liberal," in our increasingly therapeutic culture, have everywhere taken their toll. "Adequate spiritual guidance," wrote Reinhold Niebuhr, "can come only through a more radical political orientation and more conservative religious convictions than are comprehended in the culture of our era."[7] These words seem truer today than when Niebuhr first wrote them, and they may well be truer than he knew.

---

4. As Thomas F. Torrance has pointed out, in previous generations people who were brought up on the Shorter Westminster Catechism, even when not otherwise highly educated, acquired an intellectual and spiritual proficiency not easily matched by churchgoers today. See *The School of Faith* (New York: Harper, 1959), p. xxix.

5. Jürgen Moltmann, *Umkehr zur Zukunft* (Gütersloh: G. Mohn, 1970), p. 133.

6. H. Richard Niebuhr, *The Kingdom of God in America* (New York: Harper, 1937), p. 193.

7. Reinhold Niebuhr, *Reflections on the End of an Era* (New York: Scribners, 1936), p. ix.

Generous Orthodoxy: Two Samples

The new catechisms are no panacea, because of course there are no panaceas. At least three generations of ever-declining catechesis, however, have not promoted the progress of the gospel. Presbyterian churches that at the turn of the last century were reeling from distasteful heresy trials enter the new millennium with an identity crisis. Excessive and ill-conceived laxity has replaced the earlier rigidity. The promise of a generous orthodoxy might be the prospect of arresting destructive pendulum swings between unsatisfactory extremes. Here are two small samples of orthodoxy and generosity as embodied in the Study Catechism.

> **Question 52.** *How should I treat non-Christians and people of other religions?*
> As much as I can, I should meet friendship with friendship, hostility with kindness, generosity with gratitude, persecution with forbearance, truth with agreement, and error with truth. I should express my faith with humility and devotion as the occasion requires, whether silently or openly, boldly or meekly, by word or by deed. I should avoid compromising the truth on the one hand and being narrow-minded on the other. In short, I should always welcome and accept these others in a way that honors and reflects the Lord's welcome and acceptance of me.

> **Question 30.** *How do you understand the uniqueness of Jesus Christ?*
> No one else will ever be God incarnate. No one else will ever die for the sins of the world. Only Jesus Christ is such a person, only he could do such a work, and he in fact has done it.

Christians make large claims about Jesus Christ, but not about themselves. Humility, openness, and compassion are the only appropriate characteristics for those who know that through Jesus Christ they are forgiven sinners. Christians cannot disavow Christ's uniqueness without disavowing the gospel. No mere human being, no matter how praiseworthy, can be affirmed as Lord and Savior. Only because Jesus Christ is fully God as well as also fully human is he the object of Christian worship, obedience, and confession. Christ's uniqueness as confessed by faith is the foundation of generosity, not its ruin, for his uniqueness ensures that every wall of division has been removed. "One has died for all; therefore all have died. And he died for all, that those who live might live no longer for themselves but for him who for their sake died and was raised" (2 Cor. 5:14-15 RSV). Christians cannot live for Jesus Christ without renouncing a life lived only for themselves. They cannot devote themselves to him without living also for the world that he loves, indeed, the world for whose sins he gave himself to die. Remembering that they, too, are sinners whose forgiveness took place at the cross, they stand not against those who do not yet know Christ, but always with them in a solidarity of sin and grace. This solidarity is the open secret of generous orthodoxy, which knows that there is always more grace in God than sin in us. "Welcome one another, therefore, as Christ has welcomed you, for the glory of God" (Rom. 15:7).

Social Concerns: Justice, Peace, and the Integrity of Creation

Christians are called to bear social witness to Christ in two ways, first through the ordering of their common life, and second through direct action in the surrounding world. Ecclesial ordering and secular intervention comprise a unity in distinction. They are not alternatives, and may well at times blend together. Nonetheless they are ranked in a particular way. Priority belongs (in principle) to the ordering of the church's common life. The church does not have a social ethic so much as it is a social ethic. A church whose common life merely reflects the social disorders of the surrounding world is scarcely in a strong position for social witness through direct action. In such cases — and where is this not the case? — the gospel must progress in spite of the church, and against its failures. Here too there is more grace in God than sin in us. Note that social witness, whose direct action cannot always wait for the proper ordering of the church's common life, must proceed on several fronts at once. Nevertheless, social witness in discipleship to Christ requires the church to be a countercultural community with its own distinctive profile. It must stand over against the larger culture when that culture's values are incompatible with the gospel. No doubt a church that emphasizes distinctiveness at the expense of solidarity falsifies itself by becoming sectarian. A church that loses its distinctiveness, however, through conformity and capitulation, evades its essential vocation of discipleship, especially when it means bearing the cross for being socially dissident. A Christian is an unreliable partisan who knows that peace with God means conflict with the world (even as peace with the world means conflict with God). "You are the salt of the earth; but if the salt has lost its taste, how shall its saltiness be restored?" (Matt. 5:13). "You are the light of the world" (Matt. 5:14). Disciples are not above their teacher (Matt. 10:24).

The rule for social witness is that faithfulness is a higher virtue than effectiveness. Some things ought indeed to be done regardless of whether by human calculations they promise to be effective; and other things ought not to be done, no matter how effective they may promise to be. An example of the first would be things that are so evil that they need to be opposed regardless of whether they can be prevented. An example of the second would be adopting impermissible means to attain commendable ends. The latter merits special comment. Effectiveness pursued at the expense of faithfulness, which is always the church's undoing, very often arises from the allure of attaining commendable ends through impermissible means. This heedless strategy is nothing more than disobedience rooted in a basic distrust in God. It calls the divine sovereignty, wisdom, and beneficence into question. It doubts that God is faithful. At the same time it miscalculates what will actually result after impermissible means are employed. The God who brings good out of evil and life out of death is the God who requires the church to speak truth to power come what may. The God whose foolishness is wiser than human wisdom, and whose weakness is stronger than human might, is the God who calls the church into ever renewed conformity with its Lord through apparently senseless actions of compassion, noncompliance, and illustration. Note that faithfulness need not be in conflict with effectiveness. Both values are always to be maximized as much as possible. But in conflict situations, which are by no means uncommon, there can be no doubt which direction is expected of the church and commanded by its Lord. "But seek ye first the kingdom of God, and his righteousness; and all these things shall be added unto you" (Matt. 6:33 KJV). "Do not be overcome by evil, but overcome evil with good" (Rom. 12:21 RSV). "For the Son of man came not to be served but to serve, and to give his life as a ransom for many" (Mark 10:45).

With these principles in mind — the priority of the church's ordering over its direct action in the world, and the priority of faithfulness over effectiveness — the theme of social witness in the catechism may be pursued.

The Integrity of Creation

Whether the human race will survive the next century is not clear. What is clear is that the means and mechanisms of self-extinction already exist. The bane of modern technology may turn out to be greater than the boon. Ecological destruction is the slow version for which the quick version is nuclear war and its military analogues, with the intermediate version as overpopulation and the gross maldistribution of resources. Widespread devastation, falling short of self-extinction, could still be severe. At the level of technology and social policy, Christians qua Christians will have no special expertise with respect to details. What they have to offer through their social witness is an orientation and direction. Through ordering (or reordering) their common life as well as through direct action in the world, they will always stand, without neglecting the threat of divine judgment, for the possibility of repentance and the reality of hope.

They will challenge the technological imperative, which holds that "if it can be done, it must be done," as the symptom of a larger idolatry of human self-mastery and deceit. They will seek to break with destructive habits of consumption, heedless waste of earth's resources, and unrestrained pursuit of private gain at the expense of public good. How to adopt simpler, more sustainable patterns of living, not least in the ordering of the church's common life, as well as in the private lives of individual Christians, awaits serious discussion and implementation in the church.

> **Question 19.** *As creatures made in God's image, what responsibility do we have for the earth?*
> God commands us to care for the earth in ways that reflect God's loving care for us. We are responsible for ensuring that earth's gifts be used fairly and wisely, that no creature suffers from the abuse of what we are given, and that future generations may continue to enjoy the abundance and goodness of the earth in praise to God.

The catechism can do little more than establish generous orthodoxy's basic outlook. Here it undertakes a modest act of theological repentance. Widely publicized criticisms have not implausibly shown how the biblical injunction to "fill the earth and subdue it" (Gen. 1:28) has served to underwrite ecological irresponsibility more often than one would wish. What these criticisms overlook, however, in their zeal to establish blame, is not only the indeterminacy of the text, but also the larger theological resources that scriptural communities possess, not to mention the possibility of their learning from past mistakes. New occasions teach new readings — as well as new duties that were unforeseen.

Scriptural communities, whether Christian or Jewish, have always known that the earth belongs to another than themselves. "The earth is the Lord's and all that is in it, the world, and those who live in it" (Ps. 24:1). They have known that they are not the proprietors but only custodians of a world they have received as a gift. "The heavens are yours, the earth also is yours; the world and all that is in it — you have founded them" (Ps. 89:11). They have also seen that profound disorders in our relationship to God inevitably have earthly consequences: "The earth lies polluted under its inhabitants; for they have transgressed laws, violated the statutes, broken the everlasting covenant" (Isa. 24:5). Finally, they have known, to cite a specifically Christian example, that grace offers the uplifting possibility of renewal despite grievous sins of the past: "Do not be conformed to this world, but be transformed by the renewing of your minds, so that you may discern the will of God — what is good and acceptable and perfect" (Rom. 12:2). These verses as just cited are among the ones appended in the catechism to Question 19. While the limits to this approach are obvious, the catechism at least makes a beginning. It orients catechized Christians toward ecological responsibility in a way consonant with traditional faith.

Nonviolence and Peace

Modern warfare with all its horrors has been the defining experience of the twentieth century. A few statistics help tell the story. In this century more than 100 million people died in major wars — out of an estimated 149 million total since the first century. In most wars fought in the 1990s, the vast majority of deaths were civilian. In 1995 world military expenditures amounted to more than 1.4 million dollars per minute. An estimated 8 trillion dollars has been spent since 1945 on nuclear weapons. The world stockpile of nuclear weapons, despite recent reductions, still represents over 700 times the explosive power in the twentieth century's three major wars, which killed 44 million people.[8] The church urgently needs to reconsider how it can be more faithful to the gospel of peace in the midst of this unprecedented world-historical crisis.

No Power But the Power of Love

The very idea of "social witness" implies an orientation toward the centrality of God. It means that Christian social action, whether within the community of faith or the larger world, is more than an end in itself. This action does not simply aim to alleviate social misery in the form of hunger, nakedness, homelessness, terror, illness, humiliation, loneliness, and abuse. Efforts to name and oppose social injustice, no matter how important and necessary, are only one aspect of "social witness." As Aristotle has pointed out, any given action or policy can be an end in itself while also serving as the means to a greater end. As important as bread is to us, we do not live by bread alone. Human flourishing, as we know from the gospel, depends on more than the alleviation of social misery and the satisfaction of earthly needs. The main purpose for which we were created is to glorify and enjoy God forever.

This purpose is acknowledged by social witness in at least two ways. First, Christian social witness is parabolic in intent. It aims, in all its forms, to enact parables of God's compassion for the world. Although not all needs are alike,

---

8. See William Eckhardt, "War-Related Deaths Since 3000 B.C.," *Bulletin of Peace Proposals* (December 1991); Ruth Leger Sivard, *World Military and Social Expenditures 1996* (Washington, D.C.: World Priorities, 1996); Mary Kaldor, *New and Old Wars: Organized Violence in a Global Era* (Stanford, Calif.: Stanford University Press, 1999).

with some lesser or greater than others, God cares for us as whole persons in all our needs. The highest purpose for which we were created is not always remembered in this context. Being created to live by and for God, we know a need that only God can fulfill. Being creatures fallen into sin, moreover, we also endure a terrible plight, fatal and self-inflicted, from which we are helpless to free ourselves, but can be rescued only by God, without which we would be cut off from God and one another forever. According to the gospel, God has not abandoned us without hope to this plight, for God does not will to be God without us. On the contrary, God has spared no cost to rescue us. The point is this. No human action, not even by the church, can do for us what God has done, or be for us what God indeed is, at the deepest level of human need. Human action can nonetheless, by grace, serve as a witness. It can point away from itself to God. It can enact parables of compassion that proclaim the gospel. In addressing itself wholeheartedly to lesser needs, Christian social witness points at the same time to God as the only remedy for our greatest need. Christian social witness, in its efforts to alleviate social misery, is thus at once an end in itself while also serving as the means to a greater end.

Secondly, social witness cannot be parabolic in intent without also being analogical in form. It must correspond to the content it would attest. It cannot point to God without corresponding to God. Correspondence to God is the basic criterion of social witness, and it is this criterion that makes faithfulness more important than effectiveness. The validity of Christian social witness cannot be judged by immediate consequences alone. It must rather be judged, primarily, by the quality of its correspondence to God's compassion as revealed and embodied in Jesus Christ. No social witness can be valid that contradicts faithful correspondence, even when that means leaving the consequences to God. Consequences are in any case greatly overrated with respect to their predictability and controllability, just as they are also commonly misjudged when uncompromising faithfulness results in real or apparent failures.

It is no accident that the words *witness* and *martyr* are semantically related. The promise of the gospel is that faithful witness, whether successful in worldly terms or not, will always be validated by God. To believe that supposed effectiveness in violation of faithfulness is promised similar validation can only be illusory. No comprehensive policy of social action, regardless of what it is, will ever be without elements of helplessness, tragedy, and trade-off in the face of human misery. It is always a mistake for faithfulness to overpromise what it can deliver in resisting evil or effecting social change, though it may sometimes be surprisingly effective, or even compatible with maximal effectiveness, depending on the case. Social witness qua witness, in any case, cannot allow itself to be determined primarily by the question of effectiveness, but rather by faithful correspondence to the cruciform compassion of God.

The unprecedented horrors of modern warfare raise acute questions for Christian social witness with respect to nonviolence and peace. Who exactly is the God to whom Christian social action would bear witness? What forms of social action (whether in ecclesial ordering or secular intervention and participation) would correspond to the prior and determinative reality of God? How is God's power exercised in the world, and how is it related to God's love? What does it mean to say that God is omnipotent? Although these and other questions require greater treatment than can be afforded here, we are already in the vicinity of the first article of the Apostles' Creed.

> Question 7. *What do you believe when you confess your faith in "God the Father Almighty"?*
> That God is a God of love, and that God's love is powerful beyond measure.

> Question 8. *How do you understand the love and power of God?*
> Through Jesus Christ. In his life of compassion, his death on the cross, and his resurrection from the dead, I see how vast is God's love for the world — a love that is ready to suffer for our sakes, yet so strong that nothing will prevail against it.

> Question 9. *What comfort do you receive from this truth?*
> This powerful and loving God is the one whose promises I may trust in all the circumstances of my life, and to whom I belong in life and in death.

> Question 10. *Do you make this confession only as an individual?*
> No. With the apostles, prophets and martyrs, with all those through the ages who have loved the Lord Jesus Christ, and with all who strive to serve him on earth here and now, I confess my faith in the God of loving power and powerful love.

Here again, although the catechism cannot do everything, it can at least do something. By interpreting the divine power in terms of the divine love, it establishes a basic orientation and direction for social witness. It establishes the presumption that no social witness can be valid that exercises or endorses power in flagrant violation of love. Many questions necessarily remain open. In the tradition these questions circulate around the place of law, justice, and coercion in the work of love, and around the perceived need for recognizing "two realms," at least one of which (the secular realm) is thought to necessitate power structures, authorities, and policies that are not only coercive but at times inevitably and perhaps massively violent.

Without rejecting these traditional perceptions wholesale, the catechism generally places a question mark beside them (in their commonly received forms). Much depends on whether certain countervailing divine attributes (like mercy and righteousness, or love and wrath) are best understood dualistically, through a "pattern of disjunction," or else integratively, through a "pattern of mutual inclusion." In the second pattern the positive divine qualities would be seen as including and fundamentally determining the negative ones, with the latter being expressions of the former. Stronger constraints than traditional are thereby placed on adhering directly to compassion in faithful witness, on pain of severe dis-analogy to the God ostensibly attested.[9] (Note that the question of which pattern for the divine attributes is valid is logically independent of its social consequences. That question must be decided on its own merits. One of the most lamentable aspects of contemporary Christian social ethics is the unconscionable tendency to manipulate the doctrine of God in order to generate what are perceived as desirable social outcomes. Such instrumentalizing of God stands in flagrant violation of faithful witness, making God into little more than the object of wish-fulfillment and projection. T. S. Eliot is still right when he said that the greatest treason is to do the right thing for the wrong reason.)

The Nonviolent Cross

The catechism explains the first article of the creed on a christocentric basis. It appeals to Jesus Christ's incarnation, crucifixion, and resurrection to validate the conviction that God's power is immanent in God's love. Jesus Christ's life history clarifies the whole history of the covenant. It shows definitively that God knows no power but the power of love, and that God's love is powerful. It reveals how free and strong that love is — so free it is "ready to suffer for our sakes, yet so strong that nothing will prevail against it." A challenge thereby surfaces against too readily accepting any analysis that would pit "powerless love" against "loveless power," with the latter condoned as a necessary evil. Although loveless power cannot be denied as the terrible reality it is, the gospel includes

9. In other words, the constraints are definitely weaker when (with the normal Augustinian tradition) the pattern of disjunction is in force. In that case, the divine righteousness, holiness, and wrath are viewed as operating, in some strong sense, alongside and independently of the divine mercy, grace, and love. This split in God then warrants a corresponding split in earthly life between the spiritual (ecclesial) and the secular realms, with correspondingly different ethical norms supposedly applying to each domain. Representatives of this tradition, like Calvin, acknowledge that the pattern of disjunction makes it seem as though God's being is in tragic conflict with itself. Whether this is really the proper point at which to invoke, as they do, the divine inscrutability, is one of the key points disputed by those who adhere to the pattern of mutual inclusion.

the great promise that in the ultimate scheme of things there is no such thing as powerless or ineffective love.

How is the ultimate reality of love's triumph to be faithfully attested here and now? Won't the implicit constraints of love, as argued here, on the permissible uses of power have deleterious consequences? Won't preventable evils be accepted, and attainable goods be sacrificed, if social witness inordinately restricts itself to forms of suffering love? The historic differences on these matters within the broad Christian tradition will undoubtedly persist. Yet doesn't the cross of Christ seem clearly to establish a strong presumption that social witness will most fittingly take shape through actions and policies of nonviolence, not excluding resistance and direct action, even to the point, perhaps, of civil disobedience, civilian-based defense, and conscientious objection to unjust wars? Why should the grotesque sacrifices required by armed conflict automatically seem more necessary and promising than the sacrifices that undeniably would be required by alternative strategies of nonviolence? Doesn't the unprecedented world-historical military crisis call the church to re-examine whether it has fully taken the measure of the faithfulness required by its Lord? Can the church today responsibly participate in the preparations and mechanisms of mass destruction? Can it pretend that the history of the twentieth century did not occur?

The triumph of God's suffering love, as revealed and embodied in Christ, is a theme that unifies the entire catechism. The catechism conveys the basic Christian conviction that in reigning from the cross, the suffering love of God has triumphed in its very weakness over all that is hostile to itself (cf. 1 Cor. 1:25). Here is one example of this theme.

Question 41. *How did Jesus Christ fulfill the office of king?*
He was the Lord who took the form of a servant; he perfected royal power in weakness. With no sword but the sword of righteousness, and no power but the power of love, Christ defeated sin, evil and death by reigning from the cross.

Relative to historic Reformed standards, the catechism offers an interpretation of Christ's threefold office that is unique in being thoroughly christocentric. It is not the office which defines Christ, but Christ who defines the office. Here the royal aspect of the threefold office is defined as centered on the cross. The divine strategy for defeating sin, evil, and death — *regnantem in cruce* — is fulfilled in suffering love. "God does not use violent means to obtain what he desires," wrote Irenaeus (*Against Heresies*, V.1.1). God does not liberate us from our captivity, echoed Gregory of Nyssa, "by a violent exercise of force" (*The Great Catechism*, XXII). Since the greatness of the divine power is revealed disconcertingly in the form of the cross, how can Christian social witness fail to match? The basic criterion of faithful social witness (conformity to the God whose action is attested) would seem to point the church in principle toward strategies of nonviolent love.

An important test for nonviolent social witness is whether it can incorporate a strong element of justice. If this witness meant simply capitulating to evil, violence, and abuse, it would not only be deficient in itself, but also in its testimony to God. For God is not merciful without also being righteous, nor gracious without also being holy, nor loving without also being wrathful toward everything that tramples on love. Domestic and sexual violence, for example, long suppressed from the light of day in church and society, have recently emerged to illustrate how traditional pastoral counsels to submission, whether well-meaning or thoughtless, can be tragically mistaken and abused. Nonviolence is not the opposite of resistance and prudence. It is the opposite of vindictiveness, retaliation, and hatred — including policies or actions based on them. It recognizes that there is a time to resist and a time to flee as well as a time to suffer and submit. It allows for nonretaliatory initiatives of protest and self-defense. It nonetheless finds it hard to understand how one can love one's enemies by killing them. It is prepared if necessary to suffer and die for peace rather than kill for peace. Its deepest motivation is not to keep itself morally pure, but to bear faithful witness through conformity to the enacted patterns of divine love. It believes, when grounded in the gospel, that sin can be forgiven without being condoned, for this is how we are all forgiven by God.

Question 81. *Does forgiveness mean that God condones sin?*

No. God does not cease to be God. Although God is merciful, God does not condone what God forgives. In the death and resurrection of Christ, God judges what God abhors — everything hostile to love — by abolishing it at the very roots. In this judgment the unexpected occurs: good is brought out of evil, hope out of hopelessness, and life out of death. God spares sinners, and turns them from enemies into friends. The uncompromising judgment of God is revealed in the suffering love of the cross.

The social witness of the catechism to nonviolence and peace takes place mainly at the level of its affirmations about God. It affirms that as revealed and embodied in Jesus Christ, God's power is the power of love, that it reigns over all that would oppose it, and that it triumphs through the suffering of the cross. The church cannot possibly be faithful in witness without meditating on the heart of the gospel. While not all disagreements are likely to be removed, a strong presumption toward nonviolence is required by the cross. Arising from the gospel as considered in itself, this presumption seems especially urgent for the century ahead. Trusting in the sure promises of God, social witness will ever need to ponder anew that fellowship with Christ does not exclude fellowship with him in his sufferings. "God is faithful, by whom you were called into the fellowship of his Son, Jesus Christ our Lord" (1 Cor. 1:9). "I count everything as loss because of the surpassing worth of knowing Christ Jesus my Lord . . . that I may know him and the power of his resurrection, and may share his sufferings, becoming like him in his death, that if possible I may obtain the resurrection from the dead" (Phil. 3:8, 10-11).[10]

Social Justice

The catechism takes the same approach to social justice as it does toward ecological responsibility and peace. It offers an orientation and direction, no more, no less. It establishes work for social justice on the basis of traditional faith, especially as interpreted christocentrically. Six areas in particular may be noted: against social prejudice, solidarity with the oppressed, concern for the poor, social witness without resignation, full equality for women in church and society, and systemic focus.

Against Social Prejudice

A neglected theme in Holy Scripture is the interconnection between lies and violence. Where there is the one, Scripture recognizes, there is likely to be the other. Violence (as for example when perpetrated by governments or powerful social groups) commonly requires lies to conceal itself, just as lies commonly prepare the way for brutality and abuse. Lies are a form of verbal violence, just

---

10. It might be noted that the catechism acknowledges the reality of institutional violence. It thereby goes beyond traditional Reformation catechisms, for it interprets the Ten Commandments as pertaining to more than relations between individuals. For the commandment against murder, it offers this explanation:

Question 108. What do you learn from this commandment?
God forbids anything that harms my neighbor unfairly. Murder or injury can be done not only by direct violence but also by an angry word or a clever plan, and not only by an individual but also by unjust social institutions. I should honor every human being, including my enemy, as a person made in God's image.

A context is thus established (among other things) for naming institutional violence and seeking to end it.

as violence is the ultimate defamation of the other. Relevant verses from the psalms and the prophets are cited by Paul. In the long, harrowing passage on the divine wrath at the opening of his letter to the Romans, the apostle writes: "Their throats are open graves; they use their tongues to deceive. The venom of vipers is under their lips. . . . Their feet are swift to shed blood" (Rom. 3:13, 15). In explicating the commandment that forbids false witness against one's neighbor, the catechism draws attention to this scriptural insight.

> **Question 115.** *Does this commandment forbid racism and other forms of negative stereotyping?*
>
> Yes. In forbidding false witness against my neighbor, God forbids me to be prejudiced against people who belong to any vulnerable, different or disfavored social group. Jews, women, homosexuals, racial and ethnic minorities, and national enemies are among those who have suffered terribly from being subjected to the slurs of social prejudice. Negative stereotyping is a form of falsehood that invites actions of humiliation, abuse, and violence as forbidden by the commandment against murder.

No previous Reformed catechism, to my knowledge, has named social prejudice and negative stereotyping as a violation of the ninth commandment. Nor has any sought to explain how the commandments against false witness and murder are interconnected. Confessing and repenting of social sins have rarely been emphasized in church catechesis as strongly as they have been for personal sins. Finding a convincing basis within the tradition for redressing this unhappy imbalance has clear advantages for the church over other strategies. Antisemitism, misogyny, homophobia, racial prejudice, and the demonizing of enemies all stand in direct violation of the ninth commandment. They have all implicated the church in murder. It will be a wonderful day when social prejudice and negative stereotyping are disorders that the church finds only in the surrounding world. Until then actions against social prejudice belong above all in the renewing of minds within the ordering of the church's common life. How much longer, for example, will the de facto segregation of the churches in my own country continue to ratify and perpetuate the American system of apartheid? How can the churches expect to bear faithful witness to the reconciliation accomplished at the cross when they fail to be fellowships of reconciliation in themselves? Anti-racism programs recently approved for use within PCUSA congregations are a step in the right direction. "Speak out for those who cannot speak, for the rights of all the destitute. Speak out, judge righteously, defend the rights of the poor and needy" (Prov. 31:8-9).

Solidarity with the Oppressed

A recurring phenomenon in the history of Christian theology has been the displacement of central truths by lesser truths. Usually these displacements are more or less temporary. Nevertheless, they can cause great confusion while they last. Polarizations and animosities typically form between two groups — those who, in their wisdom, passionately reject one truth that they might recover the centrality of another, and those who do much the same thing only in reverse. In such cases the solution arises when central truths are allowed to be central and lesser truths are allowed to be lesser. The truth of neither is denied, and room can even be found for allowing the lesser truths, perhaps previously unnoticed or neglected, to assume the urgency of situational precedence.[11]

During the last twenty-five years or so, the church has increasingly witnessed the emergence of victim-oriented soteriologies. The plight of victims, variously specified and defined, has been urged by prominent theologians as the central soteriological problem. It can scarcely be denied that the history of the twentieth century has pushed the plight of victims to the fore. Nor can it be denied that the church has too often seemed ill-equipped to bring the plight of victims, especially victims of oppression and social injustice, clearly into focus for itself so that reasonable and faithful remedies might be sought. Victim-oriented soteriologies have undoubtedly made an important contribution to a better understanding of the church's social responsibility.

Polarizations and animosities have developed, however, to the extent that the plight of victims has displaced the soteriological plight of sinners, or even eclipsed it. Victim-oriented soteriologies have unfortunately tended to define the meaning of sin entirely in terms of victimization. Sin ceases to be a universal category. It attaches to perpetrators and to them alone. Since by definition victims qua victims are innocent of being perpetrators, they are to that extent innocent of sin. If sin attaches only to perpetrators, however, victims can be sinners only by somehow becoming perpetrators themselves (a move not unknown in victim-oriented soteriologies). Victim-oriented soteriologies, with their bipolar opposition between victims and perpetrators, display a logic with sectarian tendencies.

How the cross of Christ is understood by these soteriologies is also worth noting. The cross becomes meaningful because it shows the divine solidarity

11. This kind of flexibility between *de iure* and *de facto* considerations was recognized by Calvin. Commenting on a scriptural passage whose syntactical ordering places duties to others before duties to God, Calvin wrote: "Nor is it strange that he begins with the duties of love of neighbor. For although the worship of God has precedence and ought rightly to come first, yet justice which is practiced in human relations is the true evidence of devotion to God" (Comm. on Micah 6:6-8).

with victims, generally ceasing to find any other relevance, at least positively. (In extreme cases the theology of the cross is trashed as a cause of victimization. But such denunciations, when meant *de iure*, exceed the bounds even of heterodoxy and so cease to be of constructive interest to the church.) The cross, in any case, is no longer the supreme divine intervention for the forgiveness of sins. It is not surprising that more traditional, sin-oriented soteriologies should react with unfortunate polarization. When that happens, sin as a universal category obscures the plight of oppression's victims, rendering that plight just as invisible or irrelevant as it was before. Atonement without solidarity seems to exhaust the significance of the cross, and forgiveness supposedly occurs without judgment on oppression.

The task of generous orthodoxy in this situation is to dispel polarization by letting central truths be central, and lesser truths be lesser, but in each case letting truth be truth. No reason exists why the cross as atonement for sin should be viewed as logically incompatible with the cross as divine solidarity with the oppressed. Good reasons can be found for connecting them. The great historical ecumenical consensus remains, however, that the central significance of the cross, as attested by Holy Scripture, is the forgiveness of sins. This established consensus pervades every aspect of the church's life, not least including baptism and the Lord's Supper. It has by this time withstood all the onslaughts of unbelieving modernity (so that the only question today is not whether the ecumenical consensus will survive but whether those churches devitalized by modern skepticism will). It is reflected throughout the new catechism.[12] No ecclesial catechesis can be valid that fails to affirm the forgiveness of sins as the central truth of the cross.

Lesser truths, however, ought not to be pitted against central truths. Lesser truths, moreover, gain rather than diminish in significance when decentered, for they no longer have a role foisted upon them that they cannot possibly fulfill. Generous orthodoxy as evidenced in the catechism attempts to do justice to both central and lesser truths in themselves as well as to their proper ordering.

Question 42. *What do you affirm when you say that he "suffered under Pontius Pilate"?*

First, that our Lord was humiliated, rejected, and abused by the temporal

---

12. The treatment of our Lord's priestly office may be mentioned as an example.

Question 40. *How did Jesus Christ fulfill the office of priest?*

He was the Lamb of God that took away the sin of the world; he became our priest and sacrifice in one. Confronted by our hopelessness in sin and death, Christ interceded by offering himself — his entire person and work — in order to reconcile us to God.

authorities of his day, both religious and political. Christ thus aligned himself with all human beings who are oppressed, tortured, or otherwise shamefully treated by those with worldly power. Second, and even more importantly, that our Lord, though innocent, submitted himself to condemnation by an earthly judge so that through him we ourselves, though guilty, might be acquitted before our heavenly Judge.

The oppressed have always understood that the cross brings them consolation and hope by placing God into solidarity with their misery. The African-American spiritual is exactly right when it laments, "Nobody knows the trouble I've seen. Nobody knows but Jesus." The gospel does not obscure that our Lord was "mocked and insulted and spat upon" (Luke 18:32), that he was "despised and rejected" by others (Isa. 53:3). Admittedly, the church has not always kept pace with Scripture in recognizing that "The Lord is a stronghold for the oppressed, a stronghold in times of trouble" (Ps. 9:9). It has not always prayed fervently enough with the psalmist: "May he defend the cause of the poor of the people, give deliverance to the needy, and crush the oppressor" (Ps. 72:4), nor has it always acted conscientiously enough on the basis of such prayers. Social witness has a perpetual obligation to solidarity with the oppressed. This obligation, however, is entirely consonant with the truth (which can be displaced only at our peril) on which the entire gospel depends: "For our sake he made him to be sin who knew no sin, so that in him we might become the righteousness of God" (2 Cor. 5:21).

Concern for the Poor

When the universality of sin is recognized as the central soteriological problem, the results can be liberating. All illusions are dispelled, for example, that though others may be needy, I am not, and that I am therefore somehow above others if I am in a position to help them in their need. Acknowledging my need, conversely, brings no implication that I am beneath others who may help me. When recognition is accorded to the universality of divine grace, moreover, I am freed from moralistic forms of obligation. For when grounded in the reception of grace, social obligation is not an externally imposed duty, but a response to the needs of others in gratitude to the God who has already responded so graciously to me. My response to others is based on a solidarity in sin and grace. It occurs as an act of witness to the gospel and through participation in the grace of God. "Walk in love, as Christ has loved us and gave himself up for us" (Eph. 5:2). Question 64 in the catechism states that the mission of the church is to extend mercy and forgiveness to "the needy" in ways that point to Christ. The next question follows with a definition.

Question 65. *Who are the needy?*

The hungry need bread, the homeless need a roof, the oppressed need justice, and the lonely need fellowship. At the same time — on another and deeper level — the hopeless need hope, sinners need forgiveness, and the world needs the gospel. On this level no one is excluded, and all the needy are one. Our mission as the church is to bring hope to a desperate world by declaring God's undying love — as one beggar tells another where to find bread.

The ordering principle that distinguishes and unites our lesser needs with our central need is again in evidence. Our lesser needs are related to our central need by a unity in distinction. Concern for the poor and needy stands in inseparable unity with the forgiveness of sins, without displacing it or becoming a substitute for it. The catechism makes a similar move when it explains the fourth petition of the Lord's Prayer.

Question 130. *What is meant by the fourth petition, "Give us today our daily bread"?*

We ask God to provide for all our needs, for we know that God, who cares for us in every area of our life, has promised us temporal as well as spiritual blessings. God commands us to pray each day for all that we need and no more, so that we will learn to rely completely on God. We pray that we will use what we are given wisely, remembering especially the poor and the needy. Along with every living creature we look to God, the source of all generosity, to bless us and nourish us, according to the divine good pleasure.

Concern for the poor and the needy has a solid basis in traditional faith, as when linked with this petition of the Lord's Prayer. Through the recovery of sound catechesis, concern for the poor, among other things, could become more deeply embedded in the life of the church. A person who fears and blesses the Lord "opens her hand to the poor, and reaches out her hands to the needy" (Prov. 31:20). It will be a great day when congregations not only give money to help the poor, but also create situations in which the poor feel welcome to participate in the life and work of the congregations themselves.

Social Witness without Resignation

Hope for the next world has sometimes been thought to relieve us of responsibility for this one. The catechism connects our ultimate hope indivisibly to our smaller hopes, without confusing them. It grounds all our hopes in the gracious reconciliation accomplished at the cross. Urging constancy in work and prayer, it promotes social witness without resignation.

Question 86. *Does resurrection hope mean that we don't have to take action to relieve the suffering of this world?*

No. When the great hope is truly alive, small hopes arise even now for alleviating the sufferings of the present time. Reconciliation — with God, with one another, and with oneself — is the great hope God has given to the world. While we commit to God the needs of the whole world in our prayers, we also know that we are commissioned to be instruments of God's peace. When hostility, injustice and suffering are overcome here and now, we anticipate the end of all things — the life that God brings out of death, which is the meaning of resurrection hope.

Full Equality of Women in Church and Society

The catechism presupposes that the full equality of women in church and society is compatible with the heart of the gospel as understood by traditional faith. Although this presupposition is strongly contested today, the many complexities cannot be discussed here. From the standpoint of generous orthodoxy, however, "defecting in place," as advocated by some, is, regretfully, not always easy to distinguish from defecting from the gospel. As one avowedly post-Christian feminist theologian has shrewdly argued, Christians must at least believe that Jesus Christ is unique. She then goes on to show that this very minimal condition is not met by a number of avowedly Christian feminist theologians, some of whom are quite prominent.[13] Since she believes that feminism and the gospel cannot possibly be reconciled, she challenges these theologians to quit the church. Their responses are not always encouraging. If no better reasons can be found for not quitting the church than the merely expedient ones commonly offered for "defecting in place," feminist concerns face dismal prospects outside narrow circles.

Fortunately a younger generation of feminist theologians is emerging. (I am thinking, for example, of figures like Katherine Sonderegger of Middlebury, Judith Gundry-Volf of Yale, and Ellen Charry of Princeton.) They promise to bring a new level of sophistication to the important, though not always well-known, work of groundbreaking activist groups like Christians for Biblical Equality. Gender equality and the elimination of male privilege are too impor-

---

13. Daphne Hampson, *Theology and Feminism* (Oxford: Blackwell, 1990), pp. 59-66, 156-60.

tant to be left to the tragically confused who think they can blame constitutive elements of the gospel for women's oppression while gaining a wide hearing in the church. Both logically and psychologically, the contradiction is intolerable. It will inevitably resolve itself in one of two ways: either by reconciling feminism with biblical faith or else by choosing feminism over biblical faith and quitting the church. Halfway measures, whatever their appeal, will be abortive. A challenge to generous orthodoxy, yet to be adequately met, is how to reconcile feminist concerns with traditional faith. The direction, however, is clear: "Be subject to one another out of reverence to Christ" (Eph. 5:21). The church awaits a feminism that is both orthodox and generous.

The catechism makes its own effort, however modest, in opting for the hopeful alternative. A simple misconception is cleared up:

> **Question 11.** *When the creed speaks of "God the Father," does it mean that God is male?*
>
> No. Only creatures having bodies can be either male or female. But God has no body, since by nature God is Spirit. Holy Scripture reveals God as a living God beyond all sexual distinctions. Scripture uses diverse images for God, female as well as male. We read, for example, that God will no more forget us than a woman can forget her nursing child (Isa. 49:15). "'As a mother comforts her child, so will I comfort you,' says the Lord" (Isa. 66:13).

Beyond that, male privilege is disallowed, abuse is condemned, and women's full participation in the leadership in the church is affirmed.

> **Question 13.** *When you confess the God and Father of our Lord Jesus Christ, are you elevating men over women and endorsing male domination?*
>
> No. Human power and authority are trustworthy only as they reflect God's mercy and kindness, not abusive patterns of domination. As Jesus taught his disciples, "The greatest among you will be your servant" (Matt. 23:11). God the Father sets the standard by which all misuses of power are exposed and condemned. "Call no one your father on earth," said Jesus, "for you have one Father — the one in heaven" (Matt. 23:9). In fact God calls women and men to all ministries of the church.

Many questions remain to be addressed, but once again, in its own way, the catechism makes a start.

Systemic Focus

Although the gospel provides every reason for Christians not to be moralistic, they not only too often are moralistic, but also allow moralism to substitute for clear-sighted social analysis. They fail to inquire very deeply into the logic of incentives established by social and economic systems. Though not always free of this problem, Calvin can be an exemplary corrective. Ever alert to the disorders of the human heart, he does not restrict his social criticism to spiritual disorders alone. For example, in a comment relevant to our own day regarding the way impoverished, debt-ridden peoples are treated by affluent nations, Calvin wrote: "Trade carried on with far-off foreign nations is often replete with cheating and extortion, and no limit is set to the profits" (Comm. on Isa. 2:12, 16). Commerce is condemned by the prophet, he noted, "because it has infected the land with many corruptions" (ibid.). When abundance is accumulated by exploiting the vulnerable and defenseless, Calvin concluded, it only "increases pride and cruelty" (ibid.). Human beings "steal," wrote Calvin in another place, "not only when they secretly take the property of others, but also when they make money by injuring others, accumulate wealth in objectionable ways, or are more concerned with their own advantage than with justice" (Comm. on Exod. 20:15/Deut. 5:19).

The catechism makes explicit (modestly) the systemic consciousness that seems nascent in Calvin's ruminations. It recognizes that theft can be more than just a moral or spiritual phenomenon. In explaining the eighth commandment, it states:

> **Question 112. *What do you learn from this commandment?***
> God forbids all theft and robbery, including schemes, tricks or systems that unjustly take what belongs to someone else. God requires me not to be driven by greed, not to misuse or waste the gifts I have been given, and not to distrust the promise that God will supply my needs.

Dispositions toward greed, abuse, and waste are not merely moral disorders but also specifically spiritual ones, rooted in distrust and disobedience to God. At the same time they can also find institutionalized expression through the logic of incentives built into large-scale social and economic systems. It is this latter dimension that the church must take more seriously today than in the past in order to exercise social responsibility in the modern world. Although large areas for discussion and disagreement remain, the church can only gain by including a greater systemic focus within its concerns. Again, typical mistakes will need to be avoided that pit moral, spiritual, and institutional considerations against one another. As the catechism recognizes, they are interconnected. A systemic focus would foster a new sensitivity to forms of exploitation and oppression that the church, especially in affluent countries, cannot responsibly shrug off with cheap resignation. Large-scale, nongovernmental initiatives — modeled perhaps on the Pauline collection in apostolic times — might be among the strategies the international church could adopt in addressing the scandalous differentials of wealth and poverty within its own ranks, though broad-based and multidimensional initiatives of various kinds are urgently needed by the vast majority who constitute the world's poor.

Conclusion

This essay has sought to explain how the new catechism supports social witness on the basis of generous orthodoxy. It has argued for two principles which, though not explicit in the catechism, are consonant with it: the *de iure* precedence of ordering the church's common life so that it accords with the gospel (without discounting direct action in the surrounding world), and, more controversially, effectiveness within the limits of faithfulness alone. The chief criterion of social witness, it has been argued, is conformity to the enacted patterns of the divine compassion as revealed and embodied in Jesus Christ. The established ecumenical concern for justice, peace, and the integrity of creation was interpreted (in reverse order) within this context. The catechism promotes ecological responsibility through its instruction about the image of God. It establishes a strong presumption to nonviolence through its teachings on the cross of Christ. Last but not least, it encourages social justice in the following ways: (1) by opposing negative stereotyping on the basis of the ninth commandment, (2) by establishing ecclesial solidarity with the oppressed on the basis of the prior divine solidarity, (3) by highlighting a biblical concern for the plight of the poor, (4) by opposing weak resignation in the face of social evils, (5) by calling for women's full equality and the elimination of male privilege on a biblical basis that the entire church can take seriously, and (6) by recognizing a systemic focus for the church's social responsibility in the modern world. In these ways, an attempt was made to show how progressive political aspirations can be grounded in traditional faith, when interpreted, with the catechism, in the form of generous orthodoxy.[14]

14. The Study Catechism can be obtained in a handsome edition, which includes fully written-out Scripture references for each question, from Presbyterians for Renewal, 8134 New LaGrange Road, Suite 227, Louisville, Kentucky 40222-4679, USA. (FAX: 502-423-8329.) The cost is US $4.00 per copy. No edition of the First Catechism is currently available from this source. Versions of both catechisms — without the inclusion of written-out Scripture verses — can be obtained in cheap editions from the Presbyterian Publishing Corporation, 100 Witherspoon Street, Louisville, Kentucky 40202-1396, USA.

CHAPTER 22

The Union with Christ Doctrine in Renewal: Movements of the Presbyterian Church (USA)

P. Mark Achtemeier

The doctrine of the *Unio cum Christo* — the union of believers with Christ and their consequent life in Christ — has a theological pedigree that reaches back to the very beginnings of the Reformed tradition. For Calvin, this doctrine stands at the heart and center of his understanding of the sacraments,[1] and he also features it prominently at the start of his discussion of the Christian life in Book 3 of the *Institutes*.

> First, we must understand that as long as Christ remains outside of us, and we are separated from him, all that he has suffered and done for the salvation of the human race remains useless and of no value for us. Therefore, to share with us what he has received from the Father, he had to become ours and to dwell within us.[2]

As Calvin sees it, this union of the Head of the church with his members is absolutely necessary if believers are to have a share in the benefits of Christ:

> That joining together of Head and members, that indwelling of Christ in our hearts — in short, that mystical union — are accorded by us the high-

---

1. See Ronald S. Wallace, *Calvin's Doctrine of the Word and Sacrament* (Tyler, Tex.: Geneva Divinity School Press, 1953), chs. 12, 14, 16.
2. John Calvin, *Institutes of the Christian Religion*, trans. Ford Lewis Battles and ed. John T. McNeill (Philadelphia: Westminster, 1960), 3.1.1. Further citations will be indicated in the text.

est degree of importance, so that Christ, having been made ours, makes us sharers with him in the gifts with which he has been endowed. (3.11.10)[3]

Such union is accomplished as believers are engrafted into Christ by a work of the Holy Spirit. As Calvin sees it, this engrafting is inseparably connected with, though not identical to, faith.[4]

This understanding of the Christian life, as grounded in the believer's union with Christ, is deeply trinitarian: Through our engrafting into Christ by the power of the Spirit, believers enter into communion with the Father, indeed, become partakers and participants in the trinitarian life of God.[5] With the apostle Paul believers can declare, "It is no longer I who live, but Christ who lives in me" (Gal. 2:20).[6] Such participation involves a sharing both in the gifts of God — Christ and all his benefits — and in the mission of God to the world. In trinitarian terms, the whole of the Christian life can be seen as the process of our coming to the Father, through the Son, in the Holy Spirit; and of our sharing by the same Spirit in the life and ministry of the Son given from the Father for the sake of the world.

The biblical and patristic foundations of this doctrine, along with its waxing and waning in the attentions of the Reformed tradition, are subjects that lie beyond the scope of this essay. Our focus in the present discussion will be upon a contemporary revival of interest in this doctrine, as certain grassroots movements within the Presbyterian Church (USA) have recognized within it a helpful and timely resource for addressing a number of troublesome challenges currently facing American Protestantism. Following a consideration of the importance of the doctrine to these movements, we will close with some suggestions about its potential as a motive force in stimulating ecu-

---

3. Cf. 3.25.10: "If the Lord will share his glory, power, and righteousness with the elect — nay will give himself to be enjoyed by them and, what is more excellent, will somehow make them to become one with himself, let us remember that every sort of happiness is included under this benefit."

4. For a helpful survey of the way this doctrine functions in Calvin's theology, see "John Calvin on Mystical Union," ch. 5 of Dennis E. Tamburello, *Union with Christ: John Calvin and the Mysticism of St. Bernard,* Columbia Series in Reformed Theology (Louisville: Westminster/John Knox Press, 1994).

5. Cf. 2 Peter 1:3-4: "His divine power has granted to us all things that pertain to life and godliness, through the knowledge of him who called us to his own glory and excellence, by which he has granted to us his precious and very great promises, that through these you may escape from the corruption that is in the world because of passion, and become partakers of the divine nature."

6. Scriptural citations are taken from the Revised Standard Version (Division of Christian Education of the National Council of the Churches of Christ in the United States of America, 1952 and 1971).

menical dialogue and cooperation between Reformed and other Christian churches.

The *Union in Christ* Declaration

The theological rise to prominence of this doctrine within the life of the Presbyterian Church (USA) has come about in connection with the work of a group calling itself the Presbyterian Coalition. This movement is a loosely knit collection of over twenty unofficial, grassroots organizations each working in different areas and in different ways for the "renewal" of the church. Together these groups command a sizable constituency within the 2.6-million-member denomination, claiming direct ties and friendly relations with roughly four thousand of the eleven thousand congregations making up the church.

The movement was born over the summer of 1996 when leaders of these various groups began working together informally on cooperative strategies for dealing with denominational struggles over the ordination of self-affirming gay and lesbian persons. But while the movement initially formed itself around this particular set of concerns, its members soon realized that they shared together a sufficient range of theological and practical interests to make possible a much more wide-ranging agenda of cooperative efforts within the life of the denomination. Out of a desire to become less reactive and more proactive in meeting challenges facing the church, the Coalition formed a working group in the fall of 1997 and commissioned it to produce a statement of faith and a strategy paper that together could help to guide and focus the work of the Coalition and its member organizations.

The declaration of faith emerging from these efforts lifted up the *Unio cum Christo* as a central theme. Entitled *Union in Christ: A Declaration for the Church,* it was adopted and endorsed by a national convention of Coalition delegates in the fall of 1998, and has since been circulating informally among the churches (a copy of this declaration appears as an appendix to this paper). While lacking official denominational sponsorship or commission, the declaration has quickly garnered at least a measure of official support: A commentary and study guide was published by the church's curriculum publishing division, with an introduction by the head of the denomination's Theology and Worship Office.[7] The document is being promoted and publicized by Coalition members, and a number of presbyteries and other groups have set up meetings and conferences in which to study and discuss the text.

---

7. Andrew Purves and Mark Achtemeier, *Union in Christ: A Commentary with Questions for Study and Reflection* (Louisville: Witherspoon, 1999).

The Doctrine's Role as a Response to Contemporary Challenges

There are a number of theological challenges facing the Presbyterian Church (USA) and others of the so-called "mainline" Protestant churches in America, to which the doctrine of the believer's union with Christ offers a very helpful word. The first of these is an understanding of the Christian life that ignores or neglects the role of repentance and sanctification in Christian discipleship.

Discipleship

Recalling the concept of "cheap grace" so vigorously decried by Dietrich Bonhoeffer,[8] various sectors of American Protestantism are marked by a sanctification-less popular piety that tends to understand the Christian life in terms borrowed from market capitalism. Christian individuals are understood as consumers of religious goods and services that are "marketed" by the churches. As with any market transaction, the only relevant concern is whether the "customers" are pleased with the product being offered them — the need of personal response, much less transformation, tends not to enter the picture. The theological roots of this abandonment of the doctrine of sanctification seem often to be associated with the misappropriation of a purely forensic theory of atonement. Jesus, according to such piety, has "paid the price for our sins"; he has taken upon himself the legal penalty that was due to our faithlessness. The believer thus finds him or herself the beneficiary of a remote, legal transaction that removes all fear of punishment or guilt while leaving the person essentially uninvolved and unchanged. The organic connection between justification and sanctification is thus lost to view, and the result is, as Bonhoeffer puts it, ". . . the justification of sin without the justification of the sinner. Grace alone does everything, they say, and so everything can remain as it was before."[9] God accepts us just the way we are — and leaves us just the way we are!

The doctrine of the believer's union with Christ, by contrast, provides a way of approaching the doctrine of atonement that underscores the essential connection between justification and sanctification. Consider Calvin's understanding of the union: "Christ, having been made ours, makes us sharers with him in the gifts with which he has been endowed" (3.11.10). In this understanding, justification is founded on the believer's union with Christ, a union in

---

8. See the section titled "Costly Grace" in ch. 1 of Dietrich Bonhoeffer, *The Cost of Discipleship,* trans. Reginald H. Fuller (New York: Macmillan, 1953).

9. Bonhoeffer, *The Cost of Discipleship,* p. 37.

which Christ comes to be the possessor of all our sins while we become partakers in his righteousness (the so-called "happy exchange"). But this same union by which believers become the beneficiaries of Christ's righteousness also involves a sharing in Christ's own *life,* a participation in Christ *himself.* Christ is the true vine and the believer the branch who abides in him (John 15). Thus out of the same source from which the believer receives forgiveness of sins and righteousness in Christ, the believer also receives *life in Christ,* growth into the divine image. The organic connection between justification and sanctification is thus illumined by this doctrine in a way that reveals clearly the contradictions inherent in a discipleship that claims forgiveness while continuing to pursue uncritically and without repentance an unamended life.

Authority

A second theological challenge facing the Protestant mainline in the United States concerns the issue of scriptural authority. Traditional determinations to be a church "reformed and always to be reformed according to the Word of God" founder within a stormy chaos of conflicting "readings" of Scripture. One frequently encounters claims, both in congregational life and in the theological academy, that the "message" of Scripture is wholly the product of prior decisions concerning the hermeneutic one brings to the text. The assumption that stands behind such claims is that the choice of a hermeneutic is essentially arbitrary, a legitimating ideological construct put forward by self-interested groups striving for power and hegemony. Traditional Reformed aspirations to be a church of the Word are consequently crowded out by the cacophonous struggle for hegemony among competing "readings" of the Bible, with little expectation that anything other than the human Will to Power will be reflected in the readings that emerge finally from the struggle.

One obviously cannot plausibly deny that the message one hears coming from the scriptures is significantly determined by the hermeneutic one brings to the text. But the doctrine of the church's union with Christ can be of help in charting a course out of the present dilemma, precisely by its calling into question the assumption that the choice among hermeneutics is arbitrary. Indeed, the doctrine suggests that something well beyond the expression of power interests is at work here.

Union with Christ involves not simply a participation in the life of Christ, but also a sharing in the *mind* of Christ. "'For who has known the mind of the Lord so as to instruct him?' But we have the mind of Christ" (1 Cor. 2:16). "Have this mind among yourselves, which is yours in Christ Jesus . . ." (Phil. 2:5). Robert Jenson, citing the foundational work of Gregory Palamas in the East and

Thomas Aquinas in the West, emphasizes this aspect of the *Unio* in the first volume of his systematic theology:

> With respect to the knowledge of God, East and West are often thought to disagree drastically, but there is no disagreement on our present fundamental point. God, East and West have agreed, is not known because he is amenable to the exercise of our cognitive powers. He is known by us in that he grants us what we could never reach, or even know we could or should reach: he takes us into his own knowledge of himself. . . .[10]

Quoting Palamas, Jenson goes on to say that "The gift that transcends the mind's natural 'cognitive capacity' is 'union' with God, 'the grace of adoption, the deifying gift of the Spirit.'"[11] Union with Christ involves sharing in the mind of Christ. Faith is thus a participation in God's own knowledge of himself. If this is the case, it has a profound bearing on our treatment of the hermeneutical problem, for it establishes a uniquely privileged position for the hermeneutic that *the church* brings to its own reading of Scripture. It is within the historically persisting body of Christ, the fellowship of believers united with him in faith by grace through the power of the Spirit, that genuine knowledge of God — and thus genuine understanding of the scriptures — is available. "For we have the mind of Christ." Readings shaped within the community of faith thus occupy a hermeneutically privileged position as a matter of theological principle.

Such recognition elevates to a singular position of prominence the sympathetic and expectant dialogue with church *tradition* as an essential element in the church's attempts to interpret Scripture faithfully for our own day and time. The doctrine of the church's union with Christ, and its consequent participation in the mind of Christ, re-establishes in a compelling way the soundness of the famous Canon set forth by Vincent of Lerins: the church is to measure its life and teaching against that which has been believed and confessed *"semper, ubique, ab omnibus"* — always, everywhere, and by all believers. G. K. Chesterton once described church tradition as the democracy of the dead. Overcoming our exclusivist and prejudicial biases in favor of the living, and re-establishing the voice of the historic church as a pre-eminent partner in the contemporary dialogue with the scriptures, is the concrete manifestation of our confession that the historic church in union with Christ shares the mind of Christ. Such attentiveness to the voice of tradition will obviously not solve all of the difficulties we presently face over the proper interpretation of the Bible. The

---

10. Robert Jenson, *Systematic Theology,* volume 1: *The Triune God* (New York: Oxford University Press, 1997), p. 227.

11. Jenson, *Systematic Theology,* vol. 1, p. 227.

tradition is in many areas multivalent and, as the Reformers never tired of pointing out, subject to error. But our confession of the church's union with Christ does provide, in the form of a renewed appreciation for the significance of Christian tradition, a stable set of fixed points by which the contemporary church may navigate the turbulent seas of hermeneutical struggle. The mind of Christ rather than the Will to Power is the ultimate arbiter and determinant of the church's encounter with the scriptures.

Mission

A third theological challenge to which the *Unio* offers a much-needed word is the loss or neglect of mission at the heart of the church's life. One frequently encounters among Protestant mainline churches in America congregations that have become closed in upon themselves, church communities whose primary concern has become the maintenance of their own institutional and organizational infrastructure, along with the delivery of various services and benefits to their own established membership. Granted, one sometimes finds such congregations engaging in membership recruitment drives that are promoted under the label of "evangelism." All too frequently, however, the motivation at the heart of such work is simply the maintenance of an adequate base of financial support for the congregation's own self-serving activities.

The union of believers with Christ, and the church's existence in Christ, constitute an altogether different basis for understanding the nature of congregational life. The key insight here is that participation in the trinitarian *life* of God — which is the church's communion with the Father by her union with the Son in the power of the Spirit — involves also and at the same time participation in the *mission* of God to the world. The church's union with Christ's person makes it a participant in Christ's mission, which mission is constituted by the Father's sending of the Son into the world in the power of the Spirit. "As the Father has sent me, even so I send you" (John 20:21).

The doctrine of the *Unio cum Christo* thus brings powerfully to light the indissoluble connection between the existence of the church in Christ and her participation in Christ's mission to the world, and thus reveals every self-serving form of congregational life as a denial of the church's very nature. Not only that, but recognition of the church's participation in Christ's own mission dispels and overcomes the illusory opposition between evangelistic mission and ministries of justice, charity, and compassion: Just as Christ's own proclamation of the reign of God present in his very person was accompanied by works of compassion and wondrous signs testifying to the present reality and future consummation of the kingdom, so the church's proclamation of Christ is accompanied by works and signs that embody in a provisional way that *shalom* which will characterize God's future. The *Unio cum Christo* helps us to reclaim the missional character of the church in all its fullness.

Unity

A final theological challenge confronting American mainline Protestants involves questions about the basis of the church's unity. "Inclusiveness" as an abstract concept has frequently been lifted up as the pre-eminent foundation of the church's unity. Because this concept is an abstraction, what began as a relatively innocuous synonym for the catholicity of the church has drifted in directions leading to a thoroughgoing religious individualism and relativism. The "inclusiveness" of the mainline Protestant churches is now in danger of becoming a completely elastic concept, embracing and affirming any and every private and idiosyncratic belief system, regardless of whether it stands in any discernible continuity with historic Christian, much less Reformed, faith.

The result of this erosion has been a critical and widely observed loss of religious identity within the mainline churches, accompanied by a corresponding loss of motivation and vitality. The essence of being Reformed, I was recently told by a high-level denominational official, is being equally open to any and all religious ideas. Needless to say, this kind of principled refusal to affirm anything in particular serves to radically undermine the church's motivation to engage in mission, or even to perpetuate its own existence into the future.

Over against this debilitating loss of religious identity, the *Unio* doctrine lifts up an understanding of church unity that establishes and enhances the church's identity rather than undermines it. The unity of the church is grounded not in abstract concepts, nor in various forms of human striving, but in Jesus Christ alone. It is precisely as the Spirit engrafts believers into Christ that they find their unity with one another established by their common fellowship with him and in him. In this way the link between the unity of the church and the faith of the church is once again brought to prominence. The church receives its unity from Christ as a gift, received on the basis of the common participation of all its members in the divine life.

This affirmation helps to counter the powerful cultural forces of religious individualism and privatism that pose serious threats to the integrity of church life in the North American context. The American religious scene is marked by large numbers of people who profess Christian faith but fail to discern any positive connection between such profession and participation in the life of the Christian community. Lifting up the *Unio cum Christo* helps to furnish believers a set of theological categories for recognizing and affirming the essential connection between their individual relationship with Christ and their common life with one another in him. Life in Christ *is* life within fellowship of believers.

The recognition of the believer's union with Christ as the foundation of the church's unity also provides a powerful impetus for the church's involvement in ecumenical work. To recognize that the church's unity flows as a gift from the same source as her life and mission is to establish an ecumenical imperative no less essential or fundamental to the nature of the church than her missionary imperative. The union of believers *with* Christ entails the union of believers with one another *in* Christ: The existence of hardened divisions within the worldwide company of Christians thus appears as a blatant contradiction of the church's life in Christ, an unspeakably tragic failure of the church to manifest the truth of her essential nature and to live out the gospel in her common life. Such recognition perhaps ought to be especially troubling to those of us who are heirs of the Reformed tradition, the branches and divisions of which have multiplied almost beyond counting. Indeed, there have been times in its recent history that the Reformed movement has seemed to embrace schism as an almost routine principle of church polity, one that functions in place of the old Roman magisterium as the chief instrument in ecclesiastical disputes. Of this shameful history the Reformed churches surely must repent.

Ecumenical Prospects

The *Unio cum Christo* doctrine, in addition to highlighting the critical importance of the church's ecumenical task, itself may provide a useful basis and starting point for ecumenical dialogue in a variety of contexts. Among the Lutheran churches, one cannot help but think in this context of the groundbreaking work being carried on by the new Finnish school of Luther studies under the leadership of Professor Tuomo Mannermaa.[12] To summarize briefly, this group of scholars is investigating the hitherto unsuspected centrality of the believer's union with Christ in Luther's understanding of justification, arguing that an essential element of Luther's thought is the presence of Christ to the believer not only as grace but also as gift. Christ *himself* is born in the heart of the believer, and that union, that gift, constitutes the heart of Luther's concept of justification by grace through faith. Such a recognition perhaps opens up a new starting point for dialogue over disputed points of Christology that have in the past proven so troubling.

---

12. For a very helpful introduction to this work see Carl Braaten and Robert Jenson, eds., *Union with Christ: The New Finnish Interpretation of Luther* (Grand Rapids: Eerdmans, 1998).

Reformed understandings of the believer's union with Christ involve an understanding of Christian existence as participation in the divine life. Such a recognition could provide at least a starting point for significant dialogue with Eastern Orthodox understandings of salvation in terms of *theosis,* or "deification." The importance of these concepts to the two traditions surely provides the basis for conversation and exploration.

Finally, the *Unio* doctrine may even provide a starting point for conversation with the burgeoning Pentecostal movements that have become such a remarkable feature of Christianity worldwide in the latter part of the twentieth century. The indispensable role of the Holy Spirit in binding believers together with Christ perhaps affords to Reformed Christians a way of approaching the work of the Spirit in ecumenical conversations with a seriousness and a centrality that have not always been evident in times past, and they may with God's help allow such conversations to bear fruit.

In conclusion, the Reformed doctrine of the *Unio cum Christo* is a feature of the Reformed heritage that speaks powerfully to contemporary challenges facing the Reformed churches in America, and that also has the potential to impart new life and urgency to the church's ecumenical work. Our prayer is that God, in reminding the Reformed churches of their indissoluble connection with Christ the true vine, may cause the branches that abide in him to bear much fruit, and so prove to be his disciples.

APPENDIX

Union in Christ

A Declaration for the Church

He is before all things
and in him all things hold together.

Col. 1:17

With the witness of Scripture and the Church through the ages we declare:

I.

Jesus Christ is the gracious mission of God
to the world
and for the world.
He is Emmanuel and Savior,
One with the Father,
God incarnate as Mary's son,
Lord of all,
The truly human one.

His coming transforms everything.

His Lordship casts down every idolatrous claim to authority.
His incarnation discloses the only path to God.

His life shows what it means to be human.
His atoning death reveals the depth of God's love for sinners.
His bodily resurrection shatters the powers of sin and death.

II.

The Holy Spirit joins us to Jesus Christ by grace alone, uniting our life with his through the ministry of the Church.

> In the proclamation of the Word, the Spirit calls us to repentance, builds up and renews our life in Christ, strengthens our faith, empowers our service, gladdens our hearts, and transforms our lives more fully into the image of Christ.

>> We turn away from forms of Church life that ignore the need for repentance, that discount the transforming power of the Gospel, or that fail to pray, hope, and strive for a life that is pleasing to God.

> In Baptism and conversion the Spirit engrafts us into Christ, establishing the Church's unity and binding us to one another in him.

>> We turn away from forms of Church life that seek unity in theological pluralism, relativism, or syncretism.

> In the Lord's Supper the Spirit nurtures and nourishes our participation in Christ and our communion with one another in him.

>> We turn away from forms of Church life that allow human divisions of race, gender, nationality, or economic class to mar the Eucharistic fellowship, as though in Christ there were still walls of separation dividing the human family.

III.

Engrafted into Jesus Christ we participate through faith in his relationship with the Father.

> By our union with Christ we participate in his righteousness before God, even as he becomes the bearer of our sin.

347

We turn away from any claim to stand before God apart from Christ's own righteous obedience, manifest in his life and sacrifice for our sake on the cross.

By our union with Christ we participate in his knowledge of the Father, given to us as the gift of faith through the unique and authoritative witness of the Old and New Testaments.

We turn away from forms of Church life that discount the authority of Scripture or claim knowledge of God that is contrary to the full testimony of Scripture as interpreted by the Holy Spirit working in and through the community of faith across time.

By our union with Christ we participate in his love of the Father, manifest in his obedience "even unto death on the cross."

We turn away from any supposed love of God that is manifest apart from a continual longing for and striving after that loving obedience which Christ offers to God on our behalf.

IV.

Though obscured by our sin, our union with Christ causes his life to shine forth in our lives. This transformation of our lives into the image of Christ is a work of the Holy Spirit begun in this life as a sign and promise of its completion in the life to come.

By our union with Christ our lives participate in the holiness of the One who fulfilled the Law of God on our behalf.

We turn away from forms of Church life that ignore Christ's call to a life of holiness, or that seek to pit Law and Gospel against one another as if both were not expressions of the one Word of God.

By our union with Christ we participate in his obedience. In these times of moral and sexual confusion we affirm the consistent teaching of Scripture that calls us to chastity outside of marriage and faithfulness within the covenant of marriage between a man and a woman.

> We turn away from forms of Church life that fail to pray for and strive after a rightly ordered sexuality as the gracious gift of a loving God, offered to us in Christ by the power of the Holy Spirit. We also turn away from forms of Church life that fail to forgive and restore those who repent of sexual and other sins.

V.

As the body of Christ the Church has her life in Christ.

> By our union with Christ the Church binds together believers in every time and place.

> > We turn away from forms of Church life that identify the true Church only with particular styles of worship, polity, or institutional structure. We also turn away from forms of Church life that ignore the witness of those who have gone before us.

> By our union with Christ the Church is called out into particular communities of worship and mission.

> > We turn away from forms of Church life that see the work of the local congregation as sufficient unto itself, as if it were not a local representation of the one, holy, catholic, and apostolic Church called together by the power of the Spirit in every age and time until our Lord returns.

> By our union with Christ our lives participate in God's mission to the world:
> to uphold the value of every human life,
> to make disciples of all peoples,
> to establish Christ's justice and peace in all creation,
> and to secure that visible oneness in Christ that is the promised inheritance of every believer.

> > We turn away from forms of Church life that fail to bear witness in word and deed to Christ's compassion and peace, and the Gospel of salvation.

By our union with Christ the Church participates in Christ's resurrected life and awaits in hope the future that God has prepared for her. Even so come quickly, Lord Jesus!

In the name of the Father, and of the Son, and of the Holy Spirit.

CHAPTER 23

In Support of a Reformed View
of Ascension and Eucharist

Douglas Farrow

The windless northern surge, the sea-gull's scream,
And Calvin's kirk crowning the barren brae.
I think of Giotta the Tuscan shepherd's dream,
Christ, man and creature in their inner day.
How could our race betray
The Image, and the Incarnate One unmake
Who chose this form and fashion for our sake?

The Word made flesh here is made Word again,
A word made word in flourish and arrogant crook.
See there King Calvin with his iron pen,
And God three angry letters in a book,
And there the logical hook
On which the Mystery is impaled and bent
Into an ideological instrument.

There's better gospel in man's natural tongue,
And truer sight was theirs outside the Law
Who saw the far side of the Cross among
The archaic peoples in their ancient awe,
In ignorant wonder saw
The wooden cross-tree on the bare hillside,
Not knowing that there a God suffered and died.

The fleshless word, growing, will bring us down,
Pagan and Christian man alike will fall,
The auguries say, the white and black and brown,
The merry and sad, theorist, lover, all
Invisibly will fall:
Abstract calamity, save for those who can
Build their cold empire on the abstract man.

A soft breeze stirs and all my thoughts are blown
Far out to sea and lost. Yet I know well
The bloodless word will battle for its own
Invisibly in brain and nerve and cell.
The generations tell Their personal tale: the One has far to go
Past the mirages and the murdering snow.

Edwin Muir, "The Incarnate One"[1]

The disaffected Scottish poet, Edwin Muir, articulates as well as anyone the common perception that the Reformed tradition is one (among others) in which people may become "starved for the sheer humanity of the Son of God."[2] To ask how and why this perception arose is to raise a question requiring a highly complex historical and theological answer, much too complex to give here. It is safe to say, however, that the future health of the Reformed churches, and the value of their contributions to the wider church, depend in part upon addressing not only the perception but the underlying problems. What follows is an attempt to place one or two of these problems in a clearer light, while offering an appreciation of a vital feature of Reformed theology which — on my view, but not on that of some of my fellow Anglicans — it holds in trust for the wider church.

We begin on the familiar territory of the disputes between Rome and the German and Genevan reformers over the real presence, understood here as disputes about the *nature* of that presence rather than the fact of it.[3] Bound up

---

1. 1887-1959. *Selected Poems* (London: Faber & Faber, 1963).

2. To take a line from Thomas F. Torrance, and from a book that helped to set me thinking about all of this; see *Royal Priesthood: A Theology of Ordained Ministry* (Edinburgh: T. & T. Clark, 1993), pp. 43ff.; cf. *Space, Time and Resurrection* (Oxford: Oxford University Press, 1969).

3. "To them Christ does not seem present unless he comes down to us. As though, if he should lift us to himself, we should not just as much enjoy his presence! The question is therefore only of the manner, for they place Christ in the bread, while we do not think it law-

with those disputes, of course, were questions about the relation between Christ's offering to God and the eucharistic offering of the church, the answers to which obviously bear directly on the way in which we understand our own humanity in Christ. And both sets of questions, it was quickly realized, belong in turn to debate about another highly controversial subject, the doctrine of the ascension. Not for nothing does John 6 link faithful discipleship to communion in the eucharistic mystery, and the eucharistic mystery to the even greater mystery of the ascension:

> When his disciples heard it, they said, "This teaching is difficult; who can accept it?" But Jesus, being aware that his disciples were complaining about it, said to them, "Does this ['my flesh is true food and my blood is true drink'] offend you? Then what if you were to see the Son of man ascending to where he was before?"[4]

That the Reformation, as a unified movement of church renewal, came to grief over its failure to resolve its internal differences regarding ascension and eucharist is not an item of interest only to historians, or to ecumenists bravely trying to hold together new and somewhat tenuous *formulae* of agreement. It is a point of abiding theological interest, heightened not lessened by a knowledge that the reformers were only repeating debates that had already taken place in the western church: What is Christ's relation to the church at worship and to the symbols that structure that worship? Can one who is in heaven also be on earth? How does he impart to us his immortality or life-giving virtue? Such questions were raised in the ninth century by the Corbie controversy, and again by Berengarius. No discussion about the real presence of Christ, and no talk about participation in his body, can evade them, just as no ecclesiology can successfully evade a discussion of the presence and the absence or the obligation to help discern and identify his body. Failure here is *ipso facto* a failure to discover the theological foundations on which church renewal can be conducted.

Reformed theology ranges itself over against both the Roman settlement of the ancient debate and its Lutheran modification. By maintaining that the glorified body of Jesus Christ exists in its own place, that its place is *other* than ours, and that it remains in this place exclusively until the parousia, Reformed tradition appears to side with Ratramnus against Radbertus. In so doing, it is of course accused also of making common cause with Berengarian and Zwinglian eucharistic nominalism. That renders it entirely unsatisfactory from either a

---

ful for us to drag him from heaven. Let our readers decide which one is more correct." John Calvin, *Institutes of the Christian Religion*, trans. Ford Lewis Battles and ed. John T. McNeill (Philadelphia: Westminster, 1960), 4.17.31

4. John 6:61f. (NRSV).

Roman or a Lutheran point of view, as a movement that dislocates the humanity of Christ, effectively detaching our humanity from his. All that is left to us, then, as genuinely present here and now, is the divinity of Christ. This is a presence that does not so much affirm and enable our humanity as overpower it, pushing it to one side and leaving it to its own devices. Arguably, the effect of this tendency might be illustrated even from Cranmer's Book of Common Prayer, which consigns the worshipers' self-offering to a liturgical appendix, as it were, rendering it a mere attachment (and as such an independent response?) to the prior offering of Christ.[5]

Graham Ward, standing at the high-Anglican intersection between Roman and Lutheran criticism of Reformed theology, goes so far as to charge Calvin with having adopted a gnostic perspective. Writing in *Radical Orthodoxy*, he cleverly retrieves the dislocated by arguing that in Scripture the ascension represents the climax of a series of "withdrawals" or "assumptions" or "displacements" of the body of Jesus, by which it is actually rendered open or permeable to all other bodies, and becomes itself the divine location in which they live and move and have their being.[6] Simon Oliver likewise, writing for *Modern Theology*, thinks that Calvin produces a "spiritually rarified" form of Christianity by too sharp a distinction between the "natural" elements of the eucharistic celebration and the exalted (absent) body of Jesus. The reformer's focus on the *sursum corda* becomes an invitation to "a spiritualised and gnostic existence that lacks any genuine notion of corporeality." From this follows naturally, suggests Oliver, the privatizing of religion later witnessed in Europe and America, and the sundering of "nature" and "culture" from one another and from human participation in the life of God.[7]

Now it may well seem to Reformed readers that such criticisms are wide of the mark, both historically and theologically. Is there perhaps a failure here to reckon with the intricacies of the Reformation and post-Reformation debates? We will later touch on the uneasy relationship between the Roman and Lutheran elements of this critique, but first of all we ought to acknowledge that the charge laid is not entirely groundless. Might it not be admitted that there is a fundamental problem with Calvin's *sursum corda* and with his interpretation of the eucharistic mystery — viz., that the body of the worshiper, unlike his or her soul, appears to be uninvolved in the secret union and communion with

5. Similar effects, however, can be produced by quite different liturgical constructs.
6. Graham Ward, *Radical Orthodoxy: A New Theology*, ed. John Milbank, Catherine Pickstock, and Graham Ward (London: Routledge, 1999), pp. 63ff.
7. Simon Oliver, "The Eucharist before Nature and Culture," *Modern Theology* (July 1999). I am greatly indebted to Mr. Oliver for sending me an advance copy of his paper, which contains much of value, although (as will become clear) I do not agree with his reading of Calvin or with his contention that the Genevan reformer reduces the liturgy to "mere theatre."

Christ in the heavenlies, and that Christ himself, in Luther's sarcastic phrase, is made like "a stork in a nest in a treetop," detached from any genuinely human existence?[8] Must we not confess, in any case, that certain branches of the Reformed church have, by whatever means, developed nature/grace dualisms with disastrous consequences for human life?

Let it be said clearly, respecting this or any other element of the Reformed tradition, that it need not be preserved simply because it is already there. Reformed churches, not because they *are* reformed but because they seek reform, may entertain the suggestion that what is needed today, if they are to encourage a Christianity the humanity (and humaneness) of which is not in doubt, is to return to a more catholic conception of the eucharist than that offered by Calvin. That of course would mean reconsideration of his view of the ascension, and so of the problem of the presence and the absence, a reconsideration I myself want to encourage. No one by now will misunderstand me: I am not implying that these topics are of only minor relevance, and hence negotiable for the sake of some greater agenda. Just the reverse; to hold such a view would already betray a gnostic streak. Was it not precisely with respect to the eucharist that St. Irenaeus confronted his gnostic opponents with the inconsistency of their position, urging them to cease and desist from offering it?[9]

We will hear more from Irenaeus at another juncture, but we may take as our immediate partners in dialogue Thomas Aquinas and Martin Luther. Now Aquinas believed, like Calvin after him, in a literal bodily ascension of Jesus to the highest heaven, to that "most excellent of places" beyond all earthly space or time.[10] This certainly entails a real absence. But, by virtue of his divine omnipresence and omnipotence as the Logos, Jesus is able to provide on earth a eucharistic form of his humanity under the accidents of the bread and wine, making present (albeit nonspatially) the actual substance of his exalted body and blood. In this way and through this gift he is able also to determine his own bodily existence in the form of the church, that is, as the *totus christus*. Was Calvin, whose reservations were not primarily metaphysical, overhasty in exchanging this account of the presence of the absent Christ for one that leaves Christ strictly in heaven, and that postulates rather a secret relocation of the *worshiper* through faith and the ministry of the Spirit? Calvin may have believed that the doctrine of transubstantiation threatens the integrity of creaturely reality, that

8. Cf. J. McClelland, *Marburg Revisited: A Reexamination of Lutheran and Reformed Traditions*, ed. Paul Empie and James McCord (Minneapolis: Augsburg, 1966), pp. 42f.

9. See Irenaeus, *Against Heresies* 4.18.4.

10. Aquinas (*ST* IIIa, 57-58; cf. 76.1) is not clear what sort of place this might be, but *is* clear that Christ retains his bodily humanity. Augustine's dialectic is still in place: on the one hand, we should "no longer think of him as a man on earth but as God in heaven"; on the other, "the presence of his human nature in heaven is itself an intercession for us."

it arrogates to the church a false power over Christ's offering, and that it subtly alters the object and hence the nature of faith.[11] But is it really possible to reverse, as he wished to do, the eucharistic picture with which the medieval church was working? If we are not permitted to appeal to the miracle of transubstantiation, how are we to conceive of a real union of soul and body with the heavenly Christ? How, that is, are we to maintain a true solidarity between Christ and the Christian, or a true identity between the offering of Christ and the offering of his church? *Prima facie* it is by no means apparent that a simple appeal to the Spirit can justify such claims, if by them we mean to include our corporeal nature and with it the entire sphere of human culture.

Should we determine to take a fresh look at Aquinas and at transubstantiation, we might benefit from the recent analysis of Catherine Pickstock, though she takes as her main foil not Calvin but nihilistic postmodernism.[12] To reproduce her argument would require a lengthy digression — suffice it to say that she discovers in Aquinas's exposition of the sacrament a storehouse of epistemological treasure unavailable on a metaphorical or "Calvinist" reading — but we may extract for our own purposes the following salient points: First, is the creaturely undermined by the conversion of bread and wine into the body and blood of Christ? On the contrary, this conversion (which for Thomas *is* conversion, not annihilation) entails a direct grounding in the grace of God even of the leftover accidents of bread and wine, lending to them the power to disclose the gift-nature of *all* reality.[13] Second, does a Thomist view of the eucharist arrogate to the church a false power, "fetishising" pure presence, as she puts it? No it does not, for it is built upon a theology of desire that mediates between presence and absence. Third, does the doctrine of transubstantiation alter the object of faith, shifting our attention away from Christ? On this point we must extrapolate a little, since Pickstock does not concern herself with this, but again the answer is no, if we can agree that his body "is a nuptial body which is always already the unity of Christ with the Church, His people."[14]

I mention Pickstock's defense of transubstantiation, however, not because it convinces me that Calvin's concerns were ill-founded, but rather because (its brilliant deployment against nihilism notwithstanding) it does *not*

---

11. See Calvin, *Insitutes* 4.17.13ff.

12. I am referring primarily to "Thomas Aquinas and the Quest for the Eucharist," *Modern Theology* 15, no. 2 (1999): 159-80; but see also *After Writing: On the Liturgical Consummation of Philosophy* (Oxford: Blackwell, 1998).

13. In this connection Pickstock presses her bold thesis, articulated in *After Writing* (pp. 259ff.), that transubstantiation is "the condition of possibility for all human meaning." Cf. Jean-Luc Marion, *God Without Being* (Chicago: University of Chicago Press, 1991), pp. 149ff.

14. Signified by the mixing of water with the wine; cf. *ST* IIIa, 74.6ff.

quite convince me. Pickstock wants to overcome the dichotomy between presence and absence which, on her view, unites both modernism and postmodernism to a decadent form of Christianity with roots in late medieval nominalism. In doing so she appears to me to regularize or normalize the church's eucharistic situation, by tying it to a neo-Platonist understanding of participation in which the ontological dialectic of fulfillment and desire, that is, of ἔρως — sustained now by the miracle of transubstantiation — alters or even replaces the eschatological dialectic of the departure and return of Jesus.[15] And this first alteration is only possible because of a second: presence and absence are here understood primarily in theological rather than christological terms; the eucharist is more about "a tasting of God" than about an interim communion with the absent Christ.[16] Otherwise put, it is only possible as the historical setting of the eucharist recedes into the background, as it is forgotten that the problem of the presence and the absence is not *addressed* by the eucharist but *created* by it.[17]

How far Aquinas himself can be said to have allowed ontology to overcome eschatology, and how far (if at all) the doctrine of transubstantiation is implicated in the above objection, remain matters for debate. We will come back to that later, noting Jean-Luc Marion's rather different defense. But there is a related criticism to consider. The ontological approach inevitably carries with it the temptation to make the corporate, ecclesial sense of the term σῶμα primary, or even to elide the distinction between the corporeal and the corporate, so that to speak of the risen Christ's body is, without prior or further qualification, to speak of the church. We may pass over the irony that this effectively disallows any *non*-metaphorical interpretation of αἷμα. Much more important is the fact that the ontological approach cannot ultimately sustain itself without attempting this elision, for in taking the presence and absence of God as its problem it must take the supernatural reality of the church as its solution. Logically, only the church (as complex unity and unitary complexity) can mediate between God and the world, that is, between the One and the many. Eucharistically speaking, then, the church becomes the extension or perfection of Christ and the object of its own desire. On one level this is perfectly appropriate, of course. May we not hold with Aquinas that "Christ's actual body and blood" and his "mystical body" are respectively "the first thing and the ultimate

---

15. Pickstock's model *is* eschatologically oriented, and is *not* ontological in a strictly traditional way; she is after all critically engaged with Marion. Yet I miss in her work, as in that of her "radical orthodoxy" colleagues, proper attention to this most fundamental dimension of Christian eschatology.

16. Cf. Marion, *God Without Being*, p. 227, n. 12.

17. Or rather by the ascension, which generates the eucharistic situation as an anomaly, in the time between the times.

thing of which the eucharist is the sign"?[18] Yet where expectation of the parousia has faded or been redefined there is considerable pressure towards a conflation of the two, a conflation that becomes increasingly evident in the modern period — where we must take into account, among other things, the legacy of Luther.

The German reformer, like the Genevan, had a number of reasons for rejecting transubstantiation, not least its association with the idea of the mass as a meritorious sacrifice on the part of the church.[19] The bread and the body must not be confused lest the church become the author rather than the recipient of grace. But unlike Calvin, Luther responded to Zwingli's error — detaching or separating the body from the bread — by employing the *communicatio idiomatum* idea in conjunction with the doctrine of the ascension to argue for the ubiquity of Christ. Absence thus became hiddenness, as it had already in Scotus and Cusanus. In spite of Luther's insistence that we must by all means avoid a *nudus christus,* shorn of real humanity, Lutherans (especially those of Westphal's persuasion) were soon being charged by their Reformed counterparts that this is exactly what they could not do: their putatively human Christ, present everywhere and nowhere, was but a "monstrous phantasm." Now it has been observed that one ironic effect of Luther's teaching was to weaken badly his own eucharistic center. On the one hand, the sacramental presence threatened to become "a mere corollary of this massive cosmic presence";[20] on the other, the distinction between the hidden Christ who is always present and the revealed Christ who wills to be present *pro nobis* began to focus undue attention on the problem of self-disclosure, and especially on its linguistic mediation.[21] It might be more accurate, however, to say that the effect was to invite a strangely Pelagian reinterpretation of the eucharist. For the Lutheran construct, like the Roman, paradoxically leaves a deficit that requires to be made up: the *church* must supply the missing dimensions of Christ's humanity in order to vouchsafe the real presence.

I do not mean to take what is constitutive of the eucharistic gift — real participation in Christ, mutual coinherence with the incarnate one, hence gen-

---

18. *ST* IIIa, 73.1

19. This as much as anything drove the two reformers to regard the relationship between the body and the bread in terms of the maxim *distinctio sed non separatio,* to employ Calvin's way of putting it. Cf. Calvin, *Institutes* 4.17.5; and Benjamin Milner, *Calvin's Doctrine of the Church: A Thesis* (Leiden: Brill, 1970), pp. 190ff.

20. Jaroslav Pelikan, *The Christian Tradition: A History of the Development of Doctrine,* vol. 4 (Chicago: University of Chicago Press, 1984), p. 202.

21. On the *ubiquity/ubivoli* distinction, cf. Dietrich Bonhoeffer, *Christ the Center* (New York: Harper & Row, 1978), pp. 54ff. The significance of all this for the emergent question as to the meaningfulness of human speech deserves more notice than it generally receives.

uine communion with God — and turn it perversely into a criticism. Nor do I mean to imply that this gift is given independently of the eucharist and only witnessed to therein, as if the gift itself were not fundamentally ecclesial — as if *Christ* himself were not fundamentally ecclesial![22] But I do mean to identify a tendency, and a very ancient tendency it is, to regard the "whole Christ" as constituted by the divinity of the Word and the humanity of the church, rather than by the God-man and those who are liberated by him to become children of God with him.[23] Only a clear focus on the authentic humanity of the Word as the eucharistic *a priori* can defeat the temptation to imagine (secretly or openly) that in the sacrament it is not so much Christ who makes possible our humanity as we who make possible his; or to forget that the fullness which here accrues to Christ is a fullness *from* his fullness before it is a fullness towards it.[24] Both the Roman and the Lutheran doctrines of the eucharist, in their classical forms, attempt to rule out any such forgetfulness. This point must be underscored. But do they succeed? Among Luther's heirs, we increasingly encounter the thesis that the church itself is the true and only body of the ascended (or ascending) Christ.[25] Sometimes we even hear talk of a universal incarnation. Thus we are brought back around to the elision or conflation of which we have already spoken, unless indeed we are carried beyond it by a synthesis of defects into an even greater confusion.

As an Anglican myself I will not hesitate to illustrate the prevalence of this confusion among Anglican ranks. Had I space I might trace it in *Lux Mundi* or in the writings of Dean Inge or Archbishop Temple,[26] but let me turn once more to Graham Ward's recent piece in *Radical Orthodoxy*. According to Ward:

22. When we say "Christ," explains John Zizioulas, "we mean a person and not an individual; we mean a relational reality existing 'for me' or 'for us.'" *Being as Communion: Studies in Personhood and the Church* (Crestwood, N.Y.: St. Vladimir's Press, 1985), pp. 110f.; following Bonhoeffer, p. 47.

23. I.e., by adoption, and (in view of sin) by way of what Calvin calls the *mirifica commutatio* (*Institutes* 4.17.2). Calvin does not but perhaps should have criticized Augustine for encouraging the tendency in question; cf. e.g., *En. Ps.* 143 (142:3).

24. Cf. Eph. 1:17ff. Does the existence of the creation, and its eventual consummation, fill up the glory of God? Yet it also comes *from* that glory and in that sense adds nothing to it, for it is a genuinely free act and in no sense a necessary one. Likewise — though we certainly need here a *mutatis mutandis,* for as man God does indeed have needs — the ecclesial fullness of the incarnate one does not rectify any prior defect in his humanity, which is grounded enhypostatically in God and has gone before us into the sanctuary of God.

25. See most recently Robert Jenson, *Systematic Theology,* vol. 1 (Oxford: Oxford University Press, 1997), pp. 194ff.

26. See my *Ascension and Ecclesia: On the Significance of the Ascension for Ecclesiology and Christian Cosmology* (Grand Rapids: Eerdmans, 1999), pp. 195ff.

The withdrawal of the body of Jesus must be understood in terms of the Logos creating a space within himself, a womb, within which *(en Christoi)* the Church will expand and creation be recreated. In this way, the body of the Church and the body of the world are enfolded through resurrection within the Godhead. The body of Jesus Christ is not lost, nor does it reside now in heaven as a discrete object of veneration (as Calvin thought and certain Gnostics before him). The body of Jesus Christ, the body of God, is permeable, transcorporeal, transpositional. Within it all other bodies are situated and given their significance.[27]

In other words, for Ward — as for Augustine, though curiously Ward does not appeal to Augustine at this juncture — the ascension of Jesus is a retraction of his distracting physical presence in order that his divinity may shine more brightly through the global expansion of his body, the church. But Ward's particular spin on "body" and "church" is highly dependent, if only subconsciously, on Lutheran ubiquitarianism. "The body of the gendered Jew expands to embrace the whole of creation," he tells us, beginning with the church, which "is now the body of Christ."

Parenthetically, in the interest of fairness, we should note the protest that Ward's idea of the body of Christ does not rest on the sublation of Jesus or on the totalizing tendency of modernist philosophy, but rather on the "aporetic" as a means of grace.[28] I want to ask, however, whether this protest does not ring hollow for the simple reason that it is no longer clear how or in what way the savior can be distinguished from the church. Does he not abandon what Irenaeus called the analogy of the formation of Adam, which he received from Mary, in order to become a kind of Mary himself? Is the divine man not withdrawn in order to make room for a divine humanity — for the Logos coinhering in us, for the church as "the body of God"? No doubt Apollinarian language is necessary in order to effect this shift from the concreteness of the gendered Jew to an abstract and more malleable (polymorphous) humanity.[29] But what we are being offered, I fear, is a rather more obvious form of eschatological docetism than Ward finds in Calvin, covered over by a layer or two of that false enthusiasm for the particular invented by Teilhard de Chardin.

Teilhard himself, of course, provides a plainer illustration of the danger of combining ubiquitarianism with transubstantiation. Turning from "the man who lived two thousand years ago" to the one who now "shines forth from

27. Ward, *Radical Orthodoxy*, p. 176.

28. Cf. Ward, *Radical Orthodoxy*, pp. 13f. There is also the suggestion (p. 177) of an *analogia trinitatis*, but it is too imprecise to be of any help.

29. Cf. e.g., Elizabeth Johnson, *Freeing Theology: The Essentials of Theology in Feminist Perspective*, ed. Catherine LaCugna (San Francisco: HarperSanFrancisco, 1993), pp. 127ff.

within all the forces of the earth," he maintains that it is the function of the church to build up Christ by baptizing "all that is human in Man," and indeed by divinizing the entire creation. This is the true significance of "the onrush of the cult of the Holy Eucharist," says Teilhard. Has the church not been busy for two millennia transforming the world through its daily masses, bit by bit, into an extension of the body of Christ?[30]

> As our humanity assimilates the material world, and the Host assimilates our humanity, the eucharistic transformation goes beyond and completes the transubstantiation of the bread on the altar. Step by step it irresistibly invades the universe. . . . [For] in a secondary and generalised sense, but in a true sense, the sacramental Species are formed by the totality of the world, and the duration of the creation is the time needed for its consecration.[31]

The church is thus engaged in bringing to birth for God an immense body "worthy of resurrection" through the sublation of nature as a whole. Its arduous labor is the sanctification of brute matter by intense desire for, and adoration of, the holy offspring it is expecting: namely, a universal consciousness that will transcend the limits of all particularity. In Teilhard, the "totalizing" nature of the project is celebrated rather than denied; witness, for example, his famous Mass on the World, or his flirtation with the political ideologies of fascism and communism.

Now it is a very long way, to be sure, from either Aquinas or Luther to Teilhard! In the preceding discussion I have not been attempting to show that the former were altogether mistaken, or even that transubstantiation and ubiquity are unusable concepts. By pointing to some of the pitfalls in their respective approaches, and to the danger I see at the intersection between them (where Teilhard took his controversial stand) I have only been preparing to say this: that perhaps Calvin was not so hasty, after all, in wanting a radical reworking of the medieval framework. Perhaps he was attempting something which, though widely misunderstood even among his own followers, could eventually prove fruitful for the whole church of Christ.

In order to understand and evaluate that "something," we need to clear up

---

30. Without the church, "Christ evaporates, or crumbles, or disappears!" H. de Lubac, "Teilhard de Chardin in the Context of Renewal," *Communio* 15 (1988): 370. Cf. *Hymn of the Universe* (London: Collins, 1965), pp. 25ff., 149; *The Future of Man* (London: Collins, 1964), p. 265; *Le Milieu Divin* (London: Collins, 1960), pp. 122ff., 151ff.

31. Teilhard, *Le Milieu Divin*, pp. 124f.; cf. *Hymn of the Universe*, p. 134, where the logic and dynamic of the eucharist is fully reversed: "To allay your hunger and slake your thirst, to nourish your body and bring it to full stature, you need to find in us a substance which will truly be food for you. And this food . . . I will prepare for you by liberating the spirit in myself and in everything."

a pair of misunderstandings. The first concerns the charge that Calvin's eucharistic doctrine depends upon a mythological or gnostic view of the ascension, which dehumanizes both Christ and the church while reducing the eucharistic liturgy to mere theater or *mimesis*. This is the place to acknowledge that what we have here is a nice example of spoiling the Egyptians. For the charge of mythology and gnosticism is of course the charge Calvinists have traditionally leveled at Lutherans (and sometimes at Catholics) in order to point out that what is most at risk in their construct is the concrete humanity of Jesus, including his bodily specificity and self-identity, which he retains for the sake of priestly ministry to his church and as a divine affirmation that finite creaturely being can be the recipient of eternal life.[32] It was in order *not* to dehumanize or mythologize that Calvin insisted on ascension and parousia in the flesh, as had Irenaeus when confronted by the original, self-styled "gnostics." It was in order *not* to exchange reality for mere theater that he put Πνεῦμα in place of ἔρως, and πίστις in place of imagination, treating presence as a miraculous suspension of actual distance and absence as invoking — in that suspension — the cry *Maranatha!* That is, it was in order not to fall afoul of Scripture and creed that he suppressed a fair amount of ontological and cosmological agreement with the schoolmen, not to speak of his fellow reformers, for the sake of eschatology.

> When Scripture speaks of the ascension of Christ, it declares, at the same time, that he will come again. If he now occupies the whole world in respect of his body, what else was his ascension, and what will his descent be, but a fallacious and empty show?[33]

In my judgment, Reformed theology today would betray its vocation to serve catholic Christianity if it took any other line.[34]

---

32. See e.g., Calvin, *Institutes* 4.17.7, 17, 29f. "What is this," asks Calvin of the ubiquitarians, "but to raise Marcion from hell?"

33. Calvin, *Tracts and Treatises* 2, p. 286; cf. *Institutes* 4.17.27. As Ronald S. Wallace observes in *Calvin's Doctrine of Word and Sacrament* (Edinburgh: Oliver & Boyd, 1953), p. 225, it is one of the merits of his doctrine "that he leaves room for a more significant eschatology than would be possible on the assumption of his opponents."

34. Here it must be said that the famous American dispute between Charles Hodge and John Nevin, never really got to the heart of the problem. Cf. Brian Gerrish, *Grace and Gratitude: The Eucharistic Theology of John Calvin* (Philadelphia: Fortress, 1993), pp. 3ff.; and L. de Bie, "Real Presence or Real Absence," *Pro Ecclesia* 4, no. 4 (1995): 431ff. John Nevin's charge of gnosticism against the Princeton theologian anticipates Ward's charge against Calvin. Hodge's position was *not* Calvin's, however, but Zwingli's, as Hodge himself was forced to recognize. Unfortunately, Nevin anticipated Ward in certain other respects as well, insofar as his own line in *The Mystical Presence: A Vindication of the Reformed or Calvinistic Doctrine of the Holy Eucharist* (Garland, 1987) was arguably more Lutheran than Reformed.

It will be recalled that I spoke earlier of an uneasy alliance between the Roman and Lutheran elements of the critique I have been trying to deconstruct. One thing I had in mind is the fundamental difference (ignored by Calvin's Anglican critics, who often do not acknowledge their debt to Lutheranism) over the interpretation of the ascension as such. The simple fact of the matter is that Calvin's view is not unlike that of Aquinas — which is to say, it is an entirely orthodox view, however tainted by cosmological misinformation[35] — whereas that of Luther's disciples looks rather a lot like the unorthodox speculation of Origen, for example, or of much medieval Christ-mysticism. Might it be, then, that there is more room for a dialogue productive of real agreement between Thomists and Calvinists than between Lutherans and either Calvinists or Thomists? But for such a dialogue to begin, another misunderstanding must be addressed, a misunderstanding about method.

By insisting with Zwingli that what we say about the eucharist must be consistent with faith in Jesus' bodily departure and return, Calvin was asking us to let Christology control ecclesiology rather than the reverse.[36] But *should* Christology control ecclesiology, and can it actually do so? Let us note, first of all, that it would be a mistake to try to handle this methodological question prior to or apart from actual discussion of the eucharist. Would that not imply acceptance of Zwingli's sacramental nominalism? In my study hangs a photograph of the liturgical space of the Orthodox monastery of St. John the Baptist in Essex, which along its side walls has the usual paintings of key episodes in the life of Jesus (transfiguration, cross, resurrection, etc.), and on the east wall, above the iconostasis, the Last Supper. This iconography surely reminds us that it is only through him who sits at the head of the table that we who are "far off" are "brought near," to use the cultic language of Ephesians, having "access in one Spirit to the Father" and comprehending "with all the saints the breadth and length and height and depth" of a love that surpasses knowledge.[37] It highlights the fact that knowledge of God in Christ depends on *communion* with God in Christ. And at the center of that communion there is (as Rublev's well-known icon also reminds us) a eucharistic cup.

But does the ecclesial and sacramental context of our knowledge warrant an epistemological prioritizing of ecclesiology over Christology? That is the question we need to address. Ward, for one, appears to think so when he

35. See n. 10 above, and cf. the statement of the Council of Trent, 11 October 1551 (*Dz-Sch* 1636; noted by B. Meyer, "John Calvin's Doctrine of the Lord's Supper," Ph.D. dissertation 1967, p. 193).

36. McClelland, *Marburg Revisited*, p. 46, describes this christological orientation as "the heart of the Reformation."

37. Ephesians 2:13ff., 3:18f.

claims that "to understand the body of Jesus we can only examine *what the Church is* and what it has to say concerning the nature of that body."[38] If however we do not wish to reduce the relation between Christ and the church to one of pure identity, we will not be content to draw this conclusion or to state the matter this way. Where Christ is distinguished from the church as its head — where it is allowed that he, as the ascended one, stands over against us in order also to stand for us in God's presence and to give his own body to us — Christology can and must control ecclesiology. The hermeneutical circle between the doctrine of the ascension and the doctrine of the eucharist will be established *as* a circle, but it will turn in only the one direction. Here we may look to the seminal Roman Catholic thinker, Jean-Luc Marion, who (following the lead of Luke 24) argues that God's self-speaking and self-interpreting Word gives us the eucharist as the only authentic site for our theology. Yet in doing so the Word retains his otherness and indeed a certain reserve. The eucharistic site is an *eschatological* site, situated between the first and the final parousia.[39]

These points being made, we come at last to our reassessment of Calvin. The first part of this reassessment is little more than a rehearsal of his eucharistic teaching, which in a Reformed context may seem a bit like carrying coals to Newcastle.[40] Calvin states that "it would be extreme madness to recog-

---

38. Ward, *Radical Orthodoxy*, p. 177 (italics mine). Cf. John Milbank, *The Word Made Strange* (Oxford: Blackwell, 1997), pp. 164f. But mark the un-eucharistic presupposition: "We have no access to the body of the gendered Jew."

39. See Marion, *God Without Being*, pp. 139ff. I can't help but think that an earlier Frenchman, Jean Calvin, would have been enthusiastic about this passage. I will bring Calvin and Marion into a closer dialogue in a moment.

40. On the other hand, one meets today relatively few Reformed theologians who take the eucharist with anything like the seriousness that Calvin did. Barth, of course, has had a hand in this. When we recall with Bruce McCormack (*Karl Barth's Critically Realistic Dialectical Theology: Its Genesis and Development 1909-1936* [New York: Clarendon, 1995], p. 392) that "[i]n Luther's insistence on the literal force of the 'is' in the words of institution, Barth saw the opening of a door to every *direct* identification of revelation and history," we may find it easier to understand the great man's attempt at "a cautious and respectful demythologising" of the sacraments. But ironically we also discover hidden affinities with Hegel, through whom Barth traced a path from Luther to the German Christians, in his decision to locate his systematic treatment of the sacraments in ethics — that is, in human response to grace rather than in the christological basis of grace. Cf. G. W. F. Hegel's *The Philosophy of History* (New York: Dover, 1956), pp. 412ff. When in the last fragment of the *Church Dogmatics* Barth pulled apart what in §16 he had tried rather shakily to hold together, *viz.*, the objective and the subjective dimensions of the sacraments, and left only the latter in place, he should rather have considered more seriously his own earlier assertion that "by the law of this sphere" (baptism and eucharist) theology "must direct its methods."

nize no communion of believers with the flesh and blood of the Lord." Nevertheless, Christ is in heaven and we are on earth. The separation between us is overcome in the eucharistic meal by the incomprehensible power of the Holy Spirit, so that what is signified by the physical eating of bread and wine (effective signs not empty symbols) is actualized for the believer in "a great mystery." There is a real participation in the "substance" of the body and blood of Christ, together with all his experience, accomplishments, and life-giving virtue. "I leave no place," says Calvin, "for the sophistry that what I mean when I say Christ is received by faith is that he is received only by understanding and imagination."[41] Through the Spirit "all that Christ is and has is conveyed to us," for we must indeed "grow into one body with him."[42] So long as two principles are not violated — that nothing shall detract from the heavenly glory of Christ, and that nothing inappropriate to human nature shall be ascribed to his body — no objection may be raised to affirmations that we receive and enjoy "the thing itself as nourishment of eternal life."[43]

This eucharistic realism has, on my view, a great deal to commend it ecumenically: It avoids the staticism and authoritarianism that characterize some versions of transubstantiation while steering clear of individualist nominalism. It is neither Eutychian nor Nestorian in its christologic. It gives a prominent place to the Holy Spirit and hence, in principle, to the epiclesis. It makes room for faith (and desire too)[44] without becoming pietistic or Pelagian. It emphasizes an inclusive grace, and the sacrament as medicine for the sick and a solace for sinners, without conceding a *manducatio impiorum*.[45] Its claim that the *hoc est corpus meum* should be read metonymously is an affirmation, not a denial, that "many miracles are subsumed in these few words."[46] It does not, however, invent miracles in support of a preconceived notion of presence — miracles which, to secure a conjunction between Christ and the church, sacrifice the continuity between his humanity and ours. Instead, it maintains continuity through discontinuity and "a species of presence" in "a species of absence." That is, it insists on our need for a "*heavenly* nearness of Christ," and without abrogating mystery reaches out for a relational, christocentric, and pneumato-

---

41. Calvin, *Institutes* 4.17.11 (see 9ff.).

42. Calvin, *Institutes* 4.17.11 (cf. 4.17.2, 20). "For he has now entered heaven, not to possess it by himself, but to gather you and all godly people with him" (4.17.27).

43. See Calvin, *Institutes* 4.17.19, 32.

44. Cf. John Calvin, *Psychopannychia*, ed. Walter Zimmerli (Leipzig: A. Deichert, 1932), p. 435.

45. Cf. Calvin, *Institutes* 4.17.13f., 33, 42. Inclusive grace is the fundamental *stratum* of Calvin's doctrine of the eucharist. This does not alter the fact that faith is a *sine qua non* of authentic eating and drinking, however.

46. Calvin, *Institutes* 4.17.21, 24.

logical concept of space as an alternative to an illusory ubiquity, on the one hand, and to a de-eschatologized local presence on the other.[47] That on the epistemological level it makes possible something equally creative in linguistic philosophy I do not doubt, though I cannot here offer supportive exposition for this or any of the above claims. I must be content merely to state them.

Whence, then, the problematic character of Calvin's eucharistic theology? Do I wish now to withdraw the concession that it *is* problematic? On the contrary, it remains highly problematic. Why? Chiefly because Calvin is not radical *enough* in his attempt to turn the prevailing eucharistic framework inside out, that is, to think through "the manner of descent by which [Christ] lifts us up to himself." And in not being radical enough he fails to persuade that he really is able to say what the church has always found it necessary to say about human participation in Christ. He leaves a nagging doubt that the eucharist might after all be reduced (as later in Schleiermacher, for example, or in Hegel, and in some Catholic theologians who have fallen under their spell) to "a noetic moment."[48]

In following this up I am not going to cite against Calvin his inherited mistrust of the body, his faithfulness to the Ptolemaic cosmology and suspicion of life in the sublunar realm, or even his own christological weaknesses — particularly his instrumentalist view of the incarnation. Such things can of course be illustrated equally well in Aquinas, Luther, Zwingli, and just about anyone else among their contemporaries, and shown to color their eucharistic teaching in various ways. I am only going to observe that a shared vertical orientation made it difficult for Calvin to factor *time* into his eucharistic equation, that is, to subject temporal relations to the same christological and pneumatological reordering with which he experimented in spatial relations. As I have noted elsewhere, Calvin handled the dialectic of presence and absence almost exclusively in spatial terms, and to that extent in a *non*-eschatological fashion. Only in the Spirit can we hope to "leap the infinite spaces" separating earth from

---

47. On the one hand, *quadam absentiae specie nos ab eo disjungi* (*Tracts* 2/240). Yet we may rightly assert a *species praesentiae* (*Tracts* 2/286; cf. 3/280), for the Spirit "truly unites things separated in space" (*Institutes* 4.17.10). Unfortunately, having failed to understand "the manner of descent by which he lifts us up to himself," neither the Romans nor the Lutherans can "bear to conceive any other partaking of flesh and blood except that which consists in either local conjunction and contact or some gross form of enclosing" (4.17.15f.).

48. Kilian McDonnell, in *John Calvin, the Church, and the Eucharist* (Princeton: Princeton University Press, 1967), pp. 376ff., defends him, but Calvin himself sometimes invites such a reduction: "What then is the sum of our doctrine? It is this, that when we discern here on earth the bread and wine, our minds must be raised to heaven in order to enjoy Christ, and that Christ is there present with us while we seek him above the elements of this world." Cf. Wallace, *Calvin's Doctrine of Word and Sacrament*, p. 229; *CR* 12:728.

heaven. But is there no equally formidable barrier raised by time? Are we to suppose that the ascended one shares with us a common time, or that he exists timelessly? Surely the former idea reduces the ascension to some form of physical locomotion, while the latter fades off into the docetic and the gnostic. Neither can support a sound doctrine of the eucharist.

We do not need modern physics to see that this separation of the problems of space and time will not do. Christian eschatology has its own resources here, and arguably Calvin begins to tap them when he says:

> For as Christ's whole kingdom is spiritual, whatever he does with his church must not be subjected to the reason of this world. Or, to use Augustine's words, this mystery, like others, is performed by men, but divinely; on earth, but in a heavenly way. Such is the presence of the body (I say) that the nature of the sacrament requires a presence which we say manifests itself here with power and effectiveness so great that it not only brings an undoubted assurance of eternal life to our minds, but also assures us of the immortality of our flesh. Indeed, it is now quickened by his immortal flesh, *and in a sense partakes of his immortality.*[49]

Calvin might have done better to go behind Augustine to Irenaeus, however, whose eschatological analysis is much more thoroughgoing:

> He has acknowledged the cup (which is a part of the creation) as his own blood, from which he bedews our blood; and the bread (which is also a part of the creation) he has established as his own body, from which he gives increase to our bodies. . . . And just as a cutting from the vine planted in the ground fructifies in its season, or as a corn of wheat falling into the earth and becoming decomposed, rises with manifold increase by the Spirit of God . . . and then, through the wisdom of God, serves for the use of men, and having received the Word of God, becomes the Eucharist, which is the body and blood of Christ — so also our bodies, being nourished by it, and deposited in the earth, and suffering decomposition there, shall rise at their appointed time, the Word of God granting them resurrection to the glory of God, even the Father, who freely gives to this mortal immortality, and to this corruptible incorruption. . . .[50]

What is present here that I miss in Augustine and Calvin is the idea that the *telos* and indeed the *terminus* of the eucharistic conversion is in the resurrection, that is, in the eschaton, inasmuch as the consecrating Agent himself exists, spatially *and* temporally, in the freedom of the Spirit which constitutes the

---

49. Calvin, *Institutes* 4.17.32 (emphasis mine); cf. 4.17.24-26.
50. Irenaeus, *Against Heresies* 5.2.2f.

eschaton.[51] That this idea is at least understressed helps to explain why both friend and foe find it relatively easy to reduce Calvin's eucharistic teaching to the *sursum corda* (to the invitation to "feed on Him in your hearts by faith with thanksgiving," as the Book of Common Prayer puts it). It may also help to explain why Calvin normally prefers to talk about the body and blood of Christ quickening the *soul,* and why he thinks that the word *conversio* "ought to signify nothing more in the supper than in baptism."[52] Would we not do better justice to the *hoc est corpus meum,* without compromise to Calvin's two conditions, were we to allow that the consecration of the bread and the wine does in fact bring about a conversion, even a transubstantiation — albeit not one that leaves behind free-floating accidents[53] — which like the ascension itself is visible from our side only as far as the cloud, so to speak, but has as its outcome a share in the parousia and in the *recapitulatio mundi?*

I would like to pursue the matter a little further by citing Marion's defense of transubstantiation against what some in his own church would mistakenly call Calvinist-leaning variants (transfinalization, transignification, etc.).[54] Marion offers a powerful rebuke to the eucharistic idolatry he discerns in these variants, which arises from an (essentially Hegelian) identification of the community's self-consciousness with the real presence. At the same time he tries to show how the dogma of transubstantiation escapes this tendency, rather than anticipating it, precisely by maintaining the otherness of the one who makes himself present in the eucharistic action. And this defense, let it be noted, rests not on an ontological distance between God and creation, or on a dialectic of transcendence and immanence.[55] It rests instead on a rejection of the "here and now" — that is, of the present as a self-centered mode of temporality that competes with, rather than receives, the eucharistic gift[56] — as a starting point for

<hr/>

51. On Irenaeus's construct, see my *Ascension and Ecclesia,* ch. 3. On Calvin, cf. W. Walker, "The Doctrine of the Ascension of Christ in Reformed Theology" (Vanderbilt Ph.D. dissertation, 1968), pp. 70ff. I really ought here to engage more fully with Robert Jenson, especially *Systematic Theology,* vol. 2, ch. 28, but to show the relevant similarities and differences respecting the eschatological nature of the sacraments would require a paper in itself.

52. See Calvin, *Institutes* 4.17.14. This is a significant stumbling block ecumenically.

53. I am tempted to suggest that this is how Ward, e.g., understands the resurrection appearances of Jesus also!

54. A *little* further: I am conscious not only of the constraint of length but of the danger that explanation should end up, falsely, in a "eucharistic physics" or, for that matter, semiotics (see Marion, *God Without Being,* pp. 161ff.).

55. Catherine Pickstock, to whom I am grateful for a sympathetic reading of this paper, criticizes Marion here (*After Writing,* pp. 253ff.; cf. pp. 158ff.). I will have to engage her, and Henri de Lubac's *Corpus Mysticum,* more fully elsewhere. Cf. F. Bauerschmidt's remarks in *Radical Orthodoxy,* pp. 214f.

56. I.e., the present as something offered or presented — by Christ.

eucharistic theology. Positively, it rests on an eschatologically governed temporality that interprets and *reforms* our present as something inserted between the past and the future of Jesus Christ. In other words, for Marion the real presence cannot be judged by reference to our own false and inverted sense of reality. It carries its own judgment with it and — risking but rebuffing idolatrous manipulation — transforms its recipients into a mode of existence determined by the crucified and glorified Christ.[57] Is this not what Kierkegaard (Luther's anti-Hegelian son!) was already aiming at when he insisted that the one who has ascended on high is the absolute, that the rest can only be understood in relation to him?[58] Is it not what Calvin was trying to say (even without much insight into the temporal dimension) with his doctrine of the *mirifica commutatio?*

Now I am not convinced that Marion gets us far enough with the re-eschatologizing of eucharistic doctrine,[59] or that his understanding of transubstantiation can be made to defend all that he wants it to defend. There is room here, however, not only for meaningful dialogue but perhaps even for *rapprochement,* to which the Reformed have a great deal to contribute, it seems to me. Were Calvin's so-called "virtualism" to be modified by following the eschatological trajectory of the above passage from Irenaeus, we might at all events hope for progress on a number of fronts:

First, a concerted attack could be launched on the reduction of *eucharistia* to ethics or to personal piety that continues to weaken large tracts of the Reformed church and its Baptist offspring, which indeed (exacerbated by a too narrow notion of the church as *creatura Verbi*) undermines the foundations of a catholic ecclesiology.[60] At the same time, this would make it easier, not harder,

---

57. "Whoever fears that an idolatry of presence according to the *here and now* might ensue from the theology of transubstantiation admits by this very fact that he does not see that only the eucharistic present touches, in the consecrated host, the 'real,' and that what he fears as overvalued only plays there the role of *sacramentum*" (Marion, *God Without Being,* p. 181).

58. "If I dare to put it this way," he says, this "makes the Church's whole existence here upon earth into a parenthesis or something parenthetical in Christ's life." Søren Kierkegaard, *Practice in Christianity* (Princeton: Princeton University Press, 1991), p. 202. It was Kierkegaard who in connection with his notion of contemporaneity first made our *time* as well as our space relative to Jesus' own. The contemporaneity motif is developed over against both the notion of ubiquity and its modern correlate, progress. Like Marion and the later Augustine, Kierkegaard holds to the homogeneity of the present age: We are "situated between his abasement . . . and his loftiness," neither moving away from the one nor towards the other (see pp. 153ff.).

59. On the loss of the eschatological perspective, cf. Geoffrey Wainwright, *Eucharist and Eschatology* (London: Epworth, 1978).

60. Cf. Thomas F. Torrance, *Theology in Reconstruction* (London: Geoffrey Chapman, 1975), pp. 119ff.

to question cogently the false objectification of sacramental grace that continues, by way of an inadequate or overrealized eschatology, to support on the Roman and Orthodox side of our Lord's table a polity of exclusion.

Second, we would be better able to resist the growth of that "fleshless
word" which threatens not only the Reformed but even the more self-
consciously sacramental churches, especially those influenced by ubiquitarianism. For the identification of the body of Christ, in either the primary or the
secondary sense, would not be perpetually deferred by chasing after ever-new
configurations and permutations of human experience.[61] Rather, a plenitude of
meaning for human existence would be sought in the company and under the
lordship of the one crucified, risen, and glorified man, Jesus of Nazareth, who
through the Holy Spirit causes the community of faith to cohere around one table in anticipation of his return. The ubiquity confessed would be that for
which Irenaeus looks on the far side of the resurrection, where in the kingdom
of God the creation itself will be reconfigured for the sake of true communion,
and the savior shall be seen everywhere "according as they who see him shall be
worthy."[62]

Third, we might work more profitably towards a properly humanizing
church, in which Christ's offering and ours are understood as integrally con-
joined without being confused. Here again we may follow Irenaeus, who saw it
as humanity's fundamental task "to sanctify what has been created" by recognizing its quality as a gift and rendering thanks for it. Knowing that in our
Cain-like duplicity we cannot fulfill this role, he observed that we ourselves require a change of species through the implantation of the Word and the "voluntary rain" from above (the Spirit who turns slaves into freemen and corrupt-
ible offerings into incorruptible).[63] This change of species is a eucharistic
process, and the joy and vitality of the eucharistic community is the evidence
that it is actually taking place — an *indicium libertatis*. But is the church really a
priestly people, whose vocation it is to offer up themselves and their world to
God, in, with, and through Christ?[64] This conviction, though central to the Reformation, is difficult to maintain where Christ is sought "above the elements of

61. Ward denies (p. 176; cf. pp. 167ff.) that this is the essence or the outcome of his position, but it is not clear on what basis he can deny it; only a doctrine of the parousia of Jesus,
which he does not offer, will prevent a lapse into empty circularity or narcissism.

62. *Against Heresies* 5.36.1. Please note that Irenaeus does *not* thus reintroduce eschatological docetism, postponed to a later stage of redemption in Christ. See *Ascension and
Ecclesia*, pp. 65f.

63. *Against Heresies* 3.17.2 (cf. 5.10.1), 4.18.2.

64. Cf. W. Milligan, *The Ascension and Heavenly Priesthood of Our Lord* (London:
Macmillan, 1892); also, e.g., *Eucharistic Presidency: A Theological Statement* (London: Church
House, 1997), pp. 34ff.

this world," as Calvin has it; it is near impossible to maintain where he is made a feature *of* this world. Only where his relation to the world is eschatologically conceived is a priestly perspective on the church sustainable, and the problem of the eucharist as sacrifice resolvable.

If Reformed theology develops its historic insight into the ascension and the eucharist in this direction, it will give genuine leadership in cultivating such a perspective, and the change of mood that goes with it. It will also find itself more able to resist those who are fond of bending the Mystery "into an ideological instrument," and to work with Rome towards a genuine renewal of the western church. I suspect that Edwin Muir, who after a long pilgrimage abroad (during which Rome made a deep impression on him) was reconciled to his native land, would have welcomed the thought.[65]

65. See Edwin Muir, *An Autobiography* (London: Hogarth, 1987), pp. 276ff.

PART V

Ecumenicity and Ethical Profiles of Reformed Theology: Catholicity and Practical Contextuality

CHAPTER 24

A Cry for Life in a Global Economic Era

H. Russel Botman

L. R. L. Ntoane writes, in *A Cry for Life,* on the doctrine of justification and the role of the Holy Spirit in a comparative study of its interpretation in South African "Calvinism" and in Calvin's own thoughts.[1] He describes Calvin's understanding as a "cry for life." In a certain sense, he continues to speak of the crux of Reformed theology as "a cry for life." Rooted in life and its struggles, Reformed theology is at the same time deeply personal (never merely private), existential (never disinterested), congregational (never dislocated), ecumenical (never parochial), and contextual (never ahistoric and abstracted). This paper grows from these roots.

The Reformational Calling

The "reformational" center of Reformed theology must be pursued in concrete, historical context. By its very essence, Reformed theology will always be faced with a revisioning, reforming, or liberating critical approach to itself in light of the Word and the context. Reformed theology persistently reflects on the meaning of God's Word in context to understand the significance thereof for the church, our common witness and life, and the world.[2] Its vitality lies in the transformational integrity with which this task is fulfilled. South African scholars have participated in conferences and publications rethinking the meaning,

1. Ntoane, in *A Cry for Life* (Kampen: Kok, 1983).
2. Most recently, cf. Dirk J. Smit, "Reformed Theology in South Africa," *Acta Theologica* 1 (1992): 88-110.

calling, integrity, and vitality of Reformed theology in the 1990s.[3] As a South African I have not escaped the turbulence of revisioning the reformational and liberational center of Reformed theology.

Speaking of being Reformed in South Africa is not unproblematic. Our country has had an oppressive as well as a liberative appropriation of Reformed theology. The Alliance of Black Reformed Christians in Southern Africa (ABRECSA) gave rise to the new search for a liberative understanding of the Reformed tradition. The Alliance was established in 1981 as a broad movement of Black Reformed Christians. While the word "black" generally refers to ethnicity, it was then understood to mean a socially constructed conditioning rather than pigmentation. The term "Reformed" was meant to describe a particular confessing community in struggle rather than establishing a narrow confessionalism or traditionalism. Membership of the alliance was subject to acceptance of the theological basis in the charter. The charter of ABRECSA lamented the oppressive history of the Reformed tradition:

> The Reformed tradition in South Africa is seen as responsible for political oppressions, economic exploitation, unbridled capitalism, social discrimination and the total disregard for human dignity. . . . This represents a dilemma. . . . We ask ourselves the question: Is it a burden to be cast off or a challenge towards the renewal of the church and of our society?

In response to this dilemma, the charter stated:

> As heirs of the Reformed tradition, it has become absolutely necessary for Black Reformed Christians to come together and struggle with the question: What does it mean to be Black and Reformed in southern Africa today?

Speaking at the founding conference of ABRECSA, Allan Boesak reclaimed Reformed theology with reference to Kuyper's interpretation of the Reformed claim on things:

---

3. The 1990s alone saw a number of publications focusing on the vitality of Reformed theology, the integrity of Reformed theology, and the past and future of Reformed theology. See J. W. de Gruchy, *Liberating Reformed Theology* (Grand Rapids: Eerdmans, 1991); and J. M. Batteau, J. W. Marais, and K. Veling, eds., *The Vitality of Reformed Theology* (Kampen: Kok, 1994).

The 1980s became a contestation of studies on the transformation of Reformed theology in South Africa. The studies of J. C. Adonis, *Die afgebreekte skeidsmuur weer opgebou* (Amsterdam: Rodopi, 1982), and Ntoane, *A Cry for Life*, appeared at the time. Based on systematic theological and mission-historical arguments, Ntoane and Adonis respectively affirmed the idea that Kuyper's thinking was distorted by Afrikaner Calvinism. J. Kinghorn presented a paper at the 1984 meeting of the Theological Society of South Africa focusing on Kuyper and the theology of apartheid. A. J. Botha has written on the evolution of a Volkstheologie and Afrikaner nationalism (1985).

We believe passionately with Abraham Kuyper that there is not a single inch of life that does not fall under the lordship of Christ. . . . Here the Reformed tradition comes so close to the African idea of the wholeness of life that these two should combine to renew the thrust that was brought to Christian life by the followers of Calvin.[4]

This tenet in Reformed theology has become the crux of South African liberative theology. It has informed and continues to inform the theology and lives of many Reformed people in South Africa.

However, my own story in this process whereby Reformed thinking has been retrieved goes back to the year 1978. I was in a seminar where the professor focused our attention on the search for the theological center of apartheid. Having done in-depth reflection on the biblical witness and having focused especially on Karl Barth's understanding of reconciliation, the seminar emerged after several days with the dictum that "apartheid is essentially anti-evangelical in that it takes its point of departure in the irreconcilability of people."[5] This learning was communicated to the synod of the Dutch Reformed Mission Church in October that year. Synod then adopted the notion and opened the way for further reflection in local congregations. The most important consequence of these events was the declaration of a *status confessionis* on apartheid and the birth of the Confession of Belhar. The Confession of Belhar was drafted in 1982 and formally adopted by the synod of the Dutch Reformed Mission Church in 1986. In those years I came to understand the real meaning of the vitality of Reformed theology.

No wonder that the uniting church that emerged from these powerful events made a renewed commitment to the Reformed identity and integrity. Before unification on April 14, 1994, two very important discussions took place in both churches and again on the first day of the synod.[6] By which name shall the church be known and on which confessional basis should it be established? After a lengthy debate it was decided to dispose of the word "Dutch" in the name of the church, thereby giving more prominence to the Reformed identity of the church. It also paved the way for reconceiving the Reformed identity and integrity beyond eurocentrism and colonialism. The Uniting Reformed Church of

---

4. Allan Boesak, Report of the Founding Conference of the Alliance of Black Reformed Christians, 1984, p. 87.

5. See J. de Gruchy and C. Villa-Vicencio, eds., *Apartheid Is a Heresy* (Cape Town: David Philip, 1983), pp. 161-65.

6. The story about this struggle can be found in G. D. Cloete and Dirk J. Smit, *A Moment of Truth: The Confession of the Dutch Reformed Mission Church* (Grand Rapids: Eerdmans, 1984); and more recently in Willem A. Boesak and Pieter J. Fourie, *Vraagtekens oor Gereformeerdheid* [Questions about Being Reformed] (Kaapstad: LUS, 1998).

Southern Africa (URCSA) then went further in adopting the Confession of Belhar as of the same status as the Belgic Confession, Dort, and the Heidelberg Catechism. The word "uniting" precedes the name of the church in order to secure an open door to other Reformed churches in southern Africa, and specifically the white Dutch Reformed Church and the (Indian) Reformed Church in Africa. In this way the allegiance to a Reformed confessional base is paralleled by a commitment to a visible public expression of the church in a divided society.

The Confession of Belhar has five sections. First, it confesses faith in the triune God. Then it speaks about the unity of the church in Jesus Christ. Third, it says what the people believe regarding reconciliation. The fifth section refers to the absolute obedience to God. The fourth point states the justice question:

> We believe:
>
> - that God has revealed himself as the One who wishes to bring about justice and true peace among men; that in a world full of injustice and enmity he is in a special way the God of the destitute, the poor and the wronged and that he calls his church to follow him in this; that he brings justice to the oppressed and gives bread to the hungry; that he feeds the prisoner and restores sight to the blind; that he supports the downtrodden, protects the stranger, helps the orphans and widows and blocks the path of the ungodly; that for him pure and undefiled religion is to visit the orphans and widows in their suffering; that he wishes to teach people to do what is good and to seek the right; that the church must therefore stand by people in any form of suffering and need, which means, among other things, that the church shall witness against and strive against any form of injustice, so that "justice may roll down like waters, and righteousness like an ever-flowing stream."
> - that the church as God's possession must stand where he stands, namely against injustice and with the wronged; that in following Christ the church must witness against all the powerful and privileged who seek selfishly their own interests and thus control and harm others.
>
> Therefore we reject any ideology which would legitimate forms of injustice and any doctrine which is unwilling to resist such an ideology in the name of the Gospel.[7]

The Confession of Belhar underscores the Reformed passion for knowing God. It reaffirms Calvin's insistence that knowing God means patterning one's life according to God's own actions in this world. The Confession of Belhar is a tes-

---

7. De Gruchy and Villa-Vicencio, *Apartheid Is a Heresy*, pp. 180-81.

timony to the liberating activity of God in history and context. It challenges the church as community to follow God in these liberating actions. The poor and oppressed are identified as the interlocutors of such actions. God is a God of justice seeking and acting for justice in a world of enmity and suffering.

Finding a way between an uncritical understanding regarding "God as being a God of the poor" or an equally uncritical conservative view that God is merely a God of universal compassion, Belhar has opted for the Barthian description of this relationship. God has been revealed (in self-disclosure) as One who wishes to bring about justice and true peace among people. This revelation is embedded in a contextual understanding of how God acts. In a world full of injustice and enmity God is in a special way the God of the destitute, the poor, and the wronged. This is then extended ecclesiologically. It means that the church is called, in these actions, to follow God, standing by people in any form of suffering and need, which means, among other things, that the church shall witness against and strive against any form of injustice, so that "justice may roll down like waters, and righteousness like an ever-flowing stream." Standing with God impels the church, as God's possession in this world, to stand where God stands, namely against injustice and with the wronged. Barth's strong call for focusing on the historical-theological meaning of discipleship is then retrieved. In following Christ the church must witness against all the powerful and privileged who seek selfishly their own interests and thus control and harm others.

Having done this, the Confession has emphasized anew the nature of Reformed integrity in context. In a world of enmity, a world of the powerful over against the powerless, in which the privileged seek selfishly their own interest and power over others, the Word calls us to revisit our roots in light of the challenges of the global economy.

Globalization: A Challenge to Reformed Faith

My own personal place in the debate on how Reformed faith is challenged by global economic realities was recently redefined. In November 1997, during my first week as a resident scholar at the Center of Theological Inquiry in Princeton, New Jersey, I walked into the library. I wanted to study the relationship, dynamics, and tensions entailed by one's membership in a religious community, on the one hand, and one's citizenship in a new democracy, on the other. The first month of my exposure to that library and my discussions with people across different disciplines led to a radical revisioning of my theological paradigm. A review of my own life helped me see how much my life, my theological studies, and my personal library were engulfed by a Reformed theology defined by issues of church-state relationship.

Indeed, this background was justifiably part of our worldview. As people of faith we had to come to terms with the evil system of apartheid. You were either part of the problem or part of the solution. There was no third way. This choice determined how you would see the relationship between church and state. You read your world either by virtue of Romans 13 or of Revelation 13. You had to either resist or obey the system. I am steeped in the library of "Dokumentes eines konflikts," where "konflikts" refers to political conflicts. Comparisons of the Declaration of Barmen and the Confession of Belhar formed the heart of the debates.

As I continued my research at the Center of Theological Inquiry, I realized that both concepts, namely, "citizenship" and "religious membership" (or discipleship), were under threat. I learned that the sovereignty of the nation-state and the sovereignty of the religious sphere were being challenged by economic realities. This challenge reduces the capacity to intervene on behalf of the poor and the marginalized. This reduction in capacity impacts both one's citizenship and one's discipleship as it marginalizes the nation-state as well as faith communities. The transnational corporation becomes the new home, the new space for membership and citizenship. We are all subjected, not so much to religious institutions or states, with their accountability to God or people, but much rather to unaccountable transnational corporations and world trade organizations that often operate around the world with impunity.

The meeting of the World Council of Churches (WCC) in Harare, Zimbabwe, held in December 1998, resolved that:

> Globalisation is not simply an economic issue. It is a cultural, political, ethical and ecological issue. Increasingly, Christians and churches find themselves confronted by the new and deeply challenging aspects of globalisation which vast numbers of people face, especially the poor.

The Harare assembly then asked the pertinent question: How do we live our faith in the context of globalization?

The views on how the ecumenical community should respond to the challenge of globalization reflect once again the specific contribution of Reformed theology to the ecumenical movement. Some theologians and people in the ecumenical movement are presently struggling to come to terms with this phenomenon. The WCC could not go beyond an expression of the ethical challenges posed by globalization and subsequently issued an invitation to member churches asking them to join in the process of the World Alliance of Reformed Churches (WARC). Urged by the Southern African Alliance of Reformed Churches, WARC declared at its 1997 meeting in Debrecen, Hungary, a *processus confessionis* with regard to economic justice in the context of globalization. This resolve arose from the fundamental Reformed question: How is our faith challenged by social and economic realities? The exclusionary nature of the global socio-economic dynamic served as epicenter for this development. The decision at Debrecen took the issue beyond the bounds of the ethical. Indeed, it took ethical challenges and translated them in terms of faith affirmation. The Alliance has invited member churches and theologians to embark on a journey in which we continue to study the phenomena and their impact on people and nature, with the goal of coming to a better understanding of the global challenge and thus enabling faithful action for transformation.

Bob Goudswaard argues that globalization represents a spiritual challenge. He argues in line with the Kuyperian/Reformed worldview and Calvin's notion of the human heart being a manufacturer of idols:

> The more intense the adoration of an idol is the greater the chance that a kind of narrowing of the mind takes place. The image of reality shrinks, as if it consists of nothing else but the idol — its message of hope, fear, and terror — and the servants of the idol. . . . The battle we have to fight is, therefore, finally a spiritual one. . . .[8]

Retrieving Community

Reformed theology has always insisted on the priority of the local congregation in its confessions, ecclesiology, and church order. The Confession of Belhar is no exception to this fundamental commitment. In a global economic era this matter has become even more important than ever before. The very nature, essence, and cohesion of local communities are being challenged by the fragmenting forces of the global economy. Global people live in global villages, not closer to each other but at times further from their local communities. This has become a great threat to theology in South Africa. South African theologies, of whatever kind, thrived on a certain African anthropology that emphasized one's connectedness to others and to nature. This has been developed into a full-scale theological anthropology by Reformed theologians on the basis of the relationship in and with the triune God. Social community is in essence given with community in and with God. The latter is not what leads to the former. Community in and with God is not without social community, nor is social community without community in and with God.

Archbishop Desmond Tutu, leader of the Anglican community in South Africa, aptly worded this African understanding:

8. *Reformed World* 46, no. 3 (1996): 107.

I want to suggest that the West might consider a small gift we in Africa just could offer. It is the gift of *ubuntu* — a term difficult to translate into occidental languages. But it is the essence of being human, it declares that my humanity is caught up and inextricably bound up in yours. . . . I am because I belong.[9]

The concrete person is a web of interactions, a network of operative relationships. A person is fashioned by religious, historical, cultural, genetic, biological, social, and economic infrastructure. Humanity is constituted covenantally. Such relationships are not mechanical; they allow for the individualization of the person without damaging the dignity of the human being. The dignity of human beings emanates from the network of relationships, from being in community. This is valid for redeemed community as well as created community. A human being created by God should not be reduced to the idea of a unique and free personal ego. As African Christians we cannot ignore the importance of the social and economic problems. God's remedy for social problems is community.

Reformed theology has been working long with the notion of the marks of the true church. These marks were identified in terms of the primacy of the Word and the essential place of the sacraments. The purity of preaching the Word and serving the sacraments took center stage. However, our current global context challenges us to deepen this idea so fundamental to our ecclesiology. We are challenged to ask, more seriously and urgently than before, whether "community" *(oikos)* is not a much deeper and perhaps more central mark of the church, which indeed finds its nourishment in the proper preaching of the Word and service of communion.

As we read more about economic globalization we become aware of its cultural threat, its ability to fragment community. The free individual lives competitively in a market that has become a law unto itself. The fundamentals of the market replace the fundamentals of the community. The anti-community aspect of globalization, one of its major characteristics, must be confronted with a revisioning of ecclesiology in terms of the *oikos* narratives in the Bible. The *oikos* concept reveals God's intention for building or forming sustainable relationships of people in "households," of created reality in "ecosystems," and of churches in the "ecumene."

However, the local church is not merely a community as any other, it is a community of disciples: a people with a mission. Christianity is a missionary

9. Thomas F. Best and Günter Gassmann, eds., *On the Way to Fuller Koinonia: Official Report of the Fifth World Conference on Faith and Order* (Geneva: WCC, 1994), p. 101. M. D. Tutu, "Towards Koinonia in Faith, Life and Witness," in *On the Way to Fuller Koinonia,* ed. Best and Gassmann, p. 101.

religion, and in the twenty-first century we are challenged by economic globalization to understand the nature and character of our mission anew. We are called to revisit the habits of our mission in order to ask how we can conceive the mission of the local church in this global context.[10]

In former times, when spiritual danger was seen in a dualistic framework that tended to separate the physical from the spiritual, our earlier habits of mission focused on the soul of the individual. Later, in the ecumenical era, missionaries began to speak of holistic mission, taking the total human being as the focal point of mission. However, today we know that it is not only individual life but the entire universe that is doomed to physical decay. There is a continuum in the relationship between economic globalization, the hardening of poverty, ecological destruction, and growing social despair. A larger picture has to unfold for the sake of the mission of the community, the household of God. That picture includes these new contextual challenges. We do not yet have the theological genius to meet this challenge, but we do have hope in the grace of God that creates a new world, a new people, from the very old realities of human despair.[11]

Conclusion

The future of Reformed theology rests with its response to this global reality. The quest for such a response has now become an ecumenical search — within the broader community in which the Reformed voice wants to be heard. It locates theology again at the margins where excluded people suffer and die. South Africans, especially, should seize this moment to begin shaping an African Reformed theology that will take us beyond the cultural and liturgical masquerade of a European presence on African soil. The possible triage or economic sacrifice of a whole continent is more than just economic fate; its genesis lies in an economic theory that has lost whatever moorings it once had in ethical and moral philosophy. The vitality of Reformed theology at this time is not a statistical game, it is a matter of faith confronted by economic globalization. Its vitality is indeed centered in a worldview that affirms our lives are lived by grace and not simply by nature. This view has always been developed, for Reformed people, through the lenses of local communities in interaction with their different contexts.

10. See Max L. Stackhouse, Tim Dearborn, and Scott Paeth, eds., *The Local Church in a Global Era: Reflections for a New Century* (Grand Rapids: Eerdmans, 2000).

11. See John Polkinghorne and Michael Welker, eds., *The End of the World and the Ends of God: Science and Theology on Eschatology* (Philadelphia: Trinity, 2000).

Let me close with a word from the world of progressive Roman Catholicism. Leonardo and Clodovis Boff reminded us some time ago that:

> the banner of liberation theology, firmly set in biblical ground, waves in the winds of history. Its message is that today the history of faith is embarking on its third great period, the period of construction. In the past faith has performed a contestatory function; this was in the first century, the times of the church of the apostles, martyrs and virgins. Then, in the post-Constantinian era, faith performed a conservatory function in society, consecrating the status quo and collaborating with the powers of the world. Today, faith has decidedly taken on a constructive function, contesting the existing order — thereby referring back to the early church — but also taking a longer-range view — that is, taking its responsibility in history, which is to persuade society to conform to the utopia of the kingdom. . . . Starting from the absolute utopia of the kingdom, faith can contribute by marking out new paths to a new society — an alternative to capitalism and socialism — a fuller and more humane society, free and liberated, a society of the freed.[12]

---

12. Boff and Boff, *Introducing Liberation Theology: In Search of a Balance Between Faith and Politics* (Kent: Burns and Oates, 1989), pp. 92-93.

CHAPTER 25

Processus Confessionis

Milan Opočensky

Soon after the 22nd General Council in Seoul, the World Alliance of Reformed Churches (WARC) started to deal with global economic injustice in the context of Christian faith. Several issues of *Reformed World*[1] were devoted to this question.

In 1992 a small consultation was convened in Geneva which was supposed to design a project for the years to come. A letter addressed to WARC member churches says:

> We want to listen to the laments, the prophetic critique, the commandments, and the visionary expressions of hope for the hopeless. We want to turn to the sources of our faith in order to resist the temptation to accept a status quo that is unbearable for many and unsustainable for all in the long run. God the Creator entrusts humans, male and female equally, with responsibility to care for the earth and for each other. The Bible relates to economic questions throughout. It speaks of justice as central to God's will. Prophets call the people not to adjust to sinful structures, to repent and create institutions which protect the rights of the poor. Jesus himself, in his life and teachings, fulfilled the prophetic message of liberation in his solidarity with the poor. Likewise the church has been requested to preach this message of liberation to the present poor and marginalized. Our belief in the Holy Spirit which renews creation empowers us to keep being *ecclesia reformata* and *semper reformanda*. The Holy Spirit sustains us in the hope that that history has not ended, that the world does not end in a huge catastrophe but that Christ is the alpha and omega.[2]

1. *Reformed World* 41 (1991): 181-212; 42 (1992): 70-116.
2. *Reformed World* 42 (1992): 71f.

Later on the Executive Committee of WARC, meeting in Pittsburgh in 1994, adopted a program of regional conferences that proposed to test the working hypothesis. The first meeting of this kind took place in Manila (Philippines).

Manila (March 1995)

The meeting drew attention to rapid economic growth that benefits only a small minority. It is not possible to ignore the contradiction between growth and poverty. Seventy to eighty percent of the world's poor live in Asia. Poverty manifests itself in massive unemployment and in the painful exclusion of millions of people from the process of production. The population pays a high price for the Structural Adjustment Program prescribed by the International Monetary Fund and the World Bank. All this has consequences for the environment, which is poisoned and threatened. These facts need to be remembered by those who admire the development of the so-called Asian tigers (South Korea, Taiwan, Hong Kong, Thailand, etc.). The economies of Asian countries are marked by deregulation and privatization, and the growing influence of money has led to the commodification of life. In this situation everything becomes a commodity. The mass media create artificial needs, and economic injustice creates cultural injustice. Indigenous cultures are not respected.

The consultation in Manila appealed to churches and individual Christians in Asia to leave the mainstream of economic life and to resist the culture of prevailing trends. Christians are encouraged to develop a lifestyle that would differ from consumerism. It is necessary to open a space for the participation of women in economic life, which is usually male-dominated. It is necessary to formulate new principles of international economic order. The main question is not whether to maintain the global market but whether poverty and the deteriorating environment are effectively tackled. The competition struggle and the spirit of the market contradict the Reformation principle of grace and community. It is necessary to examine critically the connection that supposedly exists between Reformed faith and prevailing economic injustice. The question emerges: How has the Calvinist ethos contributed to the competitive trend?

The report suggests a holistic interpretation of the socio-economic situation. It recommends creating cooperatives to strengthen community spirit. The market was originally meant to promote life. Money is not the highest value. Human desire should not be manipulated at the cost of cultural identity. The ecological movements in Asia help mobilize people to strive for a sustainable economy. There is a real danger that limitless growth and competition could transform the entire planet into a desert. We should not forget that people are guided by motives other than the idea of profit. Love, compassion, justice, concern for the environment, and common sense may still influence economic decisions. In Asia many activities are still geared primarily to need, not to profit. The sources of hope are the anti-system movements: women's movements, tribal movements, farmers' movements, civic organizations. None of these people want to be passive victims, and they are becoming increasingly active.

The participants in Manila appealed to the Christians of the North to consider how their profit-oriented economies impose an unbearable burden on the world's poor. God's covenant with the earth and with its people is violated. Christians are challenged to join in the struggle for an alternative society. It is necessary to refuse the concentration of power and the recolonialization of other parts of the world by exploitation of resources and human labor.

Kitwe (October 1995)

In October 1995 a conference of church representatives in southern Africa took place in the Mindolo Centre in Kitwe (Zambia). The working hypothesis that injustice today means exclusion from the contemporary economic mechanism was examined. It seems that large parts of Africa have already been declared dead as far as the global economic plans of the G8 countries are concerned. The dreams and hopes kindled at the time of independence have turned into a long and harrowing winter of despair. Global economic worldviews contain a hidden premise that the peoples from the South have no right to the fruits of their own labor and that they should be subservient to market forces. Indigenous cultures have lost the power to reform economic practices because they have been turned into commodities. Creative elements are gradually disappearing under the weight of imported western cultures. Cultural homogenization is underway as local cultures are absorbed by a commodity culture in which everything can be bought and sold. Nation-states gradually lose the possibility of protecting their democracy and economic autonomy. Small enterprises and cooperatives cannot be developed and maintained if they are not protected by the state from the multinational corporations. Money flows from the South to the rich North to enrich the North still further. The systematic impoverishment of Africa has led to many people losing their capacity for self-help and self-employment.

The relationship between economy and faith is not obvious because the economy operates in an impersonal and abstract way. In the sixteenth century John Calvin saw the market economy as a product of human ingenuity. Today, the global market economy has been sacralized and elevated to an imperial throne, and it is taking precedence over the human beings who created it. By redefining what it means to be human it has become the creator of human character. It usurps the sovereignty of God, claiming a freedom that belongs to God alone. The idolatrous and dehumanizing nature of the contemporary global economy is seen in the exclusion of Africa and Africans from the human family. All of this is a far cry from Calvin's view that the ultimate goal of human economic activity is to promote mutual intercourse among human beings.

Managers of the world economy often talk of the "sacrifices" that must be made. Africans are among those sacrificed. They live on a crucified continent as people to be sacrificed. The humanity of Africans and the future of their children play no role in the global economy. In Africa, not only human beings are sacrificed but also nature. The southern hemisphere is considered a dumping ground for toxic waste.

The consultation in Kitwe called us back to the gospel for the poor. We need to rediscover Reformed concern for mutuality and equality. We also need to recover the traditional African resources of community and "ubuntu." According to Desmond Tutu, "ubuntu" is about the essence of being human. It is a gift that Africa can offer to the world. It includes hospitality, caring for others, willingness to go the extra mile. A person is a person through another person. "My humanity," Tutu writes, "is caught up, bound up and inextricable in yours. When I dehumanize you, I inexorably dehumanize myself." The solitary human being is a contradiction in terms.

The participants in Kitwe confess their share of guilt and responsibility for the situation today. It is necessary to decide between loyalty to mammon and faithfulness to God. The real poverty in Africa caused by the unjust economic system is not only an ethical problem. It is a theological issue, and it calls for *status confessionis*. In the mechanism of today's world economy the gospel for the poor is in jeopardy.

San José (May 1996)

The third regional meeting took place in San José (Costa Rica) in May 1996. In Latin America globalization is an obstacle to the development of relationships between people. In the economic sphere we can observe an asymmetric growth. In Latin America there is no access to the capital and technology that are needed for integral development. The gospel has often been misused by great powers as a means of conquest and for political and economic domination. Even now the relationship of the churches in the First World to the church denominations in Latin America is paternalistic and not partnership-like. The consequence of the economic situation is hopelessness and loss of capability. People who cannot envision a better future can be more easily controlled. The problems that typify the whole of Latin America can be described in the following way: the culture of corruption; monopolization by minorities that do not use land in a productive way; militarism; rapid change of technologies; and external debt that becomes "endless debt," growing steadily and making it impossible to direct financial means to other priorities.

The Old Testament contains the clear commandment of God that the land is to be distributed justly (Numbers 26:53-56). The New Testament challenges us to care for the poor and warns against the accumulation of wealth. Economy is a central theme in the ministry of Jesus, whose solidarity with marginalized groups led to conflict with the rulers and brought him to the cross. In many ways the findings of the consultation in San José are complementary to the previous meetings in Manila and Kitwe. They confirm the working hypothesis that exclusion is the principal feature of injustice today.

Geneva (May 1996)

The international consultation held in Geneva evaluated the process of the regional meetings. It prepared a study text for the delegates of the 23rd General Council. The working paper confesses the guilt of the Reformed tradition concerning the economic order, which is oppressive and causes misery and death to many. It is time to examine economic principles and activities in the light of faith. The conversion of personal relationships and lifestyle is indispensable, as well as a new direction in churches and society. It is necessary to change the world economic order and to seek a new economy that affirms life for all. The consultation declared that the affirmation of life, commitment to resistance against injustice, and the struggle for transformation are an inseparable part of Reformed faith and confession today.

With thanksgiving we acknowledge the abundance of life offered to us by God and accept our responsibilities to nurture the life of the household of God and to care for creation. With distress we view the current distortions that make the household the servant of the economy. Although it claims universality, the newly emerging global economy creates enslavement and injustice.

This situation can be compared to the unleashing of the idol Moloch. The consequence is exclusion, injustice, and death — the denial of God's blessing. Care for the household is driven out by greed and the competition for individual survival. The abundance of God's creation is limited by the demands of the market. Everything has a price that can be paid only by those with the money to become consumers. In place of care for creation we find exploitation. In place of the order of creation we find the disorder of injustice.

Hearing the pleas of the deprived and excluded, we seek to understand the mechanisms of their misfortune. We witness today a process of globaliza-tion, promoted by improvements in transportation and communications tech-nology coupled with the use of mass media to reach "new markets." Through advertising, cultures around the world are converted into markets. Autono-mous people are transformed into consumers. The trade and payments agree-ments that have facilitated this process provide the basis for the ascendency of transnational corporations over the limitations of national boundaries and cul-tures. The pressure of "competitiveness" has been loosed on the world.

The claims made for this new global economy are that it will bring the peoples of the world into the global marketplace where they can freely choose from an abundance of goods. We find, however, that globalization has been ac-companied by a denial of these expectations. There has been an institutional-ized transfer of wealth from the South to the North, leading to the exclusion of millions of people from an economy that was supposed to meet their needs.

We can no longer believe that economic globalization is merely a process of extending the structures and benefits of the economy of the industrial coun-tries of the North to the rest of the world.

The driving force of globalization is the relentless accumulation of capi-tal. Its vehicles are transnational corporations and financial institutions. Through the press and media we are told that the welfare of these corporations is more important than the welfare of the household of God.

Until the changes in 1989-90, globalization was to some extent restricted by the existence of the Soviet bloc and the Council for Mutual Economic Coop-eration (Comecon). While the system in Central and Eastern Europe was not a real alternative to the emerging global market system, for many people around the world its existence was nonetheless a source of hope because it provided employment, education, and health for all its citizens. It introduced trade rela-tions with the Third World that were fairer than those offered by western coun-tries. Globalization has resulted in a massive debt crisis for developing coun-tries. As a condition for loans with which to repay debts, the indebted countries are required to implement Structural Adjustment Programs (stipulated mostly by the World Bank and the IMF). As a consequence, national budgets for health, education, and social services are drastically reduced. Priority is given to the repayment of debts, although in fact it is only the interest that is being paid while the debt remains as a means of domination.

The sovereignty of nation-states is put into question. National control over domestic policy has been largely lost with the signing of trade agreements and the consolidation of power by transnational corporations. As governments have reduced trade barriers and other restrictions, they have also reduced their ability to act in the interests of their citizens.

Economies such as those of the island states of the Caribbean and South

Pacific, too small to be sources of wealth in and of themselves, find new roles in the global economy as money laundries as well as tourist resorts. This is a significant function, since only a small percentage of global currency flow is actually required to finance trade in real goods and services. The fact that so little capital is required for trade purposes means that there is a large and growing amount of money available for speculative purposes or political or economic leverage anywhere in the world on short notice. This results in a high degree of instability for the temporary host economies of this capital (as was the case in 1995 in Mexico).

The culture of competition created by the corporate and financial forces behind the global market economy creates a downward spiral of impoverishment and injustice as cities, regions, and states compete against each other for corporate favors in the form of investments and jobs. There is also competition for deregulation and environmental exploitation to attract capital. Eventually the poorer regions no longer have anything with which to compete, not even cheaper labor. At this point, they become excluded from the global economy altogether and consigned to the garbage dump, except for the women and children who are forced to sell themselves in the new globalized sex trade.

The globalization of advertising that accompanies the globalization of the market creates a monoculture of consumerism. It creates insatiable desires that can easily be manipulated, including the desire to exploit women. It can be described as a colonization of consciousness. As a result of the financial rewards of advertising, the media develop a symbiotic relationship with their corporate benefactors and begin to see themselves as autonomous agents shaping political choices.

What is generally referred to as "the environment" also becomes a victim of the culture of competition fostered by the global economy. It is essential that we gain a new understanding of creation, not as our "environment," as something outside and apart from us, but as the matrix of our life, both physically and socially. Creation and our household must be restored as the context of our lives and the economy once again viewed as the organization and structures of nurture.

A new beginning lies in the act of repentance. We, Christians of the Reformed tradition, have to confess our complicity in the global system and our insensitivity to the victimization of the people. WARC member churches must continue to discern the suffering of the households of the poor and the weak due to globalization. They should enter into consultations with the key actors of the global economic system. They should enter into the liturgical movements of tithing, of celebrating the Sabbath and Jubilee, and they should confess their complicity in globalization.

We cannot be silent if so many people are excluded and discriminated against. We are called to resist the mechanism that serves mammon first and requires both human and environmental sacrifices. We are challenged to search for a system that affirms and promotes life. We are inspired by God's promise: "My covenant is a covenant of life and peace" (Mal. 2:5).

Debrecen (August 1997)

At the 23rd General Council the problem of economic injustice was discussed at a forum attended by many delegates from both South and North. The question was raised whether or not it was possible to declare *status confessionis* regarding economic injustice and especially regarding the exclusion of Africa from the market mechanism. Even before Debrecen, it had been suggested that *status confessionis* should be preceded by a long *processus confessionis*. While the consultation at Kitwe discussed credibility and faithfulness, the Debrecen meeting examined the question of effectiveness. The two approaches are complementary.

In the report of Section II, "Justice for All Creation," the question of economic injustice and the alarming ecological situation are intertwined. It is obvious that these two areas are closely interconnected and that one cannot be separated from the other.

It is a significant advance for ecumenical thinking that the delegates in Debrecen adopted a *processus confessionis* in this matter. The resolution expresses the conviction shared by the General Council that it is time to write a confession of faith that rejects injustice and struggles against it. At the same time it affirmed faith in the triune God who promises a new creation in Christ.

The report states: "We now call for a committed process of progressive recognition, education and confession *(processus confessionis)* within all WARC member churches at all levels regarding economic injustice and ecological destruction."

What Does It Mean?

1. The churches should pay special attention to the analysis and understanding of economic processes.
2. The churches should educate church members at all levels on economic life and on developing a lifestyle that rejects the materialism and consumerism of our day.
3. The churches should work towards the formulation of a confession of their beliefs about economic life that would express justice in the whole household of God.
4. The churches should act in solidarity with the victims of injustice.

The report calls upon WARC and its member churches to facilitate the necessary programs, resources, and practical steps to initiate a *processus confessionis* as a matter of extreme priority.

There is no doubt that the resolution of the WARC 23rd General Council in Debrecen advances the ecumenical discussion on the issue of global economic injustice. WARC does not dwell on the analysis of the present situation, but commits its member churches to initiate a process of recognition, education, and confession. All churches in the ecumenical fellowship are invited to join this process. The study text and the report of Debrecen do not demonize the market itself or globalization. It is the inner logic of unlimited growth and expansion that contradicts and seriously impairs the well-being of people. It has been rightly pointed out that the text of Debrecen concentrates on justice and the integrity of creation but discussion of peace and reconciliation is mentioned only in connection with ethnic conflicts. However, one can imagine that the present "war" in the area of technology, industry, and economy may eventually lead to military conflict. One of the causes of war could be a merciless, unregulated globalization.

In this context is it justified to seek a confessional stance? We certainly shall continue to learn from the classic creeds and confessional books of the sixteenth century. In every era since then it has been necessary to struggle for an adequate expression of Reformed faith, and it is an important insight that the church is always in need of reform *(ecclesia semper reformanda)*. The same principle can be applied to a confession. In our current struggles we cannot be satisfied with the formulations that our ancestors made in response to the challenges of their time. As in Barmen 1934 or in Belhar 1986, in this generation we are called to react to the suffering of hungry, excluded, and oppressed people around the world. We need to respond to the groaning of creation, which suffers from the devastation and the insensitive interventions of humans. We are called to create new visions and alternatives to the dominating sociopolitical system — ideas conducive to well-being and to a full life in peace and harmony.

From Processus Confessionis to Status Confessionis

Let me briefly describe the context in which we live and carry out our work. In many parts of the world we are sharply confronted with a process of economic globalization facilitated by communication technology, rapid means of transportation, and the use of mass media. The making of financial contracts occurs with unprecedented speed. It is believed that about 90 percent of the money involved is of a speculative nature. About 50 percent of the capital stems from arms trade and drug trafficking. Cultures are converted into markets. People are being manipulated into becoming consumers. The sovereignty of nations is put seriously into question because the TNCs — transnational corporations — transcend the limits of national boundaries. The profit of these corporations seems to be more important than the welfare of the household of God. The ability of governments to act in the interest of their citizens is seriously limited by these developments. This was confirmed by a banker who said: "Politicians have now been brought under the control of the financial markets."

The victory of the globalized capitalist system was trumpeted around the world, and yet the crisis in Mexico, the crisis of the Asian tigers, in Brazil, Japan, and Indonesia, indicates how volatile and uncontrollable the present system is. The experts speak about expendable areas, about the necessity of sacrificing certain areas and regions. Because of its unpredictability, because of the situation which is getting out of control, the question may be asked whether or not our world is heading towards a crash that can be compared to the great collapse on Wall Street in 1929. A devastating debt crisis, a colonization of consciousness — all of this creates a dramatic situation that can be compared to the unleashing of the idol Moloch. This is the situation of the foreign religion of Baalism, which was characterized by exploitation, exclusion, and oppression.

Let me clarify the term *status confessionis,* which is probably better known than *processus confessionis. Status confessionis* refers to a radically challenging situation — a *Grenzsituation.* It is a matter of life and death. Such a declaration stems from the conviction that in an alarming situation of oppression, exploitation, hypocrisy, and heresy, when the boundaries between right and wrong, between good and evil are blurred, the integrity of the gospel and its proclamation are at stake. Such a declaration usually refers to the practice of the church as well as to its teaching. Although the declaration is related to a particular problem and a particular situation, it is addressed to all churches and it calls them to concur in the act of confessing. It is a clear stance and a clear decision for the truth of the gospel against false teaching and its practical consequences. Such a declaration is like a beam of light in the darkness of human errors and falsifications. The call for *status confessionis* is an outcry in an unclear situation; it is a point of orientation. A confession is like a railing over an abyss. It is an attempt to grasp afresh God's will and God's design for a given situation. In this respect we stand in the tradition of the Barmen Declaration of 1934, written and declared in a situation in which the church had been seduced by the pseudo-ideology of Nazism. In a similar way, in 1986 the Dutch Reformed Mission Church adopted the Confession of Belhar in a situation of apartheid and social injustice. These are two recent confessional statements that can guide us in the present situation.

Living in this world can be compared to life in the household of God. Humankind is called to be the family of God *(familia Dei). Oikonomia* (economy) is supposed to serve human beings, to order life in the household of God. Present injustice is the consequence of human greed, profit-making, speculation, and unjust structures. Injustice is related to the worship of idols and false gods. In the Old Testament (the Hebrew Bible) injustice and inequity have religious roots and religious dimensions. When injustice reigns, the god Baal and false gods dominate. People suffer and starve while a small elite lives in luxury. However, God is justice and challenges us to restore justice and to put our relationships in order. The biblical term *zedakah* (justice) is behavior-attitude that fosters and sustains community. The prophetic tradition is to attack injustice and social evils as an expression of a false religion and worship. In the tradition of the Old Testament, Jesus is the hope of the poor. The kingdom of God, the reign of God about which Jesus so centrally speaks, is righteousness, peace, and joy in the Holy Spirit. The poor wait for God with their entire existence. The opposite of the poor are the mighty and proud who will be put down. Therefore it is not surprising that the first Christian congregations lived in solidarity with the poor — those congregations were a new type of community in the oppressive and violent setting of the Roman Empire. The kingdom of God grows and is being built from below, where the poor and downtrodden find themselves.

The visions of the Old and New Testaments speak about the reconciliation of human beings with their environment. The false interpretation of the dominion of humans over nature led to nature's exploitation and devastation. The transformation of the human environment will be necessary, but it can be done in the spirit of communication and harmony, not of exploitation and plunder. We are called to choose between gentleness and brutality. Responsibility for the future and for the not yet born generations means the practice of empathy towards the creation. In dealing with creation and environment we are inspired by the biblical concept of the Sabbath and the Jubilee Year. The biblical call to observe the Sabbath and to keep it holy refers to a style of living. It is to stop being busy and active and to share God's delight in the beauty of all created things. Let me quote from a poem by Ruben Alves:

> And suddenly God's eyes changed —
> gone was the seriousness of the worker.
> They were the eyes of a child —
> sheer delight before the beauty of paradise.
> . . . .
> It was the body of a child —
> a winged body —
> butterfly —
> playful.
> The universe was at play with God —
> and it was Sabbath.

In spite of the great advances of science and technology, we live in a situation of overlapping crises. For example, besides the economic and social crisis, the ozone hole and climate change witness to both a deep ecological crisis and to a crisis of human attitudes towards nature.

The General Council of WARC in Debrecen (August 1997) sought to answer the present crisis adequately. For many of us the present challenge calls for a confessional stance. The survival of the planet Earth is at stake. Because of exclusion and marginalization caused by the unjust social system, millions of people suffer, starve, and die. Can we do our business as usual? Can we still be in Christ if millions of adults and children perish? The situation is dramatic and touches the very core of our faith — its credibility and integrity. This is why the General Council called for a committed process of progressive recognition, education, and confession *(processus confessionis)* within all member churches at all levels regarding economic injustice and ecological destruction.

We speak about the process to indicate that it may take a longer time to reach the goal of confessing our faith on economic and environmental matters. The immediate steps are as follows:

1. to study just alternatives to the present economic structure
2. to develop programs of economic literacy
3. to explore the meaning of Sabbath and the Jubilee Year
4. to study "the colonization of consciousness"
5. to examine economic activities in the light of Christian faith
6. to support the introduction of the Tobin Tax (tax on global foreign transactions)
7. to join the campaign for the cancellation of debt
8. to initiate a dialogue with IMF, the World Bank, and the WTO
9. to strengthen cooperation with other networks and partners: Christian World Communions, people of other faiths, and people of good will.

What is the goal of all these efforts? It is not to make our world more Christian, but to make it more habitable, more just and human, to reverse the present trends so that the economy will again serve the people in the household of God and not victimize them. In the struggle against racism we have finally been able to say that apartheid is a sin and that theological justification for it is heresy. I hope that in the process of recognition and education we shall be able to confess on the basis of our faith in Jesus Christ that a system demanding human and environmental sacrifices is sinful and that it has a bearing on our salvation — on our ultimate stance before God. How we relate to the mechanisms of the global market matters, because we all are enmeshed; we all are challenged.

The call of Debrecen is not directed only to the Reformed family. WARC has undertaken this bold step, the call for a *processus confessionis,* in a vicarious way for the church universal. WARC welcomes the resolution of the WCC Assembly in Harare (December 1998) to endorse the initiative of the WARC General Council in Debrecen and to urge the WCC member churches to join the process of education and confession.

We realize that the Reformed tradition has contributed to the values of the prevailing system (hard work, seeing God's blessing in accumulation, emphasis on success, efficiency, competition). We have to confess our complicity in an economic order that is unfair and oppressive. What is needed is a conversion in our personal attitude, a conversion of both church and society.

The affirmation of life, the commitment to resistance and struggle for transformation, is an integral part of Christian faith and confession. We call on Christians of other traditions, on churches of other Christian world communions, to join the Reformed family in the effort to create a more just world and to care for all creation.

"Now is the Kairos! Now is the day of salvation" (2 Cor. 6:2).

CHAPTER 26

Paradox Catholicity:
The Union of Identity and Difference
as a Core Problem of Christian Ecumenism

Ulrich H. J. Körtner

Theory Problems of Ecumenical Theology

The confused sense of transition, of stepping across a threshold, typical for the current state of the North American and European societies, has by now also reached the ecumenical movement. Its much bemoaned stagnation and lack of orientation partakes in a feeling of general cultural exhaustion — precisely what the term "postmodernism" is attempting to capture. In such confused times, it is almost natural to focus more sharply the ecumenical term of "unity." "Ecumenics in Transition" (Konrad Raiser) has, once again, to ponder the problem of unity and plurality.

The problem is however not only to give an ecclesiological definition of the relationship between unity and plurality of the churches, it also requires reflecting the unity and difference of churches and universal Christendom. Among the core changes that have occurred during modern times in the history of Christendom is the growing difference between the cultural heritage of modern societies

---

A more detailed and slightly different form of this paper has been published under the title of "Versöhnte Verschiedenheit: Die Einheit von Identität und Differenz als Grundproblem christlicher Ökumene," in *BThZ* 15 (1998): 77-96. See also Ulrich H. J. Körtner, *Versöhnte Verschiedenheit. Ökumenische Theologie im Zeichen des Kreuzes* (Bielefeld: Luther-Verlag, 1996); *Reformiert und ökumenisch. Brennpunkte reformierter Theologie in Geschichte und Gegenwart*, Salzburg Theologische Studien 7 (Innsbruck: Tyrolia-Verlag, 1998).

and the churches as organized forms of Christian religion. The borders of what is Christian do not coincide with the borders of any church, nor even with any ecumenical sum total of churches. This is the challenge for Christianity in its confrontation with a society not only secularized, but also multiply religious. The identity of Christendom is therefore not only the relationship among the churches, but also its relationship toward secularized society, toward the non-Christian religions, and toward the many syncretistic religious movements.

The meaning of the term "ecumenics" consequently varies considerably. The ecumenical idea has expanded from a movement within the churches to a *Weltanschauung*, a view of the world, which makes the idea of unity the guiding principle for the future of humankind as such.[1]

Thus, one can choose between conciliatory ecumenism, which strives for the transdenominational unity of the churches, but also secularized and even interreligious ecumenism; and all these variants of ecumenism do not easily harmonize with one another.[2]

Against extending the term until it becomes featureless, I want to refocus the discussion onto the problem of identity and plurality in Christianity, without intending to eliminate the important concerns of the interreligious dialogue or the secularized ecumenism and its focus on the concept of the kingdom of God. However, the problems — indicated with such key terms as "multireligious" and "multicultural" and the global endangerment of human survival — can be adequately discussed (whether they are solvable is a different issue) if one takes the pains to draw conceptual distinctions and does not constantly confuse analysis with engagement.

Therefore, I will deal less with the pragmatic discussion of changing ecumenic strategies, but will rather attempt a problem description and analysis. Before designing new ecumenical visions and considering strategies for mobilizing ecumenical forces, one must ask whether the questions as such are at all the right ones to ask. Without turning against ecumenical doing, I want to ask the question: What concepts are required to adequately deal with the issue of unity and plurality in ecumenic Christendom? And once one begins asking this question, one realizes very quickly that the main obstacle for an ecumenical theology as a theory of ecumenism is . . . the theology itself, for the concept of ecumenics does not mean a conceptually developed theory, but merely points

1. Cf. Erwin Fahlbusch, *Art. Ökumenismus* 6, Evangelisches Kirchenlexikon 3 (Göttingen: Vandenhoeck & Ruprecht, 1992), pp. 870-73; Reinhard Frieling, *Art. Ökumene*, TRE 25 (Berlin/New York: W. de Gruyter, 1995), pp. 44-76; Heinrich Petri and Heinz-Albert Raem, *Art. Ökumenismus*, TRE 25, pp. 77-86.

2. Regarding the term "ecumenism" and its different meanings, cf. André Birmele and Erwin Fahlbusch, *Art. Ökumenismus*, Evangelisches Kirchenlexikon 3 (Göttingen: Vandenhoeck & Ruprecht, 1992), pp. 861-73.

us at the still-to-be-resolved problem of unity and plurality of Christendom. Therefore, it does not suffice merely to discuss the concept of unity or how to reach it. What is needed is a theological theory that gives meaning and function to the concept of unity in the first place. Any current stagnation in the ecumenical movement may well have its causes in an exhaustion of ecumenical engagement and surely in the demarcation needs of church leaderships, which derive from an amplified need for self-preservation; but even more important is the lack of theory and the causally related tendencies toward ideology.

The concept of ecumenism therefore pinpoints the problem of plurality and unity in Christendom. And this immediately poses the question of whether the complexity of the issue at hand has been adequately sketched with this conceptual distinction, of unity and plurality. An ecumenical theology or ecclesiology utilizing this terminology typifies, epistemologically speaking, a theory and ontology that is object-oriented, a type with lasting influence on philosophy and theology and their respective histories. It is the theological variant of the model of late antiquity, of the whole and its parts, in ecclesiology associated with the metaphor of the body of Christ and its members. That model has the significant problem that it must duplicate the wholeness and unity of the church or Christendom, because it must concurrently render it as unity and as sum total of its parts. Of course one can say that the whole, the church as believed and as expressed in the traditional confessions of faith, is more than the sum of its parts. The known problem with such a theoretical approach is to show how the whole of the church can be expressed at the level of its parts as unity. Basically the problem can be illustrated already in the writings of the New Testament, where the church is the body of Christ while Christ at the same time is, as the head of the church, distinct from the body.[3] On the one hand the head is part of the body, on the other hand it is the organizing principle of the whole. At any rate, both society and epistemology (not to mention the structures of the churches) have been so fundamentally altered by modernity that one must wonder whether the metaphor of the body of Christ is at all ecclesiologically sufficient. And aside from that, despite what New Testament scholarship might say, the metaphor was never that decisive for St. Paul to begin with.[4]

3. Cf. 1 Cor. 12:1ff.; Rom. 12:4; Eph. 3:3; and Col. 3:15 with Eph. 1:22f.; 4:15.
4. Cf. Andreas Lindemann, "Die Kirche als Lieb. Beobachtungen zur 'demokratischen' Ekklesiologie bei Paulus," *Zeitschrift für Theologie und Kirche* 92 (1995): 140-65; Helmut Merklein, "Entstehung und Gehalt des paulinischen Leib-Christi-Gedankens," in *Studien zu Jesus und Paulus,* Wissenschaft Untersuchungen zum Neuen Testament 43 (Tübingen: J. C. B. Mohr, 1987), pp. 319-44; Thomas Söding, "'Ihr aber seid Christi Leib' (I Cor 12,27). Exegetische Betrachtungen an einem zentralen Motiv paulinischer Ekklesiologie," *Catholica* 45 (1991): 135-62. By the way, St. Paul only talks explicitly about the body of Christ in 1 Corinthians 12:27!

The lack of clarity of such an object-oriented theory of a whole consisting of parts becomes obvious when studying the concepts of current ecumenical discussion, *unitas* and *communio* or *koinonia* and their equally unclear interrelationships. New approaches to ecumenical theology attempt to solve the problem of the unity of wholeness and plurality with the aid of the concept of community. This attempt is part and parcel of a shift from a christological to a trinitarian foundation of ecclesiology, replacing the metaphor of the body of Christ with the metaphor of the table and house-community of God, realized symbolically in the celebration of the eucharist.[5]

Aside from the theological difficulties of translating the teaching of the immanent Trinity into the sphere of ecclesiology, which I will touch upon later,[6] there remains the question of usability of such conceptual tools. For the model of the household, whose members gather daily around the table, is equally pre-modern and has no connection with today's society.

Pre-modern society is divided into layers and coupled with the distinction between center and periphery, while modern society is characterized by the differentiation of functional systems, as in my opinion correctly described by the social theory of Niklas Luhmann — leaving aside some problematic features.[7]

Even if as a theologian one is reluctant to follow Luhmann's sociological suggestions for a future organization of Christianity, one cannot reject the validity of his analysis of the processes of transformation, which Christianity and the churches are undergoing in modern times.[8] In modern society, the self-

---

5. Cf. Konrad Raiser, *Ökumene im Übergang. Paradigmenwechsel in der ökumenischen Bewegung* (München: C. Kaiser, 1989), pp. 143ff.

6. For critical discussion, cf. Walter Schöpsdau, "Trinitarische Ekklesiologie — Ein Weg zur Heilung der Risse?," *MdKI* 45 (1994): 23-27; Dietrich Ritschl, "Paradigmenwechsel für eine ökumenische Ekklesiologie?," in Peter Neuner and Dietrich Ritschl, eds., *Kirchen in Gemeinschaft — Gemeinschaft der Kirche. Studie der DÖSTA zu Fragen der Ekklesiologie*, Beiheft zur Ökumenischen Rundschau 66 (Frankfurt am Main: Lembeck, 1993), pp. 201-14.

7. The key work is Niklas Luhmann, *Soziale Systeme. Grundriss einer allgemeinen Theorie* (Frankfurt am Main: Suhrkamp, 1987). For a critical discussion of Luhmann, cf. Werner Krawietz and Michael Welker, eds., *Kritik der Theorie sozialer Systeme. Auseinandersetzung mit Luhmanns Hauptwerk* (Frankfurt am Main: Suhrkamp, 1992).

8. For a theological treatment of Luhmann's theory of social systems and his functional sociology of religion, cf. among others Eilert Herms, "Das Problem von 'Sinn als Grundbegriff der Soziologie' bei Niklas Luhmann," *Zeitschrift für evangelische Ethik* 18 (1974): 341-59; Karl-Wilhelm Dahm, Volker Drehsen, and Günter Kehrer, *Das Jenseits der Gesellschaft. Religion im Prozess sozialwissenschaftlicher Kritik* (München: Claudius, 1975); Trutz Rendtorff, *Gesellschaft ohne Religion? Theologische Aspekte einer sozialtheoretischen Kontroverse (Luhmann/Habermas)* (München: Pieper, 1975); Hans-Eckehard Bahr, ed., *Religionsgespräche. Zur gesellschaftlichen Rolle der Religion* (Darmstadt/Neuwied: Luchterhand, 1975); H. Kaefer, *Religion und Kirche als soziale Systeme. N. Luhmanns soziologische Theorien und die*

description of the church as house-community of God and the socially describable reality are not congruent. Ecclesiastical ideal and church reality diverge considerably.

That something is missing and amiss in an ecclesiology or a theory of ecumenism that utilizes the house-community metaphor is obviously suspected by its proponents, though without any consequences for the theory. K. Raiser for example takes the ecumenical movement as an ecological movement and reads the concept of ecumenism as theological terminology for the household of life.[9] Unexpectedly, the metaphor of the household of God is replaced with talk of a "network of bi-directional relationships." The utilization of the teaching of the immanent Trinity is supposed to provide the foundation for an ecclesiology that "begins with 'relationships' and not so much with structures or teleological processes."[10] This to me is a clear attempt to link up, via the teaching of Trinity, the theory of ecclesiology with the current general systems theory, everybody's favorite epistemological foundational theory, without however either explicitly saying this or sufficiently reflecting such linkage theologically. The term "ecology" is consequently not clearly defined within the discourse of the ecumenical movement's self-interpretation.

In what follows I will argue that the ecclesiological problem of identity and difference in Christianity cannot be approached in terms of immanent Trinity or one-sided "ecumenism of the Holy Spirit," but must be couched in terms of a theology of both incarnation and crucifixion. In correspondence to the distinction between visible and invisible church, the one church of Jesus Christ exists *in faith*.[11] *The catholicity of the church of Jesus Christ must therefore be interpreted as a paradox.* That is the key insight of an ecclesiology of Helvetian-Protestant descent.[12]

Pastoraltheologie (Freiburg/Basel/Wien: Herder, 1977); Wolfhart Pannenberg, *Religion in der sekularen Gesellschaft. Niklas Luhmanns Religionssoziologie* (EK 11, 1978), pp. 99-103; Frithard Scholz, *Freiheit als Indifferenz. Alteuropäische Probleme mit der Systemtheorie Niklas Luhmanns* (Frankfurt am Main: Suhrkamp, 1982); Michael Welker, ed., *Theologie und funktionale Systemtheorie. Luhmanns Religionssoziologie in theologischer Diskussion* (Frankfurt am Main: Suhrkamp, 1985); Peter Koslowski, ed., *Die religiöse Dimension der Gesellschaft. Religion und ihre Theologie und Praxis der Kirche in der Auseinandersetzung mit den Sozialtheorien Niklas Luhmanns und Jürgen Habermas?* (Frankfurt am Main: Suhrkamp, 1985); Detlet Pollak, *Religiöse Chiffrierung und soziologische Aufklärung. Die Religionstheorie Niklas Luhmanns im Rahmen ihrer systemtheoretischen Voraussetzungen* (Frankfurt am Main: Suhrkamp, 1999).

9. Raiser, *Ökumene im Übergang*, pp. 125ff.

10. Raiser, *Ökumene im Übergang*, p. 127.

11. John Calvin, *Institutes of the Christian Religion*, trans. Ford Lewis Battles and ed. John T. McNeill (Philadelphia: Westminster, 1960), 4.1.3.

12. Cf. also Janos D. Pasztor, "Zukunft und Katholizität der reformierten Theologie," in Michael Welker and David Willis, eds., *Zur Zukunft der Reformierten Theologie* (Neukirchen-

It is the ecclesiology of Calvin in particular that combines the concentration on the christological essence of the church with ecumenical breadth, with Calvin drawing the distinction for the visible church between the universal church *(ecclesia universalis)*, which consists of the chosen group, selected from among all peoples while living spatially separated, the local congregations *(singulae ecclesiae)*, and individual human beings who belong to the church because of their faith, even though they are in reality outside of any particular church.[13] Even though Calvin lets the Trinity be the foundation of the ecclesiology, just as he did with Christology, he does so in terms of the economical Trinity with strong christological concentration. Therefore the church, according to Calvin, is the community of those, who, out of the friendliness of God the Father, have achieved communion *with Christ* through the power of the Holy Spirit.[14] Consequently, Calvin defines the *notae ecclesiae* — being the pure preaching of the gospel and the institution-conformant administration of the sacraments[15] — christologically.[16] The paradox of the theology of the cross in the ecclesiology of Calvin is his saying that the death of Christ carries fruit and that God preserves his Church in wonderful fashion as if in dark secrecy.[17]

In the following I will argue that an ecclesiology founded in the theology of the cross can derive profit for the construction of its theory by critical dialogue with current systems theory. In the following paragraphs I will therefore sound the possibilities for discussion between ecumenical theology and a theory of social systems, as developed by the recently deceased sociologist from Bielefeld, Niklas Luhmann.

Ecumenical Theology and Systems Theory

There is a possibility for overcoming the current difficulties of ecumenical theology in constructive dialogue with general systems theory, especially with Luhmann's theory of social systems, as long as one does not accept his suggestions for the future organization of Christian religion without reconsiderations. The self-interpretation and self-description of church and theology are not prefigured by their respective external descriptions from sociological

---

Vluyn: Neukirchener Verlag, 1998), pp. 39-62; Lukas Vischer, "Kirche — Mutter aller Gläubigen," in *Zur Zukunft,* pp. 295-321.

13. Calvin, *Institutes* 4.1.9.

14. Calvin, *Institutes* 4.1.3.

15. Calvin, *Institutes* 4.1.8ff.

16. For the *notae ecclesia,* cf. also Christian Link, "Die Kennzeichen der Kirche aus reformierter Sicht," in *Zur Zukunft,* pp. 271-94.

17. Calvin, *Institutes* 4.1.2.

points of view. However, it is essential that the church compare and contrast its self-description and the external description critically, to avoid any possibilities of ideologizing the ecclesiology.

A system-theoretic ecclesiology could be potentially fruitful and successful, without requiring theological founding in the doctrine of Trinity. Combined with the concept of ecology, such an ecclesiology is caught in contradictions anyway. For ecological thinking, developed in the biological sciences, uses the core distinction of systems theory, system and environment. In the context of this totality which is the world we live in, one can distinguish many systems from their respective environments, but one cannot describe the whole of the world as a system, for what would be its environment? If God is made the theological environment of such a global household of life, then we face the problem of God being both an element of the system and its environment. If God is however not the system's environment, then the quest for such an environment is reopened, with dualistic or Manichean consequences.

More helpful than conflating creation theology and ecclesiology and thus interpreting the whole world as a single system is in my mind the application of the system-theoretic distinction of system and environment for the problem of Christianity and the individual churches. These can be interpreted, sociologically, as self-referential systems, which are self-referentially closed and at the same time open toward their environment. Self-referentiality of a social system is, according to Luhmann, not merely dependent on the distinction of identity and difference. Rather, the self-referentiality of a system can become reality in its actual operations only "if a Self (be it as element, process or system) can be identified as self and placed as different toward others."[18] Self-referential systems differentiate themselves into subsystems by utilizing the whole system as environment for subsystem construction. Thus, we can reformulate the traditional distinction between whole and parts in system-theoretic terms as a theory of system-differentiation. And system-differentiation means "nothing but the repetition of the distinction between system and environment within systems."[19] This has consequences for the semantic description of the problem of unity. For the semantic required for the self-referential description of social systems must be switched from unity to difference. "This does not exclude the reflection of unity of the total system and especially of the unity of the world. But the unity is now the unity of a difference, and thus: paradox unity."[20]

If we consider the problem of unity and plurality of Christianity, as indi-

---

18. Luhmann, *Soziale*, p. 26.
19. Luhmann, *Soziale*, p. 22.
20. Niklas Luhmann, "Die Ausdifferenzierung der Religion," in *Gesellschaftsstruktur und Semantik,* vol. 3 (Frankfurt am Main: Suhrkamp, 1993), pp. 259-357; this quote on p. 262.

cated by the concept of ecumenism, in terms of system theory, then the issue appears to be the difference of identity and difference of Christianity and the paradox, because different, unity of the church differentiated into a plurality of denominations, which are again internally differentiated into subsystems. If the churches consider themselves as part of the one church of Jesus Christ, they comprehend themselves as subsystems whose environment is the whole church on the one hand and the many Christian denominations on the other hand, together with the social system and the many non-Christian denominations contained within it. And if things were not bad enough, the churches are also part of the modern differentiation, which makes the individual persons not part of the system, but of the environment. Individual belief and church membership are consequently not part and parcel, and therefore the identity of what it means to be Christian cannot be determined from either the official teachings of the churches or as the average of the individual beliefs and convictions. There is a base difference between universal Christendom and the churches, not a separation, but a fundamental distinction. And Christianity only exists in this irresolvable existence.

A theological theory of ecumenism, that is, a paradoxical one that grasps itself as a unity of identity and difference in Christianity, now has to be rethought in terms of the previously given sociological description.[21] Due to the differentiating processes of modern times, whose networkings are already global, the churches are being confronted with distinctions not of their own choosing.[22] This does not mean that they cannot handle these distinctions in an independent — and that means theological — fashion, but rather that they will have to. Theology as self-description of Christianity has the task to aid Christendom in coping with the sketched difference of identity and difference. This will not be possible from a single theological vantage point, but rather from an irreducible plurality of theological descriptions, which will render Christianity in a poly-contextual fashion.[23] Such an ecumenical theology will first have to theologically define not the concept of unity but rather the concept of difference. This definition however again requires a distinction, specifically the difference between distinction, distinctness, and separation; between differentness, plurality, and contrariety; between difference and *antithesis*. Otherwise the existence of many churches will either be interpreted — in a one-sided fashion — as mere

---

21. See also André Birmele and Harding Meyer, eds., *Grundkonsens — Grunddifferenz. Studie des Strassburger Institut für ökumenische Forschung. Ergebnisse und Dokumente* (Frankfurt: Lembeck; Paderborn: Bonifatius, 1992).

22. Cf. Niklas Luhmann, *Soziale*, p. 263. The functional theory of religion of Luhmann is described in Niklas Luhmann, *Funktion der Religion* (Frankfurt am Main: Suhrkamp, 1982).

23. For the term "poly-contextual" *(Polykontexturaliät)*, see Luhmann, *Soziale*, p. 14.

negation of the one church of Jesus Christ, that is, as the result of human sin, or, equally simplistic, exclusively as the lively plurality of living out of the spirit of God. Both interpretations are equally unsatisfying and do not do justice to the described complexity of identity and difference in Christianity.

However, part of this complexity is the distinction between church and Christianity. Modern Christendom is self-referential precisely in this distinction from itself. Therefore, we must theologically consider that universal Christendom is only existent in such irresolvable difference. Consequently, neither the ecclesiastical claim of absoluteness in the form of *"extra ecclesiam nulla sallus"* can claim unchanged validity, as long as the claim is referencing empirical single churches; nor can the proposition of the "end of the ecclesiastical age" and the post-church future of Christianity. For even though there can be appearances of extra- and post-ecclesiastical Christendom, these can only exist in difference to the churches and thus require the churches' continued existence for their own.

A theological formula for the different unity of identity and difference in Christianity describes this unity as reconciled diversity. This formula was coined in the 1970s by Lutheran theologians to describe the unity of the churches given the theologically legitimate differences of the denominations.[24] In keeping with our considerations so far, this formula must be expanded to include the difference between churches and Christianity, and at the same time saved from ideological abuse to legitimate ecumenical stagnation. Reconciliation is, as we painfully realize at the end of a century replete with cruelty, not a possession but a permanent mission, and mainly a gift that, according to Christian conviction, has been promised and therefore cannot be forced into being. If the concept of reconciliation is not to become ideologically shallow, then the duality of all differences has to be considered theologically. For this to succeed I propose to expound in new ways the christocentric aspect of ecumenical ecclesiology, criticized by some these days, and to formulate the concept of ecumenism in the sign of the cross.

The Churches and Judaism

The difference of "identity and difference" in Christianity, which requires reflection in the light of the cross, pertains in a special way to the difference and

---

24. For the ecclesiological model of reconciled diversity, cf. WCC Exchange No. 3 (1997): 4ff.; Harding Meyer, "'Einheit in versöhnter Verschiedenheit' — 'Konziliare Gemeinschaft' — 'Organische Union.' Gemeinsamkeit und Differenz gegenwärtig diskutierter Einheitskonzeptionen," *Ökumenischen Rundschau* 26 (1977): 377-400. For a discussion of the ecumenical concept of unity, see also Harding Meyer, *Ökumenische Zielvorstellungen*, Ökumenische Studienhefte 3 (Göttingen: Vandenhoeck & Ruprecht, 1996).

unity of church and Judaism, as expressed by the concept of the people of God. Thus, after differentiating church and Christianity, one needs to again differentiate between church and God's people. The relationship of the churches with Judaism is the true core issue of ecumenism, because the denominational split of Christianity already comes to the fore in the separation of church and synagogue, not in the inner-Christian schisms of the individual churches.

Every understanding of ecumenical unity that pigeonholes Judaism without drawing any distinctions among the non-Christian religions, and thus skips the difference between churches and people of God, does not do justice to the problem of identity and difference in Christianity. Considering the sorrowful history of the relationship between Christians and Jews and the Christian animosity towards Jews throughout the centuries, it is clear that the phrase "reconciled difference" can only derive its true and theological meaning from this issue. Nowhere is ecumenical reconciliation needed as painfully as between Christians and Jews. At the same time, the ideological abuse of the idea of reconciliation is equally nowhere more threateningly looming.

It is in my view a decisive failure of past concepts and books of denominational scholarship or ecumenical church sciences to have neglected this issue.[25] But equally this problem has not been recognized pervasively as the decisive issue of any ecumenical theology. However, reformatted theology has concentrated on this topic in the last decades with special emphasis.

The relationship between Christianity and Judaism is not only a historical or genetical one, but rather — by virtue of the continued existence of the Jewish people — a dogmatic question of theological prime importance.[26] For by its very continued existence, Judaism touches the self-interpretation of the churches as the people of God. It is a symptom of our ability to forget about Israel, both in past and present, when we ponder the source of the church, the reasons for denominational plurality, and the goal of a visible unity, without seeing the sources of Christianity in Judaism and the Jews' continued resistance to accepting Jesus of Nazareth as the Messiah of Judaism as a question posed for any ecumenical vision of unity.

The inclusion of Judaism in the research programs of denominational studies adds to our already discussed difference between church and Christianity, the difference between church and the people of God.[27] The very beginning of

25. For the following, see also Körtner, *Versöhnte*, pp. 29-59.

26. Cf. the essay collection of Rolf Rendtorff and Hans Hesmann Henrix, eds., *Die Kirche und das Judentum. Dokumente von 1945-1985* (München: C. Kaiser, 1989). Among the newer publications I would like to mention: *Christen und Juden II. Zur theologischen Neuorientierung im Verhältnis zum Judentum. Eine Studie der EKD* (Gütersloh: Gütersloh Verlagshaus, 1991).

27. For the use of "People of God" in ecclesiology and the discussion of the relationship between church and the people of God, cf. among others Wolfhart Pannenberg,

Christianity is connected with a quarrel private to the Jewish religion: Who belongs to the people of God and what is the true people of God? The writings of the New Testament show how severely the Christian faith in the universality of salvation (as it appeared in Jesus of Nazareth and his alleged fulfillment of Old Testament prophecies) was challenged by the separation of synagogue and church. We are not speaking here of the unity of the church, the guiding vision of the ecumenical movement, but the visible unity of the people of God — a title the church could only claim for itself by declaring Judaism at the same time as something of the past. This unity is the basic problem of ecumenism and ecumenical ecclesiology. Therefore, the typical vision of the visible unity of the churches, exemplified by the phrase "one church and one mankind, so that the World may believe," is pure ideology, as long as the continued existence of Judaism and the difference, already observed by St. Paul in Romans 9 to 11, between people of God and church is continually ignored. The aspect is especially important in light of the increased use of "people of God" as the base term of ecclesiology.

Consequently, it is necessary to include the dialogue between Judaism and Christianity as a foundational component of any project of ecumenical church science or theology. Two observations must be added, however. Just as we must criticize an ecumenical theology that ignores the difference between church and people of God, we must equally criticize a theology of Israel that skips the decisive difference St. Paul makes in Romans 9 to 11, between the people of God and empirical Judaism. Furthermore, we must understand that by including the question of Judaism in our ecclesiology we are relegating the ecumenical idea of the visible unity of the people of God once and for all into the realm of utopia. For which strategy is both imaginable and acceptable for bringing about the visible unity between Christianity and Judaism? The project of a mission among the Jews is impossible for mere historical reasons.[28] On the one hand, the approach up to now clearly has failed; on the other hand, the history of continued persecution of Jews with its horrible climax in the holocaust weights heavily on the endeavor. Yet even the theory of the "Dual Paths of Salvation,"[29] proposed by

---

Systematische Theologie, vol. 3 (Göttingen: Vandenhoeck & Ruprecht, 1993), pp. 469ff., 501ff. For the use Calvin makes of this term, cf. e.g., *Institutes* 4.1.9.

28. Concerning the issue of mission among the Jews, cf. Heinz Kremders and Erich Lubahn, *Mission an Israel in heilsgeschichtlicher Sicht* (Neukirchen-Vluyn: Neukirchener Verlag, 1985).

29. For a discussion of the theory of the dual paths to salvation, cf. Franz Mussner, *Traktat über die Juden* (München: Kösel, 1988); Norbert Lohfink, *Der niemals gekündigte Bund. Exegetische Gedanken zum christlich-jüdischen Gespräch* (Freiburg/Basel/Wien: Herder, 1989). Critically however, Erich Grässer, "Zwei Heilswege? Zum theologischen Verhältnis von Israel und Kirche," in Paul-Gerhard Müller and Werner Stenger, eds., *Kontinuität und Einheit* (Freiburg/Basel/Wien: Herder, 1981), pp. 411-29.

many theologians engaged in the dialogue between Christians and Jews, which discards any notion of a Christian mission among the Jews for theological reasons, is not helpful. For starters, it appears hard to me to find biblical evidence for such a view. And furthermore its real meaning is only that the visible unity of church and synagogue has no historical chance of realization but is at best an eschatological hope. Yet whoever views the clarification of the relationship between the churches and Judaism as a prime task for ecumenical denominational studies and theology will want to focus on more realistic goals in the interdenominational dialogue, more restrained than is usually the case in ecclesiastical press releases or ecumenical articles.

My view is that the denominations and the denominational particularity are not mere signs of the inner world of Christianity, but are already a part of Christianity's heritage in Judaism. The denominations of Christianity cannot be interpreted as mere expressions of the plurality of spiritual charismas, which would be reductionism under the cover of pneumatology. And the denominations have to be viewed in the perspective of the cross as sinful separation in dire need of redemption and resolution. This is precisely what the phrase "reconciled difference" could give us, if it is not ideologically abused as the description for a permanent state of ecumenism, but rather as a piece of hope of Christian faith.

Ecumenism under the Sign of the Cross

It is among the base insights of ecumenical theology that the unity of the churches is not for themselves but for the service of the one and indivisible humankind. More than ever the goal of the ecumenic movement today is the "rediscovery of the fundamental unity of human and extra-human world."[30] Of course, one may equally read this in the opposite direction: as part of the reality of this world, the church participates in the antagonisms and its inner tensions. The message of redemption, which she has to announce to the world in word and deed, in *martyria, diakonia,* and *leiturgia,* is first and foremost intended for her ears and has to be preached perpetually. Like the plurality of the world, the multiplicity and diversity within the church of Jesus Christ, which is believed to be whole, is very ambiguous. This state of denominations cannot be derived from the interior workings of the Trinity for the precise reason that it equally represents the destruction of living relationships by virtue of the power of sin. Therefore, the church is neither *societas perfecta* nor self-stabilized harmony.

---

30. Charles Birch, "Schöpfung, Technik und Überleben der Menschheit: . . . und füllet die Erde," in Hanfried Krüger, ed., *Jesus Christus befreit und eint,* Beiheft zur Ökumenischen Rundschau 30 (Frankfurt am Main: Lembeck, 1978), pp. 95-111, here p. 108.

It is part of the irresolvable ambivalence of the church that every effort for visible unity, no matter in what shape, leads to new problems of polarization and separation, and it eventually hits the painful wall of the separation of church and synagogue. If denominational boundaries are overcome or even become crossable, for example, then new particularities are introduced by theologies of context or traditional fundamentalisms. Neither for the ecclesiastical desire for unity nor for the shaping of the human everyday world do final solutions and conditions exist. For the same reason, the social and ecological activism of the churches is not without ambivalent consequences.

Thus, the *oikomene,* that is, the inhabited world and the church, stand below the sign of the cross of Christ, which is equally sign of God's judgment and mercy. Removed from any docetic triumphalism, such ecumenic theology founded in the cross is a theology of suffering, including the suffering of the ecclesiastical separations and the separation between Christianity and Judaism. *Koinonia,* the fellowship of the church, is, as we can learn from St. Paul, participation in the sufferings of Christ. What St. Paul wrote about the apostles is equally true of the congregation and the separated churches: "We carry at all times the death of Christ in our body, so that the life of Jesus may equally be revealed in our bodies. For we that live are eternally given unto death for Jesus' sake, so that the life of Jesus is revealed in our mortal flesh" (2 Cor. 4:10f.). We should also recall the statement of John Williamson Nevin (1803-1886), the guiding light of the so-called "Mercersburg Theology": "Jesus intervened in his praying for the unity of the church. If this was the spirit of Christ, then the spirit of the church can only convene with him. The whole of the church sighs in her fragmentation, as if Christ himself had been affected by the separation and could not find peace until the unnatural deed of violence had come to its end."[31]

In this sense of the theology of the cross one has, in my view, to interpret the *ecclesia semper reformanda* of the Reformation. For in view of the cross, the principle of *ecclesia semper reformanda* is critically positioned against any totalitarian drive for unity as well as against any pluralistic conception of ecclesiology whose spiritual enthusiasm is unable to distinguish between the fullness of the new life as it appeared in Christ and the creatural diversity of historical individuation.[32] Wherever plurality is described in a one-sided fashion as an essential feature of all communities, one needs to be reminded that

31. Retranslation into English of the German quote in Vischer, "Kirche," p. 309 (= J. H. Nichols, *The Mercersburg Theology* [New York, 1966], p. 43).

32. Cf. Friedrich Heyer, *Konfessionskunde, mit Beiträgen von Henry Chadwick* (Berlin: W. de Gruyter, 1977), p. 4: "For, one has to ask whether the term 'life,' which signals in 'signs of life,' really means the New Life in Christ, or whether it is still the term 'historical individuation,' as applied by Schleiermacher and Marheineke to explain the denominational plurality."

through the word of reconciliation God not only accepts this ecclesiastical plurality but at the same time places it under his judgment. The ambivalence of plurality, i.e., the unity of identity and difference, is that it not only signifies legitimate diversity but also sinful separation. The sinfulness of denominational pluralism is made visible by the separation of the Lord's table. Therefore the visible unity of the churches, which I criticize as too big a totality, is a necessary perspective of the ecumenical movement insofar as it means the possibility of sharing communion. True reconciliation does not intend mere reciprocal acceptance, but reciprocal atonement and renewal. This has the practical consequence that in the act of reconciliation, there is a simultaneous acceptance and transformation of the historically grown denominational identities.

Nevertheless, the denominational and contextual plurality of the church of Jesus Christ, believed to be one, will continue, for she is grounded not only in human sin but also in anthropological and sociological plurality in accordance with creation.[33] The ecclesiological conception of an organic unity, which pushes for a union of the churches, tends to ignore this reality. The comparatively more realistic model of reconciled diversity, in Europe exemplified through the *Leuenberger Konkordie,* can however be abused to pit the self-assertion of existing organizations and ecclesiastical power structures against desire for atonement and change. And while the dissolution of all denominational identities is no goal of reconciliation, neither is the persistent growth of new schisms. The model of organic unity can thus teach us that any reconciled diversity can only be obtained at the price of the "dying with Christ," which makes denominational identities not only relative, but possibly transforms them.

The phrase "reconciled diversity," which pinpoints the problem of the unity of identity and difference in Christendom, is only theologically acceptable if interpreted dynamically, not statically. This is possible, however, only if the ecclesiological consequences of the New Testament call to follow Christ are considered. As with every Christian, the churches too have equally received the word of Christ, with both its warning and its promise: "Whosoever wants to follow me, let him deny himself and take up his cross and follow me. For whosoever wants to save his life will lose it; and whosoever will lose his life for my sake and for the sake of the Gospel will save it" (Mark 8:34f.).

33. Cf. Erwin Fahlbusch, "Abschied von der Konfessionskunde? Überlegungen zu einer Phänomenologie der universalen Christenheit," in Gottfried Maron, ed., *Evangelisch und ökumenisch. Beiträge zum 110 jährigen Bestehen des Evangelischen Bundes* (Göttingen: Vandenhoeck & Ruprecht, 1986), pp. 456-93, esp. pp. 478ff., 483ff.; *Kirchenkunde der Gegenwart,* ThW 9 (Stuttgart: Kohlhammer, 1979), pp. 13ff., 274ff.

CHAPTER 27

The Openness and Worldliness of the Church

Michael Weinrich

Confession in the Life of the Church

The formula *ecclesia reformata semper reformanda,*[1] which originated within the Reformed sphere, reflects the view that the historical form of the church will never completely correspond to its destiny. Rather, the church's destiny and promise continually go beyond the form of the church — however perfect it may be — given to it by human beings. Leaving aside the basic belief that the church's fundamental destiny is to give glory to God, it can even be said that the church's knowledge of its true destiny is itself continually imperfect and provisional. What it actually means to give glory to God at this time is not at all self-evident but is mediated through a process of understanding that from

---

1. Otto Weber attributes the formula, which corresponds to the spirit of Calvin, to his comrade-in-arms and successor, Théodore Beza, but without giving any concrete evidence. Cf. Otto Weber, "Calvins Lehre von der Kirche," *Die Treue Gottes in der Geschichte der Kirche, Gesammelte Aufsätze,* vol. 2, BGLRK 29 (Neukirchen-Vluyn: Neukirchener Verlag, 1968), p. 58. Certainly, if even the explanations of the concept "reformare" do not note any evidence in the Reformers for this formulation, it seems obviously to concern a formulation that is difficult to trace to its origin but which in no way must be opposed to the possibility that it is used widely at a later point as a basic reformational formula. Cf. Wilhelm Maurer, "Reformation," in *Religion in Geschichte und Gegenwart,* vol. 5, 3rd ed. (Tübingen: J. C. B. Mohr, 1961), pp. 861ff.

This essay was first published in *Reformed and Ecumenical: On Being Reformed in Ecumenical Encounters,* ed. Christine Lienemann-Perrin, Hendrik M. Vroom, and Michael Weinrich (Amsterdam: Rodopi, 2000), pp. 1-23.

time to time is filled with conflict and in no way always leads to a satisfactory conclusion.

The *semper reformanda* is directed at this process of understanding that keeps the church moving. It is therefore not the ongoing need for reformation that applies to every organization or institution, thereby avoiding relegation to the status of museum pieces. The issue is not that the church always needs to be changed or renewed — if only to ensure its status quo. The task of continual renewal is just as self-evident for the church as it is for every other institution. But the *semper reformanda* goes beyond this, to the point where the concern is not only the optimization of the practical needs of an organization. Rather, the church is to remember that it does not live out of itself and can only be the living church if it shapes its existence and perspective as a response to the continually new address by God that it hears. The *semper reformanda* points the church not to itself but beyond itself to that Word of God which it hears, to which it has to respond, and to which it is responsible. The church is vitally reminded of the fact that it is neither grounded in itself nor capable of maintaining itself. It owes not only its calling but also its preservation and mission to its living opposite, to God, i.e., to the Word of God which is continually to be heard anew and is offered to it as gospel and command.

The church's strength lies in the knowledge that it is, in principle, weak. It is not called for its own sake or to develop a particular splendor that all too quickly tempts it toward a problematic self-consciousness. Neither does it have any special authorization or qualifications that it can summon up over against the world in order to derive a special self-consciousness. It is not an institution of salvation and does not have at its disposal means of grace that it can simply distribute. It is, indeed, called upon to absolve in the name of God, i.e., to bestow forgiveness of sins, but it does so not on its own initiative or out of its own power but in the name of God, whose will is that the church *testify* to him, to his activity and will in the world.

The church exists for the sake of the glory of God. This glory is not taken seriously if the church thinks too highly of itself and awaits its own glory. Rather, the church's witness takes a central position. This witness is also the continual expression of its own relativization, while it refers to God who has indeed called the church to make his acts for the world known but who has not entrusted the church to do his work for him on the earth. The church is to testify that Christ is our representative before God, but the church does not represent God to the world. No saint or other mediator is needed, for the content of the gospel is precisely that Christ is the mediator.

These fundamental insights into the essential relative nature of the church are mirrored in its relationship to and dealing with confessions. Because a confession is not the Word of God but the *response* of the church to that

Word, it shares in the church's relativity in its continually fluctuating state. Thus, as a church that perfectly corresponds to its destiny cannot exist historically, no confession can be a response that corresponds perfectly to the address of God. Certainly, the church hopes for the presence of the Holy Spirit in its search for a response to God's address, but it cannot simply assume that this is so, and indeed, it cannot reserve this Spirit permanently for itself. In this way it will continue to have a healthy and life-preserving skepticism towards everything that it produces, so that it can readily seize the next opportunity for formulating its response better and in a more contemporary way. Not only does the formulation of a confession remain an open process in the Reformed tradition but it must remain so. This is not a devaluation of the church's previous confessions. Rather, it is for that reason that they are viewed with the highest regard, for they serve as the theologically grounded and historically preserved orientation and guide for one's own confession. They therefore enjoy particularly high esteem, for in them a suitably condensed written form of the Christian faith can be seen. But their existence does not entail that the church no longer has any need to formulate new confessions.

Confession is not only citation or adoption out of a feeling of obligation to the tradition. Rather, it is done as a living response, i.e., as a contemporary response in which the church responds not only to the Word of God that it perceives but also to the specific challenges the church faces in its time. It is certainly conceivable that a contemporary *appropriation* — which is something completely different from a citation out of obligation to tradition — of, for example, the Apostles' Creed, can be seen as a suitable answer to the contemporary challenges to the church, but this is by no means self-evident or at all compulsory. While the confession of the church, indeed, must be directed not only inward but also outward to the surrounding world, it seems to me in many cases that it is particularly undesirable that the church render itself more incomprehensible than comprehensible through citing its old formulations over against the world. If the church had only repeated the Apostles' Creed instead of formulating the Barmen Declaration (1934) at the time of National Socialism, it could hardly have called attention to the *reformanda* that was needed precisely at that point in time. The same obtains, for example, for the Belhar Confession (1982) in connection with racism, particularly in South Africa. But the numerous other confessions that have arisen precisely in the second half of the twentieth century also clarify the concrete double-sided character of the answer in the current formulation of confessions.[2]

2. Cf. *Reformiertes Zeugnis heute: Ein Sammlung neurer Bekenntnistexte aus der reformierten Tradition*, ed. Lukas Vischer (Neukirchen-Vluyn: Neukirchener Verlag, 1985; Margit Ernst, "In Leben und Tod gehören wir Gott. . . . Aspekte heutigen Bekennens am Beispiel des

While the *semper reformanda* can also be particularly related to the confessional existence of the church, confession is included with that which belongs to human action in the church. Confession belongs to the historical life of the church. The vitality of the church is not least to be detected from its ability to confess and therefore from its participation in the process of formulating a confession. The essentially open character that is thereby included in the formulation of a confession contains on the one hand a strong temptation that always arises in the Reformed tradition. On the other hand, in this openness lies a potential that has as yet been much too timidly employed, that should obtain as decisive primarily for the future, and is to be fearlessly discovered and applied.

The temptation consists in always understanding the freedom connected with this openness as an invitation to special roads and individual views that have often led to splits and separations. The particular temptation associated with the Reformed tradition is to a considerable extent the consequence of a problematic appeal to the openness of the formulation of confessions. It is problematic insofar as it consists in the claim to a contradictory mixture of freedom and a simultaneously proclaimed exclusivity. To state the matter pointedly, the openness is employed in order to put a stop to it through the use of the freedom it provides. The decisions enjoyed in the freedom made possible by it are raised to an exclusivity that is expressed in the claim that the Christian faith or the existence of the church stands or falls with the acknowledgment of that confession. This is not an awareness of openness in the sense of *semper reformanda* but a usurpation of openness for one's own options. The tradition of ecclesiastical confessions, which also had the ecumenicity of the church in view, is thus abandoned, for the church does not witness to itself but to the one church elected by Christ: "The old Confessions did not confess in order to declare apologetically outwards the individual good of a particular church or esthetically inwards in order to experience the beautiful but in order to declare: The Church that expresses this recognition is, in its place, representative of the one, holy, catholic and apostolic Church."[3]

It is certainly easier to state the problem in so pointed a way than to solve it in a concrete case. In actuality, the necessary distinctions cannot be made so clearly and simply. It is all the more important that one be as conscious as possible of the temptations that arise with every distinction, even if it means that in

---

Brief Statement of Faith — Presbyterian Church (USA), 1991," in Christoph Dahling-Sander et al., eds., *Herausgeforderte Kirche: Anstösse, Wege, Perspektiven. Eberhard Busch zum 60 Geburtstag* (Wuppertal: Foedus, 1997), pp. 441-58; Eberhard Busch, "Die Nähe der Fernen — Reformierte Bekenntnisse nach 1945," in Michael Welker and David Willis, eds., *Zur Zukunft der Reformierten Theologie: Aufgaben, Themen, Traditionen* (Neukirchen-Vluyn: Neukirchener Verlag, 1998), pp. 587-606.

3. Busch, "Die Nähe der Fernen," p. 592.

a particular case a false road will be taken. This temptation — to which every church is susceptible — to become a particular church looms especially large in the Reformed tradition, because this tradition virtually invites a church not only to be content with the traditional confessions but also to take upon itself its own responsibility for the open formulation of confessions. The confessions must be *inclusive* with respect to the *invisible* church confessed in faith and thus keep the catholicity of the church in view. We succumb to the temptation, however, if the confession is *exclusive* with respect to the *visible* church that expresses the confession.

To be sure, in assessing the fragmented ecclesiastical landscape caution is needed. It would be very one-sided if we saw only a particularist obstinacy in this landscape. One cause for this landscape that is to be judged completely differently can also be found in the exalted significance that the nonhierarchical Reformed ecclesiology attaches to the congregation. According to the Reformed understanding, the congregation is not the smallest cell of a church that exists above it. It does not represent a church existing apart from it but is viewed as the nucleus of a church that develops out of it. The fragmentation can, at least partially, be seen as the expression of the plurality of churches. This decentralized, congregation-oriented ecclesiology is mobile enough to enter into the highly different living conditions of churches with their different challenges. It does not support any compulsion towards a homogeneity that subjects all churches to the same self-understanding and expects an identical orientation in doctrine and life. Rather, the principal openness in the formation of confessions means a desired flexibility of the churches towards a specific contextuality. It takes into account the fact that confessions, if they are not to evaporate into abstract generalities, can be continually expressed "in the relatively manageable space . . . of a concretely responsible group."[4] It is from this that the conclusion that there is no global Reformed confession receives its absolutely compelling material evidence.

This addresses the positive potential of openness, which encounters its admittedly ambivalent forms of existence in schisms within the church. The special potential of openness lies rather in the function of gathering together. It does not have an exclusive but an inclusive perspective; it grants a genuine right of existence to plurality and binds it to the common basis of the biblical witness for direction, which is sufficient to safeguard precisely the predicate of catholicity that was also highly esteemed by Protestantism. It is the same Word of God that people hear in different situations and under quite different circumstances. That is the decisive catholic basis that admits a plurality as wide as that already found in the biblical witness. It was precisely the actual ecclesiastical use of the

---

4. Busch, "Die Nähe der Fernen," p. 590.

controversial writing that was, incidentally, one of the decisive criteria in the formation of the canon — thus an aspect that was directed at the catholicity of the church.[5] This openness thus had its focus and limits in the catholicity that was to be preserved. Consequently, openness proves to be a fundamental qualification for an ecumenicity that is conceived not from the perspective of homogeneity but from that of a biblically grounded catholicity. The Reformed tradition is, in line with its essence, an ecumenical tradition directed at plurality and difference. That is, in my view, an essential dimension of the Reformed self-understanding, whose significance and range have remained undiscovered until now. The flexibility based on the individual congregations' right to self-determination represents a specifically modern acquisition that until now has not been confidently applied.

The View of the Scriptures

The Reformed annulment of the authoritative magisterium of the church and consequently its canceling of the difference between the clergy who mediated salvation and the people of the church, the laity, is connected to an incomparable revaluation of the Bible. Until then the Bible was protected by the magisterium installed by the clergy so that it stood not only over against the laity but also with the interpretative authority of the church which, on its own initiative, became dominant through appealing to its special spiritual gift. The ecclesiastical magisterium provided the desired clarity and perspicuity of the Bible and decided in cases of conflict how a disputed statement was to be understood. Indeed, the priority of Scripture was also always emphasized by the magisterium, but in fact the decision-making powers of the magisterium meant a dominance of the church over Scripture. If necessary, the authority of the church over against the Scripture was explicitly grounded in the claim that because the biblical canon was finally the work of the church inspired by the Holy Spirit, the church was also entitled to decide how it was to be correctly understood, an argumentation that is represented in the orthodox tradition up until the present as almost unapproachably obvious. The Reformation consistently placed all office-bearers within the congregation, and the specially emphasized interpretative authority of the magisterium within the church was lost, with the result that, since then, on the one hand no spiritual ranks were to be distinguished within the church and, on the other, the Bible now became the sole foundation for the orientation of the church. In the Reformation the Bible was

---

5. Heinrich Karpp, "Schrift, Geist und Wort Gottes," *Geltung und Wirkung der Bibel in der Geschichte der Kirche* (Darmstadt: Wissenschaftliche Buchgesellschaft, 1992).

given an exclusivity that was previously nowhere to be found in the church in a comparable way.[6] It is both an inevitable and far-reaching standard, to which the *semper reformanda* of the church has to be oriented. The simplicity and clarity of this standard will always be disputed, but such discussions are a fundamental element of a living church.

The inclusion of the clergy within the congregation resulted in a concentration of the full authority and normativity on the Bible, for it now assumed the whole of the authority that had been allotted to the clergy until that time. That is, it was now allotted the authority that it had had to share with the magisterium. Through its special inspiration it was exalted in principle to a position above the inspiration of the clergy and the congregation who interpreted it. It now stood alone for the presence of the Spirit in which it would be made clear and unambiguous *(sui ipsius interpres)*. The exclusivity that was hereby transferred to it can in a certain sense be understood as a sacralization of the Bible. This did not mean a transportation of the Bible to heaven or an untouchable mystification of its contents. Rather, it meant a spiritual and theological gain in authority, for now the Scripture alone, *sola scriptura,* was the source of content and the material criterion *(fons et index)* for the recognition of faith. Holy Scripture, with reference to the Holy Spirit, was no longer in competition with the ordained clergy but alone possessed the gift *par excellence* for making the Holy Spirit and his effects known. Because a trustworthy power for orientation is given only to the biblical witness and not to those — more or less pious — people who interpret it, the Bible is brought into a hermeneutically necessary proximity to the Holy Spirit, for it is finally not only the letter that convinces and brings one closer to faith, even if, as evidence, it is thought to attain an unusually high level (external clarity). It is rather through the Spirit, in whom the Bible is written as a human witness, that it is given its faith-awakening clarity and is able to help one achieve a certainty grounded in God himself.[7] The effect of the Reformation in making the congregation answerable only to Scripture was that the Bible became the preferred place for the encounter with the promised Holy Spirit. This was not a Bible that was viewed as obscure,[8] at least not generally, and clarified by a magisterium that was spiritually gifted for this task. Rather, it was a Bible that proved itself (externally and internally) to be true through itself, that is, through the Spirit of God who was con-

---

6. Michael Weinrich, "Die Bibel legt sich selber aus," in *Die Bibel. Das bekannte Buch — das fremde Buch,* ed. Hubert Frankemölle (Paderborn: F. Schöningh, 1994), pp. 43-59.

7. Martin Luther, "De servo arbitrio" [1525], WA 18, pp. 606ff.

8. First by Tertullian and finally also by Erasmus in his dispute with Luther on the interpretation of Scripture (Erasmus, *Vom freien Willen,* trans. O. Schumacher, 4th ed. (Göttingen: Vandenhoeck & Ruprecht, 1979), pp. 12f.

nected with its witness in a special way. *Sola scriptura* did not signify a paper pope, as the anti-Reformation polemic was wont to say. It comes decisively down to the Spirit who stands behind the letter, to the promise of the Spirit to turn even our contemporary explanations and imaginings into a promising undertaking. The Spirit of the inspiration of the Bible — not of the individual words or letters(!) — is precisely the Spirit who makes us expect the special nature of the Bible and its exegesis in the present time as well. That is the sacralization of the Bible that resulted from the desacralization of the church, which gave it an incomparably vulnerable place in the church.

Because the church lives out of its communication with the biblical witness, the Reformation placed the Bible not only *over against* the congregation but at the same time also *within* it in a particular way. The immediacy of the congregation's access to the Bible was also a special theological acknowledgment of the congregation as expressed particularly in the idea of the priesthood of all believers. The church must not draw its nourishment through secondary means, because it itself was considered worthy and capable of embarking on a "search for nourishment" and to judge for itself what was important and not important. The Bible itself was impressive enough to be seen and considered as actually authoritative — i.e., trustworthy and reliable — on the basis of its content.[9] This was an attack on dogma, the more or less orthodox church doctrine with its somewhat fantastic speculations. Here the Reformers had in view the logically formal scholasticism of the late Middle Ages, which had reached the point of absurdity. The witness of the Bible with all its embarrassments and surprises, with all its living drama and continual wrestling with the presence of God, its plurality and simultaneous focus on the wholly inscrutable God who guides history, stands incomparably closer to life than all the conceptually oriented teachings of dogmatics. According to the Reformed self-understanding, the Bible is the decisive instrument through which God builds up and preserves the congregation. Therefore, constant communication with the Bible is the decisive result also of the Reformation's theological recognition of the congregation. Here also it concerns an openness, a process that always refers to something beyond itself, in which the congregation above all is not preoccupied with itself but seeks to fulfill its special calling and mission correctly. Objectively, the openness of the formation of confessions sketched above remains grounded finally in the subordination of the confessions to the Scripture, which always speaks afresh.

9. This was the opposite of "authoritarian," i.e., requiring unconditional, uncritical obedience.

The Worldliness of the Church

Dietrich Bonhoeffer explicitly reminded the church of the fact that it exists not for itself but for others,[10] i.e., it exists for the world. The radicality of this *pro-existence* of the church, however, is realized only if one also keeps in mind Reformational ecclesiology, i.e., the view that the church is itself part of the world.[11] If the word 'world' is used in what follows in a somewhat cryptic way, this is not because of a Johannine inclination towards distantiation nor to a secret reproach to paganism. It simply has to do with the society still stamped by a secularized self-consciousness, by which the church in western and central Europe is surrounded and with which the church's boundaries are entirely fluctuating. The church is part of a society that does not understand itself above Christianity, from which it cannot separate itself, and to which at the same time it also finds itself to be an opposite, which is to be defined more closely. The definition of the relationship to be used here is typified somewhat by the concepts 'church' and 'world.'

If the church seeks a responsible relationship to the 'world,' it must remember its own worldliness, for without that perception the church all too easily becomes trapped in an artificial opposition to the 'world' in which it believes, on the basis of a certain superiority, that the 'world' can benefit from it in some way. If, on the contrary, it believes that it shares in the embarrassment of the 'world,' that it cannot prove the existence of God any more than the 'world' can prove his nonexistence, then its relation to the surrounding 'world' is determined by an essential connectedness and solidarity, from which every concept of above and below remains excluded. The recognition of the church's own worldliness is not in the first place an ethical question but one belonging to the field of systematic theology.

There are at least three possible ways for the church to understand its relationship to the 'world,' and to view its own worldliness. The *first* possibility consists in the church simply seeking to appropriate the self-understanding of the 'world' as its own. It acknowledges — not without high appreciation — the maturity of the 'world' and establishes the genuine agreement of the gospel with the freedom realized by the 'world,' so that it attains complete solidarity with the nonreligious world precisely where freedom is promoted. The church becomes the advocate for freedom that has in the meantime become secularized, feeling, on the basis of the gospel, also responsible for the advancement

---

10. Dietrich Bonhoeffer, *Widerstand und Ergebung,* Dietrich Bonhoeffer Werke 8 (Gütersloh: C. Kaiser, 1998), p. 560.

11. Cf. the whole section in Michael Weinrich, *Kirche glauben: Evangelische Annäherungen an eine ökumenische Ekklesiologie* (Wuppertal: Foedus, 1998), pp. 49-65.

and maintenance of this freedom. It does so above all by helping the 'world,' which is trapped in the problem of self-explanation, discover the necessary blessing of a total meaning that the church is to preserve from all ideological petrifications in which the freedom that has been gained will inevitably be squandered. The church succeeds in this through a theological interpretation of *secularization,* which it then seeks to mark off as impressively as possible from the temptation toward *secularism,* the end of which is nothing other than the loss of the freedom that was expected. In the preservation of their created freedom, in which human beings realize their destiny as beings capable of history, the salvation of human beings is completed. "Thus, the salvation that is realized by God and only by him occurs in this independence of the decision which is given to the human being in his concrete historical existence."[12] Barth speaks of such an extroverted self-understanding of the church pursuing the 'world,' and the offer that the church gives to the 'world' to become ideologically rounded off, as the "church in defect."[13]

The *second* possibility points exactly in the opposite direction, by mourning the spreading secularization as the specific danger for a society that is endangering itself. Only religion gives society an integrating center without which it falls apart. The obvious process of decline in modern society will continue to the extent that "the needed reflection on the religious foundations of Western ideas that are normative for political life and the political order is avoided or deferred."[14] In order to counteract the "devitalization and barbarization" of a secularist society tumbling downwards in an "indifferentist pluralism,"[15] a powerful reunited world-church is hoped for in which the 'world' can be given an example of unity and integrity that will serve as a model for its politics. The church that has been driven from the center of the village by secularization will once again become the center of a directionless 'world' that has shrunk to a village, in which the superiority of Christianity has already been proven historically. It is this specific superiority of the church, which has taken upon itself a specific responsibility for the 'world,' that the 'world' on its own cannot see as appropriate. If the first possibility of understanding the relation between the church and the 'world' tends in the direction of the self-dissolution of the church into the secular 'world,' this second possibility ex-

---

12. Friedrich Gogarten, *Verhängnis und Hoffnung der Neuzeit,* 2nd ed. (Gütersloh: Gütersloher Verlagshaus Gerd Mohn, 1987), p. 204.

13. Karl Barth, *Das christliche Leben.* Die Kirchliche Dogmatik IV/4. Fragmente aus dem Nachlaß., ed. H. A. Drewes and E. Jüngel (Zürich: Theologischer Verlag Zürich, 1976), pp. 227-31.

14. Wolfhart Pannenberg, *Anthropology in Theological Perspective* (Philadelphia: Westminster Press, 1985), p. 478.

15. Pannenberg, *Anthropology in Theological Perspective,* p. 484.

pects a conversion of the 'world' to the authoritative orientations as they are now to be found only within the church. It can certainly be conceded that for both Roman Catholic and Orthodox ecclesiology such orientations are to be seen as self-evident, but if Protestantism proposes such an understanding — as happens when Pannenberg argues for an isolated surpassing of all theoretical apologies of religion centering on function — one can only be extremely surprised. Obviously, clericalism seems to be the first and ineradicable temptation for the church.

The *third* possibility does not run exactly between the two possibilities sketched above, as one might imagine by way of a kind of compromise, but is independent of them, for it does not assume an opposition between the church and 'world' that determines the understanding of the relation. Rather, the church is itself part of the 'world,' continually related in a dynamic way to its environment and inconceivable apart from this relation. It is not to be distinguished in principle from the surrounding 'world' but only in that it sees the 'world' that it shares with all other people in a particular light. Because the church's starting point is that the 'world' is not self-explanatory and that its reality becomes evident only by means of a certain interpretation, it is already in discussion with the 'world' on the need for explaining the 'world.' But also because the church cannot present its particular perception of the 'world' in any way that is certain and clear (because it is not capable of demonstrating God to the 'world' simply, it can speak of God and his history with human beings in principle only in questionable ways), at the same time it shares with the 'world' the unavoidable embarrassment of not being able to prove its particular interpretation of reality as either generally evident or at all compelling. Also, if it speaks of God, it does so while standing with both feet on the ground of this 'world,' thus rendering any kind of special view into heaven impossible and every explanation subject to general skepticism and doubt. Thus, as the 'world' that does not believe in God cannot take its nonknowledge of God as compelling proof for his nonexistence, so the church that is certain of its God cannot, on its own initiative, lay the foundation of proof for his living effects. It proves to be, not last of all, a part of this 'world' in sharing with the 'world' embarrassment over the final foundation of its self-understanding.

Conversely, it witnesses to a God who is not only with the church but is active in the whole 'world.' The message that is the subject of the church's discussion with the surrounding 'world' witnesses to the completed reconciliation of *the world* with God in Christ (2 Cor. 5:19), i.e., from the start it is neither a private ecclesiastical message nor an advertisement by which the church can be distinguished as a particular entity. The difference between the church and the 'world' proves in this case to be most relative, for Christ also stands over against his church as he stands over against the 'world.' The people in the surrounding 'world' and the people in the church are created by God, who as such stand over against their Creator.

In this theological perspective, as it is presented in a specific way by *Karl Barth*, the church is bound in a constitutive way to the 'world' around it in its self-understanding, without drawing its self-consciousness from the current self-consciousness of the 'world.' The church neither curries favor with the 'world' nor gets carried away in an imposition of its will upon it. Whereas the church can only *witness* to God or *confess* him in the 'world,' it shares with the 'world' the suffering of the hiddenness of God. Its advantage consists merely in the belief that God can be called upon in Jesus Christ as the one in whom God's participation in this 'world' is actually carried out.

In the perception of its worldliness the church can and should, in fact, be an example for the 'world,' for the 'world' is in no way free from the inclination to explain itself by another religious or ideological means. Barth can say that the church is more profane than the 'world' around it:

> In the Church the limits of what is human is preserved and guarded, in the Church no gods are worshipped, in the Church no ideologies are cultivated, in the Church the human being must see and understand himself soberly. . . . The mystery of the world is, however, the non-existence of its gods. And it costs the world tears and blood enough that it must always again deny this mystery and would populate nature and history with gods. The basis for its unrest is its refusal to confess its profanity. The Church knows of this mystery of the world. It should not allow itself to be disconcerted by small reproaches and accusations. It is precisely in that that it maintains faithfulness with the world.[16]

Thus, it can in no way be a matter of the church attempting to outdo the world religiously. All too quickly it becomes lost in one of the religions forbidden by the first commandment and therewith falls back into its "heathen" past. The Reformed tradition has been particularly aware of this danger of the church — falling back into "paganism" — in distinction from the Lutheran tradition, which is more inclined to being attentive to the lurking danger of works righteousness (and therewith the fall back into Judaism).[17] If the general issue is one of surpassing the 'world,' it can be such only in humanity and worldliness. Only in that way can the church effectively resist the temptation towards a cleri-

---

16. Karl Barth, "Offenbarung, Kirche, Theologie," in *Theologische Fragen und Antworten*, Gesammelte Vorträge 3 (Zollikon: Evangelischer Verlag, 1957), pp. 169f.

17. Busch, "Die Nähe der Fernen," pp. 598f., appealing to A. Schweitzer, who maintained in his doctrinal works "that we see the Lutherans (sc. Protestantism) as turning out primarily to be anti-Jewish and the Reformed anti-pagan."

calism that attempts to unfold its ignominious power in the exercise of religious domination, which precisely is "the most fearsome, quite simply monstrous form of human domination" in that it presents "a greater or lesser domination of the conscience through external or intellectual means in the name of God."[18] Every attempt of the church to place itself over against the 'world' will make the fallenness of the church visible to the 'world.' While it wishes to demonstrate to the 'world' in this way above all the misery of the God who has fallen into the hands of men, it feeds above all the skepticism towards the message of the humanity of God.

The promise lies only in that the church actually lets itself be placed in the 'world' in order to appeal to God and to pray in the power of the Holy Spirit that it will not take part in the incessant attempts at self-sanctification and becoming unworldly with which the 'world' attempts to deceive itself about its creaturely finitude. Furthermore, in a consistent continuation in prayer there is much to do, both in the congregation and in the everyday 'world.' That is the double openness of the church, the openness of an actual contemporaneity that will not be realized without reflection on the living presence of God nor without a concrete reference to the order of the day in the 'world,' with all its difficulties and embarrassments. Both here and there it concerns our living worldly answer, which on the one hand comes out of hearing, understanding, and repeating the history that God has traveled and travels today with his people and on the other hand in living and being open to the contemporary context, with the responsibility that implies. This is one dimension of the *semper reformanda* that the Reformed tradition emphasizes particularly strongly. Here the cosmopolitan qualification of Christian existence becomes accessible through the gospel: "You are the light of the world. A city on a hill cannot be hidden. Neither do people light a lamp and put it under a bowl. Instead they put it on its stand, and it gives light to everyone in the house. In the same way, let your light shine before men, that they may see your good deeds and praise your Father in heaven" (Matt. 5:14-16).

The Distress of the Church

The Reformational demythologization of the church places the church with both feet on the ground of this world. This grounding does not only give the 'world' the status of the natural environment of the church but at the same time stresses the genuine relationship the church has with the 'world.' In the Protestant view, the church exists entirely on the grassroots level, within the horizontal dimension along with the whole of humanity.

18. Barth, "Offenbarung," p. 173.

But to be connected with humanity means above all to be acquainted with its misery, its suffering, its tears, and therefore also with its longing and hope. Whoever lives on this earth, rather than in an exalted artificial reality, hears the sighing of the creatures in distress. If we, as the most well-situated members of affluent societies, do not drown out that sighing with the noise with which we gladly surround ourselves, then we have no choice when perceiving the misery of this 'world' but to join in with this sighing ourselves. The reality of this *distress* is so evident — only acute deafness or total blindness can ignore it — that in respect to them the question of the *expectations* or of the *needs* of people that has been posed by the church for its own self-renewal suddenly fades or is even given a cynical tone. Obviously, modern people, presenting themselves as enlightened, are so successful in suppressing the actual distress that even in the church the question of the expectations and needs is in no way felt to be misplaced. A course is thus indicated that substantially exhausts speech and action in the church, so that in the church its essential openness to the actual distress of humankind needs to be recalled. The church's solidarity with the 'world' is not to be presented in the obligingness with which it offers itself for the satisfaction of this or that need[19] but in its attempt by its witness to free human beings from the apparent need to defy their finitude.

The question of expectations and needs gives rise — if actually seriously intended — to the appearance that everything is open. The self-evidence of the misery of human existence is denied or proportioned in the form of a wish that can be limited. The *great distress* of the human being, i.e., having to limit his life in view of the permanent decay into nothingness, will be drawn, by and large, by the shift in a space shaped by expectations and needs where it is trapped in a proximity — equally egalitarian and fictive — to a profusion of small inevitable needs, so that inevitably all resistant hopes that go beyond the feasible will at the least be cut off.[20] More and more we in the church are also looking at only that which can be managed, that which can be directed and guaranteed by us.

That obtains at least for that part of humanity which against the background of the high level of satisfaction of needs does not pose either first or final questions but merely inquires into optimizing a life that is already assured of its fundamental needs. In a friendly turn we can allow ourselves to be addressed by Friedrich Schleiermacher who stated: "You have succeeded in making the earthly life so rich and multifaceted that you no longer need eternity, and since you have created a universe yourself you feel no need to think about

---

19. Cf. on this Weinrich, *Kirche glauben*, pp. 21-48.

20. Cf. for a different treatment with respect to content but with a related focus Karl Barth, "Die Not der evangelischen Kirche," *Zwischen den Zeiten* 9 (1931): 89-122.

that which has created you."[21] That the fullness can become emptiness is effectively blocked through the fact that the fullness continually produces new needs and therefore keeps people busy in wanting still more and better things. In a permanent climate of increase, new perspectives of optimization are made or artificially produced. The principle of a restless life obtains, as was formulated already in the seventeenth century by Thomas Hobbes as characteristic for the modern period: "Felicity, therefore, (by which we mean continual delight), consisteth not in having prospered but in prospering."[22] The relatively assured fundamental needs and the restless activity in the service of a self-maintaining fulfillment are the prevailing conditions for the people described by Schleiermacher as content with this world, who have made themselves relatively weatherproof against the first and final questions. The expectations and needs are limited to the space that we have created for them. And thus the question of expectations and needs is immediately connected to the duties that we pursue anyway. Probably it is for that reason that the question seems so obvious. It can certainly be doubted whether we are actually aware here of the limited range of this question of needs.

The *distress* arises as the great misery of the human being, not in the space of the too optimizing self-organization by human beings but from beyond the limits of our possibilities. Its unapproachable and therefore so readily suppressed character makes a difference in that it confronts us not with our own possibilities but sets before us with our impossibilities the limitation of these possibilities that can be set in motion by us. Human self-consciousness remains challenged by the reality of their finitude. The human need that appears here can certainly be more or less successfully suppressed for a time, and this suppression can also be organized to a certain extent in society — as our postmodern experiential world brings home to us thoroughly and impressively — but it cannot be eliminated. It could be shown without difficulty that it exercises its suppression subcutaneously in defiance of a scarcely overrated power in our individual and social lives. Perhaps its power is even greater when one seeks to suppress it.

If we speak of the church, then certainly all the small needs of human beings are not unimportant, especially since they can also vary in importance. To look at this fully would require a separate paper and I will not elaborate on it here. But certainly in the church the great human misery should come into view in a special way from the knowledge that humans can only escape it tem-

21. Friedrich Schleiermacher, *Über die Religion. Reden an die Gebildeten unter ihren Verächtern*, ed. Rudolf Otto, 7th rev. ed. (Göttingen: Vandenhoeck & Ruprecht, 1991), p. 19.
22. Thomas Hobbes, *The Elements of Law, Natural and Politic*, ed. Ferdinand Tönnies, 2nd ed. (London: Frank Cass & Co., Ltd., 1969), p. 30.

porarily. The church should know that not infrequently in dealing with the minor needs the "invisible hand" of the great need also moves unnoticed in the background. It should maintain a particular, distinctive *sensorium* for all the deceptive ideas and explanations in order to remain open also to the distress to which the 'world' all too willingly attempts to turn a deaf ear.

Certainly the church also does not simply stand outside the distress that has been indicated — this distress cannot be escaped in this world. But the church contradicts the abysmal loneliness in which human beings are placed by that distress. It contradicts the eloquent monologue of the shrill silence of the violent cutting back of life's unfolding as it is present to all every day. It does not contradict it because it experiences something other than the 'world' around it. Neither does it not contradict it because it can look successfully beyond the borders of our finitude — thus as if it could see beyond — and thus could delight the 'world' with some conjectures about the beyond. It does not contradict it on the basis of some privileges that have been granted to it but because it does not see human beings as bounded by nothingness. In the place of the nothingness with which death threatens us stands God, who as Creator and Redeemer does not wish to abandon humanity to the self-depression of its empirical knowledge of the world. While the church shares in this experience, which confirms the finitude of the world, at the same time it hears the promise of God. Because it trusts this promise it has to witness to the 'world' in word and deed that it is not the distress that is the true motor of all worldly events. Rather, in the midst of the doubt and distress it confesses that the 'world' has not been abandoned to itself but has an opposite that is turned toward it, which has combined itself with the destiny of the 'world' in a simply salvific way so that in all its distress the 'world' can create courage and hope out of that.

It is certainly not given to the church — as has already been indicated — to demonstrate convincingly to the 'world' that it speaks of more than the strange self-prescription of a Baron von Münchhausen, who pulled himself out of the quagmire by his own hair. The church is and remains part of this 'world.' The church is not called to romp about in the "Beyond." The "Beyond" becomes accessible to the church only when it is recognized in the here and now, i.e., if it reveals itself, whereby this revelation cannot become simply subjected to the conditions of this world. Revelation does not authorize demonstrations; it corresponds to confession and witness. The *missio* of the church is realized in that; it is to confess and to witness to the special turning of God to the world.

And thus in this respect everything that the church can do and not do is, at bottom, never something that arises out of itself. The church is not the earthly agent of God but his worldly *witness* (Acts 1:8). The Protestant church is a worldly church in that it knows that it does not possess God's Word, does not manage it, and does not distribute it more or less generously. The church itself has to hear the Word continually anew, always has to seek it anew like manna in the desert. That is the fundamental meaning of *semper reformanda*. This does not produce any triumphalism of possession and salvation, no pleasure in religion and no guarantee of durability. Every emotionalism on the part of one who confesses is just as inappropriate as the substitution of faith for the vision of God. Rather, the world remains, even if it is caught in the living light of God, a world in which the trees do not grow into heaven. Faith remains faith and that means also that the certainty recognized by it is continually given over to the challenge of experience.[23] Faith continually transcends what one can see and that is what makes it so fragile and delicate. It is always more hope than fulfillment and thus includes, in accordance with its essence, the complaint that we do not yet see what we believe.

Confessional Existence Today

In a final intellectual turn we will, with respect to the openness of the church, direct our attention to a specific phenomenon in the currently perceptible management crisis in the church, which is in no way only a German issue but has an absolutely ecumenical dimension — particularly in the welfare societies of the so-called First World where the churches currently find themselves in a drastic crisis. In this crisis too the reference to the openness of the church can mobilize the necessary *Reformational* forces, whereas the orientation to ecclesiastical existence brings the *restorative* forces into play. With this a continually recurring fundamental problem in the perception of the *semper reformanda* is addressed.

People readily describe the crisis of the church by means of the concept of a *break with tradition*. This is intended to mean first a major loss of religious socialization in societies that have in the meantime become widely secularized. Most recently, the church has in fact become a *terra incognita* for the children of the members who have become distanced from it. In religious education those who still hope that religious education or confirmation as well as adult church education can somehow find a point of contact in existing knowledge are fighting a losing battle. The most elementary assumptions of which we until recently perhaps asserted a little boldly that they belonged to the obvious field of general education can no longer be made. If until recently, for example, teachers complained that the children knew hardly any biblical stories, many consider themselves lucky if children in general have any knowledge of keys words like "church," "Bible," or

---

23. Cf. Michael Weinrich, "Die Anfechtung des Glaubens. Die Spannung zwischen Gewissheit und Erfahrung bei Martin Luther," in Christoph Landmesser et al., eds., *Jesus Christus als die Mitte der Schrift*, BZNW 86 (Berlin: de Gruyter, 1997), pp. 127-58.

even "Jesus." An illiteracy regarding Christianity is spreading, which in no way stops at the doors of the university. Thus, for example, one can read in the notes of a German dissertation the comment that ". . . for they do not know what they are doing" (Luke 23:34) is the German title of the James Dean film *Rebel Without a Cause*.[24] This illiteracy is reflected not least of all in the extremely awkward, if not entirely distorted, press reports on ecclesiastical events or conflicts.

On another level this "break with tradition" is encountered in an almost unlimited indifference towards the confessional profile of the church. Thus, for example, the governing bodies of Protestant churches are attacked because of some statement made by the pope. Every defense of a theologically grounded position is as a rule lost on the public from the start, because obviously the level on which theological sentences are formulated and on which one is to struggle with theological sentences is completely dismissed as a relevant area of communication. The result is that every theological ethos seems to be foreign if not entirely perverse — I think here only of the theme of the virgin birth and the all-too-simple slip of the tongue, which, for example, Eugen Drewermann introduced into the discussion by insisting that the crucial emphasis of the tradition would be on Mary's intact hymen. It is easy to reject such a ridiculous position, and such a rejection will be confirmed immediately by the general public. At present the churches are constantly in the questionable situation of having to respond to one theological absurdity or another. Here they are basically fighting a losing battle before they even open their mouths, for the level of argument which is in no way without presuppositions, in which faith struggles for understanding, is more or less consistently excluded from general communication. The result is that the churches can no longer be made suitably understandable — at best major simplifications are involved that exclude every complex argument. The churches, in their notorious theological abstinence, are certainly not entirely uninvolved in this pauperization. It is easier than ever today to attack the church with all kinds of trite antipathies that have certainly not arisen without reason. But this does not mean that they are always on target. The churches are currently confronted with a radical loss of the confessional dimension and an accompanying loss of theology — putting all abstinence from theology until now in the shade — which has already had its effect on the expectations of many students of theology.[25]

The description of this situation is one thing; how it is to be interpreted

---

24. Ebach, "Das bekannte Buch — das fremde Buch. Die Bibel," in Frankemölle, ed., *Die Bibel*, p. 7.

25. As soon as the theological abstinence of the churches is critically noted, it should then be confessed, with respect to the theological abstinence of students of theology, that an academic theology, equally complacent and introverted — as is dominant at least in German-speaking areas — has contributed in no mean way to this development.

and then changed is another. One interpretation should certainly be excluded from the start, for we can get away too easily by placing the blame one-sidedly on the increasing decadence of society that also stamps our churches. In the general discussion the churches favor a different perspective for interpretation. They speak of a drastic *break with tradition* and promote a regaining of the *identity* of the church. However, this interpretation is also problematic. With respect to analysis, the concept of a break with tradition does not go far enough and with respect to constructive attempts, the concept of identity points in a false direction. Both objections should be somewhat elaborated.

Undoubtedly, far beyond the everyday praxis of the churches, there is something like a wide break with tradition in our society. Nobody will seriously deny this. However, a more accurate look reveals that in the church much more is at stake than the break with tradition. It does not only concern the loss of customs and usages, not only the passing away of traditional frameworks of orientation and lifestyles, but it also concerns the dimension of confession that is essential for the church. The loss of the confessional dimension was greeted as if it meant the overcoming of confessionalist petrifications. But the cut goes deeper and does not only concern the dissolution of formulations of the traditional confessions and the accompanying theological intellectual background. Rather, it concerns the act of confession itself. The hostility is directed not only at the recitation — that would be the break with tradition — but also beyond this at the act of confession in general. It would be exciting if the church would begin a truly beneficial discussion on the current treatment of the traditional confessions, but what I see in our culture is an attack on the confessional existence of the church and an essential questioning of the church in general.

The rhetoric of the break with tradition is a *playing down* of the situation, for it is not able to mark the critical boundary where the break with tradition and the substance of the church is the issue. One should note that it does not concern the preservation of a certain confessional tradition of the church but that which belongs to the essence of the church — that it came into being for something and can state the reasons for its existence. If it no longer wishes to confess, the church must abandon its role of witnessing to the reconciliation of the world with God. The church can forget about every substantial reflection on its mission, every speaking of a *missio* if it no longer bears the marks of unwieldiness that the promises of God entail. To avoid all misunderstanding as much as possible I will also attempt to use the word "confessionality" very sparsely and speak instead of the completion of a *confessorial* existence of the church. The accent lies on the completion of participation, on the act of entering for the witness of faith into the conflicts of the present. Confessorial existence is the expression for the church wanting to remain the church and not accepting being only one religion among others, which it admittedly is but also not only that. If the current danger of the church in its confessorial substance is taken into view, that it is not enough to speak of a break with tradition, then the term glosses over the actual explosiveness and temptation concealed in the present radical change.

The general answer to the established break with tradition in ecumenicity seems to me to be the tendency towards reconfessionalization that can be seen since the beginning of the 1990s. In the different attempts at reconfessionalization the concept of *identity* constantly reappears. This takes us to the second objection to the general diagnosis and therapy of our contemporary crisis that I wish to consider.[26]

Many of the church's efforts, particularly in theological respects, are, in my view, associated above all with the slogan: "Forward into the Past." The recollection of one's own tradition is announced as a means of salvation against the loss of the tradition. The memory of allegedly better times is recalled in order to gain promising perspectives for present problems. In those days, since the church represented something and was not timid, it could present itself in a firm way — most certainly helpful to authorities. In order to deal with the present erosion, the church should above all first gain more self-awareness. Its own identity is called the precondition for entering into dialogue with others. The retreat into itself is looked upon as a precondition for a promising participation in general discourse. This obtains for the general discussion among the churches, thus for ecumenicity — including interreligious dialogue — as well as for the discussion with the 'world,' whatever the latter may mean.

To me, the concept of identity seems to have brought with it precisely that which the church has not infrequently attacked as the modern "mania of finding oneself." In this use the extremely blurry concept of identity acquires the profile that one becomes aware of oneself and through the description of one's distinction from others is invigorated in order thus to strengthen one's own self-awareness. At the moment the fact that it concerns a search which from the point of view of the social sciences is illusory should perhaps occupy us less than the strangely ecclesiological longing that places its hope in such a process of yield-oriented identity formation.

The problem arises not only from the fact that the church wishes to be something for itself but also and primarily from the fact that it believes it can recapture this on the basis of the strengths of its particular tradition. In this process of self-renewal, one should note, mention is made not only of the rediscovery of the biblical roots or the biblical promises for the church in the world

---

26. Cf. also Michael Weinrich, "'Christian Identity': The Challenges of the Upheavals in Europe. Aspects of Christian Living in the Contemporary World," in *"Who Are We Called to Be?," Regional Reports on Reformed Self-understanding* (Geneva: World Alliance of Reformed Churches [Department of Theology], Document B 4 c. 1993).

— here indeed an actual *ecumenical* point of departure for the church presents itself — but also explicitly of the Roman Catholic tradition, the Protestant heritage, or the Orthodox way. The present ecumenical moratorium still has, in my view, its ground in this restorative tendency of reconfessionalization. The extent to which the theological imagination of an ecumenical rediscovery of ecclesiology reaches back is the extent to which theology presents itself as an advocate of the past. The theological courage for forward-looking steps in ecclesiology from an all-too-hesitant self-understanding has been strongly restrained in the ecumenical movement until now. In general only the voice of the tradition was allowed to speak; i.e., dialogue was entered into with what had been brought along and which one now attempted to place on stage in the exchange so that it agreed with other positions or at least appeared to be capable of being connected.[27] With respect to its understanding of the church, ecumenicity has not succeeded in developing its own vision which would in fact challenge the different confessions and denominations for the church, whereas it did succeed with respect to the conciliar process in the area of ethics. That has become particularly clear in the present crisis: the churches in their efforts at reform did not place their traditions in ecumenical perspective but attempted to reflect on that which they by themselves saw as tenable and capable of bearing the strain. The discovery of confessional identity can, against this background, be described as an attempt at retreat. The question of "Where did we come from?" takes precedence over the question of "Where are we going?"

Here the impression seems to be confirmed that, if confession is an issue, it is primarily a matter of retreat. This certainly does not only involve the fact that conservative Christians like to present themselves as the true keepers of the confessions. However, this retrospective use of the confessions is justified neither by the essence of the historical confessions nor by the confessional dimension of the essence of the churches. Rather, the issue in the formulation of the confessions is continually that the church has to respond to a certain contemporary challenge. It is never concerned with *preservation* of the tradition but always with the *proof* of its worth for the future. That which is obvious from, for example, the Barmen Declaration — that the church must respond to a concrete, historical challenge — obtains in specific ways for all confessions in church history. Their perspective was continually that of testing, of the direction-giving participation, which also precisely could not be completely answered by a recitation of the tradition but needed its own contemporary *instrumentarium* in which the church had to formulate its own responsibility to its time. Only in retrospect do confessions become tradition, for when they are

27. Michael Weinrich, *Ökumene am Ende? Plädoyer für einen neuen Realismus* (Neukirchen-Vluyn: Neukirchener Verlag, 1995), pp. 59ff., 67ff.

formulated their concern for the perception of the present applies with respect to the future. We would also then understand the confessions of the past much better, if the concrete challenges to which they had reacted, the conflicts they sought to resolve, or the concrete endangerment or temptation they had sought to reject were still present, so that we would have some sense of the drama behind them that has today been silenced through their liturgical recitation.

A church that gives up asking about its specific contemporary challenges, in order to react in a truly responsible way to this challenge, becomes inevitably part of a tradition which as such may perhaps have an "identity" but hardly lives out of its prescribed mission. To be church does not consist simply in being a church, and therefore the preservation of tradition and identity cannot be its decisive perspectives for reform. Rather, it belongs to its confessional existence to confess continually more than it is and than it can ever present. It is not to itself that it has to witness in the 'world' but to the reconciliation and the coming of the kingdom of God in word and deed. Only to the extent that it actually does that can it also be of interest to the 'world,' although it therefore also has to take into account that the 'world' in its inclination towards a vain self-idolization and to a nonsalvific religious explanation of itself makes a stand against the demythologization of the gospel. It also lies entirely in the interest of the 'world' to stylize the human being as a subject of needs and thereby, in fact, to make her an object of its needs. Then every reminder of the finitude and distress of those human beings is disturbing. But these human beings are suppressed and silenced only temporarily. And where people do not allow themselves to be suppressed, it does not help if the church speaks of itself and its possibilities, for the origins of the distress are beyond our possibilities. But the church is to speak of God, which we cannot do on our initiative as people of this world but which — thank God — we can do through God, not indeed as his plenipotentiary but as a witness that never points to itself but to him. If the church can find its way to its "confessorial" existence in this sense, it could also turn again decisively to its special mission.

The church then stands actually on the side of and in solidarity with the modern human being, if it actually becomes a worldly church and finds its way to its commanded sobriety and modesty instead of pursuing all tendencies in order to offer itself in all respects as a flexible agency of religion, value, or attribution of meaning. On this open and honestly traveled road the church will, in my view, also — without playing the religious strongman — be audible to modern contemporaries. People everywhere are fobbed off with self-confident solutions and presumptuous general answers. The complexity of our world does not allow any more superficial slogans. Nevertheless, whoever uses such slogans should recognize that he seeks to escape from this world into a synthetic one. Every kind of fundamentalism ignores the reality of the world, even though fundamentalism as a whole is understood as a collective aid in escape.[28] Over against the surplus of mutually silencing solutions there is to a large extent a lack of correct *questions*, a lack of space for the confessions of the weak or powerless as well as a lack of courage in mentioning the embarrassment and perplexity, and finally a lack of strong perspectives of hope in a world that in its lack of restraint in appropriating freedom to itself does everything to rob itself of that freedom step by step. In this the church can be recognizable in a special way in that it speaks up for the explanation of the world beyond itself in the light of the gospel. Beyond this it is not called to demonstrate the realization of allegedly steadfast principles and maintainable values but to the continually new search to live the humanity of human beings in solidarity with the world and its needs.

Conclusion

Ecclesia reformata semper reformanda — on all levels of ecclesiology this demand remains virulent. These considerations were focused first of all on the foundational dogmatic orientations that stamp, in the Reformed view, an ecclesiology. Certainly, it will always be so that where these foundational brief considerations end, the problems in the concrete situation only begin. It is relatively easy to say that the church needs to direct itself continually to the Word of God, but how, in cases of conflict, can we distinguish between what the Word of God says and what we would only like the Word of God to say? Where do we actually derive the certainty, if one constantly raises the question of division? Critical solidarity to the 'world' — Yes!, but to what extent does that solidarity go and where does criticism begin? And what does it mean in the situation of radical change, clearly marked by pluralism, in which many of the traditional customs are no longer meaningful? We are experiencing a high-speed social life, from which the church will also not escape unchanged, but where do the potential advances exist and how are they to be determined? One should frankly concede that the distinctions are considerably more complex in concrete, everyday life than in the horizon of theological teaching, but that does not in any way take away from the right and necessity of these fundamental considerations. It clarifies, to be sure, that in the life of the church, we are still a long way from being able to express a proper theology. It will seem, to be sure, incomparably hopeless for the concrete decisions, if the church must make do with a vague theology or even without any theology at all. It would be nice, if the worry that the latter could be the case were generally unfounded. In that case, these considerations can be left in obscurity.

28. Weinrich, *Kirche glauben*, pp. 262-302.

CHAPTER 28

Identity and Ecumenicity: How Do We Deal Theologically with So-Called "Nontheological" Factors?

Piet J. Naudé

The theme of this conference is — at least for myself — not merely an interesting academic one. I am an ordained minister of the Dutch Reformed Church in South Africa (DRC), which for many years identified itself so strongly with the aspirations and ideological interests of the Afrikaner people that it almost lost its identity as a truly Christian church by providing moral justification for apartheid policies.[1] As a young theologian I had to notice and live through the growing ecumenical isolation started in the early 1960s and only partially restored by the World Alliance of Reformed Churches after the last synod of the DRC in October 1998. My views on identity and ecumenicity below should consequently be seen in the light of this mainly negative experiential context.

One of the perennial problems in the ecumenical movement is the strained relation between churches' self-understanding and the aim ". . . to call the churches to the goal of visible unity in one faith and one eucharistic fellowship expressed in worship and in common life in Christ. . . ."[2] The problem may be

---

1. This is described and analyzed in many works, notably in John de Gruchy's outline of Afrikaner Calvinism in his *Liberating Reformed Theology: A South African Contribution to an Ecumenical Debate* (Cape Town: David Philip, 1991), pp. 1-46. For an informative overview of Reformed churches in South Africa, see Dirk J. Smit, "Reformed Theology in South Africa: A Story of Many Stories," *Acta Theologica* 12, no. 1 (1992): 88-110.

2. These words are taken from the Faith and Order Constitution, Appendix V in *On the Way to Fuller Koinonia*, ed. Thomas F. Best and Günther Gassmann (Geneva: WCC, 1994).

restated in the theme of our deliberations as that between (ecclesial) identity and (holy) communion. The great ecumenical theologian, Geoffrey Wainwright, declares: "At stake in the understanding of unity and schism, of continuity and discontinuity, of integrity and fragmentation, is precisely the *identity of the church* and therewith the nature and substance of truth and the conditions of its *authoritative expression.*"[3]

Apart from a "theological" identity (e.g., Reformed, Lutheran, Catholic), the self-understanding of a church is also shaped by "nontheological" factors like geography, language, culture, and a particular history. The role that these factors play has been alluded to in the early stages of the modern ecumenical movement. Already the Second World Conference of Faith and Order in Edinburgh (1937) refers to sociopolitical and historical factors such as nationality, race, class, and self-preservation that hinder the unification process among churches.[4]

The significance of the problematic relation between theological and nontheological factors has grown during the last two decades. Lukas Vischer observes that "(t)he divided churches live today in a state of powerful inner contradiction. Years ago they greeted the ecumenical era with enthusiasm. . . . But now years have passed and the situation has changed. Today the churches stress their own identity and tradition." The process of reception in the ecumenical movement has indeed stumbled over this negative flight into an isolationist "identity."

Frequently, confessional positions are not defended by a concern for the purity of their teaching. *The real motive is often simply preservation of one's*

3. Geoffrey Wainwright, *The Ecumenical Moment: Crisis and Opportunity for the Church* (Grand Rapids: Eerdmans, 1983), p. 190 (his emphasis); see also Wainwright, "Reception of 'Baptism, Eucharist, and Ministry' and the Apostolic Faith Study," in *The Search for Visible Unity,* ed. J. Gros (New York: Pilgrim Press, 1984), pp. 71-75.

4. See Faith and Order Papers, Old Series no. 84. I broadly follow Heinz-Günther Stobbe's historical overview (see "Konflikte um Identität. Eine Studie zur Bedeutung von Macht in inter-konfessionellen Beziehungen und im ökumenischen Prozess," in *Ökumenische Theologie,* ed. Peter Lengsfeld (Stuttgart: Kohlhammer, 1980), pp. 194ff. This issue of "nontheological factors" emerged again at the Third World Conference of Faith and Order (Lund 1952) where churches were called upon to give special attention to the schismatic influence of social and cultural factors. An interdisciplinary commission was set up to advise the Fourth World Conference in Montreal (1963) with a follow-up document, *Spirit, Order and Organization,* submitted to the Faith and Order Commission at Louvain. At that stage the Lutheran World Council set up a theological commission (1969) to study the same theme. The commission refers to misunderstandings created by the term "nontheological factors" and proposes "secular factors" as substitute. (See the report *Mehr als Einheit der Kirche,* 1970.) Specific reference is later made to the "kirchentrennende Wirkung der sekularen Faktoren" in a study entitled *Ökumenische Methodologie* commissioned by the executive committee of the Lutheran Council for its August 1973 meeting.

identity which has developed over the course of history. . . . These may be matters of language, ethnic identity, national pride, or other things. For this reason *the ecumenical movement must pay attention to these ancillary factors.* By breaking through these secondary barriers — which are no less resistant for all that — the church will win the freedom for its process of reception.[5]

Günther Gassmann refers to these "nicht-lehrhaften Faktoren" that exercise an essential influence on attempts for greater unity and communion among churches. He seeks an explanation for diverse replies to the Lima text from churches that share the same confessional (e.g., Lutheran) tradition in contextual factors: Is the church a minority — or state church? Is the main dialogue partner the Catholic or Orthodox or Protestant free churches? These all contribute to the self-understanding of a specific church — apart from its narrow "theological" character.[6]

The problem of identity-preservation, i.e., in the negative sense of self-sufficiency and exclusivity, is enhanced over time. Because, says the seasoned Anglican theologian G. R. Evans, over a longer period the habit of separateness determines the identity to such an extent that the self-definition over and against others (in-group versus out-group) *accepts separation as normal and as legitimate ground for continued or even further separation,*[7] with a resultant loss of vision for communion.[8]

A remarkable feature of this problem is referred to in passing by Stobbe: *The acuteness of "nontheological factors" has been recognized specifically in churches from the Protestant tradition.*[9] There is no room to analyze this elaborately, but it seems an almost typical Reformed feature to constantly ask "identity-questions." This may be linked to Calvin's original impulse to proclaim the Word in a socially active, world-formative manner derived from a

---

5. Lukas Vischer, "The Process of 'Reception' in the Ecumenical Movement," *Mid-Stream* 23 (1984): 221, 232 (my emphasis); see also Hartmut Loewe, "Die Kirchen vor der Aufgabe der Rezeption von Ergebnissen ökumenischer Gespräche und Verhandlungen," in *Vernunft des Glaubens. Wissenschaftliche Theologie und kirchliche Lehre,* FS W. Pannenberg (Göttingen: Vandenhoeck & Ruprecht, 1988), p. 646; Hermann Fischer, "Rezeption in ihre Bedeutung für Leben und Lehre der Kirche," in *Verständigung auf dem Prüfstand,* ed. W. Beinart and H. Fischer (Berlin: Wichern Verlag, 1989), p. 48.

6. Günther Gassmann, "Die Rezeption der Dialog," *OR* 33 (1984): 366-67.

7. See G. R. Evans, *Method in Ecumenical Theology: The Lessons So Far* (Cambridge: Cambridge University Press, 1996), pp. 42, 54 (my emphasis).

8. See my extensive analysis of this problem in relation to the DRC's inability to come to grips with the challenge posed by the Belhar Confession of the Uniting Reformed Church: "Die Belharstryd in ekumeniese perspektief," *NGTT* 38, no. 3 (1997): 226-43.

9. Stobbe, "Konflikte um Identität," p. 196.

wider vision of God's kingdom.[10] It may be the result of the dictum *theologia reformata et semper reformanda* as explained by Moltmann. What is Reformed theology? is constantly being asked:

> Das ist in gewisser Weise typisch für reformierte Theologie, denn sie gründet nicht in ein für alle Mal festgelegten Bekenntnissen wie die lutherische Theologie im Konkordienbuch und auch nich in einer Tradition unfehlbarer. . . . Lehrentscheidungen wie die römisch-katholische Theologie. Sie gründet in der 'Reformation' der Kirche 'nach dem Wort Gottes.'[11]

And this implies a constant reformation encompassing life, church, and world.

In short, where God is taken seriously as God of all spheres of life (the world as theater of God's glory) and where the Word of God is taken seriously as prophetic Word for each new situation (life as *coram Dei loquendi*), the problems related to "contextuality" and "rootedness" loom greater. The struggle for identity and therefore for ecumenicity is a broad question intensified in Reformed theology by its nature as a constantly reforming theology.[12]

The question now remains: How does one address the "nontheological," "nondogmatic," or "secular" factors to break through "secondary barriers" on the way to fuller koinonia? It depends, first, on the perspective from which one approaches this question; second, on the process followed; and third, on the normative reference point utilized.

A Theological Perspective

One may attempt to fathom the impact of "nontheological" factors by relying on any one or a combination of the social sciences like sociology, social psychology, political studies, or history and then by clarifying in which way a

---

10. Nicholas Wolterstorff, *Until Justice and Peace Embrace* (Grand Rapids: Eerdmans, 1983), p. 21.

11. Jürgen Moltmann, "Theologia reformata et semper reformanda," in *Zur Zukunft der Reformierten Theologie. Aufgaben. Themen. Traditionen,* ed. Michael Welker and David Willis (Neukirchen: Neukirchener Verlag, 1998), p. 157.

12. See W. Boesak and P. J. A. Fourie, eds., *Vraagtekens oor Gereformeerdheid* (Belhar: Lus Uitgewers, 1998), for a recent contribution on the issue of Reformed identity from a South African context. Dirkie Smit, a leading Reformed scholar, writes in the introduction: "There is apparently something in the Reformed soul that constantly impels us to ask these self-investigative questions about our own identity. . . . To ask this type of question is already part of our identity" ("As Voorwoord: Gereformeerde identiteit?," in *Vraagtekens oor Gereformeerdheid,* p. 21, my translation).

group (in this case a church) has been determined by so-called "nontheological" factors.

This approach reveals the difficulty in accepting the term "nontheological," as the latter assumes the theological perspective as point of reference with other factors as "not-from-theology." Even if a theological perspective is assumed, the "other factors" must in some way be honored in their own right. For the sake of this paper, I prefer the term "social factors" — although somewhat vague, it does avoid some of the pitfalls of hitherto used terms.

The approach to understanding the reasons for both church divisions and church union from social sources[13] must be welcomed as an important facet of contextual analysis crucial to theology. It does assist the theologian to understand the historical, economic, and cultural factors at play in the struggle for the visible unity of the local (regional) and universal church. *But these insights must be interpreted theologically to make a lasting impact on bilateral or multilateral dialogues.* I will explain this from both the global and local ecumenical perspectives.

The Catholic ecumenical theologian J. M. R. Tillard states in his discussion of the ecclesiological implications of bilateral dialogue that one should refuse ". . . to consider the so-called nontheological factors sufficient to explain the main divisions between Christians." He rightly points out that the ruptures between Rome on the one hand and Constantinople, Canterbury, and Wittenberg on the other ". . . happened not only for theological reasons, but religious, theological, racial, political, cultural and economical factors were also deeply entangled." He argues that during the process — and definitely in the mind of the next generation — "theological factors have come to the foreground and have gradually been considered the implicit cause of rupture." Therefore, it is the dogmatic factors of division that must form the essence of bilateral dialogues and not the "easy solution" of nontheological factors.[14]

13. Compare the well-known work of H. Richard Niebuhr on *The Social Sources of Denominationalism* (New York: Holt, 1929) with Robert Lee's book, *The Social Sources of Church Unity: An Interpretation of Unitive Movements in American Protestantism* (New York: Abingdon, 1960), to see two sides of the coin. For references see Stobbe, "Konflikte um Identität," p. 194.

14. J. M. R. Tillard, "The Ecclesiological Implications of Bilateral Dialogue," *Journal of Ecumenical Studies* 23, no. 3 (1986): 416, 417. It is interesting to note how Tillard moves from his insistence on dogmatic issues to an engagement with strategic (i.e., nontheological!) issues. He expresses an opinion that bilateral dialogues between the old churches of the Catholic tradition (including the Anglicans) on the one hand, and those between Protestant and new churches on the other hand, could, if successful, in fact be a tragedy. Why? Because "it would finally divide Christianity into two competitive and strong (if not hostile) camps" (p. 419). It is a clear statement on a church-political power struggle which is in itself no purely dogmatic issue.

In the local South African context, the struggle for church unification among the (Dutch) Reformed family of churches can indeed be viewed from a multitude of "social sources." Historical, political, and economic factors[15] illuminate the stumbling blocks in the way of church unification. But these must be interpreted theologically, clarifying the crucial questions about God,[16] Christ's reconciliation, the interpretation of Scripture,[17] and the nature of the church[18] and its confessional character.[19] To put it bluntly, to understand apartheid as an oppressive social system in conflict with universal human rights is politically significant; to understand apartheid as a matter of a theological *status confessionis*, sinful in its essence and not merely in its application, is what is ecumenically significant.[20] And obviously, one cannot speak of dichotomies here; rather of complementing perspectives supporting each other's validity in a complex and multifaceted interplay.

Social factors in the broad sense must be dealt with theologically, but not by way of sublimation. This exactly strengthens their power to ruin processes of dialogue and unification. When the question of preserving the Afrikaans lan-

---

15. For wide references on the intricacies of the South African situation, see de Gruchy, *Liberating Reformed Theology*, pp. 4-13, and Smit, "Reformed Theology" and "As Voorwoord," nn. 3-16.

16. The struggle for church unification in the Dutch Reformed family is an immensely theological one. See the ongoing debates about the nature of God's concern for the poor as expressed in the Belhar Confession in Smit's contribution to *'n Oomblik van waarheid*, ed. G. J. Cloete and D. J. Smit (Kaapstad: Tafelberg, 1984), and my own recent analysis, "Belhar se ontvangs in die NG Kerk, in Johan Botha en Piet Naudé," *Op pad met Belhar* (Pretoria: J. L. van Schaik, 1998), pp. 86-88.

17. The unification struggle is basically a hermeneutical struggle. For a succinct view of the matter from within the Dutch Reformed Church, see J. A. Loubser: *The Apartheid Bible: A Critical Review of Racial Theology in South Africa* (Pretoria: J. L. van Schaik, 1987).

18. It is significant that the influential and prophetic DRC systematic theologian from Stellenbosch University, Willem D. Jonker, started the ecclesiological debate in the context of mission churches as early as 1962. It is up to this day a very important aspect of the family dialogue — especially in the light of the design of a new church order. An example of the debate in the seventies is the collection of essays *Die eenheid van die kerk* with Piet Meiring and H. I. Lederle as editors (Kaapstad: Tafelberg, 1978).

19. The acceptance by the Uniting Reformed Church of the Belhar Confession as a fourth confessional document apart from the Three Symbols of Unity (including the Heidelberg Catechism) added a dramatic dimension to the unification struggle. For an overview and analysis of the Dutch Reformed reaction, see my contributions "Die Belharstryd" and "Belhar se ontvangs in die NG Kerk."

20. The World Alliance of Reformed Churches set this as a condition for re-acceptance of the DRC as member. At its last synod (October 1998) the formulation about apartheid as sinful in its essence was approved by the synod. This opened the ecumenical doors after sixteen years of isolation.

guage in a new unified Reformed church was raised by the now moderator of the Dutch Reformed Church and the Synod of the Northern Transvaal (1997), it was easy to explain from a historical, political, and cultural perspective.[21] What has, however, been crucial, is to clarify the language issue from the perspective of the church as exemplified in the Second Testament and confessed in the Reformed tradition — bearing in mind what important role language plays in the formation of a people's identity! This is pastorally sensitive, prophetically truthful, and ecclesiologically significant.

The theological perspective on social factors enables one to understand the fundamentally ambivalent nature of "context." Calvinism in its various social formats — English, Dutch, French, and Afrikaner; Reformed spirituality as Scottish Pietism, Dutch neo-Calvinism, Black and feminist theologies — all harbor within themselves the tension that has ecumenically been expressed as the relation between Tradition and traditions.[22] The root of the ambivalence lies in the walking of the tightrope to keep Tradition (for Reformed Christians primarily the scriptures) and traditions (interpretation of Scripture in one's own context) in a healthy tension. Tradition alone is silent; traditions alone are heresy.

The gospel is in its very nature linked to the "social sources" of ancient Near Eastern and Greek-Roman societies, and is ever again part of the "social sources" of societies through the ages. There is no such thing as "pure" gospel without social trappings. This is the essence of the hermeneutical struggle, and

---

21. The Afrikaans language developed from mid-seventeenth-century Dutch via the colonization of the Cape since 1652. It was suppressed by the later English governments, but gained momentum from 1880 onwards with formal recognition as one of two official languages in 1925. The rise of Afrikanerdom and Afrikaner identity was deeply shaped by this language — specifically via the translation of the Bible in 1933 (not unlike Luther's contribution to the German language). One of the historical markers in the black liberation movement is the Soweto student uprisings in 1976 directed against the forced tuition in and of Afrikaans. After the democratic elections of 1994, Afrikaans became one of eleven official languages and lost most of its previous exclusive privileges. It is understandable that the Dutch Reformed Church would be tempted to see itself as one of the vehicles for maintaining Afrikaans, which was at one point (quite unnecessarily) seen as being threatened by church unification. The theological question is one about the task and nature of the church and not about the cultural value of a specific language: the tension between a biblical vision of the church's "identity" and the temptation of a civil religion serving the needs of a *volks*-identity.

22. I do not engage in a detailed discussion on the history and technical distinctions of the Tradition/traditions theme in Faith and Order. It suffices to refer to the Montreal distinction (1963) between Tradition (the gospel itself, transmitted from generation to generation in and by the church, Christ himself present in the life of the church) and tradition (both the diversity of forms of expression and also the confessional traditions). See P. C. Rodger and Lukas Vischer, *The Fourth World Conference on Faith and Order* (London: SCM, 1964), paragraph 39, p. 59; and Alan D. Falconer, "En Route to Santiago," *The Ecumenical Review* 45 (1993): 45-47.

we have many examples where the Christian tradition in general and the Reformed tradition in particular failed to remain true to Tradition. "The Reformed tradition, like any other, *can be seduced by social and cultural forces* that undermine its witness and keep it captive."[23] Thus remarks John de Gruchy in the context of his discussion of Afrikaner Calvinism, a prime twentieth-century example of how the gospel was smothered and concealed by social sources.[24]

It is thus no wonder that most discussions of social forces in ecumenical dialogues are predominantly negative (see quotations above). The question of how to deal with these ambivalent forces now comes to the fore. *How* means in this case, what process could be suggested in cases where dialogue partners find it difficult or impossible to make progress?

A Therapeutic Process

It seems that the most fruitful approach to social factors in a "stuck" bilateral/multilateral union process, is a narrative, therapeutic one.[25] The partners should be allowed to reveal their identity by relating their story to each other via the telling of story-fragments ("Einzel-Stories"). Ritschl extensively dealt with this issue in his *Story als Rohmaterial der Theologie* (edited with Hugh Jones, 1976) and later in his *Zur Logik der Theologie* (1984). The link between Story and identity is clarified as follows:

> Mit 'Stories' kann etwas ausgedrückt werden, wofür andere Idiome ungeeignet wären. Vor allem kan durch 'Stories' die Identität eines einzelnen oder eine Gruppe artikuliert werden. Menschen sind das was sie in ihren Story über sich sagen (bzw. was zu ihnen gesagt wird) und was sie aus dieser 'Story' machen. . . . Jeder von uns hat seine unverwechselbare Story, jeder *ist* seine Story.[26]

23. De Gruchy, *Liberating Reformed Theology*, p. 13 (my emphasis).

24. The conclusion regarding faith communities as formulated by the Truth and Reconciliation Commission in South Africa reads as follows: "In most cases, faith communities claimed to cut across divisions of race, gender, class and ethnicity. . . . However, contrary to their own deepest principles, many faith communities mirrored apartheid society, giving the lie to their profession of a loyalty that transcended social divisions" (vol. 4, p. 65, paragraph 29).

25. I herewith engage in a free adaptation of some of Dietrich Ritschl's fascinating ideas based on his combination of insights from psychoanalysis, analytical philosophy, and the earlier Chomsky's theory of language acquisition. See references in text below.

26. Dietrich Ritschl, *Zur Logik der Theologie*, Kurze Darstellung der Zusammenhänge theologischer Grundgedanken (München: C. Kaiser, 1984), p. 45 (his emphasis, and sexist language!).

The narrative mode reveals[27] the perspective[28] or close-knit perspectives that determine "reality" in the act of a "seeing-as"[29] by each partner. In this process one moves in various ways from the "surface-level" to the "deep-structure" of the conflict. If the process is allowed to continue, it will unearth that which ultimately ("letzlich") steer the partners' thoughts and actions, namely "implicit axioms." "Das ist ja das Wesen von Axiomen, dass sie einfach da sind, dass sie funktionieren, ohne uns zu erlauben, sie wirklich begründet zu können, so, als stünden wir hinter oder über ihnen. Sie stehen aber hinter oder über uns, sie steüren uns."[30] Under close examination, the central axioms (normally few in number)[31] are revealed, with the possibility to understand their hierarchical ordering (some are more important than others) and reciprocal interchange ("Vernetzung").[32]

What is crucial to this process is its *dialogical nature.* Not only is one partner telling her story (revealing identity, perspectives, and implicit axioms), but her story is reciprocally *being told.*[33] In this way isolationism is overcome,

27. "Die Stories, die unser Leben ausmachen (einzeln und in Gruppen), sind die Träger unserer Perspektiven" (*Zur Logik,* p. 58).

28. "In der sozialen Wirklichkeit sind Gruppen und Gemeinschaften durch gemeinsame Perspektive-Bündel gekennzeichnet, die in gemeinsamen Stories und Lebenshaltungen Ausdruck finden können" (*Zur Logik,* p. 56).

29. A reference to the insight from phenomenology that objects are perceived "as-something" and not "in themselves." This determines Ritschl's definition of perspectives as ". . . die Weise, in der wir die Dinge sehen, denn wir sehen Dinge immer im Modus des 'Sehen-Als'" (*Zur Logik,* p. 56).

30. Dietrich Ritschl, *Konzepte: Ökumene, Medizin, Ethik.* Gesammelte Aufsätze (München: Kaiser, 1986), p. 148.

31. It is inter alia on this basis that Stephen Sykes argues that part of the link between the "essence" debate in theology and Ritschl's thinking is that both are driven by the motive of simplification. See "'Essence of Christianity' versus 'Implicit Axioms,'" in *Implizite Axiome. Tiefenstrukturen des Denkens und Handelns,* ed. Wolfgang Huber, Ernst Petzold, and Theo Sundermeier (München: Kaiser, 1990), pp. 268ff. The value of this for a complicated bilateral/multilateral union is obvious: it simplifies the various conflicting perspectives under a more fundamental and more manageable entity or entities.

32. This is such an important aspect of Ritschl's thought that he notes in brackets and in the small print on page 145: "Mit dem Wort 'Vernetzung' oder einfach 'Netze' habe ich als mögliche Titel für dieses Buch gespielt" (reference to *Zur Logik*). For an instructive discussion of implicit axioms as "Grundkonzept," see Michael Welker, "Implizite Axiome. Zu einem Grundkonzept von Dietrich Ritschls 'Logik der Theologie,'" in *Implizite Axiome,* pp. 30-38.

33. My involvement in a forum for interchurch dialogue in Port Elizabeth has taught me the value of this. White theologians who benefited from the politico-economic system and who formed a self-understanding in isolation must go through the (especially painful!) process of "being told" our own story. The therapeutic value of stories has been amply proven — especially during the submissions to the Truth and Reconciliation Commission in South Af-

because the neurosis[34] of a privatized language and world is opened up for a therapeutic resymbolization[35] that is a fundamental hermeneutical[36] (reinterpretative) process.[37]

One of the problems in ecumenical circles is to ensure that Stories are allowed to be told and thereby identities revealed in a truly dialogical process. Storytelling is no naïve retreat with romantic connotations, because it touches on the sensitive issue of power relations.[38] Mary Tanner, in her speech to the Fifth World Conference on Faith and Order, questions the very method and structures of Faith and Order, precisely to ensure that everyone is heard:

> For that we need a more inclusive community for reflection and interpretation, open to every culture and ecclesial tradition. We need to ask who is missing from our circle — and whom do we silence *within* our circle? . . . Faith and Order has a duty to represent those who have no voice in the structures of the World Council of Churches.[39]

Storytelling as therapeutic process is indeed no easy process. It does in no way imply that the dialogue partners will always come to "see" their differences as surface expressions of the same deep-structure or "Ur-Anliegen"[40] — the

rica. See the contribution of Gerald West, *Biblical Hermeneutics of Liberation* (Pietermaritzburg: Cluster, 1995), p. 213, on the issue of "speaking with" and the problem of a "hidden transcript" adapted from James Scott's "Don't Stand on My Story: The TRC, Intellectuals, Genre and Identity, *Journal of Theology for Southern Africa* 98 (1997): 6-8. See Piet Naudé, "Doxology and Praxis: The Ecumenical Significance of Religious Experience in a South Africa of the 1990's," in *The Relevance of Theology for the 1990's*, ed. J. Mouton and B. Lategan (Pretoria: HSRC, 1994), pp. 421-34, on the experiential basis of ecumenical relations.

34. Building on A. Lorenzer's *Sprachzerstörung und Rekonstruktion*, Ritschl notes ". . . dass sich z.B. Neurosen in privatisierter Sprache zeigen, nicht notwendig und sehr selten in unverständlichem Reden" (*Konzepte*, p. 159; see also *Zur Logik*, p. 142).

35. See Ritschl, *Konzepte*, pp. 158ff.

36. Ritschl does not, as far as I know, pursue the hermeneutical issue in this context. Wolfgang Huber ("Ökumenischer Realismus. Zur theologischen Bedeutung impliziter Axiome," in *Implizite Axiome*, p. 20) suggests that the transition from an analytic to a hermeneutic process occurs precisely when one's implicit axioms are questioned by a dialogue-partner.

37. Ritschl, *Konzepte*, p. 151.

38. The view "from power" in the ecumenical movement is extensively developed and defended by Heinz-Günther Stobbe. See Stobbe.

39. Mary Tanner, "The Tasks of the World Conference in the Perspective of the Future," in *On the Way to Fuller Koinonia*, pp. 26, 27 (her emphasis).

40. Dietrich Ritschl, "Ökumenische Theologie," in Dietrich Ritschl and Werner Ustorf, *Ökumenische Theologie — Missionswissenschaft* (Stuttgart: Kohlhammer, 1994), p. 58.

way in which Ritschl has mainly argued in his analysis of dogmatic differences.[41] Huber shows that it is possible to follow a type of axiomatic reasoning:

> . . . der gerade nicht auf die Tiefengrammatik mögliche Einheit, sondern auf die Tiefenstruktur von Differenz zielt. . . . Denn gerade in ihrer doppelten Verwendbarkeit hat die These von der impliziten Axiomen im Blick auf die ökumenische Situation der Gegenwart eine erhebliche diagnostische Kraft.[42]

This therapeutic process, which marks theology as wisdom, allows for both a critical and healing ("zärtliche") engagement[43] between dialogue partners. If allowed to grow, it will reveal if and how social sources (history, class, language, race) assume the status of implicit axioms that steer us, stealthily and often unconsciously, in such a way that despite dogmatic and textual[44] agreements, union still eludes us. More than that — and very difficult to untangle — a healthy therapeutic process will reveal to what extent social factors masquerade as "theological positions" rendering an ideological effect to the latter.

But what will serve as normative reference point in this therapeutic process? What leads theology to be a wisdom-theology? We turn to this in our last section.

41. Examples in his *Konzepte.*

42. Huber, "Ökumenischer Realismus," p. 29. Huber, in an ethical reinterpretation of axioms, also argues that they may not only be prelinguistic assumptions ("schön immer Vorausgesetzten"), but also the result of (ethical) reflection that in the end accepts certain basic insights as "implicit axioms" (pp. 23ff.).

43. Ritschl, *Zur Logik,* p. 340.

44. One of the most graphic examples to prove that agreement on theology and wording does not guarantee reception is my proposal to the Eastern Cape Synodical Commission on Dogma and Ethics (Leer en Aktuele Sake) that our Synod at least expresses support for the content of the Belhar Confession as accepted by the Uniting Reformed Church. One of the commission members, deeply embedded in the traumatic history of ecumenical isolation in the Dutch Reformed Church ("an attack on us from politically inspired churches"), said the following: "I stood on my knees before God and must say that not a single word of the Belhar-confession is in contrast to the Gospel. But I will never be able to sign it." My proposal was accepted by the Commission, but rejected by the Synod. This problem is also referred to by Evans in her discussion (with examples) of the errant belief that if we understand we would agree (p. 196). See my elaborate discussion on the value of liturgy and ritual in ecumenical reception processes, "Regaining Our Ritual Coherence: The Question of Textuality and Worship in Ecumenical Reception," *Journal of Ecumenical Studies* 35, no. 2 (1998): 235-56.

...

PIET J. NAUDÉ

Scripture as Reference Point

One does not have to argue the point that the heart of our Reformed identity is the centrality of the Word of God in its various manifestations as revelation, Scripture, and proclamation. This was reinforced at a recent worldwide consultation of Reformed theologians published as *Zur Zukunft der Reformierten Theologie. Aufgaben — Themen — Traditionen.* The introduction already makes very clear:

> Der ökumenische Beitrag der reformierten Theologie besteht darin, dass sie sich ruhig und beharrlich, kritisch und konstruktiv *den vielen Versuchen widersetzt, das Wort Gottes zu entleeren* und es unter die Herrschaft von Metaphysik, Moral, Mystik oder unter das Diktat eines 'Zeitgeists' zu bringen.[45]

To restate in terms of this paper: The ecumenical contribution of Reformed theology is resisting the temptation to disempower the Word by letting it fall under the spell of social sources.

This is pointedly displayed in the writings of Heidelberger systematician Michael Welker, one of the important voices in Reformed theology today. This is not the place for an extensive exposition or analysis, but in simplified terms one could argue that Welker takes up the double tasks of reinterpreting traditional faith symbols (dogmatic loci) from a strong biblical-theological perspective[46] as well as providing an orientation in the face of the highly complex modern and postmodern developments. He develops a "realistic theology"[47] that mediates between human reality and God's reality by ". . . acquiring clarity concerning those traits that are characteristic and unavoidable for the appearance of God's reality and God's power *in the midst of* the structural patterns of human life."[48]

---

45. Welker and Willis, eds., *Zur Zukunft*, p. 10 (my emphasis).

46. There are too many writings to cite here. Welker's studies on the church (*Kirche im Pluralismus* [Gütersloh: C. Kaiser, 1995]), creation theology (*Schöpfung und Wirklichkeit* [Neukirchen: Neukirchener Verlag, 1995]), sin (*Sünde. Ein unverständlich gewordenes Thema* [Neukirchen: Neukirchener Verlag, 1997]), and the Spirit (*God the Spirit* [Minneapolis: Fortress, 1994]) have mostly been translated and already assume an influential place in both Germany and the U.S.A.

47. The clearest statements about this approach are found in Welker, *Schöpfung und Wirklichkeit*, pp. 12-13, 33-34; and Welker, *God the Spirit*, pp. x-xii, 46-47, 49 n. 97. For a discussion of Welker's biblical-realistic theology see Bernd Oberdorfer, "Biblisch-realistische Theologie. Methodologische Überlegungen zu einem dogmatischen Programm," in *Resonanzen. Theologische Beiträge Michael Welker zum 50. Geburtstag*, ed. Sigrid Brandt und Bernd Oberdorfer (Wuppertal: Foedus, 1997), pp. 63-83.

48. Welker, *God the Spirit*, p. xi (my emphasis).

...

446

In this mediation the multifaceted biblical text serves as criterion and reference point: "Die Heilige Schrift ist das Wort Gottes, an dem wir unsere Traditionen, Normen und Überzeugungen *immer neu zu messen haben. . . .*"[49]

The implication of this Reformed thrust, "Reformierte Theologie ist als reformierende Theologie biblische Theologie,"[50] is that the therapeutic process discussed in the previous section cannot be seen in isolation. The Story that we *are* as Reformed Christians is to be understood in relation to the Bible in a double sense of the word: First, telling our story (revealing identity in an ecumenical encounter) is to acknowledge that the story itself has been shaped by the Bible (in its various manifestations such as preaching, worship, and catechesis) as well as various other social factors like politics, geography, sex, race, and class. But, secondly, the reference point and criterion of our story is always the Scripture as canonical Story; canon as "yardstick" of Christian authenticity and truthfulness.

This is the way pointed to by the biblical narratives[51] themselves. Two powerful passages from the Pauline literature serve as illustration:

The Christian identity of local churches in Galatia was threatened by the insistence of some that non-Jews could only be saved by keeping the prescribed Jewish customs (Gal. 3:1-14; 4:8-11). Further tensions grew due to the pluralistic background of the members and the social forces shaping society. The danger was that the church might allow these social forces — including Jewish religious legalism — to disempower the gospel message of Jesus Christ summarized in the well-known exhortation: "You are all sons of God through faith in Jesus Christ, for all of you who were baptized into Christ have been clothed with Christ. There is neither Jew nor Greek, slave nor free, male nor female, for you are all one in Christ Jesus" (Gal. 3:26-28). Faith and baptism in Christ become the criterion by which members are measured. And of crucial importance: *social forces like nationality, class, and sex are not denied, but seen relative to the new reality of life in Christ who, because he gave himself up, has the power to bring unity in the church* (Eph. 2:11-22).

If it then does emerge that a nontheological factor (even a religious one like the will to preserve Afrikaner identity via a form of Calvinism) serves as a hierarchically important implicit axiom, *its ecclesiological relativity must be shown in the light of the catholicity and biblical vision of the church.* This is one way to see the struggle among Reformed churches in South Africa: It was and is

---

49. Welker, *Zur Zukunft,* p. 176 (my emphasis).

50. Moltmann, "Theologia reformata et semper reformanda," in *Zur Zukunft,* p. 172.

51. One could interpret the convenant history in the First Testament as a struggle between being the people of God or following the gods as stated in the first of the Ten Commandments.

a hermeneutical struggle to interpret the biblical text and take it so seriously that the social forces of political allegiance, cultural identity, race, and class are "overpowered" (radically relativized) by the gospel, by Christ himself. If the biblical text, the canonical Scripture, loses this role, the Reformed — no — the Christian identity of the church is at stake.[52]

This is how one might interpret Paul's letter to the Philippians. In his explanation of righteousness through Christ, he explains his own identity-formation by enumerating an interesting mixture of theological and social factors,[53] i.e., his birth as a Benjaminite and circumcision on the eighth day (Jewish origin), his party allegiance to the Pharisees (politics), his minute keeping of the law and persecutions of Christians (religion) (Phil. 3:1-6). All these factors are then "taken into account" but dramatically relativized: "But whatever was to my profit, I now consider loss for the sake of Christ. What is more, I consider everything a loss compared to the surpassing greatness of knowing Christ Jesus, my Lord, for whose sake I have lost all things. I consider them rubbish, that I may gain Christ . . ." (Phil. 3:7-8). He then asks the Philippians to follow his example (v. 17) and not see themselves as citizens of the world: "Our citizenship is in heaven. And we eagerly await a Savior from there, the Lord Jesus Christ . . ." (v. 20).

It is clear: *nontheological/social factors in their negative determination of identity (neurosis in therapeutic terms; righteousness through the flesh in biblical terms) are only "overcome" via a radical reorientation to Christ (re-symbolization in therapeutic terms; conversion in biblical terms) that works a new self-understanding in the light of Christ's second coming (reinterpretation in therapeutic terms; expectation in biblical terms).*

The growth of various identities toward greater ecumenicity must be seen in pneumatological terms. As Welker has shown, the outpouring of the Spirit gives rise to a unity that is not so much an illusory homogeneity as a cultivation of differentiations that do not contradict justice.

> The Spirit gives rise to a unity in which the prophetic witness of women is no less important than that of men, that of the young is no less significant than that of the old, that of the socially disadvantaged is no less relevant than that of the privileged. The promised Spirit of God is effective in that differentiated community which is sensitive to differences, and in which

52. "If, for whatever reason, the trust in the Bible as God's living Word is threatened — and this is a world-wide process on various levels — the Reformed tradition itself is at stake" (Smit, "As Voorwoord," my free translation).
53. I am obviously aware of the vast "distance" between our perception of society with its various spheres and pluralisms and the pre-modern view reflected in biblical texts. The point about "identity" is, like all exegesis, merely a plausible construction!

the differences that stand in opposition to justice, mercy, and the knowledge of God are being steadily reduced.[54]

This, I believe, is the art of sound ecumenical practice, taught by the Spirit-teacher.

The Holy Spirit convinces of sin — also the sin of closed identities. The Spirit pours the charisma of love into our hearts. This promises ecumenical acceptance, not so much of texts or liturgical orders or dogmatic positions, but of one another — hopefully in full communion — as children in the one household of God.

54. Welker, *God the Spirit*, p. 22.